Handbook of Research on Wireless Multimedia:
Quality of Service and Solutions

Nicola Cranley
Dublin Institute of Technology, Ireland

Liam Murphy
University College Dublin, Ireland

T0350487

Information Science REFERENCE

INFORMATION SCIENCE REFERENCE

Hershey · New York

Director of Editorial Content: Kristin Klinger
Senior Managing Editor: Jennifer Neidig
Managing Editor: Jamie Snavely
Assistant Managing Editor: Carole Coulson
Managing Development Editor: Kristin M. Roth
Assistant Development Editor: Deborah Yahnke
Editorial Assistant: Rebecca Beistline
Copy Editor: Larissa Vinci
Typesetter: Sean Woznicki
Cover Design: Lisa Tosheff
Printed at: Yurchak Printing Inc.

Published in the United States of America by
    Information Science Reference (an imprint of IGI Global)
    701 E. Chocolate Avenue, Suite 200
    Hershey PA 17033
    Tel: 717-533-8845
    Fax: 717-533-8661
    E-mail: cust@igi-global.com
    Web site: http://www.igi-global.com

and in the United Kingdom by
    Information Science Reference (an imprint of IGI Global)
    3 Henrietta Street
    Covent Garden
    London WC2E 8LU
    Tel: 44 20 7240 0856
    Fax: 44 20 7379 0609
    Web site: http://www.eurospanbookstore.com

Library of Congress Cataloging-in-Publication Data

Handbook of research on wireless multimedia : quality of service and solutions / Nicola Cranley and Liam Murphy, editors.

    p. cm.

  Summary: "This book highlights and discusses the underlying QoS issues that arise in the delivery of real-time multimedia services over wireless networks"--Provided by publisher.
  Includes bibliographical references and index.

  ISBN 978-1-59904-820-8 (hardcover) -- ISBN 978-1-59904-823-9 (ebook)
  1. Multimedia communications--Quality control--Handbooks, manuals, etc. 2. Wireless communication systems--Handbooks, manuals, etc. I. Cranley, Nicola. II. Murphy, Liam.
  TK5105.15.H36 2009
  621.384--dc22
                 2008009105

British Cataloguing in Publication Data
A Cataloguing in Publication record for this book is available from the British Library.

If a library purchased a print copy of this publication, please go to http://www.igi-global.com/agreement for information on activating the library's complimentary electronic access to this publication.

List of Reviewers

Janet Adams
Dublin City University, Ireland

Fatih Alagöz
Boðaziçi University, Turkey

Michael Barry
University of Limerick, Ireland

Suzan Bayhan
Boðaziçi University, Turkey

Tarek Bejaoui
University of Carthage, Tunisia

Boris Bellalta
Universitat Pompeu Fabra, Spain

Janez Bester
University of Ljubljana, Slovenia

Graça Bressan
Escola Politécnica da Universidade de São Paulo, Brazil

Paolo Chini
Università degli Studi di Siena, Italy

Imrich Chlamtac
Create-Net, Italy

Nikki Cranley
University College Dublin, Ireland

Francesco De Pellegrini
Create-Net, Italy

Gheorghita Ghinea
Brunel University, UK

Giovanni Giambene
Università degli Studi di Siena, Italy

Gürkan Gür
Boðaziçi University, Turkey

Snezana Hadzic
Università degli Studi di Siena

Begoña Blanco Jauregi
University of the Basque Country, Spain

Jose Luis Jodra
University of the Basque Country, Spain

Scott Jordan
University of California, Irvine, USA

William Kent
University of Limerick, Ireland

Andrej Kos
University of Ljubljana, Slovenia

Harilaos G. Koumaras
N.C.S.R "Demokritos", Greece

Ming Li
California State University, Fresno, USA

Fidel Liberal
University of the Basque Country, Spain

Carlos Macian
Universitat Pompeu Fabra, Spain

Andreas Mäder
University of Würzburg, Germany

Michael M. Markou
University of Cyprus, Nicosia, Cyprus

Sean Mc Grath
University of Limerick, Ireland

Gabriel-Miro Muntean
Dublin City University, Ireland

Liam Murphy
University College Dublin, Ireland

Nidal Nasser
University of Guelph, Canada

John Nelson
University of Limerick, Ireland

Christos G. Panayiotou
University of Cyprus, Nicosia, Cyprus

Panagiotis Papadimitriou
Democritus University of Thrace, Greece

Dorel Picovici
University of Limerick, Ireland

Roberto Riggio
Create-Net, Italy

Tacha Serif
Brunel University, UK

Anna Sfairopoulou
Universitat Pompeu Fabra, Spain

Ronan Skehill
University of Limerick, Ireland

Dirk Staehle
University of Würzburg, Germany

Lingfen Sun
University of Plymouth, UK

Vassilis Tsaoussidis
Democritus University of Thrace, Greece

Mojca Volk
University of Ljubljana, Slovenia

Marcio Nieblas Zapater
Escola Politécnica da Universidade de São Paulo, Brazil

Peifang Zhang
University of California, Irvine, USA

Table of Contents

Section I
Network Quality of Service

Chapter XVIII

Detailed Table of Contents

Section I
Network Quality of Service

In this section Network Layer QoS solutions are presented. Critical factors affecting QoS for real-time multimedia streaming applications include reliability, efficient delivery, and end-to-end latencies. The tremendous growth and development of wireless networking technology has brought about fresh challenges in the provision of QoS for such real-time multimedia applications. This section focuses on key wireless networking technologies and presents novel solutions that have been designed to address these challenges. State of the art wireless technologies presented in this section include UMTS, HSDPA-Enhanced UMTS, 4G, and WLAN. Each of these wireless networking technologies has differing mechanisms for QoS support. Resource management schemes and admission control schemes can be used to prevent the network becoming overloaded such that poor network performance begins to negatively affect multimedia applications.

    Ronan Skehill, University of Limerick, Ireland
    William Kent, University of Limerick, Ireland
    Dorel Picovici, University of Limerick, Ireland
    Michael Barry, University of Limerick, Ireland
    Sean McGrath, University of Limerick, Ireland

This chapter introduces quality of service (QoS) in multi-access wireless networks, and demonstrates how QoS is implemented in IEEE 802.11 and UMTS. The chapter explains how these complementary technologies, when coupled together, provide a network that is greater than its individual parts. However, combining these networks brings new network management challenges, and so the impact of joint admission control strategies on QoS is evaluated. The evaluation results show that when UMTS and WLAN are tightly coupled, the end user enjoys a higher level of QoS.

Chapter II

Dirk Staehle, University of Würzburg, Germany
Andreas Mäder, University of Würzburg, Germany

This chapter gives an overview of the background and functionality of the high-speed downlink packet access (HSDPA), and provides insights into the radio resource management of integrated UMTS/HSDPA networks. The authors introduce aspects of radio resource management specific to the HSDPA like channel-aware scheduling and radio resource sharing strategies. Furthermore, the impact of radio resource management on the quality of service is analyzed and it is shown that the selection of an RRM strategy is an integral part of the network planning and deployment process.

Chapter III

Nidal Nasser, University of Guelph, Canada
Tarek Bejaoui, University of Carthage, Tunisia

Major research challenges in the next generation of wireless networks include the provisioning of worldwide seamless mobility across heterogeneous wireless networks, the improvement of end-to-end quality of service (QoS), supporting multimedia services over wide area and enabling users to specify their personal preferences. The integration and interoperability of this multitude of available networks will lead to the emergence of the fourth generation (4G) of wireless technologies. One of the 4G challenges is the user's ability to control and manage handoffs across heterogeneous wireless networks. This chapter proposes a solution to this problem using artificial neural networks.

Chapter IV

Ming Li, California State University, Fresno, USA
Roberto Riggio, Create-Net, Italy
Francesco De Pellegrini, Create-Net, Italy
Imrich Chlamtac, Create-Net, Italy

This chapter provides a comprehensive review of the architectures, algorithms, and protocols for resource management in IEEE 802.11 based wireless networks such as wireless LANs, heterogeneous wired/wireless networks, mobile ad hoc networks, and wireless mesh networks. The focus is on the approaches for bandwidth allocation in different networks, as well as how these strategies are incorporated in each specific protocol.

Section II
Application Quality of Service

In this section, application layer techniques are presented to facilitate QoS for multimedia streaming services. There are two facets to Application-layer QoS: server-side and client-side techniques. Server-side techniques cover the encoding configuration, adaptive encoding algorithms, error resilience, and preparation of the multimedia stream for delivery over the network. Client-side techniques include buffering, power saving, and decoding techniques such as error concealment and error recovery techniques. Through optimization of server-side and client-side encoding and decoding options, the application can compensate for and overcome limitations in the network and provide QoS for real-time multimedia streaming applications. This section presents novel server-side and client-side application layer solutions for voice and video streaming applications.

This chapter introduces the problems caused to voice over IP calls on 802.11 networks due to the link adaptation mechanism. It provides an overview of all the components participating in this study, with special emphasis on the multi-rate anomaly. The authors propose a codec selection mechanism as a solution to the multi-rate problem which, by changing the codec of some of the calls at the moment of the rate change, tries to maintain delay and packet loss values at acceptable levels and provide the desired QoS for the voice flows.

This chapter introduces network buffer control techniques as a means to provide QoS. This problem has been extensively studied in the context of wired networks; however, the proliferation of wireless networks and the introduction of multimedia applications has significantly changed the characteristics of the traffic mix that flows on the network. The objective of this chapter is to create a new methodology for automatically adapting the various buffer thresholds such that the network exhibits optimal or near optimal performance even as network conditions change.

When a mobile device has wireless LAN capability, multimedia content can be streamed over a wireless network to that device. However, a major disadvantage of all mobile devices is their limited battery lifetime. Multimedia streaming puts extra pressure on the battery, causing it to discharge faster. This chapter describes adaptive buffer power save mechanism (AB-PSM), a novel power saving wireless communication solution that enables an increase in battery lifetime during mobile multimedia streaming.

Chapter VIII

Jose Luis Jodra, University of the Basque Country, Spain
Fidel Liberal, University of the Basque Country, Spain
Begoña Blanco Jauregi, University of the Basque Country, Spain

This chapter introduces the principal characteristics of MANETs (mobile ad hoc networks) and shows how these may affect both QoS conditions and QoS management/provisioning systems, and therefore the capabilities of MANETs for properly providing multimedia services. The authors claim that QoS management cannot be handled only at the network layer or by applying some QoS-aware routing protocols. In fact, any end-to-end QoS provision architecture will demand QoS control mechanisms and information exchange among all the layers.

Section III
End-User Quality of Service

The ultimate goal of optimization techniques at the network and application layer is to ensure end-user perceived QoS. Often end-user perceived QoS measurement techniques are incorporated into network and application layer QoS solutions in order to provide greater insight into the users' QoS experience. It is only through accurate measurement of end-user perceived quality that QoS schemes can be developed and optimised. End-user QoS can be assessed using either objective or subjective methodologies. However, typically subjective testing results form the knowledge base and enhance the accuracy of objective metrics, so that objective metrics can then be incorporated into network and application layer QoS schemes. This section presents subjective results, targeted objective metrics and adaptive with integrated objective metrics. Moreover, since end-user perceived QoS is application and media dependent, targeted objective metrics are presented for voice, video and multimedia.

Chapter IX

Andrej Kos, University of Ljubljana, Slovenia
Mojca Volk, University of Ljubljana, Slovenia
Janez Bester, University of Ljubljana, Slovenia

Commonly understood as the next generation networks (NGN), a composite environment of proven telecommunications and Internet-oriented mechanisms has become generally recognized as the telecommunications environment of the future. However, the nature of the NGN environment presents several complex issues regarding quality assurance that have not existed in the legacy environments. In this chapter, a service-aware policy based approach to NGN quality assurance is presented, taking into account both perceptual quality of experience and technology-dependant quality of service issues.

Chapter X

Marcio Nieblas Zapater, Escola Politécnica da Universidade de São Paulo, Brazil
Graça Bressan, Escola Politécnica da Universidade de São Paulo, Brazil

This chapter discusses the quality assurance of multimedia services over IP networks from the end user standpoint and introduces the concept of quality of experience (QoE). The discussion of quality assurance includes aspects that range from the network and application layers to the end user perspective. This chapter presents quality requirements for video and TV services and performance measures that focuses on the quality perceived by the end user. This approach is broader than that oriented to quality of service (QoS), which focuses on the performance measures from the network perspective.

Chapter XI

Perceptual voice quality measurement can be defined as an objective quantification of an overall impression of the perceived stimulus. An alternative to laborious subjective testing is objective predictive modeling, which employs a perceptual model of the human auditory and cognitive system to predict the human response to a voice signal in terms of its quality. This chapter describes subjective and automated objective testing methods, and provides a test case scenario for measuring voice quality.

Chapter XII

This chapter describes an investigation into user experiences of accessing streamed multimedia content when that content is tailored according to perceptual, device, and location characteristics. We propose that multimedia transmission to mobile and wireless devices should be made based on pre-defined profiles, which contain a combination of static (perceptual, device type, CPU speed, and display specifications) and dynamic information (streamed content type location of the device/user, context of the device/user). Furthermore, we believe that using profiling technology, mobile service providers can effectively manage local network traffic and cut down their bandwidth costs considerably.

Chapter XIII

The concept of PQoS (end-to-end perceived QoS), although in general it deals with the user satisfaction with a specific delivered/requested service, is in practice significantly differentiated by the nature of each delivered service. This chapter reviews various existing PQoS assessment methods for video, VoIP, on-line games and web services that have been published in the literature. It then moves beyond the current PQoS assessment methods and presents novel techniques for predicting the PQoS of a multimedia service.

Section IV
Cross-Layered Solutions

Cross-layered solutions make use of QoS-enabling features at various layers of the wireless multimedia service chain, including aspects of the application layer and network layer. Although cross-layered solutions can greatly increase the degree of optimisation of the end-user QoS, cross-layered solutions incur higher orders of complexity since they have a larger number of axes of optimisation. This section presents a number of cross-layered solutions that include algorithms at the network, application and end-user layers.

Chapter XIV

Emerging wideband code division multiple access (WCDMA) data services will likely require resource allocation to ensure that throughput targets are met. Scheduling and access control can both be key components in this task. In this chapter, we introduce a two layer scheduler and connection access controller that attempts to balance efficiency with fairness. Through numerical analysis, the proposed joint scheduler and connection access controller is shown to achieve this.

Chapter XV

Nowadays there is an increasing need of broadband communication anytime, anywhere for users that expect to receive multimedia services with QoS. In such a scenario, the aim of this chapter is to present the satellite option to bridge the digital divide in those areas where terrestrial solutions are infeasible or too expensive. We provide a survey of the ETSI standardization framework for satellite networks, and then describe resource management schemes for both forward and return link. Finally a case study is provided for the integration of a DVB-S/DVB-RCS satellite system interconnected with a WiFi segment for local coverage.

Chapter XVI

An increasing demand for multimedia data delivery coupled with reliance on best-effort networks, such as the Internet, has spurred interest on effective quality of service (QoS) management for multimedia streams. Since today's multimedia applications are expected to run in physically heterogeneous environments composed of both wired and wireless components, we assess the efficiency of transport-layer solutions for multimedia traffic in heterogeneous networks. This chapter also describes the perceptual QoS assessment of voice and video streams.

Chapter XVII

Tarek Bejaoui, University of Carthage, Tunisia
Nidal Nasser, University of Guelph, Canada

This chapter introduces the cross layer design for resource allocation over multimedia wireless networks. Conventional layered packet scheduling and call admission control schemes are presented and a number of cross-layered protocols that are recently proposed are investigated. The chapter highlights the QoS improvement and the performance gain obtained while considering the interlayer dependencies concept for various real-time and non-real-time applications.

Chapter XVIII

Gürkan Gür, Satellite Networks Research Laboratory (SATLAB), Boğaziçi University, Turkey
Suzan Bayhan, Satellite Networks Research Laboratory (SATLAB), Boğaziçi University, Turkey
Fatih Alagöz, Satellite Networks Research Laboratory (SATLAB), Boğaziçi University, Turkey

This chapter introduces the QoS issues and support in transport protocols for wireless multimedia transmission. Some of the proposed modifications to the TCP and UDP protocols in order to improve multimedia transmission quality in wireless networks are also summarized. In particular, UDP Lite, TCP friendly rate control protocol (TFRC), and real-time transport protocol (RTP)--Real-time transport control protocol (RTCP) are discussed. Finally, we conclude with some discussions on the current trends in transport protocols for wireless multimedia transmission and on some of the ongoing research issues.

Foreword

In the past two decades, we have witnessed tremendous advances in wireless technologies, in particular those aimed at personal and mobile communications using cellular and ad hoc configurations. Cellular mobile communication, considered a luxury in the early 1990s, has become one of the everyday necessities for hundreds of millions of people all around the world in less than 20 years. Applications have changed dramatically from simple voice telephony to a wide range of multimedia applications. Exponential advancement in VLSI technology and liquid crystal display at the same time provided telecommunications engineers with an unbelievable electronic gadget in people's pockets. Ubiquitous communications has therefore become a reality and an all-in-one device is no longer a dream. Television broadcasting has found a new direction through the digital era, from large wall-mounted displays to the smaller and more private displays of mobile phones.

Wireless communications has had to develop at the same pace as its hardware and software counterparts in mobile devices so that they can be connected to content providers over the Internet and the telecommunications backbones. New wireless technologies have been added to the single cellular air interface mobile phones. These days we see smart phones with several air interfaces, all built on a tiny chip. They can connect simultaneously to wireless local area networks; second-generation networks such as GSM and GPRS; third generation networks like UMTS; and Bluetooth, in multiple frequency spectra. Those devices sometimes even come with their own satellite navigation system, which can locate the device and provide further information to users. With the inclusion of Windows-based operating systems on mobile devices, the user device is no longer just a phone but a handy personal computer with the usual myriad applications.

With all these advances, mobile multimedia is in our hands and the important issue is how the service quality can be maintained at a level similar to what we had in the past and which users have come to expect. The topic of mobile multimedia quality of service therefore remains the most important issue to be dealt with by telecommunications engineers.

In the past ten years, we have seen many works in the literature on the topic of quality of service in mobile environment. Dr. Nicola Cranley and Prof. Liam Murphy have put together an excellent edition of chapters, carefully chosen, reviewed, and edited in their book covering the technical solutions to this problem. They break down the problem nicely into three parts: network layer, application layer, and end-user layer, which can serve as the main elements in providing end-to-end quality of service to mobile multimedia applications. As quality of service provisioning requires good cooperation among communication layers and is not achievable by individual layer's attempts, the last part of the book addresses cross-layer solutions to the problem.

Nicola and Liam have selected a wide range of experts from all over the world to detail the problems and possible solutions in this harmonized edition. The book, while written by many authors, is read as a single piece of work with a focused and understandable theme right throughout the entire edition. I believe *Wireless Multimedia: Quality of Service and Solutions* will stand out as a long lasting reference book in the field of mobile multimedia for many years to come. I am confident that the tutorials and research works presented in this book will further seed new research topics in the field for a better and more efficient use of hardware and software advancements to achieve mobile multimedia communications into the future.

Abbas Jamalipour, Fellow IEEE
Sydney, Australia

Abbas Jamalipour *holds a PhD from Nagoya University, Japan. He is the author of the first book on wireless IP and two other books, and has co-authored six books and over 180 technical papers, all in the field of mobile communications networks. He is a fellow of IEEE (for contributions to next generation networks for traffic control), a fellow of Institute of Engineers Australia; an IEEE distinguished lecturer; the editor-in-chief of the IEEE Wireless Communications; and a technical editor of several scholarly journals including IEEE Communications, Wiley International Journal of Communication Systems, Journal of Communication Network, etc. His areas of research are wireless data communication networks, wireless IP networks, next generation mobile networks, traffic control, network security and management, and satellite systems. He was one of the first researchers to disseminate the fundamental concepts of the next generation mobile networks and broadband convergence networks as well as the integration of wireless LAN and cellular networks; some of which are being gradually deployed by industry and included in the ITU-T standards. Prof. Jamalipour has authored several invited papers and been a keynote speaker in many prestigious conferences. He served as the chair of the Satellite and Space Communications Technical Committee (2004-06); and currently is the vice chair of Communications Switching and Routing TC; and chair of Chapters Coordinating Committee, Asia-Pacific Board, all from the IEEE Communications Society. He is a voting member of the IEEE GITC and IEEE WCNC Steering Committee. He has been a vice chair of IEEE WCNC2003 to 2006, program chair of SPECTS2004, chair of symposiums at IEEE GLOBECOM2005 to 2007 and IEEE ICC2005 to 2008, among many conference leadership roles. He has received several prestigious awards, such as 2006 IEEE Distinguished Contribution to Satellite Communications Award, 2006 IEEE Communications Society Best Tutorial Paper Award, and 2005 Telstra Award for Excellence in Teaching.*

Preface

The rapid advances in wireless technologies have brought about a demand for high quality multimedia applications and services such as video telephony, multimedia streaming, video games, audio streaming (e.g., podcasting, IP HDTV broadcasting), and voice over IP. These advanced multimedia services bring a new set of challenges for providing quality of service (QoS) for delivering these services over wireless networks.

Wireless technologies are becoming increasingly sophisticated and efficient enabling support for higher bit rates. However, high and variable error rates and delays in wireless systems are still significant obstacles for providing QoS support for multimedia applications, especially when such variations occur on short timescales with respect to the applications being supported. Multimedia applications, in particular, impose significant resource requirements on bandwidth constrained wireless networks. Under these conditions it is difficult to provide any QoS guarantees. In particular the delay constraints associated with real-time multimedia pose the greatest challenge. Real-time multimedia is particularly sensitive to delay, as multimedia packets require a strict bounded end-to-end delay (i.e., every multimedia packet must arrive at the client device before its playout time with enough time to decode and display the contents of the packet). If the multimedia packet does not arrive on time, the packet is effectively lost and this affects the end-user perceived quality.

QoS is a crucial part of wireless multimedia design and delivery. Poor QoS results in poor service uptake by users which will result in the potential offered by recent advances in wireless and multimedia technologies not fully utilized. There are many aspects to QoS provisioning. These include network-layer QoS, application-layer QoS and ultimately end-user QoS. Network-layer QoS is concerned with the reliable and fast delivery of multimedia data over the wireless technologies. Many new and emerging wireless technologies such as IEEE 802.11e have been designed and developed with integrated QoS enabling controls. However these controls need to be configured and optimized in order to provide Application-layer QoS. Application-layer QoS on the other hand is concerned with the quality of the multimedia encoding, delivery, adaptation, decoding and play out on the client device. End-user QoS is concerned with the end-user experience in terms of audio and visual quality.

Typically these QoS layers are treated independently and in isolation yet the QoS schemes implemented at each of these layers have an effect on each other. It is essential for network managers, engineers and application developers to have an understanding of the QoS schemes that are in place at the network, application and end-user layer in order to be able to provide a fully end-to-end QoS solution. The ultimate goal of these QoS schemes is to maximize end-user QoS. With such diversity of QoS issues for multimedia and wireless technologies, there is an opportunity for novel QoS techniques to be developed at all layers.

OBJECTIVES AND STRUCTURE OF THIS BOOK

The objective of this book is to present state of the art research that tackles the challenges of providing QoS for multimedia services of wireless technologies. There are many aspects to QoS provisioning. We have identified three key layers for QoS provisioning. These include network-layer QoS, application-layer QoS, and ultimately end-user QoS. We have structured this book to represent the latest state of the art research in each of these three layers and have also included a section that covers Cross-layered solutions which touch two or more of these QoS layers.

This book is intended to:

- Identify each of these different layers of QoS and highlight the underlying QoS issues that arise and affect the performance of multimedia applications over wireless networks.
- Present the QoS issues that arise with different types of multimedia applications and services over different types of wireless technologies.
- Present novel solutions and state of the art research that has been done to address QoS issues for different wireless multimedia applications.

The first section of this book deals with the network-layer QoS. The primary characteristic of next generation wireless and mobile communication systems is heterogeneity, for example, wireless cellular networks, wireless local area networks, wireless personal area networks. It is crucial for inter-operability and seamless roaming among these different networks. Wireless technologies have a finite bandwidth capacity and are error prone media, it is important for wireless networks employ radio resource management schemes and optimized QoS handling to satisfy and meet the needs of users of multimedia services.

With the development of multimedia compression and coding technologies, more and more real-time applications, such as video and audio, and the proliferation of pervasive devices create a new demand for wireless multimedia communication systems. Multimedia services can be optimised and adapted to the challenges of wireless devices and service delivery. The second section deals with application-layer QoS. This encompasses quality-aware multimedia encoding, delivery, adaptation, decoding and buffering on the client device.

The third section of this book deals with end-user QoS. End-user QoS is concerned with the end-user experience in terms of audio and visual quality. Traditionally, a reactive approach has been adopted for engineering QoS for multimedia streaming applications. The main problem with this approach is that a poorly designed system cannot be tuned to perform as well as a system that was well designed from the outset. By integrating end-user QoS into the design of multimedia streaming systems, a more proactive approach can be adopted for the development and delivery of multimedia services over wireless networks.

Finally, the last section of this book presents cross-layer QoS solutions. Cross-layered solutions are extremely difficult since they rely on optimising QoS at two or more layers of the multimedia system, increasing the complexity of the optimisation; but also providing greater flexibility and potential to appropriately tune the network, application, and end-user layer to achieve the desired QoS.

Network QoS

With the recent advances in microelectronics, mobile devices now come equipped with a range of different wireless technologies on the one device. For example many PDA devices now come equipped with WLAN, 2.5G/3G cellular, Bluetooth, and Infrared. Often different wireless networks co-exist allowing users to switch between different wireless technologies. Switching between different wireless technologies is an important and difficult challenge since they have different physical layer, link layer and MAC layer schemes which result in a large variation in bandwidth and end-to-end delays making seamless transitions between different wireless technologies and continuous QoS difficult.

There are many performance-related issues associated with the delivery multimedia applications over wireless networks. Among the most significant are finite bandwidth resources, high channel error rates, contention between users for access to bandwidth, collisions, signal attenuation with distance, signal interference, etc. There are a number of techniques that have been developed and integrated into wireless technologies in order to facilitate the provisioning of network-layer QoS. The most well-known mechanisms are the integrated services (IntServ) and the differentiated services (DiffServ). Different wireless technologies such as general packet radio service (GPRS)/universal mobile telecommunications system (UMTS) and IEEE 802.11e have very different mechanisms for QoS support. Resource management schemes and admission control schemes can be used to prevent the network becoming overloaded such that poor network performance begins to negatively affect the multimedia applications.

In **Chapter I**, Skehill et al. describe how QoS can be provided in multi-access networks in particular UMTS and 802.11 networks. They demonstrate the new network management challenges and QoS provisioning problems posed by heterogeneous networks. To address this challenge they present their work on joint admission control strategies that can be employed to provide QoS. They demonstrate their system on an advanced test platform that replicates an integrated Release 4 UMTS network and standard IEEE 802.11b network. Their results show that by tightly coupling UMTS and WLAN technologies, the end user enjoys a higher level of quality of service.

In **Chapter II**, Staehle and Mäder describe high speed downlink packet access (HSDPA), and provide some insights into the radio resource management of integrated UMTS/HSDPA networks. The development of HSDPA was initiated as response to an increasing demand for high-speed mobile Internet access. HSDPA enables data rates of several megabits per seconds with packet latencies under 100ms. This chapter covers aspects of radio resource management specific to HSDPA such as channel-aware scheduling and radio resource sharing strategies and analyzes the impact of radio resource management on the achievable quality of service.

With pervasive and diverse wireless networks, users roam and move between heterogeneous networks.

In **Chapter III**, Nasser and Bejaoui describe the challenges for next generation of wireless networks to provide seamless mobility across heterogeneous wireless networks and QoS provisioning to support multimedia services. They describe how 4G wireless technologies offer great potential to meet the challenges posed by multimedia services and change the way mobile devices are used and can be adapted to provide a wide variety of new multimedia applications. One of the key challenges in heterogeneous network environments is the ability to control and manage handoffs. Nasser et al. describe their solution using artificial neural networks (ANNs) to identify the best existing wireless network that matches predefined user preferences set on a mobile device when performing a vertical handoff.

Multimedia applications are bandwidth hungry and resource demanding services. Providing multimedia services over bandwidth constrained wireless networks is challenging. In **Chapter IV**, Li et al. provide a rich and comprehensive overview of the architectures, algorithms, and protocols that are employed as radio resource management in IEEE 802.11 based wireless networks, mobile ad hoc networks, and wireless mesh networks. Li and Riggio demonstrate that with a successful resource management strategy, bandwidth usage can be minimized while providing maximized QoS and end-user QoS for multimedia applications.

Application QoS

There are several aspects to application-layer QoS that deal with all stages of the applications lifecycle including encoding, delivery, adaptation, decoding, error correction, and error concealment. Before multimedia can be streamed over the network, the multimedia content is encoded and prepared for transmission. The choice of the right encoding settings is crucial for the performance of the delivery of the multimedia stream over the network. For audio, voice, and video content, there are a number of different encoding schemes and encoding configuration parameters that can be used to optimally encode the multimedia content, which has an effect on the network-layer QoS requirements of the multimedia stream. When the content is ready to be delivered over the network, the encoded multimedia data is packetized with an optimal number of samples contained in each packet.

However when the network is overloaded and congested, its ability to reliably deliver the multimedia packets within the strict delay constraints is reduced. Such delays can result in packets being lost at the client device since they arrived too late to meet the network-layer QoS delay requirements. Packets can also be lost due to errors over the wireless channel. The loss of multimedia data in the network has a significant impact on the end-user perceived QoS. To overcome this, many multimedia streaming systems have adaptation capabilities whereby the offered multimedia content is adapted in a seamless and imperceptible manner in order to minimize the unwanted negative effects of poor network conditions on the multimedia stream. On the client device, the multimedia player application has a number of techniques to recover any errors or losses in the received stream. Error correction and error concealment algorithms interpolate the missing multimedia data from the received data in order and mask these errors to improve the end-user perceived quality in spite of these losses.

With the proliferation of WLAN technology, and the explosive growth of VoIP services, **Chapter V** by Sfairopoulou et al. describes their work for delivering high quality VoIP services over 802.11 networks. They describe how voice codecs can be optimized and adapted to the network conditions in order to provide the best QoS, for example, through the use of multi-rate voice codecs and link adaptation. They present a novel solution to the multi-rate and codec selection mechanism, which maintains the end-to-end delay and packet loss values within acceptable levels and provide the desired QoS for the voice flows.

Chapter VI by Markou and Panayiotou describes how network buffer control techniques can be used as a means to provide QoS. Although this solution has been applied to wired networks, with the explosive growth of wireless access technologies and the challenges posed by multimedia applications, buffer control schemes have had to significantly adapt to the characteristics wireless networks. This chapter presents a new methodology for automatically adapting the various buffer thresholds such that the network exhibits optimal or near optimal performance even as network conditions change making it ideal for wireless multimedia service delivery.

With the large number of wireless devices and their growing capabilities, power consumption and battery lifetimes are still significant obstacles in the continuous seamless play out of multimedia services on such devices. In **Chapter VII**, Muntean and Adams consider the power consumption problems presented by WLAN enabled mobile devices. Decoding and playout of multimedia services adds to the processing overhead causing it to discharge faster. In this chapter, Adams and Muntean describe an adaptive buffer power save mechanism (AB-PSM) that enables an increase in battery lifetime during mobile multimedia streaming which in turn increases the end-user QoS.

In **Chapter VIII**, Jodra et al. describe the new application scenarios for mobile ad hoc networks, including multimedia services and/or online games. They discuss how the demand for such wireless connectivity requires certain levels of quality of service. For this reason, a large effort has been carried out by both the industry and research community toward QoS provisioning in MANETs. However, when analyzing QoS aspects in MANETs, the first thing to notice is that MANETs' special characteristics prevent the use of traditional QoS mechanisms in these environments. These particularities are related not only to the wireless transmission medium itself (which is shared with other kinds of wireless networks) but also to the uncertainty derived from the mobility of the nodes and subsequent network topology variations.

Hence, major challenges to be faced while defining QoS mechanisms for MANETs include the wireless channel, multihop nature of communications, node mobility, lack of centralized control, dynamic network topology and limited device resources. These challenges result into a series of constraints to be added to QoS traditional ones (namely bandwidth, delay or jitter), such as battery power, CPU usage and stability of the routes. Most of these constraints demand different QoS mechanisms in different protocol layers, ranging from physical layer and MAC contention mechanisms to application level. However, since MANETs particularities are related to network topologies most of the efforts analyzed aimed at developing routing strategies focused on dealing with dynamic topology problems.

End-User QoS

End-user QoS is the primary goal of application-layer QoS schemes and a somewhat secondary goal of network-layer QoS schemes. Measuring end-user QoS is an extremely complicated task which draws from many knowledge domains such as psychology, cognitive science and signal analysis. There are two key methods for assessing end-user QoS; the first is through subjective assessment and testing, while the second is through the use of objective metrics. Different objective metrics exist for audio, video and voice quality analysis. The main goal of objective metrics is to measure the perceived quality of a given audio or visual signal. There are many factors that affect how users perceive quality, such as audio loudness, lip synchronization, video content, viewing distance, display size, resolution, brightness, contrast, sharpness/fidelity, and color. However, it is only through the accurate measurement of end-user QoS that QoS schemes can be developed and optimized.

In **Chapter IX**, Kos et al. present a service-aware policy based approach to next generation networks (NGN) quality assurance, considering both perceptual quality of experience and technology-dependent quality of service issues. The nature of the NGN environment presents several complex issues regarding quality assurance not faced in legacy environments, such as the multi-network, multi-vendor, and multi-operator IP-based telecommunications environment, distributed intelligence, third-party provisioning, and fixed-wireless access. The existence of multiple separately operated and interconnected domains requires intelligent interconnection mechanisms. On the other hand, real-time personalized interactive multimedia NGN services require end-to-end quality assurance regardless of the traversed domains. Meeting these two requirements is a complex task and involves careful quality-related planning in each separate domain and coordination of these on a service-aware end-to-end basis.

In **Chapter X**, Zapater and Bressan discuss the quality assurance of multimedia services over IP networks from the end user standpoint, and describe the concept of quality of experience (QoE). The focus is on video services that can be considered a significant evolution of services providers' portfolio. Traditional quality management approaches adopted by service providers are mostly focused on the network perspective rather than the user perspective. The authors present quality requirements for video and TV services, and performance measures that focus on the quality perceived by the end user. This QoE approach is broader than one based on quality of service (QoS), since it takes into account how well a service meets customer goals and expectations rather than focusing only on network performance.

Chapter XI by Picovici and Nelson describes the latest work for measuring perceptual voice quality and their application to wireless networks. They provide a review of various subjective testing methodologies and objective voice quality measures describing the target application of this metric and the performance limitations. They present the three main categories of objective voice quality measures, signal-based models, network-based (planning) models and both intrusive and single-ended monitoring based models. They have a devised a technique based on call history that can be used to predict end-user QoS for VoIP calls.

In **Chapter XII**, Serif and Ghinea investigate user experiences of accessing streamed multimedia content. Through the creation of pre-defined QoS transmission profiles, the end-user experience is enhanced. These pre-defined profiles have built-in perceptual information and are based on both static (such as device type, CPU speed, and display specifications) and dynamic parameters (such as streamed content type location of the device/user, context of the device/user). From their work, end-user perceived QoS could be maintained while requiring fewer network resources.

Chapter XIII by Koumaras et al. treats perceptual QoS (PQoS) assessment methods for multimedia applications and services. In this chapter, they describe subjective quality assessment methodologies and review the latest PQoS assessment models for multimedia services. Through their work, they present novel PQoS prediction models for Web, video, VoIP, and online gaming services. Their PQoS prediction model can be used to for the development and monitoring of PQoS-aware multimedia devices and networks for live multimedia services.

Cross-Layered Solutions

Emerging wideband code division multiple access (WCDMA) data services will probably require resource allocation to ensure that throughput targets are met, and may employ scheduling and access control to achieve this. In **Chapter XIV**, Zhang and Jordan introduce a two-layer scheduler and connection access controller that attempts to balance efficiency with fairness. Their scheduler takes advantage of variations in the wireless channel, and they propose an algorithm that offers targeted throughput for interactive nomadic data streams, by integrating connection access control and resource allocation per connection request with rate scheduling on a per frame basis adaptive to slow fading. Upon the request of a data stream connection, a target throughput is negotiated between the user and the network/base station. The network attempts to achieve the throughput targets over the duration of each individual connection by maximizing a system objective based on users' satisfaction as represented by a utility function.

There is an increasing need for broadband communications anytime, anywhere for users that expect to receive multimedia services with support of quality of service. In **Chapter XV**, Chini et al. describe the satellite option to bridge the digital divide in those areas where terrestrial solutions are infeasible or too expensive. They provide a survey of the ETSI standardization framework for satellite networks, and describe resource management schemes for both the forward and return link. Finally they present a case study on the integration of a DVB-S/DVB-RCS satellite system interconnected with a WiFi segment for local coverage.

Hybrid schemes make use the QoS-enabling features at various layers of the wireless multimedia service chain and optimise the QoS of the service using a cross-layer approach. **Chapter XVI** by Papadimitriou and Tsaoussidis presents a network and end-user QoS cross-layer approach for multimedia streaming services. In this chapter, they assess the efficiency of transport-layer solutions for multimedia traffic in heterogeneous networks. They compare the multimedia application requirements against the QoS features provided by the underlying network and present methods to measure the perceptual QoS assessment for the voice and video streams.

In **Chapter XVII**, Bejaoui and Nasser provide a cross layer design for resource allocation over multimedia wireless networks. In this chapter they show how inter-layer dependencies can bring QoS improvements and the performance gains for real-time and non-real-time applications. This chapter concentrates on the packet scheduling and admission control schemes proposed for QoS provisioning for multimedia services over next generation wireless networks. In particular this chapter focuses on the radio channel conditions and explore the novel approaches based on cross-layered radio resource management protocol.

The reliable transmission of multimedia services over bandwidth constrained error prone wireless networks is critical. In Chapter **XVIII**, Gur et al. describe the fundamental issues at the transport layer affecting the provision of QoS for wireless multimedia applications. They describe how the traditional transport layer protocols must be adapted to meet the challenges of delivering multimedia applications over best-effort wireless networks. They describe the latest trends and cross-layer solutions that rely on interaction between the different protocol layers. They show that cross layer protocol solution presents many challenges since such cross-layer schemes increase the inter-layer dependencies calling for a more complex protocol design, and present stability issues.

Summary

QoS is an important factor in the design and development of wireless multimedia applications and services. Different multimedia applications have very diverse QoS requirements in terms of bit rates, delay constraints, and loss tolerances. In a wireless environment, users are mobile and move between wireless technologies where the available resources are scarce and dynamically change over time. To complicate matters further, there is dramatic heterogeneity among end user devices in terms of latency, video visual quality, processing capabilities, power, and bandwidth. Providing QoS with both network and device heterogeneity to achieve efficiency in network bandwidth is a significant challenge. In this book we shall look at the major issues and challenges surrounding the provision of QoS for multimedia applications over wireless networks.

Nikki Cranley and Liam Murphy, editors
Dublin, January 2008

Section I
Network Quality of Service

In this section Network Layer QoS solutions are presented. Critical factors affecting QoS for real-time multimedia streaming applications include reliability, efficient delivery, and end-to-end latencies. The tremendous growth and development of wireless networking technology has brought about fresh challenges in the provision of QoS for such real-time multimedia applications. This section focuses on key wireless networking technologies and presents novel solutions that have been designed to address these challenges. State of the art wireless technologies presented in this section include UMTS, HSDPA-Enhanced UMTS, 4G, and WLAN. Each of these wireless networking technologies has differing mechanisms for QoS support. Resource management schemes and admission control schemes can be used to prevent the network becoming overloaded such that poor network performance begins to negatively affect multimedia applications.

Chapter I
Evaluating QoS in a Multi-Access Wireless Network

Ronan Skehill
University of Limerick, Ireland

Michael Barry
University of Limerick, Ireland

William Kent
University of Limerick, Ireland

Sean McGrath
University of Limerick, Ireland

Dorel Picovici
University of Limerick, Ireland

ABSTRACT

This chapter introduces quality of service in multi-access wireless networks. Specifically it demonstrates how QoS is implemented in IEEE 802.11 and UMTS. The chapter explains how these complementary technologies, when coupled together, provide a network that is greater than its individual parts. Combining these networks brings new network management challenges. To this end, the impact of joint admission control strategies on quality of service is evaluated. The evaluation is performed on an advanced test platform that replicates an integrated Release 4 UMTS network and standard IEEE 802.11b network. The results show that when UMTS and WLAN are tightly coupled, the end user enjoys a higher level of quality of service.

INTRODUCTION

Mobile network configurations are becoming increasingly complex. Wireless communication networks are migrating from a set of insular competitive technologies toward a heterogeneous or converged wireless access topology comprising a diverse range of radio interfaces. Cells from different radio technologies overlap in the same area resulting in co-existing layers of access technology. In this complicated environment, a multi-mode mobile can connect to different cells and unless there is knowledge about each cell it is difficult to optimise network performance and to manage resources efficiently.

Multi access or heterogeneous networks provide additional capacity for data traffic with the potential for load balancing of other services when the network becomes congested. This can be achieved through targeted admission of certain classes of traffic (e.g., background/interactive) when the session starts, or by forcing the handover of selected traffic.

There has been great interest recently in the convergence of distributed, mobile networks and more localised wireless access technologies. As illustrated in Figure 1, universal mobile telecommunications system (UMTS) and IEEE 802.11 Wireless LAN (WLAN) represent two wireless technologies that show great promise in terms of interoperability and integration. UMTS was built from the ground up to support high levels of quality of service (QoS) for packet-based services in addition to providing voice in a macro-cellular environment. IEEE 802.11 WLAN is a contention based wireless access technology designed to provide high data rates with a micro-cellular

footprint. The interworking approach taken in the ARES testbed embeds WLAN into the UMTS radio access network (RAN). Since foundation level QoS was not part of the initial design of WLAN, it can be viewed as a complementary source of bandwidth for non-realtime critical services such as Web and e-mail in a UMTS system. Diverting background/interactive traffic to WLAN allows UMTS to support a higher number of voice and video calls, reducing call blocking rates.

It is crucial for the pooled radio resources to be managed effectively to assure seamless interworking. Intrinsic radio resource management (RRM) relates to the management of a network's local radio resources whereas joint radio resource management (JRRM) is concerned with the management of the environment where the mobile is capable of being connected to different cells. The mobile is connected to the cell where there are the most resources or where the technology best suits the connection type. Joint radio resource management strategies identify common compo-

Figure 1. Multiple wireless technologies converged can provide improved QoS to the end user

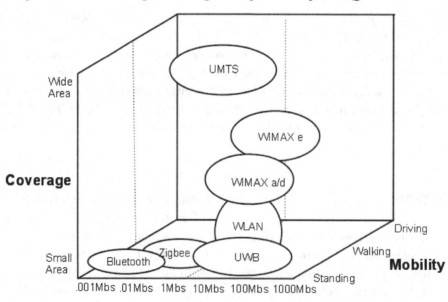

nents, algorithms and parameters from intrinsic RRM to orchestrate cross-system radio resources in a managed, coordinated manner. JRRM aims to support intelligent interworking between different access technologies by balancing load across several radio access technologies (RATs), implementing admission control strategies, joint scheduling and congestion control and essentially exploiting increased system capacity, and thus improving quality of service.

Deploying RRM strategies to marshal radio resources in multi-system networks is only part of the framework to capitalise on increased bandwidth sources. Key to the success of converged wireless networks is their ability to maintain QoS across all user sessions. In the most colloquial sense, QoS is measured by the satisfaction of the end user and how they perceive the network to be operating (i.e., can a user's call be connected, do user sessions terminate prematurely?). In a more technical sense QoS is the ability to maintain a consistent level of bandwidth, amply sufficient to provide an uninterrupted and stable service to the end user. In addition to the generation of metrics to measure QoS (e.g., call blocking rates, bit error rate, etc.) one of the mandates of the heterogeneous testbed is to provide a perceptible user experience with regard to network performance. This is achieved by using a real user terminal that experiences a populated UMTS-WLAN system. The 'reference user' terminal enables real time feedback on the QoS performance of user applications such as video conferencing, Web browsing, e-mail, and network gaming, simply by providing an interactive experience for a real end user.

In this chapter, the benefits of coupling different radio technologies are presented. Preceding the benefits is a review of different coupling strategies namely: loose, tight and very tight (ETSI BRAN TR 101 957, 2001). Following the coupling strategies review, details on how quality of service is implemented in UMTS and WLAN networks is presented. The QoS section illustrates how the different radio characteristics can be used to

complement each other in a multi-system environment. A very tightly coupled architecture is used to create the UMTS-WLAN test platform, named ARES, to evaluate the QoS benefits. Furthermore, a description of ARES and how it is used to evaluate interactive traffic over UMTS and WLAN is outlined. The results section quantifies the benefits of admitting interactive users to WLAN.

Coupling Strategies for UMTS and WLAN

Although a highly competitive industry, network operators now face the same common denominator; meeting the bandwidth requirements of global user base and providing services that match fixed line systems and satisfy or indeed exceed end user expectation. For wireless access providers then, sources of bandwidth spanning multiple technologies need to be consolidated into a system comprising multiple points of wireless access (Agusti, 2006; Niebert et al., 2004; Sachs, Wiemann, Lundsjo, & Magnusson, 2004). Often referred to as the beyond 3G vision (Romero, Sallent, Agusti, & Diaz-Guerra, 2005), this represents a shift from competition to cooperation, where wireless access systems work together to service end user needs.

A logical option then for the next wave of communications networks is the cooperative coupling of legacy systems and next generation networks, providing wireless access on top of an underlying Internet protocol (IP) infrastructure. At the heart of this development will be inter-working strategies between existing wireless networks to unlock greater pools of bandwidth and realise a heterogeneous network landscape. In this scenario wireless connectivity is provided across multiple RATs. UMTS and WLAN represent two wireless technologies that are complementary in terms of inter-operability. UMTS operates in a macro cellular environment to support a high level of QoS services across a geographically large area. WLAN provides Internet access in smaller cells that can be embedded as pockets of high-speed access with UMTS cells thus providing a complementary source of bandwidth to UMTS users.

A diversity of solutions has been put forward as to how and at what level different systems are integrated. Bodies such as the 3GPP have studied the integration of WLAN into their system, to allow WLAN users access to services within the UMTS network. Others have developed working implementations of heterogeneous systems; and have demonstrated the feasibility of handover between WLAN and cdma2000 and WLAN and general packet radio service (GPRS). Key to which network integration strategy should occur is whether the systems can be integrated within the current standards or whether modifications will be necessary.

Loose Coupling

Loose coupling (Buddhikot et al., 2003; Jaseemuddin, 2003) is the first step towards UMTS-WLAN integration. As shown in Figure 2, loosely coupled mobile networks do not have a connection at the RAN layer. Instead, the networks are connected via the core network. In these scenarios, WLAN and cellular networks are two separate access networks. The WLAN access network is attached to the Internet backbone, and the cellular network into the cellular core network.

A new component required for this coupling architecture is a WLAN gateway or a gateway GPRS serving node (GGSN) emulator. This particular option allows ownership of the WLAN network to be separate from the UMTS network. Under this type of network deployment the WLAN element has access to the authorisation, authentication

Figure 2. Loose coupling

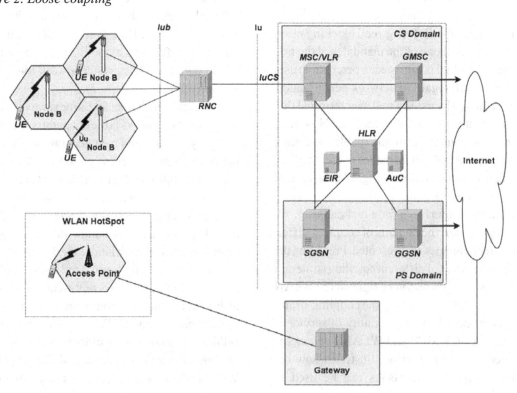

and billing mechanisms of the UMTS network (Ahmavaara, Haverinen, & Pichna, 2003). This enables the potential for common billing (3GPP TR 22.934, 2002). The WLAN network may have access to the packet switched or even the circuit switched services offered by the UMTS core network. The main benefit of this network architecture is the reuse of core network elements--one core network and two radio networks. The radio networks are, however, quite separate and distinct. Handovers from one RAT to another can be very costly in terms of signalling. Mobility may be provided by layer 3 mechanisms such as Mobile-IP (Tsao & Lin, 2002). As such, this type of network deployment does not lend itself towards the development of transparent seamless connections across multiple access technologies.

Tight Coupling

The rationale behind the tightly coupled architecture is to make the 802.11 network appear as another 3G access network, as shown in Figure 3.

Tight coupling integrates the new radio network subsystem (RNS) at the serving GPRS support node, reusing the Iu interface. By coupling at the SGSN, WLAN resources are managed separately from UMTS resources. As in the loosely coupled architecture the different networks share the same authentication, signalling, transport and billing infrastructures, independent of the physical layer protocols. This coupling architecture allows for vertical handovers, which allow the application services to transfer connections between the different networks and access technologies. However, vertical handovers can be challenging to end-to-end transport protocols, as packets often get lost, delayed or reordered during a handover. Achieving seamless handover then is a difficult task. Furthermore, path characteristics such as bandwidth, latency and the buffer size can change instantly (Korhonen & Gurtov, 2004).

Very Tight Coupling

Very tight coupling (Cristache, David, & Hildebrand, 2003) involves establishing the WLAN

Figure 3. Tight coupling

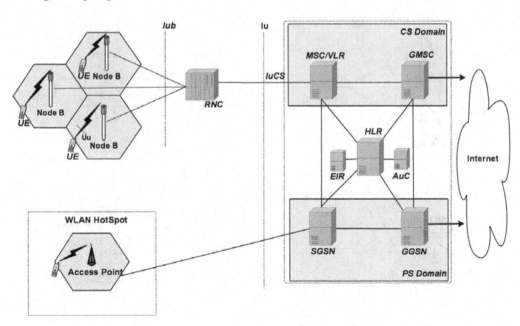

network as a second RNS, integrated at the radio network controller (RNC) as shown in Figure 4. The access point connects to the RNC through the Iub interface, presenting itself as a Node B. This mimics, quite closely, a hierarchical cellular layout. In this case, however, the micro cell RAT is of a different type to the macro cell. The benefit of this is that resource control for WLAN is co-located with the resource control for UMTS. In this way, it is possible to reuse the RRM located in the UTRAN and manage the WLAN HotSpot as a cell, or as part of a cell. The changes required in signalling are confined to the UTRAN. From a paging point of view the same RNC can retain control over locating the device in whatever RAT it is located. The underlying RAT is transparent to the core network (CN). Very tight coupling allows for the creation of joint radio resource management as information about the usage of both networks is available locally.

Very tightly coupled networks embed micro-cell RATs in macro-cells. In terms of UMTS and WLAN a true heterogeneous architecture

can be realised using tight coupling. Using tight coupling resource control for both systems can be co-located enabling WLAN HotSpots to be managed as a cell or part of a cell in the UMTS system. This is the motivation behind adopting a very tight coupling approach in the ARES integrated testbed. Using very tight coupling enables the collection of information relating to air interface conditions and network capacity, providing a logical framework for JRRM and the best approach to maintaining awareness of RRM across multiple systems. The tight coupling framework is realised in the testbed by embedding a WLAN access point in the RAN.

Trade-Off with Coupling Strategies

Inevitably there is a trade-off with each of the coupling strategies when a network operator decides to integrate or couple networks together. There are several important factors, which must be considered. Table 1 illustrates some of the key trade-offs.

Figure 4. Very tight coupling

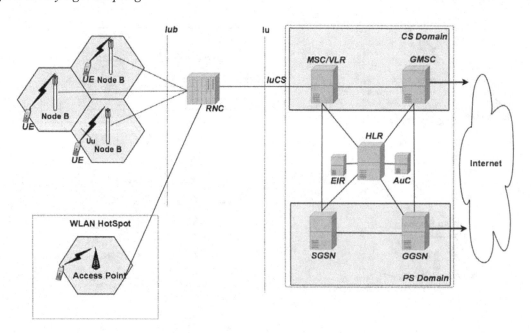

In essence, with loose coupling there is no direct link between these two networks and they are completely disjoint in operation (both data and signalling paths). There is no change in the existing architectures for cellular and WLAN networks. The only interaction between the cellular and WLAN networks is at the billing system. With tight coupling there is a direct link between cellular and WLAN networks. The WLAN network appears to be one of the access networks from the cellular core network viewpoint. A WLAN gateway is required in the WLAN network to hide the WLAN functionality from the cellular core network. With very tight coupling there is a direct link between cellular and WLAN networks. The WLAN access point becomes one of the Node B from the cellular radio network controller viewpoint. In this case, enhancements

of cellular RNC are required such that the RNC manages the radio resource for both cellular Node Bs and WLAN access points. In terms of quality of service, tight and very tight coupling provide a means of reusing cellular QoS techniques.

QUALITY OF SERVICE IN MULTI-ACCESS NETWORKS

The fundamental purpose of all communication networks is to provide a connection between end users. As networks have evolved, a multitude of services have been offered to users in the form of SMS, video conferencing, e-mail and Internet browsing. The success or failure of that network is dependent on how the user perceives performance of the service on offer. For a user to be satisfied

Table 1. Coupling trade-offs

	Loose coupling	Tight coupling
Security	Medium	High (reuse cellular security architecture)
Impact on existing cellular network architecture	None	High
Handoff speed	Slower	Faster
Session persistence	Yes	Yes
Service persistence (VOIP)	Possible	Yes
WLAN gateway required	Yes	Yes
WLAN traffic injected into cellular core network	No	Yes
QOS provisioning	Over-provisioning	Reuse cellular QOS architecture
Provisioning of the same administrative domain for WLAN and cellular	No	Possible
Mobile-initiated handoff or network initiated handoff	Mobile-initiated handoff is preferred	Both mechanisms are feasible
Standards development time	Short	Long

with a network, a number of criteria must be met. The user should be able to connect easily, the call or service should last for the intended duration without prematurely ending and with respect to interactive data services (Web browsing), speed is a factor. QoS then is a measure of the perceived quality of the service being used and an indication of user satisfaction. Rather than being a single measure of a user's satisfaction, QoS is the collective term for the quantifying of network performance from an end user point of view, and for the measures taken to ensure reliable services.

To ensure that networks are performing at the desired level, one or more measurements of desired performance and priorities of a communications system are considered as part of QoS. QoS measures may include service availability, maximum bit error rate (BER), minimum committed bit rate (CBR) and other measurements that are used to ensure quality communications service.

In heterogeneous environments (i.e., UMTS-WLAN), the ability to offer end-to-end QoS while making the different RANs interoperate with each other is an important issue. QoS management mechanisms deal with such aspects. These mechanisms include call admission control (CAC), resource reservation, policing etc. The correspondence between the QoS offered by each sub-system of the end-to-end path is also required for a seamless service. In heterogeneous networks, end-to-end path may include different RAN environments (including multi-operator scenarios) as well as the Internet environment. Services must be apportioned to RATs that best support the service and can deliver on QoS guarantees to the end user. By examining the QoS models of each constituent RAT in a multi access network, a mapping of services to technology can be defined that maintains the QoS integrity of that service.

UMTS was built from the ground up to provide a high level of QoS for the services it supports. This was done firstly by classifying the services on

offer in terms of performance related criteria, and then ensuring that the network performance was guaranteed on a per service basis. UMTS provides QoS service classifications that clearly define how each service is characterised in terms of QoS constraints and how bandwidth is provisioned to cater for that service. Time critical services such as voice and video conferencing can be delivered successfully over dedicated radio channels.

By contrast, IEEE 802.11 Wireless LAN was not designed to support a high level of QoS. IEEE 802.11 WLAN was designed as a bridging technology to provide a wireless point of connection, over a short range, to a wired backbone. The design ethos did not encompass mechanisms to provide reliable delivery of realtime services such as Voice over IP (VoIP), video conferencing or multimedia streaming. The approach to delivering packets is known as best effort i.e. no guarantees of successful packet delivery. This makes WLAN suited to cater for less time critical services such as e-mail or Internet browsing, where QoS bounds are more relaxed than those of voice or video.

UMTS Supported Services

From the outset, UMTS was designed with a diverse service environment in mind, to realise a true mobile multimedia platform. Emphasis is placed on the delivery of these services with the specification of service classes. UMTS defines four service classes:

- Conversational
- Streaming
- Interactive
- Background

The classes group services in terms of defined performance parameters such as delay and jitter, as illustrated in Table 2 (3GPP TS 23.107, 2003). The requirements of the QoS classes are met by negotiating appropriate QoS attribute values for each established or modified UMTS bearer.

Table 2. UMTS traffic classes

Traffic Class	Fundamental Characteristics	Examples of Service	Data Rates	Delay	Loss (FER)
Conversational	Preserve time variation between information entities of the stream. Conversational Pattern (stringent and low delay).	Voice Video telephony Video Games	4 -25 Kbps 32 -384 Kbps N/A	< 150 ms < 150 ms < 250 ms	< 3 % < 1 % Zero
Streaming	Preserve time variation between information entities of the stream.	Streaming Audio Streaming Video	32 -128 Kbps 32 -128 Kbps	< 10 sec < 10 sec	< 1 % < 1 %
Interactive	Request/Response pattern. Preserve payload content.	Web Browsing	4 -16 Kbps	< 4 sec	< 3 %
Background	Destination is not expecting the data within a certain time. Preserve payload.	Download of e-mails	4 -16 Kbps	Can tolerate very high delay time	Zero

The conversational class specifies realtime traffic such as voice or voice/video conferencing. These services are bi-directional and traffic is symmetric on this link. These services have very strict timing constraints in order to preserve the integrity of the traffic, both in terms of delay and packet delivery. Thus this class has the highest priority value associated with it.

The streaming class represents video/audio streaming services. Streaming information is highly asymmetric traffic, as data is continuous in one direction. Streaming services are high priority services in terms of packet loss and preserving data integrity, however data is buffered so realtime delivery is not critical.

Interactive class type refers to events such as Web browsing, database queries and FTP (i.e., information being requested by the user from a remote host). Interactive traffic is asymmetric in nature, because data is transferred mainly in one direction. Interactive traffic is not subject to strict timing requirements, but traffic is affected by round-trip delay and response time constraints.

As with other classes, transmission errors are not tolerated, however due to the more relaxed delay restrictions, the focus can be placed on packet delivery.

Background traffic is generated by e-mail and other applications without time constraints. The information is downloaded and assembled in the background without high priority, however maintaining the integrity of the data is important.

UMTS QoS Architecture

As stated in the beginning of this section, the UMTS network mainly acts as an infrastructure providing access, bandwidth, and quality for end users and the services they use. From the moment a service begins, UMTS aims to provide end-to-end QoS for that service. The service determines the level of QoS needed, and this QoS must be met throughout every stage of the connection, over the air and through wired backbones. This section introduces the QoS architecture employed by UMTS to provide bounded QoS to services.

UMTS Bearer Service

End-to-end services are carried over the UMTS network infrastructure using bearers. These bearers represent a mechanism that ensures QoS between two defined points. The end-to-end service requirements are controlled in UMTS using three bearer services: the local bearer service, the UMTS bearer service and the external bearer service, as illustrated in Figure 5 (ETSI, 2001). These bearer services ensure QoS constraints are met through every part of the network, and are sub-divided according to specific parts of the UMTS system, shown in the Figure 5. Each network subsystem contributes to bearer services and delivery of QoS.

The local bearer service contains the mechanisms to control bearers between the user equipment (UE) which consists of the terminal equipment (TE) and the Mobile Termination (MT). The UMTS bearer service governs the QoS requirements over the UMTS network comprising the UTRAN and Core network (CN). Since the UMTS network can communicate with "external" networks, the QoS requirements for mobiles connecting to other networks are handled by the external bearer service.

Within the UMTS system the QoS handling is different in the UTRAN and the CN. The UTRAN provides a transparent "fixed bearer" over the air to the CN using the radio access bearer service. The CN then in turn uses its CN bearer service to continue the QoS provisioning. This design stays true to the independence of access technology and core network functionality that is part of the UMTS modular design. The layered architecture indicates that each bearer service is enabled using the services provided by the bearer below, and in this way UMTS forms a connection through itself fulfilling the QoS requirements as dictated by the originating service request.

Essential to the establishment of end-to-end QoS, the UTRAN must provide, create, and maintain the radio access bearers (RABs) for the transfer of data between the UE and core network. A radio access bearer is defined for each data flow based on a PDP (packet data protocol) context established between the UE and the SGSN. The radio access bearer consists of two parts--the radio bearer (between the UE and UTRAN) and

Figure 5. UMTS QoS architecture

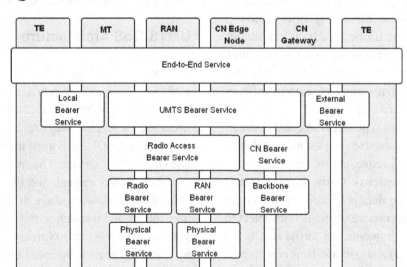

the Iu bearer (between the UTRAN and Core Network).

Radio bearers generally refer only to the transmission of user data in CS or PS mode between UE and RNC. Signalling information is carried on signalling radio bearers in the control plane. Generally, a RAB can include a combination of RBs and SRBs and data flows. The parameters of the radio bearer are based on the individual QoS classes, and can be negotiated and renegotiated depending on what QoS guarantees can be met. The UMTS architecture provides multiple possibilities for the creation of radio bearers with varying characteristics. These characteristics include a number of attributes such as traffic class, maximum bit rate, guaranteed bit rate, SDU (service data unit) error ratio, residual BER (bit error rate), transfer delay etc. Multiple radio bearers can be created over one radio connection. The allocation of resources to establish radio bearers is controlled by radio resource management (RRM) algorithms. RRM controls the actual bit rate assigned to the radio bearer, which could be lower than the specified maximum value.

PDP Contexts

In the packet switched domain, connections are known as sessions. Throughout the duration of these sessions, the packet data protocol (PDP) is responsible for packet transfer. When the UE attaches itself to the network, a tunnel is established between the terminal and the GGSN. This tunnel is known as a PDP context (3GPP TS 23.060, 2006). In order to send and receive packets, a PDP Context must be activated. The TE endpoint of this tunnel moves with the terminal and new tunnels (Secondary PDP contexts) may be dynamically activated. All the packet session attributes are handled in the PDP context; this defines the way that QoS is handled for each bearer.

As well as QoS information, a PDP context contains the access point names of the external PDP network that the user/service is trying to access as well as the PDP address of the mobile itself. The activation of a PDP context identifies the UE with the corresponding GGSN. A PDP context is set up for each packet switched service with a certain QoS class, for example video streaming and background traffic will have individual PDP contexts. If the user is accessing information in many different external networks, the mobile will have to handle as many PDP contexts.

WLAN QoS

Pioneering the development of QoS in IP networks are the Internet engineering task force (IETF). The IETF has established working groups to explore QoS frameworks for IP networks based on two approaches: resource reservation and service differentiation. The principal behind resource reservation is the requesting of IP bandwidth in advance of initiating a service. In this way, services can block book bandwidth to ensure that packets are delivered reliably. This is the premise behind the IETF IntServ model. The IntServ architecture is based on per-flow resource reservation (Wang, 2001) and uses the resource ReSerVation protocol (RSVP) (Braden, Zhang, Berson, & Jamin, 1997; Wroclawski, 1997) to reserve resources (such as bandwidth on an interface) in every intermediate router along an applications data path during session set-up.

On the other hand, a second model to come from the IETF, DiffServ (Dixit, Guo, & Antoniou, 2001), centres on the differentiation between services running on the Internet, in order to prioritise the importance of packets in the network. A barebones IP network will treat all packets the same, regardless of the service they originated from. DiffServ aims to separate the needs of Internet services based on their bandwidth requirements, quantifying this need through packet prioritisation.

Since WLAN is effectively a wireless extension to IP networks, it supports many of the services that run over IP systems and is only limited by the capabilities of the user terminal. WLANs lack of ability to natively support high QoS services remains a significant weakness in the technology, although some progress is being made to remedy this through IP QoS techniques and enhancements to the 802.11 standard, namely 802.11e. The 802.11e standard, which includes a targeted QoS solution is discussed in more detail in the following sections.

WLAN Supported Services

Since 802.11 WLAN is a derivative of the IEEE 802 standards family, conceivably WLAN can support a multitude of the services that run on IP networks. These range from Web browsing, e-mail, video-conferencing, voice over IP (VoIP), file transfer, and streaming services. Although WLAN supports a range of IP services, its capacity to support them to a high level of QoS remains a difficulty when deploying IP services on WLAN. As was referred to in the preceding introduction, 802.11 WLAN was not built with QoS as part of the standard. Therefore WLAN's capacity to support services that demand a high level of QoS is limited. In the context of time sensitive traffic, like that of video telephony or streaming, WLAN is playing catch-up with technologies like UMTS that have specific QoS infrastructures in place to guarantee service quality. Some steps have been taken through IP traffic shaping techniques and enhancements to the 802.11 standard.

For services that do not require high QoS constraints, such as Web browsing or e-mail, WLAN provides a sufficient level of connectivity to support satisfactory delivery of these services through HotSpots and Wi-Fi zones. In the context of the heterogeneous systems outline, WLAN can be viewed as a complementary source of bandwidth for interactive and background services, thus providing bandwidth relief for UMTS bearers to carry higher QoS services.

WLAN QoS Architecture

Guaranteeing resources in the fixed line IP networks is only a partial solution to providing QoS over WLAN. The fundamental differences between wired links and radio links renders some of the functionalities of QoS schemes like IntServ and DiffServ useless due to the inherently unstable nature of wireless channels. Ensuring the reliable delivery of packets over the wireless interface is paramount to the success of such schemes. 802.11e (802.11e, 2003) is an effort to map a QoS framework around wireless LANs and specifies a number of enhancements (Mangold, Choi, Hiertz, Klein, & Walke, 2003; Ni, Romdhani, & Turletti, 2004).

IEEE 802.11e

In IEEE 802.11e the DCF was extended to support QoS in the form of enhanced distributed coordination function (EDCF), which is a key part of the IEEE 802.11e proposed standard with enhancements for QoS. The main improvement of EDCF over DCF is the introduction of access categories (ACs) in which low priority traffic will get best effort service while the higher priority traffic receives "better" effort service. This concept of ordering the access to the channel is not constrained to the channel but extends into the MAC itself in the form of up to eight transmission queues, so the station can run applications of both high and low traffic priority and not run the danger of having the high priority traffic held up in the internal queue for transmission.

At the core of EDCF are access categories (ACs). MAC service data units (MSDU) are delivered through multiple backoff instances within one station, each backoff instance parameterised with AC-specific parameters. During the contention period each AC within the stations contends for a transmission opportunity. The priority of the different queues is implemented by giving the higher priority ACs shorter Arbitration InterFrame

Space (AIFS), the time the channel must be inactive before backoff begins, than the lower priority ACs. A single station may implement up to eight transmission queues, as illustrated in Figure 6.

IEEE 802.11e extends the concept of prioritisation through differing interframe space. Where IEEE 802.11b used differing interframe spaces to change the mode of the channel, contention to contention-free, IEEE 802.11e uses differing interframe spaces to prioritise traffic. Higher priority traffic uses shorter AIF spaces, to lower priority traffic, entailing that lower priority traffic must sense the medium as being idle for longer before they can begin to decrement their backoff counters. This means that the higher priority traffic is more likely to gain access to the channel over lower priority traffic.

QoS in Multi-System Networks

Supporting QoS in multi-system networks is an important issue to achieve user mobility across heterogeneous RANs with a unified service experience. Traffic management must take into account the different characteristics of each RAN to provide seamless service continuity as well as end-to-end QoS. For example, significant variation in transmission capacity can be found between RANs etc. In addition, the traffic can cross multiple domains where each of them has its own administration rendering end-to-end QoS provision even more complex. A mapping of the QoS services between different RANs is required to provide unified QoS traffic classes. It is also necessary to manage the QoS in each domain and to permit interaction between the different QoS management entities thanks to the policy-based QoS management.

In the case of UMTS services, the traffic classes and the QoS attributes are defined as previously described. As the end-to-end path in the multi-system network may include the Internet environment, the Internet QoS attributes and classes will

Figure 6. 802.11e EDCF

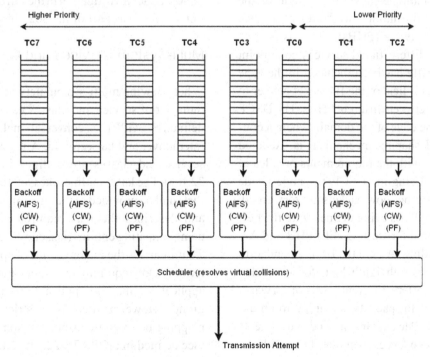

be mapped to the classes of each RAN. There are two main QoS approaches in this area, namely integrated services (IntServ) and differentiated services (DiffServ).

IntServ uses the per-flow approach to provide guarantees to individual streams. This approach adopts the resource reservation along the flow path using the resource reservation protocol (RSVP). The latter sets up some flow state (e.g., bandwidth reservations, accounting) in the routers a flow goes through. An admission control is used to guarantee the QoS. It grants or rejects the flow requests, based on availability of resources and the guarantees provided to other flows. In addition to the well known best effort service, two service classes are proposed: the guaranteed service class for the traffic requiring a firm bound on delay and the load controlled class where flow receives a quality of service closely approximating QoS that flow would receive from an unloaded network element. This is generally not seen as a scalable QoS solution for individual flows on all-IP networks due to the signalling requirements.

DiffServ follows the philosophy of the aggregation of multiple flows in the edge of the DiffServ domain into a few classes of service or per hop behaviors (PHBs). There is no reservation, but differentiated services code point (DSCP) etiquette has been included in the type of service (TOS) field of the IP packet header to differentiate between different PHBs. The DSCP is setting at the edge of the domain where a conditioning and shaping mechanism is executed in accordance with the requirements or rules of each service. Using the DSCP, the node inside network determines how packets are forwarded. There are two PHBs being defined with the best effort: expedited forwarding (EF) PHB and Assured Forwarding (AF) PHB. EF is intended to support services with tightly bounded loss, delay and jitter. AF offers different levels of forwarding assurances for packets belonging to an aggregated flow. Packets are marked with one of three drop precedence, such that those with the

highest drop precedence are dropped with lower probability than those marked with the lowest drop precedence. AF gives the customer the assurance of a minimum throughput, even during periods of congestion. The per-hop basis, lack of firm reservations and statistical nature of the guarantees given by DiffServ are seen as more scalable for Internet applications.

As DiffServ and IntServ models shall be supported for PDP contexts (3GPP TS 23.107, 2003), the mapping between Internet QoS and UMTS QoS is under investigation. For example, when DiffServ is used in the backbone of the UMTS, the conversational class is transported in the EF PHB, streaming is mapped to EF or AF. Interactive and background classes are mapped into AF PHBs.

On the other hand, end-to-end QoS guarantee should be provided in the context where WLAN is the wireless last mile of the wired Internet networks. The Wireless Internet based on DiffServ or IntServ is possible. The AC proposed in the 802.11e WLAN can be mapped to the DiffServ PHB which form a DiffServ-based WLAN. This topic is under investigation in the traffic specification (TSPEC) as part of the 802.11e standard.

Multi-System Services and Classes

When viewing multi-system networks the minimum set of service and classes can be those as defined by 3GPP (i.e., conversational, streaming, interactive, and background). An example set of service and classes are outlined in (3GPP TS 22.105). The latter outlines the QoS requirements that shall be provided to the end user/applications and describes them as requirements between communicating entities (i.e., end-to-end). Figure 7 summarises the major groups of application in terms of QoS requirements. Applications and new applications may be applicable to one or more groups. However, there is no strict one-to-one mapping between the groups of application/service defined in (3GPP TS 22.105) and the traffic

Figure 7. Multi-system applications in terms of QoS requirements

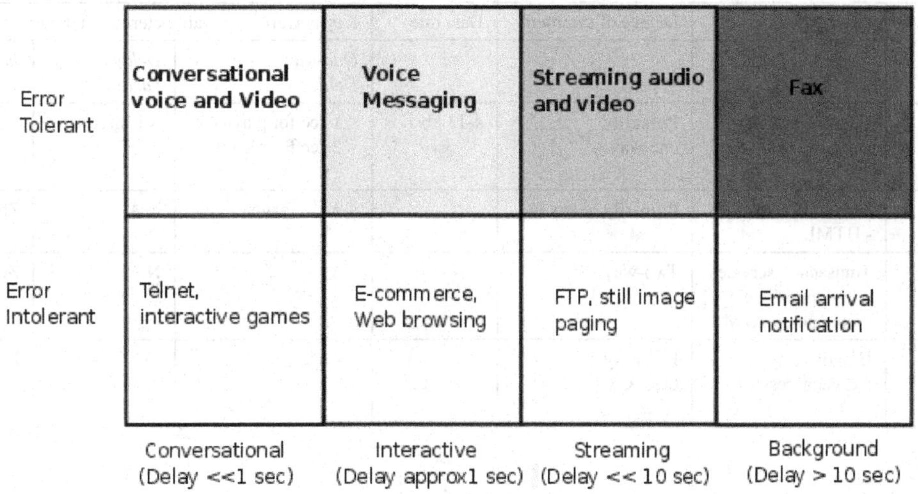

	Conversational voice and Video	Voice Messaging	Streaming audio and video	Fax
Error Tolerant	Conversational voice and Video	Voice Messaging	Streaming audio and video	Fax
Error Intolerant	Telnet, interactive games	E-commerce, Web browsing	FTP, still image paging	Email arrival notification
	Conversational (Delay <<1 sec)	Interactive (Delay approx1 sec)	Streaming (Delay << 10 sec)	Background (Delay > 10 sec)

Table 3. End-user performance expectations--Conversational/Realtime services

Medium	Application	Degree of symmetry	Data rate	Key performance parameters and target values		
				End-to-end One-way Delay	*Delay Variation within a call*	*Information loss*
Audio	Conversational voice	Two-way	4-25 kb/s	<150 msec preferred <400 msec limit Note 1	< 1 msec	< 3% FER
Video	Videophone	Two-way	32-384 kb/s	< 150 msec preferred <400 msec limit Lip-synch : < 100 msec		< 1% FER
Data	Telemetry - two-way control	Two-way	<28.8 kb/s	< 250 msec	N.A	Zero
Data	Interactive games	Two-way	< 1 KB	< 250 msec	N.A	Zero
Data	Telnet	Two-way (asymmetric)	< 1 KB	< 250 msec	N.A	Zero

classes as defined in (3GPP TS 23.107, 2003). For instance, an Interactive application/service can very well use a bearer of the conversational traffic class if the application/service or the user has tight requirements on delay.

The reference user performance expectations are presented in Table 3 for conversational services, in Table 4 for interactive services and in Table 5 for streaming services. The QoS values in the tables represent end-to-end performance, including mobile to mobile calls and satellite components. Delay values represent one way delay (i.e., from originating entity to terminating entity). The values included in the following tables are commonly accepted values from an end-user viewpoint. The delay contribution within the mobile network should be kept to minimum since there may be additional delay contributions from

Table 4. End-user performance expectations: Interactive services

Medium	Application	Degree of symmetry	Data rate	Key performance parameters and target values		
				One-way Delay	*Delay Variation*	*Information loss*
Audio	Voice messaging	Primarily one-way	4-13 kb/s	< 1 sec for playback < 2 sec for record	< 1 msec	< 3% FER
Data	Web-browsing - HTML	Primarily one-way		< 4 sec /page	N.A	Zero
Data	Transaction services – high priority e.g. e-commerce, ATM	Two-way		< 4 sec	N.A	Zero
Data	E-mail (server access)	Primarily One-way		< 4 sec	N.A	Zero

Table 5. End-user performance expectations: Streaming services

Medium	Application	Degree of symmetry	Data rate	Key performance parameters and target values		
				Start-up Delay	*Transport delay Variation*	*Packet loss at session layer*
Audio	Speech, mixed speech and music, medium and high quality music	Primarily one-way	5-128 kb/s	< 10 sec	< 2sec	< 1% Packet loss ratio
Video	Movie clips, surveillance, realtime video	Primarily one-way	20-384 kb/s	< 10 sec	<2 sec	< 2% Packet loss ratio
Data	Bulk data transfer/ retrieval, layout and synchronisation information	Primarily one-way	< 384 kb/s	< 10 sec	N.A	Zero
Data	Still image	Primarily one-way		< 10 sec	N.A	Zero

external networks. Note that the overall one way delay in the mobile network (from UE to PLMN border) is approximately 100 msec.

MULTI ACCESS TESTBED

The evaluation of QoS strategies in a multi-access network requires a suitable platform of coupled access networks and is the motivation behind the integrated UMTS-WLAN testbed. The UMTS-WLAN testbed is a large multi-user, multi-service UMTS system with WLAN hotspots embedded in the RAN. The testbed is built with the objective of creating and validating RRM algorithms for interworking in a multi-system environment and testing the affect these algorithms have on end-to-end QoS.

Figure 8. UMTS-WLAN Testbed

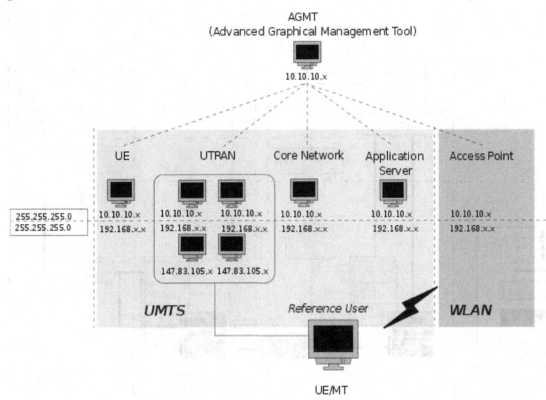

The UMTS-WLAN testbed in essence comprises two functional networks--a large multi-user, multi-cell UMTS testbed network (circa 5000 users), and a WLAN testbed network. The testbed spans nine PCs and is organised as shown in Figure 8. The important functional entities from both UMTS and WLAN technologies have been mapped to dedicated machines. From the UMTS domain there is a machine to emulate a UE, Core Network, Application Server and UTRAN. Due to the computational complexity of emulating the RAN, the UTRAN is served by four machines but can logically be viewed as a single entity. From the WLAN environment, an access point and WLAN MT (the WLAN MT and the UE are housed in the same machine creating a dual mode terminal) have been included. A 100 Mbits/s Ethernet network interconnects each testbed PC with separate address planes for testbed control (10.10.10.x) and signalling (192.168.x.x).

The UMTS and WLAN functionalities in the testbed have been distributed among the hardware platform. This distribution is made possible by the creation of software modules. Each machine runs a set of modules that replicate common UMTS-WLAN functionalities using a very specific programming philosophy (i.e., mono-task approach), common procedures for communication with other modules and well defined interfaces. The testbed is organised as a set of modules tightly connected to a control structure known as the Communications Manager. The dissemination of these modules and the interfaces connecting them is shown in Figure 9. The testbed comprises five main blocks: the UE/MT, UTRAN, access point, CN, and application server.

Figure 9. Converged wireless test platform

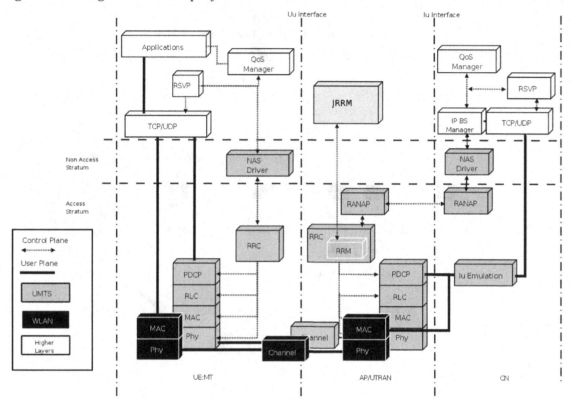

User Equipment/Mobile Terminal (UE/MT)

The UE is a real user terminal experiencing an emulated multi-user system. A user can tell perceptibly the quality of service the network is providing by simply using the applications and services on the UE. Since the network is experienced through the UE, the UE can then be called the "reference user."

The client application element refers to the QoS enabled applications, which map to the four traffic classes identified in UMTS. The QoS management of the reference user includes the IP bearer service manager (IP BS manager shown in Figure 9), which deals with QoS aspects and is responsible for translating QoS requirements from the applications point of view into UMTS QoS parameters and IP QoS parameters. The UMTS

QoS parameters are managed by the UMTS bearer service, included in the NAS driver, which interacts with the network to set up UMTS or WLAN radio access bearers (RABs) as appropriate.

The TCP/IP traffic control module manages QoS at the IP level (queuing disciplines, scheduling policies etc.) and is also in charge of tagging the user data packets with the NSAPI (network service access point identifier) which is put in the type of service (TOS) field inside the IPv4 header. This tagging allows differentiation between IP packets with different QoS requirements and transfers them to the corresponding radio access bearer in the UTRAN. The non access stratum (NAS) driver module implements the session and mobility management needed in order to establish data sessions (PDP profiles) throughout UMTS. The NAS driver in the UE makes use of the RRC signalling module to manage radio resources across the air interface.

The WLAN MT is an 802.11 enabled user device that can support multimedia applications such as Internet browsing, e-mail, streaming and VoIP. Through the extension of the UE that already exists as part of the testbed architecture, a dual mode terminal is created.

UTRAN

Three main elements can be distinguished in the UTRAN: the radio resource control and management element; the lower layers and radio channel element; and the Iu interface emulation element. As far as lower layers and the radio channel are concerned, the complete protocol stack below the network layer has been built. Thus, the data link layer (L2) and physical layer (L1) have been implemented. The emulation of the physical layer and radio channel is achieved by means of histograms of the bit error rate obtained from offline link layer simulations. These link layer simulations take into account environment parameters such as cell type (macro/micro/pico), mobile speed, transport channel type, and radio channel quality.

On the control plane there are two modules dedicated to managing and implementing radio resource algorithms: the RRC and RRM modules. The RRC module contains RRC and RANAP signalling protocols to communicate with the RRC in the UE/MT and with the RANAP module in the CN. The RRC module implements RRM algorithms like admission and congestion control, power control, handover management, and transmission parameters management.

The CRRM function is implemented in the UTRAN. It provides a load balancing function between different RATs, in this case, UMTS and WLAN. It interacts with intrinsic RRM to gather information on an admitted session and process incoming service requests from users, or to move flows between RATs. The radio resource impact

of UMTS users has been included inside the RRM module (RRM) located in the RRC in the UTRAN. UMTS emulation comprises traffic generation and radio propagation conditions for all the users in a given service area formed by several Node Bs. RRM strategies are executed inside the RRM for all the users in the system as if all users were real like the reference user. WLAN is integrated into the test platform as a combination of real and emulated parts. WLAN Access Points (AP) are much less complex and more freely available than UMTS Node Bs. Some implementations, such as HostAP, provide a facility to deploy RRM in the AP. Otherwise, RRM strategies and their impact on WLAN users can be implemented in the radio resource control (RRC) part. The use of real and emulated parts provides a great deal of flexibility to assess the impact of RRM strategies on a single real user in the testbed environment. Finally, apart from the radio interface lower layer implementation, the user plane in the Iu interface has also been emulated.

Core Network

The CN encapsulates service GPRS support node (SGSN) and gateway GPRS support node (GGSN) functionalities. The CN comprises five main elements: the RSVP (reservation protocol) signalling module, TCP/IP traffic control, IP bearer service (IP BS) management, the NAS driver, and the RANAP signalling module. The user plane inside UMTS ends at the IP bearer service module in the CN, which is responsible for connecting UMTS towards an external IP network. The RSVP signalling module and the TCP/IP traffic control have the same functionalities as detailed in the UE section. The NAS driver is in charge of the Iu interface emulation control apart from session and mobility management, and makes use of the RANAP signalling module to manage UTRAN resources.

WLAN AP

WLAN AP's are much less complex, and more freely available than UMTS node B's. For the test-bed an implementation of HostAP (Malinen, 2006) is being used to provide access point functionality. HostAP is a Linux driver for wireless LAN cards based on Intersil's Prism 2/2.5/3 chipset.

The driver sanctions a wireless card to enter a Host AP mode, which endows the card with access point functionality. Common access point duties include beacon sending and frame acknowledging, authentication (and de-authentication), association (re-association and disassociation), data transmission between wireless stations, and power saving (PS) mode. Signalling and frame buffering for PS stations are managed by the wireless card by virtue of the Host AP driver. One of the main advantages of using a Host AP driven access point in favour of a commercial, off-the-shelf component is the ability to distil key performance indicators (KPI's) from the access point. For instance, KPI's such as the number of associated station, Rx/Tx packets received/transmitted from/to the station by the access point, Rx/Tx bytes received/transmitted from/to the station by the access point among others can be more readily extracted from the HostAP driven soft access point than vendor protected technologies. Key performance indicators are crucial for implementing RRM on the AP.

IEEE 802.11 Controlled Environment

The WLAN AP and WLAN clients under test are controlled in WLAN isolated chamber. The Azimuth WLAN test platform is a wireless test network that allows automated, sophisticated and advanced testing and measurement of 802.11 wireless devices that result in repeatable, reliable and consistent test results. The Azimuth WLAN test platform allows creating an 802.11 simulated test environment in which attenuation is used to virtually distance test devices from each other. By attenuating signals in the test platform, one can virtually move the client under test (UE/MT) and the access point (HostAP) closer or further away from each other. The chamber is used in the evaluation of interactive traffic over WLAN.

Application Server

The application server is made accessible from the UMTS CN through an IP intranet with QoS capabilities. Four elements make up the application server: the RSVP signalling module, the QoS management, the TCP/IP traffic control, and the server applications. The application server provides multi-media content and services for the UE.

Open source programs were chosen as client applications due to the availability of source code and the flexibility to make changes if necessary. The services and corresponding client applications used in the testbed are:

- **Conversational class:** Audio-video telephony service; robust audio tool (RAT), and video-conference tool (VIC) applications.
- **Streaming class:** Audio-video streaming; Cisco MPEG4IP streaming client application on the UE/MT, Apple's Darwin streaming server on the server side.
- **Interactive class:** Web browsing and network gaming; Mozilla Web browser application and XPilots game. Apache Web server for Web browsing and XPilots game server.
- **Background class:** E-mail; Mozilla Web browser e-mail client on the UE/MT. QMail as the corresponding e-mail server.

EVALUATING INTERACTIVE TRAFFIC IN A HETEROGENEOUS WIRELESS NETWORK

The ARES testbed is used to evaluate and quantify the quality of service of interactive traffic over

WLAN and UMTS. The benefit of admitting interactive traffic to WLAN is twofold, firstly the reference user can achieve higher data rates on WLAN, and secondly, the radio access bearers freed up can be used to allow additional realtime users into the UMTS part of the network. The evaluation begins by considering a Joint Radio Resource Management (JRRM) policy for admitting users into the heterogeneous network and how it implemented in the ARES testbed. The evaluation continues with comparing QoS results of interactive traffic on WLAN and UMTS. Finally the evaluation concludes by demonstrating the impact of JRRM on the UMTS part of the network. The tests are repeated until statistical significance is achieved.

JRRM Admission Control Algorithm

The JRRM module in the ARES test platform makes the decision to admit interactive Requests to WLAN or UMTS based on the statistical load of the current users and endeavours to achieve highest QoS level for the end user. There is a bias to admit users to WLAN once the WLAN load is low. If the WLAN load is high the JRRM then decides to admit to UMTS. The final decision of admitting to UMTS is taken by the RRM/RRC

module in the UTRAN. The JRRM admission control process is showed in Figure 10. Mathematically, the each decision can be represented as Equation 1:

$$\eta + \Delta\eta \leq \eta_{max} \qquad (1)$$

where η is the current load factor, $\Delta\eta$ is additional load associated with the request and η_{max} is the maximum load factor for the system. Further details on this equation can be found in Skehill et al. (2007).

Scenario Setup and Evaluation Criteria

The realtime and interactive users are setup in the ARES testbed with traffic characteristics described as per Table 6. The activity and call duration are kept constant for the different realtime user scenarios. The scenarios are chosen to represent different load situations in a real network, for example:

- **Scenario *A*** represents a low load.
- **Scenario *B*** represents a medium load.
- **Scenario *C*** represents a high load.

Figure 10. JRRM decision for interactive requests with WLAN

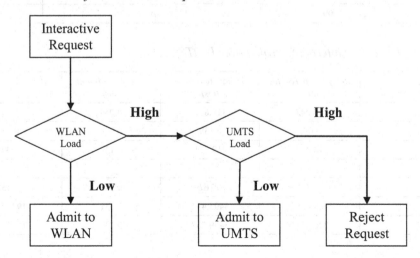

The system is populated with simulated end users to achieve these load scenarios. These users are characterised in terms of the projected impact they have on radio resources in the system, included as part of the RRM module described in Section 0. In addition to realtime and interactive users, the evaluation includes the QoS results from reference user. The user on the UE starts an interactive service by launching a Mozilla browser and loading the ARES test Website. The reference user downloads a 20Mb file over UMTS or WLAN depending on the JRRM decision. The QoS *evaluation of interactive traffic* over UMTS and WLAN is in terms of: (i) end-to-end delay and (ii) download rate/time.

Throughout the evaluation, the ARES testbed is configured so that a percentage of interactive users move from UMTS to WLAN. In order to achieve this, the JRRM algorithm is enabled and configured so that a percentage (0%, 50% and 100%) of interactive users to move to WLAN. To do this the initial load threshold η_{max} is set high,

close to 100%. This is done in order to study the best case scenario of moving all users. In reality, this threshold is set much lower. The QoS impact of moving interactive users to WLAN on *UMTS realtime traffic* users is evaluated on the ARES testbed in terms of (iii) Successful admission requests and (iv) block error rate.

Evaluating Interactive Traffic over UMTS

The goal of this test is to evaluate interactive traffic over UMTS and provide a minimum quality of service for WLAN to achieve. The results are from the reference user for Scenario B. The following results are from the UE downloading the 20Mb file from the Application server using a UMTS connection. The WLAN part of the testbed is not enabled and therefore the JRRM entity will admit users to the UMTS part only. The results in Table 7 show UMTS behaving as it should and achieving the QoS bound end-to-end delay.

Table 6. ARES configuration for realtime and interactive users

Service	Number	Activity Factor (α)		Call Duration	Intersession Time (s)	Call Rate (call/hr)
		UL	DL			
Real time (Scenario A)	1000	0.3	0.1	120 s	na	30
Real time (Scenario B)	2000	0.3	0.1	120 s	na	30
Real time (Scenario C)	3000	0.3	0.1	120 s	na	30
Interactive	1000	0.3	0.3	na	1	na

Table 7. End-to-end delay for interactive traffic over UMTS

	Delay 95th percentile (ms)	Delay Maximum (ms)	Delay Minimum (ms)	Delay Average (ms)
UTRAN (UL)	10.022	119.812	0.054	7.937
CN (UL)	0.097	0.139	0.014	0.073
End-to-End (UL)	10.092	119.821	0.134	8.009
UTRAN (DL)	9.935	105.679	0.241	6.468
CN (DL)	3204.287	3403.414	0.031	1926.841
End-to-End (DL)	3209.773	3409.767	5.727	1933.309

There is some variance in the end-to-end delay but 95th percentile is well within guidelines. The majority of the delay experienced by the reference user is in Core Network part of the system, however it never exceeds the delay outlined in the UMTS quality of service Classes (3GPP TS 23.107, 2003).

Table 8 shows that the QoS outlined for interactive traffic (i.e., resources reserved in the system) has been achieved in the UMTS part of the system. This is the minimum requirement that WLAN must achieve. However, it must be noted that from Table 8 the Uplink RAB is under-utilised indicating a waste of scarce radio resources. The nature of interactive traffic best suits WLAN and should be moved if possible. These initial results from UMTS are used to set minimum requirements for WLAN. Interactive service RABs assigned by UMTS are limited to 32kb/s or 64kb/s and these values can be used as a minimum throughput value for WLAN.

Evaluation of Interactive Traffic over WLAN

WLAN access is made available in the ARES testbed by enabling IEEE 802.11 card in the UE and activating the HostAP module. The same scenario is applied again and the reference user downloads a 20Mb file over WLAN in the presence of other competing WLAN Users and UMTS users (interactive and realtime). The reference users WLAN card and AP are connected through the controlled WLAN Azimuth environment. The other WLAN users are set to have an activity factor of 1 (i.e., always transmitting) and a TCP and UDP stream is set to produce a 32kb/s constant bit traffic. The number of other WLAN users, initially set to 1, is increased in a linear fashion until the point where the WLAN channel is saturated. Measurements again are taken from the reference user on the UE. Interactive traffic over WLAN is evaluated in terms of (i) download time, (ii) download rate and (iii) round trip time.

Comparing the total download time for the 20Mbit file in UMTS of 833 seconds, as shown in Figure 11, it is observed the reference user can achieve an improved download time using WLAN. The improvement is significant for low to medium loads--approaching a quarter of the UMTS time. For high WLAN load, the download time is still an improvement on UMTS but the margin of improvement is less. At the threshold, the download time is approaching that of UMTS and, at this point, the JRRM decision should be to no longer admit users to WLAN. The benefit is no longer substantial and cannot improve on the UMTS end-to-end QoS requirements--this threshold could be finely tuned over time to achieve slight improvements in performance.

Table 8. QoS results for interactive traffic over UMTS

	Reserved	Observed	Result
Maximum SDU (DL)	570 bytes	570 bytes	QoS Achieved
Maximum Rate (DL)	32000 bps	26666.36 bps	QoS Achieved
Average Delay End-to-End (ms) (DL)	<4000	1933.309	QoS Achieved
Maximum SDU (UL)	570 bytes	538 bytes	QoS Achieved
Maximum Rate (UL)	32000 bps	2923.89 bps	QoS Achieved
Average Delay End-to-End (ms) (UL	<4000	8.009	QoS Achieved

Figure 11. Download times for WLAN and UMTS of a 20Mb file

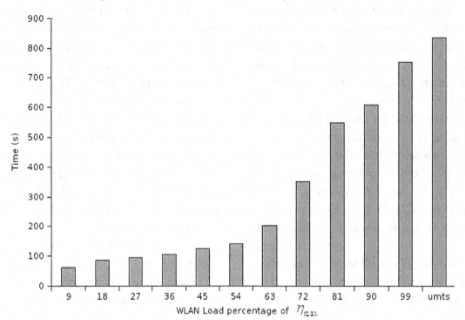

Figure 12. Download rate achieved over WLAN

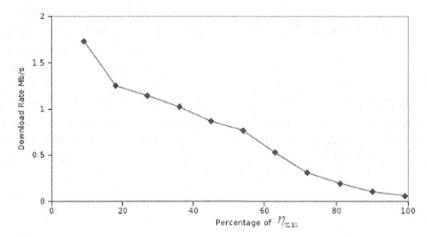

In terms of download rate, Figure 12 shows with low to medium load the reference user achieves download rates of 1.8Mb/s to 500kb/s. This is a significant improvement over a single UMTS RAB of 32kb/s.

As illustrated in Figure 13, the average round trip time (RTT) increases as load increases. This is to be expected from any wireless or wired system.

In terms of QoS requirements set out by 3GPP, interactive and background traffic does not have strict guidelines, however the end-to-end delay for interactive and background traffic should be less than 4 seconds. The results from the ARES testbed show that under low to medium load situations, the average RTT is low for the WLAN access part--in the region of 1-3 ms. As WLAN

Figure 13. WLAN average round trip time (RTT)

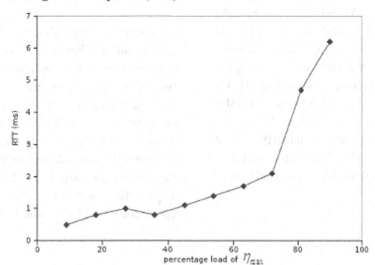

Figure 14. The rate of realtime requests per second remains constant for all scenarios

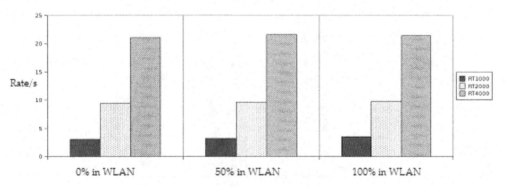

and UMTS are tightly coupled together, there is an additional delay which occurs in the core network and is the same from the UMTS results. As the load increases, the RTT rises in an exponential form, however, the delay is an improvement from the results obtained by the UMTS part. A clear reason why the RTT time is elevated in UMTS is in relation to the relationship between time-out of PDP contexts and the intersession time of interactive traffic. If the intersession time is large, the PDP context expires and thus the RAB is released. When a new session is started the RAB must be re-established, whereas in WLAN, the medium is always present and only the setup delay is waiting the back off time period.

The UMTS Benefits of Admitting WWW Users to WLAN

It has been shown that when JRRM makes the decision to send a user to WLAN, the reference user can achieve a higher quality of service level for interactive services. With interactive users camped in a WLAN cell, the UMTS has more available resources for realtime services. The following highlights the benefit of moving interactive users to WLAN on the UMTS part of the heterogeneous testbed.

Before determining the UMTS benefit in terms of unsuccessful requests and block error rates for realtime services for the different scenarios, the

ARES testbed is evaluated to ensure it can provide a level of consistency. As shown in Figure 14, the number of admission requests per second remain constant for all load Scenarios A-C and cases (i) all interactive users are admitted to UMTS, (ii) 50% of interactive users are admitted to WLAN and 50% are admitted to WLAN and (iii) 100% of interactive users are admitted to WLAN. As the rate of requests remains constant it provides a fair evaluation platform in determining the effect on unsuccessful requests, block error rate, etc.

Blocking and Reject Ratio Results

As determined by validation in the previous section, the number of admission request rate remains constant for scenarios *A-C* and thus we can evaluate the improvement in system QoS in terms of the number of realtime admission requests rejected by JRRM. As seen in Figure 15, Figure 16, and Figure 17, the number of rejects per second decreases as the number of interactive traffic users are moved to WLAN. In Scenario A the number of rejects decreased by 48%. The rejects decreased by 37% and 7% in Scenario *B*

Figure 15. Scenario A: Number of realtime rejects/s, moving 0%, 50%, and 100% interactive users to WLAN

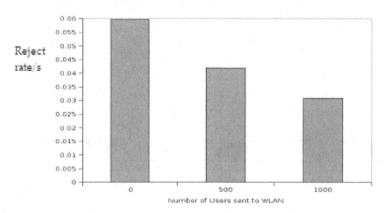

Figure 16. Scenario B: Number of realtime rejects/s, moving 0%, 50%, and 100% interactive users to WLAN

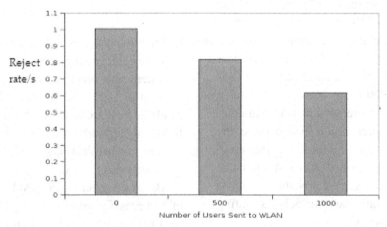

and Scenario *C* respectively. These results show that the UMTS part of the network is now enjoying higher successful admission of realtime traffic as more interactive users are sent to the WLAN. The results show that for medium to low load levels in UMTS-WLAN the UMTS system can admit up to 50% more realtime users when the majority of interactive or best effort users are admitted to WLAN.

As shown in Figure 18, the gain in terms of successful realtime requests when moving all of interactive users to WLAN is considered in the region of 50-60% for a low to medium loaded UMTS network.

As shown in Figure 19, the request-to-reject ratio shows a 33% gain when moving half of the Interactive users to WLAN, and a 56% gain when moving all of Interactive users to WLAN. The effect of moving interactive users to WLAN on block error rate (BLER) is also significant. Figure 20 shows the BLER (of the realtime users) to remain at the target BLER when the interactive users are moved to WLAN. When the users remain in the UMTS network, the BLER begins to rise

Figure 17. Scenario C: Number of realtime rejects/s, moving 0%, 50%, and 100% interactive users to WLAN

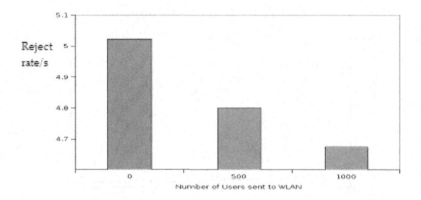

Figure 18. Percentage gain of successful realtime requests moving 100% of interactive users to WLAN

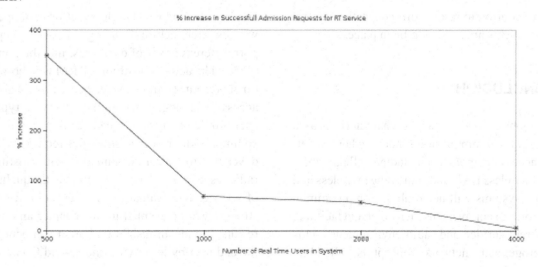

Figure 19. Realtime admission request to reject ratio

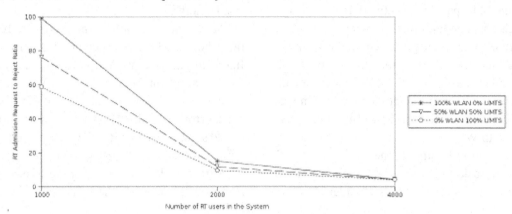

Figure 20. Block Error Rate for realtime users in the UMTS part of the ARES testbed

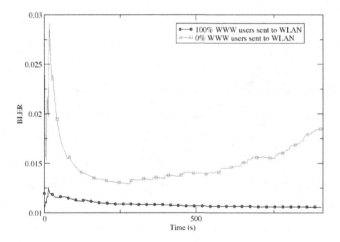

out of control, to resolve this congestion control mechanisms are needed to be in place.

CONCLUSION

4G mobile systems can be characterised as a horizontal communication model, where different access technologies including cellular, cordless, wireless LAN and short-range wireless and wired systems will be combined on a common platform to complement each other and facilitate different service and radio environments. This heterogeneous network concept is called the converged broadband wireless platform, or open wireless architecture. Converged networks support different levels of data rates, mobility, and traffic. The active role of joint RRM is to co-ordinate resources and services between available access technologies according to service type, user profile and network load. To this end, new common radio resource strategies require to be developed to work in conjunction with existing radio resource strategies that improve the quality of service. The evaluation of a new Joint RRM strategy were presented in this chapter and the results provide an insight on how it can benefit the end user by improving end-to-end QoS and for the network operator by spreading the load across multiple networks respectively

A project started in 2004 by 3GPP, called long term evolution (LTE), set goals to improve efficiency, lower costs, improve services, make use of new spectrum opportunities, and better integration with other open standards. This reflects the idea of fourth generation networks (Kyun & Prasad, 2006) (i.e., fully IP-based integrated *system of systems* and *network of networks* achieved after the convergence of wired and wireless networks). This converged network will be capable of providing 100 Mbit/s and 1 Gbit/s, respectively, in outdoor and indoor environments while providing end-to-end QoS and high security. The latest 3GPP standard is release 7 and it is envisaged that LTE will be release 8 and it is designed to complement the concept of fourth generation networks.

REFERENCES

3GPP TR 22.934. (2002). *Feasibility study on 3GPP system to wireless local area network (WLAN) interworking (Release 6).*

3GPP TS 22.105. *3GPP TS 22.105 Services and service capabilities, Release 6.*

3GPP TS 23.060. (2006). *3GPP TS 23.060 v7.1.0 General packet radio service (GPRS); Service description; Stage 2.*

3GPP TS 23.107. (2003). *3GPP TS 23.107 quality of service (QoS) concept and architecture V6.0.0 (Release 6).*

802.11e. (2003). *Draft supplement to part 11: Wireless medium access control (MAC) and physical layer (PHY) specifications: Medium access control (MAC) enhancements for quality of service (QoS): IEEE 802.11e/D6.0.*

Agusti, R. (2006). Radio resource management in beyond 3G systems. *IEEE Melecon*, Malaga, Spain.

Ahmavaara, K., Haverinen, H., & Pichna, R. (2003). Interworking architecture between 3GPP and WLAN systems. *IEEE Communications Magazine, 41*(11), 74-81.

Braden, R., Zhang, L., Berson, S., & Jamin, S. (1997). *RFC 2205--Resource ReSerVation protocol (RSVP) - Version 1 functional specification.*

Buddhikot, M., Chandranmenon, G., Han, S., Lee, Y. W., Miller, S., & Salgarelli, L. (2003). Integration of 802.11 and third-generation wireless data networks: INFOCOMM. *22nd Annual Joint Conference of the IEEE Computer and Communications Societies.*

Cristache, G., David, K., & Hildebrand, M. (2003). Aspects for the Integration of ad-hoc and cellular networks. *3rd Scandinavian Workshop on Wireless Ad-hoc Networks.*

Dixit, S., Guo, Y., & Antoniou, Z. (2001). Resource management and quality of service in third-generation wireless networks. *IEEE Communications Magazine.*

ETSI. (2001). *ETSI TS 123 107 QoS concept and architecture V4.3.0.*

ETSI BRAN TR 101 957. (2001). *Requirements and architectures for interworking between HIPERLAN/2 and 3rd generation cellular systems V1.1.1.*

Jaseemuddin, M. (2003). An architecture for integrating UMTS and 802.11 WLAN Networks. *Eighth IEEE International Symposium on Computers and Communication (ISCC03).* IEEE Computer Society.

Korhonen, J., & Gurtov, A. (2004). Effect of vertical handovers on performance of TCP-friendly rate control. *SIGMOBILE Mobile Computing and Communications Review, 8*(3), 73-87.

Kyun, K. Y., & Prasad, R. (2006). *4G roadmap and emerging communication technologies.* Artech House.

Malinen, J. (2006). Host AP driver for Intersil Prism2/2.5/3, Hostapd, and WPA supplicant.

Mangold, S., Choi, S., Hiertz, G. R., Klein, O., & Walke, B. (2003). Analysis of IEEE 802.11e for QoS support in wireless LANs: IEEE wireless communications.

Ni, Q., Romdhani, L., & Turletti, T. (2004). A survey of QoS enhancements for IEEE 802.11 wireless LAN. *Wiley Journal of Wireless Communications and Mobile Computing, 4*(5), 547-566.

Niebert, N., Schieder, A., Abramowicz, H., Malmgren, G., Sachs, J., Horn, U., et al. (2004). Ambient networks: An architecture for communication networks beyond *3G. IEEE Wireless Communications, 11*(2), 14-22.

Romero, J. P., Sallent, O., Agusti, R., & Diaz-Guerra, M. A. (2005). *Radio resource management strategies in UMTS*. John Wiley & Sons.

Sachs, J., Wiemann, H., Lundsjo, J., & Magnusson, P. (2004). Integration of multi-radio access in a beyond 3G network. *IEEE Personal, Indoor, and Mobile Radio Communications, 15th PIMRC.*

Skehill, R., Barry, M., O'Callaghan, M., Gawley, N., Kent, W., & McGrath, S. (2007). Common RRM approach to admission control for converged heterogeneous wireless networks. *Special Issue of IEEE Wireless Communications Magazine on Technologies on Future Converged Wireless and Mobility Platform.*

Tsao, S. L., & Lin, C. C. (2002). Design and evaluation of UMTS-WLAN interworking strategies. *Vehicular Technology Conference, 56th IEEE VTC.*

Wang, Z. (2001). *Internet QoS: Architectures and mechanisms for quality of service.* Morgan Kaufmann Publishers.

Wroclawski, J. (1997). *RFC 2210* - The use of RSVP with IETF integrated services.

Chapter II
Radio Resource Management Strategies for HSDPA-Enhanced UMTS Networks

Dirk Staehle
University of Würzburg, Germany

Andreas Mäder
University of Würzburg, Germany

ABSTRACT

This chapter gives an overview of the background and functionality of the high speed downlink packet access (HSDPA), and provides insights into the radio resource management of integrated UMTS/HSDPA networks. The high speed downlink packet access (HSDPA) is part of the evolution of the universal mobile telecommunication system (UMTS). It is often referred to as 3.5G system, in contrast to UMTS, which is a third generation system. The authors introduce aspects of radio resource management specific to the HSDPA like channel-aware scheduling and radio resource sharing strategies. Furthermore, the impact of radio resource management on the quality of service is analyzed and it is shown that the selection of an RRM strategy is an integral part of the network planning and deployment process

INTRODUCTION TO THE HIGH SPEED DOWNLINK PACKET ACCESS

The high speed downlink packet access (HSDPA) is part of the evolution of the universal mobile telecommunication system (UMTS). It is often referred to as 3.5G system, in contrast to UMTS, which is a third generation (3G) system. This chapter gives an overview of the background and functionality of HSDPA, and provides insights into the radio resource management (RRM) of integrated UMTS/HSDPA networks. The general goal of RRM is to provide the user with a certain quality of service (QoS), and selecting an RRM strategy is thus an integral part of the network planning and deployment process.

Background

The development of HSDPA was initiated as response to an increasing demand for high-speed mobile Internet access. In standard UMTS (as in Release '99), Internet access is realized by using dedicated channels (DCH). However, DCH radio bearers have limitations in data rate, packet latency, and resource efficiency. The maximum data rate of a DCH connection in macro-cells is 384 kbps with a one-way latency from UE to the gateway GPRS support node (GGSN), which is the gateway to the Internet, of about 100 ms (Cano-Garcia, Gonzalez-Parada, & Casilari, 2006). HSDPA enables data rates of several megabits per seconds with packet latencies of 60 to 70 ms. From the viewpoint of the providers the use of 384 kbps DCH radio bearers is problematic since they require a large amount of code resources, such that at maximum only seven 384 kbps bearers are possible in one sector if no other connections are present. With HSDPA, this limitation is avoided by using a shared channel for all HSDPA users per sector. Figure 1 illustrates the code occupancy time for "bursty" data traffic like web browsing where short times of activity are alternating with

long "idle" times, the so-called reading time. DCH connections occupy the channelization code during the lifetime of the DCH radio bearer, which is terminated only if the release timer expires--which is normally set to several tens of seconds. With HSDPA, the channelization codes are occupied only during the user activity phases.

HSDPA was first specified by the 3rd Generation Partnership Program (3GPP) in March 2002 with UMTS Release 5. Four years later at the beginning of 2006 the first HSDPA-enhanced UMTS networks were launched. The specifications define several expansion stages, which are reflected by the capabilities of the terminals. In the first deployment phase, the maximum throughput is 1.8 Mbps and 3.6 Mbps, which corresponds to UE category 11 with QPSK modulation and UE category 3 with 16QAM and a minimum scheduling interval of 2 TTIs (frames). In later phases up to 12.8 Mbps with 16 QAM will be possible, although such high bitrates require good radio conditions.

Early HSDPA-capable terminals (or user equipments (UE) in 3GPP-terminology) were mostly data cards intended for laptops, but now a wide variety of terminals are available, from small smart phones to stationary devices built as substitute for DSL modems. The increasing number of HSDPA terminals and networks is an

Figure 1. Channelization code occupation with DCH and HSDPA

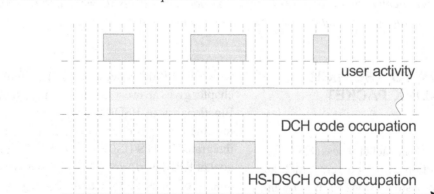

indicator of the growing acceptance and demand of this service.

HSDPA PRINCIPLES

DCH connections provide nearly constant QoS in terms of data rate by means of fast power control, which adapts the transmit power in order to keep the signal-to-interference ratio (SIR) at an appropriate target level. HSDPA breaks with this principle. Instead, HSDPA uses adaptive modulation and coding (AMC) to adapt the instantaneous data rate to the channel quality, which allows for higher data rates in case of good radio conditions. The transportation of data is done on the high speed

Figure 2. HSDPA terminal for PCMCIA slots

downlink shared channel (HS-DSCH), which implements a mixed TDMA/CDMA scheme in contrast to pure CDMA (or wideband CDMA) as for DCH radio bearers. Resource assignment is done in the NodeB scheduler (a NodeB is a UMTS base station) with help of channel quality indicator (CQI) values, which are signaled by the UEs. In order to reduce packet latency and SIR requirements, hybrid automatic repeat request (HARQ) has been introduced which handles retransmissions on MAC-layer.

In addition to the HS-DSCH, two new signaling channels have been introduced. In the downlink, the HS-SCCH (high speed signaling control channel) carries information about the UE to be scheduled in the next subframe and its code rate and modulation scheme. In the uplink, the HS-DPCCH (high speed dedicated physical control channel) carries information about the HARQ reception status, which is ACK or NACK, and the CQI values. Figure 3 gives a graphical impression of all channels involved.

HS-DSCH Transport Channel

The HS-DSCH is used for the transport of user data. The time axis is subdivided into transport time intervals (TTIs) of 2 ms length, and on the code axis in HS-PDSCHs (high speed physical

Figure 3. HSDPA data and signaling channels

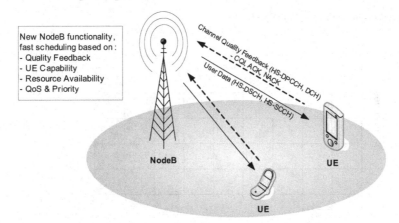

downlink shared channel), which correspond to a channelization code of fixed spreading factor SF=16. The amount of bits, which can be transported within one TTI, is given by the transport block size (TBS), which is chosen by the NodeB scheduler according to the channel quality and the HARQ retransmission number. The HS-DSCH enables a mixture between CDMA and TDMA, since the HS-PDSCHs in one TTI can be assigned to different UEs. This may be useful for very time-critical traffic where the data volume is small, but the packets arrive with small inter-arrival times. Another scenario is that if a single UE cannot use the available HS-PDCHs because of bad channel conditions, then the remaining resources could be consumed by a second UE (Kwan, Peter, Poutiainen, & Rinne, 2003). However, multi-user scheduling in one TTI leads to multiple access interference like in conventional WCDMA, so it is not always beneficial for overall performance. Therefore, and because of the increased complexity of a scheduler with code-multiplexing, scheduling is done mostly one-by-one as illustrated in Figure 4, where three UEs are scheduled one after another.

Adaptive Modulation and Coding

The perceived channel quality at each UE is constantly changing, a phenomenon which is known as fading. Fading on millisecond time scale is called fast fading and is the result of multi-path propagation. Instead of combating fast fading with fast power control as for DCH connections, the HS-DSCH instantaneously adapts the modulation and code rate to the channel quality. This scheme, called adaptive modulation and coding (AMC), enables an effective exploitation of the channel capacity (Goldsmith & Varaiya, 1997), since the number of information bits is adapted to the current theoretic capacity. Choosing the correct modulation and code rate requires knowledge of the throughput curves for different modulation orders and code rates. Since the curves are system specific, which means that they depend on the coding scheme used (for the HS-DSCH, turbo codes are used) and on implementation issues like the decoding algorithm, they are generated by extensive simulations (Döttling, Michel, & Raaf, 2002; Kolding, Frederiksen, & Mogensen, 2001).

For the HS-DSCH, this means that the number of bits which can be transported within one TTI, the transport block size (TBS), can change every 2 ms. Figure 5 shows an example trace of a slowly moving UE. The signal-to-noise ratio (SNR) varies in a range from -9 dB to 3 dB. The UE measures the SNR and signals the corresponding CQI back to the NodeB. Note the small time difference between actual SNR and measured CQI due to

Figure 4. Schematic view of the HS-DSCH

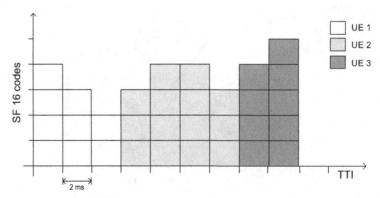

signaling delays. The NodeB then translates the CQI value to a TBS value, as seen in the lower part of the figure. The CQI values are chosen such that on average, the frame error rate of the first HARQ transmission does not exceed 10%.

Table 1 is a simplified example: the CQI value defines the transport block size, the number of HS-PDSCHs, and the modulation order. This example is an excerpt of the CQI table for UE class category 10, which allows data rates up to 12.8 Mbps with 15 codes in parallel. The UE categories describe the capabilities of the UEs and differ in the maximum number of parallel codes, the modulation order (16 QAM is optional) and the minimum inter-TTI scheduling interval. The relation between CQI and TBS is defined in the specifications (3GPP TS 25.214, 2005).

The CQI tables define the maximum number of bits per TTI, which can be transmitted with the current CQI, but this value does not necessarily represent the TBS, which is actually chosen. The reason is that the number of available codes may be lower than the number of required HS-PDSCHs, for example if some codes are already occupied by DCH connections. In that case, the

maximum TBS value for the available number of codes is selected. Another reason may be that the number of bits in the transmit buffer is lower than the TBS value. Then, the lowest TBS, which can carry the buffer content, is chosen in order to decrease the frame error probability.

Hybrid ARQ

Hybrid automatic repeat request combines error correction by retransmissions with information coding techniques. In UMTS Release '99, retransmissions are handled by the radio link control (RLC) protocol, which is one layer above MAC in the UMTS protocol stack, with end points in the radio network controller (RNC) and the UE. That means that a retransmission goes over 2 hops, making it time consuming and complex to handle. RLC retransmissions are therefore expensive and should be avoided, which in turn requires higher transmit powers to achieve lower frame error rates.

Hybrid ARQ is located on MAC layer between NodeB and UE. It is implemented as an N-stop-and-wait protocol, where N is the num-

Figure 5. CQI values and corresponding SNR (above), transport block sizes (below)

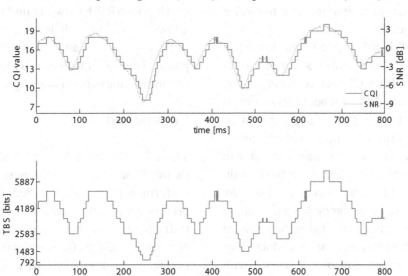

Table 1. Simplified CQI table for UE category 10

CQI value	Transport Block Size	Number of HS-PDSCH	Modulation
0	N/A	Out of range	
1	137	1	QPSK
2	173	1	QPSK
3	233	1	QPSK
4	317	1	QPSK
5	377	1	QPSK
6	461	1	QPSK
.	.	.	.
.	.	.	.
.	.	.	.
24	11418	8	16-QAM
25	14411	10	16-QAM
26	17237	12	16-QAM
27	21754	15	16-QAM
28	23370	15	16-QAM
29	24222	15	16-QAM
30	25558	15	16-QAM

ber of processes. The processes are called in a round-robin manner, such that each process is responsible for one TTI in a cycle. The number of processes (N=4) is chosen such that there is no idle time during the time required to receive an acknowledgement.

The "hybrid" in hybrid ARQ is due to the fact that it combines ARQ with forward error correction techniques. If the UE receives an erroneous packet, it does not discard it but saves a copy of the turbo-decoder output ("soft-bits") in a buffer. The second transmission is then combined with the first transmission and is again decoded, but with a much higher probability to get a correct result. At maximum, four transmissions are possible. The ratio between redundancy and information bits may be increased with the retransmission number ("incremental redundancy"), which gives a slight performance gain over a scheme with identical retransmissions ("Chase combining")

(Chase, 1985; Cheng, 2003; Frenger, Parkvall, & Dahlman, 2001). However, the total number of bits transmitted must not change during the retransmissions.

Hybrid ARQ has two main benefits: first, it allows operating with lower SNR values due to the coding gain, and second it leads to lower packet latency times since with HARQ, RLC retransmissions are seldom required.

Scheduling

The task of the scheduler in the NodeB is to assign the available resources to the users such that some performance goals are fulfilled if possible. The performance metrics depend on the carried user traffic type and on the viewpoint (network or user centric). Typical performance metrics from user perspective are throughput, packet delay, and jitter. Also, the resources should be assigned "fairly,"

Figure 6. Retransmissions in UMTS Release '99 and Release '5 with HSDPA

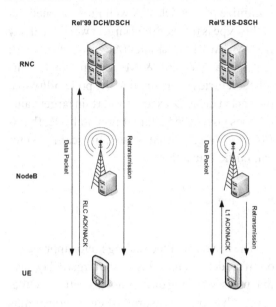

which means that the performance differences between the users should not be too large. From the viewpoint of the network, the total throughput should be optimized, which can be achieved by always serving the currently best users. These examples show that the attempt to maximize one metric may lead to lower performance for other metrics, for example in the case of total throughput and user fairness.

The scheduling disciplines can be classified into channel-aware schemes, which take the channel qualities at the UEs into account, and "blind" disciplines like round-robin. Channel-aware schedulers can exploit multi-user diversity, which describes the fact that since in HSDPA the current user data rates are random variables, the probability to see a user with good channel quality increases with the number of users in the cell (Bergren & Jäntti, 2003; Knopp & Humblet, 1995; Viswanath, Tse, & Laroia, 2002). A scheduler, which provides maximum cell throughput is therefore the MaxCQI-scheduler, which always selects the user with the currently best CQI. This scheme, often described as "riding the top," has

the disadvantage that it will lead to starvation of users, which are on the cell edge. A scheduling scheme which combines channel-awareness with user fairness is "proportional-fair" scheduling, which aims at maximizing not the sum of all users' rates, but the ratio between current and past data rate or data volume (Jalali, Padovani, & Pankaj, 2000; Kelly, Maulloo, & Tan, 1998). Thus, a user *j* is selected at TTI *t* if:

$$j = \arg\max_{j}\left\{ w_j \cdot \frac{TBS_j(t)}{\overline{TBS}_j(t)} \right\}$$

where w_j is a scaling factor, TBS_j is the current TBS and $\overline{TBS}_j$ is the average perceived TBS, which is often calculated with a sliding window approach as:

$$\overline{TBS}_j(t) = (1-\alpha) \cdot \delta_j \cdot TBS_j(t) + \alpha \cdot \overline{TBS}_j(t-1)$$

with α as weight factor and δ_j as indicator whether the current user has been served or not. In the literature, multitudes of versions and modifications exist of the proportional-fair scheduler. In Andrews (2004), several variants are analyzed which allow different sets of users to compete for a subframe: all, only the one with non-empty queue, or only the one which can use the whole TBS. Further variants differ in whether the actual TBS or the number of bits actually served is used for the average throughput update. Another question is whether the average throughput should be updated right after the scheduling decision or whether the scheduler should wait for a positive acknowledgement such that only the goodput is considered (Kolding, 2003). An important issue also is the interaction between TCP and scheduling: although the proportional-fair scheme is a good choice for best-effort traffic over TCP, the inter-scheduling times for the different users should be not too large in order to avoid TCP timeouts (Klein, Leung, & Zheng, 2004).

Round-robin and proportional-fair schedulers assign radio resources on average "fairly" to the users. However, they cannot guarantee quality of service (QoS) like a guaranteed bit rate (GBR) or delay. Multimedia traffic like voice over IP or streaming video, which requires such guarantees therefore require special schedulers, which are also often modifications of the proportional-fair principle. Schedulers, which try to guarantee data rates often, use a barrier function, which gives disproportionate priority to users who are not getting their guaranteed data rate (Aniba & Aissa, 2004; Hosein, 2002; Kolding T. E., 2006; Lundevall et al., 2004). The basic idea is to adapt the scaling factor w_j according to the difference between the guaranteed data rate and the actual received data rate. One example used in Kolding (2006) is:

$$w_j = 1 + \beta \cdot \exp\left[-\gamma \cdot (\overline{TBS}_j - TBS_j^g) \right]$$

where TBS_j^g is the guaranteed bit rate of user j, and β, γ are parameters, which control the "aggressiveness" of the barrier function. The parameters can be used to tune the trade-off between multi-user diversity gain and effectiveness of the GBR mechanism.

Multimedia traffic like Voice over IP or streaming video has more stringent requirements on the packet delay than best-effort traffic. For this type of traffic, delay-aware schedulers have been developed which try to use the benefits of AMC and to minimize packet delay. A well known scheduler of this type is the modified largest weighted delay first (M-LWDF) scheduler (Andrews et al., 2001; Ameigeiras, Wigard, & Mogensen, 2004). This scheduler tries to ensure that the probability that the packet delay D_j exceeds a certain target value D^* does not exceed a target probability ξ, that is $P(D_j > D^*) < \xi$. For that reason, the scaling factor is modified such that:

$$w_j = -\log(\xi) \cdot \frac{D_j}{D^*}$$

The last term of the scaling factor approaches one if the delay comes close to the target delay, such that users with long queues are prioritized. Other approaches try to ensure the delay constraints more aggressively, like the channel-dependent earliest deadline first (CD-EDD) scheduler (Khattab & Elsayed, 2004), or the exponential rule (ER) scheduler, which introduces a barrier function for the delays (Shakkottai & Stolyra, 2001).

All these schedulers are designed for a specific class of traffic, like best effort, streaming services, or delay-sensitive traffic. However, it is also intended to transport different types of

Figure 7. Hierarchical and flat scheduling for service class differentiation

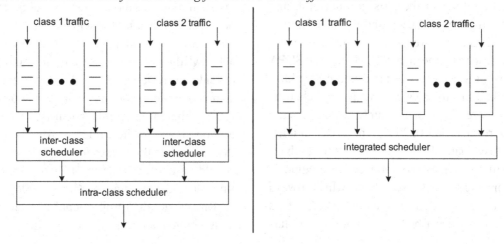

traffic and therefore different service classes over HSDPA, which makes the scheduling problem even more complex. Besides the mapping of the QoS parameters of the UMTS service classes to HSDPA as elaborated in Pedersen, Mogensen, and Kolding (2006), the question is how to design a scheduler, which meets all requirements of the different traffic types. Generally, two approaches can be distinguished. The first is a flat design in which one scheduler is responsible for the queues of all users, regardless of their service class. This implies that the scheduler can be parameterized and considers all relevant QoS variables. Although many QoS-aware schedulers have a parameter for service class differentiation, they mostly do not consider data rate and delay at the same time. Examples of such schedulers are given in Kolding (2006) and Li and Sampalli (2006). Another option is to perform hierarchical scheduling with intra-class and inter-class schedulers. The intra-class schedulers select the UE for transmission within their service class, while the inter-class scheduler selects between the classes (Necker, 2006).

Figure 7 clarifies the two concepts. The advantage of the hierarchical scheduling approach is that it allows different scheduling concepts for the different service classes, and allows easy implementation of priority scheduling (service priority is signaled via the service priority indicator--SPI--to the NodeB) by the intra-class scheduler. It is also more convenient to parameterize due to the functional split between inter- and intra-class scheduling. However, if the inter-class scheduler should take the scheduling metrics of the intra-class schedulers into account, the metrics between the classes must be comparable. Another possibility is that the inter-class scheduler evaluates the scheduling parameters for the selected packets per class of its own, as is done in the example in Figure 8. In this figure, the UDP packet delays for two inter-class schedulers for Voice over IP traffic are compared. The static priority (SP) scheduler always chooses the packet with the highest service priority, so it is a low complexity scheduler, which is very easy to implement. The dynamic earliest deadline first (DEDF) scheduler is a variant of the M-LWDF scheduler. It selects the user with the following rule:

Figure 8. Comparison between two inter-class schedulers

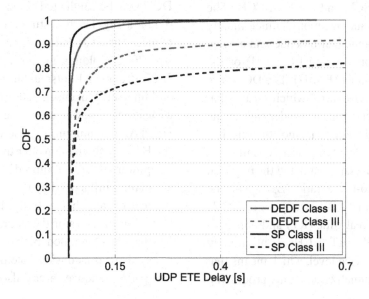

$$j = \arg\min_{j} \left\{ T_{\mathrm{HoL},j} - C_j - w_j \cdot \frac{\mathrm{TBS}_j}{\overline{\mathrm{TBS}_j}} \right\}$$

$T_{HoL,j}$ is the queuing time of the head-of-line packet of those, which are selected by the intra-class schedulers, w_j is an arbitrary constant, which determines the influence of the proportional-fair term and c_j is a class-specific constant, which describes the delay advantage one class has. We see in Figure 8 that the static priority scheduler leads to good results for the first service class, but allows the delay of the second class increase beyond acceptable values. The DEDF scheduler allows finding a more balanced prioritization of the first class, such that the second class can meet a 0.4s delay target with 90% probability.

SHARING CODE AND POWER RESOURCES BETWEEN HSDPA AND DCH

A key part of the radio resource management in HSDPA enhanced UMTS networks is the sharing of code and transmit power resources between DCHs, signaling channels, common channels, and finally channels required for the HSDPA namely the HS-DSCH and the HS-SCCH. The signaling channels and common channels mostly require a fixed channelization code and a fixed power as for the pilot channel (CPICH) or the forward access channel (FACH). The DCHs are subject to fast power control which means that their transmit power requirements depends on the cell or system load that determines the interference at the UE. The level of power consumption depends on the processing gain and the required target bit-energy-to-noise ratio (E_b/N_0) of the radio access bearer (RAB). Two types of DCHs are distinguished: real-time (RT) and non-real-time (NRT) DCHs. RT DCHs continuously require a certain service level, which means that they keep their channelization code, processing

gain, and target E_b/N_0 value throughout the connection. RT DCHs are mainly used to transport voice or video traffic. NRT DCHs are subject to a slow rate or load control, which is located in the RNC. Depending on the current system situation the RNC may change the channelization code and thus also the power consumption of a NRT DCH. Measurements in a laboratory environment (Mäder, Wagner, Hoßfeld, Staehle, & Barth, 2006) have shown that the load control of NRT DCHs takes place on the order of several seconds and is strongly vendor specific. NRT DCHs are currently used to establish a connection to the Internet over UMTS Rel99 networks and the HSDPA is mainly intended to replace them.

As discussed earlier the HSDPA uses the HS-DSCH to transport data and the HS-SCCH to signal the type usage of the HS-DSCH to slots prior to the actual data transport. Parallel scheduling of different code subsets to multiple users requires the establishment of multiple HS-SCCHs. Parallel scheduling is mainly used for services with data packets too small to utilize the possible TBS. Depending on the type of service, FTP or HTTP, two or three HS-SCCHs are sufficient (Brueck, Jugl, Kettschau, Link, Mueckenheim, & Zaprozhets, 2007).

Sharing resources between HSDPA and DCH may be conducted either semi-statically or dynamically. The first studies on HSDPA performance (Furuskär, Parkvall, Persson, & Samuelsson, 2002; Kolding, Frederiksen, & Mogensen, 2002; Pedersen, Lootsma, Stottrup, Frederikson, Kolding, & Mogensen, 2004) assume a fixed allocation of power and code resources to the HSDPA. The amount of resources allocated to the HSDPA should consider the balance of code and power resources required by the DCHs. These are mainly influenced by the spatial distribution of the users and their activity. The radio channel condition in terms of the degree of orthogonality that is maintained between channelization codes also has a considerable impact. Large soft and softer handover areas also lead to a higher increase of code consumption than of power consumption. More recent publications (Brueck et al., 2007; Pedersen & Michaelsen, 2006) assume a dynamic allocation of code and power resources which means that the HSDPA may use all resources instantaneously not occupied by CCHs or DCHs except for a certain safety margin that has to be kept due to the fluctuations in the DCH resources and the time required for adapting to these changes.

RT DCHs are mainly used for critical services like voice and video telephony, and as such should not be affected by best-effort services with lower priority. Exceptions are NRT DCH connections, which adapt their data rate and as a consequence their required power and code resources to the current system situation. NRT DCHs are intended to carry best effort traffic, which means that they carry the same kind of traffic as the HSDPA does. Consequently they should have the same priority as HSDPA connections. However, due to their slower reaction times they are often favored compared to HSDPA connections. In general, comparing NRT DCH connection and HSDPA connection is not easy due to the different kinds of resources they require: NRT DCH connections

require explicit code and power resources while HSDPA connections share a bundle of code and power resources with other connections in a dynamic and efficient way.

An adaptive, dynamic allocation of code and power resources leads to an optimal utilization of the available spectrum and optimizes HSDPA performance while the DCH achieve precisely their required service quality. As a negative consequence, the throughput of HSDPA connections diminishes in cells with high DCH load. There is no performance guarantee for the HSDPA. A fixed resource allocation leads to a certain guaranteed HSDPA throughput but also restricts the cells' DCH capacity. Additionally, resources may remain unused if only a few DCH connections are present or if the code and power resources for the HSDPA are not well balanced. We will see later that this balance strongly depends on the channel profile and the HSDPA users' locations within the cell area. The hybrid resource allocation combines the advantages of the fixed and the dynamic allocation. Allocating fixed code and power resources to the HSDPA ensures a certain HSDPA throughput. Dynamically adding unused DCH resources to the already allocated fixed

Figure 9. Radio resource management schemes for transmit power and channelization codes

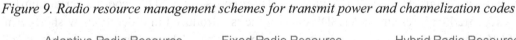

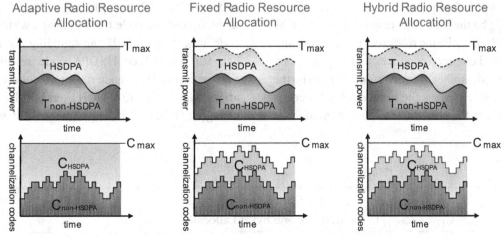

HSDPA resources avoids wasting valuable radio resources and optimizes HSDPA performance. Figure 9 sketches the idealized power and resource sharing for the three allocation schemes fixed (or semi-static), adaptive (or dynamic), and hybrid.

Code Resources

The HSDPA requires code and power resources. Codes are the channelization codes that are generated according to the orthogonal variable spreading factor (OVSF) code tree. The number of codes that is available for a certain spreading factor (SF) is equal to the spreading factor itself. A 384kbps DCH occupies a SF8 channelization code. Accordingly, the maximum number of parallel 384kbps users per sector is theoretically 8. In practice, there are only 7 parallel 384kbps users possible since the signaling and common channels also require some code resources. Figure 10 shows the beginning of the OVSF code tree for spreading factors from 1 to 8. The green nodes mark codes that are already occupied. The red nodes represent blocked codes and the yellow nodes mark available codes. An occupied code blocks all its predecessors and successors in the tree. All other codes may be used since a code is orthogonal to all codes that are located in another part of the code tree. Let us introduce an SF512 code as the basic code unit. Then, a DCH i with SF k occupies $c_i = 512/k$ code resources. A HSDPA code with SF16 requires $c_{HS} = 32$ code resources. Let C_{DCH} be the total code resources occupied by all DCHs, C_{CCH} be the resources occupied by signaling and common channels, and, $c_{HS} = n_{HS} \cdot c_{HS}$ be the total number of code resources used by the HSDPA where n_{HS} is the number of SF16 codes allocated to the HS-DSCH. The total number of

code resources is equal to $C_{tot} = 512$. Depending on the code allocation scheme, the number of codes available for the HSDPA is shown in Box 1, where n_{HS} is the number SF16 codes reserved for HSDPA in case of fixed or hybrid allocation. The call admission control for DCH ensures that the respective code resources are always available to the HSDPA.

The adaptive and hybrid allocation may be done on different time scales and additional code margins. The allocation of channelization codes to channels is done by the RNC via the NodeB application protocol (NBAP) (3GPP TS 25.433, 2007). Changing the codes allocated to the HS-DSCH does not require any radio resources since the signaling of which codes are used by which HSDPA user is signaled using the HS-SCCH. Changing the channelization code of a DCH, however, requires signaling from RNC to UE via the radio resource control (RRC) protocol (3GPP TS 25.331, 2007). Changes of the DCH codes consume radio resources and introduce longer delays than changes of HSDPA codes. Consequently, frequent changes of DCH codes should be avoided. One possibility (Pedersen & Michaelsen, 2006) is to allocate HS-DSCH codes at one end of the OVSF code tree and codes for signaling, common, and dedicated channels starting from the other end of the code tree. Between DCH codes and HSDPA codes a certain buffer zone is introduced in order to allow short-term allocation to DCH or signaling channels. Fragmentation of the code tree (i.e., gaps within the code allocation of DCH and signaling channels) can further reduce HSDPA code resources. Fluctuation of DCH code resources comes from arrival and departure of DCH users but also from changing DCH activity. The time scale on which

Box 1.

$$n_{HS} = \begin{cases} n_{HS}^* & \text{for fixed allocation} \\ \lfloor C_{tot} - C_{CCH} - C_{DCH} \rfloor & \text{for adaptive and hybrid allocation} \end{cases}$$

these activity changes take place determines whether the codes are released and available for the HSDPA or not. The delay requirement of the application determines how fast the codes have to be available again after an inactivity period. As an example, HSDPA might utilize free code resources that results from activity changes of an Internet user on a 384kbps DCH but might not utilize free code resources resulting from silence periods in voice calls.

Power Resources

The transmit power consumed by DCH is subject to power control. A DCH i with a processing gain of $\beta_i = W/R_i$ where W is the system bandwidth and R_i the DCH bit rate experiences an E_b/N_0 value of:

$$\varepsilon_i = \beta_i \cdot \sum_{p=1}^{P_{x,i}} \frac{T_{x,i} \cdot d_{x,i,p}}{W \cdot N_0 + I_{other,i} + \sum_{r=1,r\neq p}^{P_{x,i}} T_{x,tot} \cdot d_{x,i,r}}$$

The DCH i is associated with NodeB x that transmits with total power $T_{x,tot}$ and the part $T_{x,i}$ is used for DCH i. The channel between NodeB and DCH consists of $P_{x,i}$ multi-path components

and the p-th multi-path component experiences propagation gain $d_{x,i,p}$. The interference consists of the thermal noise spectral density N_0, the other-cell interference $I_{other,i}$ that depends on UE location and other-cell transmit powers and is subject to fast fading, and the own-cell interference of the p-th multi-path component that is the aggregated power received by all asynchronously arriving multi-path components. The Rake receiver combines the signals for all resolvable multi-path components. A common approximation for the average E_b/N_0 value is:

$$\overline{\varepsilon}_i = \beta_i \cdot \frac{T_{x,i} \cdot d_{x,i}}{W \cdot N_0 + I_{other,i} + \alpha_i \cdot T_{x,tot} \cdot d_{x,i}}$$

where the orthogonality α_i describes the impact of the multi-path profile for DCH i, and $d_{x,i}$ is the average path gain between NodeB x and UE i. The transmit power of the NodeB consists of a constant part T_{CCH} for common and signaling channels, a part T_{DCH} for DCHs, and a part T_{HS} for the HS-DSCH. Let T_{max} be the maximum NodeB transmit power and T_{target} be the target transmit power. Then, the HS-DSCH according to the different resource allocation schemes is shown in

Figure 10. OSVF code tree with occupied (▨) and blocked codes (▮)

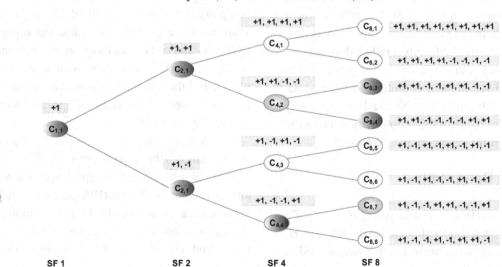

Box 2.

$$T_{HS} = \begin{cases} T_{HS}^* & \text{for fixed allocation} \\ \left\lfloor T_{target} - T_{CCH} - T_{DCH} \right\rfloor & \text{for adaptive and hybrid allocation,} \end{cases}$$

Box 2, where T_{HS}^* is the power reserved for the HS-DSCH and T_{DCH} is the total DCH power averaged over some period of time. Methods for calculating the HS-DSCH power in multi-cell networks with multi-media DCH traffic are proposed in Mäder, Staehle, and Spahn (2007).

The DCH admission control for fixed and hybrid power allocation has to take care that the DCH power does not exceed $T_{max} - T_{CCH} - T_{HS}^*$. This is achieved by keeping the average DCH power below $T_{target} - T_{CCH} - T_{HS}^*$. The margin between target and maximum power is the power control headroom reserved for fluctuations of the DCH power. In a system without HSDPA (Holma & Toskala, 2004), the target power is a factor K smaller than the maximum power. A typical value is $K = 0.5$. The introduction of the HSDPA allows for a better utilization of the power resource (Pedersen et al., 2004) even if fixed power allocation is used. As the power control headroom is chosen relative to the average DCH power ratio we obtain $T_{DCH} = K \cdot (T_{max} - T_{HS}) + T_{HS}^*$. Adaptive or hybrid power allocation tries to follow the fluctuations of the DCH power. The control of the HSDPA power can be located in the RNC or in the NodeB. If it is located in the RNC only a rather slow adaptation of the power is possible so it is beneficial to do the power adaptation directly in the NodeB. The faster the NodeB is able to adapt, especially to decrease the HS-DSCH power, the smaller the power control headroom can be chosen.

HSDPA Bandwidth

Consider an HS-DSCH with power $T_{HS} = \Delta_{HS} \cdot T_{tot}$ and n_{HS} parallel codes allocated to the HS-DSCH. Accordingly, the signal-to-interference ratio (SIR) at UE i is equal to:

$$\gamma_i = \Delta_{HS} \cdot \sum_{p=1}^{P_{x,i}} \frac{T_{tot} \cdot d_{x,i,p}}{W \cdot N_0 + I_{other,i} + \sum_{r=1, r \neq p}^{P_{x,i}} T_{x,tot} \cdot d_{x,i,r}}$$

The UE measures the SIR and maps it to the maximum CQI with a transmission format that achieves a frame error rate of 10%. In Brouwer, de Bruin, Silva, Souto, Cercas, and Correia (2004), the following relation of SIR and CQI is given:

$$CQI = \max\left(0, \min\left(30, \left\lfloor \frac{SIR[dB]}{1.02} + 16.52 \right\rfloor \right) \right)$$

The CQI reflects the maximum performance the available HS-DSCH power allows. The CQI also defines the transmission format with the number of parallel codes $n_{HS}(CQI)$. If n_{HS} is less than $n_{HS}(CQI)$, the selected TBS is the maximum TBS possible with n_{HS} parallel codes. An optimal usage of resources is only possible if the reported CQI suggests a transmission format that utilizes all available codes. If too few code resources are available power resources are wasted, and if too few power resources are available, the CQI is too small to utilize all available codes. The reported CQI value depends essentially on the multi-path profile, the users' location, the available HS-DSCH power, and the other-cell power. The number of codes required for a certain CQI value depends on the CQI category.

The above equations give the TBS for a concrete instance of the propagation gains of the multi-path component power. For a simplified simulation and evaluation of the HSDPA performance, an approximate model for the HSDPA bandwidth similar to the orthogonality factor model for DCH is required. The orthogonality factor model is not applicable to the HSDPA since it only yields the mean of the SIR. The distribution of the reported CQI values is required for evaluating the HSDPA bandwidth of a UE at a certain location value with random multi-path component powers. The essential assumption of the orthogonality factor model is that the mean SIR is a function of the ratio Σ of average other-cell received power and average own-cell received power (also called the other-to-own-cell power ratio):

$$\Sigma_i = \frac{\sum_{(y \neq x)} T_{y,tot} \cdot d_{y,i}}{T_{x,tot} \cdot d_{x,i}}$$

In Staehle and Mäder (2007) the orthogonality factor model is enhanced to yield not only the mean but also the standard deviation of the SIR in decibel scale as a function of Σ_i. Assuming that the distribution of the SIR follows a normal distribution that is entirely characterized by its mean and standard deviation, the distribution of the reported CQI values is obtained from the cumulative density function (CDF) of the distribution of the SIR. Truncating the CQI distribution according to the available codes on the HS-DSCH yields the distribution of the TBS. In Mäder and Staehle (2007) the HSDPA throughput

according to this model is determined for Round-robin, Proportional-fair, and Max-CQI/Max-TBS scheduling.

In the following, we investigate the impact and relation of different parameters like UE category, multi-path profile, HS-DSCH power, and HS-DSCH codes on the HSDPA performance expressed as the mean TBS the mobile experiences. The basic setting assumes a total NodeB power of 20W, HS-DSCH resources with 15W and 15 codes, UE category 10, and "ITU Pedestrian A" multi-path profile. The following figures show the mean TBS as a function of the own-to-other-cell power ratio Σ in decibel. Note that small values of Σ reflect locations in the cell center and large values of Σ reflect locations at the cell border. A value of Σ = 0dB shows the performance for a mobile exactly at the border between two NodeBs transmitting with equal power and no other source of other-cell interference. Values of Σ > 3dB mainly occur if the transmit power of other NodeBs exceeds the transmit power of the own NodeB and additionally multiple NodeBs contribute significantly to the other-cell interference.

Figure 11 shows the impact of the multi-path profile on the HSDPA performance. ITU Pedestrian A (PA) leads to by far the highest throughput

Figure 11. Impact of multi-path profile on HSDPA performance

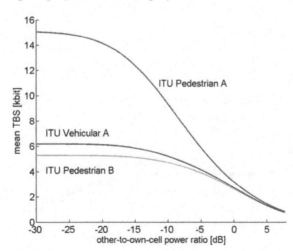

whereas ITU Pedestrian B (PB) and ITU Vehicular A (VA) show similar performance. The reason for this is that PA has a clearly dominant strongest path and hence produces little own-cell interference. PB and VA have two significant paths that mutually produce interference. For larger other-to-own-cell power ratios the difference between the multi-path profiles diminishes since the increasing other-cell interferences outweighs the difference in the own-cell interference due to the different multi-path profiles.

Figure 12 shows the impact of the different UE categories (3GPP TS 25.306) according to the CQI tables defined in (3GPP TS 25.214). The results for PA and PB are compared, VA is not considered as it shows similar performance to PB. The UE categories that allow the usage of many codes mainly show a significantly better performance for PA and small other-to-own-cell power ratios. At the cell border for other-to-own-cell power ratios above -5dB the advantage due to enhanced UE categories disappears. For PB, all UE categories that support 16QAM (categories 1-10) lead to equal performance. The categories without 16QAM (categories 11 and 12) achieve the worst performance independent of the multi-path profile. Interestingly, for UE categories 11

and 12, the multi-path profile makes almost no difference.

Figure 13 illustrates the interaction of the two HS-DSCH resources codes and power by comparing the mean TBS curves for HS-DSCH powers of 5W, 10W, and 15W and for 5, 10, and 15 available codes. Obviously, the mean TBS increases with more codes and with more power. However, the performance gain due to more codes shrinks for large other-to-own-cell power ratios. The point when the performance gain due to more codes becomes invisible depends on the HS-DSCH power. For 5W, the curves diverge at -10dB; for 10W the curves diverge at -7.5dB; and for 15W, the curves diverge at -5dB. This effect means that the area in which a large number of codes can be used shrinks with the HS-DSCH power. Analogously, the advantage of more power shrinks if not enough codes are available. As an example, with only five codes available the maximum TBS at the cell center increases only from 5800 bit to 6000bit if the HS-DSCH power is increased from 10W to 15W. The figure shows quite clearly that a certain balance between codes and power should always be maintained. Though increasing only one resource always leads to a certain performance

Figure 12. Relation between UE category and mutli-path profile

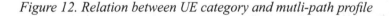
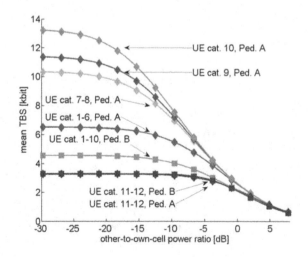

gain, it is not very effective if the other resource is not increased as well.

As a summary, we observe that many codes, much power, and an enhanced UE capability are only effective if a UE has excellent radio conditions. As soon as a mobile is located at the cell border or has two strong multi-path components, 5 codes and UE category 1-6 are sufficient to achieve an almost optimal performance.

Power Allocation for Non-Saturated HSDPA

Another issue besides the resource sharing between DCH and HSDPA is how to allocate power to a non-saturated HS-DSCH over time. If the offered load for the HSDPA is not sufficient to utilize the available HSDPA resource, periods with and without traffic on the HS-DSCH alternate. A "traffic-aware" transmit power scheme uses all available transmit power whenever there are resources to send and spends no power for the HS-DSCH when there is no data to send. The HS-DSCH power may be switched on and off in a very fast pattern, in the extreme every 2ms TTI. This poses a potential problem for the fast power control of DCH connections since it is not able

to follow the interference jumps introduced by switching the HS-DSCH power on and off. The NodeB may partially compensate for the on and off switching of its own HS-DSCH by adjusting the DCH powers accordingly. However, changes in the other-cell interference due to on and off switching of the HS-DSCH power in neighboring cells are hardly predictable and present the main source of interference for mobiles at the cell border.

An alternative is the "continuous power" scheme that keeps the HS-DSCH power constant by transmitting dummy data when no actual data is available. The advantage of this scheme is a constant interference level; the disadvantage is that this interference level is unnecessarily high, in particular if the HSDPA is little utilized. The high interference level does not concern the own cell but mainly the surrounding cells where the HS-DSCH throughput is considerably decreased.

A compromise between "traffic-aware power" and "continuous power" is the "power-ramping" scheme. It increases and decreases the HS-DSCH transmit power in small steps depending on the amount of data in the HS-DSCH buffers and thus avoids both abrupt changes in the interference and a large waste of resources due to long periods

Figure 13. Relation between HS-DSCH codes and power

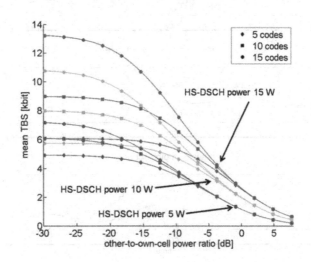

of artificially introduced interference. Figure 14 illustrates the different HS-DSCH power allocation schemes.

IMPACT OF RESOURCE ALLOCATION SCHEMES ON HSDPA AND DCH PERFORMANCE

The effect of the resource allocation schemes depends on flow level dynamics and on the interaction of traffic processes in multiple cells. In order to capture the effects of other-cell interference, scenarios with multiple cells should be simulated: typically at least a center cell with two surrounding tiers. In order to capture traffic dynamics, long simulation runs of several hours are required. Since the HSDPA is mainly used to transport best-effort traffic, a volume-based traffic model should be used, which means that the life-time of a flow is determined by a certain data volume that has to be transferred in the flow. As stated in Litjens, van den Berg, and Fleuren (2005), a

volume-based traffic model together with a location dependent throughput - which is obtained for all reasonable HSDPA scheduling disciplines – leads to a heterogeneous spatial UE distribution, though the arrivals follow a homogeneous Poisson process. This feature militates against the proper use of Monte Carlo simulations since it's hardly possible to predict the spatial HSDPA user distribution a priori. The following results are taken from Mäder et al. (2007b) and are produced according to the simulation framework presented in Mäder et al. (2007a).

Let us first study the impact of the different resource allocation schemes "fixed," "adaptive," and "hybrid" on the expected HSDPA throughput. Figure 15 shows the time-average user throughput for the three resource allocation schemes. In case of *fixed* and *hybrid*, 4 W transmit power and 5 SF=16 codes are reserved for the HS-DSCH. On the x-axis is the offered DCH load defined with the expected number of occupied code units. In the *adaptive* case, resource preemption by DCH users leads to a strong decrease of the HSDPA

Figure 14. HS-DSCH transmit power allocation schemes

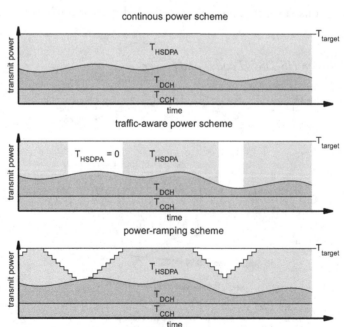

user throughput with increasing DCH load. The resource reservation of the *hybrid* strategy prevents this strong decline. The *fixed* scheme shows as expected small sensitivity to the DCH load, but the HS-DSCH also is not able to exploit the spare resources from the DCH connections, which leads to a significantly lower throughput as compared to the *hybrid* scheme. Notable is the influence of the other- and own-cell interference in the *fixed* case, which leads to a decrease of 100 kbps over the total range of the offered loads.

In the next scenario, we investigate the sensitivity of the *fixed* and *hybrid* resource allocation scheme against code and power reservation. We keep either the number of reserved codes constant and vary the power reservation, or vice versa. The range for the resource reservation is in both cases from 1 to 6 (i.e.,1 code to 6 codes or 1 Watt to 6 Watt). The constant resource is set to 3 codes and 3 W power, resp. The DCH offered load is set to 0.4, and only one service class (128 kbps) is considered.

Figure 16 shows the impact of resource reservation on the mean HSDPA cell throughput. As in the previous scenario, the *hybrid* resource

allocation scheme has a significant performance gain due to the exploitation of spare resources. The *hybrid* scheme in this scenario is not very sensitive against reservation; only in case of 6 W power reservation is an increase notable. This is in contrast to the *fixed* scheme, where especially code reservation up to 5 codes leads to an increased bandwidth. More than 5 codes are seldom required due to the chosen multipath profile (Vehicular A).

Figure 17 shows the time-average cell throughput for the three power allocation schemes "traffic-aware," "continuous," and "power-ramping." On the x-axis again the offered DCH code load is plotted. Notable is the large difference between the continuous on the one hand and the traffic-aware and power-ramping scheme on the other hand, which is around 250 kbps for lower DCH loads and then diminishes with higher loads. The following reasons can be identified: First, the higher interference caused in the continuous case generally leads to lower bit rates. Secondly, since HSDPA user behavior follows a volume-based traffic model, higher bit rates mean shorter sojourn times, which in turn leads to lower HS-DSCH activity and

Figure 15. Expected user throughput for schemes with and without reservation

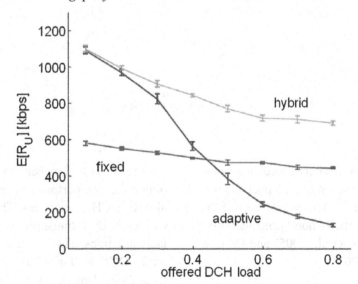

Figure 16. Effect of code and power reservation on the cell throughput

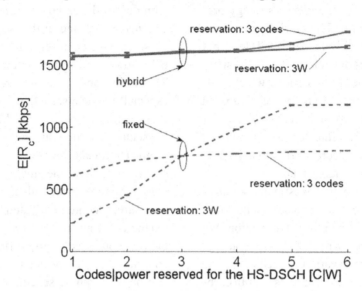

Figure 17. Cell throughput vs. offered DCH load for different power allocation schemes

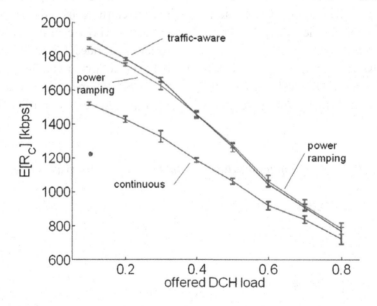

therefore again to lower interference on average for the traffic-aware scheme. This phenomenon which leads to spatial heterogeneity even if the arrival process is spatially homogeneous is also described in (Litjens et al., 2005) and (Mäder, Staehle, & Barth, 2007).

The HS-DSCH power allocation schemes not only affect the performance of the HSDPA, but also the DCH connections. The figure shows the CDF of the DCH transmit powers for two different load situations. The increase between the cases with a DCH-load of 0.2 and 0.6 is mostly due to the additional interference by DCH users, however with a load of 0.2 the benefit for the DCH users with traffic-aware and power-ramping scheme is higher than in the case with a load of 0.6, as can be seen on the steeper curve progressions in the first case. Note that if transmit power based admission control is implemented, higher power requirements also lead to higher blocking probabilities.

FUTURE DEVELOPMENTS

The development of HSDPA does not stand still. With version 7 of the specifications, 64 QAM and MIMO (multiple input multiple output) have been introduced, further increasing data rate up to 21 Mbps. These data rates are mainly intended for use in pico or femto cells (e.g., in indoor-scenarios), which enable very good radio conditions due to their small coverage area. Other improvements aim at reducing call setup times and signaling overhead, the latter especially in the uplink, where the signaling channels consume interference resources additionally to the required parallel DCH channels.

In the near future, the development of the next generation of 3GPP mobile systems will continue with the long-term evolution (LTE) project. LTE introduces a completely new air interface in the access network (universal terrestrial radio access network--UTRAN), which is based in the downlink on orthogonal frequency division multiple access (OFDMA) and in the uplink on single-carrier FDMA. The goal of this development is to increase peak rates and also to provide more fairness to users on cell edges. Peak data rates should not be lower than 100 Mbps in downlink direction and 50 Mbps in uplink direction in a 20 Mhz frequency spectrum. Packet latency of the air interface should be decreased significantly to 5 ms, since circuit-switched radio bearers like in 3G UMTS will not be supported anymore, which means that voice traffic must be transported on packet-switched bearers. A very important feature

is the scalable bandwidth concept, which allows operators to reuse existing GSM or CDMA frequency spectrums and eventually, spectrum licenses. This is achieved by allowing bandwidth "chunks" of 1.25 MHz, 1.6 MHz, up to 20 MHz (Bachl, Gunreben, Das, & Tatesh, 2007). It is planned to publish a first draft of the specifications within the next 2 years.

REFERENCES

3GPP. (2005). *3GPP TS 25.214 V5.11.0 Physical Layer Procedures (FDD)*.

3GPP. (2007). *3GPP TS 25.306 V7.4.0 UE Radio Access Capabilities*.

3GPP. (2007). *3GPP TS 25.331 V7.5.0 Radio Resource Control (RRC) Protocol Specification*.

3GPP. (2007). *3GPP TS 25.433 V7.5.0 UTRAN Iub interface Node B application part (NBAP) signalling*.

Goldsmith, A., & Varaiya, P. (1997). Capacity of fading channels with channel side information. *IEEE Transactions on Information Theory, 46*, 1986-1992.

Ahmed, D. F., & Khaled, M. F. (2004). Channel-quality dependent earliest deadline due fair scheduling schemes for wireless multimedia networks. *Proceedings of IEEE/ACM MSWiM '04*. Venice, Italy: ACM Press.

Ameigeiras, P., Wigard, J., & Mogensen, P. (2004). Performance of the M-LWDF scheduling algorithm for streaming services in HSDPA. *Proceedings of IEEE VTC Fall '04*. Los Angeles, CA, USA: IEEE.

Andrews, M. (2004). Instability of the proportional fair scheduling algorithm for HDR. *IEEE Transactions on Wireless Communications, 3*(5), 1422-1426.

Andrews, M., Kumaran, K., Ramanan, K., Stolyar, A., Whithing, P., & Vijayakumar, R. (2001). Providing quality of service over a shared wireless link. *IEEE Communications Magazine*, 150-154.

Aniba, G., & Aissa, S. (2004). Adaptive proportional fairness for packet scheduling in HSDPA. *Proceedings of IEEE GLOBECOM '04*. Montreal, Canada: IEEE.

Bachl, R., Gunreben, P., Das, S., & Tatesh, S. (2007). The long term evolution towards a new 3GPP air interface standard. *Bell Labs Technical Journal, 11*(4), 25-51.

Bergren, F., & Jäntti, R. (2003). Multiuser scheduling over Rayleigh fading channels. *Proceedings of IEEE GLOBECOM '03*. San Francisco, CA, USA: IEEE.

Brouwer, F., de Bruin, I., Silva, L. C., Souto, N., Cercas, F., & Correia, A. (2004). Usage of link-level performance indicators for HSDPA network-level simulations in E-UMTS. *Proceedings of the IEEE International Symposium on Spread Spectrum Techniques and Applications (ISSSTA)*. Sydney, Australia: IEEE.

Brueck, S., Jugl, E., Kettschau, H. J., Link, M., Mueckenheim, J., & Zaprozhets, A. (2007). Radio resource management in HSDPA and HSUPA. *Bell Labs Technical Journal, 11*(4), 151-167.

Cano-Garcia, J. M., Gonzalez-Parada, E., & Casilari, E. (2006). Experimental analysis and characterization of packet delay in UMTS networks. *Proceedings of NEW2AN '06*. St. Petersburg: Springer.

Chase, D. (1985). Code combining - a maximum-likelihood decoding approach for combining an arbitrary number of noisy packets. *IEEE Transactions on Communications, 33*(5), 385-393.

Cheng, J. F. (2003). On the coding gain of incremental redundancy over chase combining.

Proceedings. of IEEE GLOBECOM '03. San Francisco, CA, USA: IEEE.

de Angelis, F., Habib, I., Giambene, G., & Giannetti, S. (2005). Scheduling for differentiated traffic types in HSDPA cellular systems. *Proceedings of IEEE GLOBECOM '05*. St. Louis, MO, USA: IEEE.

Döttling, M., Michel, J., & Raaf, B. (2002). Hybrid ARQ and adaptive modulation and coding schemes for high speed downlink packet access. *Proceedings of IEEE PIMRC '02*. Lisboa, Portugal: IEEE.

Frenger, P., Parkvall, S., & Dahlman, E. (2001). Performance comparison of HARQ with chase combining and incremental redundancy for HSDPA. *Proceedings of IEEE VTC Fall '01*. Atlantic City, NJ, USA: IEEE.

Furuskär, A., Parkvall, S., Persson, M., & Samuelsson, M. (2002). Performance of WCDMA high speed packet data. *Proceedings of IEEE VTC Spring '02*. Birmingham, AL, USA: IEEE.

Holma, H., & Toskala, A. (2004). *WCDMA for UMTS--Radio access for third generation mobile communications* (3rd ed.). John Wiley & Sons.

Hosein, P. (2002). QoS control for WCDMA high speed packet data. *Proceedings of 4th International Workshop on Mobile and Wireless Communications Network*. Calcutta, India: Springer.

Jalali, A., Padovani, R., & Pankaj, R. (2000). Data throughput of CDMA-HDR: A high efficiency-high data rate personal communication wireless system. *Proceedings of IEEE VTC Spring '00*. Tokyo, Japan: IEEE.

Kelly, F., Maulloo, A., & Tan, D. (1998). Rate control in communication networks: Shadow prices, proportional fairness and stability. *Journal of the Operational Research Society, 49*, 237-252

Khattab, A. D., & Elsayed, K. M. (2004). Channel-quality dependent earliest deadline due fair scheduling schemes for wireless multimedia networks. *Proceedings of ACM/IEEE MSWiM*. Venice, Italy: ACM Press.

Klein, T., Leung, K., & Zheng, H. (2004). Enhanced scheduling algorithms for improved TCP Performance in wireless IP networks. *Proceedings of IEEE GLOBECOM '04*. Dallas, TX, USA: IEEE.

Knopp, R., & A. Humblet, P. (1995). Information capacity and power control in single-cell multiuser communications. *Proceedings of IEEE ICC '95*. Seattle, WA, USA: IEEE.

Kolding, T. E. (2006). QoS-aware proportional fair packet scheduling with required activity detection. *Proceedings of IEEE VTC Fall '06*. Montreal, Canada: IEEE.

Kolding, T. E. (2003). Link and system performance aspects of proportional fair scheduling in WCDMA/HSDPA. *Proceedings of IEEE VTC Fall '03*. Orlando, FL, USA: IEEE.

Kolding, T. E., Frederiksen, F., & Mogensen, P. E. (2002). Performance aspects of WCDMA systems with high speed downlink packet access. *IEEE VTC Fall '02*. Vancouver, CA.

Kolding, T. E., Frederiksen, F., & Mogensen, P. E. (2001). Performance evaluation of modulation and coding schemes proposed for HSDPA in 3.5G UMTS networks. *Proceedings of WPMC '01*. Aalborg, Denmark: IEEE.

Kwan, R., Peter, C. H., Poutiainen, E., & Rinne, M. (2003). The effect of code-multiplexing on the high speed downlink packet access (HSDPA) in a WCDMA network. *Proceedings of IEEE WCNC '03*. New Orleans, LA, USA: IEEE.

Li, J., & Sampalli, S. (2006). QoS-guaranteed wireless packet scheduling for mixed services in HSDPA. *Proceedings of ACM/IEEE MSWiM '06*. Terromolinos, Spain: ACM Press.

Litjens, R., van den Berg, J. L., & Fleuren, M. J. (2005). Spatial traffic heterogeneity in HSDPA networks and its impact on network planning. *Proceedings of the 19th International Teletraffic Congress*. Bejing, China: Elsevier.

Lundevall, M., Olin, B., Olsson, J., Wiberg, N., Wänstedt, S., Eriksson, J., et al. (2004). Streaming applications over HSDPA in mixed service scenarios. *Proceedings of IEEE VTC Fall '04*. Los Angeles, CA, USA: IEEE.

Mäder, A., & Staehle, D. (2007a). A flow-level simulation framework for HSDPA-enabled UMTS networks. *ACM/IEEE MSWiM '07*. Chania, Crete Island, Greece: ACM Press.

Mäder, A., Staehle, D., & Barth, H. (2007b). A novel performance model for the HSDPA with adaptive resource allocation. *Proceedings of the 20th International Teletraffic Congress*. Ottawa, Canada: Springer.

Mäder, A., Staehle, D., & Spahn, M. (2007). Impact of HSDPA radio resource allocation schemes on the system performance of UMTS networks. *IEEE VTC Fall '07*. Baltimore, MY, USA: IEEE.

Mäder, A., Wagner, B., Hoßfeld, T., Staehle, D., & Barth, H. (2006). Measurements in a laboratory UMTS network with time-varying loads and different admission control strategies. *The 4th International Workshop on Internet Performance, Simulation, Monitoring and Measurement*. Salzburg, Austria: Springer.

Necker, M. C. (2006). A comparison of scheduling mechanisms for service class differentiation in HSDPA networks. *AEÜ International Journal of Electronic Communication*, 136-141.

Pedersen, K. I., & Michaelsen, P. H. (2006). Algorithms and performance results for dynamic HSDPA resource allocation. *IEEE VTC Fall '06*. Montreal, CA: IEEE.

Pedersen, K. I., Lootsma, T. F., Stottrup, M., Frederikson, F., Kolding, T. E., & Mogensen, P. E.

(2004). Network performance of mixed traffic on high speed downlink packet access and dedicated channels in WCDMA. *IEEE VTC Fall '04*. Los Angeles, CA, USA: IEEE.

Pedersen, K. I., Mogensen, P. E., & Kolding, T. E. (2006). Overview of QoS options for HSDPA. *IEEE Communications Magazine, 44*(7), 100-105.

Shakkottai, S., & Stolyra, A. L. (2001). Scheduling algorithms for a mixture of real-time and non-real-time data in HDR. *Proceedings of the 17ᵗʰ International Teletraffic Congress*. Salvador da Bahia, Brazil: Elsevier.

Staehle, D., & Mäder, A. (2007). A model for time-efficient HSDPA simulations. *IEEE VTC Fall '07*. Baltimore, MY, USA: IEEE.

Viswanath, P., Tse, D., & Laroia, R. (2002). Opportunistic beamforming using dumb antennas. *IEEE Transaction on Information Theory, 48*(6),s 1277-1294.

Chapter III
Handoff Management in Next Generation Wireless Networks

Nidal Nasser
University of Guelph, Canada

Tarek Bejaoui
University of Carthage, Tunisia

ABSTRACT

Major research challenges in the next generation of wireless networks include the provisioning of worldwide seamless mobility across heterogeneous wireless networks, the improvement of end-to-end Quality of Service (QoS), supporting multmedia services over wide area and enabling users to specify their personal preferences. The integration and interoperability of this multitude of available networks will lead to the emergence of the fourth generation (4G) of wireless technologies. 4G wireless technologies have the potential to provide these features and many more, which at the end will change the way we use mobile devices and provide a wide variety of new applications. However, such technology does not come without its challenges. One of these challenges is the user's ability to control and manage handoffs across heterogeneous wireless networks. This chapter proposes a solution to this problem using Artificial Neural Networks (ANNs). The proposed method is capable of distinguishing the best existing wireless network that matches predefined user preferences set on a mobile device when performing a vertical handoff. The overall performance of the proposed method shows 87.0 % success rate in finding the best available wireless network.

INTRODUCTION

Next generation wireless networks (NGWN) will utilize several different radio access technologies, seamlessly integrated to form one access network.

This network has the potential to provide many of the requirements that other previous systems did not achieve such as high data transfer rates, effectives user control, seamless mobility, and others which will potentially change the way users utilize mobile devices. NGWN will integrate a multitude of different heterogeneous networks including (a) Cellular networks, passed through multiple generations – 1G, 2G, 3G and 3.5G; (b) Wireless LANs, championed by the IEEE 802.11 WiFi (Wireless Fidelity) networks; and (c) Broadband wireless access networks (IEEE 802.16, WiMAX). As well, multi-hop/ad hoc variable topology networks, where portable devices are brought together to form a network on the fly, are emerging as a viable alternative to enhance connectivity and flexibility.

Objective and Context

It is envisaged that next generation wireless networks will consist of multiple access technologies, integrated to form a heterogeneous network. An interesting example is the heterogeneous environment consisting of the Universal Mobile Telecommunications System (UMTS) cellular network, based on the WCDMA radio access technology and a WLAN. Both are characterized by their soft capacity and the support of multiple heterogeneous services with diverse quality requirements.

In UMTS, both packet and circuit switched services can be freely mixed, with variable bandwidth and delivered simultaneously to the same user with specific quality levels. It will support real-time and non-real-time multimedia services with data rates up to 2 Mb/s with wide coverage and nearly universal roaming. However, the costs of acquiring the necessary radio spectrum and the required network equipment upgrades are very high. This is in contrast to WLAN systems such as IEEE 802.11 a/b/g, which provide affordable services and bit rates surpassing those of 3G systems, up to 11 Mb/s with 802.11b and 54 Mb/s with 802.11a/g. However, the coverage offered by WLANs is quit limited and lacks roaming support.

Thus, each network access technology provides different levels of coverage and quality of service (QoS) as well as cost to the end user.

The complementary characteristics of 3G cellular systems (slow, wide coverage) and WLAN (fast, limited coverage) make it attractive to integrate these two technologies to provide ubiquitous wireless access. The purpose of integrating 3G systems and WLANs is to make it possible to use the best parts of both systems. High bandwidth WLANs are used for data transfer where available and 3G systems can be used where WLAN coverage is lacking.

Integrating two very different access technologies, introduced a number of technical and logistical issues that must be resolved in order to maximize the benefits reaped from such integration. Transfer an active call between access points (AP) or base stations (BS) are called horizontal handoff. The horizontal handoff has long been an issue within the wireless telecommunication field. However, a higher level of handoff complexity, and thus issues, is introduced to the differences between inter-networked heterogeneous wireless networks. This transfer between different types of wireless networks is known as a vertical handoff (Guo, 2004). Example of vertical handoff is when a mobile user moves back and forth between 3G and WLAN networks. Seamless intersystem mobility across such access heterogeneity will be the capital feature in next generation, labeled Fourth Generation (4G), wireless networks. In such networks, it will be necessary to support seamless handoffs of mobile users without causing disruption to their ongoing connections. As a result, the need for seamless handoff across the different wireless networks is becoming increasingly important.

One of the chief issues that aid in providing seamless handoff is the ability to correctly decide whether or not to carryout vertical handoff at any given time. This could be accomplished by taking into consideration two key issues: network conditions for vertical handoff decisions and connection maintenance (Yang, 2005). These two issues need to be tightly coupled in order to move seamlessly across different network interfaces. To attain positive vertical handoff, the network state ought to be constantly obtainable by means of a suitable handoff metric. In multi-network environments, this is very challenging and hard to achieve as there does not exist a single factor than can provide a clear idea of when to handoff. Signal strength, which is the chief handoff metric measured in horizontal handoffs, cannot be utilized for vertical handoff decisions due to the overlay nature of heterogeneous networks and the different physical techniques used by each network. Thus criterion of a vertical handoff is one of the chief challenges for seamless mobility.

In addition to that, 4G mobile devices will enable users to selectively choose through a combination of features of an available wireless network. This adds to the existing complexity of heterogeneity in the sense that there must exist a way to enable mobile devices to find the closest match to a predefined set of user preferences and seamlessly connect to that best match when vertical handoff is applied. Challenges are therefore so important; the solutions to these challenges are firstly to manage the scarce resources to provide better QoS for mobile users and to achieve high system utilization so that more users can be accommodated by the system; and after to allow users to control and manage handoffs across the heterogeneous networks. Sometimes, these goals are conflicting and trade-off must be made.

Developing a vertical handoff manager to provide a proper balance between system utilization and user's QoS satisfaction as to enable mobile devices to contribute to the decision of when to handoff, are the focus of this chapter.

Issues and Challenges of Handoffs in Next Generation Mobile Networks

As discussed above, handoffs can be defined as the transition of signal transmission between different cells. A handoff scheme is required to preserve connectivity as devices move about, and at the same time curtail disturbance to ongoing transfers. Therefore, handoffs must exhibit low latency, sustain minimal amounts of data loss, as well as scale to large networks. Handoff schemes have been thoroughly researched and deployed in cellular systems, also known as wireless wide area networks (WWANs), and are escalating in importance in other networks, such as wireless LANs (WLANs), as research in 4G wireless communications increases in popularity. Handoffs can be classified as either horizontal or vertical as depicted in Figure 1.

Figure 1. Horizontal and vertical handoffs

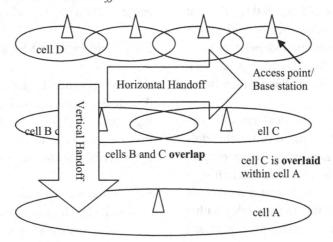

Horizontal handoff is the changeover of signal communication from one base station to a geographically neighboring base station supporting the same technology, as the user roams about. Horizontal handoff is also referred to as intra-technology handoff. Every time a mobile cellular host crosses from one cell into a neighboring cell (supporting the same technology), the network routinely and automatically exchanges the coverage responsibility from one base station to another. Each base station change, as well as the exchange procedure or method is known as horizontal handoff. In a properly operating network, handoff takes place smoothly and efficiently, without gaps in communications and without uncertainty as to which base station should be dealing with the mobile node. Mobile users need not get involved in order for horizontal handoff to take place nor do they have to sense the handoff process or identify which base station is managing the signals at any certain time.

Horizontal handoff is the most widespread definition of handoff due to the extensive research that has taken place in this field in the last several years. Vertical handoff, on the other hand, is a more recent and exciting scheme that promises to transfigure the way we communicate. While horizontal handoff is a handover among base stations in service by the same wireless network interface, vertical handoff takes place between different network interfaces that usually represent different technologies (Chen, 2004). Vertical handoff architectures and schemes will play a major role in the Multimedia Independent Handover standard (IEEE 802.21) and shall pave the road for emergence of 4G overlay multi-network environments.

There are two types of vertical handoffs: upward and downward. An upward vertical handoff (Chakravorty, 2003) is roaming to an overlay with a larger cell size and lower bandwidth such as WANs (cellular networks), and a downward vertical handoff is roaming to an overlay with a smaller cell size and larger bandwidth. Downward

vertical handoffs are less time critical, since a mobile device can always remain connected to the upper overlay and not handoff at all.

In the following sections, we present the general characteristics needed to perform successful and optimized handoffs in next generation wireless networks.

Seamless Handoff

In one of the revolutionary drivers for 4G, technologies will complement each other to provide ubiquitous high-speed wireless connectivity to mobile terminals (McNair, 2004). In such an environment, it will be necessary to support seamless handoffs of mobile terminals without causing disruption to their ongoing sessions. As a result, the need for seamless handoff across the different wireless networks is becoming increasingly important. Whereas wired networks regularly grant high bandwidth and consistent access to the Internet, wireless networks make it possible for users to access a variety of services even when they are moving. Consequently, seamless handoff, with low delay and minimal packet loss, has become a crucial factor for mobile users who wish to receive continuous and reliable services.

In the next sections we discuss desirable handoff features, horizontal and vertical handoff procedures, and newly proposed vertical handoff characteristics in detail, and explain their significance in 4G handover schemes.

Desirable Handoff Features

An efficient handoff algorithm can achieve many desirable features by trading off different operating characteristics. Some of the major desirable features of any handoff algorithm (Nasser, 2006) are described below (see Figure 2):

- **Reliable:** A handoff algorithm should be reliable. This means that the call should have good quality after handoff. Many factors

Figure 2. Desirable handoff features

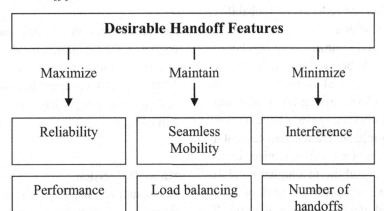

help in determining the potential service quality of a candidate base station. Some of these factors include signal-to-interference ratio (SIR), signal-to-noise ratio (SNR), received signal strength (RSS), and bit error rate (BER). Many more critical factors are discussed in the next section.

- **Seamless:** A handoff algorithm should be fast so that the mobile device does not experience service degradation or interruption. Service degradation may be due to a continuous reduction in signal strength or an increase in co-channel interference (CCI). Service interruption may be due to a "break before make" or hard handoff approach of handoff being exercised in the network.

- **Interference prevention:** A handoff algorithm should avoid high interference. Co-channel interference is caused by devices transmitting on the same channel. This is usually caused by a neighboring detrimental source that is operating on the same channel. Interchannel interference, on the other hand, is caused by devices transmitting on adjacent channels. Both CCI and interchannel interference may severely limit the transfer rates of a wireless network. WLANs suffer from interference more than WWANs; the

reason for this is the fact that most networking products available at present follow IEEE 802.11 standards, which operate in the unlicensed 2.4 and 5.2 GHz bands. As a result, devices operating in these ranges are open to all different kinds of noise and interference coming from a variety of sources such as other legitimate 802.11 networks to Bluetooth devices or cordless phones operating in the same band as the wireless network. Cellular networks have managed over the years to fix many of their interference problems, and current generations infrequently suffer from interference. Interference in WLANs has up to now been a major issue, although as WLAN technology advances interference should eventually be fully eliminated. Nonetheless, before vertical handoff from WWAN to WLAN takes place, examining the network to make certain that CCI or interchannel interference does not exceptionally degrade the network is a key concern.

- **Load balancing:** A handoff algorithm should balance traffic in all cells, whether of the same or different network type. This helps to eliminate the need for borrowing channels from neighboring cells that have free channels, which simplifies cell planning and operation, and reduces the probability of new call blocking.

- **Improving performance:** The number of handoffs should be minimized. Excessive horizontal or vertical handovers lead to heavy handoff processing loads and poor communication quality. In a handoff scenario, the more handoff attempts, the greater the chances that a call will be denied access to a channel, resulting in a higher handoff call dropping probability. A high number of horizontal handoff attempts may result in more delay in the processing of handoff requests, which will cause signal strength to decrease over a longer time period to a level of unacceptable quality. In addition, the call may be dropped if a sufficient SIR is not achieved. Handoff algorithms require network resources to connect the call to a new base station. Thus, minimizing the number of handoffs reduces the switching load. Unnecessary handoffs should be prevented, especially when the current base station is able to provide the desired service quality without interfering with other mobile devices and base stations.

In a heterogeneous networking environment the challenge of choosing the "best" network is a major issue. An internal LAN with a weak signal inside a limestone building may yield better performance than a WAN with a strong signal. Handover between the different network tiers can lead to a very different quality of service being available to the mobile terminal, such as handover from a WLAN operating at 11 Mb/s to a GSM network operating at 9.6 kb/s. There may also be other factors such as economic discrepancies that do not occur in individual networks; some networks charge per minute or byte.

Handoff Process

Both horizontal and vertical handoff processes consist of a three phases: handoff decision, radio link transfer and channel assignment (Akyildiz, 1999). In this section we discuss each phase and describe the role it plays in fourth generation handoffs.

Handoff Decision

Horizontal handoff decisions mainly depend on the quality of the channel reflected by the received signal strength (RSS) and the resources available in the target cell. Many systems are interference limited, meaning that signal strength is an adequate indication of channel quality. A handoff is made if the RSS from a neighboring base station exceeds the RSS from the current base station by a predetermined threshold value.

In vertical handoffs, many network characteristics have an effect on whether or not a handoff should take place. Most of these characteristics were not needed in horizontal handoffs. In fact (as explained above), only signal strength and channel availability are considered in horizontal handoffs (Zhu, 2004). The following characteristics are newly proposed qualities which are particularly important for vertical handoff decision:

- **Quality of Service:** Handing over to a network with better conditions and higher performance would usually provide improved service levels. Transmission rates, error rates, and other characteristics can be measured in order to decide which network can provide a higher assurance of continuous connectivity.
- **Cost of Service:** The cost of the different services to the user is a major issue, and could sometimes be the decisive factor in the choice of a network. Different broadband wireless Internet service providers (WISPs) and cellular service providers may well provide a

variety of billing plans and options that will probably influence the customer's choice of network and thus handoff decision.

- **Security:** Risks are inherent in any wireless technology. Some of these risks are similar to those of wired networks; some are exacerbated by wireless connectivity; some are new. Perhaps the most significant source of risks in wireless networks is that the technology's underlying communications medium, the airwave, is open to intruders, making it the logical equivalent of an Ethernet port in the parking lot.

- **Power Requirements:** Wireless devices operate on limited battery power. When the level decreases, handing off (or remaining connected) to a network with low power consumption can provide elongated usage time. For instance, if a device's battery is nearly exhausted, handing over from a WLAN to WWAN would be a smart decision. This is due to the fact that when operating in a cellular WWAN, the device is idle for most of the time. However, given the unpredictable and erratic nature of transmissions with WLANs, handsets are unable to standby between packet transmission since there is no set time for the arrival and transmission of data and packets arrive sporadically.

- **Proactive Handoff:** By proactive handoff, the users are involved in the vertical handoff decision and have the final decision on whether or not to handoff, regardless of the network conditions. By permitting the user to choose a preferred network, the system is able to accommodate the user's special requirements.

- **Velocity:** In vertical handoff, the velocity factor has a larger weight and imperative effect on handoff decision than in horizontal handoffs. Because of the overlaid architecture of heterogeneous networks, handing off to an embedded network when traveling at high speeds is discouraged since a handoff back to the original network would occur very shortly afterward.

Radio Link Transfer

Radio link transfer, the second part of the handoff process, refers to the task of forming links to a call at the new base station. The radio link is transferred from the old to the new base station. If the radio link transfer is within the currently serving cell, referred to as intracell handoff, no new link transfer operations are required. However, a handoff made from one cell to another, referred to as intercell handoff, requires handoff rerouting operations to link the mobile's current communication path to the new base station. Once a handoff procedure has commenced, handoff schemes can vary in the approach they take to transfer a call to a new link. The two approaches taken are known as forward and backward handoffs. In backward handoff the old serving base station prepares the handoff, and no access to the target base station is made until the control unit of the new base station has confirmed the allocation of resources. In forward handoff the process is initiated by means of the target base station without relying on the old base station during the preliminary phase of the handoff process. Each of these two methods has its pros and cons. The advantage of backward handoff is that the signaling information is transmitted through an existing radio link; therefore, the establishment of a new signaling channel is not required during the initial stages of the handoff process. The drawback, however, is that the handoff process may be unsuccessful if the link quality of the serving base station was rapidly deteriorating (e.g., due to rapid mobility). This type of handoff is used in most cellular networks to date. Forward handoff, on the contrary, is a faster handoff process, but its problem is a drop in handoff reliability.

Channel Assignment

The final handoff stage is channel assignment which consists of the allocation of resources at the new base station. If a new call is admitted to access the network, a call admission control (CAC) algorithm will make a decision to accept or reject it according to the amount of available resources vs. QoS requirements, and the effect on QoS of existing connections that may occur as a result of the new connection. Channel assignment is part of CAC and resource management, and therefore is not discussed in detail here.

Voluntary and Obligatory Handoff

Different handoff forms can be distinguished based on need. To elucidate this point, consider the following handoff scenario. A crowded town would usually contain several base stations in the city center, and there would be immense amounts of coverage overlap between neighboring base stations. Assuming that one of these base stations becomes fully overloaded to the extent that adding more nodes would degrade its performance and quality of service, it becomes beneficial for some of the terminals to be reassigned to another base station in order to relieve the jammed base station. In this situation a handoff is preferable but not mandatory. On the contrary, if a user was driving on a highway with dispersed base stations and negligible coverage overlapping, it becomes crucial for handoff to take place; otherwise, the connection will be broken.

A vertical handoff could be voluntary or obligatory, depending on the direction of handoff. When handing over from a WLAN to a cellular network, delay in the handoff transmission region must be short, so the preferred handoff point is the first time the signal strength degrades. In this case the handoff is obligatory or the connection is lost. Obligatory handoffs are also referred to as forced vertical handoffs (FVHs). On the other hand, since a cellular network covers a wide area and the handoff time is not critical, the preferred

handoff point from cellular to WLAN is the first time the signal strength in the WLAN reaches an acceptable level. The handoff is voluntary in that case, and the handoff time is not critical.

In many cases measured metrics, such as SNR and BER, will signify that a specific network is reliable and provides high quality of service.

In several of the currently proposed vertical handoff schemes (Hatami, 1999), this would routinely lead to a vertical handoff to that network. Nonetheless, one essential factor frequently neglected is the position and movement direction of the mobile node. Occasionally, this motion could indicate that the person will probably promptly leave this network's coverage area. Consequently, although the newly encountered network is in healthy condition, handoff to it would almost immediately be followed by another reverse handoff back to the original network. Such vertical handoffs are ineffectual, overwhelm the network with fruitless communications, and may at times irritate the user.

Related Work

In this section we present various handoff decisions and policy schemes that were proposed by researchers for next generation wireless networks. We deeply analyze these ideas in terms of their ability to provide QoS guarantees while meeting user and network requirements and constraints. Related works for managing the vertical handoff have been recently discussed in the literature. However, more work need to be done.

New optimizations for vertical handoff decision algorithms have been developed in (Zhu, 2004) to maximize the benefit of the handoff for both the user and the network. In (Ylianttila, 2002), the performance of horizontal handoff and vertical handoff between WLAN and GPRS networks are studied and an optimization scheme for performing vertical handoff is presented.

Janise McNair et al. (2000) introduce a new inter-system handoff protocol that uses boundary cells that allow the mobile user to roam into a different network. The mobile user receives and compares signals from the detected networks and handoff is made to a new network if it has stronger signal strength.

Makela et al. (2000) propose a handoff algorithm between WLANs and cellular networks. They argue that the vertical handoff policy is different, depending on the direction of handoff. When handing over from cellular network to WLAN, delay in the handoff transmission region must be short, so the preferred handoff point is the first time the signal strength degrades. On the other hand, when handing over from WLAN to Cellular networks, since a cellular network covers a wide area and the handoff time is not critical, the preferred handoff point from cellular to WLAN is the first time the signal strength in the WLAN reaches an acceptable level.

Hyosoon Park et al. (2003) also proposed a similar scheme that presents a seamless vertical handoff procedure between IEEE 802.11 WLANs and CDMA2000 cellular networks. In their algorithm, traffic is classified into real-time (from WLAN to CDMA) and non-real time (from CDMA to WLAN) services and a handoff decision policy similar to (Makela, 2000) is applied. These solutions are very interesting but they provide specific solutions for specific networks.

Similarly, Qian Zhang et al. (2003) propose a novel mobility management system for vertical handoff between UMTS and WLAN. The system contains a connection manager that is responsible for detecting wireless network changes when making handoff decisions. They consider two handoff scenarios. In the first scenario when moving from UMTS to WLAN, the objective of the handoff is to improve quality of service (since the handoff to WLAN is optional). They assume that WLAN would provide higher bandwidth and lower cost and therefore recommend handoff to WLAN in this case. In the second scenario, when a user steps out of a WLAN, their connection manager's goal is to switch to UMTS before the WLAN line

breaks, but at the same time, it tries to stay in the WLAN as long as possible since, again, they assume that WLAN provides lower cost and better QoS. They measure signal strength in order to determine WLAN unavailability.

Ling-Jyh Chen et al. (2004) present a smart decision model that tries to smartly perform handoff to the highest quality network at the most suitable time. Their proposed model is able to make vertical handoff decisions based on the properties of available network interfaces such as link capacity, power consumption and link cost. In another project (Chen, 2004), they propose a Universal Seamless Handoff Architecture (USHA) to deal with both horizontal and vertical handoff scenarios. USHA achieves seamless handoff by following the middleware design philosophy (Fox, 1997), and by integrating the middleware with existing Internet services and applications.

M. Ylianttila, et al. (2002) investigate the handoff characteristics in a compound vertical setting and establish the relation between the handoff delay and throughput diminution perceived by the user throughout the hand over period. An assessment of handoff decision effectiveness is suggested, but without making an allowance for the quality of service associated features. In their conclusion they assert that it is better to remain connected via WLAN as long as the data rate in WLAN is higher than in cellular UMTS, and this is true for any two systems having different rates of data transfer. Their assumption is simply invalidated in the presence of high background traffic on the WLAN.

In future mobile generations, service providers and operators may allow their customers to define their personal set of mobility parameters; these vertical handoff parameters are chosen according to user preferences and are tailored specifically for personal needs (Ylianttila, 2002). H. Wang, et al. (1999) describe a policy-enabled handoff scheme that enables users to articulate policies depending on what is the 'finest' wireless system at any instance, and make trade-offs amid network characteristics such as monetary cost, power utilization and quality of service.

In view of the fact that diverse layers of the network architecture will sustain different data rates, handoff can be achieved with virtually no delay whatsoever if applications detect the change in service level and adjust their quality of service demands accordingly. Experiments conducted on handoff performance from networks with a low bit rate to others with higher bit rates have shown that reasonably rapid handoffs can be attained with only little amount of buffering and re-transmission necessary for loss free handovers (Taylor, 1999). On the contrary, significant amounts of buffering and retransmissions are required in the case of handoff from fast to slower networks; otherwise data loss will be experienced (Chen, 2004).

M. Ylianttila et al. (1999) explain how neural networks and fuzzy logic concepts can be used to control vertical handoff procedures. They use handoff between WLAN and GPRS as an example. To enhance features such as power saving, by powering down unused interface cards, the proposed scheme allocates several levels of alerts (stable, unstable or poor WLAN), which would aid in the preparation for an upcoming handoff. M. Ylianttila et al. (2002) used several handoff factors in their proposed solution and these included the signal strength, beacon packets, signal-to-noise-ratio (SNR), bit-error-rate (BER), packet error rates and hysteresis margin of signal strength.

G. Alsenmyr et al. (2003) at Ericsson have proposed their own mechanism for vertical handoff between WCDMA and GSM. They focus on the handover mechanism, but do not give any details regarding handoff decisions. R. Heickero et al. (2002) nonetheless discusses and recommends routing traffic amongst GSM and WCDMA based on sharing.

Myers (2000) explains how an understanding of human perception and the simulation of a mobile IP network may be used to tackle the relevant issues of providing acceptable QoS for mobile multimedia. Even though this scheme doesn't explicitly discuss vertical handoff issues, it clearly discusses many of the factors such as packet delay, dropped packets and latency, which need to be analyzed for enhanced service during handoff.

Wang (2003) proposes a dynamic resource allocation model that is mainly suitable for the multimedia transmission on heterogeneous wireless networks. This model has two goals. First, it induces the resource map of the current cell using the beacon codes received from the neighbouring cells. It then extracts the mobility pattern of the mobile users from past handoff records using the backpropagation neural network. With the mobility pattern, the system then infers which cells would be possible target ones of the mobile user when it moves. Second, it uses rules of application layers (e.g., the communication cost, maximal moving velocity, maximal data rate, etc.), to select candidate cells from the target ones chosen above. It then executes dynamic resource allocations on the candidate cells for supporting the mobile user with guaranteed QoS in advance. In this way, it decreases the handoff call dropping probability and new call blocking probability, and further, increases the resource utilization on the heterogeneous wireless networks (Wang, 2003).

O. E. Falowo et al. (2005) have proposed a Joint Call Admission Control scheme for integrated UMTS-WLAN networks. Because of the fact that WLAN technologies are short-range networks, they offer lower cost to users than UMTS. Thus, the vertical handoff from UMTS to WLAN was defined as a desirable handoff. On the other hand, the mobile terminal's connection has to remain seamless as a user connected to the WLAN roams out of the WLAN domain. However, they defined handoff from the WLAN to the UMTS to be a necessary handoff, and more priority is given to necessary handoffs than desirable handoffs.

We remark that none of these studies consider the control and management of seamless vertical handoff between heterogeneous wireless networks that take into consideration user's input from within a mobile device. The decision of when to handoff will no longer be the responsibility of the network operators, however, the mobile device will greatly contribute to that decision. Therefore, a solution at the application level that takes care of the communication between the mobile device and the available networks is not efficient due to the fact that mobile devices have minimal resources (e.g. power) to be able to perform such tasks. This actually motivates us to design and develop a middleware that can act as the middleman between available wireless networks and mobile devices and needed to provide users with the ability to interact more effectively between mobile devices and registered networks.

Contributions

In this chapter we design and develop a middleware solution which we called Vertical Handoff Manager (VHM). VHM middleware is based on the use of Artificial Neural Networks (ANN). VHM will collect various mobile user preferences parameters and network information as inputs and utilizes the ANN to find the best match between what user want and what is available across these wireless networks. Once a match is found, the middleware will initiate a message between the mobile device and the chosen wireless network to execute the vertical handoff procedure. In this study, we define a vertical handoff decision function which provides handover decisions when roaming across heterogeneous wireless networks.

Organization of the Chapter

The rest of this chapter is organized as follows. Section 2 presents the middleware Vertical Handoff Manager which is a Neural Network-based solution. Numerical results are shown in Section 3. Finally, Chapter summary and open problems are presented in Section 4.

NEURAL NETWORK-BASED VERTICAL HANDOFF MANAGER

In this section, we propose a Vertical Handoff Decision Function (VHDF) and we present the architecture of the Vertical Handoff Manager (VHM) middleware solution.

A Vertical Handover Decision Function

In this section, we explain a vertical handoff decision function, VHDF, which allows the user to strategically prioritize the different network characteristics such as network performance, user preference and monetary cost. This function is simple and can be easily applied to any vertical handoff approach.

We argue that the vertical handoff decision is a composition of the following metric attributes: *cost of service (C), security (S), power consumption (P), network conditions (D) and network performance (F)*. Note that there may be additional characteristics and qualities that could be included (such as moving patterns (Hatami, 1999)); however we believe that these are the key factors for most vertical handoff decisions, regardless of the direction of the vertical handoff. The attributes can be defined as follows:

- *Cost of service* (C): The cost of the different services to the user is a major issue, and can sometimes be the decisive factor in the choice of a network.
- *Security* (S): When the information being exchanged is confidential a network with high encryption is preferred.
- *Power consumption* (P): Vertically handing off to a high power consuming network is not desirable if the mobile terminal's battery is nearly exhausted or if the battery's lifetime is relatively short.
- *Network conditions* (D): Available bandwidth is used to indicate network conditions

and is a major factor especially for voice and video traffic.

- *Network performance* (F): in some cases interference or unstable network connections might discourage a handoff decision.

As the mobile roams across different networks, VHDF is evaluated for all accessible networks. The network with the highest calculated value for VHDF is the most desirable for the user based on his specified preferences. The network quality, Q_i, which provides a measure of the appropriateness of a certain network i is measured via the function:

$$Q_i = f\left(\frac{1}{C_i}, S_i, \frac{1}{P_i}, D_i, F_i\right) \tag{1}$$

In order to allow for different circumstances, there is an apparent necessity to weigh each factor relative to the magnitude it endows upon the vertical handoff decision. Therefore, a different weight is introduced as follows:

$$Q_i = f\left(\omega_c \frac{1}{C_i}, \omega_s S_i, \omega_p \frac{1}{P_i}, \omega_d D_i, \omega_f F_i\right) \tag{2}$$

where ωc, ωs, ωp, ωd, ωf are weights for each of the network parameters. The values of these weights are fractions i.e. they range from 0 to 1. Furthermore all five weights add up to 1.0. Each weight is proportional to the significance of a parameter to the vertical handoff decision. The larger the weight of a specific factor, the more important that factor is to the user and vice versa. These weights are obtained from the user via a user interface. Even though we could add the different factors in the VHDF to obtain network quality *Qi*, that is:

$$Q_i = \omega_c 1/C_i + \omega_s S_i + \omega_p 1/P_i + \omega_d D_i + \omega_f F_i \tag{3}$$

Each network parameter has a different unit, which leads to the necessity of normalization. The final normalized equations for *n* networks are:

$$Q_i = \frac{\omega_c\left(1/C_i\right)}{\max\left((1/C_1),..,(1/C_n)\right)} + \frac{\omega_s S_i}{\max\left(S_1,..,S_n\right)}$$
$$+ \frac{\omega_p\left(1/P_i\right)}{\max\left((1/P_1),..,(1/P_n)\right)} + \frac{\omega_d D_i}{\max\left(D_1,..,D_n\right)} + \frac{\omega_f F_i}{\max\left(F_1,..,F_n\right)} \tag{4}$$

Assume that the mobile terminal detects a new network. It calculates the network quality, Q_i, for its current network and for the newly detected network. The weights would already have fixed (but different) values that assign priorities to the various characteristics. VHDF simply calculates *Qi* based on Equation 4. The network with the highest *Qi* is the preferred network. If the newly detected network receives a higher *Qi*, vertical handoff takes place; otherwise, the device remains connected to the current network.

Vertical Handoff Manager Architecture

In this section we present the architecture of the Vertical Handoff Manager (VHM) middleware solution that we propose and explain the functions of all of its components. The aim of our approach is to design an intelligent system that has the ability to select the best available wireless network by taking advantage of user preferences, device capabilities, and wireless network features. The architecture of the VHM proposed solution is shown in Figure 3. VHM is composed of three main components: (1) Network Handling Manager (NHM), (2) Feature Collector (FC), and (3) Artificial Neural Networks (ANN) Training/Selector. VHM interacts with available wireless networks and the wireless device. Each component within the VHM has a specific task. The following sections describe in detail the functionality for each of these components.

Figure 3. Vertical handoff manager (VHM) architecture

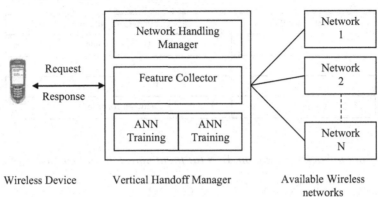

Wireless Device   Vertical Handoff Manager   Available Wireless networks

Network Handling Manager

Network Handling Manager (NHM) is mainly responsible for handling interactivity between VHM and available wireless networks as well as between VHM and wireless devices. NHM handles requests made by wireless devices when initiating a handoff, contacts available wireless networks to begin feature collection process. Once the ANN Selector defines the best available wireless network of choice, the NHM begins connecting the wireless device to the selected wireless network.

Feature Collector

Feature Collector (FC) module retrieves features that are used as attributes to feed to the neural network to be able to select the most appropriate wireless network. These features can be divided into three categories: network-specific, user-specific, and device-specific. Network-specific features are those that describe the wireless network capabilities. These features are collected from available wireless networks which can be detected by the wireless device through VHM. Network-specific features include, but not limited to: (1) Network Usage Cost: how much it costs per min (in cents), (2) Network Security: On a scale

of 1-10, how secure is the network (with 1 being low and 10 being high), (3) Network Transmission range: how wide is the network coverage (in km), and (4) Network Capacity: Data rate or speed of the connection (in Mbps). The device-specific features provide information about the mobile's device. The device specific features are used for compatibility issues and other technical information necessary when making a decision for a handoff. The user-specific features can be obtained through an application or saved locally on the wireless device. For example, a user can enter conditions such as cost per minute, specify security levels, power consumption, etc... These features are user-specific and could not be obtained without being allocated by the user. The user-specific features are used as a measure to find matches between user needs and the available wireless networks.

Handoff decision is based on the user preferences chosen and the available wireless network that best matches the VHDF function previously presented. In this study we neglect the interference effect (network performance). The four remaining preferences are summarized in Table 1.

The network quality Q_i, which provides a measure of the appropriateness of a certain network i is then measured using Equation (2). Due to the fact that each of the preferences chosen by the user has an associated unit that is different

Table 1. User preferences that can be set from a mobile device

Preference ID	Preference Name
1	Cost per minute
2	Security
3	Power consumption
4	Network conditions

Figure 4. Topology of the backpropagation ANN (a: input nodes, b: hidden nodes and c: output node)

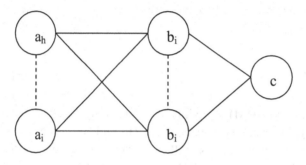

from the other (i.e., power is measured in Watts, cost is measured in cents, and others), it is necessary to find a way for Equation (2) to generate an optimized output using the associated weights. An Artificial Neural Network (ANN) is used as a possible solution to this problem. The next section demonstrates the proposed ANN solution and implementation.

Artificial Neural Network (ANN)

The ability to accurately select the appropriate features in a physical process in this study is a challenging task specially when associating it with a classification and/or selection process. There is no unique feature extraction technique that can satisfy the requirements of all types of data. Therefore, the use of Artificial Neural Networks (ANN) can significantly enhance the chances of having a higher success rate for finding an appropriate wireless network when performing a handoff across heterogeneous networks. There

are many reasons for using ANNs as a possible solution to the selection problem: (1) ANN can provide a simple representation for a physical implementation, and (2) ANN is capable of producing accurate results for inputs that are not present during the training process.

In this study, a neural network is investigated for wireless network selector using a backpropagation neural network (BPNN) algorithm. A multilayer feedforward neural network with an input layer, a hidden layer, and an output layer is shown on Figure 4.

Choosing the best wireless network is not a simple selection problem. In order to solve the network selection problem, one hidden layer is used in the feedforward neural network. In this study, all neurons use sigmoid activation function. Random values, which serve as weights, are generated for all connections from input to hidden (referenced by v_{hi}) and from hidden to output layers (reference by w_{ij}). In addition, biases are assigned random values at the hidden nodes (θ_i)

and the output node (τ_j). The activation functions at the hidden layer (referenced by b_i) are calculated using the following equation:

$$b_i = f(\sum_{i=1}^{n} a_h * v_{hi} + \theta_i)$$

(6)

The activation values at the output layer (referenced by c_j) are calculated as follows:

$$c_j = f(\sum_{i=1}^{n} a_h * w_{ij} + \tau_j)$$

(7)

In both Equations (6) and (7), $f(x)$ denotes the logistic sigmoid threshold function, $f(x) = 1/(1 + e^{-x})$. The Backpropagation neural network has been trained with moderate values for the learning rate (α) and momentum (μ). The weights are recalculated every time a training vector is presented to the network. The exit strategy or the termination condition for the network is based on the sum square error until it reaches a certain threshold assigned prior to running the network. The network should be able to choose from a given set of user preferences with the best available wireless network (selected from Table 2).

NUMERICAL RESUTLS AND DISCUSSION

Data used in this chapter was customized in a way to suit the purpose of this method. A program was written to generate a random numbers that repre-

sent a set of user preferences or weights defined in Equation (5). Each preference is represented by a percentage and then converted to a scale of 0 to 1 to be later used as weights. The weights assigned in a real-time example entered through a mobile device. Four preferences were used as shown in Table 1.

The preferences shown on Table 1 are used as inputs to the neural network. The numbers generated represent the priority set by the user on a mobile device and the sum of the four parameters equals 1 (numbers were initially entered as percentages and then normalized between 0 and 1 to be compatible with the ANN). There were ninety samples each containing four features representing user preferences and a fifth feature representing the type of wireless network. The data takes into consideration a variation of at least five different wireless networks, each with different network parameters. Note that for the purpose of testing, in our solution we limit the number of available networks to 5. In order to select a network, there exists a list of networks in which the neural network must be able to select or propose. Table 2 presents a sample list of possible wireless network types used for the data selection for each of the samples. In addition, it outlines sample network parameters that are used to propose a network for each of the samples in a dataset. These network features (parameters) are used to define the Network Definition Language (NDL) earlier discussed. The middleware determines the available wireless networks and retrieves the network parameters through the NDL.

Table 2. Sample wireless networks parameters

Network ID	Cost (cents) per minute	Network security	Network Transmission Range	Network Capacity	Classificaion
Network 1	10.00	5.00	0.01	0.80	1
Network 2	25.00	8.00	0.10	11.00	2
Network 3	30.00	10.00	0.09	5.00	3
Network 4	10.00	0.00	0.05	2.00	4
Network 5	100.00	10.00	1.00	100.00	5

Each sample in the data is classified into one of the given networks shown in Table 2. For instance, each sample in the data consists of five parameters; the first four parameters represent the user preferences and the fifth represents the type of network to select. The classification for each sample was based on an intuitive algorithm that determines the best matching network. For example, if a user gives more priority to preference id 2 (Security) 100% priority, then the algorithm would choose the network with the highest network security from Table 2 (i.e., Network 3 or 5). If the user selects 70% security and 30% for cost per minute, the algorithm would classify the sample to Network 3 since the user this time takes into consideration the security as well as the cost per minute. Therefore, the choice of Network 3 is more suitable than Network 5 since is more cost effective. In order to measure the performance of the network, an acceptable error value is used to determine if the neural network converges to a solution or not. Since the neural network uses a logistic function to detect the error for each iteration, the input must be in the range of 0 to 1 (since the sigmoid will make sure the nodes at the output layer will never be 1 or 0 but either 1-e or e). For all samples, the inputs must be normalized. To achieve this task, the first step is to (center) subtract its average, and the second step is to (scale) divide by its standard deviation. This way,

the input can still be fed into the standard logistic function and work with the backpropagation algorithm implemented. The dataset used in this chapter is extracted from 90 generated samples consisting of five types of wireless networks (as shown in Table 2). Each sample represents single user selection preferences for a wireless network with vector dimension of 5 elements. The last item in each sample is the class label or the proposed network type. In order to measure the performance of the wireless network selector defined as the performance rate, the following formula is used:

$$PR = 100 \, x \, (Correctly \, Selected \, / \, Total \, Samples)$$
$$(8)$$

where PR represents the performance rate.

Due to the fact that the number of hidden nodes when using the backpropagation algorithm must be defined before the training, the structure is not determined by the training algorithm. Therefore, a sub set of the data with equal number of samples from each network types is used to find the network configuration with highest performance. Table 3 summarizes the constants used with different network configuration.

Testing the network with the above parameters yields the results shown in Table 4.

Table 3. Constant used for the BPNN configuration

Learning Rate	0.1
Momentum	0.10.005
Acceptable Error	[-0.7 0.7]
Range	700
Number of Epochs	15
Network 1 Training Samples	15
Network 2 Training Samples	15
Network 3 Training Samples	15
Network 4 Training Samples	15
Network 5 Training Samples	15

Table 4. Results from running various configurations of the BPNN

Configuration			Performance Rate
Input Nodes	Hidden Nodes	Output Nodes	
5	4	1	85.367
5	6	1	91.925
5	8	1	96.158
5	10	1	99.215
5	12	1	95.658
5	14	1	94.245

Table 5. Results from BPNN with the performance rate

Type	Correctly Selected	# of Incorrect Selected
Network 1	21	4
Network 2	19	2
Network 3	15	3
Network 4	23	3

Figure 5. Number of epochs versus the error (Trial 1)

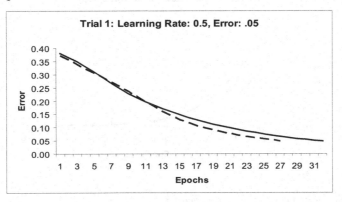

Using different network configurations, the highest performance rate is shown to be using the network configuration with 5 input nodes, 10 hidden nodes, and 1 output node yielding 99.215 % performance rate. Based on the highest performance rate of 99.215%, the network configuration of 5x10x1 was applied to training of all samples in the dataset, the 120 samples. Only 75% of the training samples were considered for the testing mode with a total number of 90 dif-ferent samples which yields a performance rate of 87.0%. Table 5 summarizes the results generated by the network.

The convergence rate based on the number of epochs and iterative decrease in the error is shown in Figure 5 (from Trial 1). Note that in Figures 5-8, the solid line represents backpropagation without momentum and the dashed line represents backpropagation with momentum.

In order to test the accuracy of the system, another trial with a different error convergence for the neural network was conducted. Figure 6 shows the obtained results. Repeating the same parameters as in trial 2 except with a lower learning rate yields the results presented in Figure 7.

To effectively test the accuracy, a test for significantly lowering the error rate yields the graph in Figure 8.

Figure 6 represents the convergence of the BPNN to a solution within an acceptable error value (Error = 0.005). Due to the fact that using momentum in a backpropagation algorithm takes into consideration the previous delta w_{ij} of the previous inter-connection, the system converges much faster than running the network without

momentum. It was noted varying the learning rate has a considerable impact on the system as well as the number of nodes. The higher the learning rate, the faster the system converges; however, there is a decrease in the performance of the system. This is due to the fact that higher learning rates allow the BPNN to learn quickly and thus does not have the enough time to adapt or learn enough to make accurate distinctions. As shown on Figure 6, the lower the acceptable error, the longer the network will converge. In addition, Figure 7 shows that learning rates affects the speed and processing time of the network in which the network will converge. Furthermore, Figure 8 shows that a very small acceptable error such as 0.00005 will take longer for the network

Figure 6. Number of epochs versus the error (Trial 2)

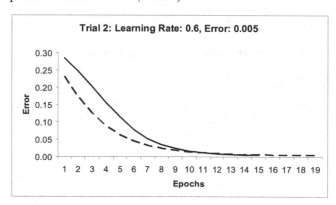

Figure 7. Number of epochs versus the error (Trial 3)

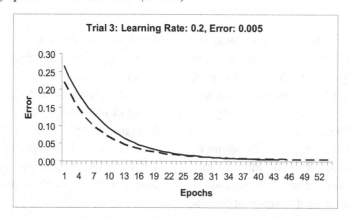

to converge and find the best wireless network match. This means the smaller the acceptable error, the longer the network will take to converge. Therefore, when choosing a neural network as an acceptable solution for selecting the best wireless network match across heterogeneous wireless networks, a use of combination of learning rates and acceptable error values must be selected with caution specially when running such system in real-time environment.

Finding the correct feature set for the selection of wireless networks can be very challenging. The four features extracted a set of possible user preferences on a mobile device appear to have solid results with a reasonable performance. However, it is important to test the effectiveness of each of the features selected for the neural network. In order to test the effectiveness for all the features, elements were removed from the neural network and tested to evaluate the performance and the selection rate success. Table 6 presents the results obtained from removing elements and testing for feature effectiveness on the overall performance of the neural network:

Results from Table 6 show that reducing the number of user preferences (parameters) in the data fed to the neural network significantly impact the overall performance of the system. For example, when removing one feature (one of the four user preferences shown in Table 1), the network performs in the 66%-74% range. However, reducing more than one preference (i.e. removing two features at the same time and thus having two features remaining), it significantly

Figure 8. Number of epochs versus error (Trial 4)

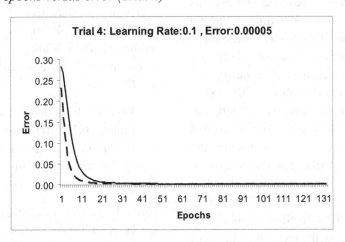

Table 6. Results from running BPNN with the performance rate (from Trial 1)

Feature Removed	Classification Rate
All Features	87.0
Feature 1	72.5
Feature 2	68.3
Feature 3	65.8
Feature 4	74.4
Feature 1,3	69.5
Feature 2,4	60.7

reduces the performance between the 61%-70% range. Therefore, the more user preferences used, the better the performance of the network. Table 6 shows the effectiveness of the features used (Table 1) to test the neural network for selecting the best available wireless network.

SUMMARY AND OPEN PROBLEMS

In this chapter, a Vertical Handoff Decision Function and a backpropagation based neural network have been proposed for the purpose of selecting the best available wireless network during vertical handoffs based on a set of predefined user preferences on a mobile device. This work can be used for applications in user control during handoff process as a starting point in which can serve as a basis for other types of neural networks. The features used from the data generated has been carefully selected and used as inputs for the neural network in order to have a high performance rate. The feature set is mainly dependent on several factors such as power consumption, cost of service, network security, and network capacity. Results show that there exists a relationship between possible user preferences although having non-uniform metrics. The use of neural networks provides a way to optimize the selection of the best available wireless network in a heterogeneous environment during a handoff process. The average performance of the neural network selection is 87%. In all of the four trials ran for testing the system, the neural network always converged to a solution which implies that the use of neural networks in selecting the best wireless network positively can be used.

The proposed method is capable of selecting the best available wireless network with a reasonable performance rate, however, there still room for improvement. It is observed that the BPNN takes long time during the training mode due to the large data size which could become an issue when implementing such system in real-time. In addition, the ability of the system configuration to adapt to current data being fed into it might become infeasible since the proposed method defined the number of hidden nodes prior in the training mode. However, results show that the proposed method can be used for applications in user control during handoff process as a starting point in which can serve as basis for other types of neural networks. The ability to use other types of neural networks such as ARTMAPs, Fuzzy ARTs, or Self Organized Map is a solution that can be explored in the future and compared against the BPNN.

REFERENCES

Akyildiz, I. F., et al. (1999, Aug). Mobility management in next-generation wireless systems. *Proceedings IEEE, 87*(8), 1347-84.

Alsenmyr, G., Bergström, J., Hagberg, M., Milén, A., Müller, W., Palm, H., Van der Velde, H., Wallentin, P., & Wallgren, F. (2003). Handover between WCDMA and GSM. *Ericsson Review no. 01.*

Chakravorty, R., Vidales, P., Patanapongpibul, L., Subramanian, K., Pratt, I., & Crowcroft, J., (2003, June). *On inter-network handover performance using Mobile IPv6.* University of Cambridge Computer Laboratory– Technical Report.

Chen, L. J., Sun, T., Chen, B., Rajendran, V., & Gerla, M. (2004). A smart decision model for vertical handoff. *4th ANWIRE International Workshop on Wireless Internet and Reconfigurability (ANWIRE 2004)*, Athens, Greece, 2004.

Chen, L. J., Sun, T., Cheung, B., Nguyen, D., & Gerla, M. (2004). *Universal seamless handoff architecture in wireless overlay networks.* Technical Report TR040012, UCLA CSD.

Falowo, O. E., & Chan, H. A. (2005). *Joint call admission control for integrated UMTS-WLAN network.* SATNAC.

Fox, A., Gribble, S., Chawathe, Y., Brewer, E., & Gauthier, P. (1997, Oct.). Cluster-based scalable network services. *Proceedings of the Symposium on Operating Systems Principles.*

Guo, C., Guo, Z., Zhang, Q., & Zhu, W. (2004, June). A seamless and proactive end-to-end mobility solution for roaming across heterogeneous wireless networks. *IEEE Journal on Selected Areas in Communications, 22*(5), 834-848.

Hatami, A., et al. (1999, Sept). Analytical framework for handoff in non-homogeneous mobile data networks. *Proceedings PIMRC '99* (pp. 760-64). Osaka, Japan.

Heickerö, R., Jelvin, S., & Josefsson, B. (2002). Ericsson seamless network. *Ericsson Review no. 02.*

Makela, Ylianttila, J., & Pahlavan, M. (2000, Sept). Handoff decision in multi-service networks. *11ᵗʰ IEEE International Symposium on Personal, Indoor and Mobile Radio Communications (PIMRC).*

McNair, J., & Zhu, F., (2004, June). Vertical handoffs in fourth-generation multinetwork environments. *IEEE Wireless Commun., 11*(3), 8-15.

McNair, J., Akyildiz, I. F., & Bender, M. (2000, March). An inter-system handoff technique for the IMT-2000 System. *Proceedings of IEEE INFOCOM 2000*, March 2000.

Myers, M. B. (2000), Predicting and measuring quality of service for mobile multimedia. *IEEE 3G Mobile Communication Technologies,* Conference Publication No. 471.

Nasser, N., & Hassanein, H., (2006). Radio resource management algorithms in wireless cellular networks. In A. Boukerch (Ed.), *Handbook of algorithms for wireless networking and mobile computing* (pp. 415-47). Chapman Hall, CRC Press.

Park, H., Yoon, S., Kim, T., Park, J., Do, M., & Lee, J. (2003). Vertical handoff procedure and algorithm between IEEE802.11 WLAN and CDMA Cellular Network. *Lecture Notes in Computer Science (LNCS)*, No. 2524, pp. 103-112.

Taylor, L., Titmus, R., & Lebre, C. (1999). The challenges of seamless handover in future mobile multimedia networks. *IEEE Personal Communications*, Special Issue on "Advanced Mobile Communication Systems – Managing Complexity in a Competitive and Seamless Environment."

Wang, C. H. (2003 June). *A dynamic resource allocation for vertical handoff on heterogeneous wireless networks.* Department and Graduate Institute of Information Management, Master's Thesis.

Wang, H., Katz, R., & Giese, J. (1999). Policy-enabled handoffs across heterogeneous wireless networks. WMCSA.

Yang, X., Bigham, J., & Cuthber, L. (2005, March). Resource management for service providers in heterogeneous wireless networks. *IEEE Wireless Communications and Networking Conference, 3*, 1305-1310.

Ylianttila, M., Mäkelä, J., & Mähönen, P., (2002, Sept). Optimization scheme for mobile users performing vertical handoffs between IEEE 802.11 and GPRS/EDGE networks. *IEEE PIMRC, 1*, 15-18.

Ylianttila, M., Mäkelä, J., & Mähönen, P. (2002). Supporting resource allocation with vertical handoffs in multiple radio network environment. *IEEE International Symposium on Personal Indoor and Mobile Radio Communications.*

Ylianttila, M., Pichna, R., Vallström, J., & Mäkelä, J. (1999). Handoff procedure for heterogeneous wireless networks. *Global Telecommunications Conference.*

Zhang, Q., Guo, C., Guo, Z., & Zhu, W. (2003, Nov.). Efficient mobility management for vertical handoff between WWAN and WLAN. *IEEE Communications Magazine, 41*(11), 102-108.

Zhu, F., & McNair, J., (2004, March). Optimizations for vertical handoff decision algorithms. *IEEE Wireless Communications and Networking Conference (WCNC)* (pp. 867-872).

Chapter IV
Resource Management in IEEE 802.11 Based Wireless Networks

Ming Li
California State University, Fresno, USA

Roberto Riggio
Create-Net, Italy

Francesco De Pellegrini
Create-Net, Italy

Imrich Chlamtac
Create-Net, Italy

ABSTRACT

This chapter provides a comprehensive review of the architectures, algorithms, and protocols in the topic of resource management in IEEE 802.11-based wireless networks such as wireless LANs, heterogeneous wired/wireless networks, mobile ad hoc networks, and wireless mesh networks. The focus is given to the approaches for bandwidth allocation in different networks as well as how these strategies are incorporated in each specific protocol. Although the issues of resource management and quality of service support in different networks highly depend on the specific network architectures and mobility patterns, existing works in the literature have shown that the key issue in 802.11 networks is how to coordinate the contention based channel access by considering channel rates, network topology, interference, and mobility. With successful resource allocation schemes, sufficient quality of services can be supported to maximize user experiences with multimedia applications such as voice and video in wireless networks.

INTRODUCTION

Next generation wireless networks will require significant flexibility on deployment so that the objective of providing seamless service to users anywhere at any time can be achieved. Having been successfully used as the ubiquitous last-mile technology in the present days, IEEE 802.11 has become the de-facto standard for providing wireless access in applications such as campus wireless LANs, wireless hotspots in hotels and airports, and military battlefields. The data rates guaranteed by the standard reach as high as 54Mbps and 11Mbps for 802.11a and 802.11b, and current research is investigating enhanced PHY layers and data aggregation techniques in order to enhance the capacity of the WLANs channels. With this availability of broadband capability in IEEE 802.11 networks, it is a natural demand that appropriate quality of service (QoS) strategies are devised so that wireless users can access multimedia data such as voice, video, and 3D animation and experience satisfactory entertainment.

Depending on the actual applications and types of networks, the issues of QoS can be quite different. For instance, in single-hop wireless LANs, it is desirable to provide sufficient quality of service for real-time flows not only within each individual wireless LAN, but also among different wireless LANs when users roam in the network. Furthermore, it is not unusual that mobile users access/exchange information in wired networks. In this case, end-to-end QoS is a must in order to better support multimedia applications such as voice over IP and online video. On the other hand, in self-organizing multi-hop mobile ad hoc networks (MANETs), it is imperative that sufficient and reliable QoS is provided from the source node to the destination node, even when significant mobility and dramatic topology change is present. In addition, the concept of multi-hop ad hoc networks can be extended to wireless mesh networks where static wireless mesh routers are installed on the top of buildings

to form what is called "mesh backbone." Existing wireless access networks can easily reach Internet via those wireless mesh routers. Since mesh routers can be equipped with multiple radios or multiple channels, the interference among different routers is reduced and thus the capacity of the mesh backbone is significantly increased. How to provide appropriate QoS by incorporating the multiple radio/channel capability is still a challenging issue.

Basically, there are two fundamental QoS issues in IEEE 802.11 based wireless networks. First, there is no QoS protocol in standard 802.11 MAC layer. Although IEEE 802.11e was proposed to prioritize the media access by stations of different priorities, how to improve the performance and provide QoS guarantee in 802.11e EDCF and HCF remains a challenge. Secondly, in multi-hop single channel wireless ad hoc networks, different links on the paths of the same flow may compete for the channel access and thus interfere with each other. In this case, it is difficult to provide high throughput. How to deal with this type of multi-hop interference and estimate the available bandwidth along a certain route is critically important for sufficient quality of service support.

Considerable works have been conducted on providing quality of service support to IEEE 802.11 wireless networks in recent years. Naturally, most approaches involve MAC layer protocol design with some approaches incorporate information at both MAC and network layers. From the network architecture aspects, these works can be classified to following categories:

- **Resource management in wireless LANs:** This work involves how to provide good QoS in the single hop wireless local area networks and can be further classified to further categories:
    o **DCF based protocols:** Since the standard distributed coordination function (DCF) only provides best-effort media access, it is important to incorporate

certain distributed approaches to achieve desirable QoS guarantee and/ or service differentiation in wireless LANs by appropriate modification of DCF. On the other hand, improvement over the centralized point coordination function (PCF) has also been proposed.

o **Extension of 802.11e standard:** With the newly proposed hybrid coordination function (HCF) MAC protocol in IEEE 802.11e standard, more efforts have been made on the improvement of 802.11e performance by addressing some of its shortcomings such as static parameter setting, starvation of low priority traffic, and limited QoS guarantee.

- **Resource management in multi-cell wireless LANs and heterogeneous wired/wireless networks:** this work involves how to provide good QoS when a mobile station roams among different wireless LANs. According to the heterogeneity of the network domains, we can classify it as follows:

o **QoS handoff in multi-cell wireless LANs:** Works in this direction usually check the resource availability before a station decides to move into another cell and gets associated with the corresponding access point (AP). Usually, certain bandwidth share is reserved for future traffic handoff.

o **QoS guarantee in heterogeneous wired/wireless networks:** Works in this direction usually address the issue of how to integrate the QoS strategies in wireless LANs such as extended distributed coordination function (EDCF) and other resource reservation protocols with QoS frameworks in wired Internet such as differentiated service (DiffServ) and resource reservation protocol (RSVP), thereby providing

an end-to-end QoS guarantee for data access that spans over both wired and wireless network domains.

- **Resource management in wireless mobile ad hoc networks:** Protocols in this direction usually involve route available bandwidth estimation by incorporating interference and traffic information, devise of QoS aware routing protocols by piggybacking QoS information along with route discovery and route collection, and design of flow reservation frameworks.

- **Resource management in wireless mesh networks:** Recent literature has focused on the design of wireless backhauls in such multi-hop scenario, and on related resources optimization problems; also, the problem of the channel allocation has to be tackled in the wireless mesh network domain. Furthermore, quite novel scenarios, which resemble similar issues arising in the peer-to-peer networks, are emerging in the field of community wireless mesh networks.

In this chapter, we focus on the resource management in IEEE 802.11-based wireless networks. Due to the broadness of the topic of QoS and wireless technologies themselves, it is impossible to cover all aspects of QoS issues in many other wireless technologies such as cellular networks, UMTS, Bluetooth, and Wi-Max. Furthermore, with a less relevance to quality of service support, issues on capacity improvement such as using different routing protocols or topology control strategies will not be discussed in details. Instead, issues on resource management such as bandwidth provisioning, service differentiation, and admission control are given more attention.

This chapter is organized as follows. Section 2 discusses representative QoS solutions based on IEEE 802.11 DCF, EDCF, and HCA. Section 3 discusses the resource management schemes in multi-cell WLANs and heterogeneous wired/ wireless networks. Section 4 discusses QoS framework, interference aware bandwidth estimation, and mobility aware QoS routing protocols in wireless mobile ad hoc networks. Section 6 describes issues of resources allocation and QoS in WMNs. Finally, Section 7 concludes the chapter with future trends.

BACKGROUND AND MOTIVATION

Compared with a wired infrastructure, wireless LAN (WLAN) has unique advantages, such as broadband bandwidth capability and low deployment cost. With these desirable advantages provided by IEEE 802.11, the wireless LAN market has experienced explosive growth in hot spots such as hotels, hospitals, and campuses, to mention just a few. With the vast deployment of wireless access points, users can access real-time and Internet services virtually anytime, anywhere, while enjoying the flexibility of mobility and guaranteed connectivity.

IEEE 802.11 is the lead standard for wireless LAN. It adopts the standard 802 LLC (logical link control) protocol but provides optimized PHY (physical layer) and MAC (medium access control) sub-layers for wireless communications. 802.11 specifies two physical layers: DSSS (direct sequence spread spectrum) and FHSS (frequency hopping spread spectrum). Based on the transmission technologies and the operating spectrum, the later revisions of 802.11 can be classified into three categories: 802.11a (OFDM-5GHz), 802.11b (HR/DSSS-2.4GHz), and 802.11g (OFDM-2.4GHz). 802.11b is based on HR/DSSS (high-rate DSSS) and operates at the 2.4 GHz ISM (industrial-scientific-medical) band with transmission rate from 1 to 11 Mbps. 802.11a is based on OFDM (orthogonal frequency division multiplexing) and uses 5GHz U-NII (unlicensed national information infrastructure) band in America with transmission rate from 6 to 54 Mbps. 802.11g is also based on OFDM but uses 2.4GHz ISM band and has been formally ratified by IEEE Standards

Association's Standard Board in June 2003. This standard specifies a maximum transmission rate of 54 Mbps, the same with 802.11a. However, since 802.11g uses the same spectrum between 2.4 and 2.4835 GHz and is inherently backward compatible with 802.11b, it may attract more attention from industry than the earlier standardized 802.11a. Nevertheless, 802.11a possesses one noteworthy advantage: the unlicensed radio spectrum (5.15-5.35 GHz and 5.725-5.825 GHz) it operates within is rarely used while the 2.4 GHz spectrum for 802.11b and g have already been taken by many home electronic devices such as cordless phones, microwave ovens, and garage door openers.

Nevertheless, IEEE 802.11 is designed for best effort services only. This lack of built-in mechanism on the support of real-time services makes it very difficult to provide quality of service guarantee for throughput-sensitive and delay-sensitive multimedia applications. Therefore, modification of existing 802.11 standards is necessary. Although IEEE 802.11e is being proposed for the upcoming standard for the enhancement of service differentiation, QoS guarantee in 802.11 is still a very challenging problem. In this chapter, we provide a detailed review of three representative IEEE 802.11 MAC protocols in the standard: distributed coordinator function (DCF), point coordinator function (PCF), and hybrid coordination function.

Distributed Coordinator Function (DCF) and Point Coordinator Function (PCF)

Distributed coordinator function (DCF) is the basic medium access mechanism in IEEE 802.11 (IEEE, 1997). DCF is contention-based and it uses carrier sense multiple access with collision avoidance (CSMA/CA) algorithm to coordinate the access to the wireless channel. To resolve the hidden terminal problem, a request-to-send/clear-to-send (RTS/CTS) handshaking procedure is required to detect the transmission collision. Before a station (STA) sends out a data frame, it first senses the channel. If the channel is idle for at least a DCF inter-frame space (DIFS), the frame is transmitted. Otherwise, a backoff time slot is chosen randomly in the interval [0, *CW*), where CW is the contention window. The contention window is incremented exponentially with the increase of the number of attempts to retransmit the frame. During the backoff period, the backoff timer is decremented in terms of slot time as long as the channel is determined to be idle. When the backoff timer reaches zero, the data frame is sent out. If a collision occurs, a new backoff time slot will be chosen and the backoff procedure starts over until some time limit is exceeded. Following the RTS/CTS, the sender STA waits for short inter-frame space (SIFS) and then sends out the data packets (DATA). Upon the receipt of the DATA, an ACK is sent from the receiver to acknowledge the success of the data transmission. After the successful RTS/CTS/DATA/ACK four-way handshaking, the contention window is reset to CW_{min}. If the data packet is larger than the MAC threshold *Frag_threshold*, multiple fragments are transmitted and immediately acknowledged separately. Furthermore, a network allocation vector (NAV) is set in RTS, CTS, and DATA. The value of NAV is the amount of the channel time the ongoing data transmission *will*

need for completion. When another STA hears any of these frames, it defers its channel access only after a time period equivalent to NAV set in the frame, thus reserving the channel for the existing data transmission. Figure 1 illustrates the CSMA/CA channel access procedure with RTS/CTS and fragmentation. DCF suffers from collision seriously under high loads, and it does not provide any traffic differentiation and quality of service.

Point coordinator function (PCF) is an optional mechanism for IEEE 802.11. PCF coexists with DCF by providing a contention free period (CFP), during which the point coordinator (PC) polls high priority stations and allocates time slots for them to transmit data frames. A STA is not allowed to transmit data packet without the permission from the PC. PCF Inter-frame Space (PIFS) is defined to make sure that low priority STAs do not interfere PCF operation. Also, DCF is supported in this case to prevent low priority stations from being starved. PCF is designed to offer QoS for real-time applications. But it is a centralized approach and suffers from location-dependent errors.

Hybrid Coordination Function (HCF)

Unlike IEEE 802.11, IEEE 802.11e standard (IEEE, 2003) proposed a single coordination

Figure 1. CSMA/CA-RTS/CTS with fragmentation access scheme

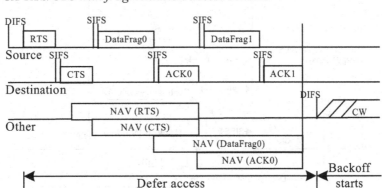

function called hybrid coordination function (HCF), which combines two mechanisms: contention based enhanced distributed channel access (EDCA) and non-contention based HCF controlled channel access (HCCA). Basically, EDCA and HCCA are extensions of DCF and PCF, respectively and EDCA is also refereed as enhanced distributed coordinator function (EDCF).

In EDCA, differentiated DCF access is provided to the wireless medium for prioritized access categories (ACs). As shown in Table 1, an EDCA station can implement at most 8 prioritized output queues, mapping to four different AC. Values for CW_{min}, CW_{max}, and arbitrary inter-frame space ($AIFS$) are set on per-AC basis. For AC i, the initial minimum contention window, maximum contention window, and arbitrary inter-frame space are $CW_{min}[i]$, $CW_{max}[i]$, and $AIFS[i]$, respectively. To make sufficient service differentiation, for AC i and j with $0 \leq i < j \leq 3$, it follows that $CW_{min}[i] \geq CW_{min}[j]$, $CW_{max}[i] \geq CW_{max}[j]$, and $AIFS[i] \geq AIFS[j]$, and at least one being "strict greater." Each station sends packets with its preferred priority, which is then mapped to a corresponding AC. By specifying smaller CW_{min} and $AIFS$ values for higher priority queues, delay and throughput of high priority flows can be ensured while minimal service is offered to lowest priority queues. Virtual collisions (Figure 2a) between competing queues within a station are resolved by granting the transmission opportunity to the highest-priority queue involved in the collision. A virtual collision happens when the backoff intervals of two or more queues within one station counts to zero

Figure 2. Channel access of EDCA (Xiao & Li, 2004). Top: Virtual collision handling; Bottom: Timing diagram

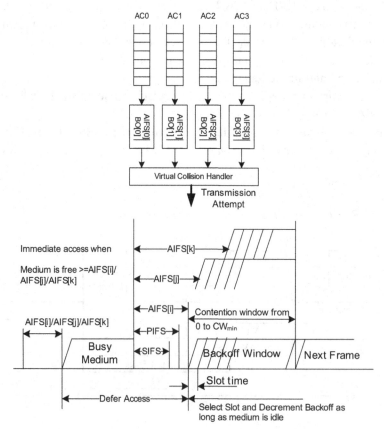

Table 1. Priority to access category mapping

Priority	Access Category (AC)	Traffic type
7	3	Voice
6	3	Voice
5	2	Video
4	2	Video
3	1	Video Probe
2	0	Best Effort
1	0	Best Effort
0	0	Best Effort

at the same time. Table 1 shows the time diagram of EDCF with three ACs: $i > j > k$. Furthermore, a new concept, transmission opportunity (TXOP) is introduced in 802.11e to represent a time period when a station wins the channel access for data transmission.

Similar to PCF, HCCA provides a central control based channel access through polling. A QoS aware hybrid coordinator (HC) is defined at the QoS access point (QAP) and uses PIFS to gain control of the channel and allocate TXOP to QoS stations (QSTAs). An interesting feature of HCCA is that it can poll stations not only during contention-free period, but also during contention period. In order to appropriately allocate TXOP, HC requests a QSTA to send a QoS reservation request with its traffic specification (TSPEC) parameters and then determine the corresponding TXOP. The major parameters (Ganguly et al., 2006; IEEE, 2003) included in TSPEC are:

- **Mean data rate (ρ):** The average bit rate for packet transmission, in bits per second;
- **Delay bound (D):** The maximum delay allowed to transport a packet across the wireless interface (including queuing delay), in milliseconds;
- **Maximum service interval (SI_{max}):** The maximum time allowed between neighbor TXOPs allocated to the same station, in microseconds;

- **Nominal MSDU size (L):** The nominal size of a packet, in octets;
- **Minimum PHY rate (R):** The minimum physical bit rate assumed by the scheduler for calculating transmission time, in bits per second.

The service differentiation in EDCA is helpful in providing better-than-best effort quality of service for multimedia data traffic under low to medium traffic load condition. However, it does not perform well under high traffic load condition. In this case, admission control and bandwidth reservation becomes a must in order to guarantee QoS of existing traffics. Otherwise, the extremely large saturation delay may lead to the failure of supporting multimedia applications. On the other hand, HCCA provides traffic protection and QoS guarantees, but it is a centralized approach. Thus, there are two major research directions on the topic of QoS in wireless LANs: (i) Modification or extension of DCF/EDCA for distributed QoS support; (ii) Improvements of HCCA for better QoS support. Basically, the approaches in the former category dominate in the literature.

However, unlike wired networks, in IEEE 802.11 wireless networks, a station has no knowledge of the network resource availability and thus cannot make accurate decision on whether or not to admit a new flow. In addition, with the contention-based CSMA/CA channel access mechanism, bandwidth provisioning is almost impossible, leading to only soft QoS guarantee. Due to these two major difficulties, admission control and bandwidth reservation in IEEE 802.11 wireless network is quite difficult.

RESOURCE MANAGEMENT IN WIRELESS LANs

Based on the ways the resource management issue is approached and addressed, we can categorize existing schemes to three general categories:

- **DCF based schemes** (Banchs & Pérez, 2002; Barry, Campell, & Veres, 2001; Chakeres & Belding-Royer, 2004; Ergen & Varaiya, 2005; Kazantzidis, Gerla, & Lee, 2001; Shah, Chen, & Nahrstedt, 2004; Valaee & Li, 2002; Zhai, Chen, & Fang, 2006): These schemes focus on how to provide sufficient quality of service without change of the legacy DCF/PCF scheduling algorithms.

- **EDCF based schemes** (Banchs, Pérez, & Qiao, 2003; Li, Prabhakaran, & Sathyamurthy, 2003; Li & Prabhakaran, 2005a; Pong & Moor, 2003; Xiao, Li, & Choi, 2004a; Xiao & Li, 2004b; Xiao & Li, 2004c): These schemes improve the performance of real-time flows in addition to the service differentiation and QoS strategies offered by the legacy EDCF/HCF scheduling algorithms.

DCF Based QoS MAC Schemes

Figure 3 shows the taxonomy of DCF based QoS MAC schemes. The common features of these schemes is to devise additional techniques to estimate the network resources such as bandwidth and delay and then enforce QoS strategy such as admission control and flow reservation to ensure the performance of real-time voice/video traffic. According to the techniques applied, these approaches can be further classified to following categories: *packet probing based approaches,*

model based approaches, and *bandwidth estimation based approach.*

Model Based Approaches

Performance modeling of IEEE 802.11 DCF has been extensively investigated (Bianchi, 2000; Wu, Peng, & Long, 2002; Xiao, 2005, Xiao et al., 2004a; Zhu & Chlamtac, 2003). These models are based on the saturation status where all stations always have packets to send in the queue. However, admission control should be enforced before saturation status is reached to avoid performance degradation of real-time traffic. Ergen et al. (2005) proposed a Markov model for DCF that incorporates carrier sense, non-saturated traffic and SNR, for both basic and RTS/CTS access mechanisms. Then, based on the performance model, a system throughput can be calculated by solving a set of non-linear equations, given the assumption that all the flows are admitted. Although significant contribution is made towards the performance modeling, especially on analysis of the non-saturation cases, using this approach for admission control has its own limitations. First, when the number of flows increases and traffic changes dynamically, the overhead of calculating system throughput is non-negligible. Second, the performance of a real network is far from ideal and the performance model does not adhere to the real conditions: In general, it is very difficult to

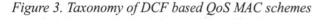

Figure 3. Taxonomy of DCF based QoS MAC schemes

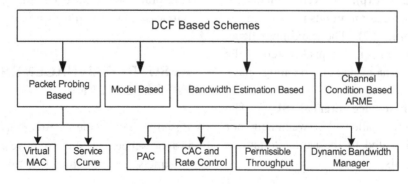

obtain an accurate throughput with performance analysis. Due to these limitations, model based approaches are usually not widely used for practical QoS protocol design. Instead, measurement based approaches have the advantage of being simple, dynamic, and practical.

Channel Condition Based Approaches

Banchs et al. (2002) proposed assured rate MAC extension (ARME) to provide assured service to multimedia applications. The core idea of ARME is to use a token bucket and a queue to change the contention window (CW) and regulate the flow transmission. The token bucket is filled at the desired transmission rate and the queue expresses the willingness of a station to transmit packets. If queue is empty (i.e., no packet to fill and the current CW satisfies the sending needs of the user), CW is increased slightly. Otherwise, CW is decreased so that a station has more frequent channel access to increase its transmission rate. On the other hand, if the length of the packets in the token bucket is smaller than a certain limit, then the CW can be increased slightly. However, it is possible that all nodes try to decrease their CWs to meet their bandwidth requirements. In this case, the channel overloading occurs due to significant channel contention. To avoid this scenario, the average number of collision per packet transmission is measured. If the collision number is greater than a threshold c, then the CW is increased over the specified value by IEEE 802.11 DCF.

Packet Probing Based Approaches

Barry et al. (2001) proposed a virtual MAC (VMAC) algorithm that passively monitors the channel by using virtual MAC frames and estimates local service level. From the observation that the wireless channel usually becomes delay limited before getting throughput limited, authors propose to estimate the MAC level delay to sense the channel condition as the basis for admission control. The idea of VMAC is that in order to accurately know how good the channel condition is, a virtually created packet is sent from the higher layer so that it will go through the channel contention and backoff procedure exactly like a real data packet, except that the virtual packet is not sent out through the air interface. Thus, VMAC does not impose traffic overhead to the network and can be executed continuously in parallel to the real applications without triggering network congestion.

VMAC works as follows. First, virtual packet is time-stamped at MAC layer and put into a virtual buffer. Then, if "virtual collision" is detected (i.e., whenever any other mobile station chooses the same slot for transmission), it will wait for a delay equal to RTS timer and then enters a backoff process. In this way, VMAC can measure MAC packet delay, loss, and collision, and can provide a very reasonable basis for admission control. Then, a Virtual Source (VS) algorithm is proposed to measure the application layer delay. Whenever a new flow is initiated, its delay requirement is compared with the measured delay. If delay requirement is satisfied, the flow is admitted, otherwise, it is dropped. With this technique, VMAC and VS work well for delay constrained voice traffics.

Instead of using virtual packet, Valaee et al. (2002) proposed to use a sequence of small size probing packets to measure the probing delay and establish the service curve, which is then used as the criteria for call admission control. The probing is a greedy manner (i.e., a new probing packet is generated once an existing probing packet is transmitted). Thus, the total delay of ith probing packet, δ_i, is approximately $\tau_i - \tau_{i-1}$, where τ_i is the time instance at which a probing packet is delivered to the destination. On the other hand, δ_i includes a waiting time in the queue w_i and the actual transmission time b that includes the duration of multiple MAC frames. Thus $w_i = \delta_i - b = \delta_i - T_{DIFS} - 3T_{SIFS} - T_{RTS} - T_{CTS} - T_{ACK} - T_{DATA}$. Thus, a sequence of total waiting time is used to obtain the service curve $S_\epsilon(t)$, which is defined as a percentile of the delay elements. Finally, call admission control (CAC) algorithm can accept a flow if the induced service curve will stay above the universal service curve and reject it otherwise.

Bandwidth Estimation Based Approaches

Probing packet usually involves algorithmic overhead (Barry et al., 2001) or traffic overhead (Valaee et al., 2002). Furthermore, the accuracy of the admission control decision largely depends on the packet sizes and frequency of the probing, especially when the network traffic is dynamic. Thus, many proposed schemes are designed to monitor the wireless channel, measure the channel utilization (or the busy ratio), and/or use existing traffic to directly estimate available bandwidth.

Chakeres et al. (2004) proposed PAC, a simple approach to estimate the channel utilization. In this approach, by monitoring the amount of time the channel is sensed busy, sending, or receiving, a node can measure not only transmissions that occur within its reception range (or transmission range), but also those within its carrier sensing range. Then, the network available bandwidth $B_{avail} = (1-U) \cdot B_{max}$, where U is the estimated channel utilization and B_{max} is an approximation of channel maximum achievable bandwidth. For 2Mbps channel rate, B_{max} is set to 1.2Mbps. Furthermore, to prevent channel congestion and make sure network is running under saturation status, a small portion of the bandwidth B_{rsv} is reserved. Then, a new flow is only admitted if $R_f < B_{max} - B_{rsv}$, where R_f is the flow rate requirement. With appropriate utilization estimation, satisfactory performance can be obtained for real-time multimedia applications. However, simply assuming a constant B_{max} may not be very desirable. With many factors such as network configuration, traffic characteristics, network topology, and mobility, the maximum

achievable bandwidth varies significantly (Bianchi, 2000).

Zhai et al. (2006) proposed two algorithms to provide QoS in IEEE 802.11 wireless LANs. In their approach, where call admission control (CAC) is used to restrict number of real time flows and rate control scheme is to regulate the transmission rates of best effort flows. The core idea of the CAC is to measure the channel utilization and then calculate the available bandwidth. Let B_U be the channel utilization corresponding to the optimal operating point and R_b be the channel busyness ratio, then the available *normalized* throughput $s_a = (B_U - R_b) \cdot T_{data}/T_{suc}$, where T_{data} is the time taken to transmit the data packet and T_{suc} is the average time period associated with one successful transmission (defined as $T_{data} + T_{ACK} + T_{SIFS} + T_{DIFS}$ without RTS/CTS). However, this estimation is too optimistic. Basically, due to overhead and collision, it is impossible to achieve normalized total throughput as high as T_{data}/T_{suc}, even with B_U considered (set as 0.9 without RTS/CTS and 0.95 with RTS/CTS). Thus, this scheme and PAC do not provide an accurate and practical method to obtain the maximum achievable channel bandwidth.

Kazantzidis et al. (2001) proposed a measurement based approach to estimate the available bandwidth. Instead of using virtual packets or probing packets, existing traffic is used to eliminate the extra overhead and algorithm complexity. In this approach, a *permissible throughput* is calculated as:

$$r_{(source,destination)} = (1-u) \cdot \frac{S}{t_q + (t_s + t_{CA} + t_{overhead}) \cdot R + \sum_{r=1}^{R} B_r}$$

where u is the link utilization, t_q is the MAC queuing time, t_s is the transmission time of S bits, t_{CA} is the collision avoidance phase time, $t_{overhead}$ is the total control overhead time such as RTS, CTS, ACK, etc, R is the number of necessary transmissions due to collision and loss, and B_r is the backoff time for rth transmission. As an approximation, a constant of 1200 μs is used for $t_{overhead}$ for simplicity. A window of 16 to 32 packets is used to smooth the estimation. However, compared to t_s, t_{CA} may not be negligible and is independent of S. Thus, this estimation scheme is affected by packet size.

Shah et al. (2004) proposed an admission control and dynamic bandwidth management scheme to provide fairness and a soft rate guarantee in single hop ad hoc networks. In this approach, a cross-layer architecture is proposed to deal with the bandwidth estimation, allocation, and adaptation of real-time flows. The architecture has the following three components: *Rate adaptor (RA)*, *total bandwidth estimator (TBE)*, and *bandwidth manager (BM)*.

- *Rate Adaptor (RA)* converts a flow's bandwidth requirements into channel time percentage (CTP) requirements and communicates it to the bandwidth manager (BM). After RA obtains an allocated CTP for the flow, it will control its transmission rate according to the allocated CTP. Let the minimum bandwidth of a flow f be $B_{min}(f)$ and the total bandwidth perception by flow f be $B_p(f)$, then the corresponding minimum CTP of f, $p_{min}(f)=B_{min}(f)/B_p(f)$.

- *Total Bandwidth Estimator (TBE)* takes advantage of the MAC layer information and makes the estimation on the total channel bandwidth. Similar to the measurement technique proposed by (Kazantzidis et al., 2001), the throughput of transmitting a packet is calculated as $TP = S/(t_r - t_s)$, where S is the

size of the packet, t_s is the time-stamp that the packet is ready at the MAC layer, and t_r is the time-stamp that an ACK has been received, as illustrated in Figure 4. This time interval $t_r - t_s$ includes the channel busy and contention time. The measurement is made for different neighboring nodes due to channel condition variation and only on active links. For inactive links, a default initial bandwidth can be set since there is no way to measure $t_r - t_s$ over non-transmitting links. Since the packet size affects the accuracy of the bandwidth estimation, authors proposed to normalize the estimated TP value by incorporating packet size. In Figure 4, we can that $T_d = S/BW_{ch}$ is the actual time for the channel to transmit the DATA packet, where BWch is the channel's bit-rate. Then, the transmission times of two packets should differ only in their times to transmit the DATA packets. Therefore, it is obvious that $(t_{r1}-t_{s1})-S_1/BW_{ch} = (t_{r1}-t_{s1})-S_2/BW_{ch} = S_2/TP_2-S_2/BW_{ch}$, where S_1 is the actual data packet size, and S_2 is a pre-defined standard packet size. With this equation, normalized throughput $TP2$ can be calculated from a standard size packet.

- *Bandwidth Manager (BM)* performs admission control at two different times: (1) when a new flow is established; (2) when an existing flow is torn down. When a new flow f is introduced and requests its $p_{min}(f)$ from RA to BM, BM checks if $1-\sum_{g\in F} p_{min}(g) \geq p_{min}(f)$. If this is true,

Figure 4. IEEE 802.11 unicast packet transmission sequence

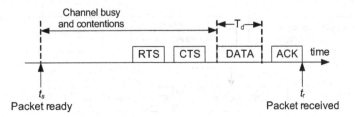

the new flow is admitted. Otherwise, it is rejected with a reply to the RA at the sender. After the admission, BM must redistribute free channel time $1 - \sum_{g \in F} p_{\min}(g)$ according to a min-max fair fashion to maximize the performance of existing flows. When a flow f terminates, the BM will eliminate the flow from the flow list, calculate the total channel time percentage, and redistribute the free channel time to existing flows through the RA.

EDCA Based Call Admission Control Schemes

With EDCA being proposed in IEEE 802.11e standard, many research works have concentrated on the resource management issues in term of how to dynamically improve the bandwidth sharing and delay guarantee by tuning the network configuration parameters. These schemes have the desirable features of good compatibility and thus are more practical. Figure 5 shows the taxonomy of EDCA based QoS MAC schemes. According to the techniques applied, these approaches can be further classified to following categories: *priority reallocation and admission control, CW and TXOP adjustment based approaches*, and *data and admission control approaches*.

Priority Reallocation and Admission Control

Li et al. (2003) proposed a general admission control and flow reservation strategy for distributed MAC schedulers in IEEE 802.11 wireless LANs such as DCF, EDCF, and DFS (Vaidya, Bahl, & Gupta, 2000). On the one hand, the approach is general since the flow reservation and bandwidth estimation work for all existing schedulers. On the other hand, they proposed a priority re-allocation scheme to improve the capacity of EDCF in the infrastructure mode.

The total bandwidth estimation technique is the same as the one proposed in Kazantzidis et al. (2001) and Shah et al. (2004). However, the flow reservation scheme ensures better QoS guarantee than the dynamic bandwidth management in Shah et al. (2004). To facilitate easy implementation and better compatibility, authors adopted a simple request/response pattern for flow reservation and admission control. No bandwidth re-negotiation is enforced because soft-QoS is offered. Since each wireless station does not have global information of the LAN, a wireless bandwidth manager (WBM) is specified for admission control and flow reservation. Every high priority mobile stations, before data transmission, must send their QoS requirements to WBM, which will accept/reject the requests according to the availability of the bandwidth in the wireless LAN.

Figure 5. Taxonomy of EDCA-based QoS MAC schemes

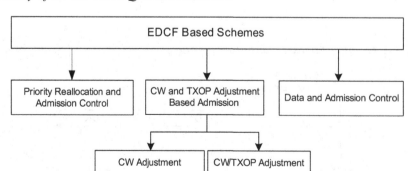

Many schemes (Aad, Ni, & Castelluccia, 2002; Romdhani, Ni, & Turletti, 2003) try to alleviate serious flow contention by dynamically changing the contention window. However, these approaches require modification of the standard. In fact, given a certain per priority contention window setting in EDCF, changing user priority also change contention window, only in a coarse scale. Thus, it is equivalently effective to assign a new priority appropriately for an incoming flow at the application layer. In this approach (Li et al., 2003; Li & Prabhakaran, 2004), flows are classified into two classes, *high priority* and *low priority*, which have priorities from 4 to 7, and 1 to 3, respectively. Correspondingly, flows are called *high priority flows* and *low priority flows*, respectively. Two flows are said to be of *the same class* (higher or lower) if they are in the same range specified. Also, *Flow_length* of a

priority p, *Flow_length*(p), is defined as the total bandwidth demands of all the flows of priority p in the network. Then, when a new flow is initiated, its priority is reassigned according to two rules: (i) A flow is assigned a priority of the same class with the smallest *Flow_length*; (ii) Among all the priorities satisfying the above condition, the one closest to the original priority is chosen. In low or medium traffic load, assigning a lower priority does not decrease the received throughput of a flow because of enough idle slots in the channel. In high traffic load, our algorithm can effectively improve the overall throughput of the network by minimizing the collision rate. Another desirable feature of this algorithm is that it can easily punish misbehaving flows by assigning a very low priority to them and protect other flows. Figure 6 compares the overall received throughput and average normalized throughput, respectively. It

Figure 6. Comparison of dynamic priority reallocation scheme with different fixed user priorities

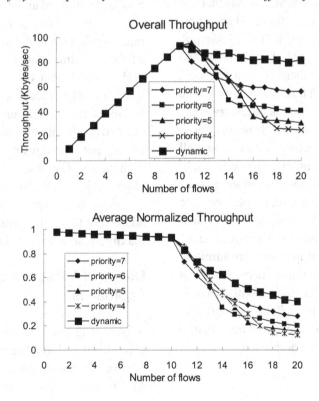

can be seen that when all flows are of the same priority, the overall throughput is decreasing after the number of flows exceeds 10. The higher the priorities, the earlier the decrease occurs. This result is consistent since that under low and medium traffic load, re-allocating priorities does not decrease the overall throughput because of the low collision rate, and when traffic load becomes high, low priority is preferred for smaller collision rate. However, high overall throughput is always obtained with even priority distribution and the improvement is up to 44%.

The previous even distribution affects the fairness of existing flows. Thus, in Li et al. (2005a), the authors proposed to only re-allocate priorities of new flows to avoid severe channel contention with existing high priority flows. In this approach, the mean MAC level delay experienced by a sender for flows of different priorities (i.e., per priority MAC delay) is measured. Let D_i^m be the average MAC delay experienced by station i on transmitting the mth priority flow packets. Correspondingly, let $D\_Max[m]$ be the maximum MAC delay that can be tolerated for mth priority flows. Then, a new flow of priority m is dropped if $D_i^m > D\_Max[m]$. Otherwise, if $D_i^m > Th_{pr} \cdot D\_Max[m]$, the flow is assigned a lower priority, where Th_{pr} is a threshold range from 0.6 to 0.8. Thus, under light traffic load, no priority reallocation is necessary since the mean MAC delay is quite low. However, under high network traffic, existing flows can be well protected with less contention from new flows. In addition, authors also proposed to enforce admission control to further guarantee the performance of admitted flows. Furthermore, a dynamic flow dropping scheme is devised to address the issue of *false admission* (i.e., multiple flows are admitted simultaneously even though the network cannot commit the service to all of them). With dynamic flow dropping, some flows will be appropriately dropped when the MAC delay is larger than a certain threshold after the admission.

CW and TXOP Adjustment Based Approaches

Similar to Banchs et al. (2002), Banchs et al. (2003) proposed a scheme to adjust CW and enforce admission control in IEEE 802.11e WLANs. In their scheme, a wireless LAN bandwidth broker (WBB) is defined at the access point. Whenever a new station $n+1$ with throughput requirements R_{n+1} arrives, the WBB first re-computes the optimal contention windows of stations from 1 to $n+1$. Then, the expected throughput of the all stations is calculated. Then, station $(n+1)$ is accepted only if for all stations, $r_i \geq R_i$, where r_i is the throughput of station i.

Pong et al. (2003) proposed a call admission control strategy for QoS of flows in IEEE 802.11e single-hop networks. In this approach, the authors adopt the analytical model proposed by Bianchi (2000) to calculate the achievable bandwidth. The probabilities in the equation can be obtained by measuring the collision rate. Then, the admission control is enforced at the Access Point (AP). Every time a new flow request arrives, the collision rate is initialized to the average collision rate of a flow with similar achievable throughput as the desired bandwidth of the new flow. Then, the AP iteratively reduces CW or increase TXOP and re-estimate achievable throughput. If the requested bandwidth is smaller than the achievable throughput after adjustment, the flow is accepted with the new CW and/or TXOP distributed to all other stations. Otherwise, the flow is rejected. The desirable feature of this approach is that it adaptively tunes the parameters to achieve the maximum admission ratio.

Data and Admission Control Approaches

Xiao et al. (2004a, 2004b, 2004c) proposed both centralized and distributed algorithms for data control and admission control in IEEE 802.11e EDCF. In centralized algorithms, the Access

Point (AP) collects all the information such as successful and failing data transmissions from each station and makes a global decision, while in distributed algorithms, each station estimates its own information locally by monitoring the channel. Basically, the ideas for the centralized and distributed algorithms are quite similar. In this section, we focus on the centralized version (Xiao et al., 2004c). Readers are encouraged to study the original papers for more details on the distributed version. Two major components are proposed:

- **Data Control:** The parameters such as CW_{min}, CW_{max} and *AIFS* of best-effort data flows are adjusted dynamically to protect the performance of existing voice and video traffic. Basically, these parameters should be increased if there are too many data transmissions, and vice versa.

- **Admission Control:** The *TXOP* budget and transmission time of all access categories are recorded as the basis of admitting/rejecting a new flow and assigning maximum transmission time for existing voice/video flows at next beacon interval.

For global data control, the key idea is how to identify the "event" of more or less data traffic. The idea in (Xiao et al., 2004c) is to use two variables: successful transmission time (STT) per AC and failed transmission time (FTT). These two variables are measured and estimated periodically during every beacon interval t. Then, the AP checks if *FTT* increases significantly. If that is the case, it will try to increase $CW_{min}[0]$, $CW_{max}[0]$, and *AIFS*[0] if $FTT(t) / (FTT(t) + sum(STT[i](t), i \in [1,3]))$ is greater than a small pre-defined threshold. The reason for this is that higher *FTT* usually indicates heavier data traffic and it is necessary to limit the channel access frequency of data flows by increasing these parameters. On the other hand, if *FTT* decreases significantly and at the same time *STT* increases significantly for at least one AC, then $CW_{min}[0]$, $CW_{max}[0]$, and *AIFS*[0] are decreased to improve the performance of data traffic.

For admission control, the idea is to maintain a transmission budget for voice/video traffic. If the budget for an AC is depleted, new stations will be rejected, while existing stations cannot increase their transmission time per beacon interval. Thus, the admission control protects admitted voice/video streams. To enforce the admission control, five variables are maintained: *TxUsed*[i] (the amount of time occupied by transmission of AC i stations), *TxCounter*[i] (time of successful transmissions of AC i stations), *TxLimit*[i] (maximum transmission time of AC i stations), *TxRemainder*[i] (transmission time of AC i stations that can be carrier over to the next beacon interval), and *TxMemory*[i] (the amount of resource that AC i of a station utilizes at a beacon interval). These variables are updated at each beacon interval. The *TXOPBudget* of a an AC i station is calculated as:

$$TXOPBudget[i] = \max(ATL[i] - TxTime[i] \times SurplusFactor[i], 0)$$

Where *ATL*[i] is the maximum amount of time that may be used for transmissions of AC i per beacon interval. If *TXOPBudget*[i] becomes zero, *TxMemory*[i] and *TxRemainder*[i] will be set to zero and new stations cannot start transmission with AC i. Otherwise, *TxMemory*[i] will be set to an initial value between 0 and *TXOPBudget*[i]/ *SurplusFactor*[i]. This time will be used for stations of AC i in the next beacon interval. In this case, new stations can possibly transmit flows of AC i. With both data control and admission control, two objectives can be achieved: (i) existing voice/video flows are not affected by the transmission of new flows of the same AC; (ii) existing voice/video flows are not affected by heavy data transmissions. Thus, sufficient protection for real-time traffic is provided in the proposed scheme.

In contrast to EDCA, no much research has been done on possible extensions of the HCCA scheme. One reason for this is that as a centrally controlled channel access scheme, HCCA can naturally enforce admission control. However, with HC being a central point, HCCA does not possess many advantages of the distributed EDCA mechanism and thus lacks its popularity in practice.

RESOURCE MANAGEMENT IN MULTI-CELL WIRELESS LANs AND HETEROGENEOUS WIRED/WIRELESS NETWORKS

IEEE 802.11 wireless LANs are being successfully used as the last-mile technology in the present-day pervasive computing environments. In many instances, wireless/mobile users need to access/exchange information stored in some servers located in wired networks. The architecture of wireless Internet is depicted in Figure 7 (revised from MIRAI architecture (Havinga & Wu, 2001)). Multiple basic service sets (BSSs) are inter-connected by a distribution system (DS) and form an extended service set (ESS). An ESS is connected to the Internet via a gateway router. In each BSS, all mobile hosts (MHs) are within

the broadcast region of their associated AP and can only access the infrastructure through the AP. All MHs can roam among different BSSs of the same or different ESSs.

In such a wired-cum-wireless network, mobile/wireless users usually access/exchange information stored somewhere on the Internet via their associated APs and the gateway routers. For multimedia applications such as audio/video streaming, end-to-end QoS guarantee is highly desirable in order to ensure user satisfaction. Basically, two requirements should be satisfied:

- Seamless roaming is supported when users move among different BSSs. With QoS handoff, ongoing multimedia traffics will not suffer from severe performance degradation due to insufficient network resource in the new cell.
- End-to-end QoS guarantee is provided through wired/wireless signaling and accurate wireless LAN admission control.

Basically, QoS handoff in multi-cell wireless LANs and end-to-end QoS signaling in wired/wireless networks are complimentary and can be combined to maximize wireless users' experience (Li, Zhu, Chlamtac, & Prabhakaran, 2006).

QoS Handoff in Multi-cell Wireless LANs

IEEE 802.11 standard (1997) specifies a procedure called *hand-off* where mobile hosts (MHs) may move between BSSs and transfer its associated AP from one cell (home cell) to another cell (target cell). In IEEE 802.11b, 11 different channels are available for use and channel 1, 6, and 11 are non-overlapping. Usually, handoff occurs when a MH moves across the boundary of two or more wireless APs and detects weak signal reception with its current associated AP or it experiences significant QoS deterioration. To facilitate the handoff, each AP broadcasts the beacon signal

Figure 7. Architecture of wireless Internet

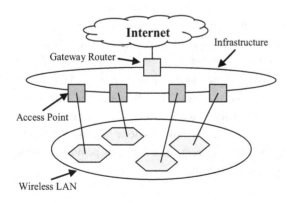

periodically and a MH scans the beacon signal and sees if there exists another AP with stronger beacon signal. Then, the MH sends authentication and reassociation request to the AP with strongest beacon signal. Upon receipt of the request, the new AP makes necessary security checking and sends the reassociation response if it accepts the handoff. The reassociation response includes information such as supported bit rates and station ID. Meanwhile, the new AP sends an Inter-access-point-protocol (IAPP) message to the old AP to inform the completion of the handoff. Figure 8 illustrates the handoff procedure in 802.11 WLANs. From a mobile user's perspective, it is desirable to have very low handoff latency. Basically, handoff latency is composed by *probe delay, authentication delay*, and *re-association delay*. Experiment results in Lo and Lin (1998) have shown that among these delays, probing delay consists of the biggest part (over 90%) of the overall handoff latency. Thus, existing research works mainly focus on techniques to reduce the probing delay.

Minimization of Handoff Delay

Shin, Forte, and Rawat (2004) proposed to two techniques to reduce the probing delay:

- *Selective scanning algorithm* that improves the scanning procedure. In this algorithm, a full channel scanning is made initially. When a station scans APs, a channel mask is built. Also, channel masks of channels 1, 6, and 11 are also set. After the stations associates with the best AP, the channel being used is removed from the channel mask since the likelihood of an adjacent AP on the same channel is very small. Then in the next handoff, if no APs are discovered with the current channel mask, the channel mask is inverted and a new scan is performed. If still no APs are discovered, a full scan on all channels is performed until some APs are found. Experiments show that selective scanning reduces the handoff latency by 30-60%, compared to the original handoff scheme in 802.11 DCF standards.

Figure 8. Illustration of the handoff procedure in IEEE 802.11 wireless LANs

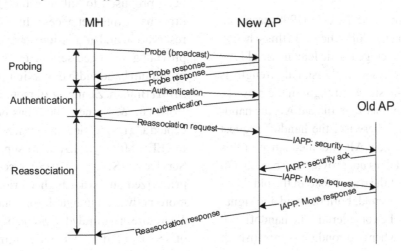

- *Caching technique* that minimizes the number of times the previous scanning procedure is needed. In this technique, an AP cache consisting of a table (with MAC address as the key) is created. With the selective scanning algorithm, multiple APs may be found and the best two APs with strongest signal strength are entered in the cache with the old AP as the key. Then, at the time of handoff, a station first checks the cache to see if there is a hit. If successful, the station sends a message to associate with the new AP. Otherwise, a selective scanning is performed. If the station fails to connect with the first entry, the second entry is tried. If both attempts fail, the selective scanning is performed to update the cache. Experiments show that caching can reduce the probing delay to very small values (5-20 ms).

Bandwidth Aware Handoff

However, the AP with strongest signal strength is not necessarily the best one for handoff. If everyone tries to move to the new cell with high bit rate, the AP is usually handling heavy network traffic. In this case, it is highly possible that a MH may move from a less crowded cell to a more crowded cell and its QoS requirements are no longer satisfied, leading to serious performance degradation.

To address this issue, Lo et al. (1998) proposed traffic load aware handoff scheme. In this scheme, if the weighted average traffic load in the old AP does exceed a threshold, the signal strength is considered. If the signal strength in the new AP is significantly higher than the old AP, the handoff is initiated. Otherwise, the handoff request to the candidate new AP is denied since in this case the handoff does not provide any benefit. On the other hand, if the traffic load in the old AP is higher than a threshold, both the load and signal strength need to be considered. The handoff will be initiated only when two conditions are satisfied:

(i) the signal strength of the new AP is higher than a threshold; (ii) traffic load in the new AP is not significantly higher than the old one. Thus, by enforcing more strict criteria, the problem of overloading due to handoff can be alleviated. However, since handoff is still allowed when traffic load is heavy, performance degradation after handoff still occurs.

To prevent QoS degradation when a node moves to a new cell, (Li et al., 2006) proposed to enforce admission control during the handoff. First, a fixed amount of channel available bandwidth (15-20%) is reserved for handoff to minimize handoff blocking probability. The actual proportion depends on the frequency of node mobility and traffic load. Second, admission control is enforced every time a node moves into a new cell with ongoing traffic. The available bandwidth estimation is similar to (Kazantzidis et al., 2001; Shah et al., 2004). If there is enough bandwidth to support the flow, the handoff is initiated. Otherwise, another candidate AP is selected for handoff attempt.

QoS Guarantee in Heterogeneous Wired/Wireless Networks

Integrated service (IntServ) (Braden, Clark, & Shenker, 1994) and differentiated service (DiffServ) (Blake, Black, & Carlson, 1998) have been proposed to enhance the QoS support in broadband Internet access. In IntServ, resource reservation and admission control is enforced to provide guaranteed service to users demanding minimum bandwidth or maximum delay. RSVP/ SBM (Braden, Zhang, & Berson, 1997; Yavatkar, Hoffman, & Bernet, 2000) has been widely accepted as a reservation scheme for flow reservation in IEEE 802 style LANs to support Integrated Service (IntServ). In DiffServ, service levels are prioritized such that higher priority users gain more network bandwidth for data transmission. Therefore, a natural idea would be the integration of RSVP or DiffServ in wired infrastructure and a QoS schemes in wireless LAN to provide end-to-end QoS support in a cost-effective manner.

Park, Kim, and Kim (2003) proposed a QoS architecture between DiffServ and IEEE 802.11e (IEEE, 2003a). The idea is that priorities in IEEE 802.1D/Q can be mapped to IEEE 802.11e to provide end-to-end service differentiation. In order to support QoS and mobility for wireless Internet, García-Macías, Rousseau, Berger-Sabbatel, Toumi, and Duda (2003) presented a hierarchical QoS architecture to extend DiffServ to WLANs with flexible mobility management.

Moon and Aghvami (2004) proposed a QoS mechanism in all-IP wireless access networks. In their scheme, re-routing of RSVP branch path toward the crossover router at every handoff event is made for reduction of resource reservation delays and signaling overheads. Also, advance reservation is made via a new BS for on-going flows to maintain QoS guarantee. Shankar and Choi (2002) proposed a MAC-level QoS signaling for IEEE 802.11e WLAN and address its interaction with RSVP and SBM. However, no effort is made to handle the specific issue of admission control in wireless LANs. Also, mobility issue is not addressed.

Based on a proposed MAC layer flow reservation and admission control protocol in IEEE 802.11 WLAN, called WRESV, (Li et al., 2006) suggested to integrate RSVP and WRESV for the support of IntServ in heterogeneous wired-cum-wireless networks. In their approach, to establish end-to-end flow reservation, signaling messages need to be sent between wireless users and wired servers through wireless AP, gateway router, and intermediate IP routers. As QoS signaling schemes for the Internet and wireless LAN, RSVP and WRESV are integrated to realize end-to-end flow reservation. Since WRESV follows the same procedure of request/response as RSVP does, mapping of signaling messages can be made between the reservation messages of Path/Resv of RSVP, and REQUEST/RESPONSE of WRESV, respectively. Features of RSVP

and the characteristics of wireless medium are carefully considered (e.g., multicast receivers in a wireless LAN can be handled by broadcasting at the AP). Message mappings at the AP are implemented by cross-layer interaction and user priorities are mapped to 802.11 MAC priorities with 802.1p. Since WRESV can work with most of the existing MAC schedulers such as DCF, EDCF, and DFS, this integration scheme is more general and leaves space for further enhancement. Advantages of this approach include: (i) Reservation based schemes can provide ensured QoS guarantee stronger than service differentiation, especially when network traffic is high. (ii) Per-flow signaling for end-to-end reservation becomes quite easy through integration of a RSVP-like flow reservation protocol in wireless LAN and RSVP. (iii) The message mapping and resource management are only needed at the access point. (iv) The overhead of the integration can be minimized by cross-layer interaction between MAC and upper layers. Furthermore, this integration scheme also considers support of both node mobility and QoS in the situation of handoff.

QoS and Mobility Management in Hybrid Wireless Networks

In addition to roaming and horizontal handoff among 802.11 WLANs, supporting QoS anytime, anywhere, and by any media requires seamless vertical handoffs between different wireless networks such as WLAN, MANET, Bluetooth, UMTS, and WCDMA. Many new architectures/schemes have been proposed recently for seamless integration of WLAN and various wireless network interfaces, which are discussed as follows:

• **Integration of WLAN and MANET:** Lamont, Wang, and Villasenor (2003) investigated the issue of maintaining session connectivity while mobiles continuously roam across multiple WLANs and MANETs. In the proposed network architecture, routing within MANETs is handled by the optimized link state routing (OLSR) protocol and handoff between WLANs and MANETs are supported through automatic mode-detection and node-switching capabilities of the mobiles. To achieve efficient mobility management, functionalities of OLSR are extended to support Mobile IPv6.

- **Integration of WLAN and Bluetooth:** Conti, Dardari, and Pasolini (2003) proposed an integrated analytical model for evaluation of the interference between IEEE 802.11 and Bluetooth. The model takes both physical layer and MAC layer into account and can be easily implemented. The performance is evaluated by packet error probability in term of the relative distances between the two systems for different conditions.

- **Integration of WLAN and 3G Wireless Networks:** An architecture for integrating UMTS and IEEE 802.11 WLANs was proposed by Jaseemuddin (2003). Since 802.11 is used primarily for high-speed best-effort service, a mobile node can maintain two connections in parallel (i.e., data connection through WLAN), and voice connection through UMTS. Park, Yoon, and Kim (2002) investigated vertical handoff between IEEE 802.11 WLANs and CDMA cellular networks. In their handoff strategy, traffic characteristics are considered in order to guarantee low handoff latency. Specifically, real-time traffic takes into account the handoff delay and best-effort traffic takes into account of throughput only. Finally, Buddhikot, Chandranmenon, and Han (2003) suggested to combine the features of wide-coverage but low-rate 3G networks, and high-rate but small-coverage WLAN, to improve the QoS and flexibility of wireless data services. A loose integration approach is realized with an IOTA gateway and a new client software in order to support seamless mobility, QoS guarantees and multi-provider roaming agreements.

With the decreasing size of cells in next generation multimedia enabled wireless networks, the number of handoffs during a call's life time increases. Thus, for integration of WLAN and 3/4-G wireless networks, an essential element of seamless end-to-end QoS guarantee is the ensuring of low call dropping probability in the 3/4-G networks. Lou, Li, and Thng (2002) proposed an adaptive bandwidth allocation scheme, termed measurement-based pre-assignment technique, to prevent handoff failure in wireless cellular networks. With periodical measurement of traffic status within a local cell, the number of channels reserved for a handoff can be adjusted, thus eliminating the signaling overhead of status information exchange between involved cells.

RESOURCE MANAGEMENT IN MANETS

In IEEE 802.11 MAC, nodes cannot transmission and receive data simultaneously. Therefore, both the reception and transmission will take the bandwidth resource of nodes. For example, in Figure 9, let node A send packets to node D, through nodes B and C. At the time when A sends to B, B may also tries to forward packet to C, and C forwards packets to D. In this case, A will sense busy channel if B's broadcast arrives A first (i.e., B's transmission consumes available bandwidth at A). Meanwhile, since A is within the carrier sense range (CS range, RCS) of C, C actually also contends with A when the flow is introduced. Thus, when a new flow is admitted, A must have available bandwidth that equals to roughly 3 times the requested flow rate due to the consumption of its available bandwidth by node B and C. Similarly, B, C, and D need 3, 3, 2 times the requested flow rate available, respectively. Furthermore, suppose node E is located within the carrier sense range of A, B, C, and D. Then, when data transmission over any of the three links occurs, E senses busy channel and has to wait. If there are ongoing

Figure 9. Illustration of channel interference

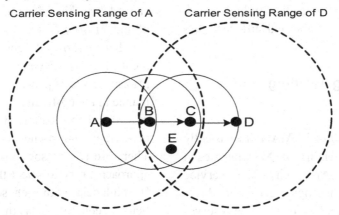

traffics going through E, those traffic may be significantly affected by the new flow due to the limited available bandwidth at E.

In single rate networks, all outgoing links of a node have basically the same physical link rate. However, when multi-rate capability is enabled, a node may have links with different possible rates. If we assume Two-ray propagation model (IEEE, 1997), then the link rate is solely dependent on node distance. For IEEE 802.11b, the possible link rates at a node A can be 2, 5.5, and 11 Mbps, depending on the perceived signal strength. Thus, different links starting from the same node may have quite different available bandwidth. To make appropriate admission decision, each node has to maintain per *link* available bandwidth information for all outgoing links. Usually, admission control schemes tend to choose high rate links for packet transmission. However, selecting high rate link usually yields longer path due to the relatively shorter transmission distance at high link rate. With more number of hops, transmission at one node may be affected by a higher number of transmissions within its CS range and the previously mentioned interference becomes more significant. Therefore, as far as the admission control decision is concerned, there is a tradeoff between choosing high rate links and short distance paths.

Node mobility also has high impact on network performance. In a MANET, the network topology is dynamically changing, leading to frequent link breaking. If a flow is being transmitted on a broken link, then route re-discovery has to be performed to smoothly forward packets along new paths. However, it is possible that the new path may not be able to support the QoS requirement of the flow. If multi-rate is enabled, node mobility affects signal strength and thus the channel transmission rate. Thus, link condition varies and a previously supported flow may not receive good QoS as it is promised. In both cases, a new path may have to be chosen for that flow.

In summary, QoS guarantee in IEEE 802.11 based MANET is a challenging issue due to its natural characteristic of shared medium access and node mobility. Successful resource management schemes demand three components:

- **Accurate available bandwidth estimation:** Given the network topology, channel status, traffic characteristics, and mobility, how to accurately estimate the available bandwidth for a specific flow along a certain path.
- **Route selection:** With the available bandwidth and other information, how to choose the best path to support a multimedia flow.

- **Mobility handling:** When nodes are moving frequently with medium or high speed, how to provide reliable and sufficient QoS support.

QoS Scheduling, Routing, and Frameworks

Early research on QoS in MANETs basically focused on either extending of QoS strategies in single-hop wireless LANs such as MAC service differentiation, or investigating network layer strategies such as routing for resource reservation and path selection. These schemes usually assume low node mobility and no consideration is given for link interference. Thus, the performance improvements for multimedia applications are quite limited.

Priority Scheduling in Multi-Hop Ad Hoc Networks

Kanodia, Li, and Sabharwal (2002) proposed a distributed priority scheduling for end-to-end quality of service guarantee in multi-hop ad hoc networks. Due to the distributed nature of wireless networks, it is difficult to coordinate channel access in an ideal fashion. In their work, a deadline based priority backoff policy is devised and the priority information is piggybacked with RTS, CTS, and ACK to minimize the extra overhead. With the priority information obtained from neighbors, each node can rank the priority of all the nodes and decide the backoff counter as follows:

$$f_l(S_j) = \begin{cases} \text{Uniform}[0, 2^l CW_{\min} - 1], & r_j = 1, l < m \\ \alpha CW_{\min} + \text{Uniform}[0, \gamma CW_{\min} - 1], & r_j > 1, l = 0 \\ \text{Uniform}[0, 2^l \gamma CW_{\min} - 1], & r_j > 1, l \geq 1 \end{cases}$$

where r_j is the rank of node j's packet in its own scheduling table S_j. α and γ are some constant and set as 1 and 2, respectively. With priority scheduling, even though a node may not be able to

overhear all packets, significant contention reduce can still be achieved to improve the performance of high priority flows.

Then, to satisfy the end-to-end delay requirement of flows, downstream stations adjust the priority levels of packets based on their performance in the upstream by a technique known as multi-hop coordination. However, the reduction of average end-to-end delay is not significant. There are two reasons for this: (i) There is no approach to try to select the lowest delay path. If a high delay path is chosen, then it is very difficult to reduce the delay through priority change. (ii) Since every node enforces priority change to improve their end to end delay, the overall effect is not very desirable among all flows.

Thus, routing should play an important role in supporting QoS in multi-hop ad hoc networks. The basic idea of QoS routing is to find a path that has sufficient bandwidth for a new flow such that its throughput and delay requirements can be satisfied. From this aspects, it is important to integrate certain QoS measures with existing routing protocols such as destination sequenced distance vector (DSDV) (Perkins & Bhagwat, 1994), dynamic source routing (DSR) (Johnson, Maltz, & Broch, 2001), ad hoc on demand distance vector (AODV) (Perkins, Belding-Royer, & Chakeres, 2003), and optimized link state routing protocol (OLSR) (Clausen & Jacquet, 2003).

QoS Routing in MANETs

Perkins and Belding-Royer (2003) proposed a QoS version of the earlier proposed on-demand routing protocol AODV. The idea of AODV-QoS is to facilitate routing based on QoS metrics, not only the number of hops. AODV-QoS adds the following fields to each routing table entries corresponding to each destination: (i) *Maximum delay*; (ii) *Minimum available bandwidth*; (iii) *List of sources requesting delay guarantees*; (iv) *List of sources requesting bandwidth guarantees*. The maximum delay extension can be appended to a route request (RREQ) by a node requesting a QoS route in order to place a maximum bound on the acceptable time delay experienced on any acceptable path from the source to the destination. Before forwarding the RREQ, an intermediate node MUST compare NODE_TRSVERSAL_TIME to the remaining Delay indicated in the maximum delay extension. If the remaining Delay is smaller than NODE_TRSVERSAL_TIME (i.e., the deadline has passed), the RREQ is simply discarded. Otherwise, the node subtracts NODE_TRSVERSAL_TIME from the Delay value in the extension and continues processing the RREQ as specified in AODV. Then, when a node forwards a route reply (RREP), it adds its own NODE_TRSVERSAL_TIME to the delay field, which is initialized to zero at the destination. Also, this information is recorded in the local route table entry for that destination. With this information, an intermediate node may be able to reply a RREQ by comparing the maximum delay field in the route table entry and the requested maximum delay in the RREQ. Similarly, the minimum bandwidth extension can also be appended to a RREQ in order to specify the minimum amount of bandwidth that must be made available along an acceptable path from the source to the destination. Before forwarding the RREQ, an intermediate node must compare its available link capacity to the Bandwidth field in the extension. If the available bandwidth is less the requested one, the RREQ is simply discarded. Each intermediate node forwarding RREP compares the bandwidth field in the RREP and its own link capacity and maintains the minimum of the two in the bandwidth field, which is initialized to infinity at the destination. Also, this information is recorded to the local route table entry for the destination. With this information, an intermediate node may be able to reply a RREQ by comparing the minimum bandwidth field in the route table entry and the requested Minimum Bandwidth in the RREQ. AODV-QoS provides a good framework for QoS support in mobile ad hoc networks for multimedia applications that

demands certain bandwidth and delay constraints. However, there are three issues to be addressed in order to enforce QoS with AODV-QoS: (i) An accurate and efficient bandwidth estimation technique is required in order for an intermediate node to be able to update the minimum bandwidth field in RREP and the local route table; (ii) How to provision the maximum delay requirement among multiple hops to make sure that the probability that a RREQ is incorrectly dropped (i.e., the total delay is smaller than the maximum delay but RREQ is dropped at an intermediate node, is minimized).

Chen and Nahrstedt (1999) proposed Ticketbased Probing (TBP) one of the first QoS routing protocols in mobile ad hoc networks. Authors assumed that the network topology does not change frequently such that soft QoS can be supported. In this work, a simple imprecision model is first proposed to estimate $\Delta D_i(t)$, the maximum change of $D_i(t)$, the delay from node i to node t before the next update, and $\Delta B_i(t)$, the maximum change of $B_i(t)$, the bandwidth from node i to node t before the next update. Then a smoothing technique is used to calculate the new $\Delta D_i(t)$ and $\Delta B_i(t)$ at each update as:

$$\Delta D_i^{new}(t) = \alpha \times \Delta D_i^{old}(t) + (1-\alpha) \times \beta \times \left| D_i^{new}(t) - D_i^{old}(t) \right|$$

and:

$$\Delta B_i^{new}(t) = \alpha \times \Delta B_i^{old}(t) + (1-\alpha) \times \beta \times \left| B_i^{new}(t) - B_i^{old}(t) \right|$$

where α and β are some constants to make sure that it is highly probable that the actual delay and bandwidth fall into the ranges $[D_i(t)-\Delta D_i(t), D_i(t)+\Delta D_i(t)]$ and $[B_i(t)-\Delta B_i(t), B_i(t)+\Delta B_i(t)]$, respectively. With these delay and bandwidth measurement, the cost of paths can be obtained.

The ticket-based probing routing protocol works as follows. For a source s and destination t, two types of tickers are issued from s every time a packet sending requests arrives:

- *Yellow tickets* that maximize the probability of finding a feasible path. Thus, yellow tickets prefer paths with smaller delays to satisfy the delay requirement.
- *Green tickets* that maximize the probability of finding a low-cost path. Thus, green tickets prefer paths with smaller costs but may have larger delay.

The strategy is to use the green tickets to find low-cost feasible path with relatively low success probability and to use yellow tickets as a backup to guarantee a high success probability of finding a feasible path. Then the total number of tickets issued at s, $N_0 = Y_0 + G_0$, where Y_0 and G_0 are the number of yellow tickets and green tickets, respectively. Basically, Y_0 depends on the delay requirement D. If D is larger than $D_s(t) + \Delta D_s(t)$, then only one yellow ticket will be sufficient to find a path to satisfy the D requirement. Otherwise, more yellow tickets are preferred to maximize the probability. However, if D is even smaller than the best expected end-to-end delay $D_s(t) - \Delta D_s(t)$, no ticket is issued and the connection request is simply rejected. G_0 also depends on the delay requirement D. Larger D usually gives a smaller G_0. However, to obtain low cost paths, $G_0 = 1$ if $D \geq \theta \times (D_s(t) + \Delta D_s(t))$ and then increase with smaller D. Similarly $G_0 = 1$ if $D \geq \theta \times (D_s(t) + \Delta D_s(t))$. A probe p from the source accumulates its delay, $delay(p)$ as it propagates along a path. When an intermediate node i receives p with a number of tickets from a node k, it determines the neighbors to forward the probes as follows. The set of candidate neighbors, $R_i^p(t)$, is defined as $\{j \mid delay(p) + delay(i,j) + D_j(t) - \Delta D_j(t) \leq D, j \in V_i - \{k\}\}$, where $delay(i,j)$ is the delay from node i to its neighbor j. and V_i is the set of neighbors of node i. Since stationary nodes provide more stable paths than mobile nodes, they are given priority for distributing probes. Among the stationary nodes, more yellow probes are sent along the paths with a smaller delay and more green tickets are sent along the paths with smaller cost.

TBP achieves desirable performance due to two advantages: (i) the proposed delay constrained routing and bandwidth constrained routing only choose qualified paths that satisfy the delay/bandwidth requirements of the applications, thus significantly improving the throughput of accepted flows; (ii) the adaptive ticket determination avoids query flooding and intelligently forwards probes along paths with high probability of satisfying the delay/bandwidth requirements.

QoS Frameworks in MANETs

Lee, Ahn, Zhang, and Campbell (2000) proposed INSIGNIA, a QoS framework for supporting adaptive services in mobile ad hoc networks. In INSIGNIA, routing, QoS signaling, and resource reservation are separated. The three interesting features in INSIGNIA are:

- **In-band signaling:** To facilitate fast reservation, in-band signaling where the control messages are carried along the data packet is adopted. In contrast, with out-band signaling, control messages are sent as separate control packets and may be sent along different data paths. The advantage of in-band routing is that it is capable of operating close to packet transmission speed and can significantly reduce the resource reservation overhead.
- **Adaptive service support:** To support adaptive service, several fields are defined in the IP header: (i) the *reservation (RES) mode* bit indicate the connection request should go through admission control procedure. If it is not set, it is considered best-effort (BE) traffic. (ii) the *payload type* identifies whether the packet is a base QoS (BQ) or enhanced QoS (EQ) packet. While BQ requires only minimum bandwidth requirements to be met along the path between a source-destination pair, EQ requires maximum bandwidth requirements to be met. Thus, the payload

type affects the admission control decision. (iii) the *bandwidth indicator* bit can be set to identify whether a max-reserved or a min-reserved should be enforced. (iv) The *bandwidth request* provides the information on how much maximum/minimum bandwidth is requested from the source. With these information included in the IP header of data packets, it is very convenient for intermediate nodes to make adaptive decision on providing sufficient QoS support for the flows.

The resource reservation protocol works as follows. Source nodes first initiate reservations by setting appropriate field of the IP option in data messages before forwarding "reservation request" toward destination nodes. Usually, such reservation request packet set service mode, payload, and bandwidth indicator to RES, BQ/EQ, and MAX/MIN, respectively. Upon the arrival of a reservation request at an intermediate node, the node will enforce admission control modules, allocate resources, and establish local state. This procedure continues until the destination receives the reservation request packet and sends back a QoS reporting message. At this time, the reservation is done. Sometimes, there are some situations that a flow is min-reserved but the payload type is EQ. To fix this conflict, all reserved packets with EQ type received at a destination will have their service level switched from RES to BE by the bottleneck node. As a result of this, all resource reserved earlier for the flow will be released. INSIGNIA also provide mechanisms to handle reservation restoration and soft state management when mobility is present.

There are three issues to be resolved in IN-SIGNIA: (i) managing the soft states at each intermediate node incurs significant overhead. When mobility is frequent, removing the state information requires additional signaling. (ii) how to accurately estimate bandwidth availability to avoid over-commitment or under-commitment is not mentioned. Without effective bandwidth

estimation, it is difficult to guarantee the performance of accepted real-time flows. (iii) When both real-time and best-effort traffic coexist, how to provision the network resource such that the performance of admitted real-time flows will not be affected significantly by heavy best-effort traffic. This usually either requires priority based access control protocols at the MAC layer, or flow control protocols at the transport layer.

Ahn, Campbell, and Veres (2002) proposed SWAN, a service differentiation framework in stateless wireless ad hoc networks. Unlike INSIGNIA, SWAN does not maintain per-flow state information at intermediate node and does not assume any prioritized MAC access protocol to do service differentiation for real-time and best-effort flows. In SWAN, three major control algorithms are implemented:

- **Rate control for best effort traffic:** Additive increase and multiplicative decrease (AIMD) rate control algorithm based on measured MAC layer delay is used to regulate the sending rate of best-effort flows. Every T seconds, each mobile device increases its transmission rate (by c Kbps) gradually until the packet delays exceed a certain threshold. When the excessive delay is detected, the rate controller reduces the sending rate by $r\%$. With this rate control, the effect of best-effort flows to real-time flows is minimized.
- **Source-based admission control for real-time traffic:** An admission controller sends a probing request packet toward the destination node to estimate the end-to-end bandwidth availability. When the source receives the probing response message, it compares the measured available bandwidth and the bandwidth requirement of the new real-time session and makes the admission/rejection decision.
- **Dynamic regulation of real-time traffic:** When mobility is present, resource availability may change due to dynamic packet rerouting. In this case, each node periodically

measures the local available bandwidth. If violation is detected (i.e., the bandwidth availability is smaller than the flow rate of the real-time traffic), the source will try to reestablish the real-time session based on its original bandwidth needs. If the session cannot be satisfied, it will be dropped.

SWAN is very practical and scalable due to its elimination of soft state of flows at intermediate nodes. Also, the regulation of best-effort traffic makes sure that good resource provisioning can be achieved for the support of real-time traffic. However, the bandwidth estimation of SWAN is not very reliable: (i) using probing packet does not provide very stable performance prediction of the real-time traffic; (ii) the multi-hop interference is not well captured, making over-commitment occur frequently.

Bandwidth Estimation-Based QoS Routing

Despite of the effort of QoS frameworks and routing protocols, how to estimate the available bandwidth is the key for the success of resource management schemes. Without good knowledge about the resource availability, it is difficult to make decision on appropriate resource allocation and admission control. However, due to various factors such as network topology, multi-hop interference, rate adaptation, and traffic characteristics, it is impossible to have an accurate performance model for mobile ad hoc networks. The majority of the research in the literature focus on measurement based approach that provide efficient and reasonable prediction on how much bandwidth is available for a new flow on a specific path.

Interference Aware Bandwidth Estimation

Xue and Ganz (2003) proposed ad hoc QoS on-demand routing (AQOR), a QoS routing protocol

with admission control enforced to support quality of service in multi-hop ad hoc networks. In their work, admission control is made based on the knowledge of the traffic at both a node itself and its neighboring nodes to account for the interference. In this approach, two different types of bandwidth are introduced:

- **Available Bandwidth at a node i** is the available bandwidth experienced locally at node i and calculated as $B_{avail,i} = B - \text{sum}(B_{self,j})$ for all neighbor j of i where B is the maximum transmission bandwidth and $B_{self,j}$ is the bandwidth consumed by traffic transmitted or received at node j.
- **Consumed Bandwidth of a flow f at a node i**, $B_{consumed,i}(f)$, is the total channel bandwidth consumed by flow f due to traffic aggregation (i.e, node i also consumes bandwidth of neighbors transmitting/forwarding packets of flow f). $B_{consumed,i}$ is calculated as $B_{uplink,i}(f) + B_{consumed,i}(f)$, which are R_f if i is the source or destination and $2R_f$ otherwise.

By comparing the available bandwidth and the consumed bandwidth, an intermediate node can decide whether or not to accept or reject a flow.

Although AQOR is more accurate than earlier approaches (Ahn et al., 2002; Chen et al., 1999) on the available bandwidth estimation by multi-hop flows, it only partially considers the multi-hop interference. To address this issue, Chen and Heinzelman (2005) improved the AODV-QoS framework with a more accurate estimation of available bandwidth. In this approach, minimum bandwidth is first calculated locally with the similar way in Chakeres et al. (2004) (i.e., the available bandwidth is the product of channel idle ratio and the channel capacity). Then, messages are broadcasted to notify neighbors to obtain a *minimum* available bandwidth, $B_{avail,min}$, among all neighbors within the communication range. Finally, they adopted the result proposed by Li, Blake, and De Couto (2001) to account for intra-flow interference as follows:

If (*HopCount* < 4)

$$B_{avail,min} = B_{avail,min}/HopCount$$

Else

$$B_{avail,min} = B_{avail,min}/4$$

This calculation provides an approximation of the upper bound of the available bandwidth for a flow along a certain path. However, it is not accurate enough, especially when multi-rate is enabled. With multi-rate MAC, the distance of a link may be much smaller due to transmission with high data rate, resulting in more intra-flow interference.

Intra-Flow Interference-Based Bandwidth Estimation

Since transmission at a node is potentially affected by transmissions of all nodes within its carrier sensing range, it is desirable that the list of those nodes on the same path that affect its transmission can be obtained at the time the available bandwidth is estimated. Li and Prabhakaran (2005b) proposed two metrics:

- **Intra-flow interference set of a flow *f* at a node *i* on path *p*** is a list of nodes (including *i* itself and excluding the destination) on *p* that reside within the carrier sensing range of *i*.
- **Route available bandwidth of a flow *f* over path *p*** is an index that indicates how much throughput a flow *f* can potentially receive if it is transmitted along a specific path *p* and is calculated based on important factors such as *intra-flow interference*, *effective link capacity*, and *channel busy time* in the MAC layer.

Intra-Flow Interference Set

Intra-flow interference set of a flow *f* at a node *N*, $IS_{N,f}$ can be obtained as follows. Let $P=\{K_1, K_2, ..., K_{L-1}\}$ with L be the number of hops of *f*.

Here K_1, K_2, through K_{L-1} are listed in the order of hops from source to destination. Note that the destination node is excluded since it does not send data packet. Let P' be the list of nodes within the carrier sensing range of node N and $P'=\{O_1, O_2, ..., O_{L'}\}$ with L' being the total number of those nodes. Then, the list of nodes on the path that affect node N is $P\cap P'$. Thus, the size of $IS_{i,f}$, $|IS_{N,f}| = |P\cap P'|$. Figure 10 illustrates intra-flow interference sets of nodes at different locations. CS range (R_{CS}) and transmission range (R_{TX}) of node A and C are represented by small and large circles, respectively. We can see that for the flow from node A to E along B, C, and D, the corresponding sizes of intra-flow interference set at node A and C are 3 and 4, respectively. While only node B and C are within R_{CS} of A, all nodes on the flow path are within R_{CS} of node C.

Obviously, the key component in intra-flow interference set is to identify all the nodes within the carrier sensing range. Although IDs of these neighbors are very easy to obtain, they consist of only a small portion of the interference set. In most network configurations, R_{CS} is more than 2 times R_{TX}, indicating that most nodes in IS are outside of the transmission range. Therefore, more nodes in the interference set must be discovered to achieve high accuracy on the estimation of the interference set. Three approaches have been proposed in the literature:

Figure 10. Illustration of intra-flow interference set

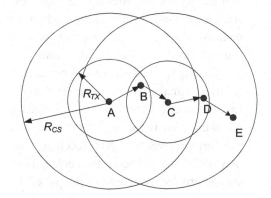

- *Two-hop approach*: Yang and Kravets (2005) proposed to collect all neighboring nodes within two hops from a node as the intra-flow interference set. This approach is easy to implement, but it is not very accurate. It is possible that many nodes within 3 or 4 hops away from a node may still reside within its carrier sensing, especially when node density is low and nodes are not uniformly distributed in the network. It is also possible to adopt three-hop approach to increase the accuracy. However, the overhead will increase significantly and it is possible that some nodes outside of the carrier sensing range may be incorrectly included in the intra-flow interference set.

- *High power approach*: Yang et al. and Kravets (2005) proposed to estimate the interference set at a node by temporarily increasing the power so that it can communicate with all nodes within the carrier sensing range and then obtain the corresponding IDs. This is a quite innovative idea. However, it is impractical for a node to increase the power to such a high level in order to facilitate the communication. If this power is available, then normal data transmission would have taken advantage of this high power to increase the channel bandwidth significantly.

- *Carrier sensing approach*: Sanzgiri, Chakeres, and Belding-Royer (2004) proposed to calculate intra-flow interference set by monitoring the channel and estimate the sizes of packets broadcasted by nodes on a path. According to their approach, when a transmission occurs at a node within carrier sensing range of the receiver node, the received signal strength is greater than the carrier-sensing threshold (CS_{thresh}) and the receiving node is able to detect the packet. Furthermore, even though the receiving node may not be able to decode the packet, it can still determine the length of the packet by

the sensing transmission duration. This is a more elegant way to estimate interference set without incurring too much overhead. To distinguish the packets from different nodes so that the number of nodes within carrier sensing range can be obtained, each node can simply broadcast a very short beacon with a *unique* length at basic transmission rate (2Mbps for IEEE 802.11b) periodically. If a node hears a packet from a neighbor or senses an error packet due to carrier sensing, it can obtain the corresponding ID of the source node and add it in its interference set.

Route Available Bandwidth

Let $b_{ava,e}$ be the experienced channel available bandwidth at station i along outgoing link e. Then, $b_{ava,e}$ can be approximated as:

$$b_{ava,e} = B_e \cdot (1 - BT_e)$$

where B_e and BT_e are the maximal achievable bandwidth and the estimated channel busy time at a link e, respectively. It should be noted that it is not easy to calculate the effective link capacity. First, for different packet sizes, B_e is different. Second, the accurate backoff time is very difficult to estimate. In Draves et al. (2004b), bandwidth is estimated using probing packets. We conduct simulations and fix B_e to be 1.2Mbps for physical link rate of 2Mbps. Then, we use the weight factors proposed in MTM (Awerbuch, Holmer, & Rubens, 2004) and then decide the corresponding B_e for different physical link rates (Table 2). It should be noted that MTM weight is proportional to channel time consumption and thus is inversely proportional to B_e weight.

Let f be a new flow that will be transmitted through link e. Then, the available bandwidth at node i along link e will be consumed by packet transmissions of flow f at all nodes belonging to intra-flow interference set of node i for flow f.

Table 2. B_e for different physical link rates

Link Rates (Mbps)	MTM Weight	B_e Weight	B_e (Mbps)
2	3	1	1.2
5.5	1.44	2.083	2.5
11	1	3	3.6

Since all links transmit with the same flow rate (we assume constant bit rate for flow f and $b_{ava,e}$ is *fairly* allocated to all contending links on path p), the *local* available bandwidth of flow f at link e, $b_{ava,e,f}$, can be expressed as:

$$b_{ava,e,f} = \frac{b_{ava,e}}{|IS|_{e,f}} = \frac{B_e \cdot (1 - BT_e)}{|IS|_{e,f}}$$

where $|IS|_{e,f}$ is the size of intra-flow interference set of flow f at link e. Then, let p be a path of flow f, we have that route available bandwidth:

$$RAB(f, p) = \min_{e \in p}(b_{ava,e,f})$$

With the estimated RAB of each path, admission control can be easily enforced at the source node by comparing the flow rate request and RAB. If RAB is sufficient, the flow is accepted. Otherwise, the flow is rejected.

Mobility Aware QoS Routing

Even though the intra-flow interference set based approach well captures the bandwidth consumption characteristics in multi-hop ad hoc networks, reliable QoS still may not be achieved when mobility is present. In most existing routing protocols such as DSDV, DSR, and AODV, whenever a link fails due to node moving out of the transmission range, an error message is sent back to the source node. Upon the receipt of the error message, the source node initiates another round of route discovery and sends packet along new path. During the transient time from link failure to the new path establishment, many packets are queued and even dropped at intermediate nodes, leading to significant throughput fluctuation and performance degradation.

Preemptive routing only chooses use the power threshold to alleviate route rediscovery and does not help much on the regular route discovery. However, when high mobility is present, most of links may not be very stable, leading to frequent packet rerouting and unreliable QoS due to the possibility of insufficient bandwidth on the new path. To address this issue, Goff, Abu-Ghazaleh, and Phatak (2001) proposed preemptive routing where a warning message is sent to the source node whenever a link has high probability of getting broken due to mobility. In PR, each node detects the probability of link failure by measuring the power of packets received from neighbors. If the received packet power is lower than certain power threshold corresponding to a distance very close to the transmission range, the link is considered highly instable. When a source node receives a warning message, it initiates route discovery immediately but eliminates all paths where at least one of the link has power below the threshold. Since the new route is discovered while an existing path is still alive, the delay due to link failure can be minimized, if not completely eliminated.

To overcome the effect of mobility on QoS in MANETs, Li et al. (2005b) also proposed the metric of route reliability (RR) that predicts how long an existing path may survive under a certain moving speed. First, let v_e be the *relative* moving speed between two nodes i, and j on a link e and L_e be the link distance, we can calculate reliability, LR_e, the estimated lifetime of link e as $(rang\text{-}L_e)/v_e$ where *rang* is the transmission range of the starting node of link e. Accordingly, let p be a path of flow f, then *route reliability RR*=$\min(LR_e)$ for all e on p. Then, similar to Goff et al. (2001), it is assumed that signal strength is solely dependent on distance and the minimum power (P_{range}) receivable by the device (i.e., the power received at the maximum transmission range), which in

Goff et al. (2001) is indicated in $3.652 \cdot 10^{-10}$ W. Similarly, the power threshold δ is defined as the ratio between the minimum allowed power level for the required RR and is calculated as:

$$\delta = \frac{P_{\min}}{P_{range}} = \left(\frac{range}{L_{e,\max}} \right)^4$$

Then, let us assume 250 meters maximum transmission range, then the power threshold for a path becomes:

$$\delta = \left(\frac{250}{250 - v_{\max} \cdot RR_{\min}} \right)^4$$

Table 3 gives the appropriate power threshold for different maximum moving speeds. It is possible that both nodes on a link move in opposite direction, so v_{max} is two times the maximum speed. RR_{min} is set to 1.5 seconds to eliminate highly unstable links. We could set this value higher but high RR_{min} might lead to the difficulty of finding an eligible path.

The work in Li and Prabhakaran (2005) integrates RAB and RR together with the dynamic source routing (DSR) for reliable QoS support in MANETs. In this approach, only paths with power higher than the corresponding threshold and RAB higher than the requested bandwidth requirement are considered for data transmission. Then, the path with highest RAB is chosen for actual data transmission. When mobility is present, preemptive routing (PR) is adopted to avoid the high cost of route reestablishment. Figure 11 shows the average delivery ratio of admitted flows for various schemes. It can be seen that with low mobility, usually 60-90% throughput can be achieved with admission control. However, "DSR" and "DSR+PR" only receive 40-60% throughput on average. With the increase of the moving speed, the benefit of using RAB alone for admission control decreases due to frequent route re-discovery and severe channel contention. With preemptive routing, better performance can be achieved due to sending of early warning messages. With "RAB+RR+PR," best performance is achieved in the case of high mobility (speed of 15 m/s and 20 m/s). Using route reliability usually results in less frequent route breaking and thus maintains higher per-flow throughput. Figure 11 compares the overall throughput of all schemes. With higher mobility, overall throughput decreases due to more frequent link failure and route re-discovery. We can see that admission control does not reduce the channel utilization, though the improvement on overall throughput is marginal when only RAB is enforced for admission. However, with "RAB+RR+PR," significant improvement (18% to 33%) on overall throughput is achieved, compared to the basic DSR protocol. This improvement should be attributed to less channel collision and link failure.

RESOURCE MANAGEMENT IN WMNS

Wireless mesh networks (WMNs) are perceived as the most promising commercial incarnation of the IEEE 802.11 standard in the multi-hop domain. As presented in Figure 12, a wireless

Table 3. Power threshold δ for different maximum moving speed (RR_{min}=1.5 second)

Moving speed (m/s)	5	10	15	20
v_{max} (m/s)	10	20	30	40
$v_{max} \cdot RR_{min}$ (m)	15	30	45	60
δ	1.281	1.667	2.212	2.997

Figure 11. Performance comparison of various QoS schemes

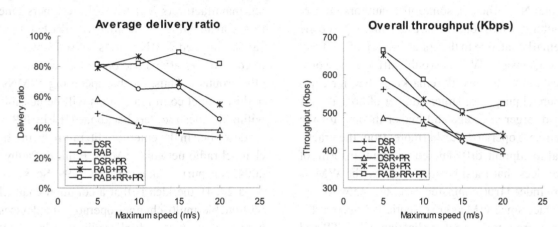

Figure 12. Left: Ad-hoc network. Right: Mesh network

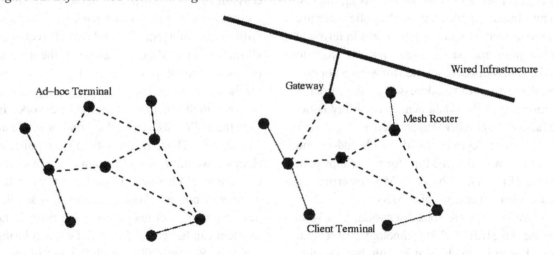

mesh network is an access network where the fixed infrastructure is reached through a gateway and the intermediate hops are sustained by fixed wireless routers. Of course, the same WMN can encompass several gateways. A WMN works in between layer 2 and layer 3, since it implements a local addressing strategy which is basically layer 2 routing, buy it is transparent to all other network trunks as it was any other AP-based IEEE 802.x LAN. In fact, the layer 2 addressing from external networks is not visible and, as in Ethernet LANs, all devices in the mesh appear directly connected to the gateway.

In brief, compared to ad-hoc networks, WMNs are IP-stack based, have a hierarchical structure, and mobility at the infrastructure level is not possible. Thus, it is clear that for WMNs, mobility and power consumption issues are less relevant, but network scalability is still a primary concern. Network scalability, in particular, was a premiere research field in ad-hoc networks, since the seminal work from Gupta and Kumar (2000). In the case of WMNs, some authors (Akyildiz, Wang, & Wang, 2005) argue that the operating hypotheses in WMNs are different, and this gives hope for tailored solutions where milder throughput decaying rates in the number of nodes are possible. Nevertheless, some other authors (Jun & Sichitiu, 2003) confirm the trend, making also the remark that, due to the concentration of traffic at the gateways, WMNs would suffer even worse scalability. It is worth remarking, that, for commercial purposes, larger number of hops means also larger coverage and higher income for the wireless operator. Furthermore, from the practical standpoint, different requirements in terms of services that must be supported by the WMNs are indeed true compared to ad-hoc networking. In fact, since WMNs are essentially IP networks, apart from traditional applications like FTP and Web Browsing are still present, current trends in Internet services show an increasing interest in multimedia application. Such applications are characterized by strict requirements in terms of delay, jitter and packet loss. Thus, in order to make WMNs a viable solution for wireless operator, the request to be addressed by the research community is the fundamental scalability issue. In fact, as the number of users increases, network performance degrades rapidly with end-to-end data rate lower than 1 Mbps for a five hops path over a IEEE 802.11-based WMN lowering the economic convenience of WMNs.

In sight of the previous discussion, in WMNs the use of the IEEE 802.11 technology over several hops has to be modulated by suitable resource allocation policies in order to obtain reasonable performance. In literature, there exist some proposals. Two of the most promising techniques are the use of a multi-channel mesh architecture and cross-layer coupling of the routing layer to the links state, respectively.

Multi-Channel WMNs

As concerns frequency allocation, the 12 available channels of IEEE 802.11 can be used in order to increase the network throughput. In particular, in the first generation WMNs, all devices, routers, gateways, and clients were adopting the same RF interface and leveraged the same channel. Later on, manufacturers and network designers, due to the availability of inexpensive IEEE 802.11 cards, equipped WMN routers with one interface to connect to stations and one interface towards other routers. Thus, in the upcoming WMNs, multi-channel communications will be possible within the mesh routers backbone (IEEE, 1998). As described in the emerging literature on multi-channel radio networks (Adya, Bahl, & Padhye 2004; Nasipuri, Zhuang, & Das 1999; So & Vaodya 2004), the idea is that a common channel will enable multi-channel operation of devices with a single and multiple radio interfaces. Of course, non-multi-channel enabled stations or access points can be integrated in the WMN using a common channel, so that backward compatibility is guaranteed. The problem of frequency allocation is a traditional issue, but, the domain is to some extent new, as proved by the interest for the general problem of the frequency allocation over multi-channel CSMA/CA networks. In fact, the IEEE 802.11 standard makes available 12 channels. Thus, the scarcity in the number of channels would represent a major problem for the allocations of channels. In particular, when the number of non-overlapping channels is smaller than the number of neighbors of a terminal, the problem can be recasted to a soft edge-coloring problem (Raman, 2006), with the aim of minimizing the number of collisions (i.e., the number of communicating nodes within 2-hops having the same assigned channel). In general, such a problem is NP-hard, but approximation algorithms exist that solve the problem with various degrees of optimality and in a distributed fashion. The rationale is that, the less conflicting channels, the less the collisions in the network. In general, the problem of efficient channel allocation in 802.11 WMNs remains hard even when only to the set of non-overlapping channels (3 out of 12) are considered (Shin, Lee, & Kim, 2006). Other authors (Ju & Rubin, 2006) consider only two channels available in the network, and provide topology construction algorithms with bounded convergence time

Link Aware Routing

In order to improve scalability of WMNs, the nature of the wireless medium has to be accounted for in order to exploit efficiently the available capacity, To this respect, as already showed in ad-hoc networks literature, cross-layer techniques are able to match routing and MAC layer parameters related to the link status. But, routing metric developed for ad hoc networks barely took into account link quality and/or bandwidth exploiting instead hop count or for example residual power at each node in order to minimize battery consumption. However, WMNs are characterized by totally different requirements in terms of power efficiency and mobility. In fact, in WMNs, relaying is performed by dedicated nodes (e.g., mesh routers), with limited or no mobility and no constraints on battery life being directly plugged to the power line.

A detailed description of the most relevant routing metrics in WMNs can be found in Draves, Padhye, and Zill (2004a, 2004b). Here we briefly summarize their key features:

- **Hop count:** Hop count is the simplest routing metric available. Exploiting a single bit of information for describing each link, this routing metric can either tell if the link exists or if it does not. Such an approach lead to poor performance especially in wireless network where a two-hops path over reliable links can easily outperforms a single hop path over a lossy link.

- **Per-hop round trip time (RTT):** This metric computes the RTT between neighbor nodes. In order to compute the RTT a node sends unicast probes to each neighbors that immediately responds with a probe ACK. Such a design is able to take into account both link quality and network congestion.

In fact, probes are delayed in each node's queue and by the IEEE 802.11 contention mechanism. As expected, over lossy links the metric will increases due to the IEEE 802.11 ARQ mechanism. It is worth noting that this metric does not take into account the link's data rate, moreover this metric require to send probes between any each pair of neighboring nodes and thus may not be suitable for dense networks.

- **Per-hop packet pair (PktPair):** This metric aims at measuring the delay between a pair of unicast probe sent to a neighbor. The two probes have different sizes (the first is Small small, while the second is large). The destination computes the delays between the two probes at report the result to the sender. Such a design is capable of taking into account both link's data rate and the loss rate. In fact, a high loss rate or a slow link will increase the metric due to respectively the ARQ mechanism or the longer time required to send the large packet, The first drawback of this metric is network overhead in that two probes must be transmitted for each pair of neighbors.

- **Expected transmission count (ETX):** This metric estimate the number of retransmission required to send unicast packets. ETX (De Couto, Aguayo, & Bicket, 2003) sends periodically a broadcast probe. This probe contains the number of probes received by each neighbors during a certain observation window. By exploiting this information each node can compute the forward and reverse loss rate for each link (the IEEE 802.11 MAC does not retransmit broadcast packets). The main advantage of ETX is that it exploits broadcast probes thus lowering the network overhead. However, according to the IEEE 802.11 standard, broadcast packets are always sent at the lowest rate (11 Mbps for IEEE 802.11b/g and 6 Mbps for IEEE 802.11a). As a result since data packets are sent typically at higher rates, they may experience higher loss rate. Moreover the ETX metric does not take into account the link rate.

- **Expected Transmission Time (ETT):** ETT is defined in Draves et al. (2004a) as a "bandwidth adjusted ETX." In fact, ETT is computed starting from ETX using this formula: $ETT = ETX \cdot S/B$ where S is the size of the probe packet and B is the link bandwidth. However, as reported in Draves et al. (2004a), computing the link bandwidth may not be trivial in real-world deployments.

- **Weighted Cumulative ETT (WCETT):** WCETT aims at minimizing interference in multi-channel WMNs. In order to achieve this goal, WCETT assumes that two hops on the same channel will always interfere (this may not be true for long routes). According to WCETT, for a n-hop path it holds that $WCETT = (1 - \beta) \sum_{i=1}^{n} ETT_i + \beta \max_{1 \leq j \leq k}(X_j)$ where X_j is the sum of ETTs of all hops on channel j and β is a tunable parameter between 0 and 1. Thus, WCETT is a weighted average of the total ETT over all channels and the maximum total ETT on each individual channel. By considering these two factors, WCETT considers both the bandwidth availability and channel diversity.

A performance comparison is described in Draves et al. (2004b) for a wide set of routing metrics are analyzed. Along this line, the link quality source routing (LQSR) is proposed as an extension to the dynamic source routing (DSR) protocol. The LQSR selects the routing path according to the link quality. Three different performance metrics are analyzed: expected transmission count (ETX) (De Couto et al., 2003), per-hop RTT, and per-hop packet pair. Such performance metrics are compared with the traditional hop-count metric. Result shows that when WMNs node mobility is required, hop-count performs better than the other

metrics. However, when WMNs nodes are fixed, and this is the case of WMN, more advanced performance metric taking into account link quality outperform hop-count.

However, exploiting link quality as only performance metric is not enough to properly support multimedia services. Instead, multiple routing metric involving delay, jitter and packet loss should be used. In this context a significant improvement of network scalability is expected as result of cross-layering techniques aimed at merging network layer and MAC layer functionalities. This is particularly true since in IEEE 802.11-based WMNs where medium access is not transparent to routing, being the transmission at a node affecting the transmission more than one-hop away.

Specific to metropolitan networks operated by wireless ISP is the need for traffic differentiation. In such a scenario the network operator is interested in providing SLA tailored to specific customer's classes (i.e., business and residential). Differentiated services (DiffServ) (Blake et al., 1998) and virtual LANs (VLAN) (IEEE, 2003c) are two reference, complementary approaches aimed at satisfying QoS requirements. DiffServ is an architecture that attempts to provide service differentiation by using a class-based approach where individual application flows with similar quality requirements are aggregated. Of course, the crucial issue in WMNs is how to decide the per-hop-behavior in order to describe the treatment of aggregated traffic to ensures the quality guarantees to the corresponding service class. Conversely, VLANs can be used in order to provide security by isolating traffic between different users. Down to the IEEE 802.11x MAC, different services can be tagged and mapped into different priority queues to achieve statistical differentiation, in the spirit of the IEEE 802.11e specification described before. Despite all the components are available, a suitable architecture for exploiting such approaches in WMNs is an open issue.

Channel Aware Aggregation for VoIP in WMNs

In order to make a concrete example of how the previously mentioned techniques increase the sustainable QoS of WMNs, a simple case study will clarify the expected improvement. In particular, in the following an example reporting of a the real testbed experiment operated for VoIP applications will demonstrate the (voice) capacity gain. Being very strict in terms of QoS guarantees for delay and jitter, in particular, VoIP services are an interesting benchmark case. Beside the probing aspect, moreover, it is well known that VoIP is per se a very well known issue in IEEE 802.11 WLANs (Ganguly et al., 2006; Garg & Kappes, 2003; Maguolo, Pellegrini, & Zanella, 2006), due to protocol overhead and to the carrier sense strategy, based on which transmission and collisions elongate backoff waiting times at each station. This translated in severe limitations in the number of sustained VoIP sessions, basically 2 orders of magnitude less than expected from the nominal link rate over VoIP session rate

ratio. Table 4 summarizes the key features of the G.729.3 VoIP codec: compared to standard data transmissions, a typical VoIP source sends typically a large number of small packets with a large penalty in terms of protocol overhead.

In order to mitigate the detrimental effect of the IEEE 802.11 MAC overhead, a natural choice is to concatenate several MAC service data units (MSDUs) to form the data payload of a larger MAC protocol data unit (MPDU) (Ganguly et al., 2006; Maguolo et al., 2006). The PHY header and the MAC header, together with the frame check sequence (FCS) are then appended in order to build the physical service data unit (PSDU). The frame format for an aggregated MSDU (A-MSDU) is sketched in Figure 13: the computational cost of the aggregation procedure is largely within the reach of commercial devices.

A typical drawback of any packet aggregation scheme is that it increases the processing delay at each node invalidating its suitability for VoIP applications: compared to the single hop scenarios, in a WMN, the aggregation policy is applied in a hop-by-hop fashion. Thus, all VoIP packets ow-

Table 4. Key features of the G.729.3 Codec

Codec	Packet Interval	Bit-rate	Payload
G.729.3	30 ms	8 kbps	30 bytes

Figure 13. Aggregated MSDU (A-MSDU) frame format

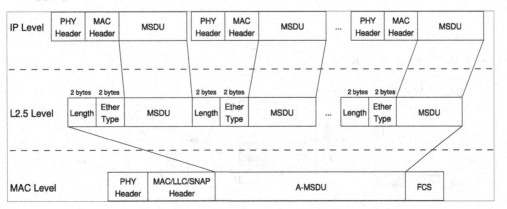

ing toward the gateway will be aggregated and de-aggregated at each intermediate mesh router. An upper bound (20ms) to the aggregation time is introduced in order to limit the processing delay at each node.

The building blocks of the MSDU aggregator and the relationships between them are sketched in Figure 14. The operations are as follows. Incoming MAC frames are first processed by the *Classifier* according to the destination address. Each flow is then fed to a different *Aggregation Queue*. For each queue, an A-MSDU is generated by the *Aggregator* when either an aggregation timer (50 ms) is expired or at least a burst of length B_{Opt} can be generated. Choosing B_{Opt} appropriately, the above scheme can be made aware of the link status. In fact, it is clear that the aggregation trades off packet length with overhead. But, over noisy channels, longer packets need to be retransmitted more due to channel errors. Thus, an optimal aggregation threshold exists: letting B_{Opt} equal to such threshold, the whole effect is to adapt the aggregation mechanism to the link conditions.

The testbed consist of a 4 nodes deployment in a typical office environment, with a two-tier structure, as sketched in Figure 15. Testbed's nodes are based on the PCEngines 1E processor board. Each node is equipped with a 233MHz CPU, 128MB of RAM, 128MB of compact flash and one IEEE 802.11a/b/g wireless interfaces with RTC/CTS disabled (the board supports up to two wireless interfaces). The testbed planimetry is illustrated in Figure 15. Node number one acts

as gateway providing Internet connectivity to the WMN. All measurements are run with the IEEE 802.11 interfaces operating in .g. mode. The testbed nodes run MIT Roofnet (MIT Roofnet Project), an experimental IEEE 802.11-based WMN. Roofnet routes packets using a modified version of DSR called SrcRR (Bicket, Aguayo, & Biswas, 2005) exploiting the ETX routing metric. Routing is implemented using the click modular router (Kohler, Morris, & Jannotti, 2000), developed at MIT; a click router is built by assembling several packet processing modules, called *elements*, forming a directed graph. Each *element* is in charge of a specific function such as packet classification, queuing, and interfacing with networking devices. Click comes with an extensive library of elements supporting various types of packet manipulations. Such a library enables easy router configuration by simply choosing the elements to be used and the connections among them. In the testbed described here, the default Roofnet configuration was added two additional elements for packet aggregation and de-aggregation.

Through measurements, one can assess the voice capacity (Maguolo et al., 2006) (i.e., the maximum number of sustained VoIP calls with high quality and related parameters). Mean opinion score (MOS) tests are the traditional choice to assess the quality of conversations sustained by the network. But, determining the voice capacity would require a prohibitive amount of work if assessed via MOS, and evaluating the MOS rate for a VoIP solution besides being a time consum-

Figure 14. MSDU Aggregator architecture

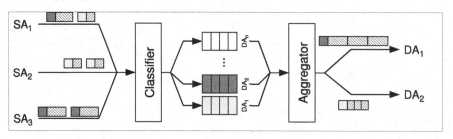

ing process, is inherently not reproducible. For this reason, the experiments can be conducted via a simple and reproducible technique. The components of the tests are a synthetic traffic probe procedure: the probes are generated using Jugi's traffic generator (JTG), a freely available synthetic traffic generator (Jugi's traffic generator) incorporating the typical characteristics of the traffic pattern of a G729.3 codec. In addition to being able of generating and injecting different traffic patterns over TCP and/or UDP sockets, in fact, JTG can read the information about packet transmission intervals and sizes from _les, allowing us to create an exact duplicate of a trace starting from a pre-recorder stream. Traffic is then collected at the receiver side where suitable tools are available for analysis. The analysis technique

is the second component of the experimental deployment. Performance can be assessed via the e-model (ITU-T, 2005), which provides an objective method to evaluate speech quality in VoIP systems. The outcome of an e-model evaluation is called R-factor (R). The R-factor is a numerical measure of voice quality, ranging from 0 to 100, where the scale is basically a logarithmic mapping of objective parameters to the quality perceived by the average listeners, namely the e-model for voice quality assessment. Parameters of interest for the R-factors are collected in dedicated ITU-T recommendations (ITU-T, 2005a, 2005b, 1996). According to such recommendations, $R = 70$ is the minimum tolerated value to obtain a VoIP call with acceptable quality.

Figure 15. Planimetry. Node number one acts as gateway providing Internet connectivity to the WMN

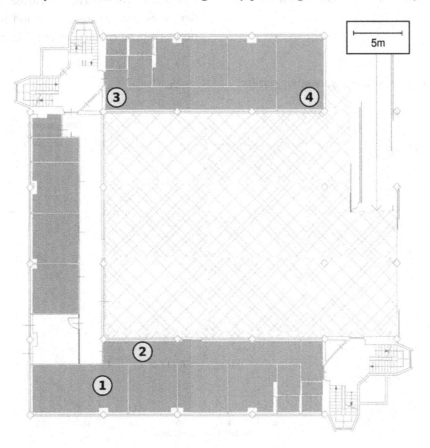

The testbed is a typical configuration for a WMN: several concurrent VoIP flows exploit the mesh nodes as their gateways towards the Internet. VoIP calls are thus UDP flows modeled according to the parameters of the G.729.3 VoIP codec (see Table. I). All mesh nodes sustain the same traffic, consisting in an increasing number of VoIP sessions. All measurements were performed over 3 minute intervals; results are averaged over 10 runs. The results in Figure 16 show clearly aggregation improves the quality of the services sustained over WMNs. The increment on the number of served VoIP flows is indicated in is almost 100% for the four nodes deployed. Hence, even a simple design as the one previously proposed doubles the number of sustained voice sessions. This measurement is in line with predictions obtained from simulations (Maguolo et al., 2006), where aggregation techniques were applied to similar but single-hop scenarios.

SUMMARY AND FUTURE TRENDS

Resource management in IEEE 802.11-based wireless networks has been extensively studied. Many QoS schemes have been proposed to support bandwidth/delay constrained multimedia applications such as voice/video in Wi-Fi-based wireless LANs, heterogeneous wired/wireless networks, mobile ad hoc networks, and wireless mesh networks. These schemes significantly improved flow performance as well as network capacity by exploring either MAC layer information such as link quality, channel diversity, and link interference, or network layer information such as neighboring nodes and collected paths, or both. Due to the contention based channel access protocol in IEEE 802.11 DCF MAC and the broadcast nature of wireless medium, it is imperative that MAC layer information should be tuned as well as incorporated to assist higher layer decisions such as route selection for maximum network performance. From this aspect, cross-

Figure 16. Performance measurements results

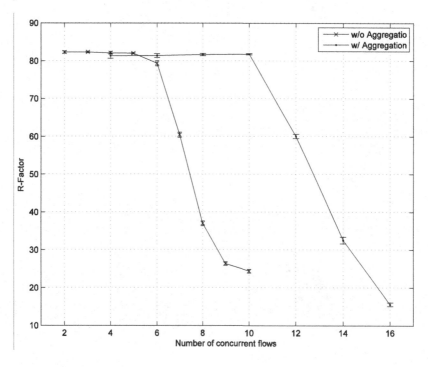

layer approaches that combine the information at both MAC layer and network layer have good potentials. On the other hand, wireless technologies have been advanced tremendously in recent years. New wireless access technologies such as Bluetooth, Wi-Max, UMTS, and UWB have gained a lot of applications and deployments. With such ubiquitous wireless network environments, how to integrate QoS schemes of different wireless network domains together so that multimedia application can be supported seamlessly is critical. Furthermore, many protocols are proposed to solve a specific issue based on certain protocols (such as AODV-QoS). Due to this type protocol dependence, the benefit to the wireless users are very limited since most protocols are designed for one specific layer or issue without considering the needs of other layers or issues. In order to maximize the contribution from the research community, it is imperative that existing protocols are combined effectively and efficiently. Being aware of the heterogeneity of wireless technologies and traffic characteristics, we feel that it is impossible to propose a unique solution for this purpose. Instead, middleware technology should be adopted with careful design.

Therefore, we expect that following research works on the topic of resource management in IEEE 802.11 based wireless networks:

- **QoS in the emerging WMNs:** Efficient schemes to provide guaranteed QoS to VoIP and video applications will be of paramount importance. More in general, several techniques are expected to mitigate the impact of lack of scalability on QoS provisioning in WMNs.
- **QoS in ubiquitous wireless access networks:** QoS and Mobility Management in hybrid mobile/wireless networks where WLAN coexists with other networks such as MANET, WMN, Bluetooth, Wi-Max, UWB, and 3G networks.

- **QoS middleware:** Given a rich set of related, architecturally similar, and loosely connected QoS protocols proposed already by the research community, a cross-layer middleware architecture will (i) significantly increase the ease of design, implementation, validation, and comparison of existing and new QoS protocols. (ii) stimulate collaboration among researchers in the same field with a generic platform. (iii) provide a built-in resource management module in the future wireless networks.

These efforts, combined, will further improve the QoS performance and make the next generation wireless access networks more suitable for the support of multimedia applications.

REFERENCES

Aad, I., Ni, Q., & Castelluccia, C. (2002). Enhancing IEEE 802.11 performance with slow CW decrease. *IEEE 802.11e working group document 802.11-02/674r0.*

Adya A., Bahl, P., & Padhye, J. (2004). A multi-radio unification protocol for IEEE 802.11 wireless networks. *Proceedings of BroadNets* (pp. 344-354), San Jose, California, USA.

Ahn, G., Campbell, A. T., & Veres, A. (2002). Supporting service differentiation for real-time and best effort traffic in stateless wireless ad hoc networks (SWAN). *IEEE Transactions on Mobile Computing, 1*(3), 192-207.

Akyildiz, I. F., Wang, X., & Wang, W. (2005). Wireless mesh networks: A survey. *Elsevier Journal of Computer Networks and ISDN Systems, 47*(4), 445-487.

Awerbuch, B., Holmer, D., & Rubens, H. (2004). High throughput route selection in multi-rate ad hoc wireless networks. *In Proceedings of 1ˢᵗ Working Conference on Wireless On-demand*

Network Systems (pp. 253-270), Madonna di Campiglio, Italy.

Banchs, A., & Pérez, X. (2002). Providing throughput guarantees in IEEE 802.11 wireless LAN. *Proceedings of IEEE Wireless Communications and Networking Conference* (Vol. 1, pp. 130-138). Orlando, Florida, USA.

Banchs, A., Pérez, X., & Qiao, D. (2003). Providing throughput guarantees in IEEE 802.11e wireless LANs. *Proceedings of 18th International Teletraffic Congress*, Berlin, Germany.

Barry, M., Campell, A. T., & Veres, A. (2001). Distributed control algorithms for service differentiation in wireless packet networks. *Proceedings of IEEE INFOCOM* (Vol. 1, pp. 582-590), Anchorage, Alaska, USA.

Bianchi, G. (2000). Performance analysis of the IEEE 802.11 distributed coordination function. *IEEE Journal of Selected Areas on Commununications, 18*(3), 535-547.

Bicket, J., Aguayo, D., & Biswas, S. (2005). Architecture and evaluation of an unplanned 802.11b mesh network. *Proceedings of ACM MOBICOM* (pp. 31-42), Cologne, Germany.

Blake, S., Black, D., & Carlson, M. (1998). An architecture for differentiated service. *RFC 2475.*

Braden, R., Clark, D., & Shenker, S. (1994). Integrated services in the Internet architecture: An overview. *RFC 1633.*

Braden, R., Zhang, L., & Berson, S. (1997). Resource reservation protocol (RSVP)-version 1 functional specification. *RFC 2205.*

Buddhikot, M., Chandranmenon, G., & Han, S. (2003). Integration of 802.11 and third-generation wireless data networks. *Proceedings of IEEE INFOCOM* (Vol. 1, pp. 503-512), San Francisco, California, USA.

Chakeres, I. D., & Belding-Royer, E. M. (2004). PAC: Perceptive admission control for mobile wireless networks. *Proceedings of the 1st International Conference on Quality of Service in Heterogeneous Wired/Wireless Networks* (pp. 18-26), Dallas, Texas, USA.

Chen, L., & Heinzelman, W. (2005). QoS-aware routing based on bandwidth estimation for mobile ad hoc networks. *IEEE Journal on Selected Areas of Communication, 23*(3), 561-572.

Chen, S., & Nahrstedt, K. (1999). Distributed quality-of-service routing in ad-hoc networks. *IEEE Journal on Selected Areas in Communications, Special Issue on Ad-Hoc Networks, 17*(8), 1-18.

Clausen, T., & Jacquet, P. (2003). Optimized link state routing protocol (OLSR). *RFC 3626.*

Conti, A., Dardari, D., & Pasolini, G. (2003). Bluetooth and IEEE 802.11b coexistence: Analytical performance evaluation in fading channels. *IEEE Journal on the Selected Areas in Communications, 21*(2), 259-269.

De Couto, D., Aguayo, D., & Bicket, J. (2003). High-throughput path metric for multi-hop wireless routing. *Proceedings of ACM MOBICOM* (pp. 134-146), San Diego, California, USA.

Draves, R., Padhye, J., & Zill, B. (2004a). Comparison of routing metrics for static multi-hop wireless networks. *Proceedings of ACM SIGCOMM* (pp. 133-144), Portland, Oregon, USA.

Draves, R., Padhye, J., & Zill, B. (2004b). Routing in multi-radio, multi-hop wireless mesh networks. *Proceedings of ACM MOBICOM* (pp. 114-128), Philadelphia, PA, USA.

Ergen, M., & Varaiya. P. (2005). Throughput analysis and admission control for IEEE 802.11a. *ACM/Springer Journal of Mobile Networks and Applications, 10*(5), 705-716.

Ganguly, S., Navda, V., Kim, K., Kashyap, A., Niculescu, D., Izmailov, R., Hong, S., & Das, S. (2006). Performance optimization for deploying VOIP services in mesh networks. *IEEE Journal* on Selected Areas in Communications, 24(11), 2147-2158.

Gao, D., Cai, J., & Ngan, K. N. (2005). Admission control in IEEE 802.11e wireless LANs. *IEEE Network, special issue on Wireless Local Area Networking: QoS provision & Resource Management, 19*(4), 6-13.

García-Macías, J., Rousseau, F., Berger-Sabbatel, G., Toumi, L., & Duda, A. (2003). Quality of service and mobility for the wireless Internet. *ACM/Springer Wireless Networks, 9*(4), 341-352.

Garg, S., & Kappes, M. (2003). Can I add a VoIP call? *Proceedings of IEEE ICC* (Vol. 2, pp. 779-783), Anchorage, USA.

Goff, T., Abu-Ghazaleh, N. B., & Phatak, D. S. (2001). Preemptive routing in ad hoc networks. *Proceedings of ACM MOBICOM* (pp. 43-52), Rome, Italy.

Gupta, P., & Kumar, P. R. (2000). The capacity of wireless networks. *IEEE Transactions on Information Theory, 46*(2), 388-404.

Havinga, P. J. M., & Wu, G. (2001). Wireless Internet on heterogeneous networks. *Proceedings of Workshop on Mobile Communications in Perspective*, Enschede, the Netherlands.

IEEE. (1997). IEEE std 802.11--Wireless LAN medium access control (MAC) and physical layer (PHY) specification. *IEEE Standard.*

IEEE 802.11e. (2003). Part 11: Wireless LAN medium access control (MAC) and physical layer (PHY) specifications: medium access control (MAC) enhancements for quality of service (QoS). *IEEE Std 802.11e/D4.3.*

IEEE 802.11f. (2003). IEEE trial-use recommended practice for multi-vendor access point interoperability via an inter-access point protocol across distribution systems supporting IEEE 802.11 ™ operation. *IEEE Standard.*

IEEE 802.1Q. (2003). Virtual bridged local area networks, *IEEE Standard.*

IEEE 802.11s. (1998). Draft amendment to standard for information technology, telecommunications and information exchange between systems - LAN/MAN specific requirements - part 11: wireless medium access control (MAC) and physical layer (PHY) specifications: amendment: ESS mesh networking, *IEEE Standard.*

ITU-T Recommendation G.107 (2005). The e-model, a computational model for use in transmission planning, *ITU-T Standard.*

ITU-T Recommendation G.113 (2005). Transmission impairments due to speech processing, *ITU-T Standard.*

ITU-T Recommendation G.729 (1996). Annex B, A silence compression scheme for G.729 optimized for terminals conforming to recommendation V.70. *ITU-T Standard.*

Jaseemuddin, M. (2003). An architecture for integrating UMTS and 802.11 WLAN networks. *Proceedings of IEEE Symposium on Computers and Communications* (pp. 716 -723), Antalya, Turkey.

Johnson, D. B., Maltz, D. A., & Broch, J. (2001). DSR: The dynamic source routing protocol for multi-hop wireless ad hoc networks. In C. E. Perkins (Ed.), *Ad hoc networking* (pp. 139-172). Addison-Wesley Press.

Ju, H. J., & Rubin, I. (2006). Backbone topology synthesis for multiradio mesh networks. *IEEE Journal on Selected Areas in Communications, 24*(11), 2116-2126.

Jugi's traffic generator. *Summary.* From https://hoslab.cs.helsinki.fi/savane/projects/jtg/

Jun, J., & Sichitiu, M. L. (2003). The nominal capacity of wireless mesh networks. *IEEE Wireless Communications, 10*(5), 8-14.

Kanodia, V., Li, C., & Sabharwal, A. (2002). Distributed priority scheduling and medium access in ad hoc networks. *ACM Wireless Networks Journal, 8(*5), 455-466.

Kazantzidis, M., Gerla, M., & Lee, S. J. (2001). Permissible throughput network feedback for adaptive multimedia in AODV MANETs. *Proceedings of IEEE International Conference on Communications* (Vol. 5, pp. 1352-1356), Helsinki, Finland.

Kohler, E., Morris, R., & Jannotti, J. (2000). The click modular router. *ACM Transaction on Computer System, 18*(3), 263-297.

Lamont, L., Wang, M., & Villasenor, L. (2003). Integrating WLANs & MANETs to the IPv6 based Internet. *Proceedings of IEEE International Conference on Communications* (Vol. 2, pp. 1090-1095), Anchorage, Alaska, USA.

Lee, S. B., Ahn, G., Zhang, X., & Campbell, A. T. (2000). INSIGNIA: An IP-based quality of service framework for mobile ad hoc networks. *Journal of Parallel and Distributed Computing, special issue on Wireless and Mobile Computing and Communications, 60*(4), 374-406.

Li, J., Blake, C., & De Couto, D. S. J. (2001). Capacity of ad hoc wireless networks. *Proceedings of ACM MOBICOM* (pp. 61-69), Rome, Italy.

Li, M., & Prabhakaran, B. (2005a). MAC layer admission control and priority re-allocation for handling QoS guarantees in non-cooperative wireless LANs. *ACM/Springer Mobile Networks and Applications, 10*(6), 947-959.

Li, M., & Prabhakaran, B. (2005b). On supporting reliable QoS in multi-hop multi-rate mobile ad hoc networks. *Proceedings of the 1ˢᵗ IEEE International Workshop on Next Generation Wireless Networks*, Goa, India.

Li, M., & Prabhakaran, B. (2004). Dynamic priority re-allocation scheme for providing quality of service in IEEE 802.11e WLANs. *Proceeding of*

SPIE/ACM Conference on Multimedia Computing and Networking (pp. 83-94), Santa Clara, CA, USA.

Li, M., Prabhakaran, B., & Sathyamurthy, S. (2003). On flow reservation and admission control for distributed scheduling strategies in IEEE 802.11 wireless LANs. *Proceedings of the 6ᵗʰ ACM International Workshop on Modeling, Analysis and Simulation of Wireless and Mobile Systems* (pp. 108-115), San Diego, CA, USA.

Li, M., Zhu, H., Chlamtac, I., & Prabhakaran, B. (2006). End-to-end QoS framework for heterogeneous wired-cum-wireless networks. *ACM/Baltzer Wireless Networks, 12*(4), 439-450.

Lo, C. C., & Lin, M. H. (1998). QoS provisioning in handoff algorithms for wireless LAN. *Proceedings of the International Zurich Seminar on Broadband Communications, Accessing, Transmission, Networking* (pp. 9-16), Zurich, Swissland.

Lou, X., Li, B., & Thng, I. (2002). An adaptive measured-based pre-assignment scheme with connection-level QoS support for mobile networks. *IEEE Transactions on Wireless Communication, 1*(3), 521-530.

Maguolo, F., Pellegrini, F. D., & Zanella, A. (2006). Cross-layer solutions to performance problems in VoIP over WLAN. *Proceedings of EURASIP EUSIPCO*, Florence, Italy.

Mishra, M. S. A., & Arbaugh, W. (2003). An empirical analysis of the IEEE 802.11 MAC layer handoff process. *ACM SIGCOMM Computer Communication Review, 33*(2), 93-102.

MIT Roofnet Project. From http://pdos.csail.mit.edu/roofnet/

Moon, B., & Aghvami, A. H. (2004). Quality of service mechanisms in all-IP wireless access networks. *IEEE Journal on Selected Areas in Communications, 22*(5), 873-888.

Nasipuri, A., Zhuang, J., & Das, S. R. (1999), A multichannel CSMA MAC protocol for multihop wireless networks. *Proceedings of IEEE Wireless Communications and Networking Conference* (pp. 1402-1406), New Orleans, Louisiana, USA.

Park, H., Yoon, S., & Kim, T. (2002). Vertical handoff procedure and algorithm between IEEE 802.11 WLAN and CDMA cellular network. *Proceedings of Mobile Communications: 7th CDMA International Conference*, Seoul, Korea.

Park, S., Kim, K., & Kim, D. C. (2003). Collaborative QoS architecture between DiffServ and 802.11e wireless LAN. *Proceedings of IEEE VTC'03-Spring* (Vol. 2, pp. 945-949), Jeju, Korea.

Perkins, C. E., & Belding-Royer, E. M. (2003). Quality of service for ad hoc on-demand distance vector routing. *Internet Draft, draft-perkins-manet-aodvqos-02.txt.*

Perkins, C. E., Belding-Royer, E. M., & Chakeres, I. (2003). Ad hoc on demand distance vector (AODV) routing. *IETF Internet draft, draft-perkins-manet-aodvbis-00.txt.*

Perkins, C. E., & Bhagwat, P. (1994). Highly dynamic destination sequenced distance vector routing (DSDV) for mobile computers. *Proceedings of ACM SIGCOMM* (pp. 234-244), London, UK.

Pong, D., & Moor T. (2003). Call admission control for IEEE 802.11 contention access mechanism. *Proceedings of IEEE GLOBECOM* (Vol. 1, pp. 174-178), San Francisco, California, USA.

Raman, B. (2006). Channel allocation in 802.11-based mesh networks. *Proceedings of IEEE INFOCOM* (pp. 1-10), Barcelona, Spain.

Romdhani, L., Ni, Q., & Turletti, T. (2003). Adaptive EDCF: Enhanced service differentiation for IEEE 802.11 wireless ad hoc networks. *IEEE Wireless Communications and Networking Conference* (Vol. 2, pp. 1373-1378), New Orleans, USA.

Sanzgiri, K., Chakeres, I. D., & Belding-Royer, E. M. (2004). Determining intra-flow contention along multihop paths in wireless networks. *Proceedings of IEEE BROADNETS Wireless Networking Symposium* (pp. 611-620), San Jose, CA.

Shah, S. H., Chen, K., & Nahrstedt, K. (2004). Dynamic bandwidth management for single-hop ad hoc wireless networks. *ACM/Kluwer Mobile Networks and Applications, Special Issue on Algorithmic Solutions for Wireless, Mobile, Ad Hoc and Sensor Networks, 10*(1-2), 199-217.

Shankar, S., & Choi, S. (2002). QoS signaling for parameterized traffic in IEEE 802.11e wireless LANS. *Lecture Notes in Computer Science, Vol. 2402,* 67-84.

Shin, M., Lee, S., & Kim, Y. (2006). Distributed channel assignment for multi-radio wireless networks. *Proceedings of International Conference on Mobile Adhoc and Sensor Systems* (pp. 417-426), Vancouver, Canada.

Shin, S., Forte, A., & Rawat, A. (2004). Reducing MAC layer handoff latency in IEEE 802.11 wireless LANs. *Proceeding of ACM MobiWAC* (pp. 19-26), Philadelphia, Pennsylvania, USA.

So, J., & Vaodya, N. (2004). Multi-channel MAC for ad hoc networks: Handling multi-channel hidden terminals using a single transceiver. *Proceedings of ACM MobiHoc* (pp. 222-233), Roppongi, Japan.

Vaidya, N. H., Bahl, P., & Gupta, S. (2000). Distributed fair scheduling in wireless LAN. *Proceedings of ACM MOBICOM* (pp. 167-178), Boston, USA.

Valaee, S., & Li, B. (2002). Distributed call admission control in wireless ad hoc networks. *Proceedings of IEEE Vehicular Technology Conference* (Vol. 2, pp. 1244-1248), Vancouver, British Columbia.

Wu, H., Peng, Y., & Long, K. (2002). Performance of reliable transport protocol over IEEE 802.11

wireless LANs: Analysis and enhancement. *Proceedings of IEEE INFOCOM* (pp. 599–607), New York, USA.

Xiao, Y. (2005). Performance analysis of priority schemes for IEEE 802.11 and IEEE 802.11e wireless LANs. *IEEE Transactions on Wireless Communications, 4*(4), 1506-1515.

Xiao, Y., Li, H., & Choi, S. (2004a). Protection and guarantee for voice and video traffic in IEEE 802.11e wireless LANs. *Proceedings of IEEE INFOCOM* (pp. 2153-2163), Hong Kong, China.

Xiao Y., & Li, H. (2004b). Local data control and admission control for ad hoc wireless networks. *IEEE Transactions on Vehicular Technology, 53*(5), 1558-1572.

Xiao Y., & Li, H. (2004c). Voice and video transmissions with global data parameter control for the IEEE 802.11e enhance distributed channel access. *IEEE Transactions on Parallel and Distributed Systems, 15*(11), 1041-1053.

Xue, Q., & Ganz, A. (2003). Ad hoc QoS on-demand routing (AQOR) in mobile ad hoc networks. *Journal of Parallel Distributed Computing, 63*(2), 154-165.

Yang, Y., & Kravets, R. (2005). Contention-aware admission control for ad hoc networks. *IEEE Transactions on Mobile Computing, 4*(4), 363-338.

Yavatkar, R., Hoffman, D., & Bernet, Y. (2000). SBM (subnet bandwidth manager): A protocol for RSVP-based admission control over IEEE 802-style networks. *RFC2814*.

Zhai, H., Chen, X., & Fang, Y. (2006). A call admission and rate control scheme for multimedia support over IEEE 802.11 wireless LANs. *ACM Wireless Networks, 12*(4), 451-463.

Zhu, H., & Chlamtac, I. (2003). An analytical model for IEEE 802.11e EDCF differential services. *Proceedings of the 12th International Conference on Computer Communications and Networks* (pp. 163-168), Dallas, Texas, USA.

Zhu, H., Li, M., Chlamtac, I., & Prabhakaran, B. (2004). Survey of quality of service in IEEE 802.11 networks. *IEEE Wireless Communications, Special Issue on Mobility and Resource Management, 11*(4), 6-14.

Section II
Application Quality of Service

In this section, application layer techniques are presented to facilitate QoS for multimedia streaming services. There are two facets to Application-layer QoS: server-side and client-side techniques. Server-side techniques cover the encoding configuration, adaptive encoding algorithms, error resilience, and preparation of the multimedia stream for delivery over the network. Client-side techniques include buffering, power saving, and decoding techniques such as error concealment and error recovery techniques. Through optimization of server-side and client-side encoding and decoding options, the application can compensate for and overcome limitations in the network and provide QoS for real-time multimedia streaming applications. This section presents novel server-side and client-side application layer solutions for voice and video streaming applications.

Chapter V
Adaptive Codec Selection for VoIP in Multi–Rate WLANs

Anna Sfairopoulou
Network Technologies and Strategies (NeTS) Research Group, Universitat Pompeu Fabra, Spain

Carlos Macián
Network Technologies and Strategies (NeTS) Research Group, Universitat Pompeu Fabra, Spain

Boris Bellalta
Network Technologies and Strategies (NeTS) Research Group, Universitat Pompeu Fabra, Spain

ABSTRACT

This chapter introduces the problems caused to voice over IP calls on 802.11 networks due to the link adaptation mechanism of them. It provides an overview of all the components participating in this study with special emphasis on the multi-rate anomaly. Furthermore, it reviews the literature on recent works on the specific area of link adaptation and codec selection. The authors finally propose as a solution to the multi-rate problem a codec selection mechanism, which, by changing codec of some of the calls at the moment of the rate change, has as an objective to maintain delay and packet loss values in acceptable levels and provide the desired QoS for the voice flows.

VOIP OVER WLANS

Voice over IP (VoIP) over wireless LANs (WLANs) has been a hot research topic during the past years due to the widespread deployment and ease-of-use of both technologies. The capacity of a wireless cell in terms of number of supported calls, as well as the quality of the voice transmis-sion over the wireless link under different channel conditions, are crucial for deciding whether this technology can be widely deployed and accepted for voice service. In spite of all the research efforts in this area, there are still unsolved issues concerning the quality of VoIP calls, most commonly caused by the specific wireless network characteristics listed below (note that the purely physical effects, such as meteorological impact on channel conditions, are beyond the scope of this chapter):

1. Unfairness between uplink and downlink streams
2. High protocol layer overheads
3. Fast VoIP degradation in presence of TCP flows
4. Variable capacity due to multi-rate transmissions

Although the first three problems have been widely analyzed in previous works, there is scarce bibliography considering the last problem. Multi-rate transmission is one of the key features of the IEEE 802.11 PHY/MAC specifications, which allows each mobile node to select its physical layer parameters (modulation and channel coding) to optimize the bit transmission over the noise/fading-prone channel. These sporadic rate changes occurring on the mobile nodes as they move around the cell due to the link adaptation algorithm of the 802.11 specification have an impact on the transmissions of all active calls and produce a general degradation of the network performance.

This chapter intends to provide an overview of the impairments observed on voice flows due to the multi-rate characteristic of 802.11, and discuss some of the solutions that have been proposed so far, with particular focus on a codec adaptation solution. Main goals are:

1. To give some background on VoIP over WLAN systems and analyze the source of the various problems and how they affect the voice transmission in terms of total cell capacity and quality of service
2. To describe what is a multi-rate wireless LAN and its impact on VoIP calls
3. To review the literature on how to best cope with the multi-rate problem and introduce the benefits of a codec adaptation solution

4. To present a cross-layer codec adaptation algorithm and demonstrate how it is able to satisfy the QoS needs of VoIP traffic
5. To examine the suitability of proposing some future enhancements to the SIP architecture to better cope with this issue

Voice over IP Systems: From Encoding to Media Transmission

What Composes a VoIP System?

In order to better understand what the impact of a multi-rate 802.11 environment on a VoIP system can be, it is necessary to review the elements that compose such a system, and which among them are prone to interact with 802.11 in order to provoke alterations on the VoIP quality. According to Figure 1, the main elements of a VoIP system are:

-   **Human voice:** Pretty obviously, the foremost element of a VoIP system is human voice, or in general an audio source (music from a CD or a stored speech, for example). Throughout this chapter, and since the main impact of 802.11 will be over real-time transmissions, as will be explained, an interactive speaker is assumed.
-   **A microphone and speakers:** Or, in general, some device to capture human voice and transform it from a pressure wave to a continuous electric signal, which can be processed by a computer. Conversely, at the reception point, the inverse procedure must take place, and hence some speakers or headsets are highly desirable.
-   **A sampling and encoding device:** In order to adapt an analog signal to be transported over a packetized data network, a dual process must occur: First, the analog signal must be transformed into a train of discrete samples, so that one or more of

Figure 1. Main elements of VoIP system

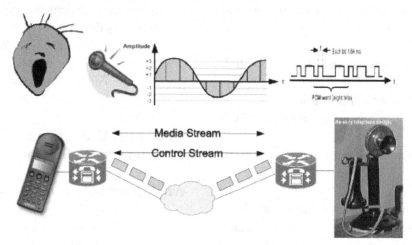

these samples can be inserted on every data packet. Additionally, in order to limit the (theoretically, infinite) range of values that the voice sample can take (from a whisper to a shout), it is advisable to reduce the value range to a pre-specified set of equispaced or nonuniform values. This procedure will allow the system to set a fixed number of bits to encode all possible values of a sample. Second, a standardized and efficient way to digitally encode such values must be agreed upon (e.g., agreeing that 00000000 will mean -1 Volt and 11111111 will mean +1 Volt, with all values in between equally spaced). Additionally, the encoding can be designed to be robust in the face of probable data loss (e.g. by introducing some redundancy between samples), or to be especially efficient in terms of capacity usage (e.g. by only encoding the difference between two consecutive samples, thus saving some bits), or in general to try to maximize some desired property. The diversity of goals and procedures designed to encode and decode voice samples has given rise to a broad number of encoding-decoding algorithms,

generally known as codecs, and which will be reviewed in section 1.1.2.

- **A media transport protocol:** If the encoded voice samples are to be transported over a data network, some protocol devised for this purpose has to be used. Since VoIP is an interactive, real-time application, the chosen protocol has to show good properties in the face of delay, jitter, and loss. As will be explained in section 1.1.4, RTP is the protocol of choice for such a purpose in the Internet.

- **A session management protocol:** Beyond transmitting the encoded voice samples, there has to be a way for the communicating parties to negotiate which codec will be used, when the interchange of voice will start and end, to which port number the samples should be addressed, etc. Besides, a VoIP transmission can involve more than one voice/sound stream, as in the case of a multi-party conference or a multi-track sound recording. Hence, a protocol is needed that manages the set up, negotiation and tear-down of media sessions among participating peers. This is the role of SIP, which is the subject of section 1.1.3.

- **An application:** So far, the corresponding elements for the capture, sampling & encoding of voice, as well as its transmission over a data network have been mentioned. But to what purpose is voice being transmitted? Is it a conversation between two humans? Is it the broadcasting of a music video clip? Is it part of a multimedia session á la Messenger, involving voice, webcam video, and chat? In general, all the elements explained up to now are merely *tools* that an application will use to provide a specific multimedia service over the Internet. As seen through the many examples mentioned above, the same set of tools serve to support a wide variety of different applications. The applications themselves are not the subject of this chapter, and will only be treated as examples of the usage of the other elements.

- **Specialized network nodes:** In the same way that the Internet uses routers and switches for its correct operation, for the correct operation of the above mentioned protocols and the associated communication architecture, as well as the applications using them, a number of dedicated network nodes will be necessary. Such nodes will implement such functions as finding users by using their VoIP identificator, storing user preferences, redirecting calls to a voicemail, translating the codec used by a peer to the one supported by another one, etc. Such nodes are not the focus of this chapter, but some reference to them will be necessary to highlight the characteristics of some of the proposed solutions. Hence, in section 1.1.3 a brief explanation of the main one, the proxy server, will be made for clarity.

Of the many elements that compose a VoIP system, only some are involved in coping with the multi-rate phenomenon. As has already been pointed out, the codecs can be designed to optimize different parameters, such as capacity usage or robustness, or they can even adapt their behaviour to the changing channel conditions. The particular characteristics of some of them will be reviewed in section 1.1.2.

The media transport protocol, RTP, was not designed to be adaptive in any way, so it cannot be used in any adaptive solution. The session management protocol, SIP, does provide a mechanism for re-negotiating the characteristics of a call if network conditions change, but it was not intended for quick reaction and repeated usage, as would be the case in WLANs. Furthermore, it does not, by itself, record or notice any changes at the PHY/MAC layer, so it can not react to rate changes. RTCP, on the other hand, since it delivers continuous quality information, provides an indirect way of detecting the effect that a PHY layer rate change has. As it is then, the only way of using SIP mechanisms to cope with the multi-rate phenomenon is by coupling it with PHY/MAC information and/or RTCP in some way. That is the subject of section 2.3.

Last, applications themselves can be designed to implement their own quality monitoring mechanisms at the application layer. They are then independent of the network and do not really take multi-rate changes into account; they simply measure any quality degradations due to any causes, and react. On the one hand, that allows to implement mechanisms that are valid for any situation and independent of any technology or specific effect. On the other, however, since they do not take into account the nature of the problem, but only its symptoms, it is much more difficult to implement an efficient response. To put it in other words, "one size does not necessarily fit all." Since such mechanisms are not specific for multi-rate environments, they will not be further considered in this chapter.

In the next sections, a brief introduction to the main elements relevant to the designed solutions of the specific multi-rate issue will be reviewed. Hence, codecs, RTP/RTCP and SIP will be presented in summary and their main characteristics reviewed, before proceeding to the solutions themselves.

Codecs

The transformation of analog speech into discrete binary-encoded samples amendable to transport through packet networks is a complex procedure, in which several degrees of liberty exist. As a consequence, a number of different algorithms have been devised. All of them have to perform the same rough steps:

1. Transform the continuous analog signal into a train of equally spaced, discrete samples. The sampling rate must conform to Nyquist's Theorem, which states that in order to be able to reconstruct the original analog signal, it must be sampled at a frequency equal to twice its bandwidth. Although human voice roughly comprises the band between 0 and 20.000 Hz, it is generally limited to the 0-3400 Hz band with the help of a low-pass filter, in order to save bandwidth. The typical sampling rate, slightly above Nyquist's minimum, is 8000 Hz.

2. The amplitude of the samples (the "volume") can take a broad range of values. Consequently, in order to be able to provide a discrete value to each one, which can then be codified in a binary word, a huge number of bits would have to be used. In order to limit the capacity needed to codify a sample, a set of limited, standardized values is chosen, and all intermediate values are rounded to those ones. As a consequence, a certain error is introduced, called the quantization noise. It is intuitively easy to see that this error is relatively more important for small amplitude values ("whispers") than for big ones ("shouts"), for the SNR is smaller in the first case, making the message difficult to understand. Hence, nonuniform quantization is used, by which the distance between

two standard values is smaller (provoking a smaller quantization error) for smaller values of amplitude.

3. Last, the resulting sample values must be transmitted across a network. Not necessarily the sample value itself must be transmitted, other more sophisticated schemes can be used: For example, the difference between two samples could be coded, potentially reducing the number of bits needed. Or even the value of a sample could be used by the receiver to predict the next one, eliminating the need to send it altogether.

Obviously, the result of filtering the voice frequency band and limiting the number of bits used to codify each sample is to reduce the overall quality, and hence also the understandability, of the message. However, the effect is far from linear, so that "intelligent" ways of coding the samples can go a long way in reducing bandwidth consumption without greatly degrading the quality. The different methods to code, predict or otherwise optimize the transmission and calculation of samples also introduce a degree of error.

In general, three codec families exist:

*   **Waveform codecs:** These codecs simply sample, quantize, and send the information, without further considerations. They are simple and provide very good quality, since they closely reproduce the original analog signal. Being so simple, they take low processing effort and hence do not introduce any additional delay into the system, which is an optimal characteristic for real-time communications. In exchange of this, they need fairly large bandwidth to provide good quality, and degrade rapidly otherwise. A well known example of a waveform codec is the G.711 codec.

*   **Source codecs (a.k.a. vocoders):** The basis of these codecs is always a mathematical model of the speech generation process at

the human voice tract. The model usually takes the form of a linear multi-parameter filter. By transmitting the adequate filter parameters, any sound can theoretically be reproduced. Furthermore, since the generation of human voice presents a fair amount of correlation among consecutive samples, it is possible to predict the next samples from previous ones, with a high degree of probability. Hence, combining sample prediction at the receiver with the sending of only the filter parameters, the overall bandwidth needed can be much reduced. The price to pay, however, is a synthetic-sounding voice, which is only fair, since it was synthetically generated. Additionally, these sophisticated algorithms need much more processing effort than waveform codecs and generally use several samples at once in order to operate and predict the next ones, so that the overall effect is introducing some additional delay, as well as necessitating more powerful (and hence more expensive) signal processors.

- **Hybrid codecs:** A mixture of both previous techniques: Hybrid codecs use a mathematical model of the voice tract, but use a number of different input vectors to compare the result with the original signal. This way, a more precise encoding can be found for every sample. In this case, not only the filter parameters are sent but also an indication of which of the standardized excitation vectors has been used in generating it. As could be expected, these codecs lie somewhat in between the previous two in terms of bandwidth usage and quality, and are widely used, like the G.728 and G.729 codecs.

A particular case of the previous family are the variable-rate codecs. By slightly changing the characteristics of the algorithm, they can trade some additional bandwidth against better quality, or higher robustness in the face of packet loss or a noisy channel. This type of codecs, although originally designed for GSM networks, can be

Figure 2. Network distortion of VoIP transmission

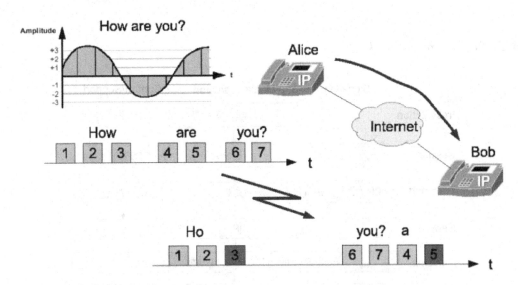

particularly interesting for a 802.11 multi-rate scenario, since this presents frequent channel changes. Adaptive codecs can change their parameters as fast as every 20ms, and could present an automatic, user-independent way of coping with the multi-rate issue. Widely used actually in 3G cellular networks, their translation to the 802.11 world seems only logical, and some of the existing proposals will be reviewed in section 2.1.

Session Management using SIP

A voice over IP call consists mainly of two parts: signalling (a.k.a. call control) and media transmission. The signalling procedure is responsible for establishing the call, authenticating users, setting up the route, controlling the status of the call and terminating the session when the call is finished. The most used signalling protocols nowadays are the session initiation protocol (SIP) (Rosenberg et al., 1998) and the H.323 standard (H.323 Rec., 1998). While H.323 is based on previous PSTN architectures, SIP was created following the guidelines of the HTTP protocol, with a request-response model, directly focused on the Internet architecture. As such, it re-uses as many existing Internet protocols and elements as possible, and

where new items are needed, it tries to keep them at a minimum, and as simple as possible.

The idea behind SIP is to provide a simple, lightweight means for creating and ending connections for real-time interactive communications over IP networks--mainly for voice, but also for video conferencing, chat, gaming, or even application sharing. Hence, it is specifically focused on call control and nothing but call control: It does *not* implement or control QoS, mobility management, media synchronization and/or mixing (e.g., such as in a multi-conference), or in general, any kind of application-specific media processing. SIP is only a tool that applications can use to support more complex functionality, like implementing a video downloading service through the Internet. But SIP only provides the call control part, nothing more, nothing less.

It was originally designed by Schulzrinne (Columbia University) and Handley (UCL) starting in 1996 (Rosenberg et al., 1998). Since then, it has been increasing in success and acceptance among the VoIP community and in November 2000 it was adopted as the 3GPP signalling protocol and a permanent element for the new IP multimedia system (IMS) (Camarillo & García-Martín, 2004).

Figure 3. The SIP protocol stack

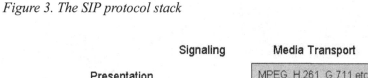

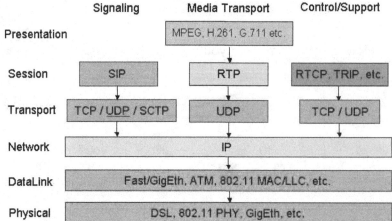

SIP packets are generally called *messages*. Every SIP request messages carries a *method* indicating the request type, and the corresponding response carries a *status code* indicating the answer. The original SIP specification had only six methods, which gives an idea of its commitment to simplicity. There is a large number of status codes, built along the lines of HTTP: each consists of a 3-digit code, the first indicating the general kind of answer, and the last two giving more concrete information, such as: 183, 1 - Informational response, 83 - Session in progress; 400, 4 - Request failure, 00 - Bad request. The most common answer to any request, if everything worked properly, is 200 OK.

The six original request methods were:

- **INVITE:** Used for initiating a session. Its two most interesting characteristics for this chapter are:
  - o That it carries the session description parameters in its body during the negotiation phase, such as which codecs the peer can support, which media types, etc.
  - o That sending further INVITEs after the session has been established, with new session parameters, serves to renegotiate the session characteristics among the peers.
- **ACK:** Confirms the session establishment, à la TCP. It can only be used with INVITE.
- **BYE:** Terminates a session.
- **CANCEL:** If an INVITE has been sent, but a response is still pending, CANCEL serves to cancel the pending INVITE.
- **OPTIONS:** It serves to enquire about a peer's capabilities prior to negotiating the session characteristics.
- **REGISTER:** This method is used for binding a permanent address (i.e., a user's SIP identifier) to a current location (i.e., an IP address).

Of these six methods, only the INVITE is of relevance here. In the body of this message, all the relevant session parameters are transported during the set up phase. Paramount among them are the codecs supported by every partner and the corresponding sampling rates, the media types (e.g., audio and/or video), and the IP addresses and port numbers to which media packets shall be addressed. The corresponding 200 OK response carries the callee's selection of codecs. Once this

Figure 4. Basic SIP call

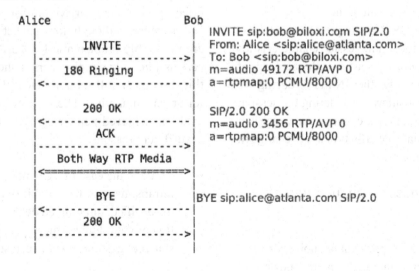

negotiation has taken place, the ACK finishes the set up and media packets can be interchanged. Figure 4 presents a schematic version of a basic SIP call.

If due to a change in the communication characteristics, such as the addition of a new media stream (e.g., a video stream on top of an existing audio stream--from audio--conference to video-conference), the session parameters should be re-negotiated, a new INVITE-OK-ACK cycle is started, without interrupting the existing media streams. It is this characteristic that can be used in the context of a multi-rate scenario to react to a rate change by negotiating a new codec, more apt for the new conditions.

Although SIP is an end-to-end protocol, and hence does not mandate the usage of any network elements, any VoIP architecture beyond the trivial one needs at least one node to find and authenticate users and to route calls: The SIP proxy. In the most common VoIP architecture, the SIP proxy receives all signalling messages from both participating peers, which gives it a privileged overview of the session state. In some cases, the proxy can even control the interchange of the data packets themselves. As will be seen in section 2.3, taking advantage of these characteristics, together with an adequate positioning of the SIP proxy co-located at the 802.11 access point can facilitate the implementation of very efficient solutions to the multi-rate issue.

Summarizing, SIP is a request/response session control protocol. The session characteristics are negotiated during set-up with the help of INVITE messages. Further INVITEs during the life of the session allow for updating the session parameters, including the codecs used, which can be used to alleviate the effects of a rate change in 802.11 environments.

Media Transmission on the Internet: RTP/RTCP

The media transport protocol of choice for most multimedia applications in the Internet nowadays is undoubtedly the real-time protocol (RTP). Originally specified in RFC 1889 (and updated in RFC 3550) (Schulzrinne, Casner, Frederick, & Jacobson, 2003), it was designed together with its companion protocol, the real-time control protocol (RTCP). The role of this second protocol was to provide feedback on communication quality to the peers, so that they could react accordingly. The most critical aspect of both protocols is that even if they provide extensive information on QoS, they themselves *do not* use that information in any way: They simply collect and transport it, and it is up to the controlling applications to implement the corresponding adaptation mechanisms. That is one of the reasons why some multimedia architectures bypass RTCP and implement themselves their own mechanisms and even protocols, tailored to their exact needs.

The rationale behind defining a new transport protocol for real-time multimedia data over IP networks derives from the strict requirements in terms of QoS, that neither TCP, nor UDP could fulfil. VoIP traffic necessitates an end-to-end delay of no more than 150 ms for good voice quality, together with a strictly bounded jitter. The reason is that interactive voice requires the sampling of the signal at very short intervals, and their reproduction at the exact same rate. Hence, beyond the samples reaching the destination in a short period of time, to avoid the "walkie-talkie" effect, packets must arrive almost periodically. Furthermore, although low packet loss ratios are not highly problematic for VoIP communications (the user simply hears a short "click"), this ratio must still remain below the 5% mark for understandability. These strict requirements could be achieved neither by TCP nor by UDP for different reasons:

- **TCP:** In the case of TCP, mainly its use of retransmissions for reliability provokes an unspecified, unbounded delay in the reception of data. Furthermore, its phases (slow start, congestion avoidance, fast retransmit) further increase the variability of both delay and jitter. Hence, TCP can by no means be used for real-time communications.

- **UDP:** UDP does not present the previous limitations, but is equally unsuited. Its purely best-effort nature brings with it a lack of mechanisms to detect packet loss, out-of-order packet delivery and unbounded delay and jitter. Hence, it is also not suitable for periodic real-time packet transmission.

RTP brings the solution by complementing UDP's weaknesses while travelling on top of it. Basically, RTP encapsulates one or more voice samples and adds a sequence number and a timestamp to it. With the sequence number, data loss can be detected (although no retransmission will be requested, obviously) and those packets skipped during retransmission. Furthermore, the sequence number also guarantees in-order playback. The timestamp permits adequate playback synchronization, even in the presence of packet loss, as well as delay and jitter calculation for QoS measurement purposes. It is precisely its simplicity, while covering UDP's main weaknesses, what has permitted RTP's widespread success.

RTCP, on the other hand, provides extra information at the cost of more complexity. But since RTCP does not transport user data, it can accept non-real-time delay and processing times. RTCP packets contain so-called *reports*, which contain the actual session QoS information, from the point of view of both the sender and the receiver. This information includes:

- A timestamp, for clock synchronization purposes, as well as delay and jitter calculations.
- The sender's and receiver's packet and octet count, for integrity checks.
- The percentage as well as the absolute number of packets lost during the session.
- The highest sequence number received to help detect lost data.
- The inter-arrival jitter.

These packets are periodically interchanged among the partners; however, in order not to waste too much capacity on them, their transmission frequency is calculated so that RTCP traffic does not exceed 5% of available capacity. With this information, as has been previously stated, both the sender and the receiver can obtain an accurate picture of the session's QoS state. However, it must be recalled that neither RTCP, nor RTP take any correcting measures, since this could take too much time and/or be inadequate for a specific application. Hence, it remains solely the application's responsibility to redress any quality degradation.

A last question still arises: How can QoS for VoIP traffic be defined? Can the user's perception of "good" or "bad" quality be accurately mapped to technical parameters like delay, jitter or packet loss? This has proven an elusive goal, and the next section reviews the most common indicators used to bridge that gap.

Measuring Quality for VoIP

Call quality can be measured using subjective testing or instrumental monitoring. In subjective testing methods, humans are asked to evaluate the quality of the service according to a standardized process and give a score, typically from 1 to 5 (MOS score). These kinds of tests are time consuming because many users have to be asked. That is why in the last few years more efforts have been focused on instrumental measurement tools, like the ITU-T E-Model. Both methods are described briefly here.

Mean Opinion Score (MOS)

One of the most used tools for measuring voice quality is the mean opinion score or MOS. Defined in ITU-T P800 standard (1996), MOS is a tool based on subjective testing, where a number of users are asked to listen to a voice sample (corresponding to a particular codec) and give a score for the received media as they perceive it after the transmission. The MOS score, calculated from the average of the users' scores, ranges from 1 for an unacceptable call to 5 for an excellent call. A typical range for acceptable Voice over IP quality would be from 3.5 to 4.2.

The relationship between the MOS score and some of the most used codecs, can be seen on the codec Table 1 (taken from Cisco Technical Document 7934 (2006)).

Although it may be the best known voice quality tool, MOS is difficult to implement since human intervention is necessary (although estimates of voice quality can be made by automatic test systems). That is why ITU-T proposed a few years ago the e-model.

E-Model

The e-model is a planning tool for estimating the overall quality of a telephone network. ITU recommendation G.107 (G.107, 2000) introduced it with the objective to determine a quality rating that incorporated the "mouth-to-ear" characteristics of a speech path. The output of an e-model calculation is a single scalar, called R factor, derived from delays and equipment impairment factors. Once the R factor is obtained, it can be mapped to an estimated MOS.

The R factor can be obtained through the following expression:

$$R = Ro - Is - Id - Ie + A \qquad (1)$$

where Ro represents the basic signal-to-noise ratio (SNR), Is represents the combination of all impairments which occur simultaneously with the voice signal, Id represents the impairments caused by delay, Ie represents impairments caused by low bit rate codecs, the so-called "equipment impairment factor", and A is the advantage factor, that corresponds to the user allowance due to the convenience in using a given technology. This means that a telephone call quality is judged different by a user if the advantage of access and use of this technology can recompense for the lower quality (cellular phone users do not expect the same call quality as in PSTN calls).

Cole and Rosenbluth (2001) give the following simplified expression for calculating the R-factor for VoIP, taking into account that many of the factors of the previous expression can be simplified to a default number:

$$R = 94.2 - Id(Ta) - Ie(codec, loss) \qquad (2)$$

where Id is a function of the absolute one-way delay (Ta) and Ie is, in short, a function of the used codec type and the packet loss rate. In Table 1, the Ie values of some of the standard codecs and considering 0% packet loss can be seen, as provided in Appendix I of G.113 ITU recommendation (G.113, 2001). For further details of the Ie/Id calculation the reader should refer to the work of Gardner, Frost, and Petr (2003).

After calculating the R factor, the equivalence between R and MOS can be determined as follows:

For R < 0 : MOS = 1
For 0 < R < 100 : MOS = 1 + 0.035 R + 7x10-6 R(R-60)(100-R)
For R > 100 : MOS = 4.5

Table 1. Codecs and their MOS score

Codec	Bit Rate (Kbps)	MOS score	Ie (0% loss)
G. 711	64	4.1	0
G.726	32	3.85	7
G.729	8	3.92	11
G.723.1	6.3	3.9	15

This method of obtaining the MOS value through the R-Factor equivalence, has the advantage of permitting a real-time calculation of the actual instant quality of service perceived by the user, as opposed to a fixed MOS value depending on the codec used and not taking into account factors that may vary during the call. Hence, the R-Factor will be used for obtaining the MOS in the simulation experiments presented later in this chapter, using the procedures described above with the loss/delay data gathered from the RTCP reports.

IEEE 802.11 Background

The success of the IEEE 802.11 technology is motivated by the similar nature, simplicity and mode of operation of the successful ethernet-based LANs. In a WLAN, the mobile stations (STAs) share the channel using a random access CSMA/CA (with carrier avoidance) MAC (medium access control) protocol (which is the wireless version of the wired well-known CSMA/CD). Moreover, new mechanisms such as an ARQ (Automatic ReQuest) protocol and an adaptive PHY layer, which are able to adapt to the channel conditions, are introduced in the IEEE 802.11 protocol stack to mitigate the channel impairments.

In the next subsection, a short description of the DCF (distributed coordination function) protocol (Std 802.11, 1999) and the EDCA (enhanced distributed channel access) (Std 802.11e, 2005) traffic differentiation enhancements are presented

in order to help the reader to understand the rest of the chapter. Here, a comprehensible justification of the reasons for the low VoIP capacity (in terms of maximum number of simultaneous active calls) is exposed.

The DCF MAC Protocol

The IEEE 802.11 layer-2 is split in two sub-layers: (i) the LLC (link layer control), which basically implements a packet fragmentation function (in order to adapt the packets to the packet length required by the MAC/PHY layers) and the ARQ (Automatic ReQuest) protocol, that tries to mitigate the high channel-error rates by retransmitting the erroneous packets, and (ii) the MAC sub-layer, which governs the transmission attempts over the channel between the set of active STAs and access point (AP).

The DCF (distributed coordination function) is based on the CSMA/CA MAC protocol. It uses a random binary exponential back off (BEB) algorithm in order to schedule the channel transmissions. The BEB algorithm is designed to provide long-term fairness in terms of the service received by each node, distributing the channel capacity among all the active nodes. For a clear and detailed explanation of the DCF protocol, including its performance analysis, refer to Bianchi (2000).

Basically, to schedule a packet transmission, each STA has a counter, which is decreased by one at each SLOT time (period of time that the channel

Table 2. Equivalence of R-factor and MOS score

User Opinion	R Factor	MOS score
Very Satisfied	90-100	4.3-5.0
Satisfied	80-90	4.0-4.3
Some Users Satisfied	70-80	3.6-4.0
Many Users Dissatisfied	60-70	3.1-3.6
Nearly All Users Dissatisfied	50-60	2.6-3.1
Not Recommended	0-50	1.0-2.6

is detected idle). Notice that the BEB counter is not decreased if other STAs are transmitting as the channel is detected busy. When the counter reaches its lower value, the packet is transmitted over the channel. If all goes well, the packet will be received by the destination node, which answers with a level-2 ACK frame to confirm its correct reception. However, if two or more nodes transmit at the same SLOT time, a collision occurs and the packet must be retransmitted until the maximum number of retransmissions is reached. The same treatment is done if the packet is received erroneously, as in both cases no ACK is transmitted (this is of crucial importance when a rate adaptation mechanism based on monitoring the correct packet transmission is used, as there is no way to differentiate between a collision and channel errors). Therefore, there are several factors, which actually increase the time required to transmit successfully a packet: the time spent in back-off, the time spent in re-transmitting the packet after a collision or a channel error and the time required to transmit the corresponding ACK to each transmitted packet. Thus, the time required to transmit a packet using the transmission rate r from the point of view of the node j is:

$$X_j(r) = \left(M_j - 1\right)\left(EB_j \cdot \gamma_j + T_{c,j}\right) + \left(EB_j \, \gamma_j + T_{s,j}(r)\right)$$

(3)

where $T_{c,j}$ is the duration of a collision (which depends on the set of data rates used by the colliding STAs), M is the average number of transmissions which require a single packet, EB is the average number of slots at each transmission and γ is the average time between two back-off counter decrements. The T_s value is the time spent in transmitting a packet and the corresponding ACK, so:

$$T_{s,j}(r) = \left(H + \frac{H_{mac} + L_{data}}{r}\right) + SIFS + \left(H + \frac{L_{ack}}{R^b}\right) + DIFS$$

(4)

where H is the time to transmit all the PHY headers (preambles) at 1 Mbps, r is the data rate used from the set of data rates R and R^b is the basic rate used by all STAs. Notice the dependence of T_s with the packet length itself but also with the data rate used. For further details about these equations refer to Bellalta, Oliver, Meo, and Guerrero (2005).

Due to its distributed access, it could be proved that $X(n) > n \cdot X(1)$, where $X(i)$ is the average service time with i nodes active. This means that the useful bandwidth decreases faster than linearly to the number of nodes.

A Multi-Rate PHY Layer

When a packet from the LLC/MAC layer is ready to be transmitted, it is sent to the PHY layer, where the bits are encoded and modulated to make possible their transmission over the wireless channel. Each MAC protocol data unit (MPDU) is transmitted at a specific rate from the set of available rates R which are obtained by combining a modulation $q \, \varepsilon \, Q$ and a channel codec rate $c \, \varepsilon \, C$, where Q and C are the set of available modulations and coding rates respectively for each STA and allowed at the BSS (basic subsystem set). The q modulation and c coding rate are announced in the PHY header (SIGNAL field), which is added to the MPDU to form the PHY protocol data unit (PPDU). The PHY header (PLCP preamble and the PLCP header) is always transmitted at the PHY rate, which is equal to 1 Mbps. Thus, the duration of that interval is equal to 192 μs. Other considerations, such as the use of the short preamble, are included in the 2003 revision of the IEEE 802.11b standard and in the IEEE 802.11a and IEEE 802.11g PHY specifications.

The use of a multi-rate PHY permits the increase of the WLAN communications range. Thus, the selection of a modulation and a codification rate satisfy the trade-off between the coverage area and the data transmission rate (e.g., when there are bad channel conditions, the transmission rate is lower than in cases when the channel conditions are good). The mechanism that selects the proper rate based on information about the channel state is called the link adaptation algorithm.

Liu and Lin (2005) show the range achievable for each rate. For example, considering the IEEE 802.11b DSSS specification, the 11 Mbps rate allows a range of about 50 meters from the AP and using the 1 Mbps rate the maximum distance from the AP is about 100 meters. Obviously, between 50 and 100 meters the other rates are scaled.

To select the transmission rate, the IEEE 802.11b standard specifies the use of the ARF (auto-rate fallback) mechanism (Std 802.11, 1999). This scheme decreases the transmission rate to a lower one when a certain number of consecutive transmitted packets are detected erroneous by missing their respective ACKs. It is worth mentioning that a performance anomaly exists when consecutive packets are not received correctly due to the occurrence of consecutive collisions. This could cause an unnecessary change to a lower transmission rate, since the cause in this case is not the bad channel conditions. Although it is very improbable, the use of low CW_{min} values in the new EDCA standard for real-time traffic (for example, VoIP) makes this a non-negligible problem.

In terms of BSS performance, the use of multiple rates in the same cell introduces an interesting unexpected result: *STAs using low rates harm STAs using fast rates* (Heusse, Rousseau, Berger-Sabbatel, & Duda, 2003). This is due to the higher channel occupancies caused by the use of slow rates (as the application data packet length remains equal). For example, with VoIP calls, STAs transmitting packets from a slow call have a higher channel occupancy than STAs transmitting at high rates, which reduce the number of packets that can be transmitted each second, increasing the packet losses and the packet transmission delay and jitter.

To give a simplified but understandable example, let us suppose that we have two nodes,

both transmitting at a data rate r. If we assume that both nodes use the same packet size L then the time each of the nodes will occupy the shared channel will be $T_s \approx L/r$. If now one of the nodes starts transmitting at lower rate r' then the time that this node will occupy the channel changes to $T_s' \approx L/r'$ where $T_s < T_s'$. Occupying the shared medium for a longer period of time means less available transmission time for the fast node resulting to less number of total packets transmitted during the same period of time, even though the fast node does not perceive any change in its channel conditions. Figure 5 presents this example; in the first case (a) both nodes transmit an equal number of 3 packets each, while in case (b) when one node starts transmitting at a lower rate the number of transmitted packets change to 2 for both the fast and the slow node.

This effect reduces the total saturation point of the cell, causing high packet losses due to buffer overflows and thus severe problems on the quality of VoIP transmission, with the effect being more evident on the fast nodes.

Throughout the analysis here, it is assumed that the data rate used is the same in the uplink and downlink flows of the call, this is, the channel is assumed to be symmetric and the same SNR / FER is observed from the AP and the STA.

QoS Enhancements: EDCA

The IEEE 802.11e (Std 802.11e, 2005) standard was released at the end of 2005 to fulfill the requirements of traffic differentiation and QoS provision in WLANs. The DCF was enhanced with the EDCA (enhanced distributed coordination access), which is able to satisfy the requirement of traffic differentiation by classifying the packets in different categories, called access categories (ACs) and giving them different channel access priorities by considering different MAC parameters for each AC. In Table 3 the MAC parameters of each queue are shown.

Figure 5. Transmission when (a) both nodes use R rate and (b) when one node changes to rate R

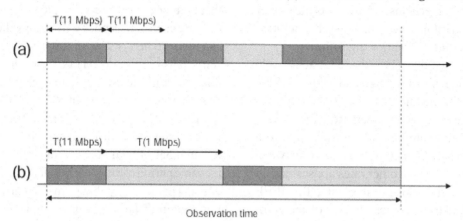

Table 3. Default EDCA parameter set element parameter values for the 802.11b specification

AC	AIFSN$_j$	TXOP$_{limit}$ (ms)	CW$_{min,j}$	CW$_{max,j}$
0 (Background: BK)	7	0	31	1024
1 (Best effort: BE)	3	0	31	1024
2 (Video: VI)	2	6.016	15	31
3 (Voice: VO)	2	3.264	7	15

The combination of these MAC parameters provides a higher priority to access the channel for the real-time traffic (low CW$_{min}$, high TXOP$_{limit}$ for the AC_VO queue). Conversely, the data ACs suffer from a low priority to access the channel (high CW$_{min}$ values and high AIFS values). Thus, EDCA is able to provide protection for the real-time traffic, increasing the number of possible VoIP calls in a WLAN hotspot, especially when the channel is shared between VoIP calls and best-effort (TCP) traffic.

Furthermore, the IEEE 802.11e standard provides other mechanisms to make more efficient the channel transmission. For example the consideration of different ACK policies, with the new Block ACK (a single special ACK packet can acknowledge several frames) and the No ACK, which avoid the transmission of ACKs for services where the information on if a packet has been received is unnecessary as the packet will not be retransmitted (for example, in VoIP applications).

The IEEE 802.11e standard also provides the basic interfaces and information to implement a call admission control (CAC) mechanism on top of the EDCA. The CAC is responsible to decide whether a new flow could be accepted or not. However, the standard does not specify how to implement it, being one of the current open problems in the deployment of a successful VoIP service in WLANs.

Voice Capacity in Hotspot WLANs

The WLAN capacity for VoIP calls has been a hot topic on research for years as VoIP is expected to be one of the killer applications, which boost the public WLAN use (Garg & Kappes, 2003; Hedge, Proutiére, & Roberts, 2005; Hole & Tobagi, 2004).

As a reference to compute the VoIP capacity in WLANs, Hole et al. (2004) present an upper limit (but enough accurate, with +0/1 VoIP call error from the exact maximum number of calls) for the number of simultaneous calls in an infrastructure WLAN. This upper limit is shown in Equation 5:

$$N = \left| \frac{1}{\frac{B}{L}\left[2\left(T_s(r) + \left(T_{slot}\frac{CW_{\min}}{2} \right) \right) \right]} \right| \quad (5)$$

where T_s was introduced in Equation 4, B / L is the rate of VoIP packets from the source and T_{slot} is the duration of an empty SLOT.

The VoIP capacity provided by this upper limit for different VoIP codecs is shown in Table 4 (considering the IEEE 802.11b MAC parameters as defined in the standard of 802.11 (1999)). An interesting first observation is that the number of calls does not increase/decrease proportionally to the data rate. For example, notice that with the G.726 codec at 11 Mbps only 10 calls could be active simultaneously. Then, it was expected that at 1 Mbps, the result would be a maximum number of 1 or 2 calls, but up to 5 calls could be in fact accepted. This is caused by the previously commented effect: *the channel bandwidth decreases sub-linearly with the number of nodes.* In this case, as the access (contention) overheads are not considered, it is caused mainly by the transmission of layer-2 ACKs that are always sent at the minimum rate (1 Mbps). Thus, a second observation is that the proportional part of time spent transmitting ACKs increases with the data rate.

Notice that, the upper limit used has not considered the extra contention overhead in spite of showing very accurate results. Therefore, for the case VoIP traffic, the channel contention should not be considered as the main cause of the low capacity and it has to be focused in the protocol overheads. In that sense, EDCA provides the No ACK policy to avoid the transmission of ACKs for packets that will not be retransmitted, such as the VoIP packets. The results without the time spent in the ACK transmission are also plotted in Table 4, showing clearly the achieved gain. However, it is still not clear how to use the No ACK policy combined with the ARF scheme, as there is no feedback about the correct or erroneous reception of the transmitted packet.

Other considerations for the low VoIP capacity in WLANs, such as the downlink starvation, the multi-rate channel and the simultaneously coexistence with TCP flows are viewed shortly next.

Downlink Starvation

Considering the case of VoIP traffic from several calls, the AP has to carry the same traffic as all active STAs together (Bellalta & Meo, 2006). However, it uses the same rules as the STAs to access the channel, so it tends to be saturated rap-

Table 4. Maximum number of calls for each data rate

	Standard ACK				No ACK			
	Data Rates (Mbps)				Data Rates (Mbps)			
VoIP codec	11	5.5	2	1	11	5.5	2	1
G.723.1	16	15	13	11	34	31	24	18
G.729	10	10	9	7	22	20	16	11
G.726	10	9	7	5	20	17	11	7
G.711	9	8	6	4	18	14	8	5

idly. EDCA allows to mitigate this effect by using *AIFS*-1 values at the AP compared with the values of the STAs, so given them a higher priority to access the channel. See the work of Cano, Bellalta, and Oliver (2007), where some elaborated EDCA parameters tuning algorithms, which contribute to mitigate this effect are evaluated.

Multi-Rate Channel

In Table 4, it is assumed that all active calls use the same data rate. However, what would happen if some calls change their rate to a lower one? For example, choosing the G.711 codec, at a data rate of 11 Mbps, a maximum number of 9 calls can perform satisfactorily. However, if some of those active calls change to a lower rate, the maximum number of acceptable VoIP calls is reduced as the new system state will become unfeasible. This is due to the higher relative bandwidth required by the calls, which have changed to a lower rate, this is, the sum of all relative bandwidths will exceed the channel capacity and all calls start to suffer from congestion.

The relative bandwidth is the real channel bandwidth required by a traffic flow. It is related with the VoIP codec and the instantaneous transmission rate used. VoIP calls using low transmission rates will require higher relative bandwidth values to transmit the same amount of voice data than calls using higher transmission rates.

Therefore, the VoIP capacity depends on the instantaneous set of rates used, fluctuating between the minimum number of active calls (at the lower transmission rate) and the maximum capacity (at the highest transmission rate). To approximate the maximum number of calls when multiple rates are used simultaneously, the upper limit shown in Equation 6 is extended to:

$$2\left[\sum_{r \in R} N_r \left(\frac{B}{L} T_s(r) + T_{slot} \frac{CW_{min}}{2}\right)\right] \leq 1 \qquad (6)$$

where N_r is the number of VoIP calls at rate r, B/L is the rate of VoIP packets from the source and $T_s(r)$ is the duration of a VoIP packet transmitted at rate r. Equation 6 reduces to Equation 5 for a single transmission rate. For example, consider the possible combinations of VoIP calls using the G.711 codec and two rates: 11 Mbps and 1 Mbps. The feasible states (n_{11}, n_1) are shown in Figure 6. Notice that nine simultaneous active calls are possible if all of them use the 11 Mbps data rate. However, a single rate change of one of the active calls to the 1 Mbps data rate reduces the maximum number of calls to 7 calls at 11 Mbps and 1 at 1 Mbps. Thus, to guarantee the system stability there are two options: i) drop the call which has changed to the lower rate or ii) drop one of the calls which continue using the data rate of 11 Mbps. Notice that when the system is unstable no call performs satisfactorily.

Simultaneously Presence of TCP Flows

A TCP flow is characterized by trying to send packets continuously until all the data associated have been transmitted. This behaviour makes a node with a TCP flow active a fierce competitor for the channel resources as it will try to use all the shared bandwidth. Bellalta, Meo, and Oliver (2007b) show how, with only few downlink or uplink TCP flows, the impact over the VoIP capacity is critical since with only 1-2 uplink/downlink flows all VoIP calls are starved.

Clearly, EDCA mitigates that problem, by providing traffic prioritization at each node (when a VoIP and TCP packets compete for access to the channel, the probability to gain the contention for the VoIP packets is higher) and therefore it provides a good solution to integrate data and VoIP traffic in the same Hotspot. Moreover, EDCA allows to modify its MAC parameters in running time, so adaptive solutions could be used in order to improve simultaneously both the VoIP protection and the TCP performance (Cano et al., 2007).

Figure 6. Maximum 11Mbps/1Mbps calls active

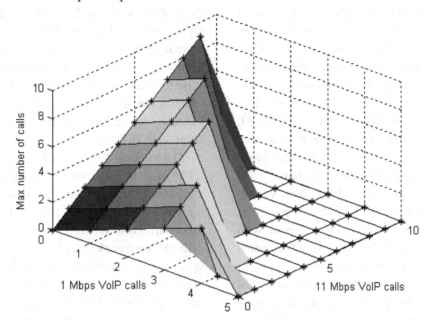

COPING WITH THE MULTI-RATE EFFECT

Although the transmission of VoIP over WLAN suffers from the problems above-mentioned, at the same time wireless 802.11 networks are becoming more and more popular, both for home-use and for hot-spots/public places, with their extension foreseen to grow during the following years.

The need for some new ideas and solutions has led the research community to study in more detail admission control techniques and capacity evaluation of such networks. One big step ahead was the evolution of the WLAN standards to the newer 802.11e, which can guarantee some minimum QoS for multimedia traffic offering different priorities for different service types, as analyzed in section 1.2.3. Nevertheless, few effort has been placed on the Link Adaptation mechanism, which remains a problematic point for voice traffic having the effects mentioned in section 1.3.2 and thus still demanding efficient solutions.

Main Approaches

There have been different ideas on how to cope with the problems that the Link Adaptation mechanism of 802.11 causes on multimedia traffic. One big group of research papers propose to change the base of the problem, the link adaptation mechanism itself. This can be done by trying to avoid unnecessary rate changes or by choosing the new rate based on more elaborated criteria, different for each type of traffic.

An example of this idea is the implementation of Haratcherev, Taal, Langendoen, Lagendijk, and Sips (2005). The decision on *when* to change rate and *which* new rate to choose is usually made by a control algorithm, based on information about the current link conditions, normally in the form of statistics-based feedback. This type of information is very slow especially in fast changing situations, so a new control algorithm is proposed, which adding signal-to-noise ratio (SNR) information can achieve less oscillation in rates. In a similar way, Kim, Tode, and Murakami

(2005) propose a new service-based rate control algorithm as an addition to the already existing throughput-based and error-based methods. The service-based algorithm can select which of the two other algorithms is more appropriate according to the service type of transmission data (best effort or real-time), on a per packet basis. Another idea can be seen in the work of Huang, Chindapol, Ritcey, and Hwang et al. (2006), where the authors try to deal with the "false link adaptation" problem, which means perform link adaptation when there is no actual need for it. What they propose is to classify packet errors (congestion-provoked or due to wireless channel error) and react with link adaptation only when necessary (i.e., when they fall into the second category).

In general these methods can optimize the link adaptation process but they normally need and/or propose changes on the core PHY/MAC layers of the 802.11 protocol. For this reason, on the opposite side there are those who propose the adaptation of the traffic parameters to the new rate, leaving the link adaptation process untouched. When talking about voice traffic parameters this most of the times is translated to adapting the codec and/or the packetization interval of the voice stream. Experimental studies like the ones of Hole et al. (2004), Wu, Tseng, and Lee (2005) and Cai, Xiao, Shen, and Mark (2006) have pointed out the important role of these two parameters on increasing the total capacity of a wireless cell. Based on this fact many works on how to best solve the link adaptation problem have turned their focus on adjusting these parameters.

This is for example the basic idea behind the works of McGovern, Murphy, and Murphy (2006a) and Trad, Ni, and Afifi (2004). The authors in the first refer directly to the link adaptation problem and the change of voice codec is applied only to the node that suffered the rate change. The new codec is chosen based on metric called channel occupancy time. A more simple solution would be to drop the problematic call, as suggested in another work of the same authors (McGovern,

Murphy, & Murphy, 2006b), which would solve the problem very fast but with a negative effect on the user's opinion of the network QoS. The second study on the other, tries to deal with congestion in general and the proposed transcoding is performed by a centralized element to all calls entering the cell. The choice of the new codec is based on round trip time information obtained from the RTCP reports.

The work presented by Chen, Lee, and Tseng (2006) uses the same basic idea (adjusting codec and packetization interval) in order to solve capacity problems mainly occurring due to the handoff procedure. By lowering the quality of some of the calls in the network can adjust the distribution of resources among existing calls and permit others to enter. In fact, this is an example of how a codec adaptation algorithm can work together with a call admission control technique in order to provide a more efficient use of the network resources.

An extension of the previous methods is to focus on multi-rate codecs, like the GSM adaptive multi-rate (AMR) (ETSI, 1998), originally designed and implemented for GSM/3G networks to cope with the channel errors characterizing these environments. The philosophy behind these codecs is to lower the codec rate as a reaction to channel conditions when the interference increases, enabling more error correction to be applied to guarantee a good speech quality (MOS) for voice calls, as mentioned by Lundberg, de Bruin, Bruhn, Hakansson, and Craig (2005) and Qiao, Sun, Heilemann, and Ifeachor (2004) among others.

Nevertheless, few bibliographies exist actually on using this codec on 802.11 networks. Servetti and De Martin, (2003) have proposed the use of the narrowband AMR for speech transmission over 802.11 WLAN networks, to change the codec rate by using shorter or larger voice packets (i.e. lower or higher bitrate), according to channel conditions. The results obtained show a big improvement comparing to a constant bit rate approach. However, in the scenario under test they refer to bad channel conditions to the ones perceived individually on each STA's channel caused by factors such as noise, fading and interference. This differs from the multi-rate channel effect, where the behaviour of other nodes (which change from *fast* to *slow* rates) is what impacts over the performance of the rest, without any channel change occurring on the fast nodes. It is quite probable then that, using the AMR codec under a multi-rate scenario, *all* mobile nodes would see the erroneous channel and change to a lower codec at the same time, so reducing the overall MOS more than necessary. So, to maximize the total MOS of the cell other solutions would be more adequate.

The Codec Adaptation Approach

The approach of the multi-rate problem presented next in detail follows the second idea of the ones previously mentioned: adapt the media transmission to the new rate. Between its main advantages is that of being a simple solution, that can be adapted to work in both centralized and distributed scenarios, with no new special server needed or modifications to the AP in the distributed case. It is based on the same simple concept that different codecs have different bandwidth needs without at the same time having an equivalent gap in the QoS they offer (in terms of MOS). Giving an example, while using the G.729 codec the bandwidth needs (8Kbps) decrease almost eight times compared with using the G.711 codec (64Kbps), the quality offered by the first codec is not eight times worse, since G.729 codec produces a MOS of 3.92, while the MOS when using G.711 is 4.1, both considered as satisfactory MOS results (see Table 1).

Another key idea behind this solution is its ability to help maintain the QoS of active calls, without interrupting or dropping them. While the main interest until now has fallen on different call admission control (CAC) techniques and on preventing congestion by restricting the incorporation of troublesome new calls *before* they join the network, the codec adaptation algorithm is focused on the calls *already* accepted at the network and how they can recover fast and without interruptions from a change on the network conditions. As a matter of fact, the two techniques can be combined and work together in order to increase the performance of the network. However, since they are focusing on different problems, they can also act independently from each other. It is therefore believed that the codec adaptation algorithm can provide the part missing from the admission control mechanism. A proposal with

Figure 7. Information flow for the proposed solution

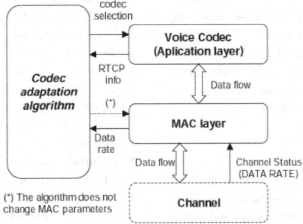

different policies combining the two techniques can be found in the work of Bellalta, Macian, Sfairopoulou, and Cano (2007a).

A Cross-Layer Codec Adaptation Algorithm Implementation

Following the above reasoning, one of the most effective solutions of the multi-rate problem on VoIP calls is to adapt the codecs of some of the active voice flows to the new cell conditions. The basic structure of this proposal can be seen in Figure 7 and the entire algorithm flow chart in Figure 10.

There are three factors that must be taken into consideration in this approach: the MAC layer, for information on the link adaptation changes, the RTCP reports, for real-time feedback on the voice quality, and the SIP protocol, for re-establishing the voice session with a different codec without interrupting the call. The main idea is to detect voice quality drops and react by evaluating the new cell conditions and proposing a new codec that is more efficient for it.

The RTCP packets, which include basic QoS metrics, such as delay, jitter and packet loss, as also the MAC layer, informing about rate changes the moment they happen, provide all the necessary information for this evaluation.

So, the basic codec adaptation algorithm is composed of three main phases: the *monitoring phase*, including the MAC monitoring function and the RTCP filtering function, the *adaptation phase*, where all the calculations and decisions on codec change are made, and the *recovery phase*, where any codec change decided previously is negotiated through SIP messages and the results of the change are measured.

Monitoring

The monitoring phase is a constant feedback gathering procedure, focusing particularly in two types of feedback: link rate changes and quality of service alarm signals.

The information over rate changes arriving from the 802.11 MAC layer is more immediate and can allow a faster reaction. Almost instantly after the rate change signal, a codec adaptation can be performed for the node that lowered its transmission rate (see Figure 8). Therefore, this method can be considered as a proactive reaction; although there is no quality decrease observed yet, knowing the negative effects of a rate change to the whole cell, a codec change is performed for the now slow node trying to prevent the predicted quality decrease. In the following adaptation phase, it can then be determined if the codec drop was helpful enough or if there is a need to adjust the codecs further. Apart from achieving a faster response, this method is also very important so as to maintain the fairness of the algorithm. In other words, the node that suffers the rate change is the first to change codec and therefore is the first to suffer the consequences of its rate change, while the rest of the nodes may avoid even noticing any alarm and thus the need to adapt to it. Note here that this procedure can work equally well both for rate increase and decrease, but since the rate decrease situation is more critical the analysis here focuses only on this case. In the case of a rate increase a codec increase would be proposed similarly to the decrease procedure, for better utilization of the network resources.

However, the second type of feedback is also necessary, since the codec change of just the slow node is not always enough. If this is the case then this will be detected from the RTCP packet filtering. In a VoIP session, when seeking quality of service metrics such as end-to-end delay or packet loss ratio, RTCP is the key. RTCP packets arrive to each of the nodes involved in a call session periodically, at a fixed interval time, usually set to 5 seconds (Schulzrinne et al., 2003). Filtering these packets, the previously mentioned QoS metrics can be obtained, necessary for calculating the R-factor of each flow using the E-model voice quality measuring tool as explained in section 1.1.5. The equivalence of this factor to the most known MOS

Figure 8. MAC monitoring process

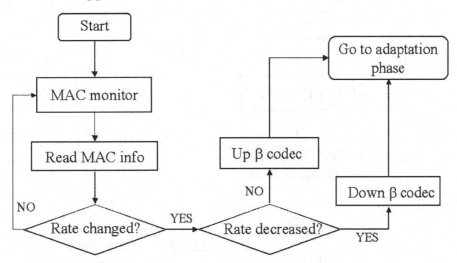

can provide a first QoS metric for the system and define a decision threshold; if R-factor value falls below 70 (equivalent to MOS 3.6) the quality of the voice flow is not satisfactory (see the R-Factor to MOS Table 2 and the algorithm triggers the adaptation phase for a new codec selection. This threshold, as also the thresholds used in the next phases of the algorithm, can be furthered tuned using more exhaustive simulations.

Adaptation

The adaptation phase is in fact a two-step procedure: evaluation and decision. The idea is to check if the alarm situation that initiated adaptation was due to a spurious error or if it still continues, and if so evaluate the extent of the problem and decide what to do in response. The duration of the adaptation phase must be as short as possible since it is in fact what determines the critical reaction time, between the alarm signals and the codec change. Therefore it must be limited by an adaptation timer, randomly chosen so as to also avoid that all nodes react and change codecs simultaneously, even if all of them perceive the alarm signals at the same instant. This way, the change of codec for more calls than necessary can

be avoided and the system is given some time to recover after every codec change.

In order to evaluate the current conditions efficiently, more feedback information is necessary. This can be obtain using again the RTCP packets data, only that this time and since the duration of this phase is limited, it is recommended to use an extension of the standard RTCP protocol, which allows to modify the interval between the transmission of two successive RTCP packets. This extension was proposed and evaluated by Ott, Wenger, Sato, Burmeister, and Rey (2004) and is referred as "immediate RTCP feedback." While in the RTP standard a minimum of 5 seconds interval is defined, using this extension the interval can be set to be lower (i.e., RTCP reports are sent more frequently), according to the needs of each scenario.

Although it may appear that the use of more (fast) RTCP packets would overload the system and thus further increase the problem, this is not true. An estimation of the total overhead that these packets would introduce at the network can be roughly calculated as follows: Based on a RTCP packet size of 90 bytes and setting the frequency of fast RTCP transmit at 1 second, the overhead provoked by the control traffic is very

Figure 9. RTCP monitoring process

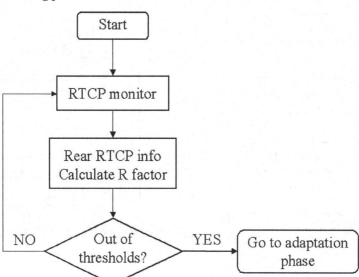

small compared with the data traffic of a VoIP call using G.711 codec (with packets of 160 bytes every 20 ms), with the control traffic occupying only around 1.3% of the total traffic generated per user, way less than the allowed 5% for control traffic according to the RTP/RTCP standard.

The frequency of the fast RTCP transmission in combination with the adaptation timer is set so as to allow the receiving of a feedback sample big enough for an efficient evaluation, while trying to minimize the total delay of the process at the same time. That means that if, for example, the RTCP interval is set to 1 sec, then the timer should be set to a random number higher than 3 sec, so as to have a minimum of N=3 fast RTCP packets (note that the numbers used here are indicative and can be further adjusted through simulations). At the same time, this leads to a lower bound of minimum 3 seconds for the delay of the evaluation phase.

After the adaptation timer expires and with the information collected during this time, the algorithm is able to decide which codec is the most appropriate for the node under the current conditions. To do so, it calculates the average of the R-factor (and from there the MOS score

equivalent), as also the average of packet loss and delay, critical voice quality metrics. The codec adaptation algorithm compares the average values as also the current values of the parameters after the timeout with a set of thresholds, chosen using the common values of permitted QoS parameters for an acceptable voice transmission (delay < 150ms, packet loss < 3%, R > 70). Having as input the result of this comparison and the node's current codec a new codec is chosen, using the following procedure (see also Algorithm 1):

a. In the case that the average value of the parameter is out of threshold then check its current value; if the current value is also out of threshold propose a codec of α steps lower in the codec ranking else propose a β steps lower codec. This way, even if the average performance of the call was not satisfactory during the fast RTCP monitoring time, if some other call has meanwhile changed codec and the system is beginning to recover (so the current value is above the threshold) then the call will suffer a smaller codec drop.

b. If on the other hand, both the average and the current value of the parameter are above the thresholds then there is no need to change codec.

This check is performed for each one of the three parameters (delay, loss, R) used in the evaluation and an average of the proposed codec of the three is chosen. Note that $\alpha > \beta$, with $\alpha = 2$ and $\beta = 1$ in the simulations, and that the codecs are ordered based on their bit rates, as shown in Table 1.

Algorithm 1: Adaptation phase.

while *timer* $\neq$ 0 **do**
  fastRTCP monitoring
  NowValue(param) $\Leftarrow$ current values of delay, loss, R
  for param $\Leftarrow$ delay, loss, R ***do***
    AvgValue(param) $\Leftarrow$ calculate average of parameter
  end for
  adaptTimer = adaptTimer - 1
end while
for *param* $\Leftarrow$ *delay, loss, R* **do**
  if *AvgValue(param) > paramThreshold* **then**
   if *NowValue(param) > paramThreshold* **then**
    change(param) $\Leftarrow \alpha$
   else
    change(param) $\Leftarrow \beta$
   end if
  else
   change(param) $\Leftarrow 0$ {No drop}
  end if
end for
changeTotal $\Leftarrow \Sigma(change(param))/3$
newCodec $\Leftarrow drop(currentCodec, changeTotal)$

Recovery

So far, the algorithm has analyzed the situation and taking into consideration all the feedback from the lower layers it has decided the most suitable codec to meet the needs of the current network conditions. Here, at the recovery phase, is where the negotiations for the new codec agreement are performed at the application layer. This can be easily done using SIP, the signalling protocol for control of the call session parameters. More specifically, the SIP re-INVITE method is used, with a structure almost identical to the initial INVITE message and with only difference the new codec proposal in the SDP audio codec negotiation field.

Hence, during the recovery phase the wireless node is asked to issue and send a SIP re-Invite message to the other end node, and re-negotiate through this the new codec. Depending on whether the other node accepts or not the new codec, the call continues normally or otherwise is dropped. In the case that the codec chosen as the most appropriate is lower than the lowest codec that a node can support, the easiest approach would be to drop the slow call in order for the others to continue with no problem. However, and depending on whether talking about a centralized or distributed implementation, there are other solutions in order to "save" the call. One idea, applying at the distributed implementation case, would be for the call to continue as it is during some stand-by time, without any codec change; If during this time some other node changes codec and the quality metrics show that the problem is solved then the call can continue successfully, otherwise the call will be then dropped. On the same line, for the centralized implementation, the AP could choose another call for codec adaptation if the call originally chosen cannot change any further. These adjustments can vary highly, as they depend on the specific needs of the implemented scenario in each case and on the trade off between capacity and quality/fast reaction and recovery. The details of the different variations of this solution are not considered here.

After the negotiations are over, the algorithm returns to the adaptation phase and continues to monitor the system using the fast RTCP messages and evaluate its performance after the change; if

Figure 10. Algorithm flow chart

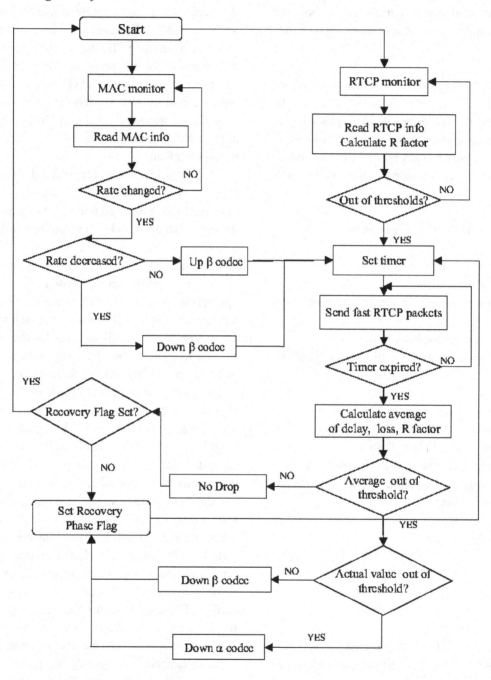

the parameters are higher than the upper thresholds then it can return to the normal monitoring phase, else it needs to perform another codec change until reaching acceptable QoS levels.

Implementation Issues (Delay)

An important parameter of any of the solutions focusing on VoIP traffic is the delay that they suppose and if this delay affects the call and is noticeable by the user. The delay during a call, translated into interruptions of the speech flow, should not be more than some hundred milliseconds so as not to be practically noticed by the user. When higher than this, the user will start to notice there is a communication problem. If this problem is solved fast enough from a human's perspective (in less than a few seconds), then it can be considered as an incidental interruption and will not affect much the rest of the communication. Otherwise, the user will most probably end up hanging up and terminating the call.

Therefore, the delay of the process mentioned above - and of any similar solution - is an important consideration when it comes to implementation. Although this delay is not as critical as in other environments, since the call is not interrupted during the process, it is essential to be able to recover from the network changes and their negative effects as fast as possible in order to avoid the user hanging up himself.

The total delay, from the moment the algorithm receives the first alarm signals until the moment that the system recovers can be represented from the following equation:

$$DelayTotal = Da + Db + Dc$$

where Da is the duration of the adaptation phase, Db the time needed for the SIP re-Invite/OK/ACK messages for the codec renegotiation procedure and Dc the general processing time of the algorithm. While Db, being 1.5 times of the round trip time, depends on variable factors, like the internet delay when working on a wired to wireless scenario, it is usually in the order of milliseconds, as is the Dc. So both these delays are negligible in comparison with the duration of the adaptation phase, and in extension the RTCP interval delay, which is what really increases the total process delay to the order of seconds. Remember that the adaptation random timer is also set depending on the frequency of RTCP packets arrival, which was

the reason for choosing the fast RTCP extension at the first place.

With the adaptation timer normally set to a value between 3 and 5 seconds, the delay should not be more than a few seconds (e.g., less than 5), which is acceptable from the point of view of human perception and taking into account that during this time the call is not dropped. From the simulations below and choosing a frequency of 1 second for RTCP interval, it can be seen that the delay is in fact not more than 3-4 seconds. Clearly, this delay can be minimized even more choosing a lower RTCP interval.

Distributed vs. Centralized Architecture

One of the main advantages of the algorithm previously presented is its flexibility when it comes to implementation. Since it is entirely based on the feedback from packets already existing and circulating in the network, like RTCP reports and MAC layer information, it does not need any specific modifications on the MAC layer, the Access Point or any of the nodes involved in the cellular architecture. In addition to this, it can be implemented both in a distributed and in a centralized mode, with minimum changes between the two versions and permitting higher flexibility depending on the specific characteristics of the working scenario.

The basic difference between the two implementations is the location of the core adaptation algorithm. In the distributed scenario, the algorithm is implemented on each node and each node is made responsible for monitoring and adapting its own state. The node, based on the information of its rate changes (from MAC) and its QoS feedback (from RTCP), should determine whether or not to change codec. On the contrary, in the centralized case, the AP is in charge of monitoring all calls, including the transmission rate and the codec used by each one. When a call passes from fast to slow then the AP must determine if there is a need for a codec change, how many calls must change codec and which ones of them in particular must change, so as to reach network stability again, based on the RTCP information exchange between the clients.

Therefore, the complexity and processing work is higher in the centralized version since the AP has to intercept all the RTCP packets in their way from one end to the other and calculate the parameters needed for the threshold comparison for all calls. Then the AP chooses the calls with the worst performance and decides according to the adaptation procedure, which calls to change and to which codec, giving more weight and priority in changing the slow calls first. The next step is to inform the nodes that there is the need to change codec, which includes suggesting to them to issue a SIP re-invite message for re-negotiating the codec with the other end. This is not a trivial process and is certainly more complex than in the distributed version, although some ideas on the interfacing issues of the AP with the nodes are given in section 3.

However, the centralized view of the problem as a whole gives much better results and more possibilities of achieving an optimal codec combination among the nodes. As it has been proved in the authors' own work (Sfairopoulou, Macián, & Bellalta, 2006), there is no need for all calls to change codec at the same time and the results are better when changing slow-rate calls than when changing fast-rate ones. This is due to slow-calls being the ones actually causing the problem, as seen in the problem statement. This priority on slow over fast calls is not possible in the distributed implementation, where each node will decide the action to be taken depending on its own limited view of the system, the call to detect first the QoS decrease will be the first to react, without knowing if there are other calls in the cell and the state (codec/rate) of each one. Additionally, since the control of the adaptation phase timer is not centralized, more nodes can coincide and change simultaneously codec, while

in the centralized implementation the AP can be set to wait during a random time between each codec change, which permits that less number of calls will have to change. But on the other hand, while the distributed approach may not be the globally optimal solution is easy to implement and it distributes the processing load of the algorithm.

Simulation results show that there is an improvement in the performance of the algorithm when used in its centralized version; less calls are changing codec, the packet loss percentage is almost zero and the overall MOS achieved is higher than in the distributed implementation. These results will be reviewed in the following section.

Performance Results

In order to test the performance of the codec adaptation solution explained above, extensive simulations was performed using the network simulator tool NS-2 (NS2, 2005). The description of the testing scenario as also the performance results are provided next.

Scenario Description

The results presented next are obtained using a hot-spot multi-rate scenario (Figure 11), with the network composed by one 802.11e (Std 802.11e, 2005) basic service set including N=9 wireless nodes and one Access Point connected to the wired network, acting also as a Proxy Server. A total number of nine bi-directional calls, established between one wired and one wireless client, are considered active during the simulations. The nodes start with a date rate of 11Mbps (fast-rate calls) and at predefined instants some flows change to 1Mbps data rate (slow-rate calls). It is assumed that all calls start with the G.711 codec, have the same duration, and change when needed to one of the lower bitrate codecs seen in Table 1.

Table 5. System parameters of the IEEE 802.11b specification

PARAMETER	VALUE	PARAMETER	VALUE
R_{data}	{11, 5.5, 2, 1} Mbps	R_{basic}	{11, 5.5, 2, 1} Mbps
R_{phy}	{1} Mbps		
DIFS	50 µs	CW_{min}	32
SIFS	10 µs	CW_{max}	1024
SLOT (σ)	20 µs	m	5
EIFS	364 µs	ACK	112 bits @ R_{basic}
RTS	160 bits @ R_{basic}	CTS	112 bits @ R_{basic}
MAC payload	[0, 18496] bits @ R_{basic}	-	
MAC header	240 bits @ R_{data}	MAC FCS	32 bits @ R_{data}
PLCP preamble	144 bits @ R_{phy}	PLCP header	48 bits @ R_{phy}
Retry Limit (R)	$R_S = 4$, $R_L = 7$	K (Queue length)	20 packets

Figure 11. Multi-rate WLAN scenario

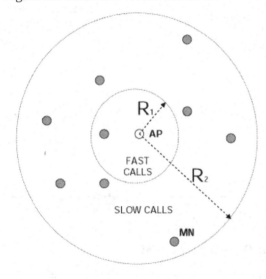

Monitoring frequency for the MAC monitor is f = 5 seconds, equal to the normal RTCP monitoring frequency. The fast RTCP transmission interval is one of the tunable parameters when using the extended RTCP version proposed by Ott et al. (2004) and is set here at δ = 1 seconds for a faster algorithm reaction time. It is assumed that all users support all codecs and there is no other traffic or other interferences in the wireless network. Each STA has a queue length of K = 50 packets. The values of the parameters set used can be found in Table 5.

The AP coverage area A and radius R is composed of two regions: FAST and SLOW areas. The FAST area, A_F is defined by a circle of radius R_1 and the rest is defined as the SLOW area, A_S (A=A_F + A_S). Mobile Nodes are uniformly distributed through the coverage area, so with probability P_F=A_F/A the STA is in the FAST region and with P_S=1-P_F the SLOW region.

Result Analysis

As explained previously in section 1.3.2, in a scenario with 9 calls, all of them using G.711 codec, when 2 calls drop to 1 Mbps rate the new state is not feasible. This can be translated in voice quality metrics as high delays and high packet loss ratio. The effect can be observed in the example presented here.

No Codec Adaptation Algorithm
When there is no codec control algorithm implemented in the network, observe the effect when two nodes start transmitting at a lower rate changing from 11 Mbps to 1 Mbps (at instants t = 95 sec and t = 105 sec on Figures 12, 13, 14 and 15. As McGovern et al. (2006a) mention *"the congestion in 802.11 is not gradual; the system has the a tendency to transition from an uncon-*

gested state delivering good performance to a congested state delivering very poor performance with the addition of little extra traffic" (p. 1). Due to this characteristic of the 802.11 networks, the observed packet loss percentage during the simulation increases almost instantly after the rate change happens to values reaching 90%. In fact, this result can be translated as a call drop since almost all packets are lost during a big part of the call. Moreover, the packet delay reaches very high values (of approx. 1 sec), as the queue

length of the AP becomes saturated (Figure 13). The congestion of the system, both in terms of loss and delay, is much more obvious in the AP, since it aggregates the traffic of *all* calls, which is the reason of the big difference observed on the results between uplink and downlink (as explained in section 1.3.1). In this case the AP acts as a bottleneck dropping queue packets and provoking a significant increase in packet loss ratio and delay. The same saturation can be also observed in the very low throughput obtained in Figure 15

Figure 12. Average aggregated packet loss percentage of VoIP flows in (a) Downlink (b) Uplink

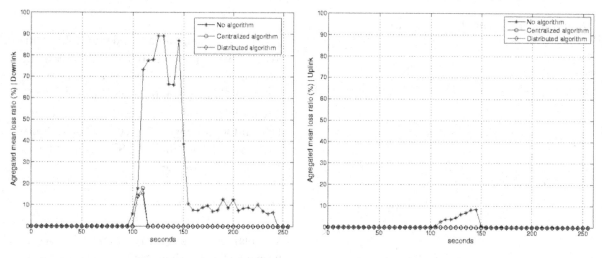

Figure 13. Average aggregated delay of VoIP flows in (a) Downlink (b) Uplink

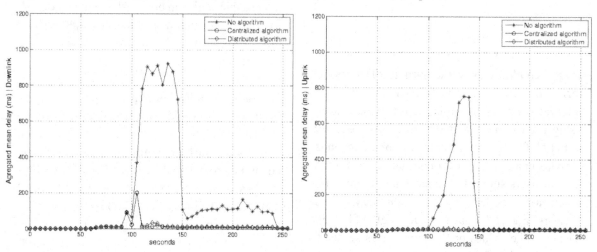

and the low quality perceived by the user in terms of MOS in Figure 14. This MOS, as calculated in real-time using the E-model, drops to values as low as 1, meaning communication breakdown according to the MOS standard definition.

The situation is corrected only when one of the two nodes that previously dropped to a lower rate changes again to a higher rate (11 Mbps) at simulation instant t = 145 sec. After this point, a decrease on delay and packet loss is observed, although they still remain higher than the desired for a correct VoIP transmission, with delay above

100ms and packet loss percentage of 10% in the downlink.

Distributed Implementation of the Codec Adaptation Algorithm

With the implementation of the codec adaptation algorithm in either of its two modalities (centralized and distributed), and since the codec of some of the calls is adjusted, the congestion level of the AP is significantly reduced, and as a result the effects of the multi-rate are barely noticed by the users. Looking at the distributed implementation

Figure 14. Average aggregated MOS obtained for VoIP flows in (a) Downlink (b) Uplink

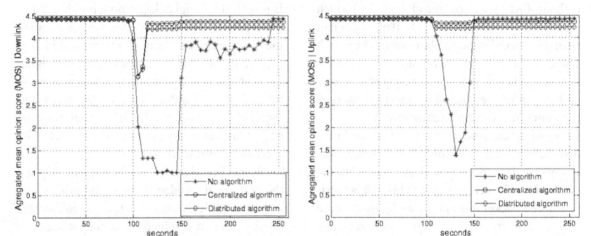

Figure 15. Average aggregated throughput of VoIP flows in (a) Downlink (b) Uplink

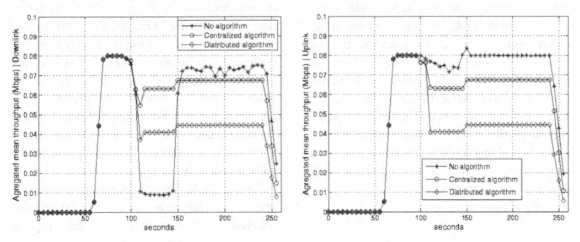

to begin with, almost instantly as the rate changes happen at t = 95 sec and t = 105 sec of the simulation, the algorithm takes action by first changing proactively the codec of the nodes that suffered the rate drop. The MAC information arrives as soon as the rate change takes place and the proactive codec change is very fast.

However, this change is not enough and the RTCP packets announce that the QoS alarm situation continues. The nodes that receive this alarm (in fact this could be *all* nodes) enter the adaptation phase and after the adaptation timer expires they decide whether to change or not the codec they use. Indeed, the throughput values of the Figure 15, indicate that only some nodes had finally changed codec; the average aggregated throughput is about 40Kbps (with overheads included) which is higher than the result would be if all nodes had changed, according to the bitrates used by each codec on Table 1. This is because, as the codec change of other nodes lowers the congestion levels bit-by-bit, after the adaptation timer the node may encounter the problem already solved.

So while the total throughput may be lower than before the rate changes, since some calls now use codecs that require less bandwidth, the system is no longer saturated. This can be verified in the packet loss and delay figures, where there is just one peak of high loss percentage reaching 20% and high delay of around 200 ms at the moment of the transmission rate changes and are corrected efficiently in less than 4 sec. The effect of the codec change observed in the packet loss ratio (Figure 12) agrees with the one expected; When using a lower bitrate codec, the offered load on the queue decreases and therefore less packet losses due to buffer overflow in the Access Point are observed. The results of MOS come to justify that the user perceived quality is maintained at very high levels, with only an instant drop at the moment of the rate change and until the nodes start reacting.

Centralized Implementation of the Codec Adaptation Algorithm

Even more impressive are the results of the centralized implementation. At the moment, the MAC monitoring receives the rate change signal, it lowers by one the codec of the affected nodes. Along with this proactive codec change, only one more codec change of a fast node's call was in fact needed during simulation, provoked from the RTCP monitoring, and the system recovers without noticing any of the negative effects mentioned above. Again, as it can be observed from the packet loss and delay figures, the peaks of high loss percentage and delay at the moment of the transmission rate change are corrected very fast. During the rest of the time packet loss is practically 0 and delay is no more than a few milliseconds. The average MOS value, indicating the user perceived quality is maintained in very high values around 4.3, as can be seen in Figure 14, with only an instant drop at the moment of the rate change and until the nodes start reacting. This shows a huge gain compared to the MOS with value less than 1.5 achieved when no algorithm is present.

By having overall control on the timing and the order of the codec changes and prioritizing more efficiently the change of the slow calls before the fast ones, it results that the total number of calls that need to change codec is lower than on the distributed implementation. Observe the total throughput obtained (Figure 15) that is higher than in the distributed mode, which is translated in more calls transmitting with higher bit rate codec. This is because since the slow calls are the ones blocking the others, it is more efficient to lower more the codec of these calls, apart from also being the most fair solution. Again, both delay and packet loss results adjust to the expected performance as in the distributed implementation and even slightly better.

To conclude, the performance of both the previous implementations, centralized and distributed, is satisfactory: no calls are dropped, the reaction of the algorithm and correction of the quality problems is quite fast and the packet loss is minimized which leads to high average MOS values. The difference in the performance between the two implementations is as expected, with the centralized giving better results since the Access Point has an overall control of the nodes and provides a more efficient combination of codecs. However, this implies higher processing effort for the Access Point and since the results of the distributed method are quite satisfactory, it can provide an easier and also effective alternative to the centralized version.

The results presented in this chapter were compared against an analytical model presented by Bellalta et al. (2005). The system behaviour was shown to match quite precisely the expected results, as foreseen by the analytical model.

OPEN ISSUES AND FUTURE GUIDELINES

This chapter has presented the impact of the multi-rate effect on VoIP communications in an 802.11 environment. Several proposed solutions have also been pointed out, namely the use of adaptive codecs, variations on the Link Adaptation mechanism and a cross-layer algorithm using MAC, SIP and RTCP information for the re-negotiation of codecs.

Along the line of this last option, a number of further enhancements can be drafted. On the one hand, an unaddressed issue regards the communication between the Access Point and/or SIP Proxy and the Mobile Station in order to interchange information about the cell state. Another open issue is which exact functionality should the Access Point take: Should every AP implement a mini-SIP proxy, in order to implement the algorithm and its associated workload? Should it intercept all traversing RTCP and SIP packets, in order to gain detailed information about current VoIP sessions, especially in the centralized case?

No definitive answers have been provided so far, but some directions can be pointed out.

First, as Camarillo, Kauppinen, Kuparinen, Ivars, and Res (2007) state, a possible mechanism for the interchange of information regarding codecs to be used for better overall session quality in the cell could be the SUBSCRIBE/NOTIFY mechanism of SIP (Roach, 2001). Although Camarillo et al. (2007) restricts its use to IMS, the basic idea is easily translated to the multi-rate scenario. Furthermore, by means of the same transactions the actual cell-wide quality could be communicated, in order for the STAs to take proactive actions in the distributed algorithm, if need be.

In principle, every AP needs not be a SIP proxy, if the algorithm is distributed and the existing SIP proxies would be multi-rate aware. Otherwise, it could certainly prove very advantageous, indeed necessary, that either every AP is co-located with a SIP proxy, or that a communication protocol exists between the two. This second options seems less feasible, for it involves strong modifications in existing proxy architectures and functionalities. The first option, however, only involves a further modification of the AP software, which must be adapted in any case to make it multi-rate aware.

The AP/SIP proxy certainly needs to be made aware of the session state in order for the algorithm to work. Hence, it must intercept all RTCP and SIP messages, or be made aware of their content (e.g., by means of SUBSCRIBE/NOTIFY messages).

An alternative avenue for further work is to consider if private extensions to the RTCP protocol, foreseen in the standard, would be useful. For example, RTCP provides application-specific reports that can be freely defined to convey extra information, relevant for a certain application only. It could be considered if certain real-time applications running on multi-rate environments, like for example online gaming, may take advantage of this to enhance their overall user experience.

However, one of the paramount characteristics of the algorithm presented in this chapter lies precisely in that it does not need any protocol extensions or modifications at any layer in order to work properly. This represents a huge practical advantage to achieve fast and effective deployment, as well as correct interworking with legacy equipment that is not multi-rate aware.

CONCLUSION

While VoIP will continue to grow in popularity and use, future wireless networks will have to come up with more efficient ways to handle traffic heterogeneity. Current WLANs introduce several performance impairments, which reduce the efficient usage of the wireless bandwidth. In this chapter, an extended analysis was performed on the problems encountered in VoIP flows due to the specific characteristics of the 802.11 WLANs, with special emphasis on the Link Adaptation mechanism and the multi-rate effect on the voice flows. The main causes of the problem as also various proposed solutions were examined and a codec adaptation algorithm was presented as an example implementation in more detail.

Having a first approach on how such a solution could work with the simulation results presented in section 2.5, such a deployment can be highly beneficial for voice traffic over multi-rate WLANs, with relative small additional cost. Further testing of this kind of solutions as also some experimental testbed and/or an enhanced AP implementation including the modifications mentioned in section 3 is highly recommended in order to have more sustainable results on the viability of these proposals and the other implementation issues that arise from them.

Adapting the parameters of the VoIP flows is the most discussed solution for coping with the multi-rate effects. The co-operation of such an algorithm with the Call Admission Control (CAC) mechanisms of 802.11 networks is the next important step from there. It has been pointed out how these two algorithms work on different

areas and how they can complement each other. As a matter of fact, any action taken by the algorithm could be communicated to the CAC so that it can immediately adapt to the new network conditions. However, the exact mechanism for the co-operation between the two modules are still to be determined.

REFERENCES

Bellalta, B., & Meo, M. (2006). Call admission control in WLANs. *Resource, Mobility and Security Management in Wireless Networks and Mobile Communications*. Auerbach Publications, CRC Press.

Bellalta, B., Macian, C., Sfairopoulou, A., & Cano, C. (2007a). Evaluation of joint admission control and VoIP codec selection policies in generic multirate wireless networks. *ITC/IEEE NEW2AN'07*, St. Pertersburg, Russia.

Bellalta, B., Meo, M., & Oliver, M. (2007b). VoIP call admission control in WLANs in presence of elastic traffic. *IEEE Journal of Communications Software and Systems, 2*(4).

Bellalta, B., Oliver, M., Meo, M., & Guerrero, M. (2005). A simple model of the IEEE 802.11 MAC protocol with heterogeneous traffic flows. In *IEEE Eurocon 2005*, Belgrade, Serbia, and Montenegro.

Bianchi, G. (2000). Performance analysis of the IEEE 802.11 distributed coordination function. *IEEE Journal on Selected Areas in Communications, 18*(3).

Cai, L., Xiao, Y., Shen, X., & Mark, J. (2006). VoIP over WLAN: Voice capacity, admission control, QoS, and MAC. *International. Journal of Communication Systems, 19*, 491-508.

Camarillo, G., & García-Martn, M. (2004). *The 3G IP multimedia subsystem (IMS): Merging the Internet and the cellular worlds*. John Wiley and Sons.

Camarillo, G., Kauppinen, T., Kuparinen, M., Ivars, I., & Res, E. (2007). Towards an innovation oriented IP multimedia subsystem [IP multimedia systems (IMS) infrastructure and services]. *IEEE Communications Magazine, 45*(3), 130-136.

Cano, C., Bellalta, B., & Oliver, M. (2007). A simple model of the IEEE 802.11 MAC protocol with heterogeneous traffic flows. In *IEEE Personal, Indoor and Mobile Radio Communications (PIMRC'07)*, Athens, Greece.

Chen, J., Lee, L., & Tseng, Y. (2006). Integrating SIP and IEEE 802.11e to support handoff and multi-grade QoS for VoIP applications. In *Proceedings of the 2nd ACM International Workshop on Quality of Service & Security for Wireless and Mobile Networks* (pp. 67-74). New York, NY, USA, ACM Press.

Cisco Technical Document 7934. (2006). *Voice over IP--Per call bandwidth consumption*. Updated February 2006. Retrieved from http://www.cisco.com

Cole, R., & Rosenbluth, J. (2001). Voice over IP performance monitoring. *ACM SIGCOMM Computer Communication Review, 31*(2), 9.

ETSI. (1998). *Digital cellular telecommunications system (Phase 2+): Adaptive multi-rate (AMR) speech transcoding (GSM 06.90)*. European Telecommunications Standards Institue (ETSI)

G.107 Rec. (2000). *The E-model, a computational model for use in transmission planning*. International Telecomunications Union (ITU-T) Recommendation.

G.113 Rec. (2001). *Transmission impairments due to speech processing*. International Teleccomunications Union (ITU-T) Recommendation.

Gardner, M., Frost, V., & Petr, D. (2003). Using optimization to achieve efficient quality of service in voice over IP networks. *IEEE Performance, Computing, and Communications Conference Proceedings* (pp. 475-480).

Garg, S., & Kappes, M. (2003). Can I add a VoIP call? *IEEE International Conference on Communications (ICC'03)*, Anchorage, Alaska, USA.

H.323 Rec. (1998). *H. 323, packet-based multimedia communications systems*. International Telecomunications Union (ITU-T) Recommendation.

Haratcherev, I., Taal, J., Langendoen, K., Lagendijk, R., & Sips, H. (2005). Automatic IEEE 802.11 rate control for streaming applications. *Wireless Communications and Mobile Computing, 5*(4), 421-437.

Hedge, N., Proutiére, A., & Roberts, J. (2005). Evaluating the voice capacity of 802.11 WLAN under distributed control. In *IEEE LAN/MAN Conference*, Megalo Arsenali, Chania, Greece.

Heusse, M., Rousseau, F., Berger-Sabbatel, G., & Duda, A. (2003). Performance anomaly of 802.11b. In *IEEE INFOCOM*, San Francisco, USA.

Hole, D. P., & Tobagi, F. A. (2004). Capacity of an IEEE 802.11b Wireless LAN supporting VoIP. In *IEEE International Conference on Communications (ICC'04)*, Paris, France.

Huang, C., Chindapol, A., Ritcey, J., & Hwang, J. (2006). Link layer packet loss classification for link adaptation. In *WLAN. 2006 40th Annual Conference on Information Sciences and Systems* (pp. 603-608).

Kim, J. O., Tode, H., & Murakami, K. (2005). Service-based rate adaptation architecture for IEEE 802.11 e QoS networks. In *IEEE Global Telecommunications Conference (GLOBECOM'05)*.

Liu, J. S., & Lin, C. H. R. (2005). A relay-based MAC protocol for multi-rate and multi-range infrastructure wireless LANs. *Wireless Personal Communications, 34*, 7-28.

Lundberg, T., de Bruin, P., Bruhn, S., Hakansson, S., & Craig, S. (2005). Adaptive thresholds for

AMR codec mode selection. In *IEEE 61ˢᵗ Vehicular Technology Conference (VTC 2005-Spring)*.

McGovern, P., Murphy, S., & Murphy, L. (2006a). Addressing the Link adaptation problem for VoWLAN using codec adaptation. In *IEEE Global Telecommunications Conference (GLO-BECOM'06)*.

McGovern, P., Murphy, S., & Murphy, L. (2006b). Protection against link adaptation for VoWLAN. In *Proceedings of the 15ᵗʰ IST Mobile and Wireless Communications Summit*.

NS2. (2005). *Network Simulator*, release 2.28. Retrieved from http://www.isi.edu/nsnam/ns/

Ott, J., Wenger, S., Sato, N., Burmeister, C., & Rey, J. (2004). *Extended RTP profile for RTCP-based feedback (RTP/AVPF)*. Internet Engineering Task Force. Technical report, Internet Draft.

P800 Rec. (1996). *P. 800: Methods for subjective determination of transmission quality*. International Telecommunications Union (ITU-T) Recommendation.

Qiao, Z., Sun, L., Heilemann, N., & Ifeachor, E. (2004). A new method for VoIP quality of service control use combined adaptive sender rate and priority marking. In *IEEE International Conference on Communications*.

Roach, A. (2001*). SIP-specific event notification*. draft-sip-events-00 (work in progress), July.

Rosenberg, J., Schulzrinne, H., Camarillo, G., Johnston, A., Peterson, J., Sparks, R., Handley, M., & Schooler, E. (1998). *SIP: Session Initiation Protocol*.

Schulzrinne, H., Casner, S., Frederick, R., & Jacobson, V. (2003). *RFC3550: RTP: A Transport Protocol for Real-Time Applications*. Internet RFCs.

Servetti, A., & De Martin, J. (2003). Adaptive interactive speech transmission over 802.11 wireless LANs. In *Proceedings of the IEEE International Workshop on DSP in mobile and Vehicular Systems*.

Sfairopoulou, A., Macián, C., & Bellalta, B. (2006). QoS adaptation in SIP-based VoIP calls in multi-rate 802.11 environments. In *ISWCS 2006*, Valencia, Spain.

Std. 802.11 (1999). *Wireless LAN medium access control (MAC) and physical layer (PHY) specifications*. IEEE Std 802.11.

Std. 802.11e (2005). *Wireless LAN medium access control (MAC) and physical layer (PHY) specifications; Amendment: Medium access control(MAC) quality of service enhancements*. IEEE Std 802.11e.

Trad, A., Ni, Q., & Afifi, H. (2004). Adaptive VoIP transmission over heterogeneous wired/wireless networks. *Lecture Notes in Computer Science, 3311* (pp. 25–36). Springer.

Wu, P., Tseng, Y., & Lee, H. (2005). Design of QoS and admission control for VoIP Services over IEEE 802.11e WLANs. In *National Computer Symposium*.

Chapter VI
Buffer Control Techniques for QoS Provisioning in Wireless Networks

Michael M. Markou
University of Cyprus, Cyprus

Christos G. Panayiotou
University of Cyprus, Cyprus

ABSTRACT

This chapter introduces the network buffer control techniques as a mean to provide QoS. This problem has been extensively studied in the context of wirelined networks; however, the proliferation of wireless networks and the introduction of multimedia applications has significantly changed the characteristics of the traffic mix that flows on the network. The objective of this chapter is to create a new methodology for automatically adapting the various buffer thresholds such that the network exhibits optimal or near optimal performance even as network conditions change. The behavior of the network (generally a discrete event system—DES) is approximated by that of a stochastic fluid model (SFM); then using infinitesimal perturbation analysis (IPA) we obtain sensitivity estimators of the performance measure(s) of interest with respect to the control parameter. These estimators are easy to compute using data observed from the DES's sample path. Finally, the computed estimators are used in stochastic approximation algorithms to adjust the thresholds.

INTRODUCTION

The emergence of advanced multimedia and other real-time applications has increased the demand for better than best effort services thus increasing the pressure on network providers to provide quality of service (QoS) guarantees. As a result, providers need to find ways to configure the parameters of their networks such that the application requirements are met. Over the past few years, QoS provisioning has been an active area of research resulting in the standardization of several architectures and protocols. Most of the past research assumed wirelined networks and that the dominant network traffic is based on the TCP (transport control protocol). However, the situation with current networks is changing. Wireless networks are becoming more popular and there is an increase of the UDP (user datagram protocol) based traffic (e.g., real-time protocol (RTP) for voice over IP). Thus, there is a need for new protocols and architectures that adopt the characteristics of the wireless channels and of the new traffic mix to provide the required QoS guarantees.

Management of different types of services such as video, voice, file transfer and email while provisioning at the same time the QoS level that each service demands is a challenging task; the analysis of large scale networks is excessively difficult and queuing theory is largely based in the Poisson assumption that does not capture the bursty nature of the realistic traffic. Furthermore, any proposed solution has to be scalable and easy to implement, adding the least possible overhead to the system's operation.

Integrated services (IntServ) is a proposed architecture for delivering QoS guarantees. In IntServ every application that requires some level of QoS guarantees has to make a resource reservation at each intermediate node along the path of the flow. The underlying protocol used for signaling to dynamically allocate resources in IntServ is the resource reservation protocol (RSVP), described by Braden et al. (1997). In this architecture, communication between a sender and a receiver is established only when every node (router) in the intermediate path between them has the necessary resources to support the QoS requirements of the new flow without affecting the QoS delivered to existing flows. A major drawback of this approach is that each router that supports a flow has to maintain information about it, making it difficult to keep track of all flows

when the network scales up. Furthermore, the overhead caused due to RSVP signaling reduces the utilization efficiency.

Differentiated services architecture (DiffServ) solves the problem by providing a framework for classification of the traffic and differentiation between the levels of service that each class will receive. In DiffServ each data packet is classified as belonging to one of a finite number of traffic classes (Blake et al., 1998). Routers in the network treat each incoming packet according to its class, enabling the protection of higher priority traffic against the lower priority, providing a more efficient and scalable traffic management mechanism. The treatment of each packet is achieved by mapping its traffic class to a per-hop behavior (PHB), which defines how a packet will be forwarded. The four available standard PHBs are: default, class-selector (Nichols et al., 1998), assured forwarding (Heinanen, Baker et al. 1999), and expedited forwarding (Jacobson et al., 1999). However, DiffServ architecture has also some disadvantages. DiffServ mechanism cannot provide individual connection QoS guarantees. Moreover, there are no clear incentives for applications to voluntarily mark their packets with a priority other than the highest. Policing mechanisms that downgrade an application's packets if it exceeds its allocated bandwidth exist however, for example, see (Heinanen & Guérin 1999; Heinanen & Guérin 1999).

In the last years, some researchers tried to combine the advantages of the two architectures and achieve an improved mechanism. A framework to apply IntServ over DiffServ was proposed by Bernet et al. (2000), whereas Zhang and Mouftah (2001) developed a sender-initiated resource reservation mechanism over a DiffServ network to offer end-to-end QoS. In addition, other frameworks that are more appropriate for wireless ad-hoc networks have been proposed, for example, flexible QoS model for mobile ad hoc networks (FQMM). FQMM is a hybrid service model that takes advantage of the per-flow granularity of IntServ and the services aggregation into a number of classes performed by DiffServ. Based on the assumption that the number of flows requiring per flow QoS guarantees is much smaller than the low priority flows, FQMM is designed to provide per flow QoS guarantees for the high priority flows while the lower priority flows are aggregated into a number of classes as in DiffServ. Although FQMM combines the advantages of both IntServ and DiffServ, it has also some unresolved issues such as the traffic classification policy, the amount of traffic that will be provided to each per flow service and the allotment of per flow or aggregated service for the given flow (Reddy et al., 2006).

In this chapter, we consider data traffic that is categorized in different priorities according to its *importance* to the end user, in order to meet the predefined QoS requirements. In the case of IntServ data traffic can be a data flow whereas in DiffServ architecture a class may consists of all packets with the same PHB. The end user may be anyone that uses the network's services at a higher network level (e.g., a client application that presents data sent from a video server or a taxi passenger that uses his or her cell phone to make a videocall while traveling on a highway). The importance of data traffic can be related directly to the application that generates it and thus the priority of each packet will be the same or it can vary between data generated from the same application. An example for the first case is voice over IP (VoIP) and file transfer applications; VoIP applications generate data with the same, strict requirements in delay whereas every FTP packet requires best effort with as low losses as possible. On the other hand, a single application may generate data with different levels of priority. For example, MPEG defines three different types of frames; the "I" frames carry more information than the "P" or "B" frames (Hoffman et al., 1998). Thus, a source may mark all packets that carry "I" frames with higher priority and the rational is that in case of congestion, a router may drop

packets that carry "P" or "B" frames increasing the probability that "I" frames will get through and thus the degradation of the quality of the received video will be minimized. Alternatively, the priorities may be set by a policing mechanism at the ingress gateway (Heinanen & Guérin 1999; Heinanen & Guérin 1999).

Several techniques for providing statistical QoS guarantees to multimedia streams can be found in the literature, each one designed to be applied in a different level of the OSI structure. For example, some higher-level techniques reduce the quality of the transmitted multimedia content in order to minimize the amount of information sent and, as a result, their transmission rate. On the other hand, some network-level techniques implement packet admission control policies in the network's buffers to control incoming traffic. The emphasis of this chapter is on the latter case (i.e., controlling the buffer of the intermediate nodes) even though similar concepts can be applied for controlling the transmission rate of the sender.

This chapter presents several buffer control techniques that have been proposed for QoS provisioning in wirelined and wireless communications. Furthermore, the chapter presents a methodology for automatically adapting the various buffer thresholds in ways such that the network exhibits optimal or near optimal performance. The methodology adopted is similar to the one in Panayiotou et al. (2004) and references therein. Namely, the behavior of the network (generally a discrete event system (DES)) is approximated by that of a stochastic fluid model (SFM). Using the SFM one can use infinitesimal perturbation analysis (IPA) (Cassandras & Lafortune, 1999) and obtain sensitivity estimators of the performance measure of interest with respect to the control parameter of interest (e.g., the buffer thresholds). The simplicity of these estimators allows us to compute them using data observed from the sample path of the real system. Finally, at the end of every observation period, the computed sensitivities can be used together with stochastic approximation type algorithms to adjust the thresholds and achieve optimal performance even as network conditions change. This chapter extends the results of (Panayiotou et al., 2004) by allowing for packet expiration due to QoS delay violations as well as by allowing for user mobility (in the context of cellular networks). The chapter is organized as follows: The next section presents relevant work on techniques for buffer management for QoS, namely tail drop and threshold policies as well as active queue management. The subsequent section proposes a framework that utilizes stochastic fluid modeling and infinitesimal perturbation analysis (SFM/IPA framework) for developing buffer control algorithms in communication systems. Finally, the chapter concludes with an outlook of future trends.

BACKGROUND

The degree of user satisfaction varies between the services that generate or receive the traffic and is reflected in their QoS requirements. Among the most common performance measures that need to be satisfied in a QoS agreement is the *average packet delay*, the *delay jitter* and the *packet loss probability*. A fundamental tradeoff in buffer management is the balance between packet delay and packet losses. On one hand, buffers are needed to limit packet losses and unnecessary retransmissions during bursts of traffic. On the other hand, large buffers may introduce excessive packet delays causing degradation of the provided QoS. Thus, providers need ways of managing their buffers to alleviate the effects of congestion and such that the best possible QoS is provided. Note that the buffer management problem is not static since it does depend on the current network conditions, which change over time. Thus dynamic mechanisms are in need that can adjust the buffer parameters such that the best possible QoS is always achieved. Due to the large size of the

current networks, the proposed solutions need to be scalable and distributed in nature.

Most of the past research on buffer management assumed that the medium of communication is reliable and that the individual flows respond to congestion by reducing their transmission rate (TCP based). In current networks, several paths exist that consist of at least a wireless link where the probability of packet error is significant due to poor transmission, interference, weather phenomena etc. As a result, in wireless networks, a packet drop does not necessarily imply congestion, which is the case in wirelined networks. This fact is very important, since until recently, all proposed solutions for congestion control assumed that a packet loss directly implies congestion and thus these solutions could not be applied in wireless networks. Furthermore, until recently, the overwhelming majority of traffic was based on TCP, which includes control mechanisms that limit the transmission rates of sources when the network becomes congested. The emergence of multimedia applications that use UDP based protocols (such as real-time transport protocol (RTP) and real time streaming protocol (RTSP)) is changing the mix of traffic that flows in the network, thus in current and future networks, it is expected that a significant number of flows will not respond to network congestion. RTP (Schulzrinne et al., 2003) defines a standardized packet format for delivering multimedia content (audio and video) over the Internet whereas RTSP is used in streaming media systems enabling the client to control the traffic transmission procedure of the streaming media server (Schulzrinne et al., 1998). RSVP can be used in conjunction with RTP to enhance the provided service in multimedia applications.

Buffer Management Techniques

A buffer management algorithm consists of two key mechanisms, the *backlog controller* that specifies *when* to drop a packet and the *dropper* that specifies *which* packet to drop.

The following paragraphs present some of the most popular queue (buffer) management and congestion control techniques. Most of these techniques that can be found in literature (e.g., (Labrador & Banerjee, 1999) discuss buffer management algorithms for IP and ATM networks) are similar to TCP in the sense that they use acknowledgments as a means to control the network traffic. The reason that the greatest portion of research work was targeted to improve TCP performance is because the overwhelming majority of the network traffic was TCP traffic. However, it is known that the share of multimedia traffic in the traffic mix grows continually, thus it is expected that both TCP and UDP traffic will coexists. Hence, more sophisticated strategies for buffer management are needed in order to improve the playback quality of the multimedia content, which is packetized in UDP-based packets.

Backlog Controllers

Random Early Detection

To overcome the reduced throughput problems that arise in TCP when network is highly loaded and improve system's performance Floyd and Jacobson proposed Random Early Detection (RED) (1993), a form of active queue management (AQM). AQM is a proactive mechanism used to inform users in a network about incipient congestions enabling them to react and avoid it.

The idea behind RED is to give indications about an oncoming congestion by probabilistically dropping (or marking) arriving packets. Users consider the packet loss (equivalently, the marked packet) as a result of congestion and reduce their sending rates; due to that, RED performs better with protocols that perceive packet losses as congestion indications (e.g., TCP). This technique can improve the end-to-end performance compared to other reactive mechanisms (which choose to drop packets only when congestion occurs) since many unnecessary packet drops are avoided. In addition, the synchronization problem is alleviated since

only a fraction of the flows drastically cut their sending rates. RED maintains an exponentially weighted moving average of the queue length:

$$Q_{avg}^{t+1} = (1-w) \cdot Q_{avg}^t + w \cdot Q^t \qquad (1)$$

where Q_{avg}^t is the weighted average of queue length at time instant t, Q^t is the queue length at time t and w is a weight factor commonly set to 0.002 (Floyd, 1997). When Q_{avg} exceeds a maximum threshold th_{max} all arriving packets are dropped. If Q_{avg} is between a minimum th_{min} and a maximum threshold th_{max}, packets are randomly dropped with a probability $p(Q_{avg})$ that increases linearly as a function of Q_{avg} up to a maximum value p_{max}, as described in Eq. (2) and shown in Figure 1. p_{min} is usually set to zero.

$$p(Q_{avg}) = \begin{cases} 0, & \text{if } 0 \le Q_{avg} < th_{min} \\ \dfrac{Q_{avg} - th_{min}}{th_{max} - th_{min}}, & \text{if } th_{min} \le Q_{avg} < th_{max} \\ 1, & \text{otherwise} \end{cases}$$

$$(2)$$

The decision which packet to drop is random in order to provide fairness between the connections which are candidates to slow down. The values of th_{min}, th_{max}, p_{min}, p_{max} and the weight w are parameters set by the network administrators and can be tuned as to avert short-lived conges-

Figure 1. RED drop function

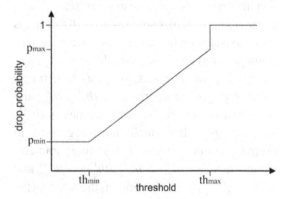

tion to exist, maintaining high throughput and low delay. However, tuning RED's parameters is not easily achievable; actually, the difficulty of its parameter tuning is one of the most important drawbacks of RED (Alemu & Jean-Marie 2004; Bonald et al., 2000; Christiansen et al., 2001). The most important factor that adds extra complication to the tuning problem is the dynamic nature of networks which may cause continuous changes of the optimal operating point for a RED enabled gateway, thus generating the need for dynamic tuning of RED parameters (Alemu et al., 2004; Chrysostomou et al., 2003; Hollot et al., 2002; Misra et al., 2000; Sirisena et al., 2002; Verma et al., 2003). Furthermore, although for long lived sessions RED seems to improve the system performance, experiments with short lived traffic such as Web traffic, don't show any clear benefits for using RED over a reactive mechanism and more specifically, tail drop (Christiansen et al., 2001).

Other AQM techniques include explicit congestion notification (ECN), used to prevent congestion and improve TCP's performance and a version of ECN that supports differentiated services (Floyd 1994; Floyd et al., 1993), random early marking (REM) that uses optimization techniques to maximize a utility function subject to the constraint that the output link has finite capacity (Athuraliya et al., 2000; Lapsley & Low 1999;) and BLUE that uses packet loss and link utilization history to manage congestion (Feng et al., 2002).

RED with In/Out bit (RIO) is an approach that incorporates mechanisms for service differentiation in multiclass traffic. RIO extends RED considering two classes of traffic: assured (high priority) and best effort (low priority) and uses two parameter sets, one for each traffic class: *in-profile* with parameters th^{in}_{max}, th^{in}_{min} and p^{in}_{max} and out-of-profile with parameters th^{out}_{max}, th^{out}_{min} and p^{out}_{max}. It is usually more aggressive in dropping *out-of-profile* packets setting parameter values such that $th^{in}_{min} > th^{out}_{min}$, $th^{in}_{max} > th^{out}_{max}$ and $p^{out}_{max} > p^{in}_{max}$. RIO also maintains the values of the

average queue length of in-profile packets (Q^{in}_{avg}) and total packets (Q_{avg}) and controls the packets rejection accordingly (Clark & Fang, 1998). As with RED, the out-of-profile thresholds can be dynamically adapted using estimates of the packet arrival rates (Chien & Liao, 2003).

RED in Wireless Networks

RED performance in wireless data networks is ineffective under self-similar traffic. As shown in a simulation study, self-similarity affects negatively the performance of the network. It is believed that this ineffectiveness comes from the channel errors and network's varying resources (Gao et al., 2002). Goodput and delay performance of TCP over 3G networks can be improved if slope based discard (SBD) algorithm is used. SBD is an AQM mechanism with easier than RED implementation and configuration (Alcaraz & Cerdan, 2006).

Multiclass RED in wireless networks uses traffic classification, RED and weighted first in first out (FIFO) scheduling, in which the scheduling rate is proportional to p_{max}. This scheme is shown to offer low loss to loss-sensitive applications and low delay to delay-sensitive applications (Gyasi-Agyei, 2002).

Threshold Policies

In this approach, the buffer space is partitioned in N partitions based on $B_1 < B_2 < \ldots\ldots < B_N$ where N is the number of priorities supported by the node. If a packet of priority i arrives, it gets accommodated in the buffer if the buffer state (i.e., the number of packets in the buffer) is less than B_i, otherwise, the packet is dropped. Such policies are very attractive because they are very easy to implement and they have been shown to better protect higher priority packets. FIFO policies (Cidon et al., 1994) have investigated several packet accepting policies for preserving the drop requirements of the premium class. In their investigation, they define a property that characterizes such policies, referred to as *M -Protective Policy*. A buffering policy is *M-protective* if the drop probability of the premium class is not affected by the lower priority streams.

The emphasis of this chapter will be on threshold type policies since they exhibit two main advantages: the FIFO policy guarantees that packets are delivered in order and it does not require any scheduler.

Droppers

Tail Drop

In this approach, packets that arrive at a full buffer (i.e., a buffer with Q_{max} packets, where Q_{max} is some threshold) are dropped. This technique is known as "Tail Drop." It is a simple and widespread technique and usually the threshold Q_{max} is set equal to the maximum queue capacity. Although this approach has been used sufficiently for years, it has some important drawbacks such as global synchronization, lockouts and full queues (Braden et al., 1998). Global synchronization is a situation at which a number of TCP senders reduce their transmission rates at the same time. This is likely to happen when a group of consecutive packets is dropped by the node's buffer, which causes the corresponding TCP senders to presume congestion and reduce their sending rates. As a result, for a significant amount of time the related links are underutilized. When a small fraction of traffic flows receives a large proportion of the bandwidth we observe a situation known as lockout. Lockouts cause unfair allocation of the network's resources. Finally, full queues lead naturally to an increase of delay; moreover, full queues can lead to an increase of jitter.

Push-Out Techniques

Other more complex techniques discard packets that are already enqueued in the buffer. The complexity of each technique depends on how it chooses the packet that will drop. One of the simpler push-out technique is "drop front on full," which drops the older packet in the buffer, which, compared to drop-tail, reduces the waiting time of the packets in the buffer (Lakshman et

al., 1996). Other techniques are: "lower priority first" (LPF), which drops packets from the lowest backlogged priority queue (Kroner et al., 1991; Lin & Silvester, 1991), "complete buffer partitioning" (CBP), which provides packet class differentiation by assigning an amount of buffer space to each class and drops traffic when the buffer space of the corresponding class is full (Lin et al., 1991) and "partial buffer sharing" (PBS, which also provides differentiation and drops packets according to the aggregated backlog of all classes (Kroner et al., 1991). Note that the partitioning of buffers in LPF, CBP, and PBS is static and hence cannot support per-class service differentiation since there is no a priory knowledge of the arrival process. A push-out technique that was designed to support relative per-class QoS is the proportional loss rate (PLR). PLR keeps track of the packet drops for each class and ensures that the ratio of two successive priority classes remains roughly constant at a predefined value. There are two variations of PLR according to the number of packets used to estimate the drop rates: PLR(n) uses only the last n packets whereas PLR(∞) uses all information received until that moment (Dovrolis & Ramanathann, 2000).

In the case of multimedia traffic (e.g., video, frames packets may be related with other packets in the stream). For example, in MPEG protocol, information contained in a "P" frame is encoded with reference to the previous frame whereas a "B" frame is encoded using information from the next and previous frames. Note that "I" frames contain the most information and are encoded with little compression. Subsequently, the rejection (or the discard due to some QoS constraints) of a packet that contains a frame immediately causes an important reduction of the amount of information that the relative frames (following or preceding) will provide; the information lost due to a packet rejection depends on the type of frame that contains. Therefore, it may be more efficient if the packets with frames connected to a dropped packet are also rejected, leaving free space for other packets to enter the buffer and reducing queuing delay. Of course, this approach adds further complication to router's operation, since it has to keep record of the rejected packets and also read higher layer packet headers.

Joint Buffer Management and Scheduling

Per-hop behavior in network routers is usually implemented by two "independent" mechanisms, *buffer management,* and *packet scheduling. Buffer management* performs admission control to all incoming packets deciding whether a packet of a certain class can enter the buffer or be dropped (such mechanisms have been presented earlier). *Packet scheduling* mechanisms decide which packet that lies in the buffer will be transmitted next. The effective cooperation of the two mechanisms is very important, since the performance of the PHB scheme is directly dependent on their performance. In this paragraph, some recent research results in the field are presented. Strategies for joint radio link buffer management and scheduling for video streaming over wireless shared channels are proposed in Liebl et al. (2005). Authors search for an optimal combination of scheduler and drop strategy providing also fairness among users. Joint buffer management and scheduling (JoBS) is a framework for providing QoS in a packet network without information on traffic arrivals. JoBS has two unique capabilities: it makes scheduling and buffer management decisions in one-step and it supports both relative and absolute QoS requirements for classes. Its operation is based on predicting delays of the currently backlogged traffic; after that it adjusts the service rate and the amount of traffic to be dropped for each traffic class (Liebeherr & Christin, 2001).

A possible solution to provide both fair resource sharing among flows and strict priority for real-time services is the integration of hierarchical scheduling and buffer management mechanisms. Under this scheme, traffic streams grouped according to certain criteria as protocol

and traffic type are allowed to share resources (Pi et al., 2004).

An alternative buffering scheme for differentiated services assigns one buffer for each class of traffic and, in addition, a shared buffer that can be used from all classes, with the priority of the shared buffer being to the higher priority class. In the case of two priority classes (higher and lower priority) is shown that using a weighted round robin scheduling policy the packet loss ratios of the high priority class are low without starving the lower priority traffic (Kamal & Hassanein 2004).

Playback and Rate Control

Even though the emphasis of this chapter is the management of the buffers of intermediate nodes, buffer management may also be applicable at the end nodes. In video streaming, there is a continuous flow of data from a media server to a set of distributed receivers in the network. Large transmission rates may cause the buffer of the client to overflow resulting to video quality degradation. On the other hand, buffer underflows may also lead to degradation of the video quality, since receiver will not have enough video data for playback resulting to image "freezing."

A common solution to the problem of multimedia presentation is to offer a framework for synchronization between the source (the multimedia server) and the destination (the multimedia client). In other words, provide means to bound jitter. There are two types of synchronization: *intramedia*, in which synchronization should be achieved among a multimedia stream and other data associated with the same stream, and *intermedia*, in which synchronization should be achieved among two different multimedia streams. Recently some new synchronization schemes were proposed, the general functions of which are described in Figure 2 (Chuang et al., 2004; Nam & Park 1999; Takahata et al., 2004).

Figure 2 shows some functions and elements that most intramedia synchronization schemes include. At the multimedia server side, a source feeds the media stream with data. This data can be extracted from a database (e.g., in video on demand applications) or even captured and decoded online (e.g., in videocalls). In some cases, data from the source are buffered in a proxy along their path to the receiver. Buffer level control allows the buffer to maintain its level within a certain range so that no underflow or overflow occurs. If its level is not in this range, the rate control unit sends feedback to server to adjust its sending rate. At the client side, another buffer is used as a reservoir to regulate the difference between source's transmission rate and application's playout rate. A rate regulator in the client provides server with feedback to change its data supply rate. The QoS broker is responsible to observe the network conditions and perform QoS negotiation when new conditions arise (i.e., due to changes in wireless link).

The methodology presented in the next section is directly applicable to the problem of dynamically controlling the thresholds that arise in the tail drop and threshold policies at intermediate routers. However, we point out that similar approaches can be used together with other policies. For example, one can use a similar approach to adjust the RED parameters. Furthermore, in the playback problem, the multimedia server can adapt the rate at which multimedia traffic reaches the receiver either by reducing its sending rate or by reducing the quality of the multimedia content. In the former case, a similar framework that enables the dynamic control of the transmission rate of a source is presented by Panayiotou and Markou (2007). In the latter case, the amount of data sent is reduced resulting in lower data per unit time received by the client (Ng et al., 1996).

BUFFER CONTROL USING THE SFM/IPA FRAMEWORK

The SFM/IPA Framework

In this section, the framework for dynamically adapting network parameters (e.g., buffer thresh-

Figure 2. A generalized function diagram for synchronization models

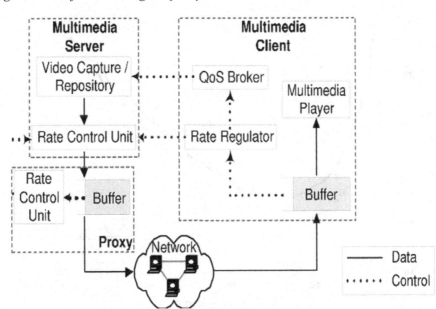

olds) to maintain the network at optimal (or near optimal) point is presented. In this framework, first the behavior of the network (generally a discrete-event system) is approximated by a stochastic fluid model (SFM). Using the SFM, one can use infinitesimal perturbation analysis (IPA) to obtain estimators of the sensitivity of the performance measures of interest (e.g., average packet loss, average delay) with respect to the parameters of interest and use them together with gradient-descent type of optimization algorithms to optimally control the network.

SFM paradigms have become increasingly attractive and have been shown to be especially useful for simulating various kinds of high-speed networks (Kesidis et al., 1996; Kumaran & Mitra 1998; Liu et al., 1999; Yan & Gong, 1999). The fluid-flow approach rests on a molecular view of packets in moderate to heavy loads over high-speed transmission links, where the effect of an individual packet in the entire traffic process is infinitesimal. It can provide either approximations to queuing-based models or primary models in their own right.

Of course, stochastic fluid modeling is not for every type of analysis. It forgoes the identity and dynamics of individual packets and focuses instead on the aggregate flow rate. Thus, fluid models may not be appropriate for metrics that depend on the identity of certain packets. Furthermore, for the purpose of performance analysis of networks with QoS requirements, the accuracy of SFMs depends on a number of parameters (e.g., traffic conditions and the structure of the underlying system). Nevertheless, Cassandras et al. (2002) and Panayiotou et al. (2004) (and references therein) show that though approximate models may not be very accurate in terms of performance evaluation, they often are very effective for control and optimization. We emphasize that in the context of this chapter, SFM is used for optimization and control rather than performance evaluation.

An illustrative example is presented in Figure 3, which shows some cost function $J(\theta)$ of a typical network node with respect to the control parameter of interest θ measured using (i) the real DES (solid line) and (ii) an SFM that models the

Figure 3. Cost function in a typical node measured in SFM and DES model

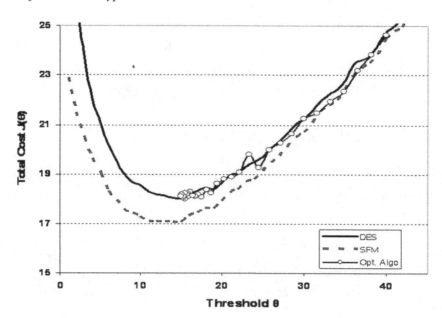

real system (dotted line). Note that though the difference between the values in two curves can be substantial, the minimum points of each curve lie very close to each other. This means that although SFM may not be appropriate for evaluating the performance of the network node, it can be used for optimization purposes. This is the main motivation for the approach presented in this section. In this approach, SFM is used to derive sensitivity estimators through IPA. These estimators turn out easy to implement from data observed at any network router. Then these estimators are used together with stochastic approximation (gradient based) algorithms (Kushner & Clark, 1978) that drive the parameters towards the optimum point. The steps of such an optimization algorithm are also plotted in the figure (solid line with points on it); starting from an initial value $\theta = 40$ the algorithm converges to an optimal value for $\theta^* = 16$.

The advantages of this approach are (a) The estimation of the sensitivities of the performance metrics is performed online. Estimators can therefore be implemented in a real system to continuously monitor and optimize the performance metrics as the operating conditions change. (b) The estimators are quite simple and easy to implement thus they can be used for real time control, and (c) they do not require any knowledge of the system's underlying stochastic processes.

Perturbation analysis (PA) is a sample path technique used in stochastic systems that analyzes their performance measures when some of the system's parameters change. The analysis provides estimators of the *sensitivity* of the performance measures of interest with respect to some parameter of the system. Specifically, let $J(\theta)$ be a system's performance measure where θ is a $n \times 1$ vector of the system's parameters of interest and n is the number of such parameters (e.g., the thresholds for the n classes of service). Let $L(\theta;\omega)$ be the sample performance function, i.e., the estimated value of the performance function after observing a realization ω, then:

$$J(\theta) = E[L(\theta;\omega)] \qquad (3)$$

The objective of IPA is to also utilize the observed data to estimate the gradient of $L(\theta;\omega)$ with respect to θ, $\nabla L(\theta;\omega)$. More information and references for PA techniques can be found in Ho and Cao (1991) and Cassandras et al. (1999). Using the SFM approximation, one can use calculus tools in order to derive the gradient $\nabla L(\theta;\omega)$. As already mentioned, it turns out that these estimators are easy to compute even using data from the sample path of the real system. Thus the system is observed for an interval of length T and an estimate of the gradient is computed. Finally, the parameter values are updated using the following stochastic approximation algorithm:

$$\theta_{n+1} = \theta_n - s_n \cdot \nabla L(\theta;\omega), \quad n = 0, 1, 2, \ldots \qquad (4)$$

where s_n is an appropriate step size sequence. Even though for the convergence of this algorithm, it is required that s_n is a decreasing sequence, for the purposes of this chapter, it will be kept constant in order to maintain the adaptability properties of the algorithm over time; If the step size approaches zero, then, even if the network conditions change, the algorithm will not be able to adjust the control parameters. Furthermore, for the convergence of this algorithm, it is required that $\nabla L(\theta;\omega)$ is an unbiased estimator of $\nabla J(\theta)$, in other words, it is required that:

$$\nabla E[L(\theta;\omega)] = E[\nabla L(\theta;\omega)] \qquad (5)$$

In the context of stochastic fluid models, one can prove that the derived $\nabla L(\theta;\omega)$ is an unbiased estimator of the $\nabla J(\theta)$. However, some simulation results have shown that when these estimators are computed with data from the sample path of the discrete event system, some bias may be introduced. Nonetheless, in all of our experiments as well as other reports from the literature, the algorithm quickly converges to the optimal or near optimal point.

In the sequel, we will present the main steps of this approach using an example where the objective is to control the threshold at a node that handles two priority classes. However, we emphasize that this approach is also applicable for controlling multiple thresholds or the packet arrival or transmission rates, see for example Wardi et al. (2002), Panayiotou et al. (2004), and Sun et al. (2004). Furthermore, for brevity the proofs of the derived estimators are omitted, however, the interested reader is referred to the references or to Cassandras et al. (2002) where a detailed and insightful analysis of the IPA estimators for a simple node is presented. This chapter extends the results of Panayiotou et al. (2004) by allowing for user mobility. Furthermore, the model accounts for packet drops at intermediate nodes due to delay constraint violations. In this context, if the node knows that a packet has violated a delay constraint, it is immediately dropped and not forwarded to its final destination. In this way, valuable resources are not wasted along the path of the packet.

A Node with Two Classes of Traffic and QoS Support

The bottleneck node in a communications network (such as a router or a base station subsystem in cellular networks) is modeled as a discrete event system, in the sense that the operation of the system is defined over a set of discrete events (e.g., packet arrival/departure, packet expiration). As shown in Figure 4, there are two priority classes of traffic (class 1 is the low priority and class 2 the high priority). For simplicity, it is assumed that the buffer has infinite capacity and it uses a threshold policy with threshold B. Thus, if a packet arrives, then it is admitted to the queue according to the following policy:

- If the packet is of priority 2 (high priority) it is admitted if there is any space at the buffer. Note that since for this chapter it is assumed that the buffer has infinite capacity, then it is always admitted.
- If the packet is of priority 1 (low priority) it is admitted only if the current queue length is less than B, otherwise the packet is dropped.

Any admitted packet can be either transmitted to the next node using a FIFO policy or it can be removed from the queue as a result of user mobility or delay constraint violation. In the context of cellular networks, when a user moves from one base station subsystem (BSS) to the next (due to roaming), unsent packets will be removed from

Figure 4. The basic DES buffer model with two classes of traffic and expiration/forwarding processes

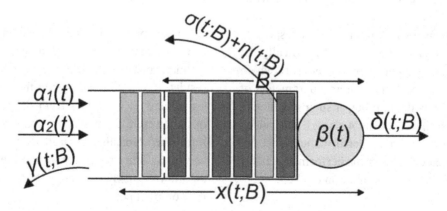

the buffer of the current BSS and be forwarded to the new BSS using some other medium (e.g., wirelined transfer). Similarly, if a packet violates a delay QoS constraint, then it can be removed from the buffer before it gets transmitted to the next node. Thus, in both cases, from the point of view of a buffer, a packet is removed before it is transmitted by the transmitter. The fact that packets are allowed to exit the buffer before being transmitted complicates the dynamics of the buffer (i.e., the control parameter B affects both, the state transition mechanism and also the exit rate from the buffer). Consequently, the results of (Sun et al., 2004) are not applicable.

For this chapter it is assumed that the processes $\alpha_1(t)$, $\alpha_2(t)$, and $\beta(t)$ are independent of the control parameter $\theta=B$. Based on these input processes, the following output processes are also defined: the buffer state, i.e., the queue length $x(t;B)$, the node's transmission process, $\delta(t;B)$, the low priority packet drop processes $\gamma(t;B)$, the packet expiration process $\sigma(t;B)$ due to QoS delay violations and the packet removal due to user mobility $\eta(t;B)$. The objective is to determine an algorithm for finding the value of the threshold parameter B that optimizes an objective function that trades off packet losses, QoS delay violations and network throughput. In this approach, the algorithm of Equation (4) will be used. During

the remaining of this section we will present the proposed approach for devising an algorithm for computing the gradient or in this case the derivative $dL(B)/dB$.

The Equivalent Stochastic Fluid Model

As already mentioned, the first step is to approximate the behavior of the DES with a SFM. In this case, the system is characterized by a number of processes, all defined in a common probability space (Ω, F, P) as shown in the single node buffer model below. All input processes are assumed piecewise differentiable functions. In this context, it is assumed that $\alpha(t)$ corresponds to the superposition of all inflow process due to packet arrivals. In other words, the inflow process is decomposed into a number of independent inflow processes, one for each traffic class, such that $\alpha(t) = \sum_{j=1}^{M} \alpha_j(t)$ where $\alpha_j(t)$ to the inflow process of the class j traffic and M is the number of traffic classes. For the example considered $M=2$. Furthermore, $\beta(t)$ is the maximum outflow due to successful transmissions. In the general case, there will be a parameter vector θ that includes all controllable parameters of interest, e.g. the buffer thresholds $b_1,\ldots, b_M$, and parameters of the inflow

Figure 5. The equivalent SFM of a node with two classes of traffic and expiration/forwarding processes (feedback mechanism)

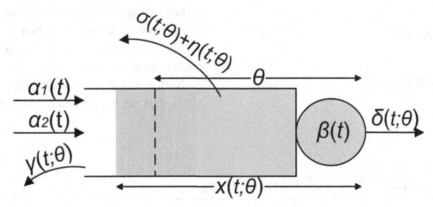

and outflow processes. In addition, the process $\eta(t;\theta)$ corresponds to the outflow process due to user mobility and $\sigma(t;\theta)$ is the process of message expiration due to QoS delay violations.

Based on the previous input processes, the following processes are derived from the system's dynamics: $x(t;\theta)$ is the buffer workload, $\delta(t;\theta)$ is the system's outflow and $\gamma(t;\theta)$ is the buffer overflow process due to the threshold policy. All processes evolve in a given time horizon $[0,T]$ for some fixed $0 < T < \infty$. Stochastic processes are classified as *defining processes*, which are all external inflow processes (e.g., $\alpha(t), \beta(t)$) and as *derived processes*, which are the ones that result from the defining processes, the system dynamics and the controllable parameters (e.g., $x(t;\theta)$ and $\delta(t;\theta)$).

To measure the system's performance and be able to map it to a certain QoS requirement, the following metrics are defined. $Q_T(\theta)$ is the cumulative workload (equivalently, the packet delay through Little's law), $G_T(\theta)$ is the low priority fluid loss volume due to the threshold policy (equivalently, the amount of media content that is lost), $P_T(\theta)$ is the fluid expiration volume (equivalently, the amount of media content dropped due to QoS delay violations), and $R_T(\theta)$ is the throughput. All above functions are defined over a time interval $[0, T]$ and are shown below. Note that strictly speaking, the functions in Equations (6)-(9) are also functions of the realization ω but the argument is omitted to ease the notation.

$$Q_T(\theta) = \frac{1}{T}\int_0^T x(t;\theta)\,dt \qquad (6)$$

$$G_T(\theta) = \frac{1}{T}\int_0^T \gamma(t;\theta)\,dt \qquad (7)$$

$$P_T(\theta) = \frac{1}{T}\int_0^T \sigma(t;\theta)\,dt \qquad (8)$$

$$R_T(\theta) = \frac{1}{T}\int_0^T \delta(t;\theta)\,dt \qquad (9)$$

As mentioned earlier, the aim is to continuously monitor and optimize the system's performance by controlling the control parameters of interest. Depending on the QoS requirements one can define an appropriate objective function that may consist of one or more terms. For example, one can define an overall sample function in Box 1, where w_Q, w_G, w_P, and w_R are appropriate weights. Of course, one would be interested in minimizing the expectation of this sample function:

In the sequel, for the sake of exposition, only a single control parameter will be considered, thus, $\theta = \theta = b_1 = b$.

IPA Derivatives

IPA is a sample path technique that we use to derive the sensitivity estimators of the performance measures defined in Equations (6)-(9). Assuming the SFM, the sample path of $x(t;\theta)$ is generated using the general dynamics given by

$$\frac{dx(t;\theta)}{dt} = \text{total inflow} - \text{total outflow} \qquad (10)$$

which means that the rate of change of the queue length is equal to the net inflow in the buffer. As already mentioned, the QoS delay violations are modeled as fluid that is removed from the queue before is transmitted to the next node. To determine the fluid outflow due to QoS delay violations we assume a Markovian system for the fluid model and approximate the expiration process $\sigma(t;\theta) = c \cdot x(t;\theta)$ where the constant c is defined as the packet expiration rate.

Notice that $dx(t;\theta)/dt$ depends on the state $x(t;\theta)$, thus the model includes a form of "feed-

Box 1.

$$L_T(\theta) = w_Q \cdot Q_T(\theta) + w_G \cdot G_T(\theta) + w_P \cdot P_T(\theta) + w_R \cdot R_T(\theta)$$

back," violating one of the assumptions in Sun et al. (2004) and thus, these results no longer hold.

To compute the IPA sensitivity estimators, we first partition and classify the sample path into several time periods. We then differentiate the relevant sample functions (Equations (6)-(9)) to obtain their sensitivity estimators. For the sake of brevity, the derivations of the IPA estimators are omitted (for more information interested readers can advice the proposed bibliography). The following paragraph describes how the sample path is partitioned. Note that the partitioning procedure is performed online, during the operation of the system; a part of this operation is the *Find_New_Period_Type* procedure of Figure 8.

Classification of Time Periods

Figure 6 shows a typical sample path of the system with two classes of traffic. The sample path can be decomposed into two types of alternating intervals: *Empty periods* (EP) during which the system is empty ($x(t;\theta)=0$) and *Non-Empty Periods* (NEP) during which the system is nonempty ($x(t;\theta)>0$). Figure 6 shows a typical NEP (the kth in the sample path) which is preceded and followed by EPs. A NEP period is further decomposed into the three types of time periods. The starting and ending points of each period is identified by three important events: (a) the buffer becomes

or ceases to be empty (b) $x(t;\theta)$ becomes (and stays) equal to θ or ceases being equal to θ, and (c) $x(t;\theta)$ crosses the threshold θ either from below or above. The occurring time of these events is denoted by $v_{k,i}$.

Each period is classified as of type:

- *No Loss (W)*, if the buffer level $x(t;\theta)$ during this time period is below the threshold and hence no loss occurs. Examples of such periods are $[v_{k,0}, v_{k,1})$, $[v_{k,2}, v_{k,3})$, $[v_{k,4}, v_{k,5})$ and $[v_{k,7}, v_{k,8})$ in Figure 6.
- *Partial Loss (U)*, if the buffer level $x(t;\theta)$ during this time period is equal to the threshold and hence some (partial) loss occurs. Periods $[v_{k,3}, v_{k,4})$, $[v_{k,5}, v_{k,6})$ in the typical sample path above are examples of such type of periods.
- *Full Loss (V)*, if the buffer level $x(t;\theta)$ during this time period is above the threshold and hence full loss occurs. Examples of V-type periods are $[v_{k,1}, v_{k,2})$ and $[v_{k,6}, v_{k,7})$.

The type of the periods is required in the procedures *Update_Sensitivity_Estimators* and *Find_New_Period_Type*. Note that in this chapter the classification of the time periods is performed using only two classes of traffic and a single threshold $\theta=b$. For models with more traffic classes the reader is referred to Sun et al. (2004).

Figure 6. A typical system sample path in SFM with two classes of traffic

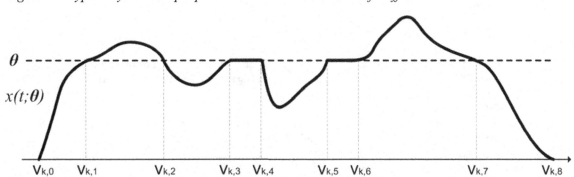

Computation of IPA Derivatives

The derivation of IPA was performed based on SFM since SFMs are simpler and allow differentiation of the sample functions. On the other hand, the estimators are computed based on information of the DES, at which we do not need to generate the sample path of the equivalent SFM; we are only interested in the three important events referred to the previous paragraph. Thus, we can obtain the required information from the sample path of the DES and proceed with the computation of the sensitivity estimators.

Under these circumstances, the computation of the new IPA sensitivity estimators of $Q_T(\theta)$, $G_T(\theta)$ and $R_T(\theta)$ from the DES sample path is described in Figure 7, Figure 8, and Figure 9. Recall that this DES has two classes of traffic, supports QoS delay violations and is controlled by a threshold policy. Again, in this section it is assumed that the controllable parameter θ is the threshold b of the threshold policy.

To deploy the algorithms either on a simulation scenario or in a real network buffer, one has to create an observer that continuously observes the sample path (i.e., the evolution of the buffer size) and record the points of the sample path needed to compute the required derivatives. What is actually needed is to record all the important events in the sample path. Each time that a period ends the observer performs the few necessary calculations and continues observing the sample path. In the pseudocode of Figure 7-Figure 9, the starting and ending points of each period are indicated by s and t respectively. The event time derivative of the end point t' is computed through an iterative algorithm at which the value of the event time derivative at the beginning of the period s' is used. In procedure *Update_Sensitivity_Estimators* the functions $A(t;\theta)$, $B(t;\theta)$ and $C(t;\theta)$ are given by:

Figure 7. Pseudocode for the structure of the observer that computes the estimators of the sample functions of Equations (6)-(9). Note that the prime notation ($\cdot'$) is used to indicate the derivative with respect to the control parameter of interest (in this case, θ)

I. Procedure: *Derivative_Estimation*

- Initialize the variables dQ, dG, dR, x, s, t, s', t' to zero   % x is the buffer state
- Set the variable that indicates the period type $pType = E$ % Empty period
- **If** an event (packet arrival/departure/expiration/forward) occurs **then**

     If the current period did not end   % Compare x with 0 and θ

         Do nothing

     else

         $t =$ current time   % Record the ending point the period

         Update_Sensitivity_Estimators

         $pType =$ Find_New_Period_Type   % Find the type of the new period

         Set $s = t$, $s' = t'$.   % End of previous period is the

     endif   % beginning of the new period

     Update system state x

   endif

- **If** $(t \geq T)$ **then**   % End of observation interval

     Set $dQ = \frac{dQ}{t}$, $dG = \frac{dG}{t}$, $dR = \frac{dR}{t}$ and $dP = \frac{c_1 \cdot dQ}{t}$

     Return dQ, dG, dR and dP

endif

$$A(t;\theta) = \alpha_1(t) + \alpha_2(t) - \beta(t) - c \cdot \theta$$
$$B(t;\theta) = \alpha_2(t) - \beta(t) - c \cdot \theta$$
$$C(t;\theta) = 1 - e^{-c \cdot (t-s)}$$

Finally, the only information missing are the various instantaneous rates, $\alpha_1(t), \alpha_2(t), \beta(t)$ and the packet expiration rate c. To estimate the arrival and service rates one can maintain an exponentially weighted moving average of the interarrival times between two successive packets of the same class. For example, let τ^{ave} be the average interarrival time between class 1 packets, then:

$$\tau^{ave} = (1-y) \cdot \tau + y \cdot \tau^{ave} \qquad (11)$$

where τ is the current sample and $0 \le y \le 1$. Then $\alpha_1(t) = 1/\tau^{ave}$. Similar algorithm can be devised for all other rates. An estimate of the rate c is obtained using the approximation for packet expiration process $\sigma(t;\theta) \approx c \cdot x(t;\theta)$. Using this approximation, the total number of expired packets can then be expressed as Box 2, where c_t is an estimation of c obtained after the system is observed for an interval of length t. Note that $lim_{t \to \infty} c_t = c$.

User mobility in the context of cellular networks is treated similarly to packet drops due

Figure 8. Pseudocode for determining the new period type for estimators. Note that the events packet expiration and packet forward can occur only in the model with packet expiration and packet forwarding processes.

II. Procedure: *Find_New_Period_Type*

- If $pType = E$ and the current event is a packet arrival **then**
    Period of type E ends and the new period is of type W
  endif
- If $pType = W$
    If $x = 1$ and the event occurred is a packet departure/expiration/forward **then**
        The new period type is E
    endif
    If $x = \theta - 1$ and the event occurred is a packet arrival **then**
        The new period type is U
    endif
  endif
- If the period type is U
    If the event occurred is a packet departure/expiration/forward **then**
        The new period type is W
    endif
    If the event occurred is a packet arrival **then**
        The new period type is V
    endif
  endif
- If the period type is V
    If $x = \theta + 1$ and the event occurred is a packet departure/expiration/forward **then**
        The new period type is U
    endif
  endif
- Return the new period type

Figure 9. Pseudocode for the computation of the estimators in the general case

III. Procedure: *Update_Sensitivity_Estimators*

- Update_Event_Time_Derivative   % Update t'
- If pType=W then
   - If this is the first period of the NEP then
       - Set $dQ = dQ + C(s) \cdot (1 - s' \cdot \mathcal{A}(s, \theta))$
   - endif
   - If this is the last period of the NEP then
       - Set $dR = dR - I_1(t) \cdot t'$
   - endif
   - endif
- If pType=U then
   - Set $dQ = dQ + c_t \cdot (t - s)$
   - Set $dG = dG - \mathcal{A}(s, \theta) \cdot s' - c_t \cdot (t - s)$
   - endif
- If pType=V then
   - Set $dQ = dQ + C(s) \cdot (1 - s' \cdot \mathcal{B}(s, \theta))$
   - Set $dG = dG + [\frac{\alpha_1(t) \cdot (1 - C(s)) \cdot \mathcal{B}(s,\theta)}{\mathcal{B}(t,\theta)} - \alpha_1(s)] \cdot s' + \frac{\alpha_1(t) \cdot C(s)}{\mathcal{B}(t,\theta)}$
   - endif

Box 2.

$$N_{\exp}(t) = \int_0^t \sigma(\tau; \theta) \approx \int_0^t c_\tau \cdot x(\tau, \theta) = c_t \cdot t \cdot Q_t(\theta) \Rightarrow c_t = \frac{N_{\exp}(t)}{t \cdot Q_t(\theta)}$$

to delay constraint violations thus it is omitted. Interested readers are referred to Markou and Panayiotou (2006).

Relation Between the Sensitivity Estimators of the Performance Metrics

Using the principle of conservation of flows, one can obtain a simple relationship between the sensitivity estimators of the different metrics. As a result, if two of the estimators are computed, then the third is immediately derived. For simplicity, assume that at the end of the observation interval, the buffer is empty. Using the conservation principle, then all arriving fluid is either transmitted to the next node or it is dropped due to the threshold policy or it is dropped either due QoS delay violation, then one can write:

$$\int_0^T \alpha(t)dt = \int_0^T \delta(t; \theta)dt + \int_0^T \gamma(t; \theta)dt + \int_0^T \sigma(t; \theta)dt$$

Dividing by T we obtain:

$$\frac{1}{T} \int_0^T \alpha(t)dt = R(\theta) + G(\theta) + c \cdot Q(\theta)$$

where for the last term the approximation $P(\theta) \approx c \cdot Q(\theta)$ is used. Differentiating both sides with respect to θ we get:

$$R'(\theta) + G'(\theta) + c \cdot Q'(\theta) = 0$$

SIMULATION AND RESULTS

In this section, we present some experimental results that show the properties of the proposed algorithms. The simulation study concerns a single node that accepts incoming traffic from different sources and each source voluntarily marks its packets as high or low priority. Furthermore, each packet is time stamped with a hard deadline by which the packet needs to be delivered to the destination. If the deadline is past, then the packet is useless thus it is dropped. The objective in this simulation study is to set the threshold parameter $\theta=b$ such that $J_T(\theta)$ is minimized, using the optimization algorithm described in this chapter. The aim of the optimization algorithm (*OptAlg*), is to dynamically adjust the parameter θ such that the average delay of high (class 1) and low (class 2) priority packets is optimally traded off with the packet losses either due to overflow of low priority packets as a result of the threshold policy or due to expiration of either high or low priority packets as a result of excessive delay. Thus, it is assumed that each node it optimizing a performance metric of the form:

$$\min_{\theta} E[J_T(\theta)] = E[w_Q \cdot Q_T(\theta) + w_G \cdot G_T(\theta) + w_P \cdot P_T(\theta)]$$

(15)

where, w_Q, w_G and w_P are constant weights, T is the length of the observation interval. For the following experiments the weights are set to w_Q=1, w_G=20 and w_P=20. The overall cost

$E[J_T(\theta)]$ represents a tradeoff between providing low delay, low packet expiration and low packet rejection probability. Note that in general one could also include a throughput term or one can assume that it is included in w_Q, w_G and w_P. The following sections present the results obtained using a DES model which actually simulates a real system.

We consider three source nodes, N^1, N^2 and N^3 where each node N^i is modeled by a pair of ON/OFF sources, N_h^i and N_l^i which correspond to the traffic generator of high and low priority packets respectively. The arrival rates from each traffic generator are random variables defined similarly: $\alpha_1^i(t)$ and $\alpha_2^i(t)$ are the arrival rates of low and high priority packets respectively generated from the ith source, $i = 1, 2, 3$. Two different scenarios are considered; the description of the six arrival processes in Scenario I and Scenario II is summarized in Table 1 and Table 2 respectively. Note also, that the instantaneous rates used in the IPA estimators are obtained using (11) with y = 0.8.

Furthermore, for both scenarios, the transmission time of the relay node is assumed exponentially distributed with mean $1/\lambda_\beta$ = 1ms. To simulate the process $\sigma(t;\theta)$, each packet is marked with a time stamp (Time To Live - TTL). If the time of a packet waiting in the buffer exceeds the TTL then the packet is considered as stale and

Table 1. The arrival processes in Scenario I

Source	ON time (ms)	OFF time (ms)	Arrival Rate (pckts/s)
N_h^1	Exponential(45)	Exponential(15)	Exponential(330)
N_l^1	Exponential(45)	Exponential(15)	Exponential(330)
N_h^2	Exponential(40)	Exponential(20)	Exponential(200)
N_l^2	Exponential(40)	Exponential(20)	Exponential(250)
N_h^3	Exponential(60)	Exponential(25)	Exponential(200)
N_l^3	Exponential(60)	Exponential(25)	Exponential(200)

Table 2. The arrival processes in Scenario II

Source	ON time (ms)	OFF time (ms)	Arrival Rate (pckts/s)
N_h^1	Exponential(45)	Exponential(15)	Deterministic(330)
N_l^1	Exponential(45)	Exponential(15)	Deterministic(330)
N_h^2	Uniform(30,50)	Uniform(10,30)	Deterministic(200)
N_l^2	Uniform(30,50)	Uniform(10,30)	Deterministic(250)
N_h^3	Exponential(60)	Exponential(25)	Deterministic(200)
N_l^3	Exponential(60)	Exponential(25)	Deterministic(200)

is removed from the buffer. TTL is set to be an exponential random variable with mean equal to $\lambda_e = 20$ms.

Figure 10 and Figure 12 present the values of the derivatives of the performance measures $G_T(\theta)$, $Q_T(\theta)$, $P_T(\theta)$ and $R_T(\theta)$ with respect to the threshold θ, when computed from the data observed from the sample path of the DES. The derivatives were evaluated using two methods: (i) IPA method presented in this chapter; the corresponding curves are *dG-IPA*, *dQ-IPA*, *dP-IPA* and *dR-IPA* respectively and (ii) the finite difference method on the performance metrics' data extracted from the brute force simulation; the corresponding curves are respectively *dG-FD*, *dQ-FD*, *dP-FD* and *dR-FD*. The simulation interval was set to $T = 100$ minutes.

As the results in Figure 10 show, in Scenario I the IPA estimators perform excellent approximation of the finite difference method curves. Figure 11 presents the steps taken by the stochastic approximation algorithm (*OptAlg*) (4). *OptAlg* uses the derived IPA sensitivities in an iterative scheme with step size $\sigma_n = 20$ for all n. The initial threshold is set to either 1 or 16. It is emphasized that for the optimization scenario the observation interval is set to just 1 minute (i.e., the IPA estimates are considerably more noisy than the ones presented

in Figure 10 and Figure 12). As seen from Fig. 10 *OptAlg* converges to the optimum value of $J(\theta^*)$ within a few iterations.

Simulation results of Scenario II are presented in Figure 12. Although the IPA derivatives of the performance metrics do not match perfectly with their finite difference counterparts, they approximate them satisfactorily. Moreover, the performance of *OptAlg* is not affected at all, since, as shown in Figure 13, the algorithm converges to the minimum value of $J(\theta^*)$ within a few iterations for both initial values of threshold (θ=1 and θ=16).

FUTURE TRENDS

Recently, the telecommunications industry is experiencing a transformation abandoning the traditional circuit switched technology and converging towards IP based services, bundling together services like high speed Internet access, television and telephony, often referred to as "triple play." Furthermore, fourth generation (4G) wireless networks are also converging all services (voice and data) over an IP based integrated network. Packet based networks, though more efficient in terms of resource utilization than

Figure 10. The sample derivatives of the performance metrics of DES model in Scenario I

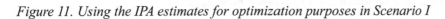

(a) Workload   (b) Packet Rejection Volume

(c) Packet Expiration Volume   (d) Throughput

Figure 11. Using the IPA estimates for optimization purposes in Scenario I

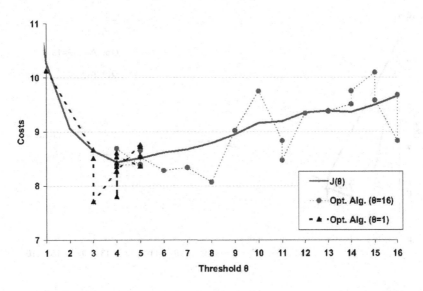

Figure 12. The sample derivatives of the performance metrics of DES model in Scenario II

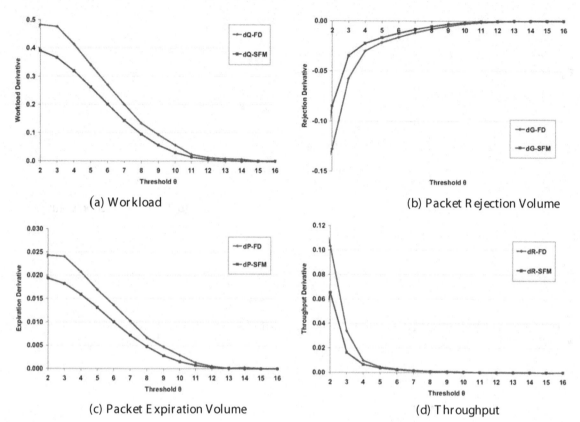

(a) Workload

(b) Packet Rejection Volume

(c) Packet Expiration Volume

(d) Throughput

Figure 13. Using the IPA estimates for optimization purposes in Scenario II

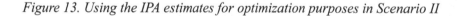

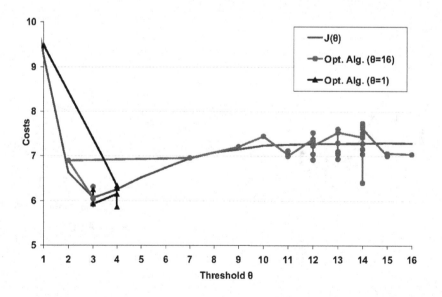

circuit switched systems, do not naturally support QoS guarantees. To successfully integrate all these systems together using IP based technology it is imperative that new mechanisms are devised that will enable the provision of various levels of QoS guarantees. Furthermore, since the provided QoS depends on the current network load conditions, providers need adaptive resource allocation mechanisms that will automatically react to the network conditions and provide the best possible QoS as perceived by the users.

QoS provisioning is a topic that was researched extensively over the past years. Most of the existing research studies assume an error free channel where packet losses are interpreted as network congestion. Furthermore, most of the existing research assumes that the majority of traffic responds to congestion by reducing its transmission rate to alleviate its effects. Both of these assumptions are valid for wirelined networks that are used to carry TCP like traffic. However, the emergence of wireless networks and the proliferation of services like voice over IP violate these assumptions. As already mentioned, in wireless networks a packet drop is not necessarily the result of congestion but it may be due to a low quality wireless channel. The current versions of TCP interpret packet drops as congestion and drastically reduce their transmission window. As a result, they can never achieve a high utilization of the available bandwidth. Furthermore, buffer management techniques have also been extensively studied (e.g., Active Queue Management (AQM)) but the underlying assumption in all these studies is that the sources respond to congestion signals by reducing their transmission rates. Even with responsive sources, the benefits of AQM approaches, such as RED, are not clear since as reported in Christiansen et al. (2001) for short lived sessions like Web traffic, RED did not provide any benefits. The question that arises is what happens when the traffic mix also includes a significant number of flows that are based on UDP that do not respond to congestion signals. Related to this question is what incentives

should be given to users to behave in ways that promote the "common" good, in the sense that they do not overload the network.

CONCLUSION

This chapter presents an overview of various buffer management approaches, such as tail drop, threshold policies and active queue management. Furthermore, it presents a framework based on stochastic fluid models and infinitesimal perturbation analysis that can be used to optimize various parameters of the buffer management techniques. Simulation results indicate that the proposed approach can lead to the optimal parameter setting within a few steps. Furthermore, the approach is simple and can be used online to continuously monitor the performance of each network node and making the necessary parameter adjustments such that the node's performance is kept close to the optimum.

REFERENCES

Alcaraz, J. J., & Cerdan, F. (2006). Using buffer management in 3G radio bearers to enhance end-to-end TCP performance. *20th International Conference on Advanced Information Networking and Applications*, 2006. AINA 2006..

Alemu, T., & Jean-Marie, A. (2004). Dynamic configuration of RED parameters [random early detection]. *Global Telecommunications Conference, 2004*. GLOBECOM '04. IEEE.

Athuraliya, S., Lapsley, D., et al. (2000). An enhanced random early marking algorithm for Internet flow control. INFOCOM 2000. The *19th Annual Joint Conference of the IEEE Computer and Communications Societies.*

Bernet, Y., Ford, P., et al. (2000). A framework for integrated services operation over Diffserv networks. *IETF RFC 2998.*

Blake, S., Black, D., et al. (1998). An architecture for differentiated services. *RFC 2475.*

Bonald, T., May, M., et al. (2000). Analytic evaluation of RED performance. *19th Annual Joint Conference of the IEEE Computer and Communications Societies (INFOCOM 2000).*

Braden, B., Clark, D., et al. (1998). Recommendations on queue management and congestion avoidance in the internet. *RFC 2309.*

Braden, R., Zhang, L., et al. (1997). Resource ReSerVation Protocol (RSVP). *RFC 2205.*

Cassandras, C. G., & Lafortune, S. (1999). *Introduction to discrete event systems.* Kluwer Academic Publishers.

Cassandras, C. G., Wardi, Y., et al. (2002). Perturbation analysis for online control and optimization of stochastic fluid models. *Automatic Control, IEEE Transactions on, 47*(8), 1234-1248.

Chien, C. H., & Liao, W. (2003). A self-configuring RED gateway for quality of service (QoS) networks. *2003 International Conference on Multimedia and Expo*, 2003. ICME '03.

Christiansen, M., Jeffay, K., et al. (2001). Tuning RED for Web traffic. *IEEE/ACM Transactions on Networking, 9*(3), 249-264.

Chrysostomou, C., Pitsillides, A., et al. (2003). Fuzzy logic controlled RED: Congestion control in TCP/IP differentiated services networks. *Soft Computing, 8*(2003) 79-92.

Chuang, H. C., Huang, C. Y., et al. (2004). On the buffer dynamics of scalable video streaming over wireless network. *IEEE 60th Vehicular Technology Conference 2004 (VTC2004-Fall).*

Cidon, I., Guérin, R., et al. (1994). On protective buffer policies. *IEEE/ACM Transactions on Networking, 2*(3), 240-246.

Clark, D. D., & Fang, W. (1998). Explicit allocation of best-effort packet delivery service. *IEEE/ACM Transactions on Networking, 6*(4), 362-373.

Dovrolis, C., & Ramanathann, P. (2000). Proportional differentiated services, part II: Loss rate differentiation and packet dropping. *2000 Eighth International Workshop on Quality of Service*, 2000. IWQOS.

Feng, W. C., Shin, K. G., et al. (2002). The BLUE active queue management algorithms. *IEEE/ACM Transactions on Networking, 10*(4), 513-528.

Floyd, S. (1994). TCP and explicit congestion notification. *ACM Computer Communication Review, 24*(5), 10-23.

Floyd, S. (1997). *RED: Discussions of setting parameters.*

Floyd, S. & Jacobson, V. (1993). Random early detection gateways for congestion avoidance. *IEEE/ACM Transactions on Networking, 1*(4), 397-413.

Gao, D., Shu, Y., et al. (2002). Evaluating RED performance in wireless base-station under self-similar traffic. *Canadian Conference on Electrical and Computer Engineering, 2002.* IEEE CCECE 2002.

Gyasi-Agyei, A. (2002). Service differentiation in wireless Internet using multiclass RED with drop threshold proportional scheduling. *10th IEEE International Conference on Networks.* ICON 2002.

Heinanen, J., F. Baker, et al. (1999). Assured forwarding PHB group. *RFC 2597.*

Heinanen, J., & Guérin, R. (1999). A single rate three color marker. *IETF RFC 2697.*

Heinanen, J., & Guérin, R. (1999). A two rate three color marker. *IETF RFC 2698.*

Ho, Y. C., & Cao, X. R. (1991). *Perturbation analysis of discrete event dynamic systems.* Boston, MA: Kluwer Academic Publishers.

Hoffman, D., Fernando, G., et al. (1998). RTP payload format for MPEG1/MPEG2 video.

Hollot, C. V., Misra, V., et al. (2002). Analysis and design of controllers for AQM routers supporting TCP flows. *IEEE Transactions on Automatic Control, 47*(6), 945-959.

Jacobson, V., Nichols, K., et al. (1999). An expedited forwarding PHB. *RFC 2598*.

Kamal, A. E., & Hassanein, H. S. (2004). Performance evaluation of prioritized scheduling with buffer management for differentiated services architectures. *Computer Networks, 46*(2), 169-180.

Kesidis, G., Singh, A., et al. (1996). Feasibility of fluid-driven simulation for ATM network. *Proc. IEEE Globecom.*

Kroner, H., Hebuterne, G., et al. (1991). Priority management in ATM switching nodes. *IEEE Journal on Selected Areas in Communications, 9*(3), 418-427.

Kumaran, K., & Mitra, D. (1998). Performance and fluid simulations of a novel shared buffer management system. *Proceedings of IEEE INFOCOM.*

Kushner, H. J., & Clark, D. S. (1978). *Stochastic approximation for constrained and unconstrained systems.* Berlin, Germany: Springer-Verlag.

Labrador, M. A., & Banerjee, S. (1999). Packet dropping policies for ATM and IP networks. *IEEE Communications Surveys & Tutorials, 2*(3), 2-14.

Lakshman, T. V., Neidhardt, A., et al. (1996). The drop from front strategy in TCP and in TCP over ATM. INFOCOM '96. The *15th Annual Joint Conference of the IEEE Computer Societies.*

Lapsley, D., & Low, S. (1999). Random early marking: An optimisation approach to Internet congestion control. 67-74.

Liebeherr, J. O. R., & Christin, N. (2001). JoBS: Joint buffer management and scheduling for differentiated services. *Lecture Notes in Computer Science, 2092,* 404.

Liebl, G., Jenkac, H., et al. (2005). Joint buffer management and scheduling for wireless video streaming. *Lecture Notes in Computer Science, 3420,* 882-891.

Liebl, G., Jenkac, H., et al. (2005). Radio link buffer management and scheduling for wireless video streaming. *Telecommunication Systems, 30*(1-3), 255-277.

Lin, A. Y. M., & Silvester, J. A. (1991). Priority queueing strategies and buffer allocation protocols for traffic control at an ATM integrated broadband switching system. *IEEE Journal on Selected Areas in Communications, 9*(9), 1524-1536.

Liu, B., Guo, Y., et al. (1999). Fluid simulation of large scale networks: Issues and tradeoffs. *Proceedings of the International Conference on Parallel and Distributed Processing Techniques and Applications.*

Markou, M. M., & Panayiotou, C. G. (2006). Dynamic control and optimization of buffer size in multiclass wireless networks. The *49th IEEE GLOBECOM Conference.*

Misra, V., Gong, W. B., et al. (2000). A fluid-based analysis of a network of AQM routers supporting TCP flows with an application to RED. *Proceedings of ACM SIGCOMM.*

Nam, D. H., & Park, S. K. (1999). Adaptive multimedia stream presentation in mobile computing environment. TENCON 99. *Proceedings of the IEEE Region 10 Conference.*

Ng, K. T., Chan, S. C., et al. (1996). Buffer control algorithm for low bit-rate video compression. *International Conference on Image Processing, 1996.*

Nichols, K., Blake, S., et al. (1998). Definition of the differentiated services field (DS Field) in the IPv4 and IPv6 Headers. *IETF RFC 2474.*

Panayiotou, C. G., Cassandras, C. G., et al. (2004). Control of communication networks using infinitesimal perturbation analysis of stochastic fluid models. In S. Tarbouriech, C. T. Abdallah, & J. Chiasson (Eds.), *Lecture notes in control and information sciences (LCNCIS): Advances in communication control networks*. Springer-Verlag.

Panayiotou, C. G., & Markou, M. M. (2007). Perturbation analysis for stochastic fluid models with respect to parameters of the fluid arrival process. *European Control Conference (ECC'07)*, Kos, Greece.

Pi, R., Song, J., et al. (2004). An integrated scheduling and buffer management scheme for packet-switched routers.

Reddy, T. B., Karthigeyan, I., et al. (2006). Quality of service provisioning in ad hoc wireless networks: A survey of issues and solutions. *Elsevier Ad Hoc Networks, 4*, 83-124.

Schulzrinne, H., Casner, S., et al. (2003). RTP: A transport protocol for real-time applications.

Schulzrinne, H., Rao, A., et al. (1998). Real Time Streaming Protocol (RTSP).

Sirisena, H., Haider, A., et al. (2002). Auto-tuning RED for accurate queue control. *Global Telecommunications Conference, 2002*. GLOBECOM '02. IEEE.

Sun, G., Cassandras, C. G., et al. (2004). Perturbation analysis of multiclass stochastic fluid models. *Journal of Discrete Event Dynamic Systems: Theory and Applications, 14*(3), 267-307.

Takahata, K., Uchida, N., et al. (2004). Optimal data rate control for video stream transmission over wireless network. *18th International Conference on Advanced Information Networking and Applications*, 2004. AINA 2004.

Verma, R., Iyer, A., et al. (2003). Towards an adaptive RED algorithm for achieving delay-loss performance. *Communications, IEE Proceedings*.

Wardi, Y., Melamed, B., et al. (2002). On-line IPA gradient estimators in single-node stochastic fluid models. *Journal of Optimization Theory and Applications, 115*(2), 369-405.

Yan, A., & Gong, W. B. (1999). Fluid simulation for high-speed networks with flow-based routing. *IEEE Transactions on Information Theory, 45*, 1588-1599.

Zhang, G., & Mouftah, H. T. (2001). End-to-end QoS guarantees over Diffserv networks. The *6th IEEE Symposium on Computers and Communications*, 2001.

Chapter VII
Power Saving in Wireless Multimedia Streaming to Mobile Devices

Gabriel-Miro Muntean
Dublin City University, Ireland

Janet Adams
Dublin City University, Ireland

ABSTRACT

Wireless networks are becoming a part of everyday life for many people. When a mobile device has wireless LAN capability, multimedia content can be streamed over a wireless network to that device. However, a major disadvantage of all mobile devices is their limited battery lifetime. Multimedia streaming puts extra pressure on the battery, causing it to discharge faster. In some cases, streaming tasks cannot be completed purely because the battery of the device becomes fully discharged, which causes significant user dissatisfaction. This chapter describes adaptive buffer power save mechanism (AB-PSM), a novel power saving wireless communication solution that enables an increase in battery lifetime during mobile multimedia streaming.

INTRODUCTION

There has been significant development in areas of both portable devices and wireless networks in recent years. It is now considered reasonable to support multimedia-streaming applications on mobile devices via wireless networks at high quality (Muntean & Cranley, 2007). However, development has concentrated on various pieces of hardware and software and has, to a large extent, neglected power. For example, although memory, CPU, and network bandwidth resources have increased exponentially in recent years, batteries have fallen behind in terms of development, improving by only about 2% per year over the last 50 years.

As it is a need to improve battery duration in order to keep up with the rising curve of application-based processing, device complexity, and wireless networking capabilities, our research proposes a novel power saving solution for wireless multimedia streaming process which enhances the existing IEEE 802.11 power save mechanism.

A typical architecture for mobile multimedia streaming includes a server, which streams multimedia content over a wireless IP network to a number of client devices. These devices could be PDAs, smartphones or any other mobile device with wireless connectivity. In relation to possible power savings, the multimedia streaming process can be described as consisting of three stages: reception, decoding and playing (Adams & Muntean, 2006). Other researchers have shown that energy savings can be made in each stage, for example by using pre-buffering in the reception stage, feedback control during decoding and backlight adjustment for playing. However, it is not a common practice to combine energy savings in the three stages in order to achieve the best overall savings. Due to the large amount of power used by the network interface card, the reception stage is the largest consumer of the battery and consequently could contribute the most in any power saving effort.

In this context, this chapter describes a novel adaptive-buffer power save mechanism (AB-PSM) that provides significant power savings in the reception stage, and hence to the overall battery life. The mechanism introduces a supplementary application level buffer and a control solution to manage when data is transmitted to wireless mobile stations. In this way, they are allowed to extend their time spent in power save mode and therefore they use less power.

The chapter starts with a description of the wireless multimedia streaming process main issues related to mobile devices, multimedia delivery, and wireless communications solutions. Related works that propose solutions for power saving in data reception, decoding and playing stages of multimedia streaming are presented and discussed in section three whereas section four gives details about the major characteristics of wireless communication solutions. The proposed AB-PSM is described in details in section five and testing setup, scenarios and results are presented in section six. The chapter ends with conclusions.

WIRELESS MULTIMEDIA STREAMING TO MOBILE DEVICES

Mobile Devices

Mobile devices are becoming smaller and more advanced in terms of processing power, memory, and communications capabilities. They are now capable of running increasingly complex applications and in particular, these devices can now play high quality multimedia clips due to improved screens and speakers. Additionally, many of these devices have wireless connectivity and can support multimedia streaming. In general, all mobile devices are battery powered, batteries, which can be recharged after depletion. However, chargers are in general heavy and require mains power supply, which may not be available while on the move. Also the charging process is lengthy and for best efficiency requires the mobile device to be switched off. These battery power limitations affect the most users' experience during mobile device usage. Examples of mobile devices with very limited battery power supply include personal digital assistants (PDA) and mobile phones. In comparison, the laptops have better batteries, but also drain more power.

Mobile devices are also becoming more popular than ever before. According to the Commission for Communications Regulation[1] in the Irish Communications Market quarterly report (Comm, 2007), mobile penetration in Ireland is now at 111% based on a population of 4.235 million. These figures are based on the number of active SIM cards, some users having more than one active card. This has increased steadily since the last quarter of 2002, when it was at 79%, reaching 100% penetration in the third quarter of 2005. In comparison with other European Union countries, Ireland is at the average, with Luxembourg and Italy at the top with over 130% and Belgium and France last with below 90% mobile phone penetration. In terms of mobile computers the situation is similar, laptops being very popular especially among the professionals and scholars.

Multimedia Streaming Process

Multimedia streaming process involves a client-server based architecture. The server and the clients communicate over a network, which for mobile device clients is wireless. A block diagram of the client-server wireless communication is shown in Figure 1.

Figure 1 clearly indicates how the wireless multimedia streaming process involves server and client sides. As the clients are battery powered mobile devices, in the quest to increase the battery life while the client wirelessly streams multimedia, three major stages can be focused on so that the highest possible power savings can be achieved. The three stages of the wireless multimedia streaming process are data reception, decoding and playing. By investigating the effect of each stage on the battery life of the device, it is possible to ascertain which stage is the most battery power intensive and hence, to know where

it will be most effective to make changes in order to save power.

The reception stage involves the reception at the client of the media data sent across the network by the server. It is a combination of all the network related tasks involved in the wireless streaming process. The decoding stage comprises the media being decoded by the client device once it has been received. The playing stage occurs once the media has been received and decoded. The nature of this stage will depend on the media type, which is received. For video, the screen and speakers will be involved, for music only the speakers and for images or silent video, it will just be the screen. The wireless multimedia streaming process is shown graphically in Figure 2.

Wireless Communication Solutions

Wireless communications have also grown in popularity in recent years. Many solutions that enable wireless access between compatible devices are available. Solutions such as WiFi, WiMax, Bluetooth, and UWB differ in terms of range, bandwidth, deployment, etc. Among them WiFi - generic term used to describe the connectivity provided by the IEEE 802.11 (IEEE80211, 2000) family of standards--is the most popular as best balances these different issues. Consequently, since the first standard ratification, WiFi growth and development has been very significant.

The majority of laptops come equipped with WiFi capability, whereas most PDAs and

Figure 1. Architecture for wireless multimedia streaming process

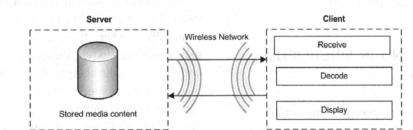

Figure 2. Major stages in the wireless multimedia streaming process

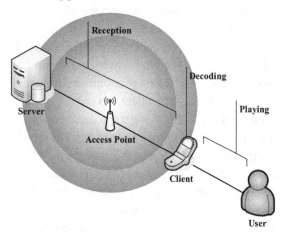

increasing number of mobile phones also have WiFi connectivity. Game consoles such as the Playstation Portable[2] and the Nintendo DS[3] have WiFi capability.

Recently it has become quite common for regular home broadband users to have a WiFi network set up in their home, whereas WiFi has also become widely used in educational institutions and in growing number of companies. The use of public WiFi hotspots has also grown. For example, Ireland has the highest number of wireless hotspots per head of population in the world at 18.3 per 100,000 people.[4]

WiFi deployment is developing so that eventually, entire cities will be covered by wireless networks, and eventually seamless handovers may be provided from one to the next so that uninterrupted wireless access can be achieved which will result in increased user satisfaction. This will in turn facilitate further growth and popularity of wireless multimedia streaming.

POWER SAVING IN MULTIMEDIA STREAMING

The area of power saving during multimedia streaming is one that has been thoroughly re-searched. There have been many different approaches to it, which can make classification difficult. However, broadly speaking, the majority of approaches fall into the following three main categories: controlling the burstiness of network traffic, memory optimization, and compiler and/or application efficiency.

In Acquaviva, Benini, and Ricco (2001), the authors focus specifically on embedded devices that are designed with multimedia streaming in mind. The authors propose to save energy by allowing an application to dynamically reconfigure the system so that the performance levels and required services are provided without wasting power. They highlight the possibility to reduce power consumption by reducing the speed and supply voltage to the minimum level necessary in order to match real-time constraints. While other researchers observe in Chandrakasan, Sheng and Brodersen (1992) that frequency scaling decreases power but not energy unless it is coupled with supply voltage scaling, Acquaviva et al. demonstrate that energy can be saved by frequency scaling, even with a constant voltage supply. They achieve this by obtaining a set of three normalized curves: the overall best frame rate, the overall worst frame rate and the overall average frame rate. These curves relate multimedia streaming application performance with processor clock frequency. The authors develop an algorithm that controls the processor speed in order to save power, while ensuring that any real-time constraints are satisfied. As the application provides the information required to set the processor speed, this is an application-driven method of frequency scaling.

Another application driven frequency scaling method can be found in Flinn and Satyanarayanan (1999), where the authors concentrate on user experience when the energy level is low and then when the energy level drops, the focus is toward energy conservation. Their results show up to 30% energy savings. Their solution is based on the Linux operating system and has not been tested on other platforms. An additional application driven frequency scaling method is presented in Sinha and Chandrakasan (2000), where the authors present an energy model for software which separates the voltage switching and voltage leaking components and predicts the total energy consumption.

Some operating-system level schemes are introduced in Krishna and Lee (2000), Ishihara and Yasuura (1998), and Martin (1999). Acquaviva et al. argue that in comparison to other frequency scaling schemes, theirs is robust and does not suffer from poor stability and poor real-time performance problems. Their results show that they can achieve up to 40% saving with respect to fixed-frequency operation while satisfying real-time playback constraints.

Korhonen and Wang study the effect of burst length and peak transmission rate for observed packet loss and delay characteristics and also potential energy savings in wireless local area networks (WLAN) (2005). They argue that power related research in the area of wireless multimedia can be divided into two principle categories: power-aware multimedia decoding, where the power save is implemented when the power level drops, such as in Pouwelse, Langendoen, and Sips (2003) and Choi, Dantu, Cheng, and Pedram (2002) and power-efficient radio communications where power-efficient methods are used from the outset, as in Zhu and Cao (2004), Havinga and Smit (2001), and Acquaviva, Lattanzi, and Bogliolo (2004). The authors state that streaming applications typically transmit a constant stream of packets with periodic arrival times. For this reason, the legacy power save mode of 802.11 is not suitable as the gaps between the packets are so short that the station would never actually enter sleep mode. To counter this problem, Korhonen et al. propose a solution that employs a layered multimedia coding scheme with a customized packet scheduler, which provides bursty traffic with a decreasing priority order of packets in each burst. The scheme allows the receiver to

sacrifice some of the enhancement layer data in order to maintain stable power efficiency. They then implement a test system incorporating this adaptive burst length. This achieves an improved trade-off between power efficiency and congestion tolerance. One of the major disadvantages of this scheme is that the role of CSMA/CA, as used in 802.11, is omitted. It is therefore very difficult to implement this solution on current 802.11 devices.

In Anastasi, Passarella, Conti, Gregori, and Pelusi (2005), the authors look specifically at streaming of audio content to a mobile device that is connected to the Internet by means of a wireless connection. They provide a solution to the power consumption problem of mobile devices dealing with multimedia streaming. Their solution allowed the wireless network interface card (WNIC) to reduce to between 9% and 24%, depending on various conditions, of the energy consumption achieved by current systems. They do this by including periodic transmission interruptions in the schedule of the frames (in their case all frames are audio) at the server so that the WNIC can be set to sleep. However, they do not integrate their solution with the legacy 802.11 PSM, instead opting to disable the legacy power save. Their reasons behind this are that the legacy PSM only performs well when used with regular traffic (Chandra & Vahdat, 2002). Although this is true, it would perhaps make more sense to improve the legacy PSM to work with burst traffic rather than omitting it completely. They conclude their paper with an interesting result: the higher the burstiness of the traffic, the more power savings their scheme achieves.

In Mohapatra, Cornea, Dutt, Nicolau, and Venkatasubramanian (2003) the interesting argument that there is a distinct lack of cross-level integration between the different power saving techniques that have been proposed in recent years is presented. The authors state that the majority of the proposed power saving techniques can be attributed to one of the following categories:

system cache, external memory access optimization and DVS (Mesarina & Turner, 2003; Pillai & Shin, 2002), dynamic power management of disks and network interfaces, efficient compilers, and application/middleware-based applications (Mohapatra & Venkatasubramanian, 2003; Noble et al., 1997). Mohapatra et al. argue that all these approaches are independent and that the power saving capabilities could be improved by combining the different techniques. In order to do this, it is necessary to investigate the trade-offs involved and the customization required. In order to address this potential cross-level integration, Mohapatra et al. devise an algorithm that takes an integrated approach to power management. They do this by combining low-level architectural optimizations, OS power-saving mechanisms and adaptive middleware techniques. The low-level architectural optimizations that they address include the CPU, the memory, and the register. The OS power-saving technique was dynamic voltage scaling and the adaptive middleware technique included admission control, optimal transcoding and network traffic regulation. All of these techniques were then combined to make the integrated power save solution. Some knowledge of the system and device characteristics was required in order for the middleware technique to adapt the video to the appropriate quality. Their results show significant improvements with energy gains up to 57.5% for the CPU and memory and 70% for the WNIC. User experience was improved by the device lasting longer.

Zhu and Cao (2005) use a scheduling algorithm at the base station called rate-based bulk scheduling which decides which flow should be served at which time. A proxy at the mobile terminal buffers data so that the WNIC can sleep for longer periods. The sleep time is adjusted based on the channel conditions.

Other power saving schemes for the WNIC have been designed at different levels of the OSI network model. For example, work proposed for the MAC layer includes Krashinsky and Bal-

akrishnan (2002), Prabhakar, Biyikoglu, and El Gamal (2001), and Zhang, Ge, and Hou (2003) as well as the legacy PSM in the IEEE 802.11 standard. Some solutions proposed for the network layer are described in Li, Aslam, and Rus (2001) and Xu, Heidemann, and Estrin (2001) whereas Stemm and Katz (1997) propose a transport layer solution. The work proposed in this chapter is a solution involving both transport and application layers.

The *reception stage* of the multimedia streaming process is related to sending and receiving of data. In general power saving in this stage involves WNIC. Best known energy-aware solutions include an application-specific server side traffic shaping mechanism proposed in Chandra et al. (2002), a buffer-based energy efficient CPU scheduler for mobile devices described in Bae, Kim, Kim, and Park (2005), a scheme that uses traffic shaping with added benefit of a proxy scheduling algorithm introduced in Zhang and Chanson (2005), and a client side energy prediction scheme is described in Wei, Bhandarkar, and Chandra (2006).

The *decoding stage* is when the device receives the data and decodes it to a playable format. However, the encoding of multimedia data will impact on the amount of battery required for this stage. Power saving solutions which have been proposed in this stage generally focus on making the decoding of the data more efficient. Solutions include two schemes based on reducing the number of memory and bus accesses by high level language optimization presented in Pakdeepaiboonpol and Kittitornkun (2005), a mechanism to reduce the multimedia decoding power by using feedback control proposed in Lu, Lach, Stan, and Skadron (2003), a scheme, which can lower the supply voltage and reduce the power consumption detailed in Lee (2005) and the results of an investigation of the effect of dynamic voltage scaling on the trade off between energy consumption and high picture quality in multimedia decoding presented in Mesarina et al. (2003).

The *playing stage* involves all activities related to displaying of the media to the user. Depending on the media type, this stage will involve the screen, the speakers, or a combination of the two. The majority of power saving in this area has focused on the screen of the device, in particular the backlight as in Pasricha, Mohapatra, Luthra, Dutt, and Venkatasubramanian (2003) and Shim, Chang, and Pedram (2004). There is no known research on the effect of the speakers on the battery.

IEEE 802.11 WIRELESS COMMUNICATIONS

IEEE 802.11 Overview

IEEE 802.11 refers to a set of WLAN standards developed by the working group 11 of the IEEE LAN/MAN Standards Committee (IEEE 802). This section briefly describes this IEEE 802.11 family of standards (IEEE80211, 2000) and highlights its power-related solutions.

The basic building block of the IEEE 802.11 architecture is the basic service set (BSS), which is defined as a set of stations (STA) controlled by a single coordination function, which could be point coordination function (PCF) or distributed coordination function (DCF). A coordination function determines when a STA can transmit within the BSS. In DCF, the same coordination function logic is active in every STA of the BSS whereas in PCF the coordination function logic is only ever active in one STA in the BSS at any one time. Both PCF and DCF can operate at the same time.

The 802.11 architecture allows for two types of operational modes: infrastructure and independent BSS (IBSS) or ad-hoc. In the infrastructure mode, in each BSS centralized data distribution exists in form of an access point (AP) and all communication goes through this AP. In IBSS direct communication between STAs is enabled

without the need for an AP and is often formed without being pre-planned and for temporary use. The work in this chapter will use the infrastructure mode.

PCF and DCF

PCF provides contention-free data transfer. In PCF, a point coordinator (PC) is present in the AP and it controls when STAs can transmit and at what time. During a contention free period (CFP), the PC will allow a STA operating in PCF mode to transmit. While a STA is transmitting, no other STA can transmit. In IEEE 802.11, PCF is optional and rarely implemented.

The principle **DCF** uses is CSMA/CA. This is implemented in all STAs within both types of configurations i.e. ad-hoc and infrastructure. When a STA wants to transmit it first senses the medium to see if another STA is transmitting. If the medium is free then the STA can commence its transmission. CSMA/CA specifies that there must be a minimum duration between adjacent frame sequences. Therefore any STA will wait for this amount of time after deeming the medium idle before commencing transmission. If the medium is busy, the STA will wait until the current transmission is complete, then select a random back off interval which will be decremented while the medium is idle.

Further to this, it is possible to also use short control frames, known as Request to Send (RTS) and Clear to Send (CTS) after determining that the medium is idle and after any waits or back offs. The RTS and CTS frames contain a duration/ID field, which defines the time required to transmit the data frame and the returning ACK frame. A station STA1 before transmitting data to station STA2 sends a RTS frame, which is broadcast to all STAs in the range and contains a field, which specifies the intended recipient of the data packet. When STA2 receives the RTS it responds with a CTS and STA1 can proceed with the transmission. To further prevent collisions, Network Allocation

Vectors (NAV) are used. When all STAs in the BSS get the RTS, they set a NAV which is basically a time in which they cannot send. This means that they will not collide with the transmission. All the STAs also get the CTS and update NAV. This is to allow for any STA that did not see the RTS to avoid collision.

When DCF is used there are some performance limitations:

- If multiple stations communicate simultaneously, then collisions will occur, which will reduce bandwidth.

- If a station that has a low bit rate receives access to the medium and can therefore transmit, all other stations must wait until it is finished, which will take a long time when bit rate is low.

- There is no prioritization of traffic or QoS guarantees.

IEEE 802.11 Amendments

The original standard needed improving as it had low data rates and a short range. Since the release of IEEE 802.11 there have been various amendments made to it. Some of them increase bitrate or range, others aim specifically at various aspects such as security, voice or quality of service (QoS).

The **IEEE 802.11b** amendment to the original standard was ratified in 1999 (IEEE80211b, 1999). 802.11b has a maximum raw data rate of 11 Mbit/s and like the legacy standard, uses CSMA/CA. Due to the overhead incurred by CSMA/CA, the actual achievable throughput is in fact lower, about 5.9 Mbit/s using TCP and 7.1 Mbit/s using UDP.

Due to the similarity that 802.11b had with the original standard, the equipment was inexpensive and easy to produce and therefore was released to the market relative quickly. As 802.11b had a high throughput (compared to original standard) and was easy to implement, it became popular very quickly. It is the most widely accepted of the WLAN standards to date and it is usually used in an infrastructure configuration. The range is approximately 150 feet indoors and 300 to 500 feet outdoors. 802.11b can operate at a maximum rate of 11Mbit/s but as the signal becomes weaker rate drops first to 5.5 Mbit/s, then 2 Mbit/s and finally to 1 Mbit/s.

IEEE 802.11a was ratified in 1999 (IEEE80211a, 1999). Using the same base protocol as the original standard, it operates in the 5GHz band and has a maximum data rate of 54Mbit/s (in reality, the achievable throughout is approximately 20Mbit/s). IEEE 802.11a is not interoperable with 802.11b unless the equipment being used is specifically designed for this purpose.

The main advantage of 802.11a is that the 5GHz band has less interference. However, the use of 802.11a is reduced to almost line of sight and because the range is not as good as 802.11b, more access points are required. The equipment for 802.11a was released after the equipment for 802.11b due mainly to the difficulty in acquiring the 5GHz components. As when 802.11a was released, 802.11b was already widely used and as it was less expensive and had a larger range, people were unwilling to change. In response to this, 802.11a was improved so that the range almost equaled that of the 802.11b and technology allowed more than one 802.11 standard to be used with the same equipment, but not at the same time. In spite of this, 802.11a it still not as popular as 802.11b.

IEEE 802.11g was introduced in 2003 (IEEE80211g, 2003). Like 802.11b, 802.11g works in the 2.4GHz range but it achieves a maximum data rate of 54Mbit/s, which is the same as 802.11a. It is backwards compatible with 802.11b and both standards work well together. The range of 802.11g is similar to that of 802.11b but to achieve the maximum advertised rate, it is necessary to be quite close to the AP. When 802.11g was ratified, the devices that had been dual band to allow for 802.11a and 802.11b became tri-band to support 802.11g as well. Although it has a higher data rate, 802.11g is subject to the same interference problems as 802.11b.

IEEE 802.11e (IEEE80211e, 2005) is an amendment to the 802.11 standard that is specifically intended for QoS enhancements. This standard is extremely important for delay-sensitive applications, particularly for the streaming of multimedia content. The enhancements are made to the MAC layer of the OSI model. 802.11e was approved in late 2005.

In 802.11e a new coordination function is used which is called the hybrid coordination function (HCF). In HCF, two methods of channel access are used: the HCF controlled channel access (HCCA) and the enhanced DCF channel access (EDCA). Traffic classes are defined within both. This allows for prioritization of traffic. Each priority level is assigned a transmit opportunity (TXOP), which is an interval of time that a STA can use to send as many frames as possible. Frames that are too large to be sent in a TXOP are fragmented. While EDCA and TXOP are mandatory for APs, all other 802.11e enhancements are optional.

The latest addition to the 802.11 family is **IEEE 802.11n** (IEEE80211n, 2006). Due to be ratified in approximately early 2008, it is reported to have a theoretical output of 540 Mbit/s making it up to fifty time times faster than 802.11b. 802.11n adds MIMO which uses multiple transmitter and receiver antennas to allow for increased data throughput. It will operate in the 2.4 and 5GHz spectrum and will have a typical range of 150 feet.

With the introduction of 802.11n, there will be three modes in which an 802.11 access point can operate:

- **Legacy:** 802.11a, 802.11b and 802.11g
- **Mixed:** 802.11a, 802.11b, 802.11g and 802.11n
- **Greenfield:** 802.11n only

The Greenfield mode gives maximum performance.

Power Saving in IEEE 802.11 Networks

The reception stage is the most significant power drainer in the wireless transmission process due to the fact that the WNIC consumes a large amount of energy. For this reason, methods to save battery power during this stage are being devised.

Within the 802.11 standard, there is a built in power save mechanism (PSM) (IEEE80211, 1999). There are two power management modes for 802.11 STAs:

- **Active Mode (AM):** STAs can receive and transmit frames and have normal energy consumption levels.
- **Power Save Mode (PS):** STAs can be in one of two possible states:
  - **Awake:** The station is fully powered and is able to transmit and receive data
  - or
  - **Doze:** The station is asleep, cannot transmit or receive and consumes very little power.

If STAs are using the power management mode, they inform the AP via the frame control field of the transmitted frames (i.e., set to 1 if power management is used and 0 otherwise). The AP maintains a power management state for each associated STA.

When using power management, a STA can enter a low power sleep state when it is not receiving traffic and this is how it saves power. If AP receives packets for a station that is in sleep mode, then it will buffer these packets in the AP buffer.

At regular intervals, AP sends to all STAs a special frame called beacon that contains control information. All STAs, including those that are sleeping, will listen to beacons to check if there is traffic for them. The STAs for which AP have buffered data are identified in a Traffic Indication Map (TIM), which is included in all beacons generated by the AP. TIM also indicates whether there is broadcast or multicast traffic waiting. If a TIM indicates that there is data for a particular STA, which is in PS mode, the STA will wake up and send a PS-Poll frame to the AP. AP will deliver data to a STA in PS mode only as a response to a PS-Poll. The corresponding buffered data will be delivered immediately or later after first an acknowledgement of the PS-Poll was sent. Once received the data, the STA sends an acknowledgement to the AP.

Every a given number of TIMs (in general three), a delivery TIM (DTIM) is sent. After DTIM, the AP transmits any broadcast or multicast traffic before transmitting the unicast traffic.

STAs in PS mode and in the doze state enter the awake state to receive selected beacons, broadcast, and multicast packets and responses to transmitted PS-Poll frames. How often STAs listen to the medium for beacons is determined by the ListenInterval parameter. This is usually set to the same value as the beacon interval (default value is 100ms), which means that STAs listen to every beacon.

Although this PSM does save power in mobile STAs, the savings are minimal as the ListenInterval is not used in the most power-efficient manner. ListenInterval determines whether or not the STAs wake up for every beacon or whether they sleep through some of them. As ListenInterval is rarely changed from the default value, STAs wake up for every beacon, consuming power.

In Kwon, Kim, Park, and Jung (2005), they carry out experiments to investigate the performance effects and energy saving of the IEEE 802.11 PSM. They measure the throughput and performance time of a STA working in PSM with various applications and in comparison with STAs working in active mode. Their results show that this PSM successfully saves energy when in a heavy and continuous traffic situation. They also illustrate that a multimedia streaming application suffers little decrease in performance when using PSM.

ADAPTIVE-BUFFER POWER SAVE MECHANISM

This section describes the newly proposed power save scheme for wireless multimedia streaming-- the adaptive-buffer power save mechanism (AB-PSM), which improves streaming device battery life while maintaining good level of end-user perceived quality. This scheme complements the legacy power save mechanism (PSM) described in the IEEE 802.11 standard as opposed to replacing it. An important advantage of the AB-PSM is that it can be implemented into current networked applications without requiring any standard adjustments.

AB-PSM Principle

As in the legacy 802.11 PSM, the AB-PSM principle relies on the fact that, in order to save power, the device will enter the low-power sleep state when it is idle. However, the device will only enter this mode once it has received all waiting traffic and there is none buffered for it at the access point (AP). In order to achieve higher power save, AB-PSM regularly hides traffic from the AP, which in turn informs the STA that there is no traffic for it. To achieve significant power savings, this must be done at least every second beacon interval. In normal 802.11 operation, the traffic would be sent so frequently that this would not occur often enough to achieve significant power savings. Therefore, the way that the traffic is sent must be changed to allow the AP to inform the device that there is no traffic and therefore, allow it to sleep for longer periods.

AB-PSM does this by introducing a second buffer called the application buffer. This is in addition to the access point (AP) buffer and it is implemented on the server. The application buffer effectively hides packets from the default AP buffer. This means that when a beacon is received, the TIM only reports traffic, which is waiting in the AP buffer and is not influenced by the data that is in the application buffer. Therefore, if this happens often enough, the device will sleep for longer periods of time. Figure 3 presents the system architecture for AB-PSM, indicating the server, AP, and client as well as the application and AP buffers.

Assuming that the ListenInterval is set to one, as is generally the case, the station will wake up at every beacon interval to listen to the beacon. If the TIM within the beacon indicates that there is buffered traffic at the AP, the station will enter the fully awake state in order to receive it, otherwise it will return to the low power sleep mode. The Application Buffer stores the packets so that when the beacon is sent, the TIM reports no traffic. The station can then return to the low power sleep mode. Once the beacon interval has passed, the Application Buffer will allow the packets to move to the Access Point Buffer so that, at the next beacon interval the station will see that there is traffic waiting for it and stay awake to receive it.

The amount of time that the packets are stored in the Application Buffer can be varied. The packets could be held so as to skip one, two or more beacon intervals, saving power and enabling the battery to last longer. However, the longer

the packets are held in the Application Buffer, the higher the probability of delay. For non-real time data applications, this may be acceptable but for real-time streaming, it will not be tolerated. For this reason, it is necessary to set a threshold time for which the packets can be hidden in the Application Buffer. This time is a multiple of the beacon interval. For example, two, three or more beacon intervals can be skipped and this number will directly relate to the threshold time. Figure 4 graphically presents two examples with one and two skipped beacon intervals.

One of the main benefits of the newly proposed AB-PSM scheme is that it requires no changes to the 802.11 standard. The station will still wake to receive beacons and in this way, will still be able to receive any broadcast or multicast packets sent on the network. AB-PSM saves power by allowing the station to sleep for a longer amount of time. It achieves this while still allowing the station to receive all beacons and to behave as defined in the 802.11 standard. The fact that the station can still receive all beacons means that, from the network point of view, the station is behaving identically whether using AB-PSM or not.

The scheme is described graphically in Figure 5. In this diagram, there are three timelines. The top one represents 802.11 with the power save mechanism disabled. The middle one shows 802.11 with the legacy power save mechanism enabled. The final one shows 802.11 with AB-PSM enabled. Notice the introduction of the Application Buffer in AB-PSM and the fact that the station only receives traffic every second beacon, on the others it can return to sleep.

AB-PSM can be controlled adaptively and the amount of time that the Application Buffer stores the packets can be adjusted based on the battery power level remaining in the device.

Scalability Issues and Solutions

Some scalability issues occur with AB-PSM when more than one client is included. For example,

Figure 3. AB-PSM architecture

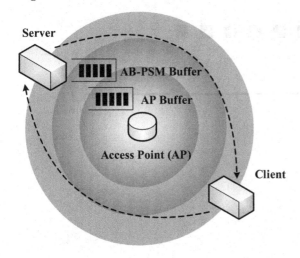

Figure 4. Transmission examples with one and two skipped beacon intervals

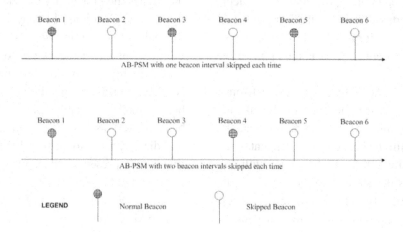

Figure 5. Graphical comparison IEEE 802.11 transmission with: No power save, legacy power save, and AB-PSM

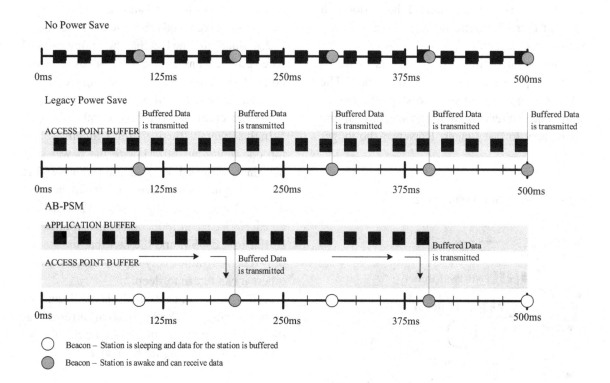

assuming that two clients synchronize (i.e., they sleep through the same beacon intervals and wake to receive traffic at the same time), this will cause inefficient and unfair usage of AB-PSM will occur. Due to the fact that both clients will not be able to receive traffic synchronously (as specified in the 802.11 standard), one client must stay awake for twice as long. This is because both clients wake at the beacon interval and see that there is buffered traffic waiting for them. Therefore, both clients will stay awake to receive this data. However, only one client will be able to receive traffic at a time, which means that the second client will have to remain awake while the first client receives its data and then while it receives its own data. This is counter-productive because

the client that must wait is using battery power when it is not doing anything and could be asleep, saving power.

This is shown in detail in Figure 6. It can be seen that the clients synchronise at the beginning and because of this, Client 2 has to remain awake until Client 1 finishes receiving its data. This is completely inefficient.

To avoid this, it is necessary to make sure that the clients do not synchronize. To do this, instead of just specifying the interval (e.g., telling the client to wake at every second interval), the starting point will also be specified. Clients will therefore sleep and wake up at different points in time and consequently any synchronization problems will be avoided.

Figure 6. AB-PSM scalability issues

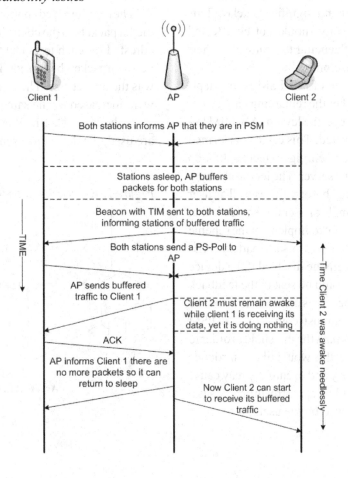

AB-PSM Advantages

AB-PSM has many benefits over other schemes. In terms of the PSM specified in the standard, AB-PSM offers better savings in a more efficient manner. It does this taking advantage of the beacons, unlike other schemes, which choose to ignore them, in spite of the fact that they are a fundamental part of the 802.11 standard. Any of these proposed schemes that do not work in conjunction with the 802.11 standard may either not work with 802.11 equipment or will not take full advantage of the 802.11 features, making them difficult to implement. AB-PSM will work without any changes to hardware, being extremely user friendly and implementable.

Another advantage is that the user will not be aware of the AB-PSM. The proposed power saving solution works in the background and ensures that there is no significant delay. This means that user quality should not be affected while positively influencing the battery of their device making it last longer.

Another advantage of AB-PSM is its adaptability. Based on either the remaining battery life or the user's preference, the level of AB-PSM being used can be adjusted. This can be performed adaptively by implementing a feedback loop from the device to the server. The feedback could contain the remaining battery life as well as user preference. An example of user preference is that the user may choose not to implement the scheme because they do not need to save battery. AB-PSM will automatically be disabled if the device is plugged in. This would be sent in the feedback loop. If the battery becomes critically low and the multimedia task is almost complete, AB-PSM could temporarily bypass the threshold in order to complete the task. As this would likely introduce a user detectable delay and eventually may cause some loss during multimedia streaming, this is a decision to be approved by the user.

EXPERIMENTAL TESTING

Test Setup and Scenarios

In order to assess the effectiveness of the newly proposed AB-PSM, tests were performed to compare it to the case when streaming is performed over IEEE 802.11 with no PSM employed and with the legacy PSM, respectively. For these tests, a 3GHz Pentium 4 desktop computer with 1GB of RAM using the Microsoft Windows XP operating system, was used as the server. The client was a personal digital assistant (PDA), with a 520MHz CPU, 64MB RAM and running Microsoft Windows Mobile 5 operating system. The multimedia content was sent from the server, to an IEEE 802.11b AP and then via the wireless network to the client. The testbed is shown in Figure 7.

The tests involved continuously sending multimedia packets to the client. Two parameters were adjusted for each test. The first was the interval between packets being sent. The second parameter was the packet size. The interval and packet size were increased by the same factor.

In the cases when no PSM and the legacy PSM are used, the data is just sent and the packet size

Figure 7. Experimental testbed

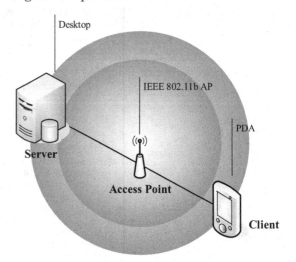

or interval length makes no difference. With no PSM, the device never sleeps. With the legacy PSM, if the device is idle, it will enter the low power sleep mode. However, as the main idea of AB-PSM is to send a larger amount of data less frequently, the tests involved increasing the packet size by the same factor as the interval, hence keeping the average data bit rate constant. The beacon interval is set to the default value of 100ms in all tests.

Comparison Between Different PSM

The goal of these tests is to see if AB-PSM had any effect on applications with a smaller bandwidth than that required for multimedia streaming. The first set of tests used smaller packets than those used for video streaming. These were performed in order to show the effect of AB-PSM on general network tasks within multimedia streaming. The interval between sent packets is represented in terms of milliseconds and ranges from 25ms to 200ms. The packet sizes, or more specifically

the size of the multimedia data chunks before lower layer fragmentation, are also shown and range from 512B(ytes) to 4096B. The first test included 802.11 with the PSM disabled, with a 25ms inter-packet sending interval and packet size of 512B. The second test used the same settings as in the first, but this time the 802.11 legacy PSM was enabled. The third test used AB-PSM with an inter-packet sending interval of 100ms and a packet size of 2048B and the final test, also using AB-PSM, had an interval of 200ms and a packet size of 4096B. As all of the intervals were increased by the same factor as the packet size, the same amount of data was sent in every case.

Testing results are presented in Figure 8. The graph shows four bars, each representing the results of one of the tests previously described. The x-axis in the graphs represents the time in minutes that battery of the device lasted.

The results show significant increases in the battery life when AB-PSM is used in comparison with both other cases: when no power saving and when the legacy PSM is employed respectively.

Figure 8. Comparison between no PSM, legacy PSM and two versions of AB-PSM

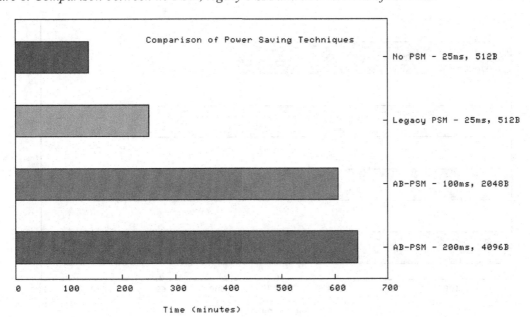

This battery life increase accounts for 140% when first AB-PSM scenario was considered and 160% in the second AB-PSM test in comparison with the same legacy IEEE 802.11 PSM.

AB-PSM: Effect of Inter-Packet Sending Interval

Further tests were performed to investigate the effect of the interval between sent on the battery power consumption rate. If in the previous tests, the average sending data rate was the same, in the following tests the amount of data being sent varies.

In these tests, AB-PSM was used. The packet size was kept constant at 2048B, and the sending interval between two data packets varied from 50ms to 200ms. The results shown in Figure 9 indicate that by adjusting the interval in 50ms increments, the battery lifetime increases. Between the first and second case, there is an increase in battery lifetime of over 150 minutes. Between the second and the third and the third and the

fourth cases respectively, there is an increase of approximately 60 minutes per each 50ms increment. The large difference in the first case can be attributed to the fact that this is the only case where the interval is less than the beacon interval, which is set to 100ms.

AB-PSM: Effect of Packet Size

This section investigates the effect that the packet size has on the battery life. For these tests, AB-PSM was used. The base values were an interval of 100ms and a packet size of 2048B.

The tests involved keeping the inter-packet sending interval constant at 100ms and varying the packet size. The same testbed as shown in Figure 7 was used. The results from Figure 10 indicate that varying the packet size has a less important effect on the battery than varying the inter-packet sending interval. This suggests that during AB-PSM a large increase in battery life can be attributed to the inter packet sending interval. However, in order for AB-PSM to work efficiently

Figure 9. AB-PSM: Effect of inter-packet sending interval on battery life span

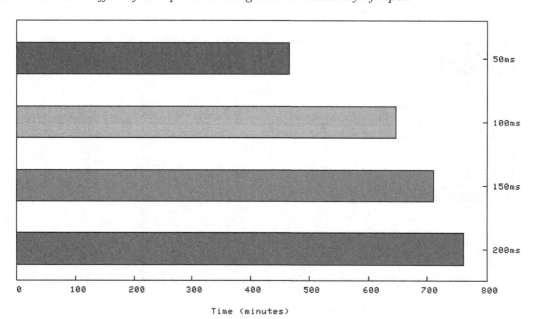

it is essential to send data in large chunks so as to force the station to return to the low power sleep mode as often as possible.

CONCLUSION

Wireless multimedia streaming process to battery powered mobile devices has three major stages: data reception, decoding, and playing. As the reception stage is the biggest consumer of power, the largest power savings can be obtained in this stage.

This chapter presents a novel power saving solution in the reception stage, the adaptive-buffer power save mechanism (AB-PSM). AB-PSM is a mechanism that makes use of an additional application buffer in order to "hide" packets temporarily from the stations they are intended for, allowing them to sleep for longer periods and consequently to save power.

Experimental tests involving wireless multimedia streaming with a client-server testbed have shown significant increases in battery life when AB-PSM is used. For example, tests presented in this chapter indicate that when AB-PSM is used,

the battery life increased by 160% in comparison with the legacy power save mode described in the IEEE 802.11 standard and over 500% in comparison with the situation when no power save mechanism was employed.

Tests were also carried out to investigate the effect on the battery duration of packet size and interval between packets sent. These tests showed that the effect of packet size on battery life span was not significant. However the inter-packet sending interval had an important effect on the battery consumption rate. The longer the period of time between sending packets, the longer the period of time the stations are allowed to sleep, saving power. Consequently the battery duration increases and so potential user satisfaction.

REFERENCES

Acquaviva, A., Benini, L., & Ricco, B. (2001). Software-controlled processor speed setting for low-power streaming multimedia. *IEEE Transactions on Computer-Aided Design of Integrated Circuits and Systems*, *20*, 1283-1292, November 2001.

Figure 10. AB-PSM: Effect of packet size on battery life span

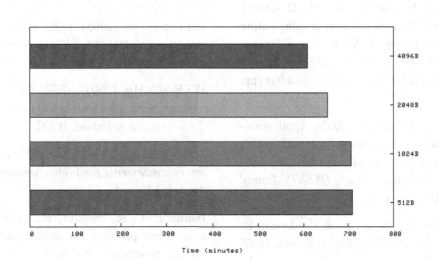

Acquaviva, A., Lattanzi, E., & Bogliolo, A. (2004). Design and simulation of power-aware scheduling strategies of streaming data in wireless LANs. *ACM MSWiM 2004 – Proceedings of the 7th ACM Symposium on Modeling, Analysis, and Simulation of Wireless and Mobile Systems* (pp. 39-46).

Adams, J., & Muntean, G. M. (2006). Power-dependent adaptation algorithm for mobile multimedia networking. *IEEE International Symposium on Broadband Multimedia Systems and Broadcasting*, April 2006.

Adams, J., & Muntean, G. M. (2007a). Power save adaptation algorithm for multimedia streaming to mobile devices. *IEEE International Conference on Portable Information Devices,* Orlando, Florida, USA, 2007.

Adams, J., & Muntean, G. M. (2007b). Adaptive-bu®er power save mechanism for mobile multimedia streaming. *IEEE International Conference on Communications (ICC07),* Glasgow, Scotland, UK, 2007.

Anastasi, G., Passarella, A., Conti, M., Gregori, E., & Pelusi, L. (2005). A power-aware multimedia streaming protocol for mobile users. *Proceedings of the International Conference on Pervasive Services 2005* (pp. 371-80).

Bae, G., Kim, J., Kim, D., & Park, D. (2005). Low-power multimedia scheduling using output pre-buffering. *13th IEEE International Symposium on Modeling, Analysis, and Simulation of Computer and Telecommunication Systems* (pp. 389-96).

Chandra, S., & Vahdat, A. (2002). Application-specific network management for energy-aware streaming of popular multimedia formats. *Proceedings of the General Track, USENIX Annual Technical Conference* (pp. 329-42).

Chandrakasan, A., Sheng, S., & Brodersen, R. (1992). Low-power CMOS digital design. *IEEE Journal of Solid-State Circuits, 27*(4), 473-484.

Choi, K., Dantu, K., Cheng, W. C., & Pedram, M. (2002). Frame-based dynamic voltage and frequency scaling for a MPEG decoder. *IEEE/ACM International Conference on Computer Aided Design. IEEE/ACM Digest of Technical Papers (Cat. No.02CH37391)* (pp. 732-737).

Commission for Communications. (2007). *Irish communications market: Quarterly key data report.* Tech. Rep., Commission for Communications Regulation, Ireland http://www.comreg.ie, 2007.

Flinn, J., & Satyanarayanan, M. (1999). Energy-aware adaptation for mobile applications. *Operating Systems Review, 33*(5), 48-63.

Havinga, P., & Smit, G. (2001). Energy-efficient wireless networking for multimedia applications. *Wireless Communications and Mobile Computing, 1*(2), 165-184.

IEEE 802.11. (2000). *IEEE 802.11: Wireless LAN medium access control (MAC) and physical layer (PHY) specification.* Standard, IEEE.

IEEE 802.11a. (1999). *IEEE 802.11a: High-speed physical layer in the 5GHz band.* Standard, IEEE.

IEEE 802.11b. (2001). *IEEE 802.11b: Higher-speed physical layer (PHY) extension in the 2.4GHz band.* Standard, IEEE.

IEEE 802.11e. (2005). *IEEE 802.11e: Medium access control (MAC) quality of service enhancements.* Standard, IEEE.

IEEE 802.11g. (2003). *IEEE 802.11g: Further higher-speed physical layer extension in the 2.4GHz band.* Standard, IEEE.

IEEE 802.11n. (2006). *IEEE 802.11n: Standard for enhancements for higher throughput.* Standard, IEEE.

Ishihara, T., & Yasuura, H., (1998). Voltage scheduling problem for dynamically variable voltage processors. *Proceedings, 1998 Interna-*

tional Symposium on Low Power Electronics and Design (pp. 197-202).

Krashinsky, R., & Balakrishnan, H. (2002). Minimizing energy for wireless Web access with bounded slowdown. *Proceedings of the Annual International Conference on Mobile Computing and Networking, MOBICOM* (pp. 119-130).

Korhonen, J., & Wang, Y. (2005). Power-efficient streaming for mobile terminals. *Proceedings of the 15th International Workshop on Network and Operating Systems Support for Digital Audio and Video. NOSSDAV 2005* (pp. 39-44).

Krishna, C., & Lee, Y. H. (2000). Voltage-clock-scaling adaptive scheduling techniques for low power in hard real-time systems. *Proceedings of the 6th IEEE Real-Time Technology and Applications Symposium* (pp. 156-165).

Kwon, D., Kim, S. S., Park, C. Y., & Jung, C. I. (2005). Experiments on the energy saving and performance effects of IEEE 802.11 power saving mode (PSM). *Lecture Notes in Computer Science* (Vol. 3391, pp. 41-51).

Lee, S. (2005). Low-power video decoding on a variable voltage processor for mobile multimedia applications. *ETRI Journal, 27*(5), 504-10.

Li, Q., Aslam, J., & Rus, D. (2001). Online power-aware routing in wireless ad-hoc networks. *Proceedings of the Annual International Conference on Mobile Computing and Networking, MOBICOM* (pp. 97-107).

Lu, Z., Lach, J., Stan, M., & Skadron, K. (2003). Reducing multimedia decode power using feedback control. *Proceedings 21st International Conference on Computer Design* (pp. 489-96).

Martin, T. (1999). *Balancing batteries, power, and performance: System issues in CPU speed-setting for mobile computing.* PhD thesis, Carnegie Mellon University, Pittsburgh, USA, August 1999.

Mesarina, M., & Turner, Y. (2003). Reduced energy decoding of MPEG streams. *Multimedia Systems, 9*(2), 202-13.

Mohapatra, S., Cornea, R., Dutt, N., Nicolau, A., & Venkatasubramanian, N. (2003). Integrated power management for video streaming to mobile handheld devices. *Proceedings of the 11th ACM International Conference on Multimedia* (pp. 582-591).

Mohapatra, S., & Venkatasubramanian, N. (2003). PARM: Power aware reconfigurable middleware. *Proceedings, International Conference on Distributed Computing Systems* (pp. 312-319).

Muntean, G. M., & Cranley, N. (2007). Resource efficient quality-oriented wireless broadcasting of adaptive multimedia content. Accepted, Special Issue on "Mobile Multimedia Broadcasting." *IEEE Transactions on Broadcasting, 53*(1), part II.

Noble, B., Satyanarayanan, M., Narayanan, D., Tilton, J., Flinn, J., & Walker, K. (1997). Agile application-aware adaptation for mobility. *Operating Systems Review, 31*(5), 276-87.

Pakdeepaiboonpol, P., & Kittitornkun, S. (2005). Energy optimization for mobile MPEG-4 video decoder. *Mobile Technology, Applications, and Systems, the 2nd International Conference on* (pp. 1-6), November 2005.

Pasricha, S., Mohapatra, S., Luthra, M., Dutt, N., & Venkatasubramanian, N. (2003). Reducing backlight power consumption for streaming video applications on mobile handheld devices. *ACM/IEEE/IFIP Workshop on Embedded Systems for Real-Time Multimedia* (pp. 11-17).

Pillai, P., & Shin, K. G. (2002). Real-time dynamic voltage scaling for low power embedded operating systems. *ACM Operating Systems Review, 35*(5), 89-102.

Pouwelse, J., Langendoen, K., & Sips, H. (2003). Application-directed voltage scaling. *IEEE Trans-*

actions on Very Large Scale Integration (VLSI) Systems, 11(5), 812-826.

Prabhakar, B., Biyikoglu, E., & El Gamal, A. (2001). Energy-efficient transmission over a wireless link via lazy packet scheduling. *Proceedings IEEE INFOCOM* (Vol. 1, pp. 386-394).

Shim, H., Chang, N., & Pedram, M. (2004). A backlight power management framework for battery-operated multimedia systems. *IEEE Design and Test of Computers, 21*(5), 388-396.

Sinha, A., & Chandrakasan, A. (2000). Energy aware software. *VLSI Design 2000, Proceedings of 13th International Conference on VLSI Design* (pp. 50-55).

Stemm, M., & Katz, R. (1997). Measuring and reducing energy consumption of network interfaces in hand-held devices. *IEICE Transactions on Communications*, E80-B, pp. 1125-1131, August 1997.

Wei, Y., Bhandarkar, S. M., & Chandra, S. (2006). A client-side statistical prediction scheme for energy aware multimedia data streaming. *IEEE Transactions on Multimedia, 8*(4), 866-874.

Xu, Y., Heidemann, J., & Estrin, D. (2001). Geography-informed energy conservation for ad hoc routing. *Proceedings of the International Conference on Mobile Computing and Networking MOBICOM* (pp. 70-84).

Zhang, F., & Chanson, S. (2005). Proxy-assisted scheduling for energy-efficient multimedia streaming over wireless LAN. *Networking 2005. Networking Technologies, Services and Protocols; Performance of Computer and Communication Networks; Mobile and Wireless Communication Systems. Proceedings of the 4th International IFIP-TC6 Networking Conference.* (LNCS vol. 3462, pp. 980-91).

Zhang, L. Y., Ge, Y., & Hou, J. (2003). Energy-efficient real-time scheduling in IEEE 802.11 wireless LANs. *Proceedings - International Conference on Distributed Computing Systems* (pp. 658-667).

Zhu, H., & Cao, G. (2004). A power-aware and QoS-aware service model on wireless networks. *IEEE INFOCOM* (Vol. 2, pp. 1393-1403).

Zhu, H., & Cao, G. (2005). On supporting power-efficient streaming applications in wireless environments. *IEEE Transactions on Mobile Computing* (Vol. 4, pp. 391-403).

ENDNOTES

[1]   http://www.comreg.ie

[2]   Playstation web site, http://ie.playstation.com/psp

[3]   Nintendo web site, http://www.nintendo.com/systemsds

[4]   Ofcom International Communications Market Report, November 2006, http://www.ofcom.org.uk/media/news/2006/11/nr_20061129

Chapter VIII
Multimedia Services Provision in MANETs

Jose Luis Jodra
University of the Basque Country, Spain

Fidel Liberal
University of the Basque Country, Spain

Begoña Blanco Jauregi
University of the Basque Country, Spain

ABSTRACT

This chapter introduces the principal characteristics of MANETs and shows how these particularities may affect both QoS conditions and QoS management/provisioning systems, and therefore the capabilities of MANETs for properly providing multimedia services. After a deep analysis of different QoS mechanisms at different layers, the authors claim that QoS management cannot be handled only at the network layer or by applying some QoS-aware routing protocols. In fact, any end-to-end QoS provision architecture will demand QoS control mechanisms and information exchange among all the layers. A clear understanding of different proposals aimed at coping with QoS requirements at different layers will not only provide researchers with valuable information for designing better multimedia capable MANETs, but will also assist them in evaluating the need for a unified cross-layer approach in order to optimize the performance of analyzed protocols.

INTRODUCTION TO MANETs

Since the 1970s, the mobile ad hoc networks (MA-NETs) have attracted a lot of interest from both the industry and the research community due to their particular conditions. It is not easy to provide a proper single definition for these networks, since multitude of them have been proposed in today's literature. Nevertheless, we can use the definition made by Internet Engineering Task Force (IETF), the body responsible for guiding the evolution of the Internet:

A mobile ad hoc network (MANET) is an autonomous system of mobile routers (and associated hosts) connected by wireless links. The routers are free to move randomly and organize themselves arbitrarily; thus, the network's wireless topology may change rapidly and unpredictably. Such a network may operate in a stand-alone fashion, or may be connected to the larger Internet.

So, a typical MANET (Maltz, 1999) is a set of potentially mobile nodes that possibly concur to share information. During that exchange of information, different nodes can be continuously moving, so that the network must be prepared to get adapted continuously. Due to the lack of infrastructure, the nodes have to organize by themselves in the network and set up routes among them without any outer help.

In general, the ad hoc networks will make possible the communication between nodes connected indirectly by jumping through other nodes (Figure 1) forming a peer-to-peer connection. In this communication intermediate nodes act like routers, so that nodes can represent both roles: router and host.

MANETs can appear in two forms in real life. The first one consists of a pure wireless ad hoc network where all nodes are mobile and have the same characteristics. The second and most common one is a mixed hybrid network with wireless and fixed nodes. The main function of the fixed nodes is to forward the traffic to the mobile nodes. Therefore, the fixed nodes must have greater capacity and reliability than the mobile ones.

Special characteristics of MANETs constitute a centre of attention for the industry as for the research community. Since they don't need any infrastructure they promote collaborative work in areas where it was unthinkable before (conferences, for the reestablishment of the communications in areas desolated by natural disasters, in the battlefield, etc.). Furthermore, there have recently arisen other new scenarios that suggest the need for reliable MANETs, such as vehicular or sensor networks and new videogames portable platforms. In addition, the evolution of PDAs, videogames, and multimedia devices in vehicles demand both higher and more stable QoS requirements from the network.

Figure 1. Mobile ad hoc network

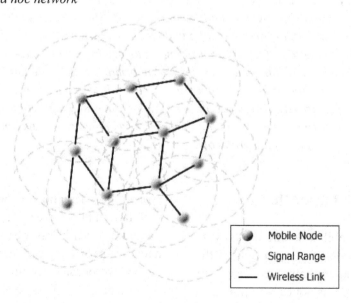

Table 1 shows different application areas for MANETs, as well as the services available in each area.

These new scenarios draw a playfield totally different to wired networks (or even "static" wireless network). Together with the problems due to providing some QoS guarantees for proper multimedia transmissions, MANETs involve several additional challenges to be addressed in order to guarantee minimum levels of *quality*. This is due the dynamic behaviour and limited resources of such networks. On the one hand, these limitations strengthen the need for some QoS support, nearly in every protocol layer. On the other hand, in this kind of environments, there appear others constraints apart from traditional QoS requirements. For example, battery life, stability, and location must also be considered.

OBJECTIVES

Taking into account this overall picture of MA-NETS the main objectives of the chapter are:

Table 1. Applications for MANET

Application area	Description/Services
Military tactical networks	-Communications and combat operations. -Use in battlefields.
Sensor networks	-A sensor network is a group of specialized devices with a communication infrastructure intended to monitor and record conditions at diverse locations. Commonly monitored parameters are wind direction and speed, power-line voltage, humidity, illumination intensity, sound intensity, vital body functions, pressure, vibration intensity, temperature, chemical concentrations, pollutant levels, etc.. -These networks may typically have between 1000 and 100,000 nodes, each one taking samples and sending them to a central node where they will be processed.
Emergency services	-Search & rescue services. -Disaster recovery. -Substitution of the fixed architecture in case of deteriorations produced by earthquakes or hurricanes.
E-Commerce	-Electronic payments from any place.
Automation	-Information of the conditions of the highway and the meteorological conditions to improve the security. -Coordination of the electronics of traffic control to improve the efficiency in the control of the traffic. -Value added services for the conductor and the passengers.
Enterprise & Business	-It foments the mobile office concept. -Wireless access to the corporative network. -It allows the extension of the network, thanks to its low cost and easy installation.
Home	-Wireless access to Internet. -Creation of personal area networks (PAN).
Communitarian networks	-They are networks formed by different blocks of buildings or neighbours to provide wireless access to Internet.
Education	-Creation of virtual conference rooms. -Wireless access to Internet.
Entertainment	-Multiplayer games.
User location based services	-The user has access to information relative to his location. -There are two different types of location services: Push: The information is sent to the network without any request. Pull: The user sends a request to the network to obtain the service.

- To describe the principal characteristics of MANETs and show how these particularities affect QoS factors and QoS management/provisioning systems and therefore, the capabilities of MANETs for providing multimedia services.
- To summarize different proposals to cope with QoS requirements for multimedia services at different layers:
  - **Transport layer:** Alternatives to traditional TCP/UDP transport protocols and their performance in MANETs.
  - **Special emphasis in the network layer:** Principal routing protocols in MANETs, as well as different metrics considered and their relationships with traditional (wired) routing protocols.
  - **Link layer:** QoS aware MAC protocols, contention, and access control mechanisms.
- To assess the need for a unified cross-layer approach in order to optimize the performance of analysed protocols.
- To introduce the reader to service discovery mechanisms and QoS management models and signalling proposals.

CHARACTERISTICS OF MANETs AND THEIR IMPACT ON MULTIMEDIA SERVICES

Mobile ad hoc networks maintain the general characteristics of wireless networks while including additional properties and restrictions. Whereas in the infrastructure wireless network there exists some fixed topology, due to the movement of the nodes in ad-hoc networks and resulting route failures and recomputation, difficulty for the maintenance of sessions, etc, their topology changes dynamically. Moreover, ad-hoc networks have no central controller and in most cases, each node is responsible for maintaining the information of delay, jitter, loss rate, stability, and distance

for each link in order to feed routing algorithms. However, this state information is inherently imprecise due to the changes in the topology and resources such as battery, bandwidth, processing, and storage are limited.

Then, these additional characteristics of a MANET that complicate QoS provision can be summarized as follows (see for example (Mohapatra, Li, & Gui, 2003) for extended analysis):

- **Dynamic network topology:** Due to the mobility of the nodes, the topology of mobile ad hoc network changes continuously. And this characteristic is the key for the performance of routing protocols and the applications located in superior layers.
- **Asymmetry:** Due to the diversity of the MANETs, the characteristic of each node will be different.
- **Multihop communication:** This characteristic worsens the quality of the communication, since several wireless connections exist in an end-to-end connection.
- **Bandwidth:** The bandwidth available in MANETs is very small in comparison with that available in fixed networks. In addition, the radioelectric interface suffers from very high error rates resulting in *worse quality* connections.
- **Energy:** All the wireless devices obtain the necessary energy from batteries, so that energy consumption plays a very important role in the development of MANETs.
- **Cooperation:** Due to the lack of infrastructure, all nodes must participate in the construction of the routes. Nevertheless, it may happen that some nodes decide not to cooperate and not to lend their resources to communications among other nodes.
- **Security:** In general, the nodes and the information in the ad hoc networks are exposed to the same threats as in the rest of networks. In addition, in MANETs other specific threats exist because of the implicit insecurity of any radio communication.

These inherent characteristics of MANETs hinder the fulfilment of the QoS requirements demanded by multimedia services. In order to cope with these requirements, different QoS provisioning architectures and protocols can be managed at different layers. Each one of these procedures will have not only an effect into overall end-to-end QoS but into other layers behaviour as well. So although it is possible to minimize the global impact of these characteristics by solving the possible problems in the suitable layer the interactions between layers must be also considered. Different alternatives will be analyzed in the following sections in a per-layer basis.

QOS MECHANISMS IN MANETs: LINK LAYER

The link layer is commonly split into two sublevels, namely MAC (medium access control) and LLC (logical link control). Since the dynamic characteristics of MANETs are a consequence of the wireless medium, the mayor enhancements to provide QoS support have been developed for the MAC layer.

The design of a suitable MAC protocol for multimedia applications should start with the deep understanding of the next strategic features:

- **Regarding channel utilization:** The main choice is between single-channel or multi-channel protocols. In single-channel protocols, all the nodes in the network share all the bandwidth for both control and data transmissions, so collisions are an implicit characteristic of these mechanisms. This is the case of CSMA contention protocol, whose performance degrades with high traffic load, increasing the transmission latency and thus being not the most suitable for multimedia applications. Some attempts to enhance CSMA performance have been developed in MACA (Karn, 1990), MACAW (Vaduvur, Alan, Scott, & Lixia, 1994) or FAMA (Chane & Garcia-Luna-Aceves, 1995). Multi-channel protocols separate a channel for the control plane and one or multiple channels for data transmissions. This separation is achieved through several techniques such as TDMA, FDMA, or CDMA. Multimedia applications give better results with TDMA access, but it implies a less efficient use of the channel as not reserved slots are not reused by other communications. Thus an optimal solution could be a hybrid approach that combines two or more of these techniques to improve channel utilization. We find examples in HRMA (Zhenyu & Garcia-Luna-Aceves, 1999) that combines TDMA and FDMA, or Bluetooth (Haartsen, 1998), that combines CDMA and TDMA.

- **Transmission initiation:** The transmission can be initiated by the sender or the receiver. In sender initiated transmissions, when a node has data to transmit, asks the receiver if it is ready to start communication (CSMA, MACA). In receiver initiated transmissions, when a receiver is ready to start a communication performs a poll to the other nodes asking for data to receive (MACA-BI (Talucci, Gerla, & Fratta, 1997)). Although sender initiated transmission is more intuitive and suits better for general traffic, receiver initiated transmission performs better in specialized high loaded environments, such as multimedia applications.

- **Topology:** The choice here is between a flat topology or a hierarchical/clustered topology. Flat topologies require less control overhead but hierarchical/clustered topologies scale better. When nodes have heterogeneous characteristics, the most powerful nodes can take charge of the cluster/hierarchy header and perform control tasks, but flat topologies are more appropriate for balancing load among similar nodes.

- **Power:** Power consumption is an essential design criteria for mobile networks, as battery live of the network nodes is limited. There are several techniques to improve power consumption behaviour at MAC layer. Some protocols adapt the transmission power to the minimum acceptable SNR. Other attempts address the possibility of idle listening avoidance through entering in sleep modes to save power when there is no data to interchange. This is the case of Bluetooth. MARCH protocol (Toh, Vassiliou, Guichal, & Shih, 2000b) saves power by maintaining the control overhead, necessary to minimize collisions, as low as possible.

On the other hand, although MANETs can be built upon different wireless technologies nowadays most MANETs actually use 802.11a/b/g wireless technology. So we will analyse briefly the enhancements that have been developed in order to provide QoS support within 802.11 MAC layer.

IEEE 802.11 (IEEE, 1999) includes two medium-access coordination functions:

- **Distributed Coordination Function (DCF):** This asynchronous basic medium access method is based on the CSMA/CA. When a station has data to send, it senses the medium to check if there is already another transmission in progress. If the medium is idle during a DIFS (Distributed InterFrame Space), the station starts the transmission. Otherwise, the node must wait a random time interval, known as the backoff interval, to retry the transmission. The backoff timer is decreased while the medium remains idle, but it is frozen when another station is transmitting. When the timer expires, the node attempts a new transmission. Nevertheless, a collision may occur when two or more stations try to start a transmission simultaneously, and that collision will not

be detected. Hence, a positive acknowledge mechanism must be implemented to notify the sender that the frame has been successfully received. Another possibility of collision of wireless networks is the hidden terminal problem that happens when a node is visible from another station, but not from other nodes communicating with that station and two or more senders collide trying to transmit to the same receiver. To avoid this situation, a RTS/CTS scheme can be introduced. Before start transmitting, a node sends a RTS frame to the receiver and, if it is ready to receive, answers the sender with a CTS frame. Then, all the nodes within the range of the receiver a aware of the ongoing transmission. This handshake mechanism improves the performance of DCF in many cases, but also introduces a control overhead that involves suboptimal utilization of the channel.

- **Point Coordination Function (PCF):** IEEE 802.11 also provides an optional centralized contention-free method that requires an access-point (AP) to coordinate the access to the medium in order to avoid collisions. The AP polls the stations within its range to later assign a transmission slot without contention.

The centralized nature of PCF makes this method not suitable for the MANET environment, distributed by definition. So, we will focus our analysis on the QoS limitations of DCF and how to overcome these limitations through DCF based QoS techniques.

Multimedia applications are time-bounded services with tight bandwidth, delay, and jitter requirements. However, DCF method by itself makes no differentiation to prioritize multimedia flows over data flows. Drabu (1999) and Qiang Ni (2004) introduce different modifications of 802.11 to provide a minimum QoS guarantee in wireless networks. Those applicable to MANETs are the following:

- **Backoff increase function:** If the backoff interval is calculated not only proportional to the size of the frame but also inversely proportional to the weight of the flow, an implicit service differentiation may be achieved.
- **Varying DIFS:** Another service differentiation can be performed simply by varying the DIFS time for each type of flow.
- **Different maximum frame length:** Assigning different frame lengths according to different priority levels, so high priority nodes can send more information than low priority nodes. However, as long frames are more likely to suffer transmission errors, this service differentiation mechanism can decrease its efficiency.
- **VMAC:** A virtual MAC level monitor estimates some QoS level statistics that can be used to tune transmission parameters in response to the dynamic channel conditions.
- **Blackburst:** This scheme uses a black burst contention interval to indicate the amount of time the station has waited to access the medium in order to minimize the delay of real-time traffic.

QOS MECHANISMS IN MANETs: NETWORK LAYER

Routing plays an important role while providing QoS in wireless ad hoc networks. Special QoS-aware routing protocols are needed in order to select those routes that best satisfies QoS requirements like bandwidth, delay, jitter, and loss rate (Baoxian & Mouftah, 2005; Chunhung Richard & Jain-Shing, 1999; Tafazolli, 2007) and make related networks more suitable for providing multimedia services (Chen, Tsai, & Gerla, 1997;

Lin & Gerla, 1997; Min & Geng-Sheng, 2005; Wang, Kurose, Shenoy, & Towsley, 2004). This is especially important in MANETs due to its instability and changing nature, so that network layer will me analyzed more in depth than others in this chapter.

Since the end of the last decade, an important amount of routing protocols has been developed for multihop ad hoc networks. Basically an ad hoc routing protocol is a standard that controls how different nodes have to route the packets within the MANET. When a node joins an ad hoc network, it has no prior knowledge about the topology of the network. So, the first task to accomplish is to discover it. The new node can optionally announce its presence and listen to the advertisements from its neighbours. This way the node will detect the other nodes of the network and receive information about how to reach them. Eventually, all the nodes will know the new topology and the available routes to get to any destination.

In order to make routing decisions any routing algorithms should:

- Maintain reasonably small routing tables
- Provide the best route for a given destination (it can be: the fastest, the most trustworthy, with the best throughput or cheapest)
- Use a small amount of messages or time to converge

In general, routing can be divided into two strategies (Lang, 2003) (Murthy & Manoj, 2004):

- **Adaptive:** Changes of the topology of the network are adapted by the routing protocol.
- **Non-adaptive:** The routing is carried out using fixed tables.

Of course chosen routing strategies in MANETs should be adaptable to the changes of the conditions of the network: such as the size of the network, the density of traffic and nodes or the partition of the network in different zones. So, In MANETs only adaptive strategies are useful.

Those routing protocols can be classified in one of the following groups:

- **Proactive:** They are based on calculating the routes to all the destinations in the initial phase, maintaining them later by means of periodic updates. Each node maintains the routing information to each node of the network, stored generally in different tables. These tables are updated either periodically, or whenever a change in the topology of the network takes place.

- **Reactive:** A route is established when required by a node, using an on-demand routing discovery. They were designed to reduce the overload of the network, only using the information of the active routes. The router discovery is performed flooding route request packets. When one of these packets reaches a node with a route to the destination (or the destination itself), this one will be in charge of sending related information back to the source by a process of link reversal (in case that the connections are bidirectional) or by flooding a reply packet otherwise.

- **Hybrid:** Hybrid routing algorithms combine the basic characteristics of the two other types of protocols. They were designed to increase the stability with respect to the previous ones. The routes between near nodes settle down and maintain by a solution of proactive type, whereas to obtain the routes to the distant nodes a reactive strategy is used.

In MANETs, the physical and logical organization of the nodes is very important in order to define the network topology.

Most typical topologies in MANETs are the following ones:

- **Flat:** The network has no hierarchy. In this case, all nodes are uniform (all nodes are considered equals).

- **Hierarchical:** Nodes are organized hierarchically in the network. This hierarchical organization reduces the interchange of routing information as nodes can only send updates to the nodes in the same hierarchical level or to their immediate superior or immediate inferior nodes. This mechanism improves the efficiency of the protocol and moderates control message overload.

- **Cluster:** Builds up a hierarchy of clusters. There are two special types of nodes for each cluster (Non-uniform nodes):
  o **Gateway-node:** Responsible for the communication between clusters.
  o **Cluster-head:** Builds up a hierarchy of clusters, manages the communication inside the cluster and the cluster itself.

This topology information can be fully distributed (full topology information) when all topology information is distributed or in a reduced way (reduced topology information) when only a fraction is distributed. Whenever a message is sent within this topology, it must follow one of the policies next:

- **Broadcast:** The network is flooded with the message to send.
- **Restricted broadcast:** The network is flooded with the message to send with a time to live value.
- **Local broadcast:** All nodes in transmission range receive the messages.
- **Local multicast:** Some nodes in transmission range receive the messages.

Finally, most of the protocols to be analyzed in this section have been developed generally only in theory, so proposed improvements to existing protocols were justified by simulations that showed enhanced capabilities. However, while the use of simulation has increased, the credibility of the simulation results has decreased (Kurkowski, Camp, & Colagrosso, 2005) due to the simulation techniques always require the simplification of real-world properties such as radio characteristics or node mobility (Wolfgang & Martin, 2007).

Historical Evolution of Routing Protocols

Since the late 90s, a lot of routing protocols for ad hoc multi-hop networks have been developed. One of the first protocols to arise, in 1987, is DBF (Varadhan, Estrin, & Floyd, 1998) a proactive flat topology protocol that suffered from serious problems, including looping and deadlocks. An enhanced version of DBF called DSDV was proposed in 1994 (Charles & Pravin, 1994). This protocol (proactive with a flat topology) offered an improvement with regard to its predecessor by avoiding deadlocks generation. This was not the only proposal of solution for the problem of deadlocks, in 1995 there appeared WRP (Shree & Garcia-Luna-Aceves, 1996), also a proactive protocol with a flat topology. WRP is table-driven, avoiding deadlocks and uses hello messages. One of the first reactive protocol with a flat topology is DSR (Johnson & Maltz, 1996) created in 1996. It uses a routing cache and it adapts quickly to routing changes when host movement is frequent, yet requires little or no overhead during periods in which hosts move less frequently. Another reactive protocol is ABR (Chai-Keong, 1997), with a flat topology and associability-based routing.

It is necessary to wait until 1997 to see the first routing protocol with hierarchical topology, such as:

- **CGSR** (Chiang, Wu, Liu, & Gerla, 1997): Proactive- and cluster-based protocol focused on minimizing routing information overload. Within each cluster, a turn-based communication is used controlled by cluster-

head. The main idea is to set up routes that alternate a cluster-head and a gateway in the path to destination in order to improve efficiency since cluster-heads have more changes to transmit and gateways are the only nodes that cluster-heads can forward messages to. CGSR uses DSDV as an underlying protocol.

- **ZRP** (Haas, 1997) (Zygmunt, Haas, Pearlman, & Samar, 2002c): One of the first hybrid protocol. Each node configures a zone that groups all the nodes within a previously determined radius. The node proactively maintains a routing table for the zone and asks for on-demand routes to communicate with other zones. Suitable for large networks with different mobility patterns.
- **GSR** (Tsu-Wei & Gerla, 1998): Proactive and link-state protocol, it uses the DBF propagation method to avoid the flooding problem of link-state algorithm, by sending the topology updates only to the neighbors.

Also in 1997 appears SSR (Dube, Rais, Wang, & Tripathi, 1997) a reactive flat topology protocol where the routes are selected according to the signal strength and the stability of the nodes and is a result of the combination of other two protocols:

- **DRP:** For routing tables' maintenance
- **SRP:** For packet processing

In 1998, the location of the node begins to be considered while forwarding the message to well-known destinations. One of these protocols is DREAM (Stefano, Imrich, Violet, & Barry, 1998), a flat-proactive protocol where nodes announce their position (gathered using a GPS) periodically. This advertisement period depends on the distance and mobility. In the same way, in 1999 appears ZHLS (Joa-Ng & Lu, 1999), a proactive protocol with hierarchical topology and geocast routing, where each node has an identifier for its own terminal and the zone where it is located. Later, in 2000 two new protocols based on DSR, appear, a proactive one GPSR (Brad & Kung, 2000) and a reactive one LAR (Ko & Vaidya) both of them with a flat topology and geocast routing. Finally, one of the latest geocast routing protocol is DFR (Lee et al., 2006), a proactive protocol with flat topology, whose primary objective consists in avoiding the problem of the expired routes.

Regarding multicast protocols, its history begins in 1998 with AMRIS (Wu, Tay, & Toh, 1998), a reactive protocol with hierarchical topology. This protocol with tree structure distinguishes each node with an identifier that indicates the logical position within the tree. Later, in 2000 ABAM appears (Toh, Guichal, & Bunchua, 2000a), a new reactive protocol with hierarchical topology. The main objective of this protocol is to reuse the concept of association stability implemented in ABR that involves a smaller overload and improves the overall delay, but it needs much space in each node in order to store all the routes. In the same year, MAODV (Royer & Perkins, 2000) turned up, a hierarchical reactive protocol based on AODV. It makes it possible the use of unicast, multicast and broadcast messages and the trees are built using distributed control in order to avoid loops. It has also the capacity of restoring broken connections. One year later, in 2001 a new reactive protocol called ADMR (Jetcheva & Johnson, 2001) with hierarchical topology is developed. Aimed at creating smaller and more dynamic trees, it requires an active participation of the nodes, which causes this protocol not to be always useful.

Other kind of routing protocols are those with power-awareness. The main objective of this protocol is to optimize power utilization in the network. One of the first protocols of this type is EADSR (Shah & Rabaey, 2002), a flat-topology reactive protocol, where the routes are selected using a probabilistic method to divide the routing overhead among all the nodes of the network. Another power-aware protocol is ISAIAH (Lind-gren & Schelen, 2002), a flat-topology reactive protocol based on AODV, the cost function used to calculate the cost of a route has been modified, there has been some changes in the way route requests are forwarded, and a power saving mode has been added. Finally, in 2005 there appears PBAR (Chi & Yuanyuan, 2005), a flat-topology reactive protocol, which reduces the throughput, in order to increase the battery life.

The rest of the protocols fall into the aforementioned two kinds of topologies (flat and hierarchical) and three types of protocols (proactive, reactive, and hybrid) with the following characteristics ordered chronologically:

- **STAR (Seet et al., 2004), 1999:** This proactive protocol looks for non-optimal routes in order to save bandwidth. STAR also reduces control overload, getting closer to the efficiency of reactive protocols. Depending on the available bandwidth of the ad hoc network it can use two routing policies:
  - **OR (optimum routing approach):** In order to calculate more optimized routes, resulting in more overload.
  - **LORA (least overhead routing approach):** It selects less optimized routes but also reduces overload.
- **TBRPF (Bellur & Ogier, 1999):** This flat-topology proactive protocol uses the link-state mechanism and hop-by-hop routing to inform only about updated neighbours. TBRPF combines periodic and differential updates to keep all nodes informed, while reducing control overhead when compared to traditional flooding mechanisms.
- **DST (Radhakrishnan, Racherla, Sekharan, Rao, & Batsell, 1999):** This hierarchical-topology proactive protocol groups the nodes in trees for stability purposes. The root node manages the tree and has to communicate with the root nodes of other trees.

- **HSR (Iwata, Ching-Chuan, Guangyu, Gerla, & Tsu-Wei, 1999; Pei, Gerla, Hong, & Chiang, 1999):** This hierarchical-topology proactive protocol handles the mobility of nodes by grouping them in clusters under two criteria:
  - **Physical:** Using the position of the nodes.
  - **Logical:** Grouping the nodes with more mobility pattern affinity.

  Compared with flat proactive routing strategies (such as DSDV) HSR is more scalable at the cost of non-optimal routing and more complexity. Compared with reactive protocols HSR provides a lower latency for non-frequently used routed and lower control overload.

- **AODV (Elizabeth & Charles, 1999):** This reactive flat protocol uses a destination sequence number for each route entry and for the route discovery and maintenance mechanisms. Whenever there are two different available routes, the one with the highest sequence number is selected. When a route is needed, the node broadcasts an RRQ message to discover the route. The range of dissemination of RREQ is limited with the TTL field of IP header. When the RREQ packet reaches either the destination node or another node with an available route to destination, an RREP is unicasted backwards. AODV was designed for MANETS with tens to thousands nodes with low or moderate mobility rates.

- **RDMAR (George & Rahim, 1999):** This reactive flat-topology protocol is based on the calculation of the distance between nodes, avoiding requests of route discovery to distant nodes using a relative distance micro-discovery (RDM) mechanism. This protocol is suitable for large mobile networks with moderate topology changes rate.

- **ROAM (Raju & Garcia-Luna-Aceves, 1999):** This reactive flat-topology protocol maintains multiple loop-free routes to a destination, preventing the search-to-infinity problem. It assumes the existence of a protocol for neighbours' discovery. It works with three tables: distances, routing and link-cost. In order to avoid obsolete routes, all the routes have a time-to-life parameter. ROAM is applicable to wireless networks with static nodes or nodes with limited mobility.

- **DDR (Nikaein, Labiod, & Bonnet, 2000):** This proactive protocol with hierarchical routing strategy is similar to DST protocol but it does not have a root node, which prevents single points of failure. The nodes are divided in zones and forests with an identifier. It offers mechanisms for the improvement of the delay and the complexity of the routing, in order to reduce maintenance cost and radio resource consumption overheads.

- **FSR (Guangyu, Gerla, & Tsu-Wei, 2000a):** It is a hierarchical proactive protocol where nodes perceive the network as divided in concentric circles around him. The size of the circle is calculated in jumps from the centre. The nearest nodes are updated more than the distant ones and when a node falls, nothing is transmitted. This way, the amount of information exchanged is reduced, resulting in a more efficient and scalable protocol.

- **LANMAR (Guangyu, Mario, & Xiaoyan, 2000b):** It is a proactive protocol with hierarchical routing strategy combining the features of Fisheye State Routing (FSR) and Landmark routing. A reference node is assigned to each group in order to reduce routing update overhead in large networks, and the exchange of neighbourhood link state. LANMAR applies to large, mobile, ad hoc environments with group mobility patterns.

- **OLSR (Jacquet et al., 2001):** This flat-topology proactive protocol is an optimization of link-state protocols and it is specially designed for the operation in MANET networks. It is particularly suitable for large and dense environments (as the technique of MPRs (multipoint relays) works well in this context). Multipoint relays are selected nodes that forward link state information during the flooding process, in order to reduce control overload. At the moment the second version 2 is being developed by IETF (Group). OLSRv2 imposes minimum requirements on the network by not requiring sequenced or reliable transmission of control traffic. Furthermore, the only interaction between OLSRv2 and the IP stack is routing table management.

- **DSRFLOW (Hu, Johnson, & Maltz, 2001):** This reactive protocol with flat topology is a extension of DSR. This extension makes it possible to compute routing without an explicit source route header in the packet, reducing the overload and preserving other advantages of DSR.

- **TORA (Park & Corson, 2001a):** This distributed flat reactive protocol is optimized for dynamic environments, providing multiple routes to a same destination. TORA minimizes the control overhead associated with adapting to topological changes. Its major disadvantage is the need of clock synchronization.

- **ADV (Boppana & Konduru, 2001):** This hybrid protocol with flat routing strategy is a distance vector routing algorithm that exhibits some on-demand characteristics by varying the frequency and the size of the routing updates in response to the network load and mobility conditions. Compared to on-demand protocols, ADV applies better to high mobility networks and reduces control overhead and lower packet latencies.

- **BSR (Song & Yang, 2002):** This flat reactive protocol is another extension of DSR that maintains backup routes in case the main falls, with the objective of minimizing broadcasts in the discovery phase. Therefore it is a suitable protocol for high mobility environments.

- **IARP (Zygmunt et al., 2002b):** This flat proactive protocol is a link-state and limited scope method. IARP is the table-driven part of ZRP protocol that proactively discovers local routes. It is based on OSPF with some modifications:

Figure 2. OLSR flooding procedure (MPR)

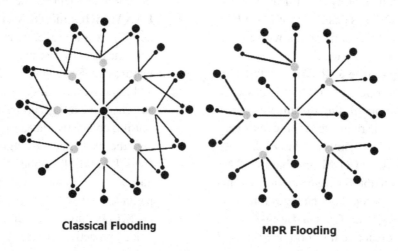

Classical Flooding　　　　**MPR Flooding**

- o Limited TTL
- o It does not consider the neighbours outside of the radio range
- o It eliminates routers that move away
- **IERP (Zygmunt J. Haas, Pearlman, & Samar, 2002a):** This reactive protocol with flat topology corresponds to the on-demand part of ZRP protocol. It takes advantage of the locally known routes (discovered with IARP) to avoid route requests for local destinations.
- **CHAMP (Valera, Seah, & Rao, 2002):** This reactive protocol uses a shorter multipath algorithm and balance of load to optimize the consumed energy. In order to avoid the overload it has two caches, one for the routes and another one for the route request packets. Therefore, CHAMP protocol reduces dropped packets as well as routing overhead, while saving energy consumption. It makes this protocol suitable for high-load-and mobility small networks.
- **LUNAR (Tschudin, Gold, Rensfelt, & Wibling, 2004):** This reactive protocol is very similar to AODV. It doesn't need any route maintenance, but, it needs a forced path rediscovery every 3 seconds. The lack of route maintenance reduces the complexity of the protocol. However, LUNAR limits itself to three hops, so it only applies to small MANET environments.
- **DNVR (Lee & Riley, 2005):** This flat reactive protocol selects a loop-free route and maintains it like other on-demand protocols. It has several new features like more stable routes and with better scalability. DNVR protocol scales well to large networks with varying traffic loads and mobility patterns.
- **DYMO (Chakeres & Perkins, 2007):** This reactive protocol offers adaptation to changing network topology and determines unicast routes between nodes within the network. It is based on AODV and avoids loops by the use of sequence numbers. It is a protocol that is expected to be the natural substitute of AODV.

Figure 3 and Table 2 show a historical evolution of routing protocols and a summary of MANET routing protocols for ad hoc networks.

Figure 3. Historical evolution of MANET routing protocols

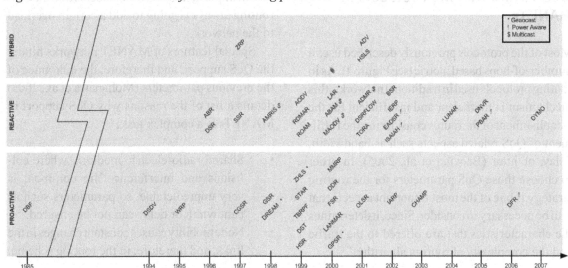

Table 2. Classification of MANET routing protocols

MANET routing protocols					
	Unicast			Multicast	
	Proactive	Reactive		Hybrid	
Flat	DBF DFR DREAM * DSDV GPSR * IARP MMRP OLSR STAR TBRPF WRP	ABR AODV BSR CHAMP DNVR DSR DSRFLOW DYMO EADSR !	IERP ISAIAH ! LAR * LUNAR PBAR! RDMAR ROAM SSR TORA	AODV CBRP DDR HARP GLS $ GPSAL HSLS	
Hierarchical	CGSR DDR DST FSR GSR HSR LANMAR ZHLS *			ZRP	ABAM ADMR AMRIS AMROUTE CAMP CBM DCMF DDM DSR-MB FGMP GEOGRID * GEOTORA *	LAM LBM * MAODV MCEDAR MOBICAST * MRGR * MZR ODMRP SOM SPBM SRMP

* Geocast
! Power Aware
$ Grid

QoS-Aware Routing Protocols in MANETs

Most of the protocols previously described uses a number-of-hops based metric (see Figure 4). As in routing protocols used in traditional networks, this mechanism is inefficient and insufficient for the establishment of the routes considering the fulfillment of QoS related aspects such as bandwidth, delay, or jitter (Baoxian et al., 2005). In order to choose those QoS parameters for the routing strategy is one of the most important aspects that will be necessary to consider. Since, it determines the characteristics that are offered to the traffic and the complexity of routing algorithm.

An important aspect to consider is that the QoS routing always is going to add a certain overload to the network.

Special features of MANET networks hinder the QoS support, and therefore, the guarantee of the previous parameters (Mohapatra et al., 2003) details a list of the reasons why QoS support in MANETs is a complex task:

* Shared radio-electric medium, where collisions and interference are common, is very unpredictable, so parameters such as bandwidth or delay can not be ensured.
* Node mobility causes constant changes in the links, and therefore, in the routing scheme.

Figure 4. Search of routes with requirements of QoS

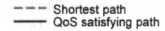

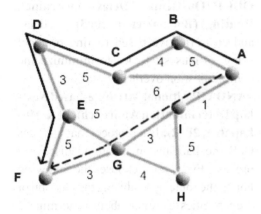

New links can have completely different features affecting the QoS of the routes.

- Routing protocols should not require excessive processing to save batteries.
- Hidden and exposed terminal problems of wireless networks may also cause interferences.
- Route maintenance and reconstruction should involve a minimum overload in the network.
- Finally, lower security of wireless links must be considered as well.

Some of proposed alternative cover one QoS constraint at a time (in order to reduce the algorithm complexity); while others use some heuristics in order to deal with more than one constraints and therefore, overcome the NP-complete complexity of multi-constraint routing problem (Xipeng & Ni, 1999).

Next a brief introduction to more important QoS aware routing protocols:

- **AAQR (Application Aware QoS Routing) (Min et al., 2005):** Is a delay and bandwidth based routing scheme for multimedia ap-

plications in mobile ad hoc networks using the real time control protocol (RTCP) to estimate the node state.

- **CAAODV (Contention Aware Ad hoc On-Demand Distance Vector routing) (Lei & Heinzelman, 2005):** Is a bandwidth estimation based routing scheme for real-time applications in mobile ad hoc networks using AODV routing protocol.
- **CACP (Contention-aware Admission Control Protocol) (Yaling & Kravets, 2005):** Is a bandwidth allocation controlling based routing protocol, which provides admission control for flows.
- **CBCCR (Clustering-based Channel Capacity Routing) (Chen et al., 1997):** Is a bandwidth based routing protocol, where "bandwidth" is a time-slotted network that is measured with the number of not reserved slots. It uses DSDV like routing protocol.
- **CCBR (Channel Capacity-Based Routing) (Chunhung et al., 1999):** Is a end-to-end bandwidth calculation and bandwidth allocation routing protocol. The source knows the bandwidth and QoS available to any destination and with these properties can efficiently support real-time applications. It uses DSDV like routing protocol.
- **CEDAR (Core Extension Distributed Ad Hoc Routing) (Sivakumar, Sinha, & Bharghavan, 1999):** Is a bandwidth based routing protocol with link state propagation where nodes are organized like a cores for performing route computations.
- **CLMCQR (Cross Layer Multi-Constraint QoS Routing) (Zhong, 2004):** Is a MAC delay (to indicate the level of interference), residual bandwidth and link reliability based routing protocol that uses a heuristic algorithm to solve the NP-complete multiple constrained routing.
- **DSARP (Delay Sensitive Adaptive Routing Protocol) (Min, Jiandong, & Yan, 2003):** Is a reliable route for delay-sensitive

traffic based routing protocol, with the next constrained condition: `*the shortest route and the lowest average delay*'. Therefore, it is assured to provide QoS guarantee and improve the performance of the network.

- **EBLLD (Entropy-Based Long-Life Distributed QoS routing) (Hui, Bingxin, Ling, & Huazhi, 2003):** Is a entropy-based routing protocol using the local multicast mechanism to reduce the message overhead. The objective is to select the long-life path to reduce the number of route reconstruction.

- **GAMAN (Genetic Algorithm-based routing for Mobile Ad hoc Networks) (Barolli, Koyama, & Shiratori, 2003):** Is a packet dropping rate and delay based routing protocol using Genetic Algorithm (GA) to define rules to find possible routes.

- **HARP (Hybrid Ad Hoc Routing Protocol) (Nikaein & Bonnet, 2001):** Is a bandwidth and delay based routing protocol combining reactive and proactive approaches depending on the routing is performed on inter-zone or intra-zone respectively.

- **IAR (Interference-Aware Routing) (Gupta, Zhanfeng, Tung, & Walrand, 2005):** Is a bandwidth based heuristic interference-aware routing protocol that chooses the path to the destination based on localized information at the source nodes.

- **LSBR (Link Stability-Based Routing) (Rubin & Liu, 2003):** Is a link stability based routing protocol to improve the QoS performance (link survival time) over AODV routing protocol.

- **MRPC (Maximum Residual Packet Capacity routing) (Misra & Banerjee, 2002):** Is a power-aware routing algorithm for energy-efficient routing that increases the operational lifetime of multi-hop wireless networks.

- **NSR (Node State Routing) (Stine & de Veciana, 2004):** Provide an alternative set of concepts for access and routing. Permit to implement real-time resource arbitration that can be calculated from link or node states to deliver QoS.

- **ODCR (On-Demand Delay-Constrained Routing) (Baoxian et al., 2005):** Is a delay and cost-effective based routing protocol using various strategies to minimize the communication overhead.

- **PANDA (Positional Attribute-based Next-hop Determination Approach)(Li & Mohapatra, 2002):** Is a protocol that includes QoS mechanisms in the route discovery process. Every node chooses the following hop in the route by analysing the location or the capacities of the neighbouring terminals. When a route request is received, instead of waiting a random time until re-broadcasting the request, the receiving node introduces a delay proportional to its capacity, so trying to cope with QoS requirements of the request. By doing so, the algorithm gives higher priority to these paths that can better satisfy QoS requirements (since neighbours retransmit route discovering messages first). The final decision regarding the selected path is made in the destination considering a series of predefined rules. This algorithm is able to satisfy the end-to-end QoS requirements whenever the route does not experience important degradation. For these cases, a discovery mechanism for new routes with QoS is defined.

- **QAODV (Quality of service for Ad hoc On-Demand Distance Vector) (Perkins & Royer, 2001):** Is a version of AODV protocol with QoS extensions. The main novelty is the introduction of some extensions into RREQ and RREP messages. A node verifies QoS requirements before retransmitting the message or sending a RREP message to the source. If after the route is established a node detects that the QoS requirements can not be fulfilled any longer, that node must send an ICMP QOS LOST message to the source. To compute the routes according to QoS requirements, four new elements are included in the structure of the routing tables: *Maximum Delay, Minimum Available Bandwidth, List of Sources Requesting Delay Guarantees,* and *List of Sources Requesting Bandwidth Guarantees.*

- **QOLSR (QoS Optimized Link State Routing) (Badis, 2006):** Is a research project targeted at the inclusion of QoS aspects in OLSR protocol. Each network node performs measurements of the bandwidth and delay of the symmetric links to its neighbours and stores the information in a table. Then it uses it to establish the MPR (multi-point relay) through heuristics. Each MPR sends topology control messages, including its measurements of bandwidth and delay. Thus, this information is spread throughout the network, to be used by each node to build the routing tables according to the QoS parameters.

- **QGUM (QoS-GPSR for Ultra-wideband MANETs) (Abdrabou & Weihua, 2006):** Is a bandwidth reservation, position information and call admission control based routing protocol using cross-layer design.

- **SIRCCR (SIR and Channel Capacity-Based Routing) (Dongwoo, Chan-Ho, & Sehun, 2004):** Is a bandwidth and signal-to-interference (SIR) based routing protocol. Bandwidth is reserved by allocating time slots and SIR reservation is made by assigning adequate powers at the intermediate nodes.

- **TBR (Ticket-Based Routing) (Shigang & Nahrstedt, 1999):** Is a bandwidth or delay based routing protocol that search multiple paths in parallel to find the most interesting in order to satisfy the requirement QoS. It uses DSDV like routing protocol.

Multimedia applications (audio and video) have much more QoS requirements than traditional applications, the last QoS-Aware brief and the following summary (Table 3) shows, how the researches are working to improve these QoS routing protocols to increase the bandwidth and decrease the delay for real-time applications.

Table 3 shows a summary of other MANET routing protocols with QoS according to Tafazolli (2007), ordered chronologically:

QOS MECHANISMS IN MANETS: TRANSPORT LAYER

Transport layer is the final responsible for providing some e2e QoS guarantees to upper layers in the theoretical OSI model. In TCP/IP networks both reliable connection-oriented and non reliable / non connection-oriented transport services are provided, through the use of TCP and UDP respectively. None of them were originally designed to ensure minimum QoS levels resulting on the "best effort" nature of TCP/IP networks. However, the simplicity and lower delays of UDP transmissions (due to its lack of error recovery and ordering mechanisms) make it apparently the best candidate for multimedia traffic. In fact, most real time protocols developed for multimedia applications such as VoIP and streaming (SIP, H323, RTP, RTPC...) were originally designed to use UDP as carrier.

On the other hand, although TCP is supposed not to be suitable for multimedia streaming actual situation is that a high percentage of today's multimedia traffic is carried over TCP connections (using HTTP streaming). This use can be admissible in wired networks since TCP behaves quite well for multimedia stream as long as obtained goodput is at least twice as large than required streaming bitrate (Wang et al., 2004).

Since providing stable bandwidth is still an open issue in MANETs TCP's real capabilities for effectively carrying multimedia traffic in

Table 3. Classification of MANET routing protocols with QoS

Year	Protocol	QoS assurance provided	Type of QoS guarantees
1997	CBCCR	Assured throughput	Pseudo-hard
1999	CCBR	Assured throughput	Pseudo-hard
1999	CEDAR	Assured throughput	Soft
1999	TBR	Assured throughput or Bounded delay	Soft
2001	QAODV	Assured throughput and delay	Soft
2001	HARP	Reduced delay & congestion; improved link longevity	No guarantees, per packet QoS improvement
2002	MRPC	Improved route lifetime; reduced energy consumption; reduced packet dropping rate	No guarantees, per packet QoS improvement
2002	PANDA	Robustness and the smallest number of hops	Soft
2003	DSARP	Reduced delay jitter; bounded delay	Soft
2003	EBLLD	Improved link and path longevity	No guarantees, per packet QoS improvement
2003	GAMAN	Bounded delay and packet dropping rate	Soft
2003	LSBR	Bounded path failure probability	Soft
2004	CLMCQR	Assured throughput, bounded delay and packet dropping rate	Soft
2004	NSR	Assured throughput or any metric that can be calculated from node and link states	Hard – as long as all movement and propagation predictions are correct
2004	SIRCCR	Assure throughput; and delay	Pseudo-hard
2005	AAQR	Bounded delay and jitter; assured throughput	Soft
2005	CAAODV	Assured throughput	Soft
2005	CACP	Assured throughput	Soft
2005	IAR	Assured throughput	Soft
2005	ODCR	Bounded delay	Soft
2005	QOLSR	Improved throughput; and delay	Soft
2006	QGUM	Assured throughput; and delay	Soft

MANETs must be carefully analyzed. In fact, performance degradation of TCP in all kind of wireless networks has been extensively analyzed in the literature (Al Hanbali, Altman, & Nain, 2005; Balakrishnan, Padmanabhan, Seshan, & Katz, 1997; Tian, Xu, & Ansari, 2005; Xylomenos, Polyzos, Mahonen, & Saaranen, 2001). Since TCP was originally conceived for nearly error-free wired networks, every packet loss is supposed to be caused by congestion. As a result of this the response of TCP to packet losses is to reduce the sending rate (by adjusting the congestion window). However, in noisy channels such as wireless links, this behaviour results in poor performance, since TCP transmitter slows down due to packet losses that are not caused by congestion but by transmission errors.

In MANETs TCP performance is even worse (Liu & Singh, 2001; Wang & Zhang, 2002) due to the effect of frequent route changes, route failures, route recomputation procedures, network partitioning and multipath routing.

On the two former ones the changing nature of MANETs can cause both losses at the intermediate nodes and out-of-order delivery, resulting in additional problems to TCP control mechanisms, apart from those caused from the wireless nature of links in MANETs.

Additionally whenever a route gets unavailable the recomputation procedure can take longer than the TCP timeout (RTO), resulting on a retransmission and subsequent triggering of congestion control mechanisms and reduction of sending rate. If route recomputations are frequent (this is quite common in MANETs) the TCP achievable throughput is quite lower than the maximum negotiated rate.

It is also quite common in MANETs that different areas of the networks get isolated during certain periods of time as a result of loss of connectivity between nodes acting as "edge routers." If this situation lasts longer than multiple TCP timeouts, all consecutive TCP retransmissions of the same packets get lost. Since the retransmission timer doubles every time a retransmission is lost these serial timeouts lead to inactivity periods up to several seconds (even longer than the partitioning period itself, because sending node continues waiting for its timeout while the area has already got connected again).

Finally, some protocols such as DSR (Johnson, Maltz, & Broch, 2001) and TORA (Park & Corson, 2001b) rely on multipath routing as a technique to ensure that at least one of available routes will make it possible to packets to reach the target and therefore reduce recomputation delays. However, this kind of approaches commonly result on out-of-order segments and, once again, poor TCP performance (Wu & Harms, 2001a, 2001b).

Another known problem of TCP in 802.11 based MANETs is that of TCP unfairness. This unfairness is caused by the interaction between TCP and 802.11 MAC protocols (due to channel capture, hidden and exposed terminal conditions, and the binary exponential backoff of IEEE 802.11 MAC) and depends on buffer size and mobility issues (Pilosof, Ramjee, Raz, Shavitt, & Sinha, 2003).

Due to this poor TCP performance, there have appeared several approaches for improving TCP both in general wireless environments (Balakrishnan et al., 1997) and specific ones for MANETs (Al Hanbali et al., 2005).

TCP performance enhancement approaches can be categorized as end-to-end, split connection and link layer (Balakrishnan et al., 1997):

- **End-to-end solutions:** These solutions are intend to modify TCP to make it more wireless-friendly. For example SACK TCP (Samaraweera & Fairhurst, 1998) is probed to behave better in noisy wireless channel than traditional Reno and Tahoe TCP implementations by minimizing total amount of retransmitted packets. Similarly in explicit loss notification (ELN) based TCP (Balakrishnan & Katz, 1998) the reason for the loss of a packet can be communicated to the TCP sender and, therefore, congestion control mechanism are only triggered when needed.
- **Split-connections:** In infrastructured wireless network dividing one TCP connection in two parts (one TCP connection from mobile node to the base station (BS) and other one between the BS and final target) can improve end-to-end performance by separating loss recovery over the wireless link from that across the wired network (see (Yavatkar & Bhagawat, 1994) and (Bakre & Badrinath, 1994) for more details).
- **Link level solutions:** Providing more robust link layer protocols (including error detection, correction, and recovery procedures) would enhance TCP performance by reducing "effective" losses.

A similar classification can be found in Charoenpanyasak, Paillassa, and Jaddi (2007), specifically for MANETs:

- **Under layer:** In those approaches new lower layer protocols are adapted to ad-hoc networks (i.e., more TCP-friendly routing and MAC protocols).
- **Intralayer:** These studies modify the transport layer only, but they sometimes take into account cross-layer information regarding lower layers. Different methods fall into this category:
  - **Protocol methods:** A new transport protocol is developed by defining additional messages (see for example (Fu, Greenstein, Meng, & Lu, 2002) for a "designing guide").
  - **Algorithm method:** There is no new protocol definition. Yet, the improvement is achieved by adapting algorithms either within the basic TCP processes (i.e., congestion window management, error recovery and timer management), or within new TCP processes.
  - **Event method:** New events are handled in order to modify the behaviour of TCP. For example an special event is specified to detect the packet loss due to a route change instead of assuming that this loss is caused by network congestion (as in traditional TCP).

In Wang et al. (2002), a detailed survey of wireless-friendly TCP variants can be found:

- **TCP-F:** During normal operation, a node uses traditional TCP protocol. However, whenever an internal node detects a route failure it notifies the sender. Then, the sender switches to an additional "snooze mode" where any TCP activity is frozen. As a result of that, internal TCP status is not affected by the route failure and, therefore, TCP performance degradation is avoided because no congestion control mechanisms are triggered. Once the route is recomputed the sender switches back to normal operation

model and traditional TCP operation continues (Chandran, Raghunathan, Venkatesan, & Prakash, 2001).
- **ELFN** follows a similar way of operation that TCP-F, by using feedback to sender to carry out congestion control mechanisms or not (Holland & Vaidya, 2002). In this case, the explicit link failure notification is carried on DSR routing messages and, instead of waiting for an additional message notifying route restoration, a keepalive or polling mechanisms is used to test the route.
- The fixed **RTO** technique does not rely on an explicit congestion/link failure notification link in previous protocols but uses an heuristic instead in order to find out the probability that a loss is due network congestion or transmission errors (Dyer & Boppana, 2001).
- In **TCP-DOOR** "the sender can distinguish route changes from network congestion by detecting out-of-order delivery, thereafter improve the performance of normal TCP by not invoking unnecessary congestion control" (Wang et al., 2002).

A similar survey is carried out specifically for MANETS in Al Hanbali et al. (2005) where, apart from aforementioned protocols following variants are described:

- **Split TCP:** In order to overcome TCP degradation due to route failure, each e2e TCP connection is split up into several "serial TCP connections,' by turning some of the internal nodes in the route into TCP proxies. These proxies act as TCP counterparts and therefore, are responsible for local error/congestion control. Thus any, loss between two proxies is handled locally and no e2e congestion control mechanisms are triggered, improving global TCP performance while maintaining TCP fairness

(Kopparty, Krishnamurthy, Faloutsos, & Tripathi, 2002).

- **A-TCP** falls into the "explicit notification" set of protocols. An additional A-TCP sublayer between TCP and IP is responsible for manipulating the state of the TCP agent (state machine) by triggering congestion control mechanisms whenever an explicit notification is received but not forwarding third ACK so that occasional losses do not degrade TCP performance (Liu et al., 2001).

- **TCP-bus:** Similarly to other notification based algorithms TCP-bus gets feedback from network layer but it also incorporates notifying and buffering capabilities in internal nodes, so that they can handle special situations (such as route failures and recoveries), notify both ends and retransmit buffered packets once route is active again (Kim, Toh, & Choi, 2001).

Regarding other analysis of multimedia transmission performance on MANETs not related to TCP in Calafate, Malumbres, and Manzoni (2004), Clausen, Jacquet, and Viennot (2002), Khorashadi, Chen, Ghosal, Chuah, and Zhang (2007), Lee, Ahn, and Campbell (2001), and Xylomenos & Polyzos, 1999) some examples of UDP performance analysis and power constraint issues can be found.

As the reader can see the activity in this area has been less intense than in TCP since UDP performance is more closely tied to network performance itself, analyzed in other section of this chapter.

CROSS-LAYER APPROACH TO QOS PROVISION FOR MULTIMEDIA APPLICATIONS OVER MANETs

The tightly layered QoS model assigns clear and differentiated functionalities to each protocol in the stack, not allowing the interaction between layers on behalf of interoperability and compatibility. Nevertheless, the objective of generality of the OSI model may not be the most efficient one in some specific scenarios such as the MANET environment. Its dynamic characteristics (i.e., scarcity of resources and unstable link state) make it even more difficult to provide QoS capabilities to multimedia applications.

The delays of TCP acknowledgements are always considered as congestion indicative, triggering a flow control mechanism that reduces transmission rate, as it is the commonest cause in wired or infrastructure networks. But in MANETs, those delays may be caused by transmission errors rather than congestion. An appropriate interaction between layers could help the transport layer take the proper flow control decision.

An interaction between physical layer and higher layers could facilitate the adaptation of transmission power to the network current conditions to safe battery in mobile devices.

Similarly, the MAC protocol could improve frame scheduling to prioritize real-time multimedia traffic, if flow differentiation is provided by higher layers.

A cross-layer approach tries to take advantage of the possibility of interaction between layers to optimize the performance of the network in order to provide QoS support to real-time traffic in hostile environments, trading off generality for performance gain.

As interaction between communication layers appears to be a plausible choice for providing QoS support to multimedia scenarios, in the next sections we will analyze cross-layer design options and some architectures that have been developed.

Two Cross-Layer Design Approaches

There are two categories of cross-layer interaction between adjacent or not adjacent layers:

- **Information sharing:** The interaction is based on shared global variables accessible to all communication protocols in the stack.
- **Layer coupling:** The layered architecture concept disappears to build new communication protocols that integrate the functionality of adjacent layers with the objective of optimizing the performance of the network.

Although layer coupling design offers higher optimization possibilities, its loss of modularity and compatibility advantages makes information sharing option to be the most applied nowadays. However, coupling design should still be highly regarded in those environments here compatibility is not an essential issue (i.e., videogame platforms).

Cross-Layer Architectures

Quality of service provision in MANET networks is usually tackled modifying just one protocol layer only, generally the routing protocols related to network layer. However, the variability of physical and link layer conditions of wireless media raises the need for exploring other alternatives that combine adjustments in various layers of the protocol stack to provide QoS support. All this leads to cross-layer models.

In MANET environments, the routing protocols should be feed-backed with metrics sampled in the lower layers, as an abstraction of physical and link layers (Masip-Bruin et al., 2006). At the same time, as the quality of a link varies rapidly, routing algorithm should be able to damp the oscillating effects of the wireless medium.

The operation of the cross-layer models is shown is the follows: while MLN (MAC layer metrics) and NLM (network layer metrics) analyze link quality to build good quality paths, ALM (application layer metrics) selects the path that better satisfies the requirements of the application.

Ideally, a cross-layer QoS model would split MLM, NLM, and ALP up. To that effect, one of the proposals suggests the definition of a set of parameters per layer that, depending on the priority class, gives emphasis to some parameters over the rest.

Next some of cross-layer architectures will be presented (Jurdak, 2007):

- **Mobile Man:** This information sharing architecture defines a network status repository that gathers network information from all the layers and makes it available for all the protocols in the stack.
- **Cross-talk:** The innovation of this architecture is the incorporation of two views of network state: a local view with information about the node collected by the layers of the communication stack, and a global view that gathers local information of remote nodes adding a small overhead in the packets transmitted. These views give nodes quite a precise notion of the network state in order to improve global performance.
- **Jurdak:** This is another information sharing framework with the novelty of providing flexible and tuneable variable specifications to adapt the behaviour of the network to the requirements of different applications.
- **LEACH:** In this architecture, the application layer communicates it requirements to the lower layers to improve performance.

As we will study in the next section, the combination of a routing protocol with a signalling mechanism for resource reservation can also be considered a cross-layer design, since network and transport layers share information to provide QoS support.

Signalling Systems

To provide QoS in MANET networks two main problems must be solved:

- **QoS routing:** Or how to find a route through the network that satisfies the requested QoS level.
- **QoS maintenance:** Or how to guarantee that, once a route is found, QoS agreement is going to be granted "regardless" the network dynamics.

The routing problem has been studied in the previous section, but route maintenance is particularly complex. Signalling protocol will perform the reservation and liberation of network resources, together with flow establishment. All the varied signalling mechanisms (Lee, Ahn, Zhang, & Campbell, 2000) are divided between those that include control information inside data packets (in-band signalling) and those that employ specific control messages (out-of-band signalling).

dRSVP

dRSVP (Mirhakkak, Schult, & Thomson, 2000) is an evolution of RSVP for providing dynamic QoS over a distributed network protocol. This approach to QoS comprises a resources reservation scheme similar to that carried out in IntServ, but with a more extended meaning of the term "reservation." Thus reservation represents an agreement with the network to provide a service level within a given range. The applications request QoS indicating the required minimum service level and the maximum level they can manage. After that, the applications complete the reservation in the range provided by the network that may vary in time.

This protocol has been created from the implementation of RSVP's ISI to obtain a dynamic RSVP protocol. The performed modifications to the RSVP protocol are the following:

- Additional information is added to RESV and PATH messages to make them able to describe traffic flow ranges.

- A new measurement specification and a new reservation notification are added to allow nodes to learn about bottlenecks.
- The admission control process has changed to allow bandwidth distribution.
- The SCRAPI API of RSVP is extended to allow bandwidth ranges.

INSIGNIA

While other QoS approximations are based on a circuit model that needs an explicit connection management and the establishment of a hard-state prior to the communication, INSIGNIA (Lee et al., 2000) proposes a new alternative network model with a higher response capacity to the changes in MANET networks.

The main objective of INSIGNIA is to provide adaptive services that support a minimum guarantee of quality to real time flows, offering better service levels when the resources become available.

The INSIGNIA components are listed below:

- **In-band signalling:** To establish, re-establish, adapt, and cancel adaptive services between source-destination pairs. Flow restoration algorithms respond to dynamic changes on routes and adaptive services respond to available bandwidth changes.
- **Admission control:** Performs the bandwidth reservation for the flows based on the maximum/minimum bandwidth range requested by the application and the capacity/occupation of the channel. New reservation requests do not affect ongoing reservations, to keep the signalling protocol light-weighted.
- **Packet forwarding:** Classifies incoming packets and forwards them to the proper module, depending on the nature of the packet (signalling or data).
- **Routing:** Tracks topology changes and provides the routes either proactively or

on-demand. ISIGNIA does not force the use of a certain routing protocol, but supposes that there is a set of suitable protocols.

- **Packet scheduling:** Schedules the packets according to the time-variant conditions of the links.
- **Medium access control:** Provides access to the wireless shared medium for adaptive and best-effort services.

The main disadvantage of INSIGNIA is the need of storing the state machines of the mobile nodes, and it may become a problem as the network grows. On the other hand, INSIGNIA only provides two service classes: real time and best effort.

Once the characteristics and architecture of the cross-layer communication have been analyzed, the possibility of collaboration among different layers helps into the provisioning the necessary QoS for each application. But how can nodes knows what kind of applications or services can be used when it joins to an ad hoc network? And how it must use those services?

Therefore, the uses of service discovery mechanisms are necessary, in order to correctly configure and use the services that offer the other nodes of the network.

In the next section, service discovery mechanisms and characteristics will be analyzed.

SERVICE DISCOVERY

Due to the mobility of the nodes in MANETs, the topology of mobile ad hoc network changes continuously. In this kind of networks one of the most relevant research problems is that of service discovery. It is really important to implement a mechanism to detect the availability of a service (multimedia services) and how to use them (Chakraborty, Joshi, & Yesha, 2006; Hannikainen, Hamalainen, Niemi, & Saarinen, 2002; Kozat & Tassiulas, 2004; Lenders, May, & Plattner, 2005;

Sailhan & Issarny, 2005; Varshavsky, Reid, & de Lara, 2005).

There are several scenarios where implementing this mechanisms, such as gateway service (a node has access to the Internet and let the rest of the nodes use that service), parking service (in public car parks announce where the free parking places are), game service (multiplayer games), database services, music services, information-oriented services, VoIP services, and video services.

At the same time, QoS support has been increased, both in wired and wireless networks and nowadays the use of Internet as a source of multimedia content using these networks it is a fact. Thus, the search of mechanisms for the discovery of services that include mechanisms that guarantee a minimum of QoS has become in the objective of many researchers (Deora et al., 2004).

In traditional networks a lot of work has been done around service discovery: service location protocol (SLP) (Guttman, Perkins, Veizades, & Day, 1999), Jini (Keith & Tom, 2001), universal description discovery and integration (UDDI) (understanding Web services: XML, WSDL, SOAP, and UDDI, 2002), universal plug and play (UpNP) (John, 1999), Bluetooth's service discovery protocol (SDP) ("Bluetooth Specification Part E, Service Discovery Protocol,"). But these works are not valid for MANETs, since they require a central administration and introduce a big overhead that ad hoc networks cannot support. And using QoS properties like (Al-Ali, Rana, & Walker, 2003) with the focus on the application layer, whereby a given service may indicate the QoS properties it can offer, or where a service may search for other services based on particular QoS properties. Or in Shuping (2003) where proposes a new Web services discovery model in which QoS is taken into account for the service discovery. Another work is Dongyan, Klara, and Duangdao (2001), where introduce the addition of QoS feedback capability to clients and the caching and propagation of discovery results with QoS.

In Francoise and Valerie (2005) service providers proactively provide QoS parameters together with the service's functional interface, to service requesters.

Recently, many works has been done on these strategies for ad-hoc networks:

- **Allia (Olga, Dipanjan, Anupam, & Timothy, 2002):** A peer-to-peer caching based and policy-driven agent-service discovery framework to facilitate cross-platform service discovery in ad hoc environments for mobile electronic commerce applications.

- **Konark (Helal, Desai, Verma, & Choonhwa, 2003):** It is a specific service discovery protocol for ad hoc networks, focused on service independent devices and oriented to m-commerce.

- **DEAPspace (Nidd, 2001):** It addresses peer-to-peer networking of pervasive devices instead of client-server networking.

- **GSR (Chakraborty et al., 2006):** It is a routing and session management protocol for ad-hoc networks as an integral part of a service discovery infrastructure. This enables GSR to accommodate service-centric routing apart from the traditional node-centric routing.

- **Service Rings (Michael, Birgitta, Nig, & Philipp, 2003):** It is a proposal to use semantic techniques to discover services based on a transport layer overlay. The main objectives are: Decentralization, easy and local adaptability to frequent topology changes, basis for effective and efficient trading mechanisms and semantic overlay to route messages by inspecting their semantical content.

- **Bluetooth SDP (Sasikanth, Anupam, & Timothy, 2002):** This Bluetooth based protocol is optimized for ad hoc networks and resource-constrained devices using universal unique identifiers (UUIDs). For

example, a hands free and cellular phone connection.

Most of these proposals place service discovery at a layer over the routing. On the other hand, some of these service discovery mechanisms assume a reactive routing protocol (Clausen & Jacquet, 2003; Engelstad, Thanh, & Egeland, 2003; Kozat et al., 2004) for the network support. These two conditions make those mechanisms not suitable for all ad hoc networks. Nevertheless, if a proactive protocol is used, this type of protocols can improve latency and data transmission delay--factors, which are critical to the performance of multimedia applications (Jodra, Vara, Cabero, & Bagazgoitia, 2006).

CONCLUSION AND FUTURE TRENDS

New application scenarios for mobile ad hoc networks, including multimedia services and/or online games, demand certain levels of quality so that a large effort has been carried out by both the industry and research community toward QoS provisioning in MANETs.

However, when analysing QoS aspects in MANETs the first thing to notice is that MANETs' special characteristics prevent the use of traditional QoS mechanisms in these environments.

These particularities are related not only to the wireless transmission medium itself (which is shared with other kinds of wireless networks) but also to the uncertainty derived from the mobility of the nodes and subsequent network topology variations.

Hence, major challenges to be faced while defining QoS mechanisms for MANETs include the wireless channel, multihop-nature of communications, node mobility, lack of centralised control, dynamic network topology, and limited device resources. These challenges result into a series of constraints to be added to QoS traditional ones (namely bandwidth, delay or jitter), such as battery power, CPU usage and stability of the routes. Most of these constraints demand different QoS mechanisms in different protocol layers, ranging from physical layer and MAC contention mechanisms to application level. However, since MANETs particularities are related to network topologies most of the efforts analysed aimed at developing routing strategies focused on dealing with dynamic topology problems.

Historically first MANET routing protocols were proactive. Hence, they reproduced the way routing tables are calculated in traditional wired networks. Both the neighbour discovering procedures and route advertisements were carried out asynchronously, whenever a new router entered the network (and after that periodically or triggered by any topology change). Although this approach works pretty well for quasi-static topologies, since network topology in MANETs may vary quite quickly most of these calculations would be useless if no node needed them at a certain time. This is the reason behind the definition of reactive protocols. In this kind of protocol, the route discovery procedures take place whenever a node requests a path to a certain destination. So, routing data exchange between nodes is triggered by real needs resulting in reduced network overload. Unfortunately this on-demand route calculation causes increasing delays in session initiation and could compromise QoS requirements.

Hybrid protocols try to take advantage of the best of both worlds by splitting the whole network topology in smaller areas, and combining local route pre-computation inside the different areas, with reactive inter-area route request to specific destinations.

Regardless prior classification some initiatives have targeted at metrics different than traditional ones. They cover specific constraints, such as battery power, CPU utilization, and/or node location in order to compute best possible route.

Although the research around routing protocols has been intensive, none of the proposed solutions fits every possible scenario. Currently, main research works are focused on OLSRv2 as the evolved version of a proactive protocol and DYMO as the reactive protocol aiming to be the natural successor of AODV. Anyway, it can be affirmed that usually, for a traffic-dense low-mobility scenario, a proactive protocol, such as OLSRv2 will suit better. On the other hand, reactive protocols such as AODV and DYMO will apply to smaller environments supporting higher-mobility-pattern nodes.

Besides the typical difficulties of MANET environments, the increasing acceptance of ad hoc mobile networks has led to the development of new applications demanding QoS support. Therefore, new solutions must be designed in order to satisfy the new QoS requirements. Some initiatives, such as QOLSR or QAODV have chosen to extend a widely accepted ad hoc routing protocol without QoS support in order to make it QoS capable. Other initiatives, such as PANDA, have been specifically designed for this kind of scenario. However, as it happens when QoS is not supported, there is no solution suitable for any environment.

So, the main question that leads to current open issues and future trends in QoS routing in MANETs could be the following one: is there any routing solution that could be applied to all the possible scenarios including different network sizes, mobility patterns and multiple constraints/metrics and, at the same time, provide guaranteed QoS levels?

The number of protocols and research initiatives analysed suggest that there is no answer yet or, at least, no one suitable for all the scenarios and constraints considered.

There already exist some approaches focused on addressing with different constraints. Nevertheless, in order to reduce the complexity associated with multi-criteria routing problems most of these alternatives use some kind of heuristics valid only for those scenarios/specific constraints. Therefore this problem-orientation prevents their use in all the scenarios MANETs are suitable for.

Genetic algorithms (i.e., multi objective evolutionary algorithms or MOEA), fuzzy logic, and other multi-criteria optimization techniques appear as the more suitable contenders in order to face the multi-purpose multi-constraint QoS routing problem in MANETs. The reduced CPU power and battery issues of actual devices will set up the upper thresholds for these algorithms and, therefore, final capabilities of associated multi-criteria routing protocols.

On the other hand, most of the initiatives have not led to any actual implementation. History told us that whenever there are so many alternatives any killer-app will probably win that race. Regarding this, any movement from major players such as mobile vendors, standardization bodies, or game industry should be carefully analyzed.

Another issue when analysing QoS aspects in MANETs will be related to the actual quality perceived by end-users (PQoS). Since QoS requirements are especially critical in this kind of environments (with low network and processing resources) calculating minimum QoS levels for acceptable user experience will become a key issue. One of the research fields focuses on incorporating PQoS assessing techniques while trying to get the highest effective performance with the minimum resource consumption.

Finally, assuring certain QoS levels cannot be handled only at the network layer or by some routing protocols. Any end-to-end QoS provision architecture will demand QoS control mechanisms and information exchange among all the layers. So, the issue of cross-layer QoS architectures and both intra-layer and inter layer signalling mechanisms will gather increasing interest.

REFERENCES

Abdrabou, A., & Weihua, Z. (2006). A position-based QoS routing scheme for UWB mobile ad hoc networks. *IEEE Journal on Selected Areas in Communications, 24*(4), 850-856.

Al-Ali, R. J. S., Rana, O. F. Walker, D. W. (2003). Supporting QoS-based discovery in service-oriented grids. *Proceedings of the International Parallel and Distributed Processing Symposium, 2003.*

Al Hanbali, A., Altman, E., & Nain, P. (2005). A survey of TCP over ad hoc networks. *IEEE Communications Surveys & Tutorials*, 22-36.

Bakre, A., & Badrinath, B. R. (1994). *I-TCP: Indirect TCP for mobile hosts.* Rutgers University, Dept. of Computer Science, Laboratory for Computer Science Research.

Balakrishnan, H., & Katz, R. H. (1998). *Explicit loss notification and wireless web performance.* Paper presented at the EEE Globecom Internet Mini-Conference, Sydney, Australia.

Balakrishnan, H., Padmanabhan, V. N., Seshan, S., & Katz, R. H. (1997). A comparison of mechanisms for improving TCP performance over wireless links. *IEEE/ACM Transactions on Networking (TON), 5*(6), 756-769.

Baoxian, Z., & Mouftah, H. T. (2005). QoS routing for wireless ad hoc networks: Problems, algorithms, and protocols. *Communications Magazine, IEEE, 43*(10), 110-117.

Barolli, L., Koyama, A., & Shiratori, N. (2003). *A QoS routing method for ad-hoc networks based on genetic algorithm.*

Bellur, B., & Ogier, R. G. (1999). *A reliable, efficient topology broadcast protocol for dynamic networks.*

Bluetooth specification part E, service discovery protocol. Retrieved from http://www.bluetooth.com

Boppana, R. V., & Konduru, S. P. (2001). *An adaptive distance vector routing algorithm for mobile, ad hoc networks.*

Brad, K., & Kung, H. T. (2000). *GPSR: Greedy perimeter stateless routing for wireless networks.* Paper presented at the Proceedings of the 6th Annual International Conference on Mobile Computing and Networking.

Calafate, C. T., Malumbres, M. P., & Manzoni, P. (2004). *Performance of H.264 compressed video streams over 802.11b based MANETs.* Paper presented at the 24th International Conference on Distributed Computing Systems Workshops, 2004. Proceedings.

Cesar, A. S., & Ram, R. (2001). Hazy sighted link state routing protocol (HSLS). *BBN Technical Memorandum, 1301.*

Clausen, T., Jacquet, P., & Viennot, L. (2002). Comparative study of CBR and TCP performance of MANET routing protocols. *Workshop MESA.*

Chai-Keong, T. (1997). Associativity-based routing for ad hoc mobile networks. *4*(2), 103-139.

Dynamic MANET On-demand (DYMO) routing, (2007).

Chakraborty, D., Joshi, A., & Yesha, Y. (2006). Integrating service discovery with routing and session management for ad-hoc networks. *Ad Hoc Networks, 4*(2), 204-224.

Chandran, K., Raghunathan, S., Venkatesan, S., & Prakash, R. (2001). A feedback-based scheme for improving TCP performance in ad hoc wireless networks. *IEEE Personal Communications, 8*(1), 34-39.

Chane, L. F., & Garcia-Luna-Aceves, J. J. (1995). Floor acquisition multiple access (FAMA) for packet-radio networks. *SIGCOMM Comput. Commun. Rev. %@ 0146-4833, 25*(4), 262-273.

Charles, E. P., & Pravin, B. (1994). Highly dynamic Destination-Sequenced Distance-Vector routing (DSDV) for mobile computers. *24*(4), 234-244.

Charoenpanyasak, S., Paillassa, B., & Jaddi, F. (2007). *Experimental study on TCP enhancement interest in ad hoc networks.* Paper presented at the 3rd International Conference on Wireless and Mobile Communications, 2007. ICWMC '07, Guadeloupe, French Caribbean.

Chen, T. W., Tsai, J. T., & Gerla, M. (1997). *QoS routing performance in multihop, multimedia, wireless networks.*

Chi, M., & Yuanyuan, Y. (2005). *A prioritized battery-aware routing protocol for wireless ad hoc networks.* Paper presented at the Proceedings of the 8th ACM International Symposium on Modeling, Analysis, and Simulation of Wireless and Mobile Systems.

Chiang, C. C., Wu, H. K., Liu, W., & Gerla, M. (1997). *Routing in clustered multihop, mobile wireless networks with fading channel*: Computer Science Department, University of California, Los Angeles.

Chunhung Richard, L., & Jain-Shing, L. (1999). QoS routing in ad hoc wireless networks. *IEEE Journal on Selected Areas in Communications, 17*(8), 1426-1438.

Deora, V., Shao, J., Shercliff, G., Stockreisser, P. J., Gray, W. A., & Fiddian, N. J. (2004). Incorporating QoS specifications in service discovery. *Web Information Systems – WISE 2004 Workshops* (pp. 252-263).

Dimitri, B., & Robert, G. (1987). *Data networks.* Prentice-Hall, Inc.

Dongwoo, K., Chan-Ho, M., & Sehun, K. (2004). On-demand SIR and bandwidth-guaranteed routing with transmit power assignment in ad hoc mobile networks. *Vehicular Technology, IEEE Transactions on, 53*(4), 1215-1223.

Dongyan, X., Klara, N., & Duangdao, W. (2001). *QoS-aware discovery of wide-area distributed services.* Paper presented at the Proceedings of the 1st International Symposium on Cluster Computing and the Grid.

Drabu, Y. (1999). A survey of QoS techniques in 802.11.

Dube, R., Rais, C. D., Wang, K. Y., & Tripathi, S. K. (1997). *Signal stability based adaptive routing (SSA) for ad-hoc mobile networks.*

Dyer, T. D., & Boppana, R. V. (2001). A comparison of TCP performance over three routing protocols for mobile ad hoc networks. *Proceedings of the 2nd ACM International Symposium on Mobile Ad Hoc Networking & Computing* (pp. 56-66).

Elizabeth, M. R., & Charles, E. P. (1999). *Multicast operation of the ad-hoc on-demand distance vector routing protocol.* Paper presented at the Proceedings of the 5th Annual ACM/IEEE International Conference on Mobile Computing and Networking.

Engelstad, P., Thanh, D. V., & Egeland, G. (2003). *Name resolution in on-demand MANETs and over external IP networks.* Paper presented at the ICC '03. IEEE International Conference on Communications, 2003.

Francoise, S., & Valerie, I. (2005). *Scalable service discovery for MANET.* Paper presented at the Proceedings of the 3rd IEEE International Conference on Pervasive Computing and Communications.

Fu, Z., Greenstein, B., Meng, X., & Lu, S. (2002). *Design and implementation of a TCP-friendly transport protocol for ad hoc wireless networks.* Paper presented at the 10th IEEE International Conference on Network Protocols, 2002., Paris, France.

George, A., & Rahim, T. (1999). *RDMAR: A bandwidth-efficient routing protocol for mobile ad hoc networks.* Paper presented at the Proceedings of the 2nd ACM International Workshop on Wireless Mobile Multimedia.

Grace, K., & Corporation, M. (2000). *Mobile mesh routing protocol (MMRP).* Retrieved from http://www.mitre.org/tech_transfer/mobilemesh

Group, I. I. E. T. F. M. W. Mobile Ad-hoc Networks. Retrieved from http://www.ietf.org/html.charters/manet-charter.html

Guangyu, P., Gerla, M., & Tsu-Wei, C. (2000a). *Fisheye state routing: a routing scheme for ad hoc wireless networks.*

Guangyu, P., Mario, G., & Xiaoyan, H. (2000b). *LANMAR: Landmark routing for large scale wireless ad hoc networks with group mobility.* Paper presented at the Proceedings of the 1st ACM International Symposium on Mobile Ad Hoc Networking & Computing.

Gupta, R., Zhanfeng, J., Tung, T., & Walrand, J. (2005). *Interference-aware QoS routing (IQRouting) for ad-hoc networks.*

Guttman, E., Perkins, C., Veizades, J., & Day, M. (1999). *Service Location Protocol, Version 2:* RFC Editor.

Haartsen, J. (1998). BLUETOOTH—The universal radio interface for ad hoc, wireless connectivity. *Ericsson Review.*

Haas, Z. J. (1997). *A new routing protocol for the reconfigurable wireless networks.*

The Interzone Routing Protocol (IERP) for Ad Hoc Networks, (2002a).

The Intrazone Routing Protocol (IARP) for Ad Hoc Networks, (2002b).

The Zone Routing Protocol (ZRP) for Ad Hoc Networks, (2002c).

Hannikainen, M., Hamalainen, T. D., Niemi, M., & Saarinen, J. (2002). Trends in personal wireless data communications. *Computer Communications, 25,* 84-99.

Helal, S., Desai, N., Verma, V., & Choonhwa, L. (2003). *Konark: A service discovery and delivery protocol for ad-hoc networks.* Paper presented at the Wireless Communications and Networking, 2003. WCNC 2003. 2003 IEEE.

Holland, G., & Vaidya, N. (2002). Analysis of TCP performance over mobile ad hoc networks. *Wireless Networks, 8*(2), 275-288.

Flow State in the Dynamic Source Routing Protocol for Mobile Ad Hoc Networks, (2001).

Hui, S., Bingxin, S., Ling, z., & Huazhi, G. (2003). *A distributed entropy-based long-life QoS routing algorithm in ad hoc network.*

ANSI/IEEE Std 802.11

Part 11: Wireless LAN Medium Access Control (MAC) and Physical Layer (PHY) Specifications, (1999).

Iwata, A., Ching-Chuan, C., Guangyu, P., Gerla, M., & Tsu-Wei, C. (1999). Scalable routing strategies for ad hoc wireless networks. *IEEE Journal on Selected Areas in Communications, 17*(8), 1369-1379.

Jacquet, P., Muhlethaler, P., Clausen, T., Laouiti, A., Qayyum, A., & Viennot, L. (2001). *Optimized link state routing protocol for ad hoc networks.*

The Adaptive Demand-Driven Multicast Routing Protocol for Mobile Ad Hoc Networks (ADMR), (2001).

Joa-Ng, M., & Lu, I. T. (1999). A peer-to-peer zone-based two-level link state routing for mobile ad hoc networks. *IEEE Journal on Selected Areas in Communications, 17*(8), 1415-1425.

Jodra, J. L., Vara, M., Cabero, J. M., & Bagazgoitia, J. (2006). *Service discovery mechanism over OLSR for mobile ad-hoc networks.* Paper presented at the 20th International Conference on Advanced Information Networking and Applications, 2006. AINA 2006.

Johnson, D. B., & Maltz, D. A. (1996). *Dynamic source routing in ad hoc wireless networks.*

Johnson, D. B., Maltz, D. A., & Broch, J. (2001). DSR: The dynamic source routing protocol for multi-hop wireless ad hoc networks. *Ad Hoc Networking, 1*, 139-172.

Jurdak, R. (2007). *Wireless ad hoc and sensor networks: a cross-layer design perspective* (1st ed.). Springer.

Karn, P. (1990). *MACA--A new channel access method for packet radio.* Paper presented at the ARRL/CRRL Amateur Radio 9th Computer Networking Conference.

Keith, E., & Tom, R. (2001). *Jini Example by Example.* Prentice Hall PTR.

Khorashadi, B., Chen, A., Ghosal, D., Chuah, C. N., & Zhang, M. (2007). Impact of transmission power on the performance of UDP in vehicular ad hoc networks. *IEEE International Conference on Communications, 2007. ICC'07* (pp. 3698-3703).

Kim, D., Toh, C. K., & Choi, Y. (2001). TCP-BuS: Improving TCP performance in wireless ad hoc networks. *Journal of Communications and Networks, 3*(2), 1.

Ko, Y. B., & Vaidya, N. H. *Optimizations for Location-aided Routing (LAR) in Mobile Ad Hoc Networks (A brief note).*

Kopparty, S., Krishnamurthy, S. V., Faloutsos, M., & Tripathi, S. K. (2002). *Split TCP for mobile ad hoc networks.* Paper presented at the IEEE Global Telecommunications Conference, 2002. GLOBECOM'02.

Kozat, U. C., & Tassiulas, L. (2004). Service discovery in mobile ad hoc networks: an overall perspective on architectural choices and network layer support issues. *Ad Hoc Networks, 2*(1), 21.

Kurkowski, S., Camp, T., & Colagrosso, M. (2005). *MANET Simulation Studies: The Incredibles.*

Lang, D. (2003). *A comprehensive overview about selected ad hoc networking routing protocols.* München: Department of Computer Science, Technische Universität München.

Lee, L., Gerla, M., Chen, J., Chen, J., Zhou, B., & Caruso, A. (2006). "Direction" forward routing for highly mobile ad hoc networks. *Ad Hoc & Sensor Wireless Networks.*

Lee, S. B., Ahn, G. S., & Campbell, A. T. (2001). Improving UDP and TCP performance in mobile ad hoc networks withINSIGNIA. *Communications Magazine, IEEE, 39*(6), 156-165.

Lee, S. B., Ahn, G. S., Zhang, X., & Campbell, A. T. (2000). INSIGNIA: An IP-based quality of service framework for mobile ad hoc networks. *Journal of Parallel and Distributed Computing, 60*(4), 374-406.

Lee, Y. J., & Riley, G. F. (2005). *Dynamic nix-vector routing for mobile ad hoc networks.*

Lei, C., & Heinzelman, W. B. (2005). QoS-aware routing based on bandwidth estimation for mobile ad hoc networks. *IEEE Journal on Selected Areas in Communications, 23*(3), 561-572.

Lenders, V., May, M., & Plattner, B. (2005). Service discovery in mobile ad hoc networks: A field theoretic approach. *Pervasive and Mobile Computing, 1*(3), 343-370.

Li, J., & Mohapatra, P. (2002). *PANDA: An Approach to Improve Flooding Based Route Discovery in Mobile Ad hoc Networks*: CSE.

Lin, C. R., & Gerla, M. (1997). *Asynchronous multimedia multihop wireless networks.*

Lindgren, A., & Schelen, O. (2002). *Infrastructured ad hoc networks.* Paper presented at the Proceedings. International Conference on Parallel Processing Workshops.

Liu, J., & Singh, S. (2001). ATCP: TCP for mobile ad hoc networks. *IEEE Journal on Selected Areas in Communications, 19*(7), 1300-1315.

Maltz, D. A. (1999). *Resource Management in Multi-hop Ad Hoc Networks.*

Masip-Bruin, X., Yannuzzi, M., Domingo-Pascual, J., Fonte, A., Curado, M., Monteiro, E., et al. (2006). Research challenges in QoS routing. *Computer Communications, 29*(5), 563-581.

Michael, K., Birgitta, K., Nig, R., & Philipp, O. (2003). *Service rings--A semantic overlay for service discovery in ad hoc networks.* Paper presented at the Proceedings of the 14th International Workshop on Database and Expert Systems Applications.

Min, S., Jiandong, L., & Yan, S. (2003). Routing protocol with QoS guarantees for ad-hoc network. *Electronics Letters, 39*(1), 143-145.

Min, W., & Geng-Sheng, K. (2005). *An application-aware qos routing scheme with improved stability for multimedia applications in mobile ad hoc networks.*

Mirhakkak, M., Schult, N., & Thomson, D. (2000). *Dynamic quality-of-service for mobile ad hoc networks.*

Misra, A., & Banerjee, S. (2002). *MRPC: maximizing network lifetime for reliable routing in wireless environments.*

Mohapatra, P., Li, J., & Gui, C. (2003). QoS in mobile ad hoc networks. *IEEE wireless communications (IEEE wirel. commun.) ISSN 1536-1284*

Institute of Electrical and Electronics Engineers, New York, NY, ETATS-UNIS (2002) (Revue), 10, 44-52.

Murthy, C. S. R., & Manoj, B. S. (2004). *Ad Hoc Wireless Networks.* Prentice Hall International.

Nidd, M. (2001). Service discovery in DEAPspace. *Personal Communications, IEEE [see also IEEE Wireless Communications], 8*(4), 39-45.

Nikaein, N., & Bonnet, C. (2001). HARP-Hybrid Ad Hoc Routing Protocol.

Nikaein, N., Labiod, H., & Bonnet, C. (2000). *DDR-distributed dynamic routing algorithm for mobile ad hoc networks*. Paper presented at the Mobile and Ad Hoc Networking and Computing, 2000. MobiHOC. 2000 First Annual Workshop on

Olga, R., Dipanjan, C., Anupam, J., & Timothy, F. (2002). *Allia: Alliance-based service discovery for ad-hoc environments*. Paper presented at the Proceedings of the 2nd international workshop on Mobile commerce.

Optimized Link State Routing Protocol (OLSR), (2003).

Park, V., & Corson, S. (2001b). *Temporally-ordered routing algorithm (TORA) Version 1 Functional Specification*. Retrieved from http://www.ietf.org/internet-drafts/draft-ietf-manet-tora-spec-04.txt

Park, V. D., & Corson, M. S. (1997). *A highly adaptive distributed routing algorithm for mobile wireless networks*.

Pei, G., Gerla, M., Hong, X., & Chiang, C. C. (1999). *A wireless hierarchical routing protocol with group mobility*.

Quality of Service for Ad hoc On-Demand Distance Vector Routing, (2001).

Quality of Service for Ad hoc Optimized Link State Routing Protocol (QOLSR), (2006).

Pilosof, S., Ramjee, R., Raz, D., Shavitt, Y., & Sinha, P. (2003). *Understanding TCP fairness over wireless LAN*. Paper presented at the INFOCOM 2003. The 22nd Annual Joint Conference of the IEEE Computer and Communications Societies.

Qiang Ni, L. R. T. T. (2004). A survey of QoS enhancements for IEEE 802.11 wireless LAN (Vol. 4, pp. 547-566).

R.John. (1999). *UpnP, Jini and Salutation. A Look at some popular Coordination Frameworks for*

Future Network Devices: California software Labs.

Radhakrishnan, S., Racherla, G., Sekharan, C. N., Rao, N. S. V., & Batsell, S. G. (1999). *DST-A routing protocol for ad hoc networks using distributed spanning trees*.

Raju, J., & Garcia-Luna-Aceves, J. J. (1999). *A new approach to on-demand loop-free multipath routing*.

Multicast Ad hoc On-Demand Distance Vector (MAODV) Routing, (2000).

Rubin, I., & Liu, Y. C. (2003). *Link stability models for QoS ad hoc routing algorithms*.

Sailhan, F., & Issarny, V. (2005). *Scalable Service Discovery for MANET*.

Samaraweera, N. K. G., & Fairhurst, G. (1998). Reinforcement of TCP error recovery for wireless communication. *ACM SIGCOMM Computer Communication Review, 28*(2), 30-38.

Sasikanth, A., Anupam, J., & Timothy, F. (2002). Enhanced service discovery in bluetooth (Vol. 35, pp. 96-99): IEEE Computer Society Press.

Seet, B. C., Liu, G., Lee, B. S., Foh, C. H., Wong, K. J., & Lee, K. K. (2004). A-STAR: A Mobile Ad Hoc Routing Strategy for Metropolis Vehicular Communications: Springer.

Shah, R. C., & Rabaey, J. M. (2002). *Energy aware routing for low energy ad hoc sensor networks*.

Shigang, C., & Nahrstedt, K. (1999). Distributed quality-of-service routing in ad hoc networks. *IEEE Journal on Selected Areas in Communications, 17*(8), 1488-1505.

Shree, M., & Garcia-Luna-Aceves, J. J. (1996). An efficient routing protocol for wireless networks. *Mob. Netw. Appl. %@ 1383-469X, 1*(2), 183-197.

Shuping, R. (2003). A model for web services discovery with QoS (Vol. 4, pp. 1-10): ACM Press.

Sivakumar, R., Sinha, P., & Bharghavan, V. (1999). CEDAR: A core-extraction distributed ad hoc routing algorithm. *IEEE Journal on Selected Areas in Communications, 17*(8), 1454-1465.

Song, G., & Yang, O. W. (2002). *Performance of backup source routing in mobile ad hoc networks.*

Stefano, B., Imrich, C., Violet, R. S., & Barry, A. W. (1998). *A distance routing effect algorithm for mobility (DREAM).* Paper presented at the Proceedings of the 4th Annual ACM/IEEE International Conference on Mobile Computing and Networking.

Stine, J. A., & de Veciana, G. (2004). A paradigm for quality-of-service in wireless ad hoc networks using synchronous signaling and node states. *IEEE Journal on Selected Areas in Communications, 22*(7), 1301-1321.

Tafazolli, L. H. I. A. R. (2007). A survey of QoS routing solutions for mobile ad hoc networks.

Talucci, F., Gerla, M., & Fratta, L. (1997). *MACA-BI (MACA By Invitation)--A receiver oriented access protocol for wireless multihop networks.* Paper presented at the The 8th IEEE International Symposium on Personal, Indoor, and Mobile Radio Communications, 1997. 'Waves of the Year 2000'. PIMRC '97.

Temporally-Ordered Routing Algorithm (TORA) Version 1, (2001a).

Tian, Y., Xu, K., & Ansari, N. (2005). TCP in wireless environments: Problems and solutions. *Communications Magazine, IEEE, 43*(3), S27-S32.

Toh, C. K., Guichal, G., & Bunchua, S. (2000a). *ABAM: On-demand associativity-based multicast routing for ad hoc mobile networks.*

Toh, C. K., Vassiliou, V., Guichal, G., & Shih, C. H. (2000b). *MARCH: A medium access control protocol for multihop wireless ad hoc networks.*

Paper presented at the MILCOM 2000. 21st Century Military Communications Conference Proceedings.

Topology Dissemination Based on Reverse-Path Forwarding (TBRPF), (2004).

Tschudin, C., Gold, R., Rensfelt, O., & Wibling, O. (2004). LUNAR: a Lightweight Underlay Network Ad-hoc Routing Protocol and Implementation.

Tsu-Wei, C., & Gerla, M. (1998). *Global state routing: a new routing scheme for ad-hoc wireless networks.*

Understanding Web Services: XML, WSDL, SOAP, and UDDI. (2002). Addison-Wesley Longman Publishing Co., Inc.

Vaduvur, B., Alan, D., Scott, S., & Lixia, Z. (1994). *MACAW: A media access protocol for wireless LAN's.* Paper presented at the Proceedings of the Conference on Communications Architectures, Protocols and Applications.

Valera, A., Seah, W. K. G., & Rao, S. V. (2002). *CHAMP: A highly-resilient and energy-efficient routing protocol for mobile ad hoc networks.*

Varadhan, K., Estrin, D., & Floyd, S. (1998). *Impact of network dynamics on end-to-end protocols: case studies in reliable multicast.*

Varshavsky, A., Reid, B., & de Lara, E. (2005). *A cross-layer approach to service discovery and selection in MANETs.* Paper presented at the Mobile Adhoc and Sensor Systems Conference, 2005. IEEE International Conference.

Wang, B., Kurose, J., Shenoy, P., & Towsley, D. (2004). Multimedia streaming via TCP: An analytic performance study. *Proceedings of the 12th Annual ACM International Conference on Multimedia* (pp. 908-915).

Wang, F., & Zhang, Y. (2002). Improving TCP performance over mobile ad-hoc networks with out-of-order detection and response. *Proceed-*

ings of the 3rd ACM International Symposium on Mobile Ad Hoc Networking & Computing (pp. 217-225).

Wolfgang, K., & Martin, M. (2007). A survey on real-world implementations of mobile ad-hoc networks (Vol. 5, pp. 324-339): Elsevier Science Publishers B. V.

Ad hoc Multicast Routing protocol utilizing Increasing id-numberS (AMRIS) Functional Specification, (1998).

Wu, K., & Harms, J. (2001a). On-demand multipath routing for mobile ad hoc networks. *Proceedings of EPMCC.*

Wu, K., & Harms, J. (2001b). *Performance study of a multipath routing method for wireless mobile ad hoc networks.* Paper presented at the IEEE Int'l Symposium on Modeling, Analysis and Simulation of Compute and Telecommunication Systems (MASCOTS).

Xipeng, X., & Ni, L. M. (1999). Internet QoS: A big picture. *Network, IEEE, 13*(2), 8-18.

Xylomenos, G., & Polyzos, G. C. (1999). *TCP and UDP performance over a wireless LAN.* Paper presented at the INFOCOM'99. The 18th Annual Joint Conference of the IEEE Computer and Communications Societies, New York, USA.

Xylomenos, G., Polyzos, G. C., Mahonen, P., & Saaranen, M. (2001). TCP performance issues over wireless links. *Communications Magazine, IEEE, 39*(4), 52-58.

Yaling, Y., & Kravets, R. (2005). Contention-aware admission control for ad hoc networks. *IEEE Transactions on Mobile Computing, 4*(4), 363-377.

Yavatkar, R., & Bhagawat, N. (1994). Improving end-to-end performance of TCP over mobile internetworks. *Mobile Computing Systems and Applications, 1994. Proceedings., Workshop on,* 146-152.

Young-Bae, K., & Nitin, H. V. (2000). Location aided routing (LAR) in mobile ad hoc networks. *Wireless Networks, V6*(4), 307-321.

Zhenyu, Y., & Garcia-Luna-Aceves, J. J. (1999). *Hop-reservation multiple access (HRMA) for ad-hoc networks.* Paper presented at the INFOCOM '99. The 18th Annual Joint Conference of the IEEE Computer and Communications Societies. Proceedings. IEEE.

Zhong, F. (2004). *QoS routing using lower layer information in ad hoc networks.*

APPENDIX A: COMPREHENSIVE GLOSSARY

Acronym	Name	Reference
AAQR	Application Aware QoS Routing	(Min et al., 2005)
ABAM	On-demand Associativity-Based Multicast	(Toh et al., 2000a)
ABR	Associativity-Based Routing	(Chai-Keong, 1997)
ADMR	Adaptive Demand-Driven Multicast Routing	(Jetcheva et al., 2001)
ADV	Adaptive Distance Vector Routing	(Boppana et al., 2001)
AMRIS	A Multicast Protocol for Ad Hoc Wireless Networks	(Wu et al., 1998)
AODV	Ad Hoc On-Demand Distance Vector Routing Protocol	(Elizabeth et al., 1999)
BSR	Backup Source Routing Protocol	(Song et al., 2002)
CAAODV	Contention Aware Ad hoc On-Demand Distance Vector routing	(Lei et al., 2005)
CACP	Contention-aware Admission Control Protocol	(Yaling et al., 2005)
CBCCR	Clustering-based Channel Capacity Routing	(Chen et al., 1997)
CCBR	Channel Capacity-Based Routing	(Chunhung et al., 1999)
CEDAR	Core Extension Distributed Ad Hoc Routing	(Sivakumar et al., 1999)
CGSR	Cluster-Head Gateway Switch Routing Protocol	(Chiang et al., 1997)
CHAMP	CacHing And MultiPath Routing Protocol	(Valera et al., 2002)
CLMCQR	Cross Layer Multi-Constraint QoS Routing	(Zhong, 2004)
DBF	Distributed Bellman-Ford	(Dimitri & Robert, 1987)
DDR	Distributed Dynamic Routing Algorithm	(Nikaein et al., 2000)
DFR	Direction Forward Routing	(Lee et al., 2006)
DNVR	Dynamic Nix-Vector Routing	(Lee et al., 2005)
DREAM	Distance Routing Effect Algorithm for Mobility	(Stefano et al., 1998)
DSARP	Delay Sensitive Adaptative Routing Protocol	(Min et al., 2003)
DSDV	Highly Dynamic Destination-Sequenced Distance-Vector	(Charles et al., 1994)
DSR	Dynamic Source Routing	
DSRFLOW	Flow State in Dynamic Source Routing Protocol	(Hu et al., 2001)
DST	Distributed Spannig Tree Protocol	(Radhakrishnan et al., 1999)
DYMO	Dynamic MANET On-demand	(Chakeres et al., 2007)
EADSR	Energy Aware Dynamic Source Routing Protocol	(Shah et al., 2002)
EBLLD	Entropy-Based Long-Life Distributed QoS routing	(Hui et al., 2003)
FAMA	Floor Acquisition Multiple Access	(Chane et al., 1995)
FSR	Fisheye State Routing	(Guangyu et al., 2000a)
GAMAN	Genetic Algorithm-based routing for Mobile Ad hoc Networks	(Barolli et al., 2003)
GPSR	Greedy Perimeter Stateless Routing	(Brad et al., 2000)
GSR	Global State Routing	(Tsu-Wei et al., 1998)
HARP	Hybrid Ad Hoc Routing Protocol	(Nikaein et al., 2001)

continued on following page

Appendix A. (continued)

HRMA	Hop Reservation Multiple Access	(Zhenyu et al., 1999)
HSLS	Hazy Sighted Link State Routing Protocol	(Cesar & Ram, 2001)
HSR	Hierarchical State Routing	(Iwata et al., 1999)
IAR	Interference-Aware Routing	(Gupta et al., 2005)
IARP	IntrAzone Routing Protocol	(Zygmunt J. Haas et al., 2002b)
IERP	IntErzone Routing Protocol	(Zygmunt J. Haas et al., 2002a)
ISAIAH	Infra-Structure AODV for Infrastructured Ad Hoc Networks	(Lindgren et al., 2002)
LANMAR	Landmark Routing Protocol	(Guangyu et al., 2000b)
LAR	Location-Aided Routing Protocol	(Young-Bae & Nitin, 2000)
LSBR	Link Stability-Based Routing	(Rubin et al., 2003)
LUNAR	Lightweight Underlay Network Ad hoc Routing	(Tschudin et al., 2004)
MACA	Multiple Access Collision Avoidance	(Karn, 1990)
MACA-BI	MACA By Invitation	(Talucci et al., 1997)
MACAW	MACA for Wireless LANs	(Vaduvur et al., 1994)
MANET	Mobile Ad hoc NETwork	(Group)
MAODV	Multicast Ad Hoc On-Demand Distance Vector Routing	(Royer et al., 2000)
MARCH	Media Access with Reduced Handshake	(Toh et al., 2000b)
MMRP	Mobile Mesh Routing Protocol	(Grace & Corporation, 2000)
MRPC	Maximum Residual Packet Capacity routing	(Misra et al., 2002)
NSR	Node State Routing	(Stine et al., 2004)
ODCR	On-Demand Delay-Constrained Routing	(Baoxian et al., 2005)
OLSR	Optimized Link State Routing Protocol	(Jacquet et al., 2001)
PANDA	Positional Attribute-based Next-hop Determination Approach	(Li et al., 2002)
PBAR	Prioritized Battery-Aware Routing	(Chi et al., 2005)
QAODV	Quality of service for Ad hoc On-Demand Distance Vector	(Perkins et al., 2001)
QGUM	QoS-GPSR for Ultra-wideband MANETs	(Abdrabou et al., 2006)
QOLSR	QoS Optimized Link State Routing	(Badis, 2006)
RDMAR	Relative-Distance Micro-discovery Ad hoc Routing protocol	(George et al., 1999)
ROAM	On-demand loop-free multipath routing	(Raju et al., 1999)
SIRCCR	SIR and Channel Capacity-Based Routing	(Dongwoo et al., 2004)
SSR	Signal Stability Routing Protocol	(Dube et al., 1997)
STAR	Source-Tree Adaptative Routing Protocol	(Seet et al., 2004)
TBR	Ticket-Based Routing	(Shigang et al., 1999)
TBRPF	Topology Broadcast Based on Reverse Path Forwarding	(Ogier, Templin, & Lewis, 2004)
TORA	Temporally-Ordered Routing Algorithm	(Park & Corson, 1997)
WRP	Wireless Routing Protocol	(Shree et al., 1996)
ZHLS	Zone-Based Hierarchical Link State Protocol	(Joa-Ng et al., 1999)
ZRP	Zone Routing Protocl	(Haas, 1997)

Section III
End–User Quality of Service

The ultimate goal of optimization techniques at the network and application layer is to ensure End-user perceived QoS. Often end-user perceived QoS measurement techniques are incorporated into network and application layer QoS solutions in order to provide greater insight into the users' QoS experience. It is only through accurate measurement of end-user perceived quality that QoS schemes can be developed and optimised. End-user QoS can be assessed using either objective or subjective methodologies. However, typically subjective testing results form the knowledge base and enhance the accuracy of objective metrics, so that objective metrics can then be incorporated into network and application layer QoS schemes. This section presents subjective results, targeted objective metrics and adaptive with integrated objective metrics. Moreover, since end-user perceived QoS is application and media dependent, targeted objective metrics are presented for voice, video and multimedia.

Chapter IX
Quality Assurance in the IMS–Based NGN Environment

Andrej Kos
University of Ljubljana, Slovenia

Mojca Volk
University of Ljubljana, Slovenia

Janez Bester
University of Ljubljana, Slovenia

ABSTRACT

Commonly understood as the next generation networks (NGN), a composite environment of proven telecommunications and Internet-oriented mechanisms has become generally recognized as the telecommunications environment of the future. However, the nature of the NGN environment presents several complex issues regarding quality assurance that have not existed in the legacy environments (e.g., multi-network, multi-vendor, and multi-operator IP-based telecommunications environment, distributed intelligence, third-party provisioning, fixed-wireless and mobile access, etc.). In this chapter, a service-aware policy-based approach to NGN quality assurance is presented, taking into account both perceptual quality of experience and technology-dependant quality of service issues. The respective procedures, entities, mechanisms, and profiles are discussed. The purpose of the presented approach is in research, development, and discussion of pursuing the end-to-end controllability of the quality of the multimedia NGN-based communications in an environment that is best effort in its nature and promotes end user's access agnosticism, service agility, and global mobility.

INTRODUCTION

In the past decade, the value of information and communication has grown beyond all expecta-

tions. The ability to communicate in general is no longer limited to the time-critical transfer of vital information but has become an overall lifestyle, tightly interlaced within the social system of mankind.

The communications are no longer limited to the choice of voice, data, or video: their multimedia nature presumes an enhanced end user's experience engaging various services and contents within a single convergent session. Commonly understood as the next generation networks (NGN), a composite environment of proven telecommunications and Internet-oriented mechanisms is established, enabling agile service creation, access agnosticism, and global mobility of end users. The NGN environment is based on the Internet protocol (IP) transport platform and adopts a model of a transparently separated service provisioning platform above a heterogeneous transport and access platform, employing various technologies to accomplish the IP connectivity. Unlike legacy solutions, the NGN tends to be access agnostic; from the functional viewpoint it consists of subsystems—logical groupings of entities that perform precisely defined functionalities—which originate from both fixed and wireless domains and promote unlimited choice of access possibilities (e.g., fixed—DSL, cable—or wireless —UMTS, WiMAX, WiFi). The key objective of the NGN environment is to converge and turn to advantage the benefits of the two communications worlds by combining the controllability, reliability, and quality of telecoms with the flexibility, ease of operation, creativeness, and end users' involvement of the Internet.

Throughout the evolution of communications systems, the issue of quality assurance has been a key measure of successful system operation in order to meet the end user's expectations. However, the nature of the NGN environment presents several complex issues regarding quality assurance that have not existed in the legacy environments (e.g., multi-network, multi-vendor, and multi-operator IP-based telecommunications environment, distributed intelligence, third-party provisioning, fixed-wireless and mobile access, etc.). The existence of multiple separately operated and interconnected domains requires intelligent interconnection mechanisms. On the other hand, the real-time personalized interactive multimedia NGN services require end-to-end quality assurance regardless of the traversed domains. Meeting these two requirements is a complex task and involves careful quality-related planning in each separate domain and harmonization of these on a service-aware end-to-end basis.

QUALITY MECHANISMS

The measure of system performance represents one of the basic evaluation criteria of a successful network, solution or a service from nearly all viewpoints: deployment, operation, and customer satisfaction. In general referred to as the quality, there are basically two approaches to defining, measuring and assessing the success of meeting a specific set of requirements or an expected behaviour (DSL Forum, TR-126, 2006).

The measure of performance from the network perspective is known as the quality of service (QoS) and involves a range of QoS mechanisms that are implemented for the purpose of meeting the defined conditions in the network. Typically, QoS metrics include network operation parameters (i.e., bandwidth, packet loss, delay, and jitter). On the other hand, the measure of performance as perceived from the end user is known as the quality of experience (QoE) and addresses the overall satisfaction of the end user and the ability to meet their expectations.

While the QoS is rather objective approach to assessing the success of performing within a specified network subsection, the QoE is subjective, measured on an end-to-end basis, and involves human-related criteria, based on which certain descriptive indexes of performance are set. Some examples of QoE metrics are the mean opinion score (MOS), degraded seconds, errored seconds, unavailable seconds, etc.

In essence, there are three layers of a service environment that should be considered in terms of quality in any type of telecommunications environment:

- The service exposure layer, representing the final point of QoE measurements toward the end user.
- The application layer, realizing and shaping the service through various application layer service parameters (i.e., media resolution, codec types, bit rate, error correction mechanisms, etc.).
- Transport (network) layer, potentially inducing various impairments (i.e., losses, delay, jitter, and employing the respective QoS mechanisms).

Regardless of the layer, there are generally two dimensions of quality-related issues. Control-related issues address foremost the delays (e.g., zapping time, application response time, user interface friendliness), while the data-related issues are reflected through losses, jitters, echoes, distortions, and latencies (e.g., blurring, audio or video noise, loss of synchronization).

When the network, service, or solution engineering is discussed from the quality viewpoint, there are generally two approaches available:

- The user-perceived QoE is defined, based on which the QoS parameters are negotiated and set.
- The QoS parameters are negotiated and set, based on which an assessment of possible QoE metrics is defined.

With regards to service-oriented and user-centric approach of today's telecommunications environments, the former approach is more applicable. However, the most important prerequisite of any professional engineering procedure is an exact definition of the engineered service. The latter is the issue of priority, real-time operation, interactivity, personalization, and the employed media (the stage of the multimedia nature of the service, i.e., voice, data, and video).

Based on these aspects, the QoE/QoS measures and mechanisms could be specified. Once the performance targets are defined, the contributing factors and dependencies should be established. These are many, addressing nearly all aspects of service delivery and performance. While from the end user's perspective the key issue is the effort the end user is required to invest or willing to perform throughout the service usage, from the service and network viewpoint it is the issue of the expected responsiveness and level of quality of the end user's perceived service. Moreover, the fidelity of the information or the content, the security requirements and the availability of the services should also be resolved from the network perspective.

Resulting from these two phases, the basic system performance requirements are defined: maximum delay, jitter, packet loss, application decomposition, client-server interaction, etc.

From this point further, the QoE engineering is directly followed by the architecture definition, QoS mechanisms and configuration definition and deployment. Service level guarantees are defined, scheduling, policing, queue management and admission control are set. Once the solution is put into operation, traffic engineering and resource allocation are conducted to satisfy the previously defined requirements and meet the chosen parameters.

THE NGN ENVIRONMENT

The issues of NGN environment have been considerably addressed, foremost in ITU-T (ITU-T Rec. Y.2001, 2004; ITU-T Rec. Y.2011, 2004), 3GPP (3GPP TS 23.228, 2006) and ETSI/TISPAN (ETSI ES 282.007, 2006), as well as in recent telecommunications research work. Different logical architectures have been proposed based on the common principles but vary among each other in the logical organization, the services focus and the communications domains.

The generic NGN architecture and its functionalities are represented in Figure 1. A two-layer model is adopted, logically decoupling the transport from the service control functionalities and the services. Four principal groups of functionalities within the NGN architecture can be identified, as follows:

- **Service-layer application functionalities:** The upper-most entities of the service layer represent various general or dedicated ap-

plication servers (AS), where service logic is hosted and operated. Additionally, the developer-friendly interface functionalities and secure gateway functionalities for third party service provisioning are enabled. The openness and the support for various technologies result in considerable complexity of this NGN segment, and the blended service offering requires mutual engagement and coherent functioning of many application servers simultaneously, therefore orchestration application servers are needed.

- **Service-layer control functionalities:** In this segment, session control, service

Figure 1. The generic IMS-based NGN model

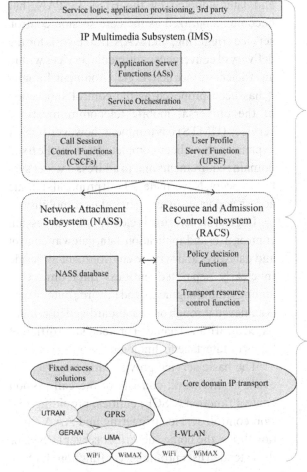

Service layer
IP Multimedia Subsystem (IMS)
- core session control (CSCFs)
- service triggering (CSCFs, UPSF)
- authentication, authorization, accounting
Services and applications
- application servers (ASs)
- service orchestration

Transport layer
Network Attachment Subsystem (NASS)
- access network control and configuration
- end-user's attachment procedures
Resource and Admission Control Subsystem (RACS)
- policy enforcement
- admission control
- transport resource management

triggering, and authentication, authorization, and accounting mechanism (AAA) are implemented. Service-layer profiles are sustained here, incoming requests are routed to the appropriate entities and services are triggered. Recently, the IP multimedia subsystem (IMS) (3GPP TS 23.228, 2006; ETSI ES 282.007, 2006) has become the recognized standard for service-layer functionalities and is today incorporated into the majority of recommendations. For this reason, the remainder of this paper assumes the IMS as the core of the service layer. The IMS provides the core session control, service triggering, and authentication and authorization mechanisms for the NGN environment.

- **Service-layer to transport-layer arbitrator functionalities:** In order to have transparently decoupled service and transport layer, specialized arbitrator functionalities are needed to implement the inter-layer communications and transport control logic. The network attachment subsystem (NASS) is needed that enables the end users admission to the NGN ecosystem and the NGN services, and sustains transport-layer profiles. The resource and admission control subsystem (RACS) performs policy-based resource allocation and appropriate QoS assurance. The two subsystems are addressed foremost in ITU-T (ITU-T Rec. Y.2111, 2006) and ETSI (ETSI ES 282.004, 2006; ETSI ES 282.003, 2006).

- **Transport-layer functionalities:** The IP-based transport platform spans through core and various types of fixed and mobile access networks. It operates under the control of the arbitrator functionalities. The key objective of this group of functionalities is to provide IP connectivity for the purpose of accessing the service-layer functionalities. At this level, the QoS is ensured by using the corresponding mechanisms for the trans-

portation of the media and the reservation, quality, and security accomplishment, which are outside of the scope of NGN.

Note that the presented generic NGN model comprises core functionalities that represent the enabling infrastructure for session handling, service triggering, admission control, user management, and quality assurance, whereas additional functionalities are required for specific features, e.g., application-related issues, management, real-time streaming support, access termination, etc., that are outside of the scope of this chapter.

The IP Multimedia Subsystem

The IP multimedia subsystem (IMS), defined by the Third Generation Partnership Project (3GPP) and later adopted by the ETSI TISPAN, has become recognized as the core session control, service triggering, and AAA framework for the delivery of convergent multimedia services within an efficient service delivery environment. Initially it has been proposed as the control subsection of the universal mobile telecommunications services (UMTS) environment, however further expansions have been completed to meet the fixed domain requirements and to address a wider system concept. Nevertheless, both proposals pursue access agnosticism and general user mobility.

Logical structuring is clearly defined; session control, user and application data, gateway control and gateways and service environment all reside in clearly separated entities. Interconnection amongst these segments and towards outer world is achieved through open standardized interfaces based on SIP and Diameter protocols and different types of interface technologies.

The basic service provisioning triangle, relevant to this work, consists of the call session control function (CSCF) entities, providing session control, service triggering and AAA functionalities, the home subscriber server (HSS), or the extended user profile server function (UPSF), representing the subscriber profile database and an extended AAA and mobility server, and the application server (AS), hosting the service logic and providing the convergent service delivery environment. Other entities are also defined for the IMS (e.g., media server functionalities, interworking, and gateway functionalities, etc.).

The inherent nature of the IMS as the core session control subsystem is global mobility of end users, services and the ability of these to be independent of the selected access domain and terminal equipment. The IMS-based NGN environment is applicable to both fixed and mobile domains regardless of the initial mobile origin of the IMS subsystem. However, there are notable mobile characteristics that should be considered that affect the performance of the system as a whole and condition the quality-related issues.

For the purpose of quality assurance procedures within the IMS-based NGN environment, the profile entity is important, incorporating relevant subscriber, service and content information. The HSS/UPSF entity of the IMS subsystem sustains the service-layer profile repository, as depicted on Figure 2.

QUALITY ASSURANCE IN THE NGN

The Service-Aware Quality Assurance Approach

The process of quality assurance in the NGN environment is a challenging task due to several factors. The IP-based next generation environment, originating from Internet domain, is best effort and therefore requires several additional mechanisms to meet the appropriate quality and availability levels. The issue is even intensified due to an extensive range of different media-rich services, which presents a challenge to resource allocation in terms of diverse performance needs (e.g., real-time or near-real-time delivery, priority treatment). In the NGN environment a single session operates across many conceptually and technologically unfamiliar networks, operated by different operators; moreover, the operators do not have full control over the environment as in the legacy telecommunications solutions and each end user is increasingly involved in the shaping of the operation of the environment through the usage of intelligent end user's devices and service personalization.

Figure 2. The key quality-related IMS entities and the service-layer profile repository information

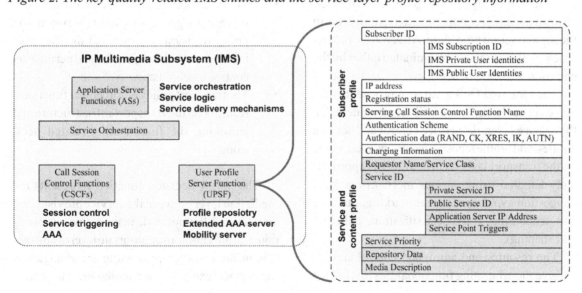

There are numerous recommendations and guidelines on how to ensure the appropriate IP network level performance objectives (ETSI TS 185.001, 2005). However, for complete service delivery, a systematic QoE and QoS assurance is required (ITU-T Rec. Y.1291, 2004; Kapov & Matjasevic, 2006) that spans through all layers of the solutions and approaches the issue of end user's satisfaction from the services viewpoint rather than from the network viewpoint. Moreover, the notion of multiple separate interconnected domains enforces dynamically changing conditions that imply the usage of dynamic quality assurance mechanisms.

The NGN QoS mechanisms are technology dependent and extend vertically across transport layer and transport control functionalities of the service layer. On the other hand, NGN QoE mechanisms are technology independent and involve service control and application functionalities as well as the mapping of these to transport-layer quality assurance. Only overall integrity and orchestration of all functionalities in all subsystems and layers brings systematic quality assurance in all aspects of service delivery. Based on these prerequisites, the following approach is generally recognized for the NGN environment.

The procedure of quality assurance occurs in two stages. First, dynamic negotiation is conducted to set the initial communications parameters in the session set-up procedure. Afterwards, further renegotiations are possible, initiated either by the end user, network, or services.

The QoE and QoS assurance procedures involve vertically the entire NGN environment. On the service layer, the service control and service entities, and profile repositories are engaged, while on the transport layer the user traffic is appropriately handled using various mechanisms (e.g., congestion avoidance, packet marking, queuing and scheduling, traffic classification, policing, and shaping).

The resource and admission control entities enforce the arbitrating functionalities that bridge

the service and the transport layers. While the entire system is indirectly involved in the QoE and QoS assurance, these functionalities directly enforce the dynamic service-aware admission control and resource reservation, as follows.

The Resource and Admission Control

The resource and admission control subsystem (RACS) has become generally recognized as the subsection of the NGN responsible for the policy control, resource reservation and admission control. Standardization efforts of ETSI TISPAN NGN and ITU-T have addressed the issue of policy-based admittance of the end user to the resources based on a rather complex service-aware procedure of negotiation. The proposals vary in the defined entities and logical organization but are conceptually similar and extend horizontally across access and core domain and vertically across service and transport layers.

As depicted in Figure 3, the generic RACS comprises:

- The policy decision function, negotiating with the session control and application functions via northbound interfaces.
- The transport resource control functions, representing the mediator between the policy decision function and the transport infrastructure through dedicated permission control mechanisms.
- The transport policy enforcement functions, residing on the transport infrastructure and enforcing the final quality-related decisions.

The policy decision function represents the mediation layer between the service provisioning domain and the network resource provisioning domain, providing an appropriate level of abstraction of the resource processing technologies to the service execution technologies. The policy

Figure 3. Resource and admission control subsystem (RACS)

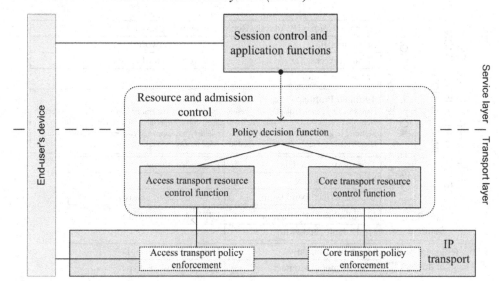

decision function issues a request for resource authorization and reservation, indicating the QoS characteristics (negotiated with the service provisioning domain). The resource control function is in charge of the permission control mechanisms and informs the policy decision function of the successful resource allocation. In general, separate resource control functions exist for the core network and for each type of access network, taking into account specific characteristics and management policy. In the process of the resource allocation it consults the network attachment subsystem (NASS) for the access and transport-layer QoS profile.

Other functionalities of the RACS are the border gateway functions and the resource control enforcement functions that perform the gate control, packet marking, resource allocation, network address translation, policing and usage metering, etc. In general, the resource control functions act as the local policy decision points in terms of subscriber access admission control and resource handling control, whereas the policy decision function represents the final policy decision point.

The resource control function derives and installs the Layer 3 and Layer 2 traffic policy, indicating the traffic control handling (e.g., gate control, packet marking, etc.). In the process of granting the resources the network QoS parameters of the Layer 3 and Layer 2 are mapped to the respective policy.

The operation of the RACS is generally application agnostic but supports traffic control for the purpose of application delivery with uni-/bidirectional, a-/symmetric, uni-/multicast, up-/downstream traffic patterns.

The Network Attachment

The network attachment subsystem (NASS) has also been considered for the NGN-based environment within the standardization efforts of ETSI TISPAN NGN and ITU for the purpose of consistent and controlled registration and attachment of the end users accessing the NGN services through various access networks. The NASS is responsible for the registration procedures within the access domain and the initialization of the end user's terminal equipment when accessing the

Figure 4. Transport-layer access, session, and subscription information

TRANSPORT-AYER ACCESS, SESSION AND SUBSCRIPTION INFORMATION	**ACCESS SESSION DECRIPTION**	Globally Unique IP Address/Realm	Logical Access ID
		Subscriber ID	Access Networky Type
		Physical Access ID	RACS Point of Contact
		Privacy Indicator	
		Terminal Profile Hardware (e.g., model, display size, resolution, processor & memory info, sound capabilities) Network Connectivity (e.g., supported interfaces, current interface, DL and UL capabilities) Software (e.g., OS, browser info, supported media types, supported content protection) User Preferences (e.g., desired/acceptable service quality, time&budget constraints)	
	QoS profile	Transport Service Class	Requestor Name
		Maximum Priority	Media Type
		UL Subscribed bandwidth	DL Subscribed bandwidth
Initial Gate Settings		List of allowed destinations	UL Default bandwidth
		DL Default bandwidth	
Physical and logical access ID		Location Information	Derault Subscriber ID
		RACS Point of Contact	Access Network Type

NGN services, providing identification and authentication on the network level, management of IP addressing scheme within the access networks and authentication of the access sessions.

The following key functionalities are provided through the NASS:

- Dynamic allocation of IP addresses and other relevant parameters for the end user's terminal equipment configuration
- IP-layer authentication before or within the procedure of IP address allocation
- Network access authorization based on the subscriber profile
- Access network configuration based on the subscriber profile
- IP-layer location management

The functionalities are provided through several logical entities. Among these, the functionality responsible for session description and transport-layer profile maintenance is actively involved in the quality assurance procedure (referred to as the NASS database—NASS DB). It communicates with the RACS subsystem to relay the relevant transport-layer access, session and subscription information, involved in the quality assurance procedures. An example of the information model of the NASS is represented in Figure 4.

SERVICE-AWARE IMS-BASED NGN QUALITY ASSURANCE PROCEDURE

Referring to Figure 5, within the generic session set-up procedure, the following steps are involved in complete NGN QoE and QoS assurance:

- Service authentication procedure based on the requesting user and the requested service
- Parameter negotiation and resource authentication
- Determination of final feasible service configuration and final application operation point based on resource allocation capabilities
- Final profile confirmation and delivery of the requested service to the end user

Figure 5. The generic NGN quality assurance procedure

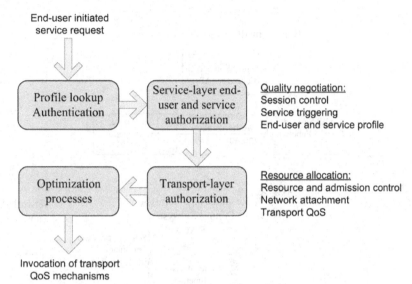

According to ITU-T Rec. Y.2111 (2006), there are three basic scenarios for QoS provisioning, as follows:

1. The end user is only aware of the services they may request and is unaware of the QoS signalling mechanisms, while it is the responsibility of the service control functionalities to determine the QoS service requirements and issue the respective requests to resource authorization functionalities. The latter perform resource authorization and reservation procedures.

2. The end user's device is capable of signalling and managing its QoS resources, however prior authorization via the service control functionalities is required. After the initial service request, the service control functionality determines the QoS service requirements and requests the network authorization. If approved, the end user's device receives the authorization token and requests resource reservation.

3. The end user's terminal is capable of issuing QoS requests over signalling and manage-

ment protocols without prior authorization.

These scenarios are heavily dependent of the operator's policy standpoint, defining the strictness of the resource allocation and the service-awareness of the transport-layer operation. The notion of heterogeneous access domain, user and service mobility, and support of various end users devices in a multimedia-oriented NGN environment requires a generalized approach that assumes any of the above scenarios. From the end user's terminal devices viewpoint the first scenario is most general, while the remaining two scenarios could be understood as simplified cases of the first scenario. Therefore, any further discussions are in terms of the first scenario.

Based on the IMS-based NGN architecture presented before and the dynamic service-aware approach to quality assurance for the NGN, the following model is applicable as shown on Figure 6.

The quality assurance procedure consists of two consecutive sections. The first section involves service-layer IMS-based service provisioning and

Figure 6. The admission control procedure using RACS subsystem for the IMS-based NGN environment

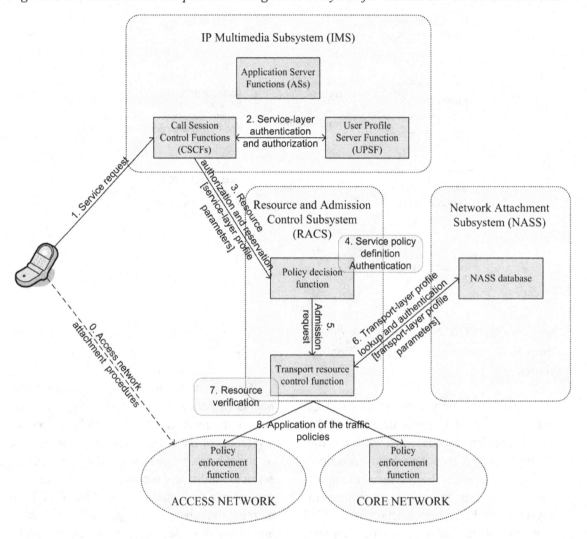

user authentication and authorization procedures. Based on the service request, issued by the end user's device, the IMS CSCF entities perform authentication and authorization procedures based on the information, retrieved from the UPSF (1-2). If successful, the CSCF entities issue a request for resource authorization and reservation to the RACS policy decision function, containing the parameters of the requested transport control service (i.e., priority and QoS parameters) (3). The second section involves transport-layer RACS-

based service policy definition and resource allocation procedures.

The policy decision function receives the request, chooses the service policy and performs an authentication procedure (4). The authentication procedure is based on the process of matching the requested parameters against the chosen service policy.

If successful, the policy decision function is in charge of forwarding the request to the resource control functions that have been chosen through the service policy (5).

The resource control function performs the admission control in three steps:

- The function compares the received request against the access and transport-layer subscriber profile, retrieved from the NASS (6).
- Based on the resource requirements from both the service-layer request and the NASS profile, the function verifies the available resources on Layer 2 or Layer 3 in accordance with the current network conditions (7).
- The policy enforcement functions are instructed to apply the respective traffic policies (8).

Based on the successfully completed admission control procedure, the transport resource control functionalities apply the appropriate traffic conditioning mechanisms for Layer 2 and Layer 3 QoS assurance. For guaranteed QoS the traffic parameters are enforced, while for relative QoS an IP QoS policy is used, based on which the dynamic QoS update is triggered.

If the admission control procedure is successfully completed and granted, the resource control function replies to the policy decision function (including the ID of the allocated resources). The resulting parameters are forwarded to the session control functions (i.e., CSCF, UPSF, AS) and to the end user's terminal device. From this point forth, further negotiations are possible in case the parameters do not fully comply on either service or transport layer. Also, further renegotiations may be invoked based on session modification requests from end user or service side or due to resource availability changes. If further negotiations with the service control and application layer entities occur within the session set-up procedure, the previously described "push" model is extended into the "pull" model.

Figure 7. The transport-layer QoS-related parameters within the resource allocation procedure

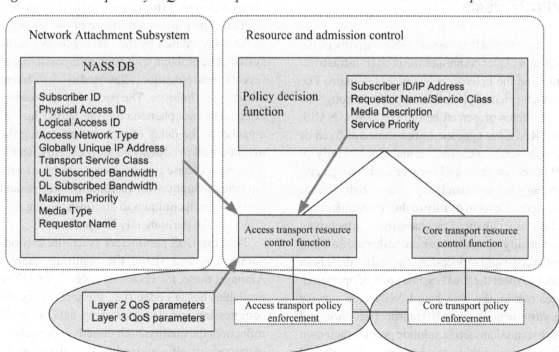

Indicated with (0), prior to connecting to the IMS, the end user is required to attach to the chosen access network and successfully complete the required procedures (e.g., context activation, authentication and authorization, security procedures, etc.). This step is outside of the scope of the IMS-based provisioning of services and is therefore not discussed in detail; however the quality-related steps of the attachment procedure involve RACS and NASS functionalities (i.e., the NASS provides the access user profile, the RACS functionalities apply the respective traffic policies for the chosen access network). The access network QoS assurance acts completely independently, however it affects the negotiation procedure of deciding whether the environment is capable of completing the requested service in accordance with the expected quality.

The transport-layer QoS-related parameters within the above procedures are presented in Figure 7.

TRANSPORT-LAYER QOS MECHANISMS

In the presented IMS-based NGN environment, the transport layer comprises the core IP infrastructure and the heterogeneous access domain. The service-oriented platform, established through the subsystems presented before (i.e., IMS, NASS, and RACS) is agnostic to the choice of fixed or mobile access technologies and requires only an IP-based connectivity. However, the heterogeneity and agnosticism should not cause a reduction in the agreed level of quality of the communication. Therefore, enhanced mechanisms of attachment and quality assurance are needed that are aware of both access and service domains and mediate both sides to meet the final feasible point of operation. Meanwhile, the IMS-based NGN core service environment, the core IP transport network, and each standalone access solution provide their own independent quality mechanisms: these should be harmonized.

Conceptually, modern QoS mechanisms are based on the active control and management of traffic flows and queuing. Aside from admission control, the techniques use classification, shaping and policing, marking, scheduling and queuing to provide the appropriate levels of QoS.

Traffic admission is based on the priority/importance of the service, service level agreement, and current conditions of the network (i.e., the current state of the network resources). According to IETF RFC 2475 (1998), the Service Level Agreement (SLA) is a bi-lateral agreement between two parties that specifies the forwarding service a customer should receive. Conditions are defined through metrics; most important are:

- Throughput
- Delay
- Jitter
- Packet loss

There are various reasons for different types of delays in the network. The end-to-end delay, also known as the latency, is the time taken for the packet to pass from its source to its final destination. The jitter is a measure of the variation in the delay, caused by the varying delays in the system. The problem with jitter is the possibility of loss of synchronization, alleviated using different buffering techniques. The packet loss represents effectively two phenomena: the actual loss of a packet or the delay of a packet exceeding the maximum allowed delay for the packet to enter the processing. These two issues are addressed with buffering techniques to overcome the latencies and concealment techniques to diminish the negative effects of the permanently lost packets.

Network QoS parameters aside, the network parameters also shape the resulting quality. Amongst these, the choice of codec is vital. The available/chosen codec (i.e., the technology for compressing and decompressing data, strongly influences the quality, both directly—the quality of the codec itself—and indirectly—the response of the codec to the induced impairments).

Other mechanisms should also be in place for echo control, signal level maintenance, etc. Each of the discussed factors could be measured independently, however it is the cumulative effect of all these factors that affect the overall level of quality and should therefore be considered relatively.

Based on the traffic characteristics, there are four basic groups of NGN services:

- Voice
- Interactive video
- Streamed video
- Data applications

The metrics values for the guaranteed quality delivery of the respective service groups are presented in Table 1.

There are two basic models of QoS-aware NGN service delivery:

- The delivery of NGN services with a guaranteed QoS, where absolute numerical bounds are defined for some or all of the relevant QoS parameters (e.g., bandwidth, delay, loss, jitter, etc.).
- The delivery of NGN services with a relative QoS, in this case absolute numerical bounds are not defined, however the operation should be consolidated with the network level services differentiation mechanisms.

The provisioning of QoS unaware networks (i.e., best effort networks) and statically provisioned QoS networks do not require the resource and admission control functionalities.

Core IP Network Quality Assurance

Traditionally, the core IP networks have been established as a best-effort transport infrastructure for the purpose of data transfer and transport of Internet traffic. Initially, no SLA has been set and only one service class has been defined, whereas statistical multiplexing and the over-subscription have been used for better exploitation of the available network resources. With the introduction of more complex and mission critical real-time multimedia services (e.g., Voice over IP (VoIP), IP TV, and business applications), the issues of quality, availability, and reliability have arisen, resulting in additional intelligent quality-related functions.

On the IP transport layer, the traffic conditioning mechanisms are used to enforce the negotiated and allocated QoS conditions. These are available for the network layer (Layer 3) and the data layer (Layer 2).

On the network layer, two traffic conditioning mechanisms are in use: resource reservation model based on integrated services (IntServ) and traffic prioritization model based on differentiated services (DiffServ).

The integrated services (IntServ, IETF RFC 1633, 1994), standardized by the Internet Engi-

Table 1. The network quality metrics values for the four basic groups of NGN services

	Ear-to-mouth delay	Jitter	Packet loss	Bandwidth
Voice	150 ms	30 ms	0,25 %	21 – 88 Kbit/s Codec dependant
Interactive video	Under 150 ms	30 ms	0,25 %	Codec dependant
Streamed video	Under 5 s	Resolved through buffering	Under 2 %	2 – 20 Mbit/s Codec dependant
Data applications	Under 150 ms	Resolved through buffering	Application dependant	Application dependant

neering Task Force (IETF), RFC 1633, is based on the Internet service model with best effort behaviour, real-time service and controlled load. IntServ assumes strict management of resources and applies resource reservation and admission control along the entire service path. The QoS requirements are signalled on a per-flow basis using the RSVP reservation mechanisms.

The differentiated services (DiffServ, IETF RFC 2475, 1998) represents a QoS framework, also proposed by the IETF, RFC 2475, enabling the engineering of the IP networks to support tight SLA commitments. The DiffServ distinguishes different service classes, described through exact and assured SLA metrics, and defines the forwarding path behaviour for IP packets, known as the per-hop behaviour. DiffServ is commonly used within the scalable quality-assured IP deployments, implementing the per-flow traffic classification, marking, metering, and conditioning. Scheduling and queuing mechanisms are applied to the defined service classes to meet the respective SLA requirements. These mechanisms are not prescribed with the DiffServ, instead it defines the possible per-hop behaviour patterns, applied to the traffic:

- The expedited forwarding (EF) for traffic with strict delay, jitter, and loss requirements
- The assured forwarding (AF) in the case of traffic with assured bandwidth requirements
- The default per-hop-behaviour class for all other traffic, not belonging to the EF and AF classes

Operator-grade data-layer technologies incorporate native QoS mechanisms. Multi protocol label switching (MPLS) represents an extended DiffServ concept for data layer, introducing the usage of packet labels. The Ethernet standard specifies additional QoS-related mechanisms for QoS handling on Ethernet switches (i.e., the

usage of virtual local area networks (VLAN) and mechanisms for service classes). In the case of ATM technology, the virtual path (VP) and virtual channel (VC) concept is in use for the definition of four traffic classes with fixed QoS parameters.

The *de facto* standard for most QoS IP NGN solutions is DiffServ. The principal drawback of this technology is the lack of admission control, severely diminishing the reliability of the QoS framework. For this reason various additional mechanisms are considered. The principal approach involves careful network traffic and application planning, which is an extremely challenging task due to the nature of the NGN environment and its services. Also, a combinational approach with IntServ in the access section and DiffServ in the core section seems promising; however there is the issue of end user's terminal equipment not supporting the IntServ mechanisms.

These mechanisms previously described are independently provided through each technology and therefore cumulatively contribute to the final QoS operation of the network. There is however a challenging task of appropriate interworking procedures between various quality domains. The horizontal interworking should provide the network-level mechanisms of interworking between DiffServ, Ethernet QoS, ATM QoS, MPLS QoS and access-network QoS mechanisms, while the vertical interworking addresses the solicitation between network-level QoS and service-level QoS/QoE (i.e., the service-aware policy-based quality assurance procedure). The issues of interworking remain un-standardized and are left open to the vendors' practical implementations and operators' solution configurations, which presents a complex challenge for further work.

Access Network Quality Assurance

Due to evolutionary reasons, most typical access solutions for environments, based on IMS, are wireless. Amongst many available choices, the following are typical:

- GPRS core network inside a packet-switched mobile system with GERAN/UTRAN radio access network (GSM/Edge Radio Access Network/UMTS Terrestrial Radio Access Network) or Unlicensed Mobile Access (UMA), exploiting WiFi or WiMAX.
- Interworking WLAN based on WiFi or WiMAX.

From the quality viewpoint, each of these applies a different QoS approach, as follows. The approaches are relevant to the overall end user-experienced quality (i.e., the QoE); the resulting quality-related parameters are considered in the processes of service-aware admission control in the RACS, as described before, taking into account the final QoS applied through mechanisms of the respective access solution.

Universal Mobile Telecommunications System (UMTS)

In UMTS, the end-to-end QoS is guaranteed through wireless and wired QoS mechanisms provided on all levels of the solution, as specified in the 3GPP standards (Dixit, 2001). It comprises Bearer Services, whereas the UMTS Bearer Service consists of Radio Access Bearer Service and Core Network Bearer Service. The GPRS Packet Data Protocol (PDP) context is used for the negotiation of the QoS parameters defining the channel between the subscriber station and the Gateway GPRS Support Node (GGSN). The Core Network Bearer Service is based on the DiffServ framework, while for the Radio Access Bearer Service QoS techniques are used between the subscriber station and the Serving GPRS Support Node (SGSN). In the GGSN, a QoS Management Module (QMM) is deployed, acting as a policy decision point for the management of services using DiffServ framework. Moreover, the QMM

supports resource management and allocation procedures. The SLA is negotiated and established to define the subscriber requirements.

Services in the UMTS are divided into four classes based on the delay sensitivity of the traffic, i.e., conversational class, streaming class, interactive class and background class. For the purpose of end-to-end quality assurance, mappings are needed between the DiffServ per-hop behaviour classes, UMTS service classes and the PDP context.

WiFi

With the pervasiveness of broadband access solutions and a growing need for mobility the 802.11 Wireless Local Area Network (WLAN) has become the prevailing broadband wireless technology. The technology is based on a best-effort principle; however, the IEEE 802.11e standard enhances the best-effort environment with additional QoS mechanisms on the air interface between the subscriber station and base station (Park et al., 2003). The QoS extension enables a differentiated and distributed channel access based on the definition of eight priority classes depending on the traffic type (best effort, video probe, video, and voice), used by the enhanced distributed coordination function (DCF) and assigned to each MAC frame header as the traffic category identification (TCID). The enhanced QoS mechanism implements a non-DiffServ environment on the air interface and should be mapped to the DiffServ mechanisms implemented in the wired portion of the solution.

The IEEE 802.11e extensions are seldom implemented and the WiFi-based solutions are left to the quality-related assurance provided by the basic standard.

WiMAX

For WiMAX access solution, QoS mechanisms are guaranteed based on the IEEE 802.16 standard defining four service classes (Cicconetti, Lenzini, & Mingozzi, 2006):

- Unsolicited grant services, providing constant bit rate, foremost for services such as T1/E1 simulation and VoIP.
- Real-time polling services for real-time services requiring variable bit rate (e.g., transmission of MPEG-encoded video contents, VoIP with enabled silence suppression).
- Non-real-time polling services for services that do not require real-time transmission, however require a certain level of QoS.
- Best effort

Within the session set-up procedure, one of the defined service classes is selected for the connection between the subscriber station and the base station. Multiple simultaneous active connections with different QoS guarantees are possible. The mechanisms for the application of the defined service classes are not defined within the standard and are left open to the implementation. Similarly to previous cases, the non-DiffServ QoS mechanisms should be mapped to the commonly implemented DiffServ mechanisms in the wired portion of the solution.

CONCLUSION

Within the NGN, the policy-based quality assurance seems to be the reasonable approach. The characteristics of the NGN environment present challenges to quality assurance for several reasons, such as general support of mobility, access agnosticism, multi-domain environment, best-effort technologies, etc. While mechanisms and technologies for the transport-layer core and access quality assurance are well defined, the issues of interconnection and interworking need to be resolved in order to achieve dynamic service-aware end-to-end user-perceived quality experience. The proposal presented here is an approach that engages all layers of the environment via parameterization, profiling, negotiation, and arbitrating mechanisms, pursuing the end-to-end controllability of the quality of the respective communications.

Further challenges arise from this concept. The complexity and the performance requirements of the rather complex signalling procedures are an issue that would present a substantial load to the entire environment, and the required level of intelligence needed to perform the quality negotiation and enforcement with the respective security issues is challenging. Further standardization efforts would be required to resolve the interconnection and interworking of the traversed access and transport domains as well as with the service-layer mechanisms. Once the various proposals are harmonized and the standardization is completed, the NGN services can be considered as a collection of specialized services implemented with the already available functionalities of the NGN environment in a standardized fashion and with ensured operator-grade quality.

REFERENCES

3GPP TR 23.802 (2005). Technical Specification Group Services and System Aspects – Architectural enhancements for end-to-end Quality of Service (QoS).

3GPP TS 23.228 (2006). Technical Specification Group Services and System Aspects: IP Multimedia Subsystem (IMS), Rel. 7.

Ban, S. Y., Choi, J. K., & Kim, H. S. (2006). Efficient end-to-end qos mechanism using egress node resource prediction in NGN network. *ICACT 2006, 1*, pp. 480-483.

Cicconetti, C., Lenzini, L., & Mingozzi, E. (2006). Quality of service support in IEEE 802.16 Networks. *IEEE Network, 20*(2), 50-55.

Dixit, S., Guo, Y., & Antoniou, Z. (2001). Resource management and quality of service in third-generation wireless networks. *IEEE Commun. Mag.*, *39*(2), 125-133.

DSL Forum TR-126. (2006). Triple-play Services Quality of Experience (QoE) Requirements.

ETSI ES 282.003 (2006). TISPAN – Resource and Admission Control Sub-system (RACS): Functional Architecture.

ETSI ES 282.004 (2006). TISPAN – NGN Functional Architecture: Network Attachment Sub-System (NASS).

ETSI ES 282.007 (2006). TISPAN – IP Multimedia Subsystem (IMS): Functional architecture.

ETSI TS 185.001 (2005). TISPAN - Next Generation Network (NGN) - Quality of Service (QoS) Framework and Requirements.

IETF RFC 1633 (1994). Integrated Services in the Internet Architecture: an Overview.

IETF RFC 2475 (1998). An Architecture for Differentiated Services.

ITU-T Rec. Y.1291 (2004). Internet protocol aspects – Architecture, access, network capabilities and resource management: An architectural framework for support of Quality of Service in packet networks.

ITU-T Rec. Y.2001 (2004). Next Generation Networks – Frameworks and functional architecture models: General overview of NGN.

ITU-T Rec. Y.2011 (2004). Next Generation Networks – Frameworks and functional architecture models: General principles and general reference model for Next Generation Networks.

ITU-T Rec. Y.2111 (2006). Next Generation Networks – Quality of Service and Performance: Resource and admission control functions in Next generation Networks.

Kapov, L. S., & Matjasevic, M. (2006). End-to-end QoS signaling for future multimedia services in the NGN. *LNCS*, Vol. 4003. Springer.

Park, S. et al. (2003). Collaborative QoS architecture between DiffServ and 802.11e wireless LAN. *VTC 2003*, *2*, pp. 945-949.

Chapter X
Quality of Experience for Video Services

Marcio Nieblas Zapater
Escola Politécnica da Universidade de São Paulo, Brazil

Graça Bressan
Escola Politécnica da Universidade de São Paulo, Brazil

ABSTRACT

This chapter discusses the quality assurance of multimedia services over IP networks from the end user standpoint and introduces the concept of quality of experience (QoE). The discussion of quality assurance includes aspects that range from the network and application layers to the end user perspective. The focus of the discussion presented in this chapter is oriented to the video services delivery that can be considered a significant evolution of services providers' portfolio. This chapter presents quality requirements for video and TV services and performance measures that focuses on the quality perceived by the end user. This approach is broader than that oriented to quality of service (QoS), which focuses on the performance measures from the network perspective. QoE takes into account how well a service meet customers goals and expectations rather than focusing only on the network performance.

INTRODUCTION

Many telecommunications service providers around the world are moving toward integrated service offerings by combining voice, video, and high-speed data services. IP-based technology plays an important role on this scenario by enabling the delivery of such services over a com-

mon multiservice IP network. A variety of access technologies can be used to reach the end user. The recent advances in wireless technologies in terms of throughput and quality assurance make them an alternative to the traditional wired line technologies for multimedia services delivery.

The multimedia services delivered to the end user using broadband networks include broadcast

TV, video on demand (VOD), video telephony, voice over IP (VoIP), multiplayer games, and audio streaming among others. Such services bring additional challenges in terms of quality assurance because of their intensive network resources utilization and stringent performance requirements.

This chapter discusses the quality assurance of multimedia services over IP networks from the end user standpoint and introduces the concept of quality of experience. The discussion of quality assurance includes aspects that range from the network and application layers to the end user perspective. The focus of the discussion presented in this chapter is oriented to the video services delivery that can be considered a significant evolution of services providers' portfolio.

The video services represent a relatively new element introduced into the traditional telecommunications services portfolio offered to mass markets that already includes voice and, more recently, high-speed data services. IP-based technology is being used by the majority of service providers to support such video services, commonly known as Internet protocol television (IPTV) services. In this context, it is important to make a distinction between IPTV and Internet TV (Heavy Heading, 2006). Both are delivered over IP networks using a broadband connection, but with different control and quality assurance levels. IPTV is a video service offered by a service provider that owns the network infrastructure and controls content distribution to its customers, generally using an IP set-top box. Internet TV encompasses content sourced from anywhere on the Internet that can be streamed or downloaded by the end user generally using a PC or, more recently, a set-top box.

As service providers roll out IPTV services, they face a new set of challenges (Heavy Heading, 2006). Their top priority is to deliver an enhanced experience to their customers. IPTV services must meet or exceed quality levels currently offered by traditional TV players, such as over the air, satellite, or cable providers. Providing such service quality levels is even more complex when delivering video using a multiservice IP platform where multiple services share same resources. Current quality of service (QoS) practices are focused on network aspects to implement quality management and metrics such as network delay, jitter, packet loss and throughput are used to indicate the services performance. Such metrics can be effective for traditional data services but are not adequate to support multimedia services quality assurance.

IPTV services require a more comprehensive quality management approach to ensure customer experience (Heavy Heading 2006, Kerpez, Waring, Lapiotis, Lyles, & Vaidyanathan, 2006). User perception is far beyond network aspects. It encompasses all the interaction between the user and the service. The concept of quality assurance focusing on the end-user QoS has been ultimately referred as quality of experience (QoE) (Jain, 2004). There is a need to ensure quality on an end-to-end basis and at a higher abstraction layer by combining traditional QoS and QoE in one integrated framework. The concepts of QoE discussed here and illustrated with the video services are also valid for other IP services.

QUALITY OF SERVICE (QOS) AND QUALITY OF EXPERIENCE (QOE)

The term quality of service (QoS) is broadly used today and it is commonly associated to broadband, wireless, and multimedia services that are IP-based. Networks and systems are gradually being designed in consideration of end-to-end performance required by user applications.

However, the term QoS is usually not well defined and frequently misused. The definitions of QoS are very comprehensive and most publications use the term QoS but do not define it. The ITU-T Recommendation E.800 provides a definition of QoS: "the collective effect of service performance which determines the degree of satisfaction of a user of the service" (ITU-T, 1994).

In general terms, QoS is understood as a measure of how well the network does it job and satisfies the end-user requirements, which means how quickly and reliably it transfers many kinds of data (Dutta-Roy, 2000). When the networks were circuit switched and designed to deal only with voice traffic, the QoS issues were not so critical considering that the network needed to support and satisfy the requirements of a single service: voice telephony. With the evolution to packet-switched networks and the introduction of new services and applications, the networks need to satisfy various sets of requirements associated to different services sharing the same infrastructure. Then, the quality of service has become a hot topic.

Even though the QoS definitions focus on the end user perspective, historically, the concept of QoS applied to IP-based services is highly associated with the network and systems themselves. QoS is typically understood as a measure of performance from the network perspective at the packet level (DSL Forum, 2006). It represents the set of parameters, technologies, and mechanisms that should be implemented in the network infrastructure in order to meet the service performance requirements.

Service performance is then managed through a set of network parameters. Such metrics do not represent the entire QoS from the user perspective. Instead, they represent the network performance parameters that may affect user experience. The key network performance parameters used to manage service performance are (Dutta-Roy, 2000):

- **Throughput:** The effective data transfer rate measured in bits per second and a minimum rate of throughput is usually guaranteed for specific services and applications.

- **Delay:** The time taken by data to travel from the source to the destination.

- **Jitter:** It represents the delay variation and their causes may include: variations in queue length, variations in the packets processing, packets traveling through different paths, among others.

- **Packet loss:** It represents the information losses at the network level that may occur for many reasons including network congestion, link failures and transmission errors, for example.

- **Availability:** The percentage of the time that the network is available to provide services to the end users.

Different services have distinct QoS requirements that are directly mapped to network performance parameters (Dutta-Roy, 2000). For example, a bulk data transfer associated to a file transfer requires high throughput and low packet loss, but can accept higher levels of delay and jitter. On the other hand, a video conferencing needs high throughput but is very sensitive to delay and jitter. Table 1 presents some examples of different services and their sensitivity to different network performance parameters (Dutta-Roy, 2000).

To provide adequate QoS for the different services over wireline and wireless IP-base networks, it is needed to understand their detailed performance requirements. The starting point for deriving such requirements must be the end user (ITU-T, 2001). A typical user is not concerned with network impairments such as packet losses, or bandwidth constraints. The user cares about characteristics that belong to a higher abstraction layer and that represent the service. That is the concept of QoE (Siller & Woods, 2003). The ITU-T Recommendation G.1010 (Patrick et al., 2004) provides guidance on the key factors that influence QoS from the perspective of the end-user and outlines that service performance should be expressed by parameters that:

Table 1. Quality of service requirements

Service	Sensitivity to network performance parameters			
	Throughput	Packet Loss	Delay	Jitter
File Transfer	High	Medium	Low	Low
E-mail	Low	High	Low	Low
Browsing	Low-Medium	Medium-High	Medium-High	Low
E-business	Low	High	High	Low
Voice	Low-Medium	Medium	High	High
Gaming	Medium	High	High	High
Video on demand	High	High	Medium	Medium
Live TV and Video-conferencing	High	High	High	High

Source: Adapted from Dutta-Roy (2000)

- Consider all aspects of the service from the user's perspective
- Focus on user-perceivable aspects, rather than their causes within the network
- Are independent of the specific network architecture or technology
- Can be objectively or subjectively measured
- Can be easily related to network performance parameters

Such considerations are direct related to the concept of QoE. Let us take the example of TV broadcast service. The performance parameters observed by the end user include audio and video quality, the zapping delay when changing broadcast channels, the audio-to-video synchronization delay, among others (Heavy Heading, 2006). Measurements of network impairments can be used to estimate the impact on video quality, but do not represent an exhaustive set of metrics to enable an end-to-end quality management focusing on the user experience. Network statistics alone will not mirror user perception (Siller et al., 2003). For example, higher packet losses rates within the network may cause different effects on video quality. Although packet loss rate is a parameter relatively easy to obtain, it is not accurate for video evaluation, and only evaluates network layer impacts (DSL Forum, 2006).

In order to achieve the required multimedia service quality levels, the service providers need to consider a broader management quality framework. Such framework must provide an end-to-end service management and must consider measurements from a higher abstraction layer, under a QoE perspective.

The term QoE can be considered relatively new to multimedia understanding. Different flavors of QoE definitions are stated throughout the literature. The DSL Forum (2006) defines that "QoE is the overall performance of a system from the point of view of the users. QoE is a measure of an end-to-end performance levels at the user perspective and an indicator of how well this system meets the user needs." DSL Forum (2006) also makes a distinction between QoS and QoE in a sense that QoE stands on the user perspective while QoS pays respect to the network perspective.

Siller et al. (2003) define QoE as "the user's perceived experience of what is being presented by the Application Layer, where the application layer acts as a user interface front-end that presents the overall result of the individual quality of services."

Patrick et al. (2004) defines QoE as "the characteristics of the sensations, perceptions, and opinions of people as they interact with their environments. These characteristics can be pleasing and enjoyable, or displeasing and frustrating."

All those definitions point out that QoE stands on a higher abstraction layer when compared to QoS. It could be considered a perceptual pseudo-layer (Siller et al., 2003), which is concerned with the end user experience, as an extension to the application layer defined in the OSI Model (Bauer & Patrick, 2004).

QoE and QoS terminology are often used interchangeably but can be defined as two complementary concepts. QoE can be defined as an extension of the traditional QoS in the sense that QoE provides information regarding the delivered services from an end-user point of view (DSL Forum, 2006). Some metrics used to performance management may be helpful to illustrate this concept. One example of QoE measurement metric is the mean opinion score (MOS), which is a subjective method to quantify the impact of various forms of service degradation on the user's perception. On the other hand, QoS metrics may include network layers measurements such as packet loss, delay, or jitter to indicate service performance. In general, the relation between QoE and QoS metrics is not directly determined and is typically observed empirically because there are several QoS metrics that may impact the overall QoE (DSL Forum, 2006).

INTEGRATED QOS AND QOE MODEL

Model Definition

Considering the drawbacks and limitations of the traditional QoS approach to ensure multimedia service quality, it is possible to use QoE concepts in addition to QoS by combining both in one layered QoE/QoS model (DSL Forum, 2006; Siller et al., 2003; Zapater & Bressan, 2007). QoE as experienced by the end user is the only way to understand what a customer really wants. Then it is possible to figure out how QoE relates with traditional QoS approach oriented to the network. By combining those two domains, a service provider can determine how to improve and assure customer experience. This approach does not substitute the QoS oriented to the network. Instead, user and network perspectives are both complementary and are combined in one integrated QoE/QoS model as shown in Figure 1.

Multiple layers impact the overall user experience for any service. The key layers from a QoE/QoS (DSL Forum, 2006; Siller et al., 2003; Zapater et al., 2007) perspective can be defined as:

- **Service layer:** It represents the perceptual pseudo-layer on top of the application layer. It is the layer exposed to the user, and where the QoE is measured. QoE metrics are typi-

Figure 1. Layered QoE/QoS model

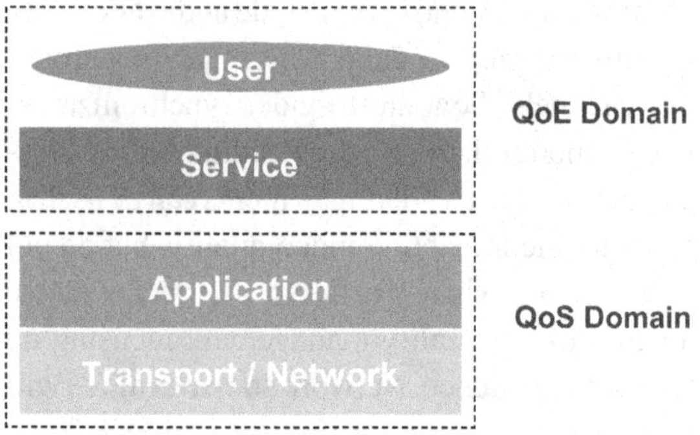

cally measurements of user opinion of the service quality such as mean opinion score (MOS) or approximations of user opinions measured via objective means.

- **Application Layer:** Where parameters related to the application (e.g., for video services: resolution, frame rate, color, video/audio codecs) are managed in order to achieve expected QoE levels.
- **Transport/Network layer:** Where parameters related to the transport and network performance (e.g., jitter, delay, packet loss) are managed in order to meet the adequate QoE levels.

Three main aspects of service delivery should be considered to identify factors that underlie QoE for a new service (DSL Forum, 2006):

- **Session set up:** The process of session establishment including, for example, logging on, dialing a number, and requesting a service.
- **Service operation:** It describes how the service operates once a session is established.
- **Session finalization:** The process of finalizing a session including, for example, logging off and system shutting down.

When a service is not session oriented, the quality of experience will be restricted to the service operations aspects.

EXAMPLE: IPTV SERVICES

This section exemplifies the application of the layered QoE/QoS model to IPTV services. The DSL Forum Technical Report TR-026 (2006) presents a detailed description of QoE requirements for video, voice, and broadband Internet services. Based on this report, some examples of IPTV QoE requirements will be given for each layer presented in Figure 1.

The IPTV services may include a wide variety of components besides traditional video distribution services, for example, online gaming, video telephony, e-commerce, among others. The analysis presented here focuses only on video services, which encompass the distribution of broadcast TV channels and video on demand (VOD). These services consist of video streams of standard or high definition targeted to television terminals using a set-top-box.

A generic high-level end-to-end IPTV delivery system is depicted in Figure 2 and its main blocks are identified according to the application and transport layers defined in the layered QoE/QoS model. The application layer includes the entire video service infrastructure: video acquisition systems (for broadcast TV or VOD), encoding, set-top box (STB), middleware, digital rights management (DRM), conditional access, and display devices. The transport and network layer includes all the network elements that carry the video streams: core, aggregation, access, and home networks.

First of all, it is important to note that QoE dimensions for IPTV services are not limited to video and audio quality. The dimensions include (DSL Forum, 2006; Kerpez et al., 2006):

- **Fidelity of information:** Audio and video picture quality.
- **Responsiveness:** Low response time after user commands (e.g., channel zapping time).
- **Usability:** User interface manipulation (e.g., ease of use of the electronic program guide (EPG)).
- **Security:** User authentication and video source protection.
- **Availability:** "Always on" service expectations from users.

Many parameters can be used to define, monitor, and evaluate the performance of IPTV services at the different layers presented in Fig-

Figure 2. IPTV delivery system (Source: adapted from DSLForum, 2006)

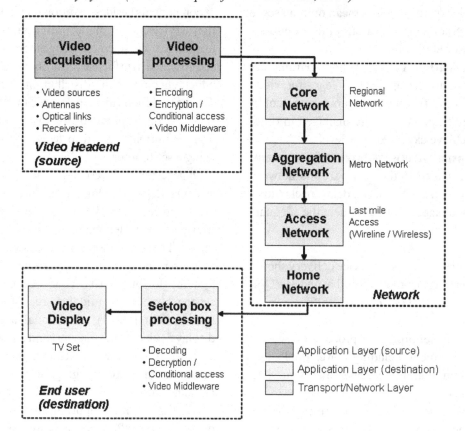

ure 1. Such parameters are defined from an end user perspective and are agnostic to the type of implementation, network architecture, protocols, or technologies used. Those parameters are meant to set the minimum requirements at each layer for a satisfactory user experience. Some key parameters of each layer are exemplified based on the DSL Forum TR-026 (2006) through the next 3 sections.

Service Layer

The key parameters associated to the service layer include (DSL Forum, 2006):

- **Data plane (video/audio quality):** It typically includes parameters for evaluat-

ing video quality subjectively or objectively from the end user perspective. The section 0 provides detailed information about video quality measurement approaches.

- **Control plane (interactive responsiveness):**
  o System start-up time (time from set-top box power until video content exhibition): < 10s.
  o Channel change time (also known as zapping time, it represents the time from remote control button push until a new channel is displayed): < 2 s.
  o User interface actions: <200 ms:
    > EPG navigation responsiveness
    > VOD control time responsiveness such as: play, fast forward, pause, and rewind.

o **Availability:** Traditional voice telephony services offer 99.99% availability. Recently, VoIP service has targeted 99.94% annual end-to-end availability. Similar availability levels could be assumed to video services.

Application Layer

The key parameters associated to the application layer include:

- **Data plane (video/audio quality):** Specific parameters that determine the quality of the content displayed and are primarily associated to compression schemes used.
  - o Quality of source displayed
  - o Codec standard used (MPEG-2, MPEG-4 AVC or SMPTE VC-1)
  - o *Resolution* (horizontal vs. vertical lines and pixels) and *frame rate*: Standard definition (SD) or high definition (HD)
  - o *Bit rate*: Constant bit rate (CBR) vs. variable bit rate (VBR)
  - o Audio channels and audio sample rate
  - o Encoder quality and settings
- **Control plane (interactive responsiveness):**
  - o *System start up time*: STB boot time, middleware server initialization and authentication
  - o *Channel change time*: STB command processing delay (time to identify and process the remote control command), STB layer delay (time to process the incoming streaming and deliver it to the decoder – includes conditional access and decrypting processing), STB jitter buffer delay (time to fill out the STB buffer) and STB decoder delay.
  - o *VOD control*: STB command processing delay, VOD server delay, STB layer

delay, STB jitter buffer delay and STB decoder delay

o *EPG navigation*: STB command processing delay and middleware server processing time

Transport/Network Layer

The transport/network layer parameters presented are measured after any application layer mechanisms to overcome the network impairments. The key network parameters include (DSL Forum, 2006):

- **Data plane (video/audio quality):** Key network performance indicators include: throughput, packet loss, delay, and jitter. Video streams require higher bandwidth when compared to traditional data or voice applications and video traffic flows have continuous and real time characteristics making intensive use of network resources. The bandwidth required for each video stream depends on the codec standard and encoding configurations defined at the application layer. In general, end-to-end delay and jitter are not problematic to IPTV services due to STB de-jitter buffers, which can store about 100-500 ms of video. Such buffers are responsible to match network and video elements performance. However, the video delay should not be such higher so that it makes the end user uncomfortable when comparing a common IPTV signal to other sources of TV signal (cable TV or off-the air). However, video streams are highly sensitive to packet losses due to their characteristics of continuous and real time traffic flows. If the network does not support the required packet losses requirements, alternative techniques can be used (e.g., forward error correction at network or application layers, loss concealment, automatic repeat request, etc.). The QoE impact of information losses depends on:

o *Type of data lost*: Losses of different frames produce different impairments on video. Let us consider the MPEG encoding algorithm. When an I-frame[1] is lost, the effect on video is propagated until the arrival of another I-frame.

o Type of codec standard used

o Transport stream packetization used

o *Encoding bit rate*: The higher the bit rate, the more vulnerable the stream becomes to packet loss impairments. More packets per second are transmitted and each one has the same loss probability.

o *Decoder concealment mechanisms*: May minimize the impact of some losses.

Table 2 outlines some examples of network performance parameters to support broadcast TV services defined by the DSL Forum (2006).

• **Control plane (interactive responsiveness)**: One of the most important aspects of the IPTV services performance is the responsiveness. The channel change is one of the responsiveness characteristics that can be related to the network performance due

to the utilization of multicast mechanisms to optimize resources utilization. Several factors influence the zapping delay: the application layer factors are listed in section 0 and the network layer factors include the time of join and leave messages[3] processing in the network and the delay for the new stream to reach the set-top box. Some experiments in fixed networks indicate that zapping delay is primarily determined by the time required to have an I-frame available at the set-top box to start decoding the new channel and, therefore, is mainly associated to the application layer. Such time depends of the configuration of the distance between two I-frames, which is configured in the encoding systems and may range from 500 to 1,000 ms depending on the encoding bit rate and I-frames distance. Figure 3 illustrates both application and network factors affecting channel change delay and shows the application layer dominance on the overall zapping delay.

It is important to mention that those network performance parameters reflect the network requirements on an end-to-end basis, considering all the network segments shown in Figure 2: core, aggregation, access, and home networks.

Table 2. Network performance parameters - IPTV (Source: DSL Forum, 2006)

Resolution	Encoding Rate (Mbps)[2]	Delay	Jitter	Maximum duration of a single error	Loss period (IP packets lost in one error event)	Loss distance (error events per hour)	Average IP video packet loss rate
SDTV	1.75	< 200 ms	< 50 ms	≤16ms	4	1	≤ 6.68E-06
SDTV	2.0	< 200 ms	< 50 ms	≤ 16ms	5	1	≤ 7.31E-06
SDTV	2.5	< 200 ms	< 50 ms	≤ 16ms	5	1	≤ 5.85E-06
HDTV	8	< 200 ms	< 50 ms	≤ 16ms	14	0.25	≤1,28E-06
HDTV	10	< 200 ms	< 50 ms	≤ 16ms	17	0.25	≤1,24E-06
HDTV	12	< 200 ms	< 50 ms	≤ 16ms	20	0.25	≤1,22E-06

Figure 3. Example of channel zapping delay influencing factors (Source: DSL Forum, 2006)

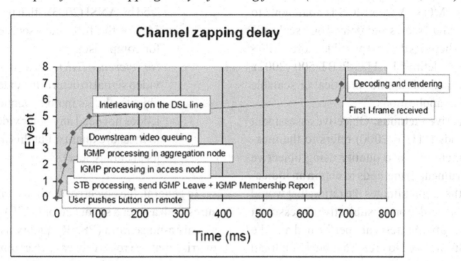

Such parameters are also independent of the network architectures and technologies adopted by the service provider. For example, the access networks can use either wireline or wireless technologies as long as the end-to-end requirements are guaranteed.

Each network segment must implement its QoS mechanisms in order to meet such end-to-end performance requirements. Traffic management techniques are used with IP networks to support a wide variety of services with diverse QoS requirements while ensuring efficient sharing of network resources. Those techniques include, for example, functions such as policing, buffer management, scheduling, shaping, backpressure flow control, admission control, route selection, and node/network monitoring.

VIDEO QUALITY MEASUREMENT

The main video quality measurement approaches will be briefly presented in this section due to its importance to IPTV services quality assurance. Considering all the different QoE/QoS dimensions of IPTV services mentioned previously, video

quality is one of the most important from user perspective. There are several impairments that can affect video quality. The most common impairments (Ashourian, Zhu, & Lambadaris, 2004) include blocking (or tiling), blurring, color errors, edge busyness, mosquito noise, error blocks, jerkiness (or jerky motion), object persistence, object retention, quantization noise, lip sync, pixilation, and smearing among others.

Basically, there are two ways to measure and verify the video quality delivered to the end user in order to identify such impairments: subjective or objective methods. They both aim to arrive at video quality metrics (VQM), which are intended to provide calculated values that are strongly correlated with viewers' quality assessments (ITU-T, 2004a).

- **Subjective methods:** Subjective assessment methods (ITU-T, 1998) are used to establish the performance of TV systems using measurements that more directly anticipate user perceptions. They require a group of people to watch a video and give it a quality score. The results of the tests are statistically treated and the output is often an average of the quality ratings known as Mean Opinion Score (MOS). Video MOS is analogous to voice MOS scores and is rated on a scale of 1 to 5, where 5 is the best possible score--MOS scale is defined by ITU-R BT 500 (2002). Such methods are not practical or scalable for live applications.

- **Objective methods:** Objective assessment methods (ITU-T, 2000) refers to the measurement of video quality using objective (instrumental) methods to obtain an indication that approximates the rating that would be obtained from a subjective assessment test. Numerous tests are performed and the results are used to create a model of human perception of quality--the human visual system. This model provides objective measures of quality (VQM) calculated algorithmically that can be integrated into automated test and analysis routines. Although objective methods may not reflect exactly users' perceptions, they have valuable characteristics to support the monitoring of large-scale IPTV deployments: they are repeatable and can be performed very quickly. The objective measurements can be performed using one of the following approaches (ITU-T, 2000):

  o *Full Reference (FR)*: The input or reference video at the input of the system, and the processed signal at the output of the system are available for comparison and to determine video quality objectively. It is considered to be the most accurate approach. ITU-T J.144 defines a set of VQM of digital television with FR (ITU-T, 2004b).

  o *Reduced Reference (RR)*: This approach differs from FR because only selected parameters are extracted from input and output to be compared. They try to keep accuracy while optimizing the transport of additional information. National Telecommunications and Information Administration (NTIA)

defined a RR model--later standardized by ANSI (2003)--that needs about 14% of the full video source channel for comparison.

  o *No reference (NR)*: Uses only received video signal to determine video quality objectively. Its main advantage is that it does not need any other video source to measure quality, but this may affect its accuracy level.

In general, the objective methods utilize measures such as mean square error (MSE), and peak signal-to-noise ratio (PSNR) quality assessment metrics that are relatively easy to compute. Both measures are indicative of the difference between the received video and a reference signal--valid for FR and RR approaches.

Moving picture quality metrics (MPQM) and v-factor (a particular MPQM implementation) are examples of single ended measures. V-factor is a particular implementation specifically designed for IPTV, and leverages MPQM research that several labs have developed over the last years. Just like MPQM, v-factor provides the video quality score but also some extra information needed for monitoring and diagnosing the root cause of problems.

A simpler approach for an objective method uses packet network parameters to extrapolate the video quality. It is not the most accurate method and will not provide a complete characterization of QoE but can provide an indication of video quality at a cost effectively manner. That is the case of another measurement method named media delivery index (MDI).

The selected approaches for video measurement depend on a case-by-case analysis. In general, objective methods are preferred to subjective ones considering the complexity and costs associated with the latter. Objective methods for video are still evolving when compared to voice quality evaluation techniques. While there is no definite solution that totally eliminates the need of a reference, a possible strategy is the combination of various objective methods to measure video quality, and including network parameters approach.

QOE ASSURANCE GUIDELINES FOR IPTV SERVICES

This section presents some high level directions from planning to operations of IPTV services for service providers aimed to deliver a differentiated customer experience. Based on the layered QoE/QoS model and the need to provide the desired customer experience, high level guidelines can be mapped throughout the traditional lifecycle of service delivery infrastructure deployment from a service provider perspective (Zapater et al., 2007) as shown in Figure 4.

Plan and Design

Methods here included are related to the engineering practices of IPTV technology infrastructure from a service provider standpoint. It is a top-down design approach (Zapater et al., 2007) as depicted in Figure 5. It starts with the QoE requirements identification based on the IPTV service offerings definition. Once QoE requirements are mapped, it is possible to identify QoS requirements at the network and application layers. The last step encompasses the definition of the technology architecture--from network to application perspectives--and all the mechanisms associated to meet QoS requirements.

Some key relevant aspects of an IPTV service infrastructure planning and design oriented to QoE assurance (Heavy Heading 2006) can be grouped into: capacity planning and service assurance, and they are summarized as follows.

Capacity Planning

Capacity planning is critical to infrastructure optimization and QoE guarantee. When designing the infrastructure, it is mandatory to keep in mind that a well dimensioned network and service infrastructure is essential to achieve the expected QoE level. The understanding of utilization and adoption trends is mandatory for

Figure 4. Service delivery infrastructure deployment lifecycle

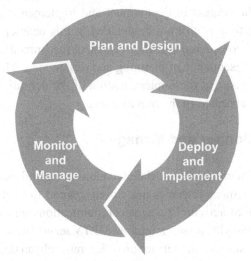

Figure 5. Plan and design steps for QoE assurance

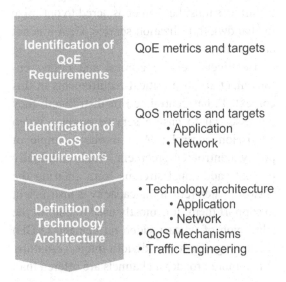

adequate capacity planning and to anticipate the demand for services.

Several mechanisms contribute to optimize the IPTV infrastructure without over-provisioning resources. Such mechanisms include enhanced QoS techniques, policy control, multicast, video admission control (VAC), and flexible content insertion at most economical infrastructure points.

Service Assurance

Originally, service assurance is not part of planning and design activities. However, assurance considerations play an important role when designing IPTV technology architecture. It is essential to be aware of the mechanisms and technologies that can help service assurance during the design phase.

Congestion avoidance is one of the key issues for IPTV services. Several approaches can minimize impacts of resource constraints on service quality. Sophisticated QoS mechanisms must be supported by the network so that differentiated treatment is given to services with conflicting QoS needs and sharing the same network resources. Almost a deterministic QoS concept must be applied to IPTV so that each subscriber is guaranteed with the bandwidth required. Intelligent QoS techniques must be then considered to optimize the bandwidth utilization service when it is not entirely in use.

Intelligent service control and policy enforcement are also critical requirements in this context. Either centralized or distributed, they are essential to ensure service quality. Video admission control (VAC) is one example of policy control enforcement. VAC essentially prevents additional streams from entering the network when remaining capacity is insufficient to support them. It is mostly used to control the admission of unicast video on demand (VOD) sessions, given its bandwidth-intensive nature. When more broadcast channels are offered than

can be concurrently viewed, multicast VAC may also be considered.

Such control policies must rely on accurate intelligence on resource availability reporting. The adequate set of tools and techniques to accurately report available resources is essential to support service requests and to enforce the appropriate policies based on service level agreements (SLA's).

It is important to consider that denial of service requests due to insufficient service resources must be considered the exception, not the rule. User expectations of always available services are based on former cable and satellite TV performance. In order to meet those expectations, high availability and reliability considerations must be applied to all key infrastructure components on an end-to-end basis.

While adequate QoS mechanisms, policy control, and high availability considerations may help service quality assurance, the only way to ensure QoE from user perspective is by placing tools to measure and verify video and audio quality, zapping delay, and other significant parameters. That subject will be further discussed throughout this chapter.

Deploy and Implement

Methods for maximizing IPTV services QoE on the context of deployment and implementation activities will not be detailed in this chapter. It is considered that they represent the immediate consequence of planning and design step. They consist of the implementation of the definitions elaborated in the previous step.

Monitor and Manage

The methods associated to monitoring and management activities are closely related to operations activities on a telecommunications service provider. In order to achieve IPTV service quality assurance the service provider must rely on three main categories of enablers (Zapater et al., 2007) as shown in Figure 6.

Processes

Well defined and repeatable processes must exist to support an end-to-end IPTV service quality management. The TeleManagement Forum's enhanced Telecom Operations Map (eTOM) (2005) is considered the standard reference for business process modeling on telecommunications service providers.

eTOM defines a set of required processes to ensure customers satisfaction. Those processes can be customized and adapted to cope with IPTV services and to reflect particular services providers' characteristics. Such eTOM processes referred are mostly part of a group of processes devoted to assurance, which is part of a major group focused on operations.

A central point underlying management processes is monitoring of any pre-defined metrics. Several variables can be used to define, monitor, and evaluate the performance of an IPTV services at the different layers presented in Figure 1 and some of them were highlighted. The definition of the metrics to be used as a management dashboard

Figure 6. Service assurance management enablers

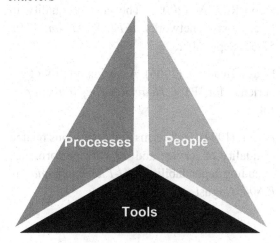

(Kerpez et al., 2006) can be done according to the top down approach presented in Figure 5. Besides, there are many measurement approaches to cope with video quality monitoring as presented previously.

There is no unique set of metrics for quality evaluation. Each service provider must define the best metrics to evaluate their IPTV services quality focusing on the user perspective requirements and considering the available measurement methods and tools.

Tools

Like other management processes, quality assurance processes need to be supported by a set of tools (also known as operating support systems (OSS) and business support systems (BSS)). By introducing a higher automation degree, tools help to increase the processes agility, accuracy, and efficiency. They include monitoring, test and measurement tools as part of a set of integrated systems focused on quality management (Kerpez et al., 2006).

Essentially, such category of tools is composed of a central management system and probes. Several probes distributed all over the service infrastructure—from the head-end to the set-top-box and through the network--are responsible for measuring service quality by extracting the relevant parameters at each level. One example of measurement architecture for IP video is described in the recommendation ITU-T J.241 (2005).

All those measures alone and not processed are useless to the service provider. They must be correlated, normalized, and aggregated so that they can be displayed on a dashboard that reflects the quality of IPTV service at its different instances--from an individual user to a region.

This function is performed by a service quality management (SQM) system that enables a service provider to model and analyze metrics from service performance (application and transport/network) to user experience (Kerpez et al., 2006).

People

People represent one key aspect of telecommunications service operations. Skilled and trained people are supposed to support and run the operations processes using the available management tools. Usually, a separate operations structure is created to support an IPTV service offering in a service provider because of its different intrinsic characteristics when compared with traditional voice and data services. Such separate operations structure is commonly named video operations center (VOC) and is integrated to the existing network operations center (NOC) that supports the telephony and data connectivity services. The development of specific skills and training programs should not be limited only to the VOC staff, but also extended to the NOC staff due to the fact that the introduction of IPTV services also have major impacts in the network infrastructure.

FINAL CONSIDERATIONS

A major challenge for wireline and wireless IP-based networks is to provide adequate quality of service (QoS) for different services. Changes in the telecommunications industry have driven integrated service offerings that include voice, high speed Internet and video, namely IPTV. As the industry moves forward with IPTV deployments, service assurance, and emphasis on QoE are mandatory to make IPTV services an attractive alternative to traditional TV offerings.

Traditional QoS management approaches adopted by service providers are mostly focused on the network perspective rather than the user perspective. Such approaches are limited for multimedia services that require a consistent QoE delivery. This chapter aims to expand the scope of such QoS approach by introducing an approach that encompasses a higher abstraction layer and provides an end-to-end quality focus.

The proposed approach combines QoE and QoS and gives some high level directions ranging from design to management of IPTV service delivery infrastructure. Such directions aim to help service providers to meet customers Quality of Experience requirements and to transition IPTV from small-scale deployments to the mass market successfully.

REFERENCES

ANSI, (2003). Digital transport of one-way video signals--parameters for objective performance assessment. *ANSI T1.801.03.*

Ashourian, M., Zhu, J., & Lambadaris, I. (2004). A review on online quality measure for videos. *TENCON 2004, IEEE Region 10 Conference* (pp. 363-366). November.

Bauer, B., & Patrick, A. S. (2004). *A human factors extension to the seven-layer OSI reference model.* Retrieved December 2, 2007, from http://www.andrewpatrick.ca/OSI/10layer.html

DSL Forum. (2006). *Triple play services quality of experience (QoE) requirements.* DSL Forum Technical Report, TR-126, December.

Dutta-Roy, A. (2000). The cost of quality in Internet-style networks. *IEEE Spectrum, 37*(9), 57-62, September.

Heavy Heading. (2006). Assuring quality of experience for IPTV. *HeavyReading Whitepaper,* July.

ITU-T. (1994). QoS terms and definitions related to quality of service and network performance including dependability. *ITU-T Recommendation E.800,* August.

Jain, R. (2004). Quality of experience. *IEEE Multimedia, 11*(1), 96-97.

Kerpez, K., Waring, D., Lapiotis, G., Lyles, J. B., & Vaidyanathan, R. (2006). IPTV service assurance. *IEEE Communications Magazine, 44*(9), 166-172.

ITU-T. (1998). Subjective picture quality assessment for digital cable television systems, *ITU-T Recommendation J. 140*, March.

ITU-T. (2000). User requirements for objective perceptual video quality measurements in digital cable television. *ITU-T Recommendation J.143*, May.

ITU-T. (2001). End-user multimedia QoS categories. *ITU-T Recommendation G. 1010*, November.

ITU-T. (2002). Methodology for the subjective assessment of the quality of television pictures, *ITU-T Recommendation BT.500*, June.

ITU-T. (2004a). Method for specifying accuracy and cross-calibration of video quality metrics (VQM). *ITU-T Recommendation J.149*, March.

ITU-T. (2004b). Objective perceptual video quality measurement techniques for digital cable television in the presence of a full reference. *ITU-T Recommendation J.144*, March.

ITU-T. (2005). Quality of service ranking and measurement methods for digital video services delivered over broadband IP networks. *ITU-T Recommendation J.241*, 2005.

Patrick, A. S., Singer, J., Corrie, B., Noel, S., El Khatib, K., Emond, B., Zimmerman, T., & Marsh, S. (2004). A QoE sensitive architecture for advanced collaborative environments. *Proceedings of the 1st International Conference on Quality of Service in Heterogeneous Wired/Wireless Networks* (pp. 319-322). IEEE.

Siller, M., & Woods, J. (2003). Improving quality experience for multimedia services by QoS arbitration on a QoE framework. *Proceedings of the 13th Packed Video Workshop 2003*, Nantes, France.

TeleManagement Forum. (2005). Enhanced Telecom Operations Map (eTOM): The business process framework for the information and communications services industry, Release 6 v6.1, *TeleManagement Forum GB921*.

Zapater, M. N., & Bressan, G. (2007). A proposed approach for quality of experience assurance for IPTV. *Proceedings of the 1st International Conference on the Digital Society 2007,* Guadeloupe, French Caribbean.

ENDNOTES

[1] I-frame is a key frame used in the compression of subsequent P and B frames and it depends exclusively on its own information to be reconstructed and presented to the end user.

[2] Considers the utilization MPEG-4 AVC as a codec standard.

[3] Join and leave are messages of the Internet Group Management Protocol (IGMP) used to implement multicast mechanisms in the network.

Chapter XI
Perceptual Voice Quality Measurements for Wireless Networks

Dorel Picovici
Institute of Technology Carlow, Ireland

John Nelson
University of Limerick, Ireland

ABSTRACT

Perceptual voice quality measurement can be defined as an objective quantification of an overall impression of the perceived stimulus. An alternative to laborious subjective testing is objective predictive modelling, which employs a perceptual model of the human auditory and cognitive system to predict the human response to a voice signal in terms of its quality. This chapter describes subjective and automated objective testing methods, and provides a test case scenario for measuring voice quality.

INTRODUCTION

Wireless communications have opened up a range of new opportunities for telecommunication companies and service providers. In particular, wireless local area networks (WLANs), continue to provide increasing data bandwidth at lower cost, and now enable support for advanced mobile services. Although most existing wireless LANs based on the IEEE 802.11 specifications (the popular Wi-Fi networks) are predominantly targeted at best effort data traffic, there has been a very strong interest in integrating support for voice traffic using VoIP. Given the performance limitations of these wireless systems, assessing and addressing the perceptual voice quality is of major importance for both service providers and telecommunication system designers.

Perceptual voice quality measurement can be defined as an objective quantification of an overall impression of the perceived stimulus. Until the 1990s, the most reliable method for obtaining true perceptual measurement was to conduct a subjective test, which gives the group's mean opinion score (MOS) of the quality of a voice signal under evaluation. Subjective tests are, however, slow and expensive to conduct, making them accessible only to a small number of laboratories and unsuitable for long-term or large scale voice quality monitoring.

An alternative to the subjective tests is represented by objective predictive modelling techniques. This approach employs the use of a perceptual model of the human auditory and cognitive system to predict the human response to a voice signal in terms of its quality. Such approaches are reported to be highly effective as the aim of the perceptual models is to simulate the response of listeners (end-users) participating in a subjective test. This has made the objective predictive modelling techniques very attractive for meeting the demands for perceptual voice quality measurements. Objective measurement techniques can be sub-divided into two types of predictive models:

a. **Intrusive models:** Compare an original voice signal with its degraded version that has been processed by a network under test. Due to their use of both signals (original and distorted) for processing such models are also known as comparison-based or full-reference.

b. **Non-intrusive models** can be used in mainly two configurations: (1) *Non-intrusive signal-based models* (also termed as no-reference, or single-ended models) where only the distorted voice signal is required for measuring its perceptual quality and (2) *non-intrusive parametric models*. Here, instead of using voice signals, several properties of the underlying transport and/or terminal, such as echo, delay, noise, network characteristics and reception measures are used to estimate the subjective MOS.

Following this introduction, Section 2 details the tests and methods used during subjective determination of voice quality. Due to their high price and time consuming subjective testing is not always practical. Automated objective models that can replace the subjective testing are reviewed in Section 3. Methods that are widely used for voice quality measurements for wireless networks are identified in Section 4. In addition, a test case scenario for measuring voice quality using the first wireless test platform for IEEE 802.11 wireless networks is also presented. Section 5 concludes the chapter and discusses future trends.

SUBJECTIVE DETERMINATION OF VOICE QUALITY

Voice quality assessment measures that are based on ratings by human listeners are called subjective measures (ITU-T Recommendation P.800, 1996). These tests seek to quantify the range of opinions that listeners express when they hear voice transmission of systems that are under test. Properly designed subjective tests provide the most accurate way of assessing voice quality. However, the results of subjective tests are influenced by the conditions of the tests such as (ITU-T Recommendation E. 800, 1994):

•   **Speech material:** Perception of a speech signal depends on the gender of talkers, their particular pronunciation, the language, content, and length of the signal.

•   **Test set-up:** Results for the same test can vary depending on the listener's previous experience with listening tests, nationality, the duration of the test, and the level of understanding.

•   **Listening conditions:** The individual ratings during the test are influenced by the loudness of the presented speech signals and choice of equipment used (i.e. headphones/telephone handset).

There are several methods to assess the subjective quality of voice signals. In general, they are divided in two main classes:

a. Conversational tests
b. Listening-only tests

Conversational tests, whereby two subjects have to listen and talk interactively via the transmission system under test, provide a realistic test environment. However, they are time consuming, and often suffer from low reproducibility, therefore listening-only tests are recommended where the subject listens to, and evaluates, recordings with various degradations.

All subjective methods involve the use of large numbers of human listeners to produce a statistically valid subjective quality indicator. The indicator used is the discussed mean opinion score, which is the average value of all the rating scores registered by the subjects. For telecommunications purposes, the most commonly used assessment methods are those standardised and recommended by the International Telecommunication Union, Telecommunication Standardisation Sector (ITU-T):

*   Conversational opinion method
*   Absolute category rating method
*   Quantal-response detectability method
*   Degradation category rating method
*   Comparison category rating method

The first method in the previous list represents a conversational type test, while the rest are effectively listening-only tests. Although as previously shown, there are five different subjective speech quality methods, the most used one is the "absolute category rating (ACR) method." The test introduced by this method is well established and has been applied to analogue and digital telephone connections and telecommunication devices, such as digital codecs. Category ratings are applied to short groups of unrelated sentences, each of which has been passed through a number of standard

processes as well as the processes under test. Subjects taking part in these listening tests must be chosen randomly with the following criteria:

*   It is their first time of getting involved in work connected with assessment of the performance of telephone circuits, or related work such as voice coding.
*   They did not participate in any subjective test for at least the previous six months, nor in a any listening-opinion test for at least one year.
*   They have never heard the same sentence lists before.

For a given sample of subjects the test is limited in size by the maximum possible length of a session without fatigue. If the experiment is too large to be finished in one session then it is recommended to sub-divide into two or more sessions. In practice each session would have duration of maximum 20 minutes. For rating, the opinion scales outlined in the following subsections are approved and recommended by ITU-T.

Listening Quality Scale

Listening-quality scale is a five-point category-judgment scale representing perceptual impression to voice quality as shown in Table 1.

The arithmetic mean of the listening-quality scale accumulated from all the subjects is known as the mean listening-quality opinion score, or

Table 1. Listening-quality scale

Quality of voice	Score
Excellent	5
Good	4
Fair	3
Poor	2
Bad	1

simply the mean opinion score and is represented by the symbol MOS.

Listening Effort Scale

Typical layout and wording of the listening effort scale is given in Table 2. The quantity evaluated from the scores accumulated (mean listening-effort opinion score), is represented by the symbol MOS_{LE}.

Loudness Preference Scale

The layout and wording of the loudness-preference scale is given in the Table 3. The quantity evaluated from the scores (mean loudness-preference opinion score) is represented by the symbol MOS_{LP}.

Amongst all the scales presented the most used one is "listening-quality scale" as shown in Table 1. In May 2003. ITU-T approved recommendation P800.1 (ITU-T recommendation P.800.1, 2003) that provides a new terminology to be used in conjunction with voice quality expressions in terms of MOS.

As shown in Table 4, this terminology is motivated by the intention to avoid misinterpretation as to whether specific values of MOS are related to listening quality or conversational quality, and whether they originate from subjective tests, from objective models or from network planning models.

As indicated above, the following identifiers are recommended to be used together with the abbreviation MOS in order to distinguish the area

Table 2. Listening-effort scale

Effort required to understand the meaning of sentence	Score
Complete relaxation possible; no effort required	5
Attention necessary; no appreciable effort required	4
Moderate effort required	3
Considerable effort required	2
No meaning understood with any feasible effort	1

Table 3. Loudness-preference scale

Loudness preference	Score
Much louder than preferred	5
Louder than preferred	4
Preferred	3
Quieter than preferred	2
Much quieter than preferred	1

Table 4. Recommended MOS terminology

Measurement	Listening-only	Conversational
Subjective	MOS-LQS	MOS-CQS
Objective	MOS-LQO	MOS-CQO
Estimated	MOS-LQE	MOS-CQE

of application: LQ to refer to *Listening Quality*, CQ to refer to *Conversational Quality*, S to refer to Subjective testing, O to refer to Objective testing using an objective model, and E to refer to Estimated using a network planning model.

OBJECTIVE DETERMINATION OF VOICE QUALITY

Until the 1990s, the standard way to assess the voice quality was to conduct one of the above-detailed subjective tests. However, employing subjective testing in a controlled environment is expensive and slow, so while using human subjects is the ideal way to make particular system decision for a codec for an international standard, they are unsuitable for the day-to-day voice quality assessment. In order to reduce the necessity for time consuming subjective testing, much effort has been spent on the development of alternative objective models capable of predicting the MOS. Several methods for measuring the voice quality of a network or its components have been proposed. Most of them address the measurement of voice quality in terms of "evaluation" and "assessment." Evaluation determines the fitness of a system for a particular purpose (similar to validation in software engineering). Assessment, likewise corresponding to verification, determines the performance of the system against the requirements or against similar systems or implementations.

Objective voice quality measurements can be further classified according to the application domain:

a.   Signal-based models
b.   Network-based (planning) models
c.   Monitoring models

Each of the above will now be addressed in detail.

Signal-Based Models

The development of the signal-based models started with the use of signal-to-noise ratio (SNR) and segmental SNR (SNRseg) (Quackenbush, Barnawell, & Clements, 1988). As these measures have been considered susceptible to the occurrence of time misalignments and phase shift between the signals under test more reliable measures have been proposed. Examples of such measures are the *log likelihood ratio* and the *Itakura-Saito distortion measure* (Itakura & Saito, 1978). The log likelihood ratio (LLR) measure or Itakura distance measure is based on the difference between the speech production models such as all-pole linear predictive coding models of the original and distorted speech signals. The Itakura-Saito measure (IS) is a variation of the LLR that includes in its computation the gain of the all-pole linear predictive coding model. Linear prediction coefficients (LPC) can also be used to compute a distance measure based on cepstral coefficients known as the cepstral distance measure. Unlike the cepstrum computed directly from a speech waveform, one computed from the predictor coefficients provides an estimate of the smoothed speech spectrum.

All signal-based models described above use the parameters of speech production models used in codecs, therefore their performance is usually limited by the constraints of those models. They base their voice quality assessment on the comparison of the clean (transmitted) signal as the reference with the signal distorted by the system under test. After pre-processing and time-alignment, both signals (clean and distorted) are transformed into a perception-based domain using concepts of the psychophysics of hearing (Quatieri, 2002). During the final steps, difference or similarity vectors are determined from the two representations, which are time-averaged and mapped onto a final quality estimate such as MOS. Figure 1 illustrates the principles of signal-based measures.

Figure 1. Principle of signal-based measures

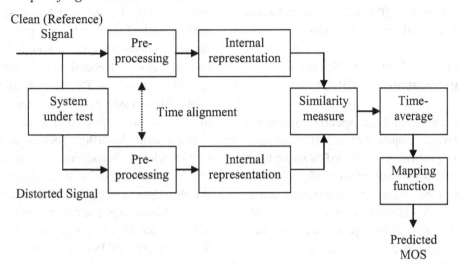

The evolution of the perceptual signal-based objective models is given in the following sub-sections.

Bark Spectral Distortion Measure (BSD)

The Bark spectral distortion (BSD) measure was developed by Wang, Sekey, and Gersho (1992) as a method of calculating an objective measure for signal distortion based on the quantifiable properties of auditory perception. The overall BSD measurement represents the average squared Euclidian distance between spectral vectors of the original and coded speech signals. The main aim of the measure is to emulate several known features of perceptual processing of speech sounds by the human ear, especially:

- Frequency scale warping, as modelled by the Bark transformation, and critical band integration in the cochlea.
- Changing sensitivity of the ear as the frequency varies.
- Difference between the loudness level and the subjective loudness scale.

BSD works well in cases where the distortions in voice regions represent the overall distortion because it processes voiced regions only; for this reason, voiced regions have to be detected. It also uses a traditional metric, Euclidean distance, in the distance measure module, but the developers did not validate the use of this metric.

Modified Bark Spectral Distortion Measure (MBSD)

The MBSD (Yang, Benbouchta, & Yantorno, 1997) is a modification of the BSD in which the concept of a noise-masking threshold is incorporated that differentiates audible and inaudible distortions. The modified Bark spectral distortion measure (MBSD) uses the same noise-masking threshold as that used in transform coding of audio signals (Johnson, 1998). There are two differences between the conventional BSD and MBSD. First, noise-masking threshold for determination of the audible distortion is used by MBSD, while the conventional BSD uses an empirically determined power threshold. Secondly, the distortion is computed in a different way between the two measures. BSD defines the distortion as the average squared Euclidian distance of estimated loudness, while the MBSD defines the distortion as the difference of estimated loudness.

Enhanced Modified Bark Spectral Distortion Measure (EMBSD)

Enhanced modified bark spectral distortion (EMBSD) is a development of the MBSD measure where some procedures of the MBSD have been modified and a new cognition model has been used. These modifications involve the following: the amount of loudness components used to calculate the loudness difference, the normalisation of loudness vectors before calculating loudness difference, the inclusion of a new cognition model based on post masking effects, and the deletion of the spreading function in the calculation of the noise masking threshold (Yang, 1999).

Perceptual Speech Quality Measurement (PSQM)

To address the continuous need for an accurate objective measure, Beerends and Stemerdink from KPN Research-Netherlands, developed a speech quality testing measure, which takes into account clarity's subjective nature and human perception, called the Perceptual Speech Quality Measurement or PSQM (Beerends & Stemerdink, 1994). In 1996 PSQM was approved by ITU-T Study Group 12 and recommended by the ITU as Recommendation P.861 (ITU-T. Recommendation P.861, 1996)

Perceptual Speech Quality Measurement Plus (PSQM+)

Taking into account the observed drawbacks of the PSQM, Beerends, Meijer, and Hekstra developed an improved version of the conventional PSQM measure. The new model became known as PSQM+, was reviewed by ITU-T Study Group 12 and published in 1997 under COM 12-20-E

(Beerends et al., 1997). PSQM+, which is based directly on the PSQM model, represents an improved method for measuring speech quality in network environments. Although for systems comprising speech encoding only, both methods give identical scores. PSQM+ technique is more applicable to a system, which experiences severe distortions due to time clipping and packet loss. When a large distortion, such as time clipping or packet loss is introduced (causing the original PSQM algorithm to scale down its score), the PSQM+ algorithm applies a different scaling factor that has an opposite effect, and the algorithm will produce higher scores that correlate better with subjective MOS than PSQM.

Measuring Normalising Blocks (MNB)

In 1997, ITU-T published a proposed annex to Recommendation P.861 (PSQM), which was approved in 1998 as appendix II. Based on a report by Voran of the Institute for Telecommunication and Science, it describes an alternative technique to PSQM for measuring the perceptual distance between the perceptually transformed input and output signals. This technique is known as measuring normalising blocks (MNB) (Voran, 1994). It was suggested that "listeners adapt and react differently to spectral deviations that span different time and frequency scale" (Atkinson, 1997). Taking into consideration this issue, MNB defines a new perceptual distance across multiple time and frequency scales. The model is recommended for use for measuring the impact of the followings:

- Transmission channel errors
- CELP and hybrid codecs with bit rates less than 4 Kb/s
- Vocoders

There are two types of MNBs: time measuring normalising blocks (TMNB) and frequency measuring normalising blocks (FMNB) (Voran,

1999). TMNB and FMNB are combined with weighting factors to generate a nonnegative value called Auditory Distance (AD). Finally, a logistic function maps AD values into a finite scale to provide correlation with MOS scores.

Perceptual Analysis Measurement System (PAMS)

PsyTechnics, which was initially a research group within British Telecommunications, developed in August 1998 an objective speech quality measure called Perceptual Analysis Measurement System (PAMS) (Rix & Hollier, 2000). The measure is based on a different model than PSQM+ but has the same goal: to objectively predict results of a subjective speech quality test for systems in which coding distortion as well as time-clipping and packet loss are potentially problems. PAMS uses a model based on factors of human perception to measure the perceived speech clarity of an output signal as compared with the input signal. Although similar to PSQM in many aspects, PAMS uses different signal processing techniques and a different perceptual model (Anderson, 2001). The results of the PAMS comparison are scores that range from 1-5 and that correlate on the same scale as MOS testing. In particular, PAMS produces a listening quality score and a listening effort score that correspond with the ACR opinion scale in ITU-T Recommendation P.800 (ITU-T Recommendation P.800, 1996).

Perceptual Evaluation of Speech Quality (PESQ)

In 1999, KPN Research-Netherlands improved the classical PSQM to correlate better with subjective tests under network conditions. The new measure is referred to as PSQM99. The main difference between the PSQM99 and PSQM concerns the perceptual modelling where they are differentiated by the asymmetry processing and scaling. PSQM99 provides more accurate correlations with subjective test results than PSQM and PSQM+. In a new study period, ITU-T recognised that both PSQM99 and PAMS had significant merits and that it would be beneficial to the industry to combine the merits of each one into a new measurement technique. A collaborative draft from KPN Research and British Telecommunications was submitted to ITU in May 2000 describing a new measurement technique called perceptual evaluation of speech quality (PESQ). Later in February 2001 ITU-T approved the new technique under the Recommendation P.862 (ITU-T Recommendation P.862, 2001).

PESQ is directed at narrowband telephone signals and is effective for measuring the impact of the following conditions:

- Waveform and non waveform codecs
- Transcodings
- Speech input levels to codecs
- Transmission channel errors
- Noise added by system (not present in input signal)
- Short and long term warping

PESQ combines the robust time-alignment techniques of PAMS with the accurate perceptual modelling of PSQM99. It is designed for use with intrusive tests: a signal is injected into the system under test, and the distorted output is compared with the input (reference) signal. The difference is then analysed and converted into a quality score. As a result of this process, the predicted MOS as given by PESQ varies between 0.5, which corresponds to a bad distortion condition, and 4.5, which corresponds to no measurable distortion. In order to align with the new MOS terminology, a new ITU-T Recommendation, Rec. P.862.1 (ITU-T. Recommendation P.862.1, 2003) was published. This Recommendation defines a mapping function and its performance for a single mapping from raw P.862 scores to the MOS-LQO (ITU-T. Recommendation P.800.1, 2003). The average correlation between PESQ score and MOS-LQS for the 22 subjective tests used in training was 0.935. The average correlation for eight unknown tests used for model validation was also 0.935. For an extended data set of 40 subjective tests including the training and validation sets, 93.5% of conditions were, after mapping, within 0.5 MOS, and 99.9% of conditions were within 1.0 MOS after mapping. Recently the PESQ was also modified to be suitable to wideband telephone signals (WPESQ).

Network-Based Models

Network-based models are based on computational models that have been used for several years for planning telecommunications networks without conducting time-consuming subjective tests. The approach has been recently been applied to measurements of wireless networks parameters such as echo and delay and to real-time voice assessment where the dominant distortions, packet loss, jitter and the codec, can be modelled by a relatively small number of statistical measures.

E-Model

The currently recommended model for use in transmission planning is the so-called E-model (ITU-T. Recommendation G.107, 2005). As shown in Figure 2, the model is a parameter-based algorithm based on 20 parameters related to terminal factor, environment factor and network factor. The primary output of the E-model is a quality-rating factor R on a 0-100 scale (0 corresponding to worst quality and 100 to excellent). The underlying assumption of the E-model is that different degradations can be transformed onto a particular scale and these degradations are

Figure 2. Reference connection of the E-model (According to ITU-T Rec. G.107)

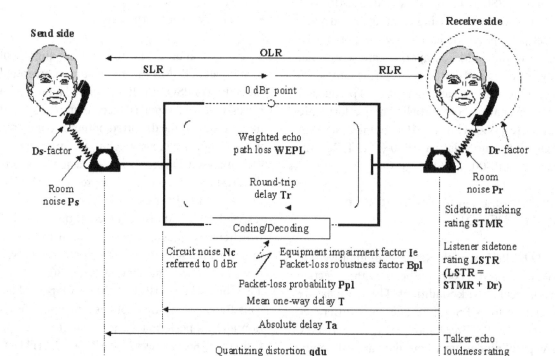

additive. The input parameters are grouped into different classes of impairments:

$$R = Ro - Is - Id - Ie,eff + A \qquad (1)$$

The classes of degradations are represented as follows (the complete set of formulae, parameter explanations, and degradation mapping to factors is given in the ITU-T Standard (ITU-T. Recommendation G.107, 2005)): *Ro* represents in principle the basic signal-to-noise ratio, including noise sources such as circuit noise and room noise. The factor *Is* is a combination of all impairments which occur more or less simultaneously with the voice signal. Factor *Id* represents the impairments caused by delay and the effective equipment impairment factor *Ie-eff* represents impairments caused by low bit-rate codecs. It also includes impairment due to packet-losses of random distribution. The advantage factor *A* allows for compensation of impairment factors when there are other advantages of access to the user.

An estimated mean opinion score (MOS-CQE) for the conversational situation in the scale 1-5 can be obtained from the *R*-factor using the formulae:

MOS-CQE = 1 for $R <= 0$

MOS-CQE= $1+0.035R + R(R-60)(100 - R)7 \cdot 10^{-6}$
for $0 < R < 100$

MOS-CQE = 4.5 for $R > 100$ \qquad (2)

The relation between the calculated quality-rating factor using the equation (1) above, the MOS-CQE using equation (2), and user satisfaction is detailed in Table 5.

In some cases, transmission planners may not be familiar with the use of quality measures such as the quality-rating factor *R* obtained from planning calculations, and MOS-CQE. Hence, provisional guidance for interpreting calculated *R* factors and MOS-CQE for planning purposes is given in Table 5.

Extensions of the E-Model

As the transmission of VoIP becomes more and more common in telephony, new quality issues were considered important. Loss of packets, delay, jitter are particular important to network operators due to their load-dependency and are considered difficult to characterise even in cases when traffic management is used. In order to address these difficulties two main approaches have been proposed. The first one has been proposed by Clark and is referred to us as "VQmon" (2003). The method extends the E-model by incorporating the effects of time varying packet loss distortions. The time distribution of packet loss during a VoIP call is modelled by a 4 state Markov model. From estimates of the Markov model parameters computed from the RTP stream a new equipment impairment factor *Ie* is computed. In addition, Clark also proposed E-model modifications to take account of time-varying perception of voice

Table 5. Relation between R-value, MOS-CQE and user satisfaction

R-value (lower limit)	MOS-CQE (lower limit)	User satisfaction
90	4.34	Very satisfied
80	4.03	Satisfied
70	3.60	Some users dissatisfied
60	3.10	Many users dissatisfied
50	2.58	Nearly all users dissatisfied

quality. The second approach has been proposed by Broom and Hollier (2003) and is known as PsyVoIP. This model is based on multiple parameters extracted from the packet stream and is calibrated for a specific VoIP device. The calibration is achieved by performing speech quality measurements of the device under test (DUT) and then training a numerical model to predict the MOS scores for each condition. At the core of PsyVoIP is a software module (probe), which combines all the software components that capture packets, extract call-streams, parameterise VoIP degradations, and predict voice quality. The architecture of the probe is depicted in Figure 3. Packets that are captured from the network by a capture module are passed to the call identification module (call_id). Following this, the pre-process module retains the relevant information to the probe and out of sequence packets are reordered by a re-sequence processing module. The voice activity detection (VAD) module enables packet identification as carrying either voice samples or non-voiced samples. Finally, relevant voice-quality parameters are extracted from the packet stream and a MOS prediction is made.

Both of the above-described models have been subject to standardisation by ITU-T. Instead of selecting a winner, a new ITU-T standard, P.564 is currently being considered by ITU-T study group 12 (Rix, Beerends, Kim, Kroon, & Ghitza, 2006). Under the working title P.VTQ (voice quality transmission) the standard is expected to recommend a method of performance assessment similar to the calibration process used by PsyVoIP. This method could then be used to determine the accuracy of a VoIP objective model.

There are several other network-based models proposed that are based on the ITU-T E-model. Amongst them are those proposed by Takahashi, Kurashima, and Yoshino (2006), Aoki, Kurashima, and Takahashi (2006), Meddahi and Afifi (2006), Masuda and Hayashi (2006), Sun and Ifeachor (2006), Picovici, Raja, and Flanagan (2006), and Narbutt and Pomy (2007). However, at least one of the following problems is associated to all of them:

- The impact of different types of packet loss distributions on voice quality is not addressed. The proposed models either employ the tabulated data available in ITU-T standards, or are based on a large number of curve-fitting parameters, and make the model applicable only to random packet loss.

- The additive assumption underlying the ITU-T E-model is not questioned. It is important to mention that the E-model was developed for stationary degradations and not for time-varying ones like packet loss.

- Most of the models assume that the only types of degradations to be expected are based on delays and codecs under packet loss conditions.

- In several cases some of the model parameters themselves are estimated using signal-based models such as PESQ. This approach may be valid for cases when errors based on packet loss are not present. The PESQ accuracy has been questioned several times especially with regard to bursty packet loss.

Figure 3. PsyVoIP probe architecture

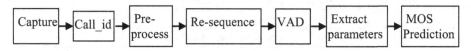

Recently the authors proposed a new model (currently under review) for time-varying VoIP quality estimation for wireless networks. The model is extending the ITU-T legacy E-model in order to count for the perceptual relevance of the packet loss distortions. Evaluation results for VoIP over IEEE 802.11 wireless networks indicate that the proposed model outperforms the ITU-T legacy E-model and ITU-T PESQ for the investigated testing conditions.

Monitoring Models

Monitoring models can be used to control the performance of an existing network, to identify and solve in advance possible problems before the network's users are dissatisfied. Depending on the nature of monitoring, these models can be further classified as intrusive and non-intrusive.

Intrusive measurements use specific test calls and measurement signals such as noise or voice are transmitted across the network. From a comparison of the input (undistorted) signal and output (distorted) signal, a direct quality estimate or quality-relevant network parameters can be obtained. Most of the signal-based models described above can be used as intrusive monitoring models.

Non-intrusive measurements can connect at a specific point of the network and acquire a measurement signal during normal network operation. From this signal, network or other parameters relevant to voice quality can be derived. However, due to non-availability of the original (or input) voice signal such a measure is very difficult to realise. In general, there are two different approaches to realise a non-intrusive objective voice quality measure (Veaux & Barriac, 2002) *priori-based* and *source-based*.

Priori-Based Approach

This approach is based on identifying a set of well-characterised distortions and learning a statistical relationship between this finite set and subjective opinions. An example of such a non-intrusive approach is the speech quality measure known as ITU Rec. P.562, which uses in-service, non-intrusive measurement devices (INMD) (ITU-T Recommendation P.562, 2000). An INMD is a device that has access to the voice channels and performs measurements of objective parameters on live call traffic, without interfering with the call in any way. Data produced by an INMD about the network connection, together with knowledge about the network and the human auditory system, are used to make predictions of call clarity in accordance with ITU-T Rec. P.800 (ITU-T Recommendation P.800, 1996).

In 2000, Gray, Hollier, and Massara (2000) reported a novel use of the vocal-tract modelling technique, which enables the prediction of the quality of a network degraded speech stream to be made in a non-intrusive way. However, although good results were reported, the technique suffers from the followings drawbacks (Gray et al., 2000): (a) its performance seems to be affected by the gender of the speaker, (b) its application is limited to speech signals with a relatively short duration in time, (c) its performance is influenced by distorted signals with a constant level of distortions, and (d) the vocal-tract parameters are only meaningful when they are extracted from a speech stream that is the result of glottal excitation illuminating an open tract. More recently, a number of non-intrusive voice quality measures based mainly on statistical models have been reported (Chen & Parsa, 2005; Kim, 2005, 2006). All the previously described methods can be used with confidence for the types of well-known distortions. However, none of them have been verified with very large numbers of possible distortions.

In 2004, the ITU-T approved a new model as Recommendation. P.563: "Single ended method for objective speech quality assessment in narrow-band telephony applications" (ITU-T Recommendation P.563, 2004). The P.563 approach is the first recommended method for single-ended non-intrusive voice quality measurement applications that takes into account the full range of distortions occurring in public switched telephony networks (PSTN) and is able to predict the voice quality on a perception-based scale MOS–LQO according to ITU-T Recommendation P.800.1 (ITU-T Recommendation P.800.1, 2003). For this model the reference signal is generated from the transmitted speech signal using linear predictive coding techniques. As illustrated in Figure 4, the artificial reference signal is used in a similar manner as the real reference signal. Several issues such as high additional noised, time varying characteristics, unnatural voices are addressed by a parametric analysis processing block and are considered in the final time-averaging and mapping process.

The reported experimental results indicate that this non-intrusive measure compares favourably with the first generation of intrusive perceptual models such as PSQM. ITU-T recommended that P.563 should be used for voice quality measurement in 3.1 kHz (narrow-band) telephony applications only. As the case with PESQ, the ITU-T emphasises that the P.563 algorithm cannot be used to replace subjective testing but it can be applied

for measurements where auditory tests would be too expensive or not applicable at all. However, the current P.563 model seems to yield limited performance compared to the PESQ (Kim, 2006). The average correlation between the MOS_LQS and MOS_LQO estimated by the P.563 is about 0.88 even for the 24 known MOS test databases used in the development of the model, whereas the PESQ shows 0.93 correlation for the same task. In addition, it has recently been reported that the performance of P.563 is quite unsatisfactory for some MOS test conditions that were not included in the model development, such as test data containing selectable mode vocoder for which a correlation of as low as 0.7 was obtained (Kim, 2006).

Source-Based Approach

This approach represents a more universal method that is based on a prior assumption of the expected clean signal rather than on the distortions that may occur. The approach handles an ample range of distortion types, where the distortions are characterised by comparing some properties of the degraded signal with a priori model of these

Figure 4. Principle of non-intrusive signal-based measures (Raake, 2006)

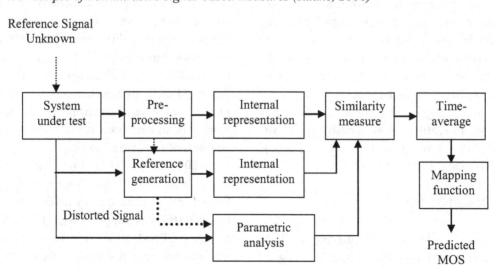

properties for clean signal. One attempt to implement such an approach was reported by Jin and Kubichek (1995). The proposed method is based on an algorithm, which uses perceptual-linear prediction (PLP) model to compare the perceptual vectors extracted from the distorted speech with a set of perceptual vectors derived from a variety of non degraded clean source speech material. However, the method reported is computationally involved since it was based on the use of a basic Vector Quantization technique.

Recently, Picovici and Mahdi (2004) proposed a new perception-based measure for voice quality evaluation using the source-based approach. Since the original speech signal is not available for this measure, an alternative reference is needed in order to objectively measure the level of distortion of the distorted speech. The method is based on computing objective distances between perceptually-based parametric vectors representing degraded speech signal to appropriately matching reference vectors extracted from a pre-formulated reference codebook, which is constructed from the database of clean speech records. The computed distances provide a reflection of the distortion of the received speech signal. In order to simulate the functionality of a subjective listening test, the system maps the measured distance into MOS_LQO. Its performance has been compared to that of both the ITU-T PESQ and ITU-T Recommendation P.563 (Picovici et al., 2004; Picovici et al., 2006). Reported evaluation results revealed that the proposed method offers a sufficiently high level of accuracy in predicting the MOS-LQS scores and outperforms the PESQ in a large number of test cases particularly those related to distortion caused by channel impairments and signal level modifications. It also provides similar accuracy to that of the ITU-T Recommendation P.563, while offering superior performance in terms of computational efficiency. It should be noted that the accuracy of a system of this nature normally depends on the coverage of the codebook with regards to speaker variation and number of clean

speech signals. This, in turn, would determine the size of the codebook and hence the processing time and the memory requirements of the system. Thus, a trade-off between accuracy and processing time for the target application has to be worked out.

VOICE QUALITY FOR WIRELESS NETWORKS

Despite the fact that existing telecommunications telephone companies are loosing customers to mobile (cellular) service providers, there is a constant perception that the voice over a mobile connection would deliver inferior voice quality and therefore it is not a realistic alternative to the traditional copper wires of the PSTN. In reality for mobile service providers, this is rarely the case as the systems were designed and managed from the outset to support voice. On the other hand, as wired service providers and network administrators have constantly found, until the recent improvements in routers and bandwidth availability, that voice is one of the hardest services to provision even on a totally wired IP network.

The cost effectiveness of accessing the Internet through a combination of the Wi-Fi Wireless LANs and broadband has resulted in a growing commercial interest in supporting Wireless VoIP telephony. This, together with developments such as Unlicensed Mobile Access (UMA) to allow a single handset to roam between mobile and Wireless LAN network types, provide the necessary impetus to find ways of improved provisioning and better management of voice quality. Progress in the voice over wireless networks industry, point to some exciting developments (addressing delay, jitter, bandwidth and packet loss) that overcome the primary objections to voice over wireless networks (Ohrtman, 2004).

As the VoIP industry matures, existing and new means of measuring the difference in voice quality between a voice over wireless network and

PSTN have been proposed. Currently there are two tests available (subjective and objective) that provide the necessary metrics for voice over wireless networks quality assessment. The first one is using subjective testing and has been detailed in Section 2 (subjective determination of voice quality). The second one is based on objective models that has emerged with the increasingly popularity of VoIP. Amongst all models reviewed and presented in Section 3 (Objective determination of voice quality) the most used ones are: PSQM, PESQ, ITU-T Recommendation G.107 (E-model) and its extended versions, and ITU-T Recommendation P.563. To put this in context the next subsection describes state of the art in the associated test equipment.

Testing Voice Quality in Wireless Networks

An example of voice quality assessment in wireless networks (IEEE 802.11) given below is using the comprehensive wireless LAN test platform devised by Azimuth. The Azimuth WLAN Test Platform (www.azimuthsystems.com) is a wireless test network that allows automated, sophisticated,

and advanced testing and measurement of 802.11 wireless devices that result in repeatable, reliable, and consistent test results. The Azimuth W-Series WLAN Test Platform allows the creation of an 802.11 simulated test environment in which attenuation is used to virtually distance test devices from each other. By attenuating signals in the Azimuth W-Series WLAN Test Platform, one can virtually move stations, access points (APs) and application specific devices (ASDs) closer or further away from each other. By using attenuation to virtually position devices, and by customizing traffic using the internal traffic generator, it is possible to create a wide variety of test scenarios such as roaming stations, overlapping/non-overlapping BSSs, and hidden stations.

Internal traffic generators in the Azimuth Systems solution facilitate the determination of the origin and destination of traffic and customized frame patterns, frame lengths, numbers of frames, and test duration. It is possible to generate traffic originating from either a wireless station or Ethernet port, and to designate the destination of that traffic. The traffic generator sends user-selectable frame patterns and frame lengths. The duration of traffic generation testing

Figure 5. VoWiFi handset range test. (Reproduced by permission of Azimuth Systems)

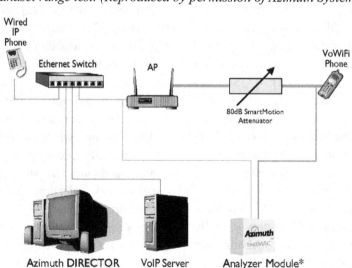

is also user-selectable; the traffic can be generated continuously, according to a set duration (in milliseconds), or according to a designated number of frames. As illustrated in Figure 5, the quality of voice transmission over Wi-Fi as a function of path loss, roaming, and traffic load test has the following features:

- Automatically validates voice over Wi-Fi performance
- Standard benchmark test to analyze rate adaptation of handset and AP pair
- Determines the e-model's r-factor and MOS performance of real time voice stream: measures packet loss, delay, and jitter to formulate MOS score
- Precise RF control allows for measurement of true range performance based on actual WiFi-enabled handsets

The test functionality is as follows: The WiFi phone is associated with the access point (AP) over an 80 dB SmartAttenuator. The AP is connected to a wired IP phone using a standard 10/100Mbs Ethernet switch. The Azimuth testMAC (TMM)

module captures the traffic from both wireless and wired channels. In addition, the analyser part of the module extracts some of the network-based parameters such as delay, packet loss, and jitter. Preliminary results of these parameters are detailed in Figure 6, Figure 7, and Figure 8. In addition, Figure 9 illustrates the topology view of the VoWiFi Handset Range Test at 80 dB attenuation. This attenuation is equivalent to a distance of 104 meters between the two phones (as shown in Figure 10) using the conversion from dB to meters using the Azimuth's outdoor model.

Figure 6 illustrates the VoWiFi handset range test, delay vs. range. As previously shown, the maximum average delay is 60 ms, which represents an acceptable value for VoIP quality. The maximum acceptable value for delay in VoIP is 150-200 ms.

Figure 7 shows the VoWiFi handset range test, packet loss vs. range. Results indicates that for upstream traffic, after 50 dB there is a 100% packet loss, which is not acceptable in a normal VoIP transmission.

Figure 8 illustrates the VoWiFi handset range test, average jitter vs. range. The downstream

Figure 6. VoWiFi delay vs. range

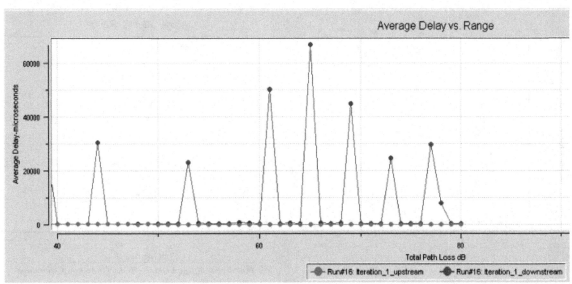

traffic indicates jitter variations with a maximum value of just over 25 ms.

Figure 9 shows the topology view for the VoWiFi Handset Range Test. As can be seen in the previous figure, there is a 80dB attenuation between the two phones.

Figure 10 indicates that at 80 dB attenuation the distance between the two phones is equivalent to 92 meters using the outdoor conversion model.

Although in a normal VoIP telephone conversation some of the results shown above are not acceptable, Figures 6 to 10 are shown here to give an insight of how the results are presented in

Figure 7. VoWiFi packet loss vs. range

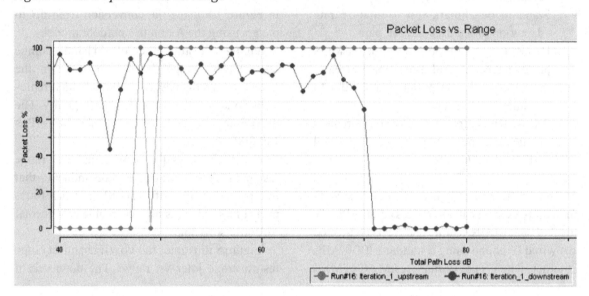

Figure 8. VoWiFi jitter vs. range

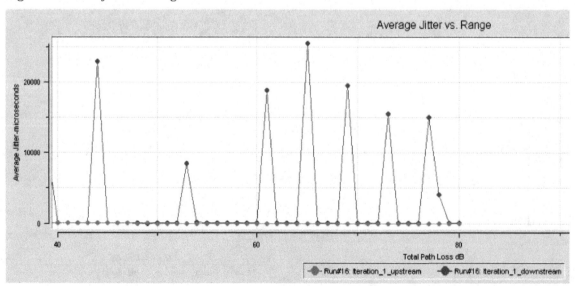

Figure 9. Topology view of the VoWiFi handset range test at 80 dB attenuation

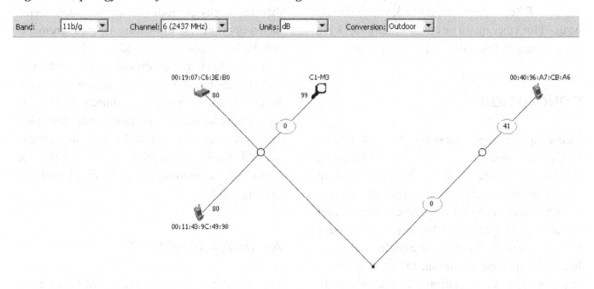

Figure 10. Topology view of the VoWiFi handset range test in meters using the outdoor conversion model

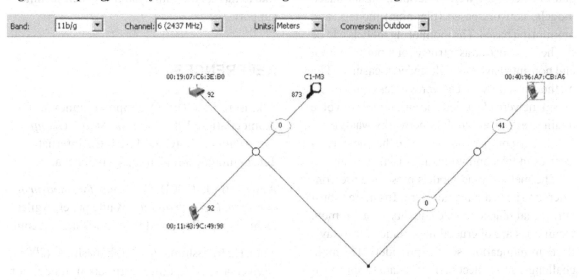

a VoWiFi handset range test using the Azimuth WLAN Test Platform.

MOST WIDELY USED METHODS

Although Sections 2 &3 have provided a detailed review of most existent perceptual voice quality measurement, this section presents a comparison between the most used metrics and their performance.

The first most used metric is represented by the ITU-T Recommendation, Rec. P.862, which specifies the Perceptual evaluation of speech quality (PESQ).

The second most used metric is represented by the ITU-T Recommendation P.563, which should be used for voice quality measurement in 3.1 kHz (narrow-band) telephony applications only.

CONCLUSION

This chapter presented a detailed review of currently used methods and metrics for measuring the perceptual voice quality and their application to wireless networks. The tests and methods recommended by ITU-T for subjective determination of voice quality were detailed. A comprehensive review of various objective voice quality measures highlighting their evolution, target application and performance limitation was also given. In particular, three main categories of objective voice quality measures were described: signal-based models, network-based (planning) models, and monitoring based. The monitoring models can be further categorised as intrusive or input-to-output and non-intrusive or single ended measures. The methods used for voice over wireless quality assessment were identified and an example of voice quality testing in wireless networks was given. Finally, a comparison between the most used metrics in telecommunications is also given.

The methods and models presented are considered to be in a transition period as more robust perceptual objective voice quality measurement techniques are of crucial importance for today's telecommunications service providers. The main challenge is to collect sufficient data to appropriately model the very wide range of types of errors that may occur in current mobile (cellular) and wireless channels, such as data rate variation, codec-related errors and various types and levels of interference. Currently, the main effort is improving the E-model and its extended versions to overcome the simplified assumptions thereby ensuring wider applicability. Nevertheless, the intrusive and non-intrusive perceptual models are continuously improving and are favoured

given their use of real voice samples. Given the distinct merits of both the network and signal based approaches, the future in measurements will be based upon combined models.

Given the characteristics of wireless networks and driven by service level agreements, call-by-call monitoring will be required, and results stored and classified. In addition, prediction based upon previous results will be used to estimate the call quality in advance, in order to provide cost-effective network selection and voice quality management.

ACKNOWLEDGMENT

This work has been funded by SFI under the NCNRC project 03/CE.2/I315. The authors would like to thank Azimuth System for their technical support.

REFERENCES

Atkinson, D. J. (1997). Proposed annex to recommendation P.861. *ITU-T Study Group 12 Contribution 24* (Com 12-24 E), International Telecommunication Union, CH-Geneva.

Anderson, J. (2001). *Methods for measuring perceptual speech quality*. White paper, Agilent technologies. Retrieved from www.agilent.com

Aoki, H., Kurashima, A., & Takahashi, A. (2006). Conversational quality estimation model for wideband IP-telephony services. *International Conference on Spoken Language Processing* (pp.1069-1072).

Broom, S., & Hollier, M. (2003). Speech quality measurement tools for dynamic network management. *Measurement of Speech and Audio Quality in Networks Conference*, Czech Technical University.

Beerends, J., & Stemerdink, J. (1994). A perceptual speech quality measure based on a psychoacoustic sound representation. *Journal of Audio Eng. Soc.*, 115-123.

Beerends, J. G., Meijer, E. J., & Hekstra, A. P. (1997). Improvement of the P.861 perceptual speech quality measure. *Contribution to COM 12-20 ITU-T Study Group 12*, International Telecommunication Union, CH-Geneva.

Clark, A. D. (2003). *Description of VQMON algorithm*. International Telecomm. Union Del. Cont. COM12-D105.

Chen, G., & Parsa, V. (2005). Bayesian model based non-intrusive speech quality evaluation. *IEEE International Conference on Acoustics, Speech, and Signal Processing* (pp. I-385-388).

Gray, P., Hollier, M. P., & Massara, R. E. (2000). Non-intrusive speech quality assessment using vocal-tract models. In *IEEE Proc.-Vis. Image Signal Process* (pp. 493-501).

ITU-T Recommendation E. 800. (1994). *Terms and definitions related to quality of service and network performance including dependability*. International Telecommunication Union CH-Geneva.

ITU-T Recommendation P.800. (1996). *Methods for subjective determination of transmission quality*. International Telecommunication Union CH-Geneva.

ITU-T. Recommendation P.861. (1996). *Objective quality measurement of telephone-band (300-3400 Hz) speech codecs*. International Telecommunication Union, CH-Geneva.

ITU-T Recommendation P.562. (2000). *Analysis and interpretation of INMD voice-service measurements*. International Telecommunication Union CH-Geneva.

ITU-T Recommendation P.862. (2001). *Perceptual evaluation of speech quality (PESQ), an objective method for end-to-end speech quality assessment of narrowband telephone networks and speech codecs*. International Telecommunication Union CH-Geneva.

ITU-T. Recommendation P.862.1. (2003). *Mapping function for transforming P.862 raw result scores to MOS-LQO*. International Telecommunication Union, CH-Geneva.

ITU-T. Recommendation P.800.1. (2003). *Recommendation P.800.1, mean opinion score (MOS) terminology*. International Telecommunication Union CH-Geneva.

ITU-T Recommendation P.563. (2004). *Single ended method for objective speech quality assessment in narrow-band telephony applications*. International Telecommunication Union, CH-Geneva.

ITU-T Recommendation G. 107. (2005). *The E-model, a computational model for use in transmission planning*. International Telecommunication Union CH-Geneva.

Itakura, F., & Saito, S. (1978). Analysis synthesis telephony based on the maximum likelihood method. *Proceedings 6th Int. Congr. Acoust.*, (pp. c17-c20).

Johnson, J. (1998). Transform coding of audio signals using perceptual noise criteria. *IEEE J. Select. Areas Comm.*, 314-323.

Jin, C., & Kubichek, R., (1995). Output-based objective speech quality using vector quantization techniques. *Proc. ASILOMAR. Conf. On Signals, Systems and Computers* (pp. 1291-1294).

Kim, D. S. (2005). ANIQUE: An auditory model for single-ended speech quality estimation. *IEEE Trans. Speech and Audio Process* (pp. 821-831).

Kim, D. S. (2006). Enhanced perceptual model for non-intrusive speech quality assessment. *IEEE Intl. Conf. Acoustics, Speech, and Signal Process* (pp. I-829-832).

Meddahi, A., & Afifi, H. (2006). Packet E-model: E-model for VoIP quality evaluation. *Journal of Computer Networks*, 2659-2675.

Masuda, M., & Hayashi, T. (2006). Non-intrusive quality monitoring method of VoIP speech based on network performance metrics. In *IEICE Transactions Communications* (pp. 304-312).

Narbutt, M., & Pomy, J. (2007). The e-model based quality contours for predicting speech transmission quality and user satisfaction from time-varying transmission impairments. *Appendix I to ITU-T Recommendation G.109*.

Quackenbush, S. R., Barnawell, T. P., & Clements, M. A. (1988). *Objective measures of speech quality*. Prentice Hall Press.

Quatieri, T. E. (2002). *Discrete-time speech signal processing: Principles and practice*. Prentice Hall Press.

Ohrtman, F. (2004). *Voice over 802.11*. Arthec House Inc. Press.

Picovici, D., & Mahdi, A. E. (2004). New output-based perceptual measure for predicting subjective quality of speech. *IEEE International Conference on Acoustics, Speech, and Signal Processing* (pp. 633-636).

Picovici, D., Raja, A., & Flanagan, C. (2006). Real-time non-intrusive VoIP evaluation using second generation network processor. *IEEE International Conference on Acoustic, Speech, and Signal Processing Proceedings,* published on DVD, IEEE Cat No.:06CH37812C.

Picovici, D., Mahdi, A. E., & Murphy, T. (in press). New output-based objective measure for non-intrusive speech quality evaluation. *Digital Signal Processing Journal*. Elsevier.

Raake, A. (2006). *Speech quality of VoIP assessment and prediction*. John Wiley & Sons, Ltd Press.

Rix, A., Beerends, J. G., Kim, D. S., Kroon, P., & Ghitza, O. (2006). Objective assessment of speech and audio quality-technology and applications. *IEEE Transactions on Audio, Speech, and Language Processing* (pp. 1890-1901).

Rix, A. W., & Hollier, M. P. (2000). The perceptual analysis measurement system for robust end-to-end speech quality assessment. *IEEE International Conference on Acoustics, Speech, and Signal Processing* (pp. 1-4).

Sun, L., & Ifeachor, E. C. (2006). Voice quality prediction models and their application in VoIP networks. *IEEE Transactions on Multimedia* (pp. 809-820).

Takahashi, A., Kurashima, A., & Yoshino, H. (2006). Objective assessment methodology for estimating conversational quality in VoIP. *IEEE Transactions on Audio, Speech, and Language Processing* (pp. 1984-1993).

Voran, S. (1999). Objective estimation of perceived speech quality--Part I: Development of the measuring normalizing block technique. *IEEE Trans. On Speech and Audio Process* (pp. 371-382).

Voran, S. (1994). Techniques for comparing objective and subjective speech quality tests. *Proc. IEEE Workshop on Speech Quality Assessment* (pp. 59-64).

Veaux, C., & Barriac, V. (2002). Perceptually motivated non-intrusive assessment of speech quality. In *Proceedings On-line Workshop on Measurement of Speech and Audio Quality in Networks*. Retrieved from http://wireless.feld.cvut.cz/mesaqin 2002/full11.pdf

Wang, S., Sekey, A., & Gersho, A. (1992). An objective measure for predicting subjective quality of speech coders. *IEEE J. Select. Areas Comm.*, 819-829.

Yang, W., Benbouchta, M., & Yantorno, R. (1997). Performance of a modified bark spectral distortion measure as an objective speech quality measure. *IEEE Proc. International Conference on Acoustics, Speech, and Signal Processing* (pp. 541-544).

Yang, W. (1999). *Enhanced modified bark spectral distortion (EMBSD)*. PhD Thesis, Temple University, Philadelphia.

Chapter XII
Enhancing the Multimedia Tour Guide Experience:
Transmission Tailoring Based on Content, Location, and Device Type

Tacha Serif
Brunel University, UK

Gheorghita Ghinea
Brunel University, UK

ABSTRACT

This chapter describes an investigation exploring user experiences of accessing streamed multimedia content, when that content is tailored according to perceptual, device and location characteristics. It builds upon the findings of our user perception evaluations by harnessing the results together to create pre-defined profiles based on QoP requirements, device type, and location for context-aware multimedia content streaming, and, in so doing, enhance the concept of context to include perceptual requirements. In the light of the findings, we propose that multimedia transmission to mobile and wireless devices should be made based on pre-defined profiles, which contains a combination of static (perceptual, device type, CPU speed, and display specifications) and dynamic information (streamed content type location of the device/user, context of the device/user). Furthermore, we believe that using profiling technology mobile service providers can effectively manage local network traffic and cut down their bandwidth costs considerably.

INTRODUCTION

As computing environments become mobile and information access on the move commonplace, computing research has extended to cover contextual information such as a user's location, situation, and circumstances. Although multimedia has been previously tailored according to user location (Abowd, Atkeson, Hong, Long, & Pinkerton, 1996; Burigat & Chittaro, 2005) and device (Buyukkokten, Garcia-Molina, Paepcke, & Winograd, 2000; Fox et al., 1998; Freire, Kumar, & Lieuwen, 2001), such tailoring until now has ignored perceptual quality considerations, even though, as we have shown in previous work (Ghinea & Thomas, 2005) bandwidth--scarce resource in a ubiquitous computing environment--could be more efficiently utilized this way. Nonetheless, to the best of our knowledge, no research has explored user multimedia perception and experiences when supported by a GPS (global positioning system) based, location aware, mobile guide--the focus of our study, described in this chapter.

CONTEXT AWARE COMPUTING

Advances in computing hardware and software technologies are key factors behind the proliferation of mobile computing. However, the initial ideas on mobile technologies and devices came from Weiser, according to whose vision the most profound technologies are the ones that weave themselves into the fabric of everyday life until they are undistinguishable from it (1991). Weiser in his articles identifies two crucially important issues, namely location and communication, which are necessary to initiate the "disappearance" of wired computing and create the conditions necessary for the birth and growth of location and context-aware computing (Want et al., 1995; Weiser, 1991, 1993, 1998).

Following the introduction to the concept of context-aware computing and its definition, some example studies will now be reviewed. One of the earliest was ParcTab (Want et al., 1995), which was implemented at the Xerox PARC Research Labs based on the vision of Mark Weiser. The main objectives of this project were:

- To design a mobile hardware device, the PARCTAB, that enables personal communication
- To design an architecture that supports mobile computing
- To construct context-sensitive applications that exploit this architecture
- To test the entire system in an office community.

As part of this prototype application, devices such as a palmtop computer, an electronic notepad, and an electronic whiteboard were used. The result of this work was a digital office facilitated with some intelligent electronic gadgets. All the devices in use as part of this project were connected to the local area network using infrared (IR) connections, which also enabled the location management of the users. Knowing the location of the user, the relevant communications (e.g., emails and phone calls) were then routed accordingly to the user's physical location or computer terminal.

The active badge project conducted at Olivetti Research Laboratories in Cambridge, UK, in the late 90s significantly affected context-aware computing through the implementation of the first indoor positioning system (Want, Hopper, Falcao, & Gibbons, 1992). The system was initially implemented as a substitute for the pager system that was used to locate members of staff and assist receptionists with their switchboard operations and is facilitated with wearable badges, sized 55x55x7mm and weighing 40grams, to produce a unique code for approximately a tenth of a second every 15 seconds. These transmissions are then picked up by receivers, which are scattered around the host building. The received signal is then relayed to a location server processing the location of the user.

One of the earliest examples of combining indoor and outdoor positioning technologies is the Cyberguide (Abowd et al., 1996). This system was initially implemented as a building guide for the department open days at the Georgia Institute of Technology and then improved to guide its users throughout the whole city of Atlanta. The core functionality of the system is divided into four components:

- **Map component:** This contains cartographical data about the physical surroundings of the user, such as the location of the buildings, interesting sights within a building, or pathways that the user can access.
- **Information component:** This provides information about the sights that a tourist might encounter during his or her visit. The users of the system can get information about the building and the people associated with these areas. This component is also responsible for answering specific questions of the user such as "Who works in this office?" or "Who painted this picture?"
- **Navigator component:** This identifies the location of the user within a given area. This service is facilitated using a positioning module that delivers accurate information on the user's location and orientation.
- **Messenger component:** The user of the guide can interact or leave a message to the tour leader. Additionally, this module can broadcast messages to other tourists in the surrounding area.

Evaluation of the system with users highlighted issues with respect to the positioning at indoor locations and on-screen map representations. During the 10-day evaluation of this system, the incidence of telephone calls not reaching the correct person dropped substantially. Receptionists had a much easier time, since they were able to avoid many wasted trips, up and down corridors, trying to find members of staff. On the other hand, the perception of clients telephoning the laboratory was one of good organization, since the receptionist was able to say with great certainty where somebody was or when they were last seen, or indeed the likelihood that they had just taken a lunch break, all without the need to be explicitly informed by the staff.

In related work, Simcock, Hillenbrand, and Thomas (2003) implement a location-based tourist guide application, using a personal digital assistant (PDA) and a GPS connection, and examine the associated design and usability issues. The main aim of this project was to use off-the-shelf hardware and software components, create a simple and easy to use interface, as well as a simple and easy to update map, and an energy efficient tool that can operate for one fully working day. The main tasks undertaken by the system were to display attraction information in the form of HTML pages relevant to the user's position and to display the user position graphically on a tour map based on co-ordinates received from a GPS device. The user interface had three main modes of interactions: *Map view*, where the user can see his/her location and the surrounding buildings on a map; *Guide view*, where the user is provided with a path of interesting attractions, and finally the *Attractions view*, where the user is streamed audio-visual tourist information. All the color schemes and map annotations are designed in a manner so that they are visible to the user on the move.

From a different perspective, Munoz, Rodriguez, Favela, Martinez-Garcia, and Gonzalez (2003) implemented a context-aware instant messenger system in a hospital environment to share information among the members of staff and provide information about the patients. The context sensitive structure of this system enables the doctors to download the medical records about the patient near them and register time sensitive information regarding the patient to his/her colleague in the next shift. The prototype system evaluation by 13 physicians, 8 nurses, and 7 support staff showed that functionalities such as context-based messaging, user positioning, and access to the patient records on the move was useful and that 91% of the participants would use the system.

MOBILE INFORMATION ACCESS

Improvements in respect of mobile technologies and the affordability of mobile units have made it possible for a large range of clientele to experience mobile information access. Today, according to the figures of National Statistics, 75% of adults in the UK own a mobile phone (National Statistics, 2006). This therefore makes for a huge market for mobile service and content providers, where the estimated multimedia content download value was about £600 million pound sterling in 2005 (eTForecasts, 2005). Also, if one adds wireless enabled PDAs and smartphones to the scene, with 58.5 million unit sales projected by 2008 (eTForecasts, 2005), the conclusion can only be that the trend for accessing information "on the go" is here to stay and will experience a dynamic growth in future years.

Device Impact

Mobile devices generally are compact with small screens and have relatively limited battery, memory and processing capacity, which is why early research in mobile computing concentrated on enhancing the user's mobile information access experience using various techniques and technologies. However, recent advances in hardware technology have made it possible for researchers to explore new application areas of mobile computing (e.g., patient monitoring system, real-time stock brokering). In the following part, existing research and implementations are detailed.

The Event Horizon User Interface model (Taivalsaari, 1999) was proposed to overcome some of the limitations of small screen mobile devices, such as personal digital assistants, by compressing and expanding objects radially farther away or closer to an event horizon in the middle of the screen.

In related work, Kim and Albers (2001) explored how the amount of text presented on a PDA affects a person's ability to retrieve information and identified factors which may affect the user's ability access and use the information on a PDA screen. To evaluate the information search burden caused by the PDA size and identify the difference between the normal computer monitor and a small PDA screen, they implemented a questionnaire in conjunction with a set of tasks that require the user to make search on 650-word Web page. Contrary to their initial hypothesis that the participants would exhibit more errors when searching for information on the small screen, repeated MANOVA (multivariate analysis of the variance) measures showed that differences between two conditions were not significant. The main experimental hypotheses on participants taking more time when searching, locating information in the middle and end of the Web pages rather than in the beginning and locating textual information rather than numerical information on a small screen, were also proven to be wrong.

In a similar study, Jones, Marsden, Mohd-Nasir, N., Boone, and Buchanan (1999) compared the Web browsing experience difference between small and traditional computer monitors. The main aim of this study was to quantify the effect of small display space on Web-based task completion and to gain qualitative impressions on how reduced displays might affect the ways users approach Web-based information retrieval. Participants in this experiment were 20 computing science staff and students, made up of both males and females ages ranging between 18-45. As part of the experiment, participants were divided into two groups, normal screen and small screen users, and asked to complete two sets of tasks on a Website. The normal screen experiments were conducted on a browser with its display resolution set to 1074x768 pixels. On the other hand, the small screen device users were asked to complete the tasks on a 640x480 pixels screen resolution to simulate the size of a small display device.

Results showed that the large screen group answered twice as many questions correctly as the small screen group. Also, questionnaire results highlighted that the smaller screen size impedes task performance – 80% of small screen users indicated that they felt screen size impacted on their ability to complete the tasks; this compares with 40% of large screen users.

To enhance the user's Web browsing experience on a low bandwidth, small display and slow CPU, Buyukkokten et al. (2000) propose the use of *power browser*. In this system, there are five main elements, namely the client PDA, wireless modem, power browsing proxy server, WebBase and the Web content (Figure 1).

The connection between the PDA and the Proxy Server is established through a wireless modem. The server has a wired link to the Web, and therefore downloads the pages faster. It processes the data and sends only a small fraction of it to the client at a time. The proxy server uses local tools, such as an HTML parser, and an incremental

crawler, which can recursively fetch the linked Web pages to the user's current page. The main functionality of the WebBase in this structure is its knowledge base in ranking the Web page content and summarising them according to the user's mobile device. To evaluate the system, 10 participants were asked to perform a total of six tasks with and without using the Power Browser prototype system. The results showed that the Power Browser system average helped user on average to save 45% of browsing time and 42% of pen action.

For the same purpose, Fox et al. (1998) implemented an adaptive middleware proxy which re-formats traditional Web pages and their content to improve the user's Web browsing experience on a Palm Pilot PDA. The proposed system is structured in a way that all browsing requests sent by the PDAs are relayed to a proxy server, which acts as a gateway to the internet via a fast wired connection. The proxy server itself has the capability of transformation, aggregation, caching and customization to tailor personalised content based on the user's profile. These functionalities are facilitated using three main units that reside within the proxy server:

- **Image and HTML Processor:** The image processor reads GIF and JPEG images (the

Figure 1. The Power Browser Architecture (Buyukkokten et al., 2000)

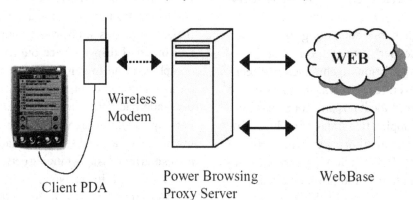

two most common Web formats), converts them to an intermediate bitmap form, optionally scales, color-quantizes and dithers, and finally outputs the result in either the Palm Pilot's native image format.

- **The HTML Processor:** This parses HTML markup, maps HTML tags to supported font attributes, and generates an intermediate-form page layout. Because the HTML processor knows the client's font metrics and display properties, it can wrap text, flow text around inline images.

- **Aggregators:** An aggregator queries one or more Web sites for specific content and collates and formats the results for presentation to the client.

Additionally Zip, PalmOS, and Doc support in the case the client fetches a Zip file (a popular format for PalmPilot software archives), the zip processor formats a listing of the archive contents in HTML, such that following the link for a particular archive member will cause the zip processor to return the selected member. Performance comparison showed that despite the fact the comparative examples were text-only proxies, the proposed system was still faster overall.

In related work, Freire et al. (2001) facilitate the user's access of Web information, entertainment and e-commerce on the go. The proposed system, called WebViews, is a solution for creating customized views of Web content and services. The main idea is to let end-users easily create and maintain simplified views of Web content and services, from news headlines to bank balances by allowing users to create their own Web views, customised for specific devices. In addition, since these Web views provide a simpler view of sites and services, they are considerably simpler to transcode into other languages (or formats).

There are two main steps involved in creating Web views: retrieving a Web page that contains the desired information, and extracting relevant content from the retrieved page. On a desktop computer, using a browser and the WebViews Recorder applet (Figure 2), a user can create a Web view by simply browsing the desired page and selecting on that page the components of interest. After a Web view is created, its content can then be accessed through a WebViews server, using any one of the access devices such as a WAP-enabled phone, Palm PDA or conventional phone.

Chandrasekaran and Joship (2002) in their work address issues related to mobility, personalization and asynchronous operation to support efficient access to the World Wide Web. As a solution they propose a prototype, called MobileIQ, which performs mobility management at the application layer. In this system the authors aim to exploit the Web caching by dynamically migrating the user to the nearest replica Web content. Thus, users no longer need to maintain a constant connection to the original source.

MobileIQ is a proxy-based system that aggregates Web content on the wired side based on user profiles and provides it to the user when they connect to the proxy. The system has also been designed to offer personalization and asynchronous operations to support wireless access to the Web. MobileIQ builds on proxy analogy to add mobility management features, content pre-fetching and location-based information. Using MobileIQ, a given user, while away from his/her home site, does not have to connect to the home proxy server for personalized services, but can use the closest proxy to him/her without having to create a new profile. Wherever the user might be roaming, his/her profile is replicated and sent to the new foreign proxy server. The system also performs local server discovery, user authentication, profile synchronization, content caching, and geographic location based information retrieval.

The scalability evaluation results of the proposed system showed that the general purpose PCs running the MobileIQ proxy server could handle about eight user migrations/second in its best case. The authors believe that by tuning the implementation with dedicated hardware and

Figure 2. WebViews Architecture (Freire et al., 2001)

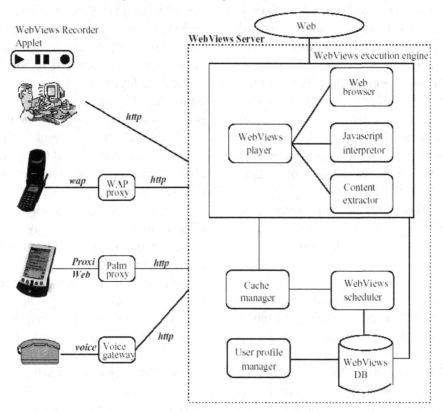

local disks, a proxy can potentially serve a large number of user migrations at a given time.

TV-Anytime applications (TV-Anytime, 2003) allow users to access their profiles remotely with a personal digital assistant and wireless Internet access (Kazasis, Moumoutzis, Pappas, Karanastasi, & Christodoulakis, 2003). Logged in users can search the online database for relevant television programs, documentaries, and movies and download to their home appliances. Using the application, programme previews can be watched online. Moreover, the user can also set the length of the clip according to the network bandwidth and battery lifetime of the personal digital assistant.

Hung and Zhang (2003) have utilized the wireless application protocol (WAP) mobile communication protocol to implement a patient monitoring system. This system consists of three main devices: the WAP-enabled mobile phone, WAP gateway and the content server. The WAP phone initially connects to the gateway and sends requests, which are then converted and sent to the content server. Upon receiving the requests, the content server sends the related data to the gateway, which is then relayed to the end user.

Using this approach, the prototype system provides patient information on the following: ECG browsing heart rate-estimation, blood pressure browsing, patient record browsing, clinic and hospital information inquiry, and doctors appointment browsing. The implemented system was then emulated for usability and functionality evaluation. The results showed that the response time was too long and the security was loose between the device and the content server. The researchers believed, nonetheless, that all these problems could be resolved using the newer version of WAP specifications on third-generation mobile phones.

Understanding the User Mobile Experience

The user's mobile information access experience is of great importance to the continued take-up and proliferation of mobile computing--users will not use mobile devices if the device and/or information access experience is frustrating. This chapter has so far reviewed the diverse range of studies that have been conducted to explore and improve the user mobile information access experience. To this end, even though user perception of multimedia-based information access has been previously explored (Ghinea, 2000; Gulliver & Ghinea, 2003), such work has mainly focused on single, non-mobile devices.

Moreover, while researchers such as Jones et al. (1999) and Buranatrived and Vickers (2004) have explored the impact of small screen devices on the user Web browsing experience and the effect of software applications on mobile devices, respectively, such work was undertaken in a laboratory setting and did not explore the user information access experience in a real-world context. Furthermore, such studies focused on at most two devices, thus ignoring interconnectivity matters, as well as the wider range of mobile devices currently available, and thus issues that might arise when a comparative analysis of the user experience is undertaken.

We also mention that while multimedia content has been previously tailored with respect to device (Buyukkokten et al., 2000; Fox et al., 1998; Freire et al., 2001) and location (Abowd et al., 1996; Burigat et al., 2005), this has not been done through the prism of perceptual requirements. Lastly, it also has to be emphasized that that these issues have not been explored in an integrated manner

and all the related work in this area has been undertaken in an isolated fashion.

PERCEPTUAL-BASED MULTIMEDIA PROFILING

The main aim of our study was to evaluate the user experience of accessing streamed multimedia content tailored according to perceptual requirements as well as location and device type. It seems natural to include perceptual-based considerations in the wireless transmission of multimedia, for user take-up will be reduced, if the perceived quality is deemed to be low.

Recognizing that all multimedia content is situated somewhere along an *infotainment* continuum, we have devised the quality of perception (QoP) metric (Ghinea & Thomas, 1998), which assesses subjective multimedia quality and has two components, both expressed as percentage measures: QoP-IA (information assimilation), representing informational analysis and synthesis, and QoP-S (satisfaction), representing subjective satisfaction with multimedia content. The impact of a multimedia clip on the user experience is then expressed as:

$$Overall \; QoP_{Clip} = Information_{Clip} \; x \; QoP\text{-}IA + Entertainment_{Clip} \; x \; QoP\text{-}S \qquad (1)$$

where:

$$Information_{Clip} = \overline{D} \; x \; W_{I,D} + \overline{A} \; x \; W_{I,A} + \overline{V} \; x \; W_{I,V} + \overline{T} \; x \; W_{I,T} \qquad (2)$$

$$Entertainment_{Clip} = \overline{D} \; x \; W_{E,D} + \overline{A} \; x \; W_{E,A} + \overline{V} \; x \; W_{E,V} + \overline{T} \; x \; W_{E,T} \qquad (3)$$

Here, $\overline{D}$, $\overline{A}$, $\overline{V}$ and $\overline{T}$ stand for the average dynamism, audio, video and textual content respectively of the clip in question, as determined through subjective tests (Ghinea, 2000), while

$W_{I,X}$ and $W_{E,X}$ reflect the relative importance of multimedia component X for information and entertainment, respectively.

We have taken the view that clips, which are highly dynamic tend to imply that they contain predominantly entertainment material, as extracting informational content out of highly dynamic clips has proved to be problematic, whilst fast-paced, dynamic content usually has a high entertainment factor (Ghinea et al., 1998). At the other end of the spectrum, it is relatively unlikely that the appearance of text in content watched predominantly for entertainment purposes adds to the entertainment factor of the clip. Of course, textual information is usually important in content watched mainly for informational purposes. Thus, in our work we have chosen the weights $W_{E,D}=3$, $W_{E,T} = 1$ for entertainment purposes, with $W_{I,D}=1$, $W_{I,T} = 3$ for informational purposes. Previous research (Kawalek, 1995; Watson & Sasse, 1997) has shown the importance of audio cues over video ones, in informational tasks, hence $W_{I,A} = 2$ and $W_{I,V} = 1$. On the other hand, true to the dictum "*that a picture is worth a thousand words,*" we have decided that the video stream has primacy over the audio, when content is viewed for entertainment purposes. Thus, we have $W_{E,V} = 2$, $W_{E,A} = 1$.

In previous works of ours (Ghinea et al., 2005; Gulliver et al., 2003; Gulliver, Serif, & Ghinea,

2004), we have determined frame rates which lead to optimal QoP values, for a wide variety of multimedia infotainment content, and it is these values which make up the perceptual transmission profiles used in our study.

CAMPUS GUIDE APPLICATION

In our study, we developed a campus guide application, which the user ran on a WiFi and GPS-enabled device (Figure 3). Initially the application connects to the content server via the university's wireless Internet access points and downloads a brief description about the buildings within the campus and their locations, using the HTTP (hypertext transfer protocol). Following this, it activates a GPS connection with a satellite and reads the current geographic coordinates of the user. Based on the location data sent by the satellite, the system provides the user with textual information about the surrounding buildings or areas. Whenever the user is around a building recognised by the system, the application updates its interface and enables the audio-visual streaming for the specific location. Upon receiving the streaming request, the content server parses the parameters and identifies the type of device and the location of the user. Accordingly, the server

Figure 3. Application structure diagram

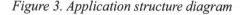
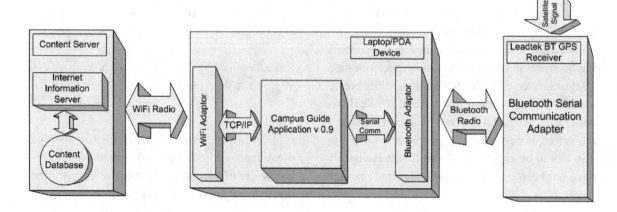

selects suitable content using a knowledge base of pre-defined perceptual transmission profiles, which resides in its backend database, and streams the multimedia content to the user.

APPLICATION WALKTHROUGH

In the course of our experiments, we have used three different display devices and implemented a specialized user interface for each one of them. In the following section, we explain each of the interfaces in detail.

PDA

The campus guide application for the handheld has two main user interface windows, which are the main application and the external video player. The main application window is relatively simple, and contains a university banner at the top of the screen, a textual reminder of the user's current location in bold characters, a textbox with description of the current location and a *Watch Video* button (Figure 4a). Unless the user is around a recognized building or area (such as *St John's Building*) (Figure 4b), the interface disables the

Watch Video button and only reports to the user whether he or she is within the university campus or not.

As soon as the *Watch Video* button is tapped in a recognized location, the main application minimizes itself and runs the local default media player (Figure 4c), which plays the streamed multimedia file in full screen to get as close as possible to the original size of the clip (320x240 pixels).

Laptop

The laptop user interface of the campus guide differs considerably from the PDA version of the same application. The screen resolutions of laptop PCs are considerably higher than the PDAs, thus full screen mode is not essential for original size playback of the multimedia clips. Accordingly, we have designed the window so that it contains all the data in an organized manner by splitting it into two panels. The information panel (left) contains mainly location related data, such as longitude, latitude, satellite time, location banner, description textbox, and play video button. The video panel (right) has an embedded video player, which plays the presentation clip in its original size (Figure 5).

Figure 4. PDA Campus Guide application interface

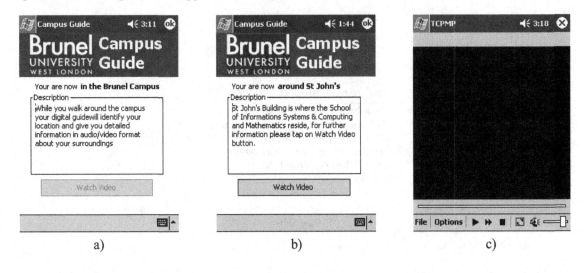

a)   b)   c)

Head Mounted Display

The head-mounted display version of the application is similar to the laptop version with the exception of the video player panel. The panels that do co-exist in the same window in the laptop design had to be split into two full screen windows due to the resolution limitations imposed by the HMD device (Figure 6).

EXPERIMENTAL STUDY

Two experimental variables were manipulated in our study--these were type of device and user location. Accordingly, three types of display devices were considered in our experiments (representing varying levels of user mobility).

Figure 5. Laptop Campus Guide application interface

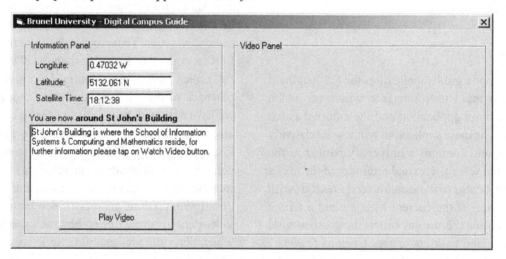

Figure 6. HMD Campus Guide application interface

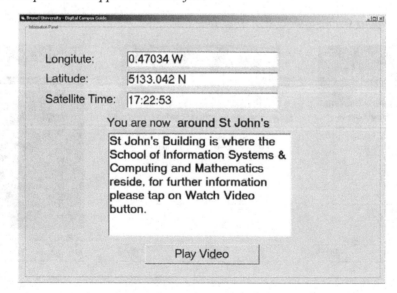

Experimental Devices

A laptop, a PDA, and a head-mounted display were used in our study. The laptop PC used in our experiments was selected from the inventory of the School of Information Systems, Computing, and Mathematics. The selection was made among a Toshiba Satellite P35-S611, a considerably heavy HP Compaq NX9020s and an IBM T20s with a low processing and memory specifications. Accordingly, we picked a Toshiba Satellite P35-S611 Notebook PC, which ran Microsoft Windows XP Professional, and had a 3.33GHz Pentium IV processor, 512MB memory, 100GB hard drive, 17-inch XGA TFT Active Matrix Display and 64MB graphics adapter memory.

The HP iPAQ 5450 PDA has 16-bit touch sensitive transflective thin film translator (TFT) liquid crystal display (LCD) that supports 65,536 colours. The display pixel pitch of the device is 0.24 mm and its viewable image size is 2.26 inch wide and 3.02 inch tall. It runs the Microsoft Windows for Pocket PC 2003 operating system on an Intel 400Mhz XSCALE processor and allows the user complete mobility. Furthermore, it comes with a full wireless connectivity suite, which is made of WiFi (802.11b/g), Bluetooth and Infrared. By default it contains 64MB standard memory and 48MB internal flash ROM. Additionally in the course of some of our experiments a 128 MB secure digital memory card was used for multimedia data storage purposes.

The Olympus Eye-Trek FMD 200 head-mounted display uses two 0.55-inch LCD displays and simulates a display view that is equivalent to a 52-inch screen at a distance of 2 meters. Each one of the displays contains 180.000 pixels and the viewing angle is 30.0° horizontal, 27.0° vertical. It supports phase alternating line (PAL) format and has a display weight of 85grams.

Experimental Material

Three different locations for multimedia access were selected: an information intensive one, an entertainment intensive one, and one which users accessed an equal mix of information and entertainment. In our study, these were given by the Departmental Building (St John's), the University Library (Bannerman Centre), and the university lawn, respectively.

In our experiment, we had to create context-sensitive content for each of the three identified locations. Whilst for St. John's and the Bannerman Centre new clips had to be produced (as previous QoP clips did not contain any information relevant to these locations), for the entertainment-intensive location (the university lawn) we had to identify, from previous QoP content, the clip with the highest entertainment component. We thus calculated the clip infotainment scores, according to Equation (2) and Equation (3), for all 12 QoP clips in light of our previous results (Table 1). From these, we chose the Animation clip, which had the highest entertainment score, as the entertainment intensive clip for the university lawn.

However, as previously remarked, for the St John's Building and the Bannerman Centre, we created, for each of these locations, three different presentation clips. In keeping with the length of previous clips used for QoP experiments, all the newly created clips were 32-second long and in

Table 1. Clip infotainment scores

Clip	$Information_{clip}$	$Entertainment_{clip}$
Commercial	50%	50%
Band	43%	57%
Chorus	47.7%	52.3%
Animation	43%	60.9%
Forecast	56%	44%
Documentary	44.7%	55.3%
Pop Music	52%	48%
News	53.5%	46.5
Cooking	49.6%	50.4%
Rugby	46.3%	53.7%
Snooker	59%	41%
Space	39.1%	57%

320x240-pixel MPEG-1 format. Each of these clips was then evaluated for their overall QoP scores with a pilot study of eight participants. In line with QoP methodology (Ghinea & Thomas, 2000), we also asked each participant to categorize on a scale of {1, 2, 3} the importance, within each of the newly created clips, of its dynamism, as well as of the video, audio, and textual content and in calculating the QoP-IA scores eliminated the questions for which participants fared best and respectively, worst. Ultimately we chose the clip with highest resulting informational component for the St. John's location, and the one with the most balanced informational and entertainment components for the Bannerman Centre clip. The number of questions for each clip targeting the video, audio, and textual components is given in Table 2 and the full listing of the questionnaires can be found in the Appendix.

The clips themselves are (Figure 7):

- **St John's building clip:** Contains a walk-through presentation of the Department of Information Systems and Computing; it has extensive information regarding the number of professors, number of research students, location of lecturers and administration staff, and student facilities.

- **Bannerman Centre clip:** Is a walk-through presentation of the Brunel University, Uxbridge Campus Library. This clip is entertaining as much as it is informative, providing basic information about the library services, and mixing it with more dynamic content such as student union facilities (bar/café shop/refectory) located in the same building.

- **Animation clip:** Features a disagreement between two main characters. Although dynamically limited, there are several subtle nuances in the clip, for example: the correspondence between the stormy weather and the argument.

Table 2. Quality of perception question distribution--video, audio, and textual

Location Video	Video (Number of Questions)	Audio (Number of Questions)	Text (Number of Questions)	Duration (Sec)
St John's (SISCM)	4	4	5	32
Bannerman Centre (Library)	5	4	4	32
Lawn	6	4	0	32

Figure 7. Video clips used in our experiments – in brackets, the (Information, Entertainment) breakdown

Information Intensive (59,41) Clip   Infotainment (50,50)Clip   Entertainment Intensive (39,61)Clip

The frame rate quality for each of the devices was specifically tailored inline with the frame rate, which resulted in highest QoP score for a particular device--described in detail in our previous paper (Gulliver et al., 2003). Accordingly, the frame rate combinations used, based on device type and location, in the course of this experiment are as shown in Table 3.

Participants

Thirty-six users, of average computing ability, took part in the study. These were split into three equal-sized groups, corresponding to the particular device used, with each user employing that device to access streamed multimedia content in each of the three locations considered in our study.

The whole process took on average 49 minutes per participant. Participants were firstly provided with a one-page Campus Guide experiment how-to manual, a QoP questionnaire, and the guide device. In the manual participants were also provided with an approximate route to follow to reach their targeted destinations, thus ensuring that they went through all the key locations where streamed content was provided. At each such location, after requesting and watching the streamed video using their specific devices, participants then answered the QoP questions (in terms of information assimilation and enjoyment) for each of the location-specific clips. Specifically:

- **QoP-IA** was expressed as a percentage measure, which reflected a user's ability to assimilate specific information from visualized multimedia content. Thus, after watching a particular multimedia clip, the user was asked a standard number of questions, which examined information being conveyed in the specific clip that had just been presented to the participant. The level of information assimilation was then calculated as being the proportion of correct answers that users gave to these specific questions.

- **QoP-S** was polled by asking users to express, on a six-point Likert scale of 0-5, how much they enjoyed the presentation (with scores of 0 and 5 representing 'complete dislike' and, respectively, 'absolute enjoyment' with the multimedia video presentation). A six-point Likert scale was used to exclude a mid-point decision, preventing a completely neutral subjective opinion. This information was used to determine whether a user's ability to assimilate information has any relation to his or her level of perceived enjoyment.

RESULTS SUMMARY

For brevity, we present the main results obtained in our study. These highlighted that device type had no significant impact on either user QoP-IA or QoP-S (Figures 8 and 9). However, what can be observed from Figure 9 is that QoP-S is consistently highest for the PDA, irrespective of the location in which our experiment was conducted. We believe that this is due to the fact that the resolution of the PDA screen was consistent with

Table 3. Device, location, and frame rate matrix

	St John's Building	Bannerman Centre	University Lawn
PDA	25	15	15
HMD	5	25	15
Laptop	25	5	25

Figure 8. Overall quality of perception information assimilation (QoP-IA) based on device type

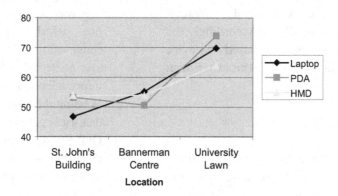

Figure 9. Average perceived satisfaction based on device type

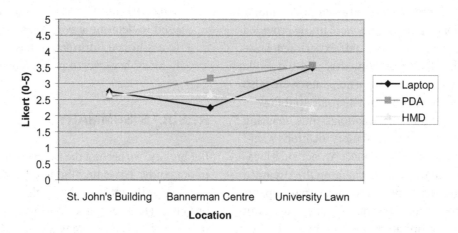

that of the displayed video clips, which was not the case with the HMD or the laptop, in which the video content was subjected to virtual enhancements so that the display size was adapted to the screen sizes of the two respective devices. Nonetheless, no clear trend could be reflected in QoP-IA, as reflected in Figure 8, and confirmed by our analysis.

This therefore shows that the user experience of using small screened devices is not necessarily detrimentally affected, if the content is appropriately tailored according to perceptual-

location and technical requirements. On the other hand, when comparing the results obtained from the study described in this paper, with that of a control group, in which no tailoring took place (Gulliver et al., 2004), analysis revealed statistically significant influences of experiment type and device type on user overall QoP (QoP was higher in the tailored scenario), thus highlighting the benefits of streaming perceptually tailored multimedia content.

We believe that the significance in user overall QoP due to the type of the experiment is natural.

The tailored experiment content was explicitly designed based on the user perspective quality evaluation of the non-tailored experiment so that it suits best to the device that is streamed at. Indeed, the overall QoP results of the tailored experiment, with the exception of Laptop-university lawn clip, are either equal or better than the non-tailored experiment. We believe that the reason for having a low overall QoP when the animation clip was streamed to the university lawn is due to the cartoon characteristics and low clip audio volume which made it hard to follow in an environment surrounded by noisy distractions.

CONCLUSION

In this chapter, we describe an investigation exploring user experiences of accessing streamed multimedia content, when that content is tailored according to perceptual, device and location characteristics. To this end, we have created pre-defined transmission profiles and stream perceptually tailored multimedia content to three different locations, each characterized by different infotainment requirements.

Although previous research (Buyukkokten et al., 2000; Freire et al., 2001) has employed profiling methods to facilitate services based on device type, screen size, processor speed, battery amount and connection speed, however, to the best of our knowledge, no-one has incorporated perceptual preferences to build pre-defined QoS transmission profiles to enhance the user experience. In this study, we have developed profiles that contain perceptual information and act as a guideline in the selection of suitable QoS transmission parameters (in our case suitable frame rate).

Results thus far have highlighted the benefits of this approach and have shown that better network resource usage could result when performing such matching in practice. In the light of our results, we propose that multimedia transmission to mobile and wireless devices should be made based on pre-defined profiles, which contains a combination of static (perceptual, device type, CPU speed, and display specifications) and dynamic information (streamed content type location of the device/ user, context of the device/user). The evaluation of such a system showed that the users and service providers can gain from such an approach considerably, as user perceptions of quality were not detrimentally affected by QoS degradations. Consequently, service providers can utilize this information to effectively manage local network traffic and bandwidth. It would thus be opportune for communication standards to recognize the importance of incorporating user requirements in the dissemination and tailoring of media rich information, and this certainly forms one of our future avenues of pursuit.

REFERENCES

Abowd, D. A., Atkeson, C. G., Hong, J., Long, S. & Pinkerton, M. (1996). Cyberguide: A mobile context-aware tour guide. *Wireless Networks, 3*(5), 421-433.

Buranatrived, J., & Vickers, P. (2004). A study of application and device effects between a WAP phone and palm PDA. *6ᵗʰ International Symposium (MobileHCI 2004)* (pp. 192-203).

Burigat, S., & Chittaro, L. (2005). Location-aware visualization of VRML models in GPS-based mobile guides. *Proceedings of the 10ᵗʰ International Conference on 3D Web Technology* (pp. 57-64).

Buyukkokten, O., Garcia-Molina, H., Paepcke, A., & Winograd, T. (2000). Power brower: Efficient Web browsing for PDAs. *Proceedings of ACM CHI 2000* (pp. 430-437), The Hague, Amsterdam.

Chandrasekaran, P., & Joshi, A., (2002). MobileIQ: A framework for mobile information access. *3ʳᵈ International Conference on Mobile Data Management (MDM'02)* (pp. 43-52).

eTForecasts (2005). *Worldwide PDA and smartphone forecasts*. Retrieved April 8, 2006, from http://www.etforecasts.com/products/ES_SP-PDA.htm

Fox, A., Goldberg, I., Gribble, S. D., Lee, D. C., Polito, A., & Brewer, E. A. (1998). Experience with top gun wingman: A proxy-based graphical Web browser for the 3Com PalmPilot. *Proceedings of Middleware '98*, Lake District, England.

Freire, J., Kumar, B., & Lieuwen, D. (2001). WebViews: Accessing personalized web content and services. *Proceedings of the 10th International Conference on World Wide Web* (pp. 576-586).

Ghinea, G. (2000). *Quality of perception: An essential facet of multimedia communications*. PhD thesis, Department of Computer Science, The University of Reading, UK.

Ghinea, G., & Thomas, J. (2005). Improving perceptual multimedia quality with an adaptable communication protocol. *Journal of Computing and Information Technology, 13*(2), 149-161.

Ghinea, G., & Thomas, J. P. (2005). Quality of perception: User quality of service in multimedia presentations. *IEEE Transactions on Multimedia, 7*(4), 786-789.

Ghinea, G., & Thomas, J. P. (1998). QoS impact on user perception and understanding of multimedia video clips. *Proceedings of ACM Multimedia '98* (pp. 49-54), Bristol UK.

Ghinea, G., & Thomas, J. P., (2000). Impact of protocol stacks on quality of perception. *IEEE International Conference on Multimedia and Expo*, New York (Vol. 2, pp. 847-850).

Gulliver, S. R., & Ghinea, G. (2003). How level and type of deafness affects user perception of multimedia video clips. *Universal Access in the Information Society, 2*(4), 374-386.

Gulliver, S. R., Serif, T., & Ghinea, G. (2004). Pervasive and standalone computing: The perceptual effects of variable multimedia quality. *International Journal of Human Computer Studies, 60*, 640-665.

Hung, K., & Zhang, Y. (2003). Implementation of a WAP-based telemedicine system for patient monitoring. *IEEE Transactions on Information Technology in Biomedicine, 7*(2), 101-107.

Jones, M., Marsden, G., Mohd-Nasir, N., Boone, K., & Buchanan, G. (1999). Improving Web interaction on small displays. *8th International WWW Conference* (pp. 51-59).

Kawalek, J. A. (1995). User perspective for QoS management. *Proceedings of the QoS Workshop aligned with the 3rd International Conference on Intelligence in Broadband Services and Network (IS&N 95)*, Crete, Greece.

Kazasis, F. G., Moumoutzis, N., Pappas, N., Karanastasi, A., & Christodoulakis, S. (2003). Designing ubiquitous personalized tv-anytime services. In J. Eder, R. Mittermeir, & B. Pernici (Eds.), *The CAISE'03 Workshops* (pp. 136-149). Slovenia: University of Maribor Press.

Kim, L., & Albers, M. J. (2001). Web design issues when searching for information in a small screen display. *ACM SIGDOC'01* (pp. 193-200). University of Memphis.

Munoz, M. A., Rodriguez, M., Favela, J., Martinez-Garcia, A. I., Gonzalez, V. M. (2003). Context-aware mobile communication in hospitals. *IEEE Computer, 36*(9), 38-46.

National Statistics Website. (2006). *Social trends*. Retrieved January 10, 2006, from http://www.statistics.gov.uk/STATBASE/Expodata/Spreadsheets/D7202.xls

Simcock, T., Hillenbrand, S. P., & Thomas, B. H. (2003). Developing a location based tourist guide application. *Australasian Information Security Workshop Conference on ACSW Frontiers* (Vol. 21, pp. 177-183).

Taivalsaari, A., (1999) *The event horizon user interface model for small devices* (Tech. Report No. SMLI TR-99-74). Sun Microsystems.

TV-Anytime. (2003). *TV anytime forum Web site*. Retrieved June 15, 2003, from http://www.tv-anytime.org

Want, R., Hopper, A., Falcao, V., & Gibbons J. (1992). The active badge location system. *ACM Transactions on Information Systems, 10*(1), 91-102.

Want, R., Schilit, B. N., Adams, N. I., Gold, R., Petersen, K., Goldberg, D., Ellis, J. R., & Weiser, M. (1995). *The ParcTab ubiquitous computing experiment* (Tech. Report No. CSL-95-1). Xerox Palo Alto Research Centre, March 1995. Also appears in Korth, H. F., & Imielinski, T. (Eds.), *Mobile computing*. Kluwer Academic Press, 1996.

Watson, A., & Sasse, M.A. (1997). Multimedia conferencing via multicasting: Determining the quality of service required by the end user. *Proceedings of AVSPN '97* (pp. 189-194). Aberdeen, Scotland.

Weiser, M. (1998). The future of ubiquitous computing on campus. *Communication of the ACM, 41*(1), 41-42.

Weiser, M. (1993). Some computer science issues in ubiquitous computing. *Communications of the ACM, 36*(7), 74-84, July 1993.

Weiser, M. (1991). *The computer for the 21st century*. Scientific American, September 1991.

APPENDIX: CAMPUS GUIDE QUESTIONNAIRE

Details	
Name:	*Age:*
Device: PDA / HMD / Laptop	*Sex: M / F*
Start Time:	Finish Time:

Computer Background	
How long have you been using desktop computer?	_____ Months _____ Years
How long have you been using mobile computers (Laptop/ PDA)?	_____ Months _____ Years
Do you regularly use electronic mail (e-mail)?	Yes ☐ No ☐
Do you regularly use search engines (Google, AltaVista)?	Yes ☐ No ☐
Do you regularly use word processing applications (Ms Word, WordPerfect)?	Yes ☐ No ☐
Do you regularly use spreadsheet applications (Ms Excel, Lotus)?	Yes ☐ No ☐
Have you ever successfully installed software on a computer?	Yes ☐ No ☐
Have you ever written and successfully run a computer program?	Yes ☐ No ☐
Do you know how much RAM your computer has? (amount orally)	Yes ☐ No ☐
Do you know what a USB port is? (mention orally)	Yes ☐ No ☐

Location: Department	
Where is SISCM located?	....
How many floors does the building have?	....
What color is the background of the ground floor corridors?	....
How many vending machines are there in the student study room?	....
What kind of monitors is used in the computer lab?	....
How many MPhil/PhD students are there in the department?	....
How many professors are there in the department?	....
On which are floor the lecturer offices and administrator offices located?	Lecturer offices:............................ Administrator Offices:......................
What was the RAE grade of the department in 2001?	....
What are the main research themes of Information Systems & Computing?	....
Quality: 0 – 1 – 2 – 3 – 4 – 5	Enjoyment: 0 – 1 – 2 – 3 – 4 – 5

continued on following page

Appendix A. (continued)

Location: Bannerman (Library)	
What is the color of the hat of the student who waves in the clip?	....
How many computers were on the table in the clip?	....
What color were the office chairs next to the computer desk?	....
What is the shape of the tables in the refectory/food court?	....
What time does the library open and close on weekdays?	....
Can you please name three services provided by the library?	....
On which areas do the Twickenham and Osterley libraries provide resources?	....
How many days of the week is the library open during term-time?	....
What facilities are there in the Student Union?	....
Quality: 0 – 1 – 2 – 3 – 4 – 5	Enjoyment: 0 – 1 – 2 – 3 – 4 – 5
Location: Lawn	
What sort of character does the woman in the fur coat have?	....
What do the man and the dog have in common?	....
Is the woman in fur coat fat or slim?	....
What is the weather outside like?	....
How many insults does the woman in the fur coat use?	....
How many characters talk in the clip? Which ones?	....
How many characters behave happily? Which ones?	....
Does the woman in the fur coat get her bag when she leaves?	....
Name an element of the clip, which is similar to the temperament of the woman in the fur coat?	....
How many scared people are there in the clip?	....
Quality: 0 – 1 – 2 – 3 – 4 – 5	Enjoyment: 0 – 1 – 2 – 3 – 4 – 5

Chapter XIII
PQoS Assessment Methods for Multimedia Services

Harilaos Koumaras
National Center of Scientific Research, "Demokritos", Greece

Fidel Liberal
University of the Basque Country, Spain

Lingfen Sun
University of Plymouth, UK

ABSTRACT

The concept of PQoS, although in general it deals with the user satisfaction with a specific delivered/ requested service, is in practice significantly differentiated by the nature of each delivered service. This chapter reviews various existing PQoS assessment methods for video, VoIP, online games, and Web services that have been published in the literature. It then moves beyond the current PQoS assessment methods and presents novel techniques for predicting the PQoS of a multimedia service.

INTRODUCTION

The term quality of service (QoS) has been widely used in various IT services throughout time, from traditional ones, such as those related to telephony to more recent ones (e.g., those provided over IP networks). Although multiple definition of QoS concept exists (one such a detailed compilation can be found in (ITU-T, 2004a)), most of the proposed definitions agree on considering quality of service as "a set of characteristics related to the performance of the elements that provide the services that have an effect into final end users perception."

Since different services may be affected by a different set of parameters, some kind of categorization of QoS is necessary. This has led to the definition of the traffic and service classes, with each of them corresponding to a different subset of parameters. However, most of traditional

QoS assessment and management architectures handle a **technical only** subset of these parameters (only network performance is considered here) (Xilouris, Kourtis, & Stefanou, 2005).

On the other hand, as early as 1994, ITU-T E.800 recommendation (ITU-T, 1994) included a more user-centric definition of Quality of Service as "*the collective effect of service performance, which determines the degree of satisfaction of a user of the service.*"

Therefore, the term QoS makes a step beyond pure performance-related concepts, such as network performance (NP) or service performance (SP). Yet, when Internet services are the focus point, NP is found to be one of the most significant factors due to the high variability of the performance parameters in data networks today. Inherent characteristics of these networks, such as non-connection-oriented or best effort properties, make the provision of a minimum level of guaranteed NP a complex issue. As a result, the research community has focused, during the last two decades, on the so-called "*Technical QoS*" *(TQoS) or "Network QoS" (NQoS)*, trying to solve the problem of assuring an accurate performance level to end-users.

The QoS perceived as user satisfaction has received less effort from the research community through past years. One of the first formal inclusions of QoS as perceived by users of Internet services was in ETSI ETR 003, (ETSI, 1994) wherein a quality matrix was proposed to relate network and service performance to the quality of service perceived by end users. This approach was later adopted by ITU-T (ITU-T, 2004a). In both recommendations, ETSI and ITU-T brought together objective aspects related to Network Performance and their subjective impact on user satisfaction.

Thus, NP parameters are key issues in QoS, however, these parameters have to be considered together with other factors (such as codecs, source/terminal mechanisms) for an overall user satisfaction or an end-to-end perceived QoS (PQoS).

Furthermore, a common vision of the future communication networks is the provision of multimedia or audiovisual content at a variety of quality and price levels (Seeling, Reisslein, & Kulapala, 2004). The evaluation of the PQoS will provide an end user with a range of potential choices, covering the possibilities of low, medium, or high quality levels. This PQoS evaluation will also give the service provider and network operator the capability to minimize the storage and network resources by allocating only the ones that are necessary to maintain a specific level of user satisfaction (Gardikis, Kourtis, & Constantinou, 2003).

Further, the success of providing novel multimedia services over wired/wireless networks depends on how good the quality of the service is and whether it meets or not an end user's satisfaction standards. Thus, it is critical for equipment manufacturers, network operators and service providers to assess, predict and possibly control the end-to-end perceptual multimedia (e.g., voice and video) quality for commercial and technical reasons. Developing accurate, efficient and robust PQoS models for multimedia services remains a challenging research target both in academia and industry.

In this context, the chapter deals with PQoS assessment methods for modern multimedia applications/services. The objectives of the chapter are (1) to describe general subjective quality assessment models, (2) to review the up-to-date PQoS assessment models for multimedia services such as Web, video and VoIP services; (3) to propose and present novel PQoS prediction models for Web, video, VoIP, and online gaming services, and (4) to present future trends on PQoS models. The work and the PQoS models presented in the chapter will be useful in developing and monitoring PQoS-aware multimedia devices and networks, and for PQoS monitoring, prediction, and control of live multimedia services over IP and mobile networks.

BACKGROUND

This section describes and analyzes a wide-range of general QoS models. Most of these models have been previously used in other industrial application areas for evaluating and quantifying the satisfaction degree of end-users/consumers.

Figure 1 depicts the general framework proposed in (ITU-T, 2004b) for the management of QoS in Internet services. According to the figure, the proposed methodology can be mainly summarized in four viewpoints:

- End-user QoS requirements
- QoS offered by service providers
- QoS achieved in the provision of the service
- QoS perceived by end-users

Oodan, Ward, and Mullee (1997) proposed four quality cycles and a series of gaps that should be analyzed in order to accurately evaluate the provision of QoS as perceived by end-users. These gaps correspond to the miscellaneous requirements of QoS between the diverse four QoS perspectives of ITU framework. Based on this work, several authors have proposed the implementation of wide-ranging quality assessment methodologies in order to research the real impact of networked communications parameters on the perception of services by end-users (Babulak, 2004).

Likewise, different authors have stated that the QoS should be assessed as a function of the difference between users' expectations and quality perceived by end-users (Cronin & Taylor, 1994; Gronroos, 1983; Parasuraman, Zeithaml, & Berry, 1985)). In this context, one of the most useful methods to evaluate QoS as perceived by users is general purpose SERVQUAL model (Parasuraman, Berry, & Zeithaml, 1988) (Parasuraman, Zeithaml, & Berry, 1991). This model, which has been previously applied to several areas, is based on the assertion that users identify the quality of a service as the difference between their previous expectations and perceived quality after usage:

$$Q = P - E$$

This expression can be associated to the gap identified in Figure 1 between "customers' QoS requirements" and "customers' perception of QoS." So it can be established this gap as the key issue for an accurate evaluation of QoS as experienced by users (i.e., PQoS).

The difference between users' expectations and perceived quality for networked services can be described as a composition of:

Figure 1. Quality cycles in Oodan et al., 1997

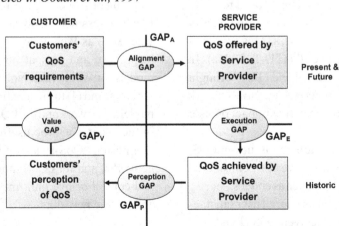

1. The difference between what users need and what providers understand and offer
2. The difference between compromised NP levels and achieved NP in the provision of the service
3. The difference between expected QoS provided a NP level and actual QoS perceived by users: $Q = GAP_A + GAP_E + GAP_P$

The analysis of the GAP_A (QoS requirements vs. QoS offered) concerns to two main areas of knowledge: how to identify and represent users' service requirements and how to include them in the service contracts. For quality control purposes, **critical to quality (CTQ) criteria** for a service should be first identified. This set of indicators allows the evaluation of end users' satisfaction in an *objective* and *comparable* manner.

One of the most common processes when obtaining final customers' requirements is the voice of the customer (VOC). This process is based on getting in touch with the customers in order to retrieve the feedback necessary to identify their necessities, which should have been covered by the product or service offered. The term *voice of the customer* includes the explicit requirements and those that are not expressed by the consumers but that can be retrieved from the consult process.

Similarly SERVPERF is a variant of SERVQUAL model developed by Cronin et al. as a result of an empirical analysis of eight different service companies (Cronin & Taylor, 1994). The authors argued that SERVQUAL was not the most suitable model for assessing QoS since the liability of using GAPs for measuring QoS was not proven. They proposed an alternative model based on clients' perceptions only.

However, although all these models allow researchers to identify CTQ parameters, they do not provide methods in order to quantitatively assess the relative importance of different criteria or the overall satisfaction of users. As a result, through the last years different alternatives have been initiated to numerically evaluate QoS experienced by

diverse services, including the subjective component. The most important ones are summarized as follows (an extensive classification can be found in Bouch, Sasse, & DeMeer, 2000):

- Mean opinion score (MOS)
- Continuous assessment
- Qualitative methods
- Perceived quality estimation from performance measurements

The **mean opinion score (MOS)** method is based on the analysis of the customers' perceptual opinion about one service. This method was proposed in ITU-T (1997) for application on voice communications, in order to evaluate the quality of the sound, coming from different samples. Each user's rating is done using a unique arithmetic mark, showing the customer satisfaction level about a service. The MOS is determined as the mean value of the marks given by all the individual participants, in a scale ranging from 1 to 5.

Since subjective evaluations depict directly the quality perceived by the user, they have been used for protocols, transmission lines, and coding algorithm evaluation as well. However, MOS method has some flaws. Bouch et al. (2000) argue that applying MOS to the evaluation of multimedia services is insufficient since it does not specify the factor that is responsible for the quality degradation. Moreover, in Koumaras et al. (2004) and Hammer, Reichl, and Ziegler (2004) authors state that this technique is high time/resource consuming. Similarly in Prasad et al. (2001) the method is proved not to be applicable for real time services.

Furthermore, in environments where transmission is time varying, such as the wireless transmission channels, PQoS evaluations and user surveys in a certain moment are practically inadequate, since the perceived quality is not equally distributed for the rest of the service duration.

In such highly varying environments, specific tools are preferred, which are called **continuous**

assessment methods. As an example, QUASS (quality assessment slider) proposed in Bouch and Sasse (1999) was a tool for retrieving user opinions continuously in closed/controlled environments. In order to do so, the users had to move a sliding bar in real time according to their evaluation of quality at this time. Similarly, in **qualitative assessment methodology** users are asked to provide qualitative/textual descriptions of the quality they are experiencing. This methodology offers a higher level of detail in subjective quality measurements.

However, all the aforementioned methods suffer from the same drawback: they need real users in order to evaluate their actual perception. This is a time and resource consuming requirement that can not be automated. In order to overcome the "human factor" researchers have developed a series of methods for estimating end-user PQoS from traditional NP parameters (in a per-service basis).

This methodology for objective evaluation of the perceived quality is based on applying certain models that try to retrieve existent relations between quality perceived by an end-user and quality that can be measured in an objective way. These relation models are obtained from empirical experiences carried out with users. In these trials their perceptions about the PQoS under different conditions are collected and then compared with objective NP parameters in the following way:

- Perform empirical studies to gather final user evaluations related to a new service. These results will highly depend on the user profile.
- From obtained results, develop models to estimate final user's perception. In this phase the resulting quality estimations are linked to the tests conditions.
- Finally, a methodology is established, including a series of performance measurements with regard to the set of interesting parameters in order to estimate the quality as it is perceived by the users.

These instruments allow the continuous evaluation of the QoS based on objective performance measurements of the parameters identified as critical for the quality. Most of the resulting expressions are oriented to certain services only, because each type of service has special features that affect in a different way the parameters considered as critical. In this framework, the following sections summarize PQoS assessment models for Web, video and VoIP services.

PQOS ASSESSMENT MODELS FOR WEB-BASED SERVICES

The first step for analyzing the quality of the Web service is the analysis of the subjective quality perception by the end-users. There are a number of studies that cover **functional parameters (i.e., a subjective approach)**, such as characteristics of the content, accessibility, security, ease of use, etc., and **non-functional parameters (i.e., an objective approach)**, more related to the performance in the provision of the service.

Subjective Quality Evaluation Methods

WebQUAL Model

Barnes and Vidgen (2000a) use the **quality function development (QFD) quality model** for detecting **critical quality parameters in a Web service** (resulting in the so-called **WebQual** model). Among them, authors identify aspects such as "ease of use, aesthetic appearance, fast navigation, etc...."

From this parameters set, the authors try to classify them in categories resembling the SERVQUAL model in order to *"adapt the SERVQUAL instrument to assess Website service."*

With regards to the nature of the parameters, most of them depend on the content of the Web pages, although some of them are directly dependent on performance parameters of service provision (i.e., "reasonable load time," "fast navigation through the pages," and "fast access to the information"). While the former must be measured using qualitative methodologies, for the latter quantitative methodologies can be used. Thus, in order to develop a comprehensive system for the evaluation of Web PQoS, there arises the need for integrating and linking both types of measurements in order to consolidate the obtained results.

Application of TAM Model and Extensions

The original version of the Technology Acceptance Model (TAM) was based on the Theory of Reasoned Action (TRA) (Davis, 1989; Davis, Bagozzi,

& Warshaw, 1989) as a tool for estimating users' acceptance of the new information systems. The TAM model states that mainly two parameters (i.e., "perceived usefulness" and "perceived ease of use") determinate the attitude of a user toward one specific technology and its potential success. Since the features of a system have influence on the user, the customer experiences different perceptions in relation to the utility of the system and the ease of use. These perceptions have also an impact on the user's attitude to the acceptance of the system. So, the TAM model and its extensions take into consideration a series of factors that have great influence to the user's final satisfaction. When evaluating QoS in an integral way, one user may not have the ability to distinguish among the causes of dissatisfaction. According to this, the application of the TAM model can help to identify the causes that make a service not attractive by one user (see Figure 2).

Figure 2. Adaptation of the TAM model to Web sites

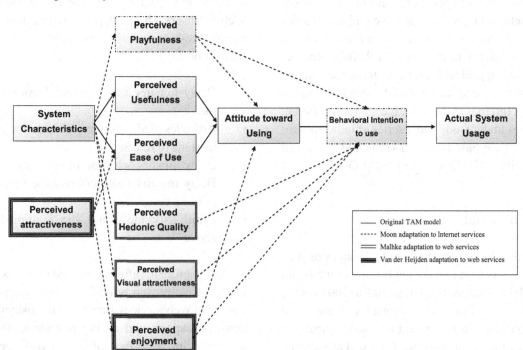

Moon and Kim (2001) extend the TAM model by adding the term playfulness as a new factor that affects the attitude to the use of an Internet service.

Other studies such as Mahlke (2002) and van der Heijden (2003) distinguish between the visual attraction of a Web site and the satisfaction a service produces. The difference between these two works is that, while Mahlke establishes the visual attraction and the perceived pleasant quality at the same level as the perceived utility and the perceived ease of use, van der Heijden establishes the perceived attractiveness influences directly over the following terms: perceived utility, perceived ease of use, and perceived pleasure.

EWAM Model

The extended Web assessment model (EWAM) was introduced by Schubert (Schubert, 2002) (Petra Schubert, 2003) as an extension of previous TAM-based models for Web services. Although the original TAM model is based on Fishbein's psychological behavior it does not include the social aspects of Schubert's model. The EWAM model considers the subjective and social sides in electronic commerce, as a criterion relevant to the confidence of the system. EWAM defines an evaluation grid with a set of criteria, focusing on consumer perspectives and the specific features of the Internet as medium. It comprises different phases under study and a series of indicators for each phase based on metrics such as perceived usefulness (USEF), ease of use (EOU) and trust (TRUST).

Kano Model

Another tool proposed in order to analyze Web services is based on the application of the **Kano model** (Zhang & von Dran, 2001a, 2001b). One of the most important advantages of the Kano model is that it identifies those quality features that fulfill unstated needs and those that make the

products and services the market leaders. Zhang et al. collect a series of these features, related to categories such as information content, cognitive outcomes, enjoyment, privacy, user empowerment, visual appearance, technical support, and other content-related aspects, such as creditability and confidentiality for example.

However, there also exist some limitations to this extended Kano model:

- It is unlikely that all the features have the same relevance for all the users. The first study does not distinguish features by weight of importance.
- There is no evidence on whether the quality expectations for features are the same for different domains.
- Methodologically, the original list of features was constructed with a top-down approach without being constrained to a particular domain.

Finally, Galletta, Henry, McCoy, and Polak (2004) propose a model, which is directly related to the delay impact on the perception of QoS by Websites users. This work presents an exhaustive experience-based study and presents a series of conclusions:

- Delay impairs attitudes (satisfaction with the site)
- Attitudes predict behavioral intentions (intentions to return)
- Delay impairs behavioral intentions
- Delay impairs task performance (number of tasks completed)
- Familiarity moderates the relationships above

Although all the aforementioned methods and models have proven reliability while assessing quality in Web services, they all deal mostly with aesthetic aspects and do not provide methods for evaluating the effects of the network performance into users' satisfaction. In order to do so, it must be established the relationships between objective Web-related NP parameters and users satisfaction.

Objective Quality Evaluation Methods

In the case of Web browsing, most of the studies associated to user-satisfaction have traditionally faced the subjective part, concerning usability, ease of use, and aesthetic aspects (Aladwani & Palvia, 2002; Barnes & Vidgen, 2000b; D'Ambra & Rice, 2001; Fogg et al., 2001; Lavie & Tractinsky, 2004; Liu & Arnett, 2000; Mahlke, 2002; Ranganathan & Shobha, 2002; Petra Schubert & Dettling, 2001; Schubert & Leimstoll, 2001; Selz & Schubert, 1997). So, they consider the contents but not directly the effect of the transmission over them.

Nevertheless, in Aladwani et al. (2002), it is scored the "speed of page downloading" as the third most important factor, just after "valid links" and "ease of navigation." Similarly, in Barnes et al. (2000b), some of obtained parameters (e.g., fast navigation to pages, reasonable response time or fast access to the information) are not only affected by the contents but also directly by the transmission. In the same way, in Petra Schubert and Dettling (2001), Schubert et al. (2001), and Selz et al. (1997) among pure subjective parameters they consider "interactivity" and "quick access to data," which are affected by network conditions.

So, although several papers can be found in the bibliography around the perceived quality regarding Web contents, it is clear that network performance does have an impact on users' perception regarding overall Web browsing. In fact interdependencies appear between usability and network conditions. For instance, fewer clicks would result on poorer perception in a slow site than more hops in a faster site. In the same sense, in Ramsay, Barbesi, and Preece (1998) and Sears,

Jacko, and Borella (1997) authors claim that Web pages retrieved faster are judged to be significantly more interesting than their slower counterparts.

In order to establish a mathematical relationship between users satisfaction towards Web browsing and network performance, the objectively measurable parameter with the greatest influence must be identified. In Muntean and McManis (2004) authors develop a QoS-aware adaptive Web-based system by considering four different performance metrics: download time, client's throughput, round-trip-time (RTT) and HTTP version. From all these parameters, the download time appears to be the main parameter of the end-to-end performance, directly perceived by users. In Cherkasova, Fu, and Tang (2002), the authors conclude that it is the user satisfaction along with Web site response that influences how long the user stays at the Web site, determining the user's future visits to the site. Likewise, in Bhatti, Bouch, and Kuchinsky (2000b) and Bouch, Kuchinsky, and Bhatti (2000), the authors (across several users' surveys, which include questionnaires, verbal protocols and group discussions) show that latency has a clear impact on users' satisfaction. This impact does not only affect users' perception about Web performance, but even users' perception of the content itself. Finally in Woolley (2000), the author points out that there is a threshold for downloading time, so that if the waiting time is greater than this threshold, users usually abort the connection and go elsewhere.

From all these criteria the most important factor affected by network performance in Web browsing seems to be associated to page downloading time (DT) (Olshefski & Nieh, 2006) also called "Web latency." This conclusion is also statistically obtained through correlation and ANOVA tests in Aladwani et al. (2002), Saliba, Beresford, Ivanovich, and Fitzpatrick (2005), and Zviran, Glezer, and Avni (2006).

Since end-to-end downloading time (DT) may depend on several factors, many authors have analysed the sources of Web latency (Habib &

Abrams, 2000; Ludmila Cherkasova, Fu, Tang, & Vahdat, 2003; Krishnamurthy & Wills, 2000; Woolley, 2000). For example, Krishnamurthy et al. (2000) consider that the DNS resolution time should be taken into account because it can introduce significant delays in DT. Thus, no single technical QoS parameter (such as delay or losses like in VoIP and video models) seems to be suitable for measuring the satisfaction toward Web browsing and an end-to-end particular measurement (DT) must be used.

All aforementioned studies do not provide a quantitative method to assess the PQoS from QoS parameters. This kind of studies will be described in the following sub-section.

Fun Factors

Charzinski (2001) describes the use of some mathematical calculus defined as fun factors as a way for evaluating the perception.

Charzinsky proposes four different analytical expressions for the definition of fun factors with a value between 0 (minimum quality) and 1 (maximum quality). The fun factors do not assess PQoS directly but the ability to take advantage of the capacity of the connection. Those users that get the highest performance ratio from their connection are supposed to be satisfied. However it seems quite difficult that all kind of users know the capabilities of their Internet access or whether they will be satisfied with a low but fully used connection.

Failure Rate

In Cherkasova et al. (2002), they introduce a new technical factor that has an important influence in Web service users' PQoS analysis: The frequency of the failed tries to connect to Web pages. In this case, it is interesting to differentiate from the total set of failures to those due to the fulfillment of the maximum waiting time for the page loading.

Web PQoS as a Function of Downloading Time

One of the aspects that has inspired a number of studies is the difference between the latency introduced by different network elements. In Woolley (2000) the global delay is analyzed considering different contributions: (local network time, network time between the access point and the destiny, processing time in the browser ,processing time in the server, processing time in the application servers and processing time in the databases).

In a similar way, Cherkasova et al. propose in Ludmila et al. (2003) a system oriented to distinguish between the delay introduced by the network and the delay associated to the server behavior. Based on this distinction, it is emphasized the influence of requesting dynamic pages to the server instead of static pages.

Another important research that deeply analyzes the division of the total delay into its different components is the one proposed by Krishnamurthy et al. (2000). In this case, the important factors retrieved are network delay, server load, number of objects, and total size in bytes, resolution time of the DNS, redirection, and caching effects and specific options of the protocol.

These specializations of delay causes are not trivial, since different delays do not contribute with the same weight to end users' satisfaction. For example, it is considered that the time associated to the name resolution in the DNS can be important in relation to the total time for loading the page, while the number and size of the objects that are part of a Web page, determine the total loading time, which set the end-to-end downloading speed as another key factor.

PQOS ASSESSMENT MODELS FOR ENCODED VIDEO SERVICES

The advent of quality evaluation in video field was the application of a pure mathematical error sensitive framework between the encoding and the original/uncompressed video sequence. These primitive methods, although they provided a quantitative approach about the quality degradation of the encoded signal, do not provide reliable measurements of the perceived quality, because they miss out the characteristics of the human visual system.

Towards this, more complicated methods have been proposed, which are in accordance to the sensitivities of the human visual system. The methods and techniques that have been proposed in the bibliography can be sorted into two groups:

- The assessment methods whose scope is the determination of the encoding settings (i.e., resolution, frame rate, bit rate), which are required in order to carry out successfully the communication task of a multimedia application (i.e., video conference). In other words, the scope of these methods is the estimation of the adequate video quality level for a particular multimedia communication task.

- The assessment methods whose aim is the evaluation of the quality level of a media clip based on the detection of artifacts on the signal caused by the encoding process. In contrast with the methods of the previous category, the scope of these methods is not the determination of the adequate level, but the classification of a video content at a perceived quality scale.

The methods of the first group take under consideration a great number of parameters and metrics that depend on the task nature and the user emotional behavior (Mullin, Smallwood, Watson, & Wilson, 2001) in order to determine the adequate quality level for a specific multimedia application. For example the classification of the task as foreground or background in correlation with its complexity (Buxton, 1995), is a param-

eter that differentiates the quality demands of a multimedia application. On the other hand, the emotional content of a multimedia communication task alters the required quality level of the specific communication service (Olson, 1994). Due to this, various parameters are measured in order to estimate the appropriate minimum quality level of a multimedia application. Such parameters are:

- The user characteristics (i.e., knowledge background, language background, familiarity with the task, age)
- The situation characteristics (i.e., geographical remoteness, simultaneous number of users, distribution of users)
- The user behavior (i.e., eye tracking, head movement)

However, these methods have still some issues to solve on technical, theoretical and practical level. A user that participates in such an assessment procedure is wired at so many points on the body (even on the head may wear the eye tracking equipment), which causes uncomfortable feelings and affects its behaviour. Technical issues, such as the eye tracking loss and the manual calibration/correction by a human operator, affect the reliability of the methods in real time environments (Mullin et al., 2001).

The most widely used primitive methods and quality metrics that used an error sensitivity framework are the peak signal to noise ratio (PSNR) and the mean square error (MSE):

$$PSNR = 10\log_{10}\frac{L^2}{MSE}$$

where L denotes the dynamic pixel value (i.e., equal to 255 for 8bits/pixel monotonic signal).

$$MSE = \frac{1}{N}\sum_{i=1}^{N}(x_i - y_i)^2$$

where N denotes the total pixels and x_i/y_i the ith pixel value in the original/distorted signal.

Currently, the evaluation of the PQoS is a matter of objective and subjective evaluation procedures, each time taking place after the encoding process (post-encoding evaluation). **Subjective picture/audio quality evaluation processes** require large amount of human resources, establishing it as a time-consuming process (e.g., large audiences evaluating video/audio sequences). **Objective evaluation methods**, on the other hand, can provide PQoS evaluation results faster, but require large amount of machine resources and sophisticated apparatus configurations. Towards this, objective evaluation methods are based and make use of multiple metrics, which are related to the content's artifacts (i.e., tilling, blurriness, error blocks, etc.) resulting during the encoding and transmission process.

These two categories of PQoS evaluation methods will be analyzed and discussed in the following sections.

Subjective Quality Evaluation Methods

The subjective test methods, which have mainly been proposed by International Telecommunications Union (ITU) and Video Quality Experts Group (VQEG), involve an audience who watch a video sequence and score its quality as perceived by them, under specific and controlled watching conditions. Afterwards, the statistical analysis of the collected data is used for the evaluation of the perceived quality. The mean opinion score (MOS) is regarded as the most reliable method of quality measurement and has been applied on the most known subjective techniques.

Subjective test methods are described in ITU-R Rec. BT.500-11 (2002) and ITU-T Rec. P.910 (1999), suggesting specific viewing conditions, criteria for observers and test material selection, assessment procedure description and statistical analysis methods. ITU-R Rec. BT.500-11 described subjective methods that are specialized for television applications, whereas ITU-T Rec. P.910 is intended for multimedia applications.

The most known and widely used subjective methods are:

- **Double Stimulus Impairment Scale (DSIS):** In this method, observers are shown multiple references and degraded scene pairs. The reference scene is always first. Scoring is on an overall impression scale of impairment: imperceptible, perceptible but not annoying, slightly annoying, annoying, and very annoying. This scale is commonly known as the 5-point scale with 5 being imperceptible and 1 being very annoying.
- **Single Stimulus Methods:** Multiple separate scenes are shown. There are two approaches: SS with no repetition of test scenes and SS where the test scenes are repeated multiple times. Three different scoring methods are used:
  - *Adjectival*: The aforementioned 5-grade impairment scale, however half-grades may be allowed.
  - *Numerical*: An 11-grade numerical scale, useful if a reference is not available.
  - *Non-categorical*: A continuous scale with no numbers or a large range (e.g., 0–100).
- **Stimulus Comparison Method:** Usually accomplished with two well matched monitors, where the differences between scene pairs are scored in one of two ways:
  - *Adjectival*: A 7-grade, +3 to -3 scale labelled: much better, better, slightly better, the same, slightly worse, worse, and much worse.
  - *Non-categorical*: A continuous scale with no numbers or a relation number either in absolute terms or related to a standard pair.
- **Single Stimulus Continuous Quality Evaluation (SSCQE):** According to this

method, the viewers watch a program of typically 20-30 minutes without the original reference to be shown. The test program has been processed by the system under test. The subjects/viewers using a slider continuously rate the instantaneously perceived quality on scale from "bad" to "excellent," which corresponds to an equivalent numerical scale from 0 to 100.

- **Double Stimulus Continuous Quality Scale (DSCQS):** At DSCQS the viewers watch multiple pairs of quite short (i.e., 10 seconds) reference and test sequences. Each pair appears twice, with random order of the reference and the test sequence. The viewers/subjects are not aware of the reference/test order and they are asked to rate each of the two separately on a continuous quality scale namely ranging from "bad" to "excellent," which corresponds to an equivalent numerical scale from 0 to 100. This method is usually used for evaluating slight quality differences between the test and the reference sequence.

The aforementioned methods are described in the ITU-R Rec. BT.500-11 document and are mainly intended for television signals. Based on slight modifications and adaptations of these methods, some other subjective evaluation methods namely absolute category rating (ACR), degradation category rating (DCR) and so on for multimedia services are described in ITU-T Rec. P.910

Objective Quality Evaluation Methods

The preparation and execution of subjective tests is costly and time consuming and its implementation today is limited to scientific purposes, especially at Video Quality Experts Group (VQEG) experiments.

For this reason, a lot of effort has recently been focused on developing cheaper, faster, and easier applicable objective evaluation methods. These techniques successfully emulate the subjective quality assessment results, based on criteria and metrics that can be measured objectively. The objective methods are classified, according to the availability of the original video signal, which is considered to be in high quality.

The majority of the proposed objective methods in the literature require the undistorted source video sequence as a reference entity in the quality evaluation process, and due to this are characterized as **full reference methods**. The methods perform multiple channel decomposition of the video signal, where the proposed objective method is applied on each channel, which features a different weigh factor according to the characteristics of the human visual system. The basic block diagram of the full reference methods with multiple channels is depicted on Figure 3. These methods emulate characteristics of the human visual system (HVS) using contrast sensitivity functions (CSF), channel decomposition, error normalization, weighting, and finally Minkowski error pooling for combining the error measurements into single perceived quality estimation (Wang, Sheikh, & Bovik, 2003).

Similarly, in the bibliography it has been proposed full reference methods of single channel, where the proposed objective metric is applied on the video signal, without considering varying weight functions. The block diagram of these methods is depicted on Figure 4. However it has been reported (VQEG, 2000; Wang, Bovik, & Lu, 2002) that these complicated methods do not provide more accurate results than the simple mathematical measures (such as PSNR). Due to this some new full reference metrics that are based on the video structural distortion, and not on error measurement, have been proposed by Wang et al. (2003).

On the other hand, the fact that these methods require the original video signal as reference

Figure 3. Full reference methods with multiple channels

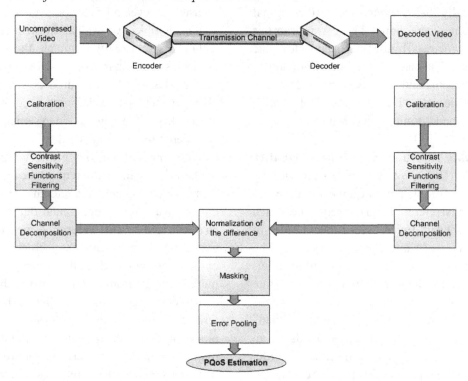

deprives their use in commercial video service applications, where the initial undistorted clips are not accessible. Moreover, even if the reference clip is available, then synchronization predicaments between the undistorted and the distorted signal (which may have experienced frame loss) make the implementation of the full reference methods difficult and impractical.

Due to these reasons, the recent research has been focused on developing methods that can evaluate the PQoS level based on metrics, which use only some extracted structural features from the original signal (reduced reference methods) (Gunawan & Ghanbari, 2003). The block diagram of the reduced reference methods is depicted on Figure 5.

Finally, some methods and techniques have been proposed in the bibliography that do not require any reference video signal (no reference methods) (Lu, Wang, Bovik, & Kouloheris, 2002).

Nevertheless, due to the fact that the 3G/4G vision is the provision of audiovisual content at various quality and price levels (Seeling et al., 2004), there is great need for developing methods and tools that will help service providers to predict quickly and easily the PQoS level of a media clip. These methods will enable the determination of the specific encoding parameters that will satisfy a certain quality level. All the previously mentioned post-encoding methods may require repeating tests in order to determine the encoding parameters that satisfy a specific level of user satisfaction. This procedure is time consuming, complex and impractical for implementation on the 3G/4G multimedia mobile applications.

Towards this, recently it has been performed research in the field of pre-encoding estimation

Figure 4. Full reference methods with single channel

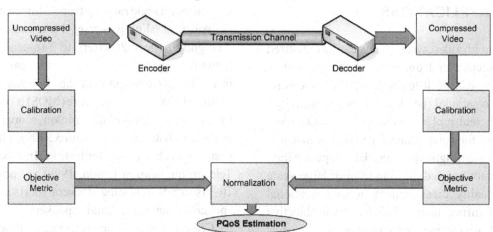

Figure 5. Reduced reference methods

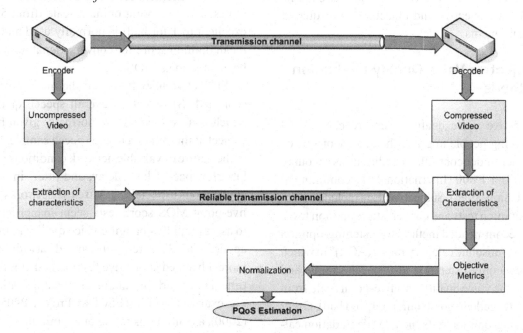

and prediction of the PQoS level of a multimedia service as a function of the selected resolution and the encoding bit rate (Koumaras et al., 2004; Koumaras, Kourtis, & Martakos, 2005). These methods provide fast and quantified estimation of the PQoS, taking into account the instant PQoS variation due to the spatial and temporal (S-T) activity within a given encoded sequence.

Quantifying this variation by the mean PQoS (MPQoS) as a function of the video encoding rate and the picture resolution, it is finally used the MPQoS as a metric for pre-encoding PQoS assessment based on the fast estimation of the S-T activity level of a video signal.

PQOS ASSESSMENT MODELS FOR VOIP APPLICATIONS

Similar with video, voice quality can be measured by subjective and objective methods. Subjective tests can be listening only (i.e., one-way) or conversational (i.e., it involves interactivity). The inherent problem in subjective MOS measurement for voice (same for video) is that it is time-consuming, expensive, lack repeatability, and cannot be used for long-term or large-scale voice quality measurement in an operational network infrastructure. This has made objective methods very attractive for meeting the demands for voice quality measurement in communication networks. This section summarizes existing work on subjective and objective voice quality measurements.

Subjective Voice Quality Evaluation Methods

Subjective voice quality tests are carried out by asking people to grade the quality of speech samples under controlled conditions as set out in the ITU-T P.800 (International Telecommunication Union, 1996). Subjective tests include listening-opinion tests and conversation-opinion tests. The recommended method for listening-opinion tests is "absolute category rating (ACR)" in which subjects only listen to a test speech sample and grade the voice quality on a five-point scale from 5 to 1 (excellent, good, fair, poor, and bad). Other listening-opinion tests include "degradation category rating (DCR)" and "comparison category rating (CCR)." In DCR tests, subjects are required to compare the quality of a test speech sample with that of a reference speech sample and give opinion score at a five-point scale from 5 (inaudible), 4 (audible but not annoying), 3 (slightly annoying), 2 (annoying) to 1 (very annoying). In CCR tests, a pair of speech samples (including reference and degraded samples without a particular order) are presented to subjects who will judge the quality of the 2nd sample to the 1st one at a seven-point scale ranging from -3 (much worse), -2 (worse), -1 (slightly worse), 0 (about the same), 1 (slightly better), 2(better), to 3 (much better). Listening-opinion tests are normally carried out in a controlled environment (e.g., in a soundproof room). The mean opinion score (MOS) is obtained by averaging individual opinion scores for a number of listeners (e.g., from 32-100). The suggested speech samples for testing (International Telecommunication Union, 1998) are normally 10-30 seconds consisting of several short sentences spoken by male and female speakers.

Conversation-opinion tests required two subjects seated in two separate soundproof rooms/cabinets to carry out a conversation test on selected topics. The five-point opinion scale (from 5 for excellent to 1 for bad) is normally used and the mean opinion score for conversational tests can be expressed as MOSc.

Subjective tests based on the mean opinion score (MOS) reflect an overall speech quality, which is an opinion score normally given by a subject at the end of a tested speech sample. Due to the nature of variable network conditions (e.g., bit-error, packet loss, delay, and jitter) in VoIP applications especially in wireless networks, the five-point MOS score tests seem inappropriate to assess rapidly changing voice quality in these applications. Researches are carried out to develop more advanced subjective test methods for multimedia networking and/or mobile applications. For example, in EURESCOM Project P905-PF (2000), a continuous rating of a 1-minute sample is proposed to assess quality for voice signal over Internet and UMTS networks. Instead of voting at the end of a test sentence (as in ITU-T P.800), a continuous voting is carried out at several segments of the test sentence to obtain a more accurate assessment of voice quality. In Watson and Sasse (1998), an unlabelled continuous rating scale is used to assess variable voice quality instead of five-point listening quality scale.

In addition to the mean opinion score (MOS) for an overall quality opinion, voice quality can also be expressed by a score or an index to reflect intelligibility, loudness, naturalness, listening effort, and/or pleasantness of tone.

Objective Voice Quality Evaluation Methods

Objective measurement of voice quality can be intrusive, which needs an injection of a reference signal (similar as reference methods in video) or non-intrusive, which is a passive method and does not need a reference signal (similar as no reference methods in video). Figure 6 depicts a conceptual diagram of different voice quality assessment methods for VoIP applications. All the terms—MOS-LQS (MOS Listening-only Quality Subjective) or MOS-LQO (MOS Listening-only Quality Objective)—follow ITU-T P.800.1 standard (International Telecommunication Union, 2003b).

The ITU-T P.862, perceptual evaluation of voice quality (PESQ) (International Telecommunication Union, 2001) is the most commonly used intrusive perceptual-based voice quality measurement method which predicts MOS score by comparing a reference speech with a degraded speech as shown in Figure 6. The PESQ score from P.862 (ranging from -0.5 to 4.5) is normally mapped to MOS-LQO (ranging from 1 to 5) according to ITU-T P.862.1 (International Telecommunication Union, 2003a). This value has been widely used for VoIP applications in industry. Normal VoIP applications are default for narrow-band (300 – 3100 Hz) applications. When wideband telephony (50-7000 Hz) is considered, the PESQ raw score can be further extended to the PESQ-WB (PESQ-WideBand) score according to ITU-T P.862.2 (International Telecommunication Union, 2005a).

The ITU-T E-model (International Telecommunication Union, 2005b) is a passive, computational model which was originally developed for network planning. It takes into account all possible impairments for an end-to-end speech transmission such as equipment-related impairment (e.g., codec, packet loss), delay-related impairment (e.g., end-to-end delay and echo), impairments that occur simultaneously with speech (e.g.,

Figure 6. Conceptual diagram of voice quality assessment methods for VoIP applications

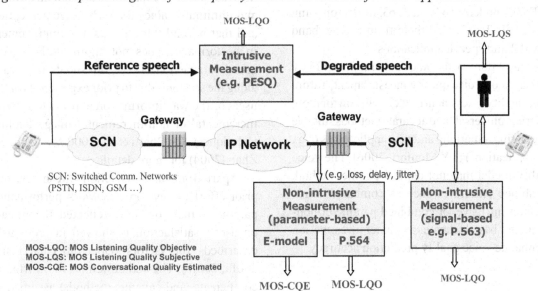

quantization noise, speech level). It can be used to predict (narrow-band) voice quality from network parameters (e.g., packet loss rate, burst loss length, and delay) and other system parameters (e.g., codec type) non-intrusively. The score obtained from the E-model is referred as MOS-CQE (MOS conversational quality estimated).

Similar as e-model which is parameter-based and non-intrusive, P.564 (International Telecommunication Union, 2006) can predict (narrow-band) voice quality from only IP network impairments by analysing the header of IP/TCP/RTP during a VoIP call. It can be used for monitoring of transmission quality for operations and maintenance purposes, and for measurements in support of service level agreements (SLAs) between service providers and their customers. The MOS-LQO score can be obtained from P.564 models.

ITU-T P.563 (International Telecommunication Union, 2004), on the other hand, can be used to estimate the MOS score non-intrusively by extracting speech and distortion features from the degraded (narrow-band) voice signal itself. It is based on models of the human vocal tract and the human perception of abnormalities (e.g., unnatural speech, noise, interruptions). It can predict MOS-LQO.

For E-model, P.564 and P.563, work is ongoing in the ITU-T to extend them from narrow-band to wideband speech applications.

In addition to the above mentioned ITU-T standards on voice quality measurement, future voice quality assessment models will aim for more generic, "universal" and accurate methods suitable for existing, emerging and new applications (e.g., 3G applications) (J-Y Monfort, 2006). The voice quality model may not depend on one method. Combined structures such as combined intrusive/non-intrusive, or combined parameter/non-parameter based schemes are under investigation to enhance voice quality prediction accuracy.

BEYOND ASSESSMENT: PREDICTING MODELS

In previous section, the state-of-the-art of subjective and objective quality assessment for Web, voice and video services over modern telecommunication networks have been reviewed. In this section, we further investigate novel prediction models for Web, voice, video and online game services. These models can be used for quality prediction and control in telecommunication networks.

Modeling/Predicting Web PQoS

Regarding page downloading time (DT) impact on satisfaction, there are no unanimous criteria for modelling the relationship between DT and user perception. There have been identified satisfaction thresholds (Muntean et al., 2004; Sevcik, 2002; Woolley, 2000), so that a bunch of "# seconds rules" have appeared. In Nah (2004) author collects five different Web downloading time tolerating thresholds and carries out a series of empirical investigations in order to provide an additional one, establishing 2 and 15 seconds thresholds. Then, although there are no standardized values, most authors agree that there are both maximum and minimum values for Web usage perception and that beyond these points any improvement in performance does not significantly affects users' satisfaction. These thresholds may vary along the sessions, due to prior experiences of the users or the way information appears (e.g., with incremental or non-incremental image loading techniques). See Bhatti et al. (2000b), Chung and Zhao (2004) for more details.

Apart from the satisfaction thresholds, one prior effort to develop a network performance parameter that somehow reflected the impact on users' satisfaction is showed in previously described "fun factors" (Joachim Charzinski, 2001a, 2001b). The author defines four different coefficients (and calculus methods) assumed to describe user perceived quality with an arithmetic value:

$$\Phi_1 = \frac{1}{2}\left(\min\left\{1, \frac{R_L}{r_t}\right\} + \min\left\{1, \frac{d_t}{T_D}\right\}\right)$$

$$\Phi_2 = \min\left\{ \min\left\{1, \frac{R_L}{r_t}\right\}, \min\left\{1, \frac{d_t}{T_D}\right\}\right\}$$

$$\Phi_3 = \min\left\{1, \sqrt{\frac{R_L \cdot d_t}{r_t \cdot T_D}}\right\}$$

$$\Phi_4 = \min\left\{1, \frac{d_t + B_L / r_t}{T_D + T_L}\right\}$$

being:

- T_D = initial time before beginning the download of an object
- B_L = the size of the object
- T_L = downloading time observed for the object
- $RL = B_L / T_L$, downloading rate observed during T_L
- r_t = target downloading rate
- d_t = target downloading delay

However, both the notation and the calculus process behind each one of these "fun factors" concern users' satisfaction about making the most out of their connection, not about the service performance itself. Thus, any slow but fully used connection would get better rates than other high bandwidth but underused connection. The author justifies the relationship between fun factors and users' satisfaction arguing that users expect certain performance levels out of their connections. Nevertheless, many users do not know this performance either because they do not have enough technical knowledge or because they have not tried any other similar connection for comparison purposes. All these drawbacks make "fun factors" not a very practical tool for Web PQoS prediction.

On the other hand, there exist alternative analytical formulations for more usable utility functions relating Web PQoS vs. downloading time derived from empirical tests. Some of them can be found in Johnson (1998), Lee, Lehoczky, Siewiorek, Rajkumar, and Hansen (1999), Okamoto and Hayashi (2002), and Van der Mei (2004). In these papers authors analyse the users' perception about Web browsing in a mean opinion score (MOS) scale, approximated as a logarithmic expression like the following one:

$$MOS = 6 - \log 2 \left(TDT\right) \mid\ 1 < MOS < 5$$

The truncated logarithmic shape of the utility function fits the characteristics of users' perception towards downloading time. In fact, logarithmic functions have been usually considered as a typical utility or cost function in studies related to minimizing cost (Chen Lee, 1999) or analyzing users' willingness to pay (Yamori & Tanaka, 2004) both for Web and other types of services (Luna, Kondi, & Katsaggelos, 2003).

Such a final analysis is further elaborated with more detailed approaches of the Web quality perception relation to the latency in different conditions. In Bhatti, Bouch, and Kuchinsky (2000a), it is studied in detail how users' tolerance to latency varies in function of the time the user has stayed in the Web site until that moment.

An experimental measurement of the valuation of the quality perceived by the users, based on the delay contributes with the following results, which are depicted on Table 1.

Furthermore, this study concludes that, when the session time raises, users' tolerance to delay decreases. Equally, the feedback obtained by the user during the waiting time for the page load favors a higher tolerance to delay. As it can be observed in the values in the Table 1, an increasing load makes possible the growth of the waiting times without a decrease in the quality perception. Another important element, in this sense, is the browser, depending on the type of information

Table 1. Impact of delays in users' perceptions

Satisfaction	Non increasing load	Increasing load
High	0-5 sec	0-39 sec
Medium	> 5 sec	> 39 sec
Low	> 11 sec	> 56 sec

provided when a Web page is being received. This effect is analyzed in Galletta et al. (2004), "Model of Immediate Reactions to Delay:"

A sensitivity analysis implies that decreases in performance and behavioral intentions begin to flatten when the delays extend to 4 seconds or longer, and attitudes flatten when the delays extend to 8 seconds or longer. Future research should include other factors such as expectations, variability, and feedback, and other outcomes such as actual purchasing behavior, to more fully understand the effects of delays in today's Web environment.

Finally in Riva, Saarto, and Kojo (2004), it is carried out an exhaustive analysis of HTTP performance using different variants of the protocol over diverse transport protocols. More complex models about load generation and the internal operation of the clients can be consulted in Irnich (2000).

Modeling/Predicting Video PQoS

In digital video encoding the discrete cosine transformation (DCT) is exploited, since it exhibits very good energy compaction and decorrelation properties. Regarding this property of DCT, it has been shows that DCT is an asymptotic approximation to the optimal Karhunen-Loeve transform. In this section, we use the following conventions for video sequences: Every real NxN frame f is treated as a N^2x1 vector in the space R^{N^2} by lexicographic ordering by either rows or columns.

The high compression during the MPEG-related encoding process is mainly based on the quantization of the DCT coefficients, which in turn results in loss of high frequency coefficients. Within a MPEG block/macroblock, the luminance differences and discontinuities between any pair of adjacent pixels are reduced, by the encoding and compression process. On the contrary, for all the pairs of adjacent pixels, which are located across and on both edge sides of the border of adjacent DCT blocks, the luminance discontinuities are increased by the encoding process. Thus, after the quantization:

$$F_n^{'} = Q[F_n]$$

where $Q[]$ denotes the quantization process and F_n the DCT encoded frame f_n, before the quantization process.

So, at the decoder side, the final reconstructed frame (after motion estimation and compensation modules) will be given by:

$$f^{'} = \sum_{n=1}^{N^2} F_n^{'} e_n$$

Thus, an error based framework in the luminance domain Δf_Y between the original and the decoded frame will quantify the perceived quality degradation per frame due to the encoding and quantization process:

$$\Delta f_Y \propto f_Y - f_Y^{'}$$

An average of the PQoS level for the whole encoding signal can be derived by the following equation:

$$< PQoS >_{video} = \frac{1}{N} \sum_{i=1}^{N} \Delta f_{Y_i}$$

An objective perceived quality metric, which provides reliable assessment of the video quality is the *SSIM* metric. The *SSIM* is a FR metric for measuring the structural similarity between two image sequences, exploiting the general principle that the main function of the human visual system is the extraction of structural information from the viewing field. If x and y are two video signals, then *SSIM* is defined as:

$$SSIM(x,y) = \frac{(2\mu_x \mu_y + C_1)(2\sigma_{xy} + C_2)}{(\mu_x^2 + \mu_y^2 + C_1)(\sigma_x^2 + \sigma_y^2 + C_2)}$$

where μ_x, μ_y are the mean of x and y, σ_x, σ_y, σ_{xy} are the variances of x, y and the covariance of x and y, respectively. The constants C_1 and C_2 are defined as:

$$C_1 = (K_1 L)^2 \quad C_2 = (K_2 L)^2$$

where L is the dynamic pixel range and $K_1 = 0.01$ and $K_2 = 0.03$, respectively (Wang & Bovik, 2004; Wang, Bovik, Sheikh, & Simoncelli, 2004).

The concept of the average *SSIM* for the whole video duration can be exploited for deriving a single perceived quality measurement, which is more practical, especially for the service providers. However, for long duration videos, where the spatial and temporal activity level of the content may differ significantly, the deduction of just one measurement of the perceived quality will not be accurate. In such a long sequence, the proposed average metric can be combined along with a scene change detector algorithm, which will lead to calculating partial average PQoS for the various scenes and then pooling them into a common estimation. However, this case is not within the purposes of the current paper and it is not examined. The sequences under test of this paper are either reference videos or movie trailers with limited durations and therefore practically constant spatial and temporal activity level.

In order to specify the dependence of the <PQoS> on the encoding bit rate various test signals, which are representative of specific spatial and temporal activity levels, were used. Each test video clip was transcoded from its original H-264 format with Hi-Def resolution (i.e., 720p) to ISO H.264 Baseline Profile, at different VBR bit rates. For each corresponding bit rate, a different H.264 compliant file with CIF (common interface format) resolution (352x288) was created. The frame rate was set at 25 frames per second (fps) for the transcoding process in all test videos.

Each H.264 video clip was then used as input in the *SSIM* estimation algorithm. From the resulting *SSIM* vs. time graph, the <PQoS> value of each clip was calculated. This experimental procedure was repeated for each video clip in CIF resolution. The results of these experiments are depicted in Figure 7.

Referring to the curves of Figure 7, the following remarks can be made:

1. The minimum bit rate, which corresponds to the lowest <PQoS>$_{SSIM}$ depends on the S-T activity level of the video clip.
2. The variation of the <PQoS>$_{SSIM}$ vs. bit rate is an increasing function, but non linear. Moreover, the quality improvement of an encoded video clip is not significant for bit rates higher than a specific threshold. This threshold depends on the S-T activity of the video content.

Moreover, each <PQoS>$_{SSIM}$ vs. bit rate curve can be successfully described by a logarithmic function of the general form:

$$< PQoS >_{SSIM} = C_1 \ln(BitRate) + C_2$$

Figure 7. The <PQoS>$_{SSIM}$ vs. bit rate curves for various test signals

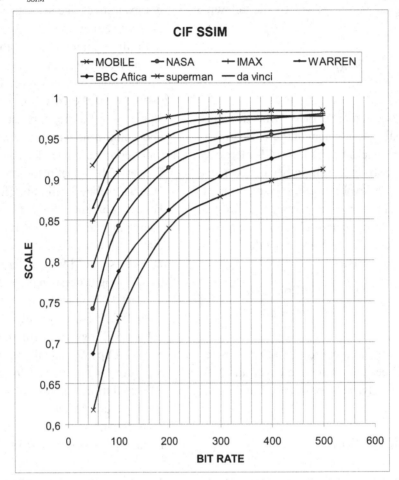

where C_1 and C_2 are constants strongly related to the spatial and temporal activity level of the content. Table 2 depicts the corresponding logarithmic functions for the test signals of Figure 7 along with their R^2 factor, which denotes the fitting efficiency of the theoretical graph to the experimental one.

Based on the aforementioned analysis, we can describe the derived <PQoS>$_{SSIM}$ vs. bit rate curve of each test signal with N total frames, which is encoded at bit rates with values from *BitRate$_{min}$* to *BitRate$_{max}$* as a set C, where each element F_n is a triplet, consisting the <PQoS>$_{SSIM}$, the constant C_1 and C_2 of the specific bit rate, which is derived

by the analytical logarithmic expression of Table 2, found in Box 1. In this equation:

- *SSIM* is the functions that calculates the perceived quality of each frame according to the *SSIM* metric.
- -N the total number of frames f_i that consist the movie *m*.

Thus deriving the sets C_n at various encoding bit rates for contents, ranging from static to very high spatial and temporal ones, a group of reference hyper sets *RS*, containing various C_n sets can be deduced:

Table 2. Logarithmic fitting functions of test signals depicted on Figure 7

Test Signal	Logarithmic Function	R² factor
Mobile	0.1295ln(x)+0.1274	0.9759
Imax	0.0563ln(x)+0.6411	0.9514
Da Vinci Code	0.0474ln(x)+0.6974	0.8833
Warren	0.0738ln(x)+0.5210	0.9528
Nasa	0.0950ln(x)+0.3892	0.9595
BBC – Africa	0.1098ln(x)+0.2702	0.9875
Superman Returns	0.0282ln(x)+0.8167	0.8859

Box 1.

$$C_n \triangleq \{m : (\frac{1}{N} \sum_{i=1}^{N} SSIM(f_i), C_1, C_2)_n = F_n, \forall n \in [BitRate_{min}, BitRate_{max}]$$

Box 2.

$$ADV = | F_{BitRate_i} : (\frac{1}{N} \sum_{i=1}^{N} SSIM(f_i)) - F'_{BitRate_i} : (\sum_{i=1}^{N} SSIM(f'_i)) |$$

$$RS_{S-T_{Low}} = \{C_{BitRate_{min}}, ..., C_{BitRate_{max}}\}$$
$$\vdots$$
$$RS_{S-T_{High}} = \{C_{BitRate_{min}}, ..., C_{BitRate_{max}}\}$$

Hence, considering an unknown video clip, which is uncompressed and we want to predict its corresponding RS_{S-T} hyper set that better describes its perceived quality vs. bit rate curve before the encoding process, we define the absolute difference value between the first parameter of each triplet element of the sets C_n and an experimental measurement of the average *SSIM* for the test signal at a specific encoding bit rate, for which we want to predict its PQoS curve as shown in Box 2.

Due to the fact that the additive property is valid, it is concluded that when the absolute difference between reference $F_{BitRate_i}$ and experimental $F_{BitRate_i}$ triplet elements of the video under test (the F_n are unique triplet elements of a specific $C_{BitRate_i}$

set), which for the needs of the proposed method it has been encoded once at specific BitRatei, is minimum, then the hyper set RS_{S-T} that contains the specific $C_{BitRate_i}$ describes better the specific video. By defining a specific hyper set RS_{S-T}, which minimizes the ADV, then we have successfully approximated the PQoS vs. Bit rate curve of the specific video with actual cost only one testing encoding at a specific bit rate. Then the service provider can predict analytically through the logarithmic expression the bit rates that satisfy specific perceived quality levels, without requiring any other testing encoding processes.

Thus, one only test measurement/estimation of the average SSIM at a specific encoding bit rate is adequate for the accurate prediction of the PQoS vs. Bit Rate curve for a given video clip. Regarding video transmission, we consider that the initial encoding quality is not degraded and it is finally delivered to the end-user.

Modeling/Predicting VoIP PQoS

For VoIP applications, PQoS modeling/predicting can be performed either on listening-only one-way voice quality or on two-way conversational voice quality, which takes into account interactivity. In earlier work (Sun & Ifeachor, 2006), it is demonstrated how to derive conversational MOS model from end-to-end packet loss and delay based on a combined ITU-T PESQ and e-model structure. A similar route is followed in this section to develop PQoS model (in terms of MOS) based on PESQ-LQO, which is closer to subjective MOS score when compared to PESQ. For explanatory purposes, adaptive multi-rate (AMR) codec is chosen as an example to develop PQoS models.

AMR speech codec was developed by ETSI and has been standardized for GSM. It has been chosen by 3GPP as a mandatory codec and is widely used in current 3G mobile handsets. AMR is a multi-mode codec with eight modes (MR475 to MR122) with bit rates between 4.75 Kb/s to 12.2 Kb/s. In current 3G mobile handsets, a fixed bit rate AMR codec (e.g., 12.2 Kb/s) is normally used. Research is on going to develop adaptive 3G mobile handsets based on adaptive AMR codec. AMR can also support mode switching based on each speech frame (in a length of 20 ms). As there are no PQoS models in the public domain for AMR applications over IP or mobile networks, we aim to develop PQoS models for adaptive AMR codec in this section. These models will help to develop PQoS-aware 3G mobile handsets in the near future.

A VoIP simulation system is built up to simulate a VoIP flow, which includes encoder, packet loss simulator, and decoder. For AMR codec, 8 modes (MR122, MR102, MR795, MR74, MR67, MR59, MR515 and MR475) are used in the simulation respectively. The reference speech is taken from the ITU-T data set (ITU-T, 1998). Packet loss is generated from 0% to 30%, in an incremental step of 3% and Bernoulli loss model is used for simplicity. Packet size is set as one. ITU-T PESQ (ITU-T, 2001) is used for evaluating end-to-end voice quality by comparing the reference and the degraded speech samples.

For each speech sample in the ITU-T data set for British English, a MOS (PESQ) score is obtained by averaging over 30 different packet loss locations (via using different random seeds) in order to remove the influence of packet loss location. Further, the MOS score for a packet loss is obtained by averaging over all male and female speech samples in the ITU-T date set (consisting of eight males and eight females) in order to remove the gender impact. At the end, the overall MOS score (from PESQ) is mapped to MOS (PESQ-LQO) score according to the following mapping function (International Telecommunication Union, 2003a):

$$y = 0.999 + \frac{4.999 - 0.999}{1 + e^{-1.4945*x + 4.6607}}$$

PESQ-LQO is regarded closer to subjective MOS score when compared to PESQ, as the PESQ-LQO value is in the range of 1 to 5 (similar to a five-point MOS scale), whereas, the PESQ score is in the range of -0.5 to +4.5.

The results of MOS (PESQ-LQO) vs. packet loss rate for AMR codec are shown in Figure 8. The gap of MOS scores between the highest bit rate codec (12.2. Kb/s) and the lowest bit rate codec (4.75 Kb/s) decreases with the increase of packet loss rate. When packet loss rate reaches 30%, all eight modes of AMR codec have similar MOS scores (between 1.5 to 1.6). For AMR codec, the higher the sender bit rate, the better the voice quality (in the term of MOS score).

The relationship between the MOS (PESQ-LQO) vs. packet loss rate can be converted to the Equipment Impairment factor, I_e (which represents effects of equipment such as VoIP systems and codecs on the quality of speech signal), vs. packet loss rate via the following equations (Sun et al., 2006):

Figure 8. MOS vs. packet loss rate for AMR codec

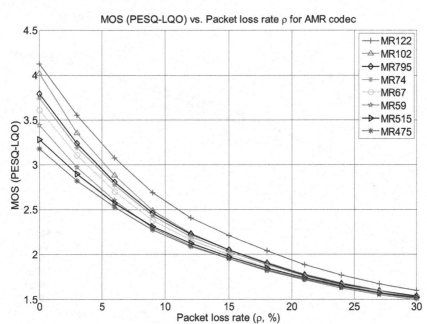

Box 3.

$$MOS = \begin{cases} 1 & for\ \ R \leq 0 \\ 1 + 0.035R + R(R-60) \times (100-R)7 \times 10^{-6} & for\ \ 0 < R < 100 \\ 4.5 & for\ \ R \geq 100 \end{cases}$$

$$R = 3.026MOS^3 - 25.314MOS^2 + 87.060MOS - 57.336$$
$$I_e = R_0 - R = 93.2 - R$$

The derived curves for I_e vs. packet loss rate are shown in Figure 9. A logarithm fitting function of I_e vs. packet loss rate (ρ in percentage) for each mode of AMR codec can be derived in the following form:

$$I_e = a\ln(1 + b \cdot \rho) + c$$

The fitting parameters for the above logarithm function for the eight modes of AMR codec can be obtained by nonlinear least-square curve fitting and are shown in Table 3. The R^2 factor for the Goodness of fit is also listed.

The delay impairment, I_d, representing all impairments due to delay of voice signals, can be derived from end-to-end delay (d) using the following equation (Cole & Rosenbluth, 2001):

$$I_d = 0.024d + 0.11(d - 177.3)H(d - 177.3)$$
$$where \begin{cases} H(x) = 0, & if\ \ x < 0 \\ H(x) = 1, & if\ \ x \geq 0 \end{cases}$$

Based on I_e and I_d, the R-factor from the E-model can be derived by:

$$R = R_0 - I_d - I_e = 93.2 - I_d - I_e$$

From the R-factor, the MOS value can be obtained by Box 3 (International Telecommunication Union, 2005).

Figure 9. I_e vs. packet loss rate ρ for AMR codec

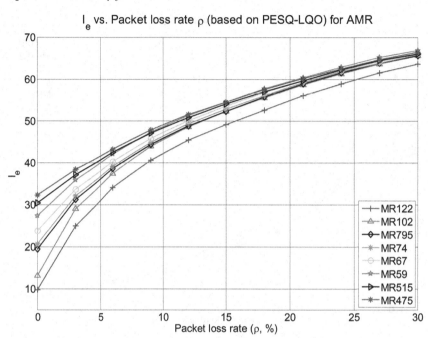

Table 3. Fitting parameters for I_e vs. packet loss for AMR codec (based on PESQ-LQO)

Para.	MR122 (12.2kb/s)	MR102 (10.2kb/s)	MR795 (7.95kb/s)	MR74 (7.4kb/s)	MR67 (6.7kb/s)	MR59 (5.9kb/s)	MR515 (5.15kb/s)	MR475 (4.75kb/s)
a	22.98	21.14	22.8	22.63	22.86	23.41	25.83	26.46
b	0.3054	0.362	0.2198	0.2113	0.1799	0.148	0.1002	0.0879
c	10.07	13.23	19.5	20.76	23.79	27.36	30.45	32.42
R^2	0.9997	0.9999	0.9998	0.9999	0.9999	0.9999	0.9999	0.9998

These models can be directly used for predicting voice quality under different network conditions and for QoS control to achieve a best tradeoff between packet loss and delay for the AMR codec. The method can also be used to develop PQoS models for other voice codecs under IP and mobile networks.

Modeling/Predicting Online Games PQoS

Due to the success of latest online gaming platforms, the research community has carried out an intensive work in order to identify the NP related parameters that have the highest impact on gamers' satisfaction.

Initially researches devoted to analyze the behavior of a certain platform/game. For example in Farber (2002), the traffic generated during Counter Strike® popular game was analytically modeled. Likewise in Henderson and Bhatti (2001) the authors studied the characteristics of gamers sessions including arrival time, session duration, etc. All these studies aimed at deriving mathematical models from real traces in order to reproduce users' behavior in simulation environments.

Once the behavior was evaluated and the effect of the variation of NP parameters into gamers satisfaction was analyzed in most of the cases authors concluded that latency was the most relevant factor (Pantel & Wolf, 2002; Schaefer, Enderes, Ritter, & Zitterbart, 2002; Sheldon, Girard, Borg, Claypool, & Agu, 2003; Zander & Armitage, 2004). In fact, many online games provide information regarding the so-called "ping time" or application level delay, so that gamers chose the servers with lowest ping times. Regarding this ping time, some researchers (Armitage, 2001a, 2001b) have analyzed for example the maximum delay gamers stand: 150 ms or as high as 250 ms if there is no nearer server for the *Quake III®* game. The impact of the delay may vary according very heterogeneous and game-dependant factors (such as, for example the kind of weapon used (Svoboda & Rupp, 2005)). However, most of the studies simply identify a maximum tolerable delay threshold that users can stand. In order to provide a detailed relationship the minimum and maximum delay thresholds as parameters can be used to build up a family of utility functions as in Johnson (1998) and Richards, Rogers, Antoniades, and Witana (1998) with the expressions in the following equations. The resulting figures, truncated logarithmic functions, are consistent with subjective experiments.

$$s(x) = 5 - 4 \cdot a \cdot \ln(b \cdot x + c),$$

$$a = \frac{1}{p - 10} \quad b = \frac{\left(\exp\left(\frac{1}{a} \right) - 1 \right)}{\left(S_{max} - S_{min} \right)}$$

$$c = \frac{\left(S_{max} - S_{min} \cdot \exp\left(\frac{1}{a} \right) \right)}{\left(S_{max} - S_{min} \right)}$$

where:

- S_{max} is the maximum tolerable delay threshold.
- S_{min} is the minimum noticeable delay threshold.

- p is often called "sensitivity factor," since it controls the sensitivity of satisfaction to variations in x.

With a minimum noticeable delay of 20 ms. and maximum tolerable delay threshold of 150 ms the family of utility functions in Figure 10 is obtained. Depending on the value of the p parameter the researcher can choose between more or less "tolerant" users in a similar way as the classification of complainers and optimistics in Dick, Wellnitz, & Wolf, 2005).

FUTURE TRENDS: INTEGRATED PQOS FRAMEWORKS

PQoS assessment and predicting models presented in this chapter bring researchers the possibility to evaluate the impact of certain QoS conditions on users' satisfaction in an accurate and automated way. However, all the proposed models are service specific, so that obtained results and resulting mathematical models cannot be applied in a universal way (i.e., out of the scope that they were designed for).

Yet currently most of the users consume several diverse multimedia services simultaneously so that a holistic evaluation of PQoS regarding multiple services becomes absolutely necessary.

There have been recently some initiatives concerning the evaluation of holistic satisfaction. These include regulatory recommendations such as the ITU-T G. 1000 (ITU-T, 2004a) that brought together prior recommendations like P.800 (International Telecommunication Union, 1996), I.350 (ITU-T, 1993) and Y.1540 (ITU-T, 2002) regarding the relationships between subjective QoS and NP issues. G.1000 proposed a theoretical matrix to be used in order to identify the most important criteria for certain telecommunication services.

In this research field, in Gbaguidi, Verscheure, and Hubaux (1997) the authors propose an extension of the typical OSI model in order to include

Figure 10. Online games utility functions family

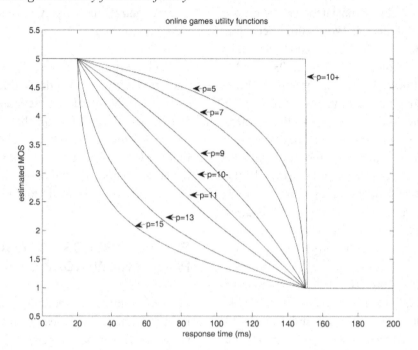

an additional layer (the end user layer). Similarly, in Patrick et al. (2004) the OSI model is extended with up to three additional layers (display, human performance, and human needs), as an attempt to include subjective interactions and human factor in the protocol definitions.

These initiatives however do not provide specific algorithms to quantitatively estimate the relative importance. In order to do so multiple subjective and objective criteria for different services must be evaluated. So, the problem resembles traditional multi-criteria decision problems, which have been widely analyzed (from an objective only aspect) in several industrial fields.

Regarding multimedia services, one of the first attempts for providing such a kind of multiple criteria evaluation technique was Ghinea and Magoulas (2001a). The authors evaluate different criteria for video PQoS evaluation by using neural networks and analytic hierarchy process (AHP) multicriteria decision tool.

Similarly, one of the latest approaches towards an holistic PQoS evaluation framework can be found in Liberal, Ferro, Jodra, and Fajardo (2005). The authors presented an holistic PQoS assessment model based on a matrix structure similar to quality function deployment (QFD) (Akao, 1990) quality methodology and ITU-T G.1000 Recommendation (ITU-T, 2004a), the proposed matrix displays the complex relationships between the agents involved in the multimedia distribution chain (in rows) and user perceptions for different services (in columns). Once this abstract representation is fulfilled with the particular characteristics of the services under study, authors use analytic hierarchy process (AHP) multicriteria decision tool as done in Bodin, Gordon, and Loeb (2005) and Ghinea and Magoulas (2001b) to estimate both the relative weights of each service in the overall users satisfaction and the relative importance of each kind of perception within a service itself.

In order to complete the whole PQoS evaluation, the impact of every QoS condition into a specific perception for a service is evaluated by using the results of the studies collected in this chapter (in a per service basis). So, proposed model takes advantages of detailed PQoS analysed carried out previously for each service and evaluates the composed behaviour using multicriteria decision tools. The objective part can be provided by simulation tools such as ns2 (NS2, 2007) or Opnet® (OPNET, 2007) or by studying the protocol in charge of content delivery and finding an analytical solution to these relationships and using performance simple metrics as in Alkahtani, Woodward, Al-Begain, and Alghannam (2002).

CONCLUSION

One of the visions of the future communication networks is the provision of audiovisual content at various quality and price levels. There are many approaches to this issue, one being the perceived quality of service (PQoS) concept for multimedia services. The evaluation of the PQoS will provide a user with a range of potential choices, covering the possibilities of low, medium, or high quality levels. Moreover, the PQoS evaluation gives the service provider and network operator the capability to minimize the storage and network resources by allocating only the resources that are sufficient to maintain a specific level of user satisfaction.

The concept of PQoS, although in general it deals with the user satisfaction from a specific delivered/requested service, practically it is significantly differentiated by the nature of each delivered service.

For example, regarding multimedia applications that distribute audiovisual content over communication networks, the use of video encoding techniques (e.g., MPEG-4/H.264), which achieve high compression ratios by exploiting the spatial and temporal redundancy in original uncompressed video sequences, cause image artifacts, which in turn result in perceived quality

degradation. Due to the fact that the parameters with strong influence on the video quality are normally those set at the encoder (with most important the bit rate, the frame rate and the resolution), the issue of the PQoS for video encoded services, considering flawless video transmission, is expressed as the deduced encoding video quality in correlation with the selected encoding parameters (e.g., codec type, picture resolution, bit rate, frame rate etc.).

Similarly, for VoIP applications, the PQoS expresses the voice quality, which is affected by applications related parameters (e.g., codec type, FEC, loss concealment, and playout buffer algorithms).

Both in video and VoIP applications, if impaired wireless or congested wired network is involved, then possible transmission impairments (e.g., packet losses) have to be considered into end-to-end PQoS evaluation. Thus, it is crucial for content providers, network operators and service providers to assess, predict, and possibly control the end-to-end perceptual voice/video quality for commercial and technical reasons. Developing accurate, efficient, and robust PQoS models for voice and video remains a challenging and interesting research target both in academia and industry.

On the other hand, although video/voice services play one of the most important roles in communication networks, the PQoS concept can be successfully applied/adapted on other type of services as well. For instance, as newest game consoles (i.e., another form of multimedia) include out-of-the box communication facilities, online gaming is becoming one of the most spread QoS demanding services, making online-gamers one of the most QoS-conscious group of users. However, their vision of PQoS is quite often reduced just to one single parameter, namely: The application level delay. This limited vision is explained through two main causes: On the one hand, the delay is considered the parameter with deepest impact on gamers' satisfaction. On the other hand, most of the games provide "ping time" estimation tools, which are then used to select "the best game server" available. However, there has been an increasing research effort towards evaluating the real impact not only of the delay but also of other factors on gamers satisfaction. This effort has provided researchers with a wider range of methods for predicting quality in online games.

Similarly, although traditional elastic services, such as Web browsing do not have so rigid PQoS constraints as real time services, they are also affected by network conditions. Therefore, the impact of different QoS parameters into users' perceived quality must be considered.

So, both multimedia services including voice, video as well as online games and general data services are main applications for today and future's packet networks (e.g., the Internet). Assessing/evaluating perceived quality of these services is an important/critical issue for a successful deployment of multimedia services and for a normal operation of these services, since the most significant parameter in the multimedia market is the user satisfaction. Furthermore, in the upcoming mobile communication systems, an end user will have access simultaneously at various services, ranging from simple Web access up to a combination of video, VoIP and Web (e.g., push to talk service, triple play services etc.). In such a complicated converged environment, there is a need to study how a PQoS assessment/management method can combine all types of services (e.g., voice, video, data) and identify the most suitable QoS-sensitive service and network-oriented parameters in order to satisfy a specific level of user satisfaction.

Within this framework, this chapter has reviewed the various existing PQoS assessment methods for video, VoIP, online games and Web services that have been published in the literature. Afterwards, it presented novel techniques for predicting the PQoS of a multimedia service, making a step beyond the current assessment

methods. In this context, the authors have extensively discussed:

- The various underlying QoS issues that arise and affect the performance of multimedia applications (i.e., video, VoIP, Web, online gaming).
- The PQoS issues that arise with different types of multimedia applications and services.
- Novel solutions and state of the art research.

Finally, a generic PQoS assessment framework for different types of services is discussed as the main future trend of this research field.

ACKNOWLEDGMENT

The work in this chapter has been performed within the research framework of FP7 ICT-214751 ADAMANTIUM Project.

REFERENCES

Akao, Y. (1990). *Quality function deployment: Integrating customer requirements into product design.* Productivity Press Inc.

Aladwani, A. M., & Palvia, P. C. (2002). Developing and validating an instrument for measuring user-perceived Web quality. *Information and Management, 39,* 467-476.

Alkahtani, A. M. S., Woodward, M. E., Al-Begain, K., & Alghannam, A. (2002). *Enhanced best effort QoS routing with multiple prioritised metrics using the analytic hierarchy process (AHP) concept.* Paper presented at the ICAI 2002, Canary Islands. Spain.

Armitage, G. (2001a). *Lag over 150 milliseconds is unacceptable.* Retrieved from http://gja.space4me.com/things/quake3-latency-051701.html

Armitage, G. (2001b). *When does the QuakeIII community play?* Retrieved from http://gja. space4me.com/things/quake3-when-051401. html

Babulak, E. (2004, Dec). Quality of service provision assessment for campus network. *Journal of Electrical Engineering, 55*(7-8), 221-224

Barnes, S., & Vidgen, R. (2000a, July 3-5, 2000). *WebQual: An exploration of Web-site quality.* Paper presented at the Proceedings of the 8th European Conference on Information Systems, Viena, Austria.

Barnes, S., & Vidgen, R. (2000b, July 3-5). *WebQual: An exploration of Web-site quality.* Paper presented at the 8th European Conference on Information Systems, Viena.

Bhatti, N., Bouch, A., & Kuchinsky, A. (2000a). Integrating user-perceived quality into Web server design. *Proceedings of the 9th international World Wide Web Conference on Computer Networks: The International Journal of Computer and Telecommunications Networking* (pp. 1-16). North-Holland Publishing Co.

Bhatti, N., Bouch, A., & Kuchinsky, A. (2000b). Integrating user-perceived quality into Web server design. *Proceedings of the 9th International World Wide Web Conference on Computer Networks: The International Journal of Computer and Telecommunications Networking* (pp. 1-16). North-Holland Publishing Co.

Bodin, L. D., Gordon, L. A., & Loeb, M. P. (2005). Evaluating information security investments using the analytic hierarchy process. *Communications of the ACM, 48*(2), 79-83.

Bouch, A., Kuchinsky, A., & Bhatti, N. (2000). *Quality is in the eye of the beholder: meeting users' requirements for Internet quality of service.* Paper presented at the SIGCHI Conference on Human factors in computing systems, The Hague, The Netherlands.

Bouch, A., & Sasse, M. A. (1999). Network quality of service: What do users need? *Proceedings of the 4th International Distributed Conference (IDC'99)* (pp. 78-90).

Bouch, A., Sasse, M. A., & DeMeer, H. (2000, 5-7 June 2000). *Of packets and people: A user-centered approach to quality of service.* Paper presented at the International Workshop on Quality of Service (IWQOS 2000).

Buxton, W. (1995). Integrating the periphery and context: A new taxonomy of telematics. *Proceedings of Graphics Interface* (Vol. 95, pp. 239-246).

Cole, R. G., & Rosenbluth, J. H. (2001, May). Voice over IP performance monitoring. *ACM SIGCOMM Computer Communication Review, 31*(2), 9-24.

Cronin, J. J., & Taylor, S. A. (1994). SERVPERF vs. SERVQUAL: Reconciling performance-based and perceptions-minus-expectations measurement of service quality. *Journal of Marketing, 58*, 125-131.

Charzinski, J. (2001a, Dec 2001). *Measured HTTP performance and fun factors.* Paper presented at the ITC 2001, Salvador, BA, Brasil.

Charzinski, J. (2001b). *Web performance in practice: Why we are waiting?* Paper presented at the AEÜ International Journal of Electronics and Communications.

Cherkasova, L., Fu, Y., & Tang, W. (2002). Measuring end-to-end Internet service performance: Response Time, caching efficiency and QoS.

Cherkasova, L., Fu, Y., Tang, W., & Vahdat, A. (2003, Dec). Measuring and characterizing end-to-end Internet service performance. *ACM Trans. Inter. Tech., 3*(4), 347-391.

Chung, H., & Zhao, X. (2004). Effects of perceived interactivity on Web site preference and memory:

Role of personal motivation. *Journal of Computer-Mediated Communication, 10*(1).

D'Ambra, J., & Rice, R. E. (2001). Emerging factors in user evaluation of the World Wide Web. *Information and Management, 38*, 373-384.

Davis, F. D. (1989). Perceived usefulness, perceived ease of use, and user acceptance of information technology. *MIS Quarterly, 13*(3), 319-340.

Davis, F. D., Bagozzi, R. P., & Warshaw, P. R. (1989). User acceptance of computer technology: A comparison of two theoretical models. *Management Science, 35*(8), 982-1003.

Dick, M., Wellnitz, O., & Wolf, L. (2005). Analysis of factors affecting players' performance and perception in multiplayer games. *Proceedings of 4th ACM SIGCOMM Workshop on Network and System Support for Games.* Hawthorne, NY: ACM Press.

ETSI. (1994). *Network Aspects (NA); General aspects of Quality of Service (QoS) and Network Performance (NP).* ETSI.

EURESCOM Project P905-PF (2000, August). *AQUAVIT - Assessment of quality for audio-visual signals over Internet and UMTS - Deliverable 2: Methodology for subjective audio-visual quality evaluation in mobile and IP networks.*

Farber, J. (2002). Network game traffic modelling. *Proceedings of the 1st Workshop on Network and System Support for Games* (pp. 53-57). ACM Press.

Fogg, B. J., Jonathan, M., Othman, L., Alex, O., Chris, V., Nicholas, F., et al. (2001). What makes Web sites credible? A report on a large quantitative study. *Proceedings of the SIGCHI Conference on Human Factors in Computing Systems.* Seattle, WA: ACM Press.

Galletta, D., Henry, R., McCoy, S., & Polak, P. (2004). Web site delays: How tolerant are users? *Journal of the Association for Information Systems, 5*(1), 1-28.

Gardikis, G., Kourtis, A., & Constantinou, P. (2003). Dynamic bandwidth allocation in DVB-T networks providing IP services. *IEEE Transactions on Broadcasting, 49*(3), 314-318.

Gbaguidi, C., Verscheure, O., & Hubaux, J. P. (1997, Julio 1997). *A new flexible and modular QoS mapping framework based on psychophysics.* Paper presented at the MMNS 97, IFIP/IEEE Conference on Management of Multimedia Networks, Montreal, Canada.

Ghinea, G., & Magoulas, G. (2001a). Neural network-based interactive multicriteria decision making in a quality of perception-oriented management scheme. *Joint Conference on Neural Networks* (pp. 2536-2541).

Ghinea, G., & Magoulas, G. D. (2001b). Quality of service for perceptual considerations: An integrated perspective. *IEEE International Conference on Multimedia and Expo* (pp. 752-755).

Gronroos, C. (1983). *Strategic management and marketing in the service sector.* Boston: Marketing Science Institute.

Gunawan, I. P., & Ghanbari, M. (2003). *Reduced-reference picture quality estimation by using local harmonic amplitude information.* Paper presented at the London Communications Symposium 2003.

Habib, A., & Abrams, M. (2000). *Analysis of sources of latency in downloading web pages.* Paper presented at the WebNet 2000.

Hammer, F., Reichl, P., & Ziegler, T. (2004). *Where packet traces meet speech samples: An instrumental approach to perceptual QoS evaluation of VoIP.* Paper presented at the IWQOS'04.

Henderson, T., & Bhatti, S. (2001, October 5, 2001). *Modelling user behaviour in networked games.* Paper presented at the ACM Multimedia 2001, Ottawa, Canada.

International Telecommunication Union. (1996). Methods for subjective determination of transmission quality. *ITU Recommendation P.800.*

International Telecommunication Union. (1998). Objective measuring apparatus, Appendix 1: Test signals. *ITU-T Recommendation P.50.*

International Telecommunication Union. (2001). Perceptual evaluation of speech quality (PESQ), an objective method for end-to-end speech quality assessment of narrow-band telephone networks and speech codec. *ITU Recommendation P.862.*

International Telecommunication Union. (2003a). Mapping function for transforming P.862 raw result scores to MOS-LQO. *ITU Recommendation P.862.1.*

International Telecommunication Union. (2003b). Mean opinion score (MOS) terminology. *ITU Recommendation P.800.1.*

International Telecommunication Union. (2004). Single-ended method for objective speech quality assessment in narrow-band telephony applications. *ITU-T Recommendation P.563.*

International Telecommunication Union. (2005). The E-model, a computational model for use in transmission planning. *ITU Recommendation G.107.*

International Telecommunication Union. (2006). Conformance testing for narrowband voice over IP transmission quality assessment models. *ITU-T Recommendation P.564.*

Irnich, T. (2000). *Measuring and modelling WWW traffic characteristics in access networks.* Thesis. Aachen University of Technology.

ITU-T. P.862.1 (11/2003). *Mapping function for transforming P.862 raw result scores to MOS-LQO.*

ITU-T. (1993). General aspects of quality of service and network performance in digital networks, including ISDNs. In *Rec. G.1000.* Vol. Rec. I.350, (ITU).

ITU-T. (1994). *E.800: Terms and definitions related to quality of service and network performance including dependability.*

ITU-T. (1997). *Methods for subjective determination of transmisión quality.*

ITU-T. (1998). Objective measuring apparatus, appendix 1: Test signals. *ITU-T P.50 (2/1998)*

ITU-T. (2001). Perceptual evaluation of speech quality (PESQ), an objective method for end-to-end speech quality assessment of narrow-band telephone networks and speech codecs. *P.862. (02/2001).*

ITU-T. (2002). *Internet protocol data communication service - IP packet transfer and availability performance parameters*: International Telecommunication Union.

ITU-T. (2004a). *Handbook on quality of service and network performance.* ITU Press.

ITU-T. (2004b). *Handbook on quality of service and network performance.* ITU Press.

ITU-T. (2005a). Wideband extension to recommendation P.862 for the assessment of wideband telephone networks and speech codecs. *P.862.2 (11/2005).*

ITU-T. (2005b). The E-model, a computational model for use in transmission planning. *G.107 (03/2005).*

ITU-T. (2006). Conformance testing for narrowband voice over IP transmission quality assessment models. *P.564 (07/2006).*

Johnson, C. (1998). *Why CHI (computer-human interaction) has failed to improve the Web.* Retrieved from www.dcs.gla.ac.uk/~johnson/papers/Web98.html

Koumaras, H., Kourtis, A., & Martakos, D. (2005). Evaluation of video quality based on objectively estimated metric. *Journal of Communications and Networks, 7*(3), 235-242.

Koumaras, H., Pallis, E., Xilouris, G., Kourtis, A., Martakos, D., & Lauterjung, J. (2004). *Pre-encoding PQoS assessment method for optimized resource utilization.* Paper presented at the HET-NETs04, Ilkley, West Yorkshire, U.K.

Krishnamurthy, B., & Wills, C. E. (2000, May 2000). *Analyzing factors that influence end-to-end web performance.* Paper presented at the Ninth International World Wide Web Conference, Amsterdam, Netherlands.

Lavie, T., & Tractinsky, N. (2004). Assessing dimensions of perceived visual aesthetics of Web sites. *International Journal Human-Computer Studies, 60*(3), 269-298.

Lee, C. (1999). *On quality of service management.* PhD thesis. Carnegie Mellon University.

Lee, C., Lehoczky, J., Siewiorek, D., Rajkumar, R., & Hansen, J. (1999). *A scalable solution to the multi-resource QoS problem.* Paper presented at the 20th IEEE Real-Time Systems Symposium.

Liberal, F., Ferro, A., Jodra, J. L., & Fajardo, J. O. (2005). *Application of general perception-based QoS model to find providers' responsibilities. Case study: User perceived Web service performance.* Paper presented at the Joint International Conference on Autonomic and Autonomous Systems and International Conference on Networking and Services (ICAS/ICNS 2005), Tahiti.

Liu, C., & Arnett, K. P. (2000). Exploring the factors associated with Web site success in the context of electronic commerce. *Information and Management, 38*, 23-33.

Lu, L., Wang, Z., Bovik, A. C., & Kouloheris, J. (2002). *Full-reference video quality assessment considering structural distortion and no-reference quality evaluation of MPEG video.* Paper presented at the IEEE International Conference on Multimedia.

Luna, C. E., Kondi, L. P., & Katsaggelos, A. K. (2003). Maximizing user utility in video streaming applications. *IEEE Transactions on Circuits and Systems for Video Technology, 13*(2), 141.

Mahlke, S. (2002). Factors influencing the experience of Web site usage. *CHI '02 Extended Abstracts on Human Factors in Computing Systems* (pp. 846-847): ACM Press.

Monfort, J. Y. (2006). *Voice quality assessment, ITU-T Study Group 12.* Retrieved from http://www.etsi.org/plugtests/History/2006STQ_Asia/JYMonfort_SG12_QoSMeasurement.pdf

Moon, J. W., & Kim, Y. G. (2001). Extending the TAM for a World-Wide-Web context. *Information and Management, 38*(4), 217-230.

Mullin, J., Smallwood, L., Watson, A., & Wilson, G. (2001). *New techniques for assessing audio and video quality in real-time interactive communications.* Paper presented at the 3rd International Workshop on Human Computer Interaction, Lille, France.

Muntean, C. H., & McManis, J. (2004, June 20-24, 2004). *A QoS-aware adaptative Web-based system.* Paper presented at the IEEE International Conference on Communications.

Nah, F. (2004). A study on tolerable waiting time: How long are Web users willing to wait? *Behaviour and Information Technology, 23*(3), 153-163(111).

NS2. (2007). NS2. *The network simulator.* Retrieved from http://www.isi.edu/nsnam/ns/

Okamoto, T., & Hayashi, T. (2002). *Analysis of service provider's profit by modeling customer's willingness to pay for IP QoS.* Paper presented at the Globecom 2002.

Olshefski, D., & Nieh, J. (2006). Understanding the management of client perceived response time. *SIGMETRICS Perform. Eval. Rev., 34*(1), 240-251.

Olson, T. (1994). *In a framework about task-technology fit, what are the tasks features.* Paper presented at the CSCW '94: Workshop on video mediated communication: Testing, Evaluation & Design Implications, North Carolina, US.

Oodan, A. P., Ward, K. E., & Mullee, A. W. (1997). *Quality of service in telecommunications.* The IEE press.

OPNET. (2007). *OPNET* [http://www.opnet.com/].

Pantel, L., & Wolf, L. C. (2002). *On the impact of delay on real-time multiplayer games.* Miami, FL: ACM Press.

Parasuraman, A., Berry, L. L., & Zeithaml, V. A. (1988). SERVQUAL: A multiple-item scale for measuring consumer perceptions of service quality. *Journal of Retailing, 64*(1), 12-40.

Parasuraman, A., Zeithaml, V. A., & Berry, L. L. (1985). A conceptual model of service quality and its implications for future research. *Journal of Marketing, 49*(4).

Parasuraman, A., Zeithaml, V. A., & Berry, L. L. (1991). Refinement and reassessment of the SERVQUAL scale. *Journal of Retailing, 67*(4), 420-450.

Patrick, A. S., Singer, J., Corrie, B., Noël, S., El Khatib, K., Emond, B., et al. (2004, Oct. 18-20, 2004). *A QoE sensitive architecture for advanced collaborative environments.* Paper presented at the 1st International Conference on Quality of Service in Heterogeneous Wired/Wireless Networks (QSHINE 2004), Dallas, US.

Prasad, A. R., Esmailzadeh, R., Winkler, S., Ihara, T., Rohani, B., Pinguet, B., et al. (2001). *Perceptual quality measurement and control: Definition, application, and performance.* Paper presented at the 4th International Symposium on Wireless Personal Multimedia Communications, Aalborg, Denmark.

Ramsay, J., Barbesi, A., & Preece, J. (1998). A psychological investigation of long retrieval times on the World Wide Web. *Interacting with Computers, 10*(1), 77-86(10).

Ranganathan, C., & Shobha, G. (2002). Key dimensions of business-to-consumer Web sites. *Information and Management, 39*, 457-465.

Richards, A., Rogers, G., Antoniades, M., & Witana, V. (1998, Nov). *Mapping user level QoS from a single parameter.* Paper presented at the International Conference on Multimedia Networks and Services (MMNS '98).

Riva, O., Saarto, J., & Kojo, M. (2004). *Performance analysis on HTTP traffic and traffic mixtures with competing TCP and UDP flows.* University of Helsinki - Department of Computer Science.

Saliba, A. J., Beresford, M. A., Ivanovich, M., & Fitzpatrick, P. (2005). User-perceived quality of service in wireless data networks. *Personal Ubiquitous Comput., 9*(6), 413-422.

Schaefer, C., Enderes, T., Ritter, H., & Zitterbart, M. (2002, April 2002). *Subjective quality assessment for multiplayer realtime games.* Paper presented at the Workshop on Network and System Support for Games.

Schubert, P. (2003). Evaluation of electronic commerce applications from the customer's viewpoint. *International Journal of Electronic Commerce, 7.*

Schubert, P., & Dettling, W. (2001). *Web site evaluation: Do Web applications meet user expectations? Music, consumer goods and e-banking on the test bed.* Paper presented at the 14th International Bled Electronic Commerce Conference, Bled, Slovenia.

Schubert, P., & Leimstoll, U. (2001). *The extended Web assessment method (EWAM) applied: Do Web sites for consumer goods stand the test?* Paper presented at the Eighth Research Symposium on Emerging Electronic Markets RSEEM 01, Maastricht, The Netherlands.

Schubert, P. D. W. (2002, January 07-10). *Extended Web assessment method (EWAM): Evaluation of e-commerce applications from the customer's viewpoint.* Paper presented at the 35th Annual Hawaii International Conference on System Sciences (HICSS'02), Big Island, Hawaii.

Sears, A., Jacko, J. A., & Borella, M. S. (1997). *Internet delay effects: How users perceive quality, organization, and ease of use of information.* Atlanta, GA: ACM Press.

Seeling, P., Reisslein, M., & Kulapala, B. (2004). Network performance evaluation using frame size and quality traces of single layer and two layer video: A tutorial. *IEEE Communications Surveys & Tutorials, 6*(3), 58-78.

Selz, D., & Schubert, P. (1997). Web assessment: A model for the evaluation and the assessment of successful electronic commerce applications. *Electronic Markets, 7*(3).

Sevcik, P. J. (2002). Understanding how users view application performance. *Business Communication Reviews--Net Forecasts, 32*(7).

Sheldon, N., Girard, E., Borg, S., Claypool, M., & Agu, E. (2003). *The effect of latency on user performance in Warcraft III.* Paper presented at the 2nd Workshop on Network and System Support for Games. Redwood City, California.

Sun, L., & Ifeachor, E. (2006). Voice quality prediction models and their application in VoIP networks. *IEEE Transactions on Multimedia, 8*(4), 809-820.

Svoboda, P., & Rupp, M. (2005). *Online gaming models for wireless networks.* Paper presented at the 9th IASTED International Conference, Internet and Multimedia Systems and Applications, Grindelwald, Switcherland.

van der Heijden, H. (2003). Factors influencing the usage of Web sites: The case of a generic portal in The Netherlands. *Information and Management, 40*(6), 541-549.

van der Mei, R. D. (2004). *Performance analysis of communication networks.* Course syllabus, Faculty of Science: Vrije Universiteit.

VQEG. (2000). *Final report from the video quality experts group on the validation of objective models of video quality assessment.* Retrieved from http://www.vqeg.org

Wang, H., & Bovik, A. C. (2004). Video quality assessment based on structural distortion measurement. *Signal Processing: Image Communication, special issue on Objective video quality metrics, 19*(2), 121-132.

Wang, H., Bovik, A. C., Sheikh, H. R., & Simoncelli, E. P. (2004). Image quality assessment: From error visibility to structural similarity. *IEEE Transactions on Image Processing, 13*(4), 1-14.

Wang, Z., Bovik, A. C., & Lu, L. (2002). *Why is image quality assessment so difficult?* Paper presented at the IEEE International Conference on Acoustics, Speech, and Signal Processing.

Wang, Z., Sheikh, H. R., & Bovik, A. C. (2003). Objective video quality assessment. In B. Furht & O. Marqure (Eds.), *The handbook of video databases: Design and applications* (Vol. 41, pp. 1041-1078). CRC Press.

Watson, A., & Sasse, M. A. (1998). *Measuring perceived quality of speech and video in multimedia conferencing applications.* Paper presented at the ACM Multimedia.

Woolley, R. D. (2000). *Web performance measurement & capacity planning: Briefing paper.* Chief Information Officer's Section. Office of the Governor. State of Utah.

Xilouris, G., Kourtis, A., & Stefanou, G. (2005). A mesh topology DVB-S network architecture for node interconnection, featuring QoS capabilities. *Computer Networks, 48*(1), 45-56.

Yamori, K., & Tanaka, Y. (2004, August 2004). *Relation between willingness to pay and guaranteed minimum bandwidth in multiple-priority service.* Paper presented at the 10th Asia-Pacific Conference on Communications (APCC 2004), Beijing, China.

Zander, S., & Armitage, G. (2004). *Empirically measuring the QoS sensitivity of interactive online game players.* Paper presented at the Australian Telecommunications Networks & Applications Conference 2004 (ATNAC 2004), Sydney, Australia.

Zhang, P., & von Dran, G. (2001a, January 03-06). *Expectations and rankings of Website quality features: results of two studies on user perceptions.* Paper presented at the 34th Annual Hawaii International Conference on System Sciences (HICSS-34).

Zhang, P., & von Dran, G. (2001b). User expectations and rankings of quality factors in different Web site domains. *International Journal of Electronic Commerce, 6*(2), 9.

Zviran, M., Glezer, C., & Avni, I. (2006). User satisfaction from commercial Web sites: The effect of design and use. *Information and Management, 43*(2), 157-178.

Section IV
Cross–Layered Solutions

Cross-layered solutions make use of QoS-enabling features at various layers of the wireless multimedia service chain, including aspects of the application layer and network layer. Although cross-layered solutions can greatly increase the degree of optimisation of the end-user QoS, cross-layered solutions incur higher orders of complexity since they have a larger number of axes of optimisation. This section presents a number of cross-layered solutions that include algorithms at the network, application and end-user layers.

Chapter XIV
Scheduling and Access Control for Wireless Connections with Throughput Guarantees

Peifang Zhang
University of California, Irvine, USA

Scott Jordan
University of California, Irvine, USA

ABSTRACT

Emerging wideband code division multiple access (WCDMA) data services will likely require resource allocation to ensure that throughput targets are met. Scheduling and access control can both be key components in this task. In this chapter, we introduce a two-layer scheduler and connection access controller that attempts to balance efficiency with fairness. We first propose a scheduler that takes advantage of variations in the wireless channel—both channel fluctuations in time for each user, and channel variations among multiple users at a particular time. By mixing a max-min policy with a policy of serving users with relatively good channels, the scheduler can achieve individual average throughput targets in a manner that encourages system efficiency. We then propose a two-layer algorithm that offers targeted throughput for interactive nomadic data streams, such as video or music streaming. The design purpose is to provide users with service differentiation, which lays the groundwork for network optimization in terms of capacity or utility, and can be easily extended to revenue maximization. Upon the request of a data stream connection, a target throughput is negotiated between the user and the network/base station. The network attempts to achieve the throughput targets over the duration of each individual connection by maximizing a system objective based on users' satisfaction that is represented by a utility function. We assume that a users' utility function depends not only on the throughput target but also on final achieved throughput. The algorithm integrates connection access control and resource allocation per connection request with rate scheduling on a per frame basis adaptive to slow fading. Through numerical analysis, the proposed joint scheduler and connection access controller is shown to achieve the design goals.

INTRODUCTION

In recent years, wireless networks have been evolving rapidly, driven by emerging multimedia applications and supported by advanced technologies. Code division multiple access (CDMA), one of the most widely applied technologies for cellular wireless networks, is undergoing a fundamental transition from providing voice only service to wideband CDMA (WCDMA) that accommodates convergence between data, audio and video (Holma & Toskala, 2004).

Much research has addressed the extremes of traffic that requires constant bit rate and traffic that can accept best effort service. However, there is an intermediate class of interactive traffic that does not require constant bit rate but requires more predictable throughput than that provided by best effort service. Relatively few papers have addressed connection access control (CAC) and rate scheduling (RS) for such interactive traffic. For such interactive traffic, we would hope that the network could support soft performance guarantees to match the limited tolerance of these applications to variations in performance, and enhance radio resource efficiency and aggregate network capacity as well.

An impediment so far to addressing CAC and RS for such traffic has been the lack of the ability to allow interactive connections to communicate a performance goal and to allow the network some flexibility in achieving these goals. In this chapter, we first focus on the scheduler, which allocates power and rate in real-time among competing data streams. Efficiency depends on how well the scheduler takes advantage of variations among users. Fairness depends on how well the scheduler achieves the throughput targets of individual data streams. The two are related, as higher efficiency makes throughput targets easier to achieve. We then consider joint CAC and RS for connections, which can specify a target throughput. The target is interpreted as an average to be achieved over the lifetime of the connection. A user's evaluation

of the throughput achieved over the connection is represented by a utility function that depends not only on the throughput target but also on the connection's achieved throughput, thus allowing satisfaction to depend on the degree to which the target was achieved. There is a balance to be achieved between the number of connections accepted into the network and the throughput achieved for each accepted connection. We therefore jointly consider CAC and RS, and propose a two-layer structure that separates these functions by time scale and that communicates vital information between these two layers.

Related Work

There is a vast literature on quality of service (QoS) provisioning in wireless networks, and we only survey a very limited portion that is throughput or rate oriented. In the scheduling literature, a number of proposals focus primarily upon system efficiency, and incorporate rate scheduling into power control of wireless CDMA networks. Typical approaches in this genre exploit channel variations among multiple users at a particular time (here called *multi-user diversity*) in such a way that users with better channels are assigned higher transmission rates (Berggren & Kim, 2004; Jafar & Goldsmith, 2000; Kim & Honig, 2000; Knopp & Humblet, 2000; Li & Ephremides, 2005). However, such approaches do not take fairness (e.g., throughput targets) into account, and consequently do not take full advantage of channel fluctuations in time for each user (here called *temporal diversity*). Fairness is often implemented through schedulers that explicitly consider the cumulative throughput achieved by each connection (e.g., max-min policies) (Bertsekas & Gallager, 1987; Kelly, 1997). However, such policies typically do not strongly consider efficiency.

A relatively small portion of the literature does consider both efficiency and fairness. The well known and widely deployed algorithm in this category is the proportional fairness algorithm (Holtzman, 2000; Kelly, 1997), to which a comparison of our proposed scheduling algorithm will be made later in this chapter. Song and Mandayam (2001) used utility functions to construct a SIR and rate control algorithm that can tradeoff between static system throughput and fairness. However, this static scheme does not allow for heterogeneous throughput targets and temporal diversity. Liu (2002) and Xiao, Shroff, and Chong (2003) exploited both multi-user diversity and temporal diversity with utility-defined efficiency and QoS constraints. Han and Liu (2004) also took both diversity dimensions into account using a signal to interference and noise ratio (SINR) defined fairness constraint. Tong and Ramanathan (2004) proposed a method to satisfy the constraints on SINR and the minimum deviations from throughput targets over a specified time interval, with the second objective of maximizing the overall throughput, which is achieved by switching between throughput optimization and feasibility. In contrast in this chapter, we exploit both diversity dimensions and consider both efficiency and fairness without any QoS constraint, since QoS constraints usually degrade the system efficiency significantly.

The application of a utility function to represent the satisfaction of mobile users for resource allocation has been studied in various contexts. Most relevant perhaps are papers, which optimize power allocation in cellular networks in order to maximize aggregate utility, see, for example, Goodman and Mandayam (2000), Xiao et al. (2003), Liu, Zhang, Jordan, and Honig (2004), and Zhou, Honig, and Jordan (2005). Designs, which cross layers or address multiple time scales have been considered to integrate various QoS provisioning functions. Grossglauser and Tse (2003) proposed a time-scale decomposition between measurement-based admission control and reservation of spare bandwidth for wired networks. Berry and Yeh (2004) surveys several cross-layer approaches to integrated power alloca-

tion and rate scheduling. Wang (2004) proposes an integration of CAC, RS, and bit error rate (BER) scheduling for time division CDMA (TD-CDMA). Wong, Mark, and Chua (2003) considered joint satisfaction of connection level and packet level QoS. Kwon and Choi (2003) coordinate CAC and RS through cell overload probability.

Overview of this Chapter

In this chapter, we propose a dynamic scheduling scheme with a goal that combines efficiency and fairness. Efficiency is implemented in a manner that exploits both channel fluctuations in time for each user (temporal diversity) and channel variations among multiple users at a particular time (multi-user diversity). Fairness is defined as achieving the target average throughput for each data stream. This fairness criterion is advantageous, since it may be utilized for service definition in the application layer of wireless networks.

The efficiency component is implemented using an opportunistic policy in part of the scheduler. This policy allocates higher transmission rates to those users who are currently experiencing less fading than average. The fairness component is implemented using a max-min policy in part of the scheduler to guarantee heterogeneous throughput targets. The motivation for a max-min policy is to offer a hard connection-scale throughput guarantee for packet-switched wireless data traffic, given a feasible set of throughput demands. The max-min component grants priority to users who are not meeting their throughput targets. This particularly helps users who have suffered from unusually bad channels for a period of time, and therefore comes at the cost of degraded system efficiency. However, since cumulative throughput over the connection lifetime is considered, temporal diversity is exploited in a manner that matches the elasticity of data applications. By mixing a max-min policy with a policy of serving users with relatively good channels, the scheduler can achieve individual average throughput targets in a manner that encourages system efficiency.

We then focus on coordination of CAC and RS for connections, which can specify a target throughput. We consider interactive data sessions in a WCDMA network. The interactive data sessions may be initiated and terminated by the user at will. When a connection is established, a throughput target is negotiated between the network and the user. Upon termination of the connection, the utility is evaluated on the basis of the target throughput and the achieved throughput. This interactive data service is supported by the implementation of a cross layer measurement-based connection access control and resource scheduling architecture.

The rest of the chapter is organized as follows. In section 2, we present the scheduler. In section 3, we present the connection access controller. Finally the performance of the two is evaluated in section 4.

SCHEDULING

System Model

We consider data streams offered through a single WCDMA cell (Holma et al., 2004). We only model the downlink, since it is usually the bottleneck for data applications. We consider a fixed number, M, of users with arbitrary connection durations.

We start by modeling frame-scale dynamics, where multiple users are multiplexed with frame-by-frame power and rate adaptation. In the duration of a frame, we assume that the system observes flat fading channels, consisting of distance-based pathloss and slow log-normal shadowing, which are assumed to be accurately and rapidly estimated from pilot symbols. Let $h_i(t)$ denote the channel of user i at a frame t:

$$h_i(t) = (\frac{d_i}{d_0})^n \psi_i(t),$$

where d_0 and d_i are the far-field reference distance and user i's distance to the base station respectively, n is the pathloss exponent (typically between 2 and 4), and $\psi_i(t)$ is log-normal shadowing with zero mean and variance $\sigma^2_{\psi_{dB,i}}$ in the dB scale. We assume that users are stationary (i.e., $\sigma^2_{\psi_{dB,i}}$ is constant), but that both parameters vary by user. We further assume that the channels vary independently both among simultaneous users and frame by frame for a user.

Based on the channel (and other information), the scheduler assigns a set of power and rate ($p_i(t)$, $r_i(t)$) to user i at frame t. With the assumptions of fixed thermal noise, N_0, and fixed other-cell interference, I_0, there is a mapping between data rate, bit error rate, and signal to noise plus interference ratio (SINR) that depends on the WCDMA physical layer design. For instance, using Orthogonal Variable Spreading Factor, a user's SINR might be expressed as:

$$\xi_i(t) = \frac{p_i(t)}{h_i(t)(I_0 + N_0)} \frac{W}{b_i(t)},$$

and hence let:

$$r_i(t) = \frac{b_i(t)\xi_i(t)}{W}(I_0 + N_0)$$

we have:

$$p_i(t) = h_i(t)r_i(t) \tag{1}$$

where W, $b_i(t)$, and $r_i(t)$ are the spreading bandwidth, bit rate, and the (normalized) rate respectively. Note that the SINR target $\xi_i(t)$ is maintained through underlying fast power control to achieve the target bit error rate, and the rate $r_i(t)$ is adopted to summarize all the physical layer concerns.

We assume rates of all users at each frame are continuous and bounded. Without loss of generality, we normalize all rates by the maximum rate for the proposed data service, so that:

$$0 \leq r_i(t) \leq 1 \qquad (2)$$

We also assume that the total downlink transmission power in the cell is limited at each frame, namely:

$$\sum_{i=1}^{M} p_i(t) = \sum_{i=1}^{M} h_i(t) r_i(t) \leq P \qquad (3)$$

where P is the power supply in a single frame.

We are interested in the average throughput achieved by user i in her connection period, consisting of T_i frames, which we denote by:

$$E[r_i](T_i) = \frac{1}{T_i} \sum_{t=1}^{T_i} r_i(t)$$

Finally let X_i denote user i's throughput target (or equivalently, throughput demand), similarly normalized between 0 and 1. The goal is thus that $E[r_i](T_i) = X_i$ for each user i.

Opportunistic Scheduler

The goal of the scheduler is to combine efficiency and fairness, and to support heterogeneous throughput targets. In this subsection, we consider efficiency, and in the next subsection we consider fairness.

The efficiency component is implemented using an opportunistic scheduler. The idea is to allocate higher transmission rates to those users who are currently experiencing less fading than average. We recognized above that there are two sources of variation: channel fluctuations in time

for each user (temporal diversity), and channel variations among multiple users at a particular time (multi-user diversity). Temporal diversity can be exploited by assigning user i higher rates when it has a relatively good channel. In the literature, this is often posed as a power minimization problem. Multi-user diversity is often similarly exploited using a variation of opportunistic scheduling in which users with the best absolute channels are assigned the highest rates. We combine these opportunistic policies into a single simpler algorithm that orders users during each frame based on the user's fading (not channel), *relative to that user's fading variance*, as described in Box 1.

Max-Min Scheduler

The fairness component of the scheduler is implemented using a max-min scheduler to guarantee heterogeneous throughput targets. The motivation for a max-min policy is to offer a hard connection-scale throughput guarantee for packet-switched wireless data traffic, given a feasible set of throughput demands. We denote the ratio of the achieved throughput for user i over a time interval of T_i frames to the target throughput for user i by:

$$g_i(T_i) = \frac{E[r_i](T_i)}{X_i}$$

We call this QoS measure the *throughput ratio* of user i at frame T_i. We propose a greedy policy that considers information available only in the current frame and $g_i(t)$ accumulating the history:

Box 1. Scheduler OS

i) Sort users according to increasing normalized shadowing, $e_i = \psi_{dB,i}(t) / \sigma_{\psi_{dB,i}}$
ii) The full rate, $r_i(t) = 1$, is assigned to users in this order as long as (3) is satisfied.
iii) Any residual rate is assigned to the next user in order.
iv) $r_i(t) = 0$ is assigned to any other users.

Scheduler MM:

$\max_{\{r_i(t)\}} \min_{\{i=1,2,...,M\}} g_i(t),$ s. t. (2) & (3)

The throughput ratio of user i at frame t, $g_i(t)$, can be explicitly found using:

$$g_i(t+1) = \frac{g_i(t)a_i(t)}{a_i(t+1)} + \frac{r_i(t)}{X_i a_i(t+1)}$$

where $a_i(t)$ is the number of frames in which user i has been active by frame t (called the *age* of user i).

The greedy policy thus grants priority to users who are not meeting their throughput targets. This particularly helps users who have suffered from unusually bad channels for a period of time, and therefore comes at the cost of degraded system efficiency. However, since cumulative throughput over the connection lifetime is considered, temporal diversity is exploited in a manner that matches the elasticity of data applications.

Combined Scheduler

We now combine the proposed opportunistic scheduling policy with the greedy max-min policy to form a hybrid scheduler. Each policy is assigned a fixed proportion of the total available power. Specifically, a parameter $0 \le \theta \le 1$ is fixed; the opportunistic policy is given a power budget θP, and the greedy max-min policy is given the remaining power. The resulting hybrid scheduler can be described by Box 2.

At $\theta=0$ therefore, the hybrid policy reduces to the max-min scheduler, while at $\theta=1$ it reduces to the opportunistic scheduler. Heavier use of the opportunistic scheduler will increase efficiency but reduce fairness. We call θ the *efficiency index*.

Additional details regarding the development of this scheduler can be found in Zhang and Jordan (2006).

ACCESS CONTROL

System Model and Problem Formulation

We now consider nomadic users with user arrivals and departures. The users arrive according to a Poisson process with a rate of λ users/frame. User i's connection is independent and Exponentially distributed with a mean connection time of $1/\mu_i$ frames. Upon arrival, a user is either admitted into the system or blocked by the network. Blocked users leave the system completely, and admitted users enter the system immediately. The location of a new user is assumed to be uniformly distributed within the cell, and fixed during the connection, and thus channel variations stem from wireless environment.

Box 2.

1. Initialization: Initialize arriving users with $a_i = 0$ and $g_i = 0$.
2. Opportunistic phase: Run Scheduler OS above, with P replaced by θP. Update $\{g_i\}$, and pass any leftover power to the max-min phase.
3. Max-min phase: Run Scheduler MM above, with P replaced by power remaining after the opportunistic phase. Update $\{g_i\}$.
4. Departures: Remove any users who depart at the end of the current frame, update the frame time $t=t+1$, update ages of remaining users $a_i = a_i + 1$.

We start with the formulation of a utility function. In order to offer a soft throughput guarantee to interactive data traffic, we propose a utility function where we assume that users' satisfaction depends not only on a pre-negotiated throughput target, but also on the final achieved throughput. Let X_i and $x_{f,i}$ denote the throughput target and achieved throughput of user i respectively. Then her *utility function* can be expressed as $U(X_i, x_{f,i}/X_i)$, or equivalently $U(X_i, g_{f,i})$, with $g_{f,i}$ denoting the achievement ratio $x_{f,i} / X_i$. We propose that the utility function $U(X_i, g_{f,i})$ should have the following properties:

1. $U(X_i, g_{f,i})$ is increasing both in X_i and in $g_{f,i}$

2. $U(X_i, g_{f,i})$ is concave in X_i, as shown in Figure 1(a);

3. $U(X_i, g_{f,i})$ is convex in $g_{f,i}$ if $g_{f,i} < 1$, and concave in $g_{f,i}$ otherwise, as shown in Figure 1(b)

4. For fixed $X_i g_{f,i} = C$, $U(X_i, g_{f,i})$ is maximum at $X_i = C$ (i.e. $g_{f,i} = 1$), as shown in Figure 1(c)

5. $\dfrac{\partial U(X_i, g_{f,i})}{\partial X_i} \Big|_{X_i=0}$ is finite.

The first property assumes that user satisfaction is increasing with achieved throughput and with the ratio of achieved throughput to target throughput $g_{f,i}$. The mixed convexity and concavity expressed in the third property reflects a

Figure 1. Assumed properties of the utility function

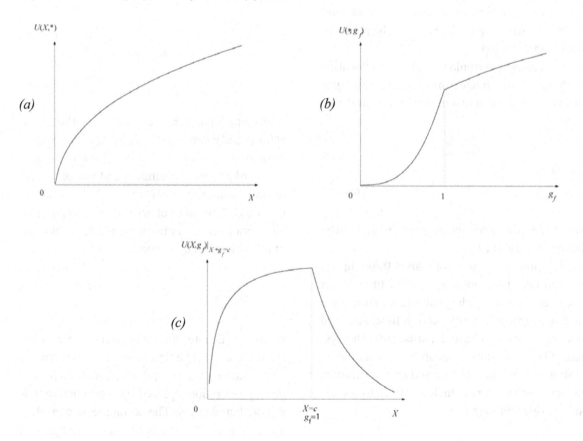

throughput target. The fourth property ensures that per user utility is maximized when achieved throughput equals target throughput, and is consistent with the rationality of the user behavior. The last property is required to ensure that the blocking probability of new connection requests is positive, given that blocking occurs if the negotiated $X_i = 0$. For the sake of simplicity, in the following we assume that all users have the same utility function.

Evaluation of utility requires measurement of achieved throughput. We define user i's average throughput at time t, denoted by $x_i(t)$, as:

$$x_i(t) = \frac{\sum_{\tau=s_i}^{t} r_i(\tau)}{a_i(t)}, \forall s_i \leq t \leq o_i$$

where s_i and o_i denote user i's arrival and departure times respectively, $r_i(\tau)$ denotes user i's assigned transmit rate at time τ, and $a_i(t) = t - s_i$ denotes the *age* of user i up to time t. Thus the achieved throughput is $x_i(o_i)$.

We can now formulate a resource allocation problem to maximize time-average aggregate utility subject to transmission power and rate constraints:

$$\max_{\{X_i, \{r_i(t), \forall t\}, \forall i\}} \lim_{T \to \infty} \frac{\sum_{i=1}^{N(T)} U(X_i, g_{f,i})}{T},$$
s. t. (2) & (3)   (4)

where $N(T)$ denotes the number of users who depart during $(0, T]$.

The problem is to choose target throughputs, X_i, and rate allocations, $r_i(t)$, at all times t, for each admitted user. The goal is to maximize the average aggregate utility per unit time, summed over all users who have departed from the system. The constraints apply an upper limit on the instantaneous rate per user and on the summed power over all users (which is related to the assigned rates through (1)).

Note, however, that in such a formulation the decision variables can potentially depend not only on current and past system states but also upon the future, in particular upon future channel conditions, arrivals and departures. As a result, the problem can only be solved off-line. In the next subsection, we formulate an online version of the optimization problem by considering a greedy objective subject to a stationary Markov decision policy set.

Connection Access Control and Resource Allocation

To convert the main problem objective into a greedy analogy with stationary Markov decisions on resource allocation, we replace the terms in (4) which depend on the future by predictions based on current and past system states. Our prediction for $g_{f,i}$ is:

$$\hat{g}_{f,i} = g_i(t)\frac{a_i(t)}{a_i(t) + 1/\mu_i} + \frac{y_i}{X_i}\frac{1/\mu_i}{a_i(t) + 1/\mu_i}$$
       (5)

where $g_i(t)$ denotes the measured throughput ratio at time t and y_i denotes the predicted time-average throughput of user i in the duration $(t, t + 1 / \mu_i)$.

In order to decouple the dependence of current resource allocation decisions with the effect of users who have not yet arrived, for purposes of connection access control we replace the objective in (4) with a greedy version:

$$\max_{\{y_i, X_i\}} \sum_{i \in A(t)} \left[U(X_i, \hat{g}_{f,i}) + \mathbf{I}_{X_j > 0} U(X_j, 1) \right]$$

where $A(t)$ denotes the set of users who have arrived by time t. The first term in the objective is a summation over current users, with their final throughput ratios replaced by their corresponding predicted ratios. The second term considers admission and throughput target assignment for a new arrival, denoted user j. X_j denotes the throughput target of the new user, and admission is granted only if $X_j > 0$. Optimistically, we assume that future decisions will result in an achieved throughput ratio for the new user equal to 1. Rate assignments for current users are summarized by the future time-average throughputs of all current users, y_i, which are now treated as decision variables.

The power constraint (3) is replaced by:

$$\sum_{i \in A(t)} m_{h_i} y_i \leq \phi_P(\Pi) P \qquad (6)$$

where Π and $\phi_P(\Pi) > 1$ denote a rate scheduler and its *power efficiency factor*. The value $\phi_P(\Pi)$ can be estimated by simulation. Similarly the rate constraint (2) is replaced by:

$$0 \leq y_i \leq \phi_R(\Pi)$$

where $0 < \phi_R(\Pi) < 1$ is called the *rate fluctuation factor*, which can be estimated by numerical analysis.

This problem transformation allows us to decompose the problem into separate connection access control and rate scheduling layers. The functionality of each layer and the communication between layers is illustrated in Figure 2, where i, j and k are used to denote the indices of current, arriving, and departing users.

On the frame scale, rate scheduling operates as outlined in the previous section. On the connection scale, CAC operates. Upon user arrivals

and departures, the goal is to maximize the system efficiency, in terms of expected aggregate utility, by assigning a connection level throughput target X_j to arrivals, and assigning future throughput targets y_i to current users.

The information flow is as follows. Upon arriving users, the system roughly estimates the first two moments of their channel during the network entry phase. The CAC layer informs the RS layer of the connection level and future throughput targets for each active user. Fast power control (at a lower layer) provides frame-level channel information to the RS layer. In turn, the RS layer informs the CAC layer of the achieved throughput ratios for each active user.

This separation of functionality by layer implements a negative feedback loop. If the CAC layer sets a throughput target X_j or y_i unrealistically high, the RS layer will achieve a low throughput ratio $g_i(t)$ in the period before the next arrival or departure. This low $g_i(t)$ will be fed back to the CAC layer, which will increase the priority of this user and lower future throughput targets, resulting in an increase in future values of $g_i(t)$. This effect will be seen in numerical analysis below.

The joint connection access control and rate allocation problem becomes **Problem CAC**:

$$\max_{\{y_i, X_j\}} \sum_{i \in A(t)} \left[U(X_i, \hat{g}_{f,i}) + \mathbf{I}_{X_j > 0} U(X_j, 1) \right], \qquad (7)$$

$$\text{s. t.} \sum_{i \in A(t)} m_{h_i} y_i + \mathbf{I}_{X_j > 0} m_{h_j} X_j \leq \phi_P(\Pi) P, \qquad (8)$$

Figure 2. Cross layer algorithm structure

$m_{h_j}, \sigma^2_{h_j}$	$\max_{\{y_i, X_j\}} \sum_{i \in A(t)} \left[\begin{matrix} U(X_i, \hat{g}_{f,i}) \\ + \mathbf{I}_{X_j > 0} U(X_j, 1) \end{matrix} \right]$	$\{X_i, \hat{g}_{f,i}\}$	$\max_{\{X_i, \hat{g}_{f,i}\}} \min_{\{i\}} \left\{ \dfrac{g_i(T_{k+1})}{\hat{g}_{f,i}} \right\}$	$\{h_i(t)\}$
$m_{h_k}, \sigma^2_{h_k}$	$s.t. \sum_{i \in A(t)} m_{h_i} y_i + \mathbf{I}_{X_j > 0} m_{h_j} X_j \leq \phi_P(\Pi) P$	$\{g_i\}$	$s.t. \sum_i h_i(t) r_i(t) \leq P$	
	$0 \leq y_i, X_j \leq \phi_R(\Pi)$		$0 \leq r_i(t) \leq 1$	

$$0 \le y_i, X_j \le \phi_R(\Pi), \forall i \in A(t). \qquad (9)$$

The optimization metric in (7) is to maximize the expected utility to be gained by current users plus a new arrival, by appropriate choice of the target future throughputs for each. Equations (8) and (9) constrain these target throughputs by relating them to a sum power limit and an individual rate limit. Since the utility function is of a sigmoid-shape, the optimization problem is not a concave program, and hence simple gradient-based searches are not guaranteed to converge to the global optimum. We therefore look for a heuristic algorithm.

We begin by focusing on a pair of users. We start with a tentative assignment of resources, and consider assignment of a rate increment. Recall that by assumption $U(X_i, \hat{g}_{f,i})$ is convex in $\hat{g}_{f,i}$ when $\hat{g}_{f,i} < 1$ and concave in $\hat{g}_{f,i}$ when $\hat{g}_{f,i} < 1$. We first consider the case in which both users are in the concave portion of the utility curve. G_i, which we call the *gradient priority*, is the marginal utility that can be earned per unit future throughput target, normalized by the user's mean channel. It can be expressed separately for current and new users:

$$G_i = \begin{cases} \dfrac{1/\mu_i}{a_i(t)+1/\mu_i} \dfrac{1}{m_{h_i}X_i} \dfrac{dU(X_i,\hat{g}_{f,i})}{d\hat{g}_{f,i}}, & \hat{g}_{f,i} \ge 1 \\[2ex] \dfrac{1}{m_{h_j}} \dfrac{dU(X_j,1)}{dX_j}, & \hat{g}_{f,j} = 1 \end{cases}$$

$$(10)$$

It can be shown that if both users have $\hat{g}_{f,i} \ge 1$, or if one user has $\hat{g}_{f,i} \ge 1$ and the other is a new arrival, then it is optimal to assign an infinitesimal rate increment to the user with the higher G_i (Zhang, 2005).

We now consider two users who are both in the convex portion of the utility curve. Again assume that a tentative resource assignment has been made and consider an incremental power assignment of δ. In this case, the increment need not be infinitesimal, so we can consider a chord of the utility function. We call this chord the *arch gradient priority*, and define it as:

$$G_i^\delta = \frac{U(X_i,\hat{g}_{f,i}+\dfrac{1/\mu_i}{a_i+1/\mu_i}\dfrac{\delta}{m_{h_i}X_i})-U(X_i,\hat{g}_{f,i})}{\delta}$$

$$(11)$$

It can be shown that if both users satisfy $\hat{g}_{f,i}+\dfrac{1/\mu_i}{a_i+1/\mu_i}\dfrac{\delta}{m_{h_i}X_i}<1$, then it is optimal to assign the incremental power δ to the user with the higher G_i^δ (Zhang, 2005).

We formulate an admission control algorithm based on these observations. The algorithm is based on iterative incremental assignment of power, based on the gradient priority users in the concave portion of the utility curve and on the arch gradient priority for users in the convex portion. In the resulting algorithm, a high priority is associated with a good channel (low $m_{h,i}$), a low throughput target, a young user (small a_i), a long expected holding time (large $1/\mu_i$), and/or $g_{f,i}$ close to 1 (large $\dfrac{\Delta U(X,g)}{\Delta g}$). The resulting CAC algorithm is shown in Box 3.

Additional details regarding the development of this CAC algorithm can be found in Zhang (2005).

NUMERICAL ANALYSIS

In this section, we evaluate the performance of the cross-layer connection access control and resource allocation (CAC) and rate scheduler (RS) architecture through numerical analysis using Matlab. We start by studying the performance of the rate scheduler in isolation. After this, we proceed to the performance of the combined CAC and RS architecture.

The following parameters are used throughout this section: far-field reference distance $d_0 = 0.1$,

Box 3.

1) Event identification and initialization: Identify a user arrival or departure, and save or remove their channel statistics. Initialize the residual power supply $P_{res} = \phi_P(\prod)P$, and update active user set $A(t)$ (subset of $\{1, ..., M(t)\}$. Let $X_i = 0$, $y_i = 0$ and $\hat{g}_{f,i} = g_i, \forall i = 1, ..., M(t)$.
2) Priority measure calculation: For all the active users with $\hat{g}_{f,i} < 1$, calculate G_i^{δ} according to equation (11). For all the active users with $\hat{g}_{f,i} \geq 1$, calculate G_i according to equation (10). If the event is an arrival, then calculate G_j according to equation (10).
3) Resource allocation (equalizing gradient priorities by water-filling): 3a. Order all the active users in $A(t)$ according to decreasing priorities. 3b. Pick the first user in $A(t)$. If it is an active user with $\hat{g}_{f,i} < 1$, then assign an increment $\Delta_i (y_i \leftarrow y_i + \Delta_i)$ chosen so that the updated $\hat{g}_{f,i} = 1$, $y_i = \phi_R$, or $P_{res} = 0$; If it is a new user, or an active user with $\hat{g}_{f,i} \geq 1$, then assign to y_i the smaller of a fixed increment $\overline{\Delta}$ or the increment Δ_i so that $y_i = \phi_R$. 3c. Update $\hat{g}_{f,i}$ according to equation (5), update G_i according to equation (10), reduce P_{res} by $m_{h,i}\Delta_i$, and remove the users with $y_i = \phi_R$ from $A(t)$. 3d. Re-sort the users in $A(t)$ according to updated priorities, and repeat steps 3b and 3c, until either $P_{res} = 0$ or $A(t)$ is empty.
4) Admission: If the event is an arrival and $X_j > 0$, then admit the new user. Otherwise, wait for an arrival or departure, and return to step 1.

distance from base station d_i uniformly distributed in (0.1,1), and path-loss exponent n=3.71. We define the *load* as the ratio of normalized power demand, $\frac{\lambda}{\mu} \frac{E[m_h]}{2}$, to the normalized power supply P.

Performance of the Rate Scheduler

In this subsection, the RS algorithm is isolated and evaluated. The following parameters are used throughout this subsection: 100 simultaneous users with target throughputs X_i uniformly distributed in (0,1], connection duration of 3000 frames, shadowing variance $\sigma_{\psi_{dB}} = 6$, and *load* = 2. We judge the performance of the RS online algorithm by users' throughput achievement ratios, $g_{f,i}$, and the corresponding minimum and mean throughput achievement ratios over all users, denoted by g_{min} and m_g respectively.

We start by examining the effect of the hybrid scheduler upon each user's achieved throughput over the duration of its connection, when the normalized power supply P=0.5 and the efficiency index θ=0.4. The achieved throughput ratio g_i for each user at the time of departure is shown in Figure 3(a).

The efficiency of the scheduler can be judged by the average throughput ratio; greater efficiency results in a higher average. The fairness of the scheduler can be judged by the variation of the throughput ratio; tightly clustered throughput ratios imply that users are achieving throughputs close in proportion to their throughput targets. In this example, all users meet or exceed their targets using our hybrid scheduler, since $g_i \geq 1, \forall i$. A few users achieve significantly higher throughput ratios, because they either have lower throughput targets, or have lower pathloss (or higher average channel gain).

Figure 3. Achieved throughput ratio for each user

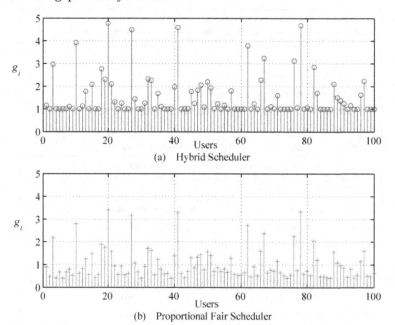

(a) Hybrid Scheduler

(b) Proportional Fair Scheduler

Another measure of the success of the scheduler is the lowest achieved throughput ratio; indeed maximizing this quantity was our original motivation for using a max-min component. For this example, the users with the lowest ratios achieved throughputs equal to their targets (i.e., $g_i = 1$).

We now turn to the effect of varying the efficiency index θ. In Figure 4, the lowest throughput ratio and the average throughput ratio (measured at the completion of each call) is shown as a function of the efficiency index.

When the efficiency index $\theta=0$, the hybrid scheduler reduces to a max-min scheduler. This gives the maximum amount of fairness but the lowest efficiency; the achieved throughput ratios for all users are tightly clustered around 0.55. As the efficiency index increases, heavier use is made of the opportunistic scheduler. Correspondingly, the average achieved throughput ratio monotonically increases from 0.55 to 2.0.

One might expect that the minimum achieved throughput ratio might be monotonically decreasing with the efficiency ratio. It is not; indeed the minimum achieved throughput ratio at first *increases* with the efficiency ratio on $0<\theta<0.4$ and then decreases on $0.4<\theta<1$. When the efficiency ratio is low and increasing, an increase in the use of the opportunistic scheduler results in quickly rising average throughput ratios. This increase in the average dominates the corresponding increase in variance, and the minimum throughput ratio increases (i.e., the increase in efficiency affects the worst user more than the decrease in fairness). In contrast, when the efficiency ratio is high and increasing, an increase in the use of the opportunistic scheduler results in slowly rising average throughput ratios. Now this increase in the average is dominated by the corresponding increase in variance, and the minimum throughput ratio decreases.

Next we compare our hybrid scheduler with the proportional fair scheduler. The achieved throughput ratio for each user under the proportional fair scheduler, at the time of departure, is shown in Figure 3(b). For this set of parameters, the proportional fair scheduler does not meet

Figure 4. Minimum and average throughput ratios vs. the efficiency index

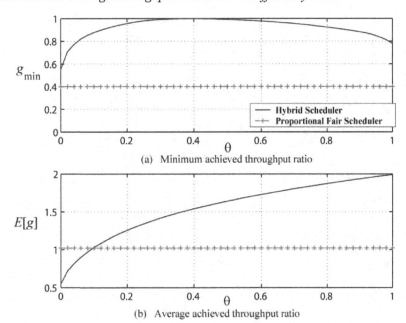

(a) Minimum achieved throughput ratio

(b) Average achieved throughput ratio

the target throughputs of most users, unlike the hybrid scheduler. Indeed, a close inspection of the results shows that the hybrid scheduler provides higher achieved throughput ratios *for every user* than does the Proportional Fair scheduler. This domination occurs because the hybrid scheduler takes advantage of both multi-user diversity and temporal diversity more efficiently than proportional fair scheduler, and holds true for a range of θ around 0.4.

A comparison of minimum and average achieved throughput ratios under the two schedulers is shown in Figure 4. (The proportional fair scheduler does not use the efficiency index, and hence its minimum and average throughput ratios are shown as constants.) The proportional fair scheduler achieves an average throughput ratio of 1, but a minimum of only 0.4. The hybrid scheduler dominates the proportional fair scheduler with respect to average throughput ratio when $\theta > 0.1$, and it dominates with respect to minimum throughput ratio over all efficiency ratios.

It can generally be argued that the max-min scheduler is more fair than the proportional fair scheduler, which is in turn more fair than the opportunistic scheduler. However, the reverse is true with respect to efficiency: the max-min scheduler is less efficient than the proportional fair scheduler, which is in turn less efficient than the opportunistic scheduler.

The hybrid scheduler, however, allows for an intermediate choice of fairness and efficiency. At the cost of the work involved to make an intelligent choice of the efficiency index, the hybrid scheduler can achieve both higher fairness and higher efficiency than the proportional fair scheduler; in this example, there is a wide range of θ for which this is true. This is possible because the hybrid scheduler takes advantage of both multi-user diversity and temporal diversity of wireless fading channels, while the Proportional Fair scheduler only takes advantage of the former.

We now analyze the effect of the power supply P upon the hybrid scheduler. In Figure 5, we show the minimum and average achieved throughput

Figure 5. Minimum and average throughput ratios vs. the power supply

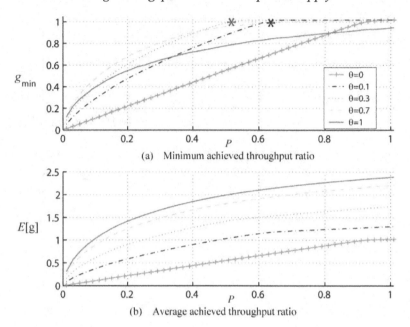

(a)   Minimum achieved throughput ratio

(b)   Average achieved throughput ratio

ratios vs. the power supply *P*, for a few choices of efficiency index θ. As expected, the average throughput ratio is monotonically increasing with the power supply. As we observed previously, higher values of the efficiency index result in higher average throughput ratios.

The minimum throughput ratio is nondecreasing with the power supply. The curves for different efficiency indices cross since, as observed previously, the minimum throughput is not monotonic with respect to efficiency index. At some efficiency indices, the minimum throughput ratio is constant above some threshold power supply (denoted by an asterisk in Figure 5(a)); the threshold depends on the efficiency index. Below this threshold, the power constraint (3) is binding; we call this case power-limited. Above this threshold (if it exists), there is more power than the users can consume, and the rate constraint (2) becomes binding for the users who have high throughput targets; we call this case rate-limited.

It follows that under the hybrid scheduler that system is power-limited when the power supply

is below the threshold and rate-limited when the power supply is above the threshold. A similar observation has been made for other wireless systems (Liu et. al., 2004; Zhou, Zhang, Honig, & Jordan, 2004).

Finally, we further explore the relationship between fairness, efficiency index, and power supply by examining the coefficient of variation of the throughput ratio. The coefficient of variation is defined as the standard deviation divided by the mean, $\sigma_g / E[g]$, and thus is a measure of the fairness of the scheduler (with lower values indicating higher levels of fairness). In Figure 6, we show the coefficient of variation of the throughput ratio vs. the power supply *P* for various choices of the efficiency index θ. When $\theta=0$, the throughput ratios for all users are nearly equal under any power supply, since the max-min policy attempts to equalize them. As a consequence, the coefficient of variation is nearly 0, indicating maximum fairness. As the efficiency index increases (under a fixed power supply), the coefficient of

Figure 6. Coefficient of variation of the throughput ratio vs. the power supply

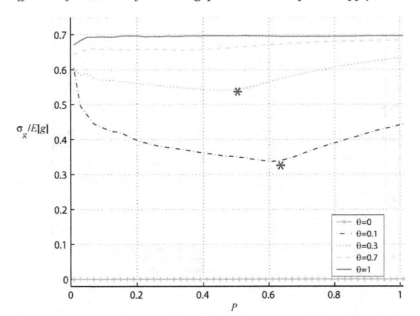

variation increases monotonically, representing decreasing fairness.

As the power supply increases, both the mean and standard deviation of the throughput ratio increase. When the system is power-limited, an increase in the power supply results in a decrease in the coefficient of variation of throughput ratio, since the increase in the mean dominates the increase in the standard deviation. However, when the system is rate-limited, an increase in the power supply results in a increase in the coefficient of variation of throughput ratio, since the increase in the mean is now dominated by the increase in the standard deviation.

We now explore variants of the static-θ policy in which θ is dynamically adapted according to real-time measurements. One variant is to set θ at any time according to the mean ($E[g]$) and standard deviation (σ_g) of users' achieved throughput ratios, as $\theta = 1/(1+c_\theta \sigma_g/E[g])$, where c_θ is a tuning parameter from 10^{-3} to 10^3. Its performance is shown in Figure 7 by asterisk marks. The second variant is to set θ to be the ratio of the minimum

throughput ratio to the maximum throughput ratio at any time, as $\theta = g_{min}/g_{max}$, and is shown in Figure 7 by squares. The last variant is to set θ to be uniformly distributed in $[0, 1]$, and results in a localized cluster of plus marks in Figure 7.

We see that in the plane of ($E[g]$, g_{min}), the constellation trajectory of the static-θ scheduling overlaps with the g-based adaptive policies. This is because the max-min component limits the variation of g in a low level, as shown in Figure 6. The random-θ policy performs worse as a result of an interpolation of the above trajectory. Therefore, we conclude that ($E[g]$, g_{min}) can be used to characterize the hybrid scheduler, and static-θ policies are the right candidate policy set for the hybrid scheduler.

Performance of the Scheduler with Access Control

In this subsection, the hierarchical two-layer algorithm is evaluated with an emphasis on cross layer coordination. The following parameters are used

Figure 7. Performance characterization of the RS scheduler in terms of (E[g], gmin)

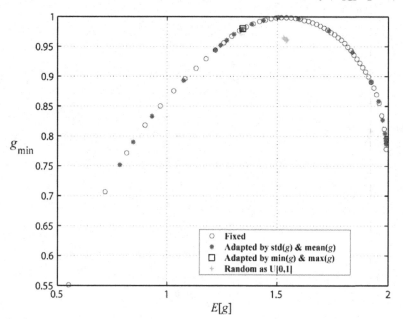

throughout this subsection: dB-scale shadowing standard deviation $\sigma_{\psi_{dB}}$ is uniformly distributed in [5, 12], $\lambda = 10^{-2}$, $\mu_i = 10^{-4}$, and $\phi_R = 0.9$.

We judge the performance of the combined CAC and RS online algorithms by blocking probability (defined as the ratio of the number of blocked users to the total number of arrivals), average aggregate utility U_{tot}, average throughput target m_X, minimum and average throughput achievement ratios g_{min} and m_g, and the percentage of maximum throughput target. All metrics other than blocking probability apply only to admitted users.

The algorithm requires estimation of the power efficiency factor, which characterizes the efficiency of the RS in the CAC perspective, now denoted $\phi_P(\theta)$ to stress its dependence on the RS efficiency factor θ. For this purpose, two users are associated with randomly generated channel statistics, $\{m_{h_i}, \sigma_{h_i}, i = 1, 2\}$, and varying throughput targets, $\{X_i \in (0,1), i = 1,2\}$. These two users are imported to the RS scheduler, where other users

with complete information, including known channel statistics, are present.

Under a fixed power supply, the resulting achieved throughput vectors, $(x_{f,1}, x_{f,2})$, are plotted in Figure 8(a) for various choices of θ. As expected, the efficiency of the scheduler increases monotonically with θ. A scheduler efficiency curve, $\phi_P(\theta)$, is fitted using a fourth degree polynomial, shown in Figure 8(b). This curve is used to incorporate the efficiency into the sum power constraint using (6).

We now examine the performance of the two layer structure under a fixed load. Given $\theta = 0.4$ and *load* = 6, Figure 9(a) illustrates the distribution of the throughput targets $\{X_i, \forall i\}$ chosen by the algorithm, and the achieved throughput ratios.

We observe that throughput targets Xs have a distribution with heavy ends, especially around the maximum *max* (0.9), and throughput achievement ratios cluster around 1 as desired. The distribution of X can be explained as follows. From the global power constraint (6), we should expect an approximately inverse relationship between

Figure 8. (a) Feasible region of two users for a power supply P. (b) Data fitting for scheduling efficiency in power $\phi_p(\theta)$

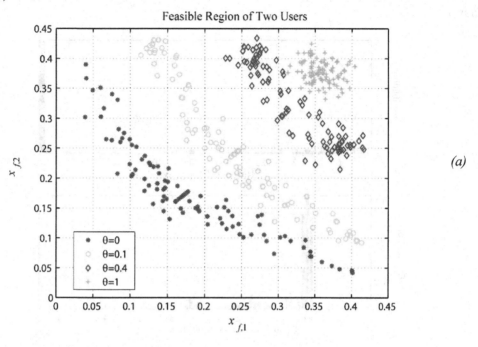

(a)

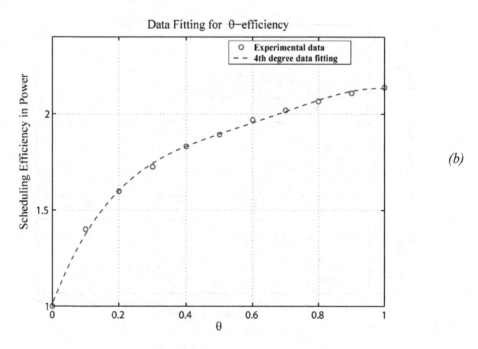

(b)

Figure 9. (a) Distribution of throughput targets X and throughput achievement ratios g when load=6 and θ=0.4. (b) Relationship of X, g, and m_h over 60 out of 100 users. In the subplot of m_h, a linear fit is shown

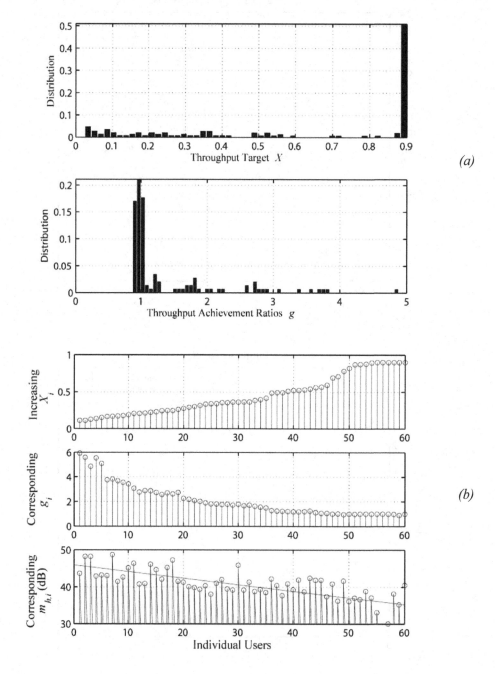

(a)

(b)

a user's throughput target and her mean channel condition. Indeed, in the CAC layer, a user's gradient priority is inversely proportional to her mean channel condition. The relationship is further illustrated in Figure 9(b), where the 60 users at the high end of channel attenuation are selected. Users with the worst channels are blocked. Users with slightly better but poor channels are assigned target throughputs less than the maximum. Users with decent channels are assigned target throughputs of the maximum.

In summary, the online algorithm largely achieves the target throughputs, since the peak density occurs near $g=1$. Users with low target throughputs X are likely induced by high mean channel attenuations m_h and usually achieve high throughput ratios g.

Figure 10. (a) Average throughput targets, percentage of maximum throughput target and average throughput ratio, for varying loads with θ=0.4, (b) Utility per unit power (normalized utility), blocking probability, and minimum throughput ratio

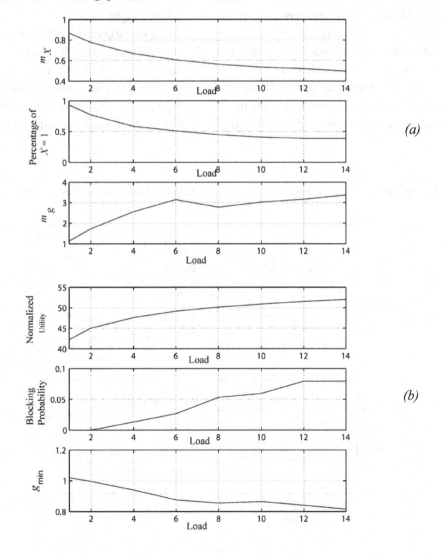

We examine the effect of variations in load, illustrated in Figure 10. Recall that *load* is defined as the ratio of normalized power demand:

$$\frac{\lambda}{\mu} \frac{E[m_h]}{2}$$

to the normalized power supply P. Hence, an increase in load can be associated with an increase in arrival rate, an equivalent increase in mean connection duration, or an equivalent decrease in the power supply. Here, we decrease the power supply to increase the load.

As load increases, the blocking probability increases monotonically. This is an indication that the CAC layer is tightening the admission control, setting 0 target throughputs for an increasing number of arrivals in an attempt to satisfy the target throughputs of those arrivals that have already been accepted into the system. Users who are admitted are assigned lower targets; the mean throughput target m_x decreases and the proportion

who are assigned the maximum throughput target $X=0.9$ also declines.

The decrease in power, however, makes it more difficult to achieve the targets of all users, and a lower degree of fairness is observed. The distribution of the achieved throughput ratio widens, as evidenced by the simultaneous decrease in the minimum throughput ratio g_{min} and the increase in the average throughput ratio m_g. Nevertheless, the hybrid algorithm acts effectively even under very high load, maintaining g_{min} above 0.8.

Finally, the aggregate utility per unit power supply increases with load. This is an indication that the system is using the limited power supply more efficiently, allocating it to users that can achieve higher utilities.

To investigate the effects of varying scheduling efficiency index θ, a series of experiments is conducted and results in Figure 11. At fixed θ, average aggregate utility and blocking probability increases, and average throughput demand and minimum throughput ratio decreases with load.

Figure 11. Performance metrics for different scheduling efficiency index θ and varying loads

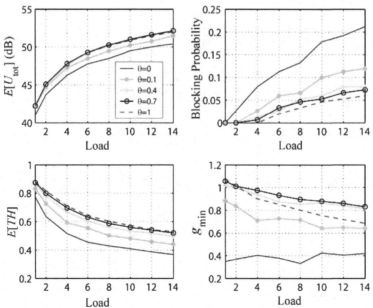

At fixed load, as θ increases, the system generally performs better, in terms of all the measures, because higher resource efficiency is achieved by higher θ. Furthermore, the efficiency improvement diminishes as θ rises (e.g., the improvement corresponding to the change of θ=0 to θ=0.1 is similar as that corresponding to the change of θ=0.1 to θ=0.4, and the improvement beyond θ=0.4 is far less significant than above improvements).

Now we turn to g_{min}, which doesn't decrease with load at θ=0, and is lower at θ=1 than at θ=0.4. At θ=0, the RS scheduler is purely max-min and achieves $g_{min} \approx 0.4$ independent of load; the CAC blocks users with high m_h as the load increases, and this is sufficient to shield the scheduler from

decreases in g_{min}. For θ>0, the presence of the opportunistic scheduler component increases g_{min}; however, the CAC can not completely shield the scheduler from increases in the load.

In summary, as the scheduling efficiency index θ varies, the system is stabilized at different balance points between efficiency and fairness. The former effect is reflected by blocking probability, $E[U_{tot}]$, $E[TH]$, $E[g]$, etc, and the latter one is represented by g_{min}.

We now explore a non-utility-based variant of the CAC algorithm. With the same RS scheduler, the new CAC algorithm is sketched in Box 4.

With the parameter setting, θ=0.4 and *load*=6, both the proposed CAC algorithm and the vari-

Box 4.

> 1. Sort all the active users in $A(t)$ according to increasing $g_{f,i}$, and serve them one by one, beginning with the first one.
>
> 2. If residual power is available and a new arrival is present, assign the highest possible throughput demand with the residual power.

Figure 12. Performance metrics for the proposed utility-regulated CAC and its analogy without utility regulation at θ=0.4

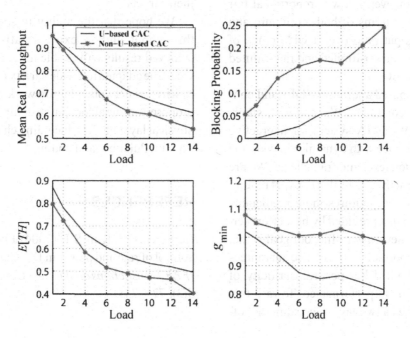

ant are evaluated in terms of all the performance metrics, as shown in Figure 12.

The non-utility-based CAC variant results in a higher blocking probability, lower throughput demands, lower real throughput, and higher minimum throughput ratio. We conclude that the use of utility in CAC provides useful information that can result in a more intelligent trade off decision between efficiency and fairness.

CONCLUSION

We have proposed a hybrid scheduler for elastic wireless data streams in WCDMA networks. The scheduler combines a greedy max-min component, which attempts to maximize fairness, with an opportunistic component, which attempts to maximize efficiency. Together, this hybrid policy takes advantage of both multi-user diversity and time diversity of the channel, in order to try to achieve a target throughput for each user. The analysis illustrated the effects of variation in the efficiency index, used to tradeoff fairness with efficiency, and the effect of the power supply. In numerical examples, the hybrid policy was shown to outperform the well-known proportional fair scheduler both in terms of both minimum and average throughput ratio over a wide range of efficiency ratios. Power-limited and rate-limited phases were discovered.

We then proposed a joint scheduler and connection access controller. We studied a single cell downlink WCDMA system for interactive nomadic data service with dynamics in two time scales, connection level and frame level. We are focused on interactive traffic that does not require constant bit rate but requires more predictable throughput than that provided by best effort service. For such interactive traffic, our goal is that the network support soft performance guarantees to match the limited but positive elasticity of these applications to performance. Toward that goal, we proposed a two layer algorithm that of-

fers targeted throughput for interactive nomadic data streams. Upon the request of a data stream connection, a target throughput is negotiated between the user and the network/base station. The network attempts to achieve the throughput targets over the duration of each individual connection by maximizing a system objective based on users' satisfaction that is represented by a utility function. We assume that a users' utility function depends not only on throughput target but also on final achieved throughput.

The online algorithms for the two layers were formulated by adopting greedy objective functions and stationary Markov control policies. In the physical layer, a hybrid rate scheduler combines a greedy max-min component, which attempts to maximize fairness, with an opportunistic component, which attempts to maximize efficiency. In the link layer, an access control and resource allocation problem is sub-optimally solved with relative priorities assigned to users based on marginal utilities. Coordination between two layers forms a closed loop, which encourages both efficiency and stability. Numerical results show that the closed-loop feedback is successful, with most users receiving throughput near or above their targets.

We hope that the ability to specify a target throughput and to express satisfaction with achieved results will enable interactive data service to be adapted to a wide variety of applications in wireless networks. Future work may apply the proposed online algorithm structure with varying physical layer models, including channel correlation, modulation, and coding.

REFERENCES

Berggren, F., & Kim, S. L. (2004). Energy-efficient control of rate and power in DS-CDMA systems. *IEEE Transactions on Wireless Communications, 3*(3), 725–733.

Berry, R., & Yeh, E. (2004). Cross-layer wireless resource allocation. *IEEE Signal Processing Magazine, 21*, 59-68.

Bertsekas, D., & Gallager, R. (1987). *Data networks*. Prentice Hall.

Goodman, D., & Mandayam, N. (2000). Power control for wireless data. *IEEE Personal Communications, 7*, 48-54.

Grossglauser, M., & Tse, D. (2003). A time-scale decomposition approach to measurement-based admission control. *IEEE/ACM Transactions on Networking, 11*(4), 550-563.

Han, Z., & Liu, K. R. (2004). Joint adaptive link quality and power management over wireless networks with fairness constraint and space-time diversity. *IEEE Transactions on Vehicular Technology, 53*, 1138-1148.

Holma, H., & Toskala, A. (2004). *WCDMA for UMTS: Radio access for third generation mobile communications* (3rd ed.). John Wiley & Sons.

Holtzman, J. M. (2000). CDMA forward link waterfilling power control. In *Proceedings of the IEEE Vehicular Technology Conference* (pp. 1663-67).

Jafar, S. A., & Goldsmith, A. (2000). Optimal rate and power adaptation for multirate CDMA. In *Proceedings of the IEEE Vehicular Technology Conference* (pp. 994-1000).

Kelly, F. P. (1997). Charging and rate control for elastic traffic. *European Transactions on Telecommunications, 8*, 33-37.

Kim, J. B., & Honig, M. L. (2000). Resource allocation of multiple classes of DS-CDMA traffic. *IEEE Transactions on Vehicular Technology, 49*(2), 506-519.

Knopp, R., & Humblet, P. A. (2000). Information capacity and power control in single-cell multiuser communications. In *Proceedings of the IEEE International Conference on Communications*.

Kwon, T., & Choi, Y. (2003). QoS provisioning in wireless/mobile multimedia networks using an adaptive framework. *Wireless Networks, 9*, 51-59.

Li, Y., & Ephremides, A. (2005). Simple rate control for fluctuating channels in ad hoc wireless networks. *IEEE Transactions on Communications, 53*, 1200-1209.

Liu, P., Zhang, P., Jordan, S., & Honig, M. (2004). Single-cell forward link power allocation using pricing in wireless networks. *IEEE Transactions on Wireless Communications, 3*, 533-543.

Liu, X. (2002). *Opportunistic scheduling in wireless communication networks*. Unpublished doctoral dissertation, Purdue University.

Song, L., & Mandayam, N. B. (2001). Hierarchical SIR and rate control on the forward link for CDMA data users under delay and error constraints. *IEEE Journal on Selected Areas in Communications, 19*, 1871-1882.

Tong, L., & Ramanathan, P. (2004). Adaptive power and rate allocation for service curve assurance in DS-CDMA network. *IEEE Transactions on Wireless Communications, 3*(2), 555-564.

Wang, X. (2004). Wide-band TD-CDMA MAC with minimum-power allocation and rate- and BER-scheduling for wireless multimedia networks. *IEEE/ACM Transactions on Networking, 12*, 103-116.

Wong, T., Mark, J., & Chua, K. C. (2003). Joint connection level, packet level, and link layer resource allocation for variable bit rate multiclass services in cellular DS-CDMA networks with QoS constraints. *IEEE Journal on Selected Areas in Communications, 21*, 1536-1545.

Xiao, M., Shroff, N. B., & Chong, E. K. (2003). A utility-based power-control scheme in wireless cellular systems. *IEEE/ACM Transactions on Networking, 11*, 210-221.

Zhang, P. (2005). *Utility-based resource alloca-tion in wireless multimedia CDMA networks.* Unpublished doctoral dissertation, University of California, Irvine.

Zhang, P., & Jordan, S. (2006). Throughput guar-antee targeted hybrid scheduling for downlink WCDMA data networks. In *Proceedings of the IEEE Wireless Communications and Networking Conference.*

Zhou, C., Honig, M., & Jordan, S. (2005). Util-ity-based power control for a two-cell CDMA data network. *IEEE Transactions on Wireless Communications, 4,* 2764 - 2776.

Zhou, C., Zhang, P., Honig, M., & Jordan, S. (2004). Two-cell power allocation for downlink CDMA. *IEEE Transactions on Wireless Com-munications, 3,* 2256-2266.

Chapter XV
Broadband Satellite Multimedia Networks

Paolo Chini
Università degli Studi di Siena, Italy

Giovanni Giambene
Università degli Studi di Siena, Italy

Snezana Hadzic
Università degli Studi di Siena, Italy

ABSTRACT

Nowadays there is an increasing need of broadband communication anytime, anywhere for users that expect to receive multimedia services with support of quality of service. In such a scenario, the aim of this chapter is to present the possibility of the satellite option that is particular attracting to bridge the digital divide in those areas where terrestrial solutions are unfeasible or too expensive. This chapter provides first a survey of the ETSI standardization framework for satellite networks. Then, resource management schemes for both forward and return link are described. Finally a suitable case study is provided for the integration of a DVB-S/DVB-RCS satellite system interconnected with a WiFi segment for local coverage; examples and results permit to understand different resource management implications.

INTRODUCTION

Satellite communication systems represent an adequate solution for providing high bit-rate services to users over wide areas. Important advantages of the satellite approach are: (*i*) easy support for both broadcast and multicast high bit-rate multimedia services; (*ii*) backup communication services for third-generation (3G) cellular users on a global scale; (*iii*) efficient support of high-mobility users (e.g., users on trains, planes, etc.). For many isolated areas on earth, satellites are the only solution to be connected to local Internet service providers.

When interconnected together with local or geographical networks, satellites can be the bottleneck of the entire system because of the delay and throughput that they entail. For these reasons, getting the maximum performance out of the satellite segment is very important.

The ETSI TC-SES/BSM (*satellite earth stations and systems / broadband satellite multimedia*) working group had the task to focus on IP layer interworking for satellite networks. This working group has defined a reference *broadband satellite multimedia* (BSM) network architecture as in Figure 1. The interest here is on *geostationary orbit* (GEO) satellites. They are on an equatorial plane at an altitude of about 35,800 km. They have synchronous motion with respect to a point on the earth (i.e., 24-hour orbital period), so that they are stationary with respect to a user on the earth. Three GEO satellites would be enough to cover all the earth except Polar Regions. Due to their distance from earth, communications with these satellites is affected by a significant delay for the propagation of the electromagnetic signal (at least 250 ms for each hop).

From the protocol stack standpoint, a BSM network can involve different layers (ETSI - TR 101 985, 2002):

* The BSM network interconnects with ground network elements at layer 2, like a *bridge*.
* The BSM network interconnects with ground network elements at layer 3, so that the satellite earth stations are *routers*.
* The BSM network operates at a layer above the 3rd one: the satellite earth stations are *gateways*. In this case, these stations can perform a more accurate routing based not only on the IP datagram header, but also on information of the higher layer headers. The earth station can implement special functions, like *performance enhancing proxies* (PEP) that are important in order to improve the *transmission control protocol* (TCP) performance in satellite networks (note that a significant problem in the provision of TCP/IP services through GEO satellites is the propagation delay of the signal from the earth station to the satellite and back).

Figure 1. BSM reference network architecture

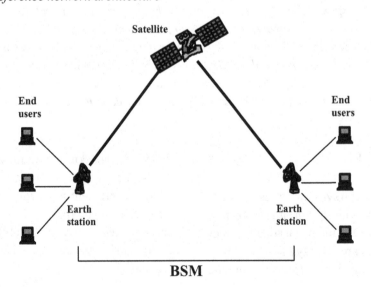

BSM

The DVB-S standard (and its variants) has gained momentum for the provision of different services in satellite networks. DVB-S has been conceived for primary and secondary distribution (*fixed satellite service*, FSS) and *broadcast satellite service* (BSS), operated in Ku (11/12 GHz) and Ka (20/30 GHz) bands (ETSI - EN 300 421, 1997). Moreover, the DVB-RCS standard (ETSI - EN 301 790, 2002) defines a two-way DVB satellite system (i.e., also a return path is considered). We refer here to a start (or mesh) topology where terminals [sometimes known as *satellite interactive terminals* (STs) or *return channel satellite terminals* (RCSTs)] communicate via a GEO bent-pipe (or regenerating) satellite to a central earth station -hub- (or directly each other). An RCST can even represent the aggregation point of multiple users. The DVB-RCS system envisages a *multi-frequency time-division multiple access* (MF-TDMA) transmission in the return link and employs the DVB-S standard (using a form of time division duplexing transmission) for the forward link traffic. The ground segment is composed of the following elements:

- *Earth stations* for the interconnection to other network segments (i.e., the earth station is the hub) and user terminals (i.e., earth stations are RCSTs).
- *Network control center* (NCC) that operates acquisition/synchronization, *radio resource management* (RRM), alarm management, security management, performance management, billing, and accounting.

MF-TDMA is a multiple access technique where RCSTs transmit their data using a range of carrier frequencies (with potentially different bandwidth sizes), each of them organized in superframes, frames and time-slots. In terms of bandwidth and duration, time-slots can have fixed or dynamic characteristics. In the latter case, besides bandwidth and time-slot duration, both transmission rate and code rate can be changed

in consecutive slots. Below the transport layer and the IP layer, the *multi protocol encapsulation* (MPE) data link layer protocol (defined by DVB) provides segmentation & reassembly functions for the generation of *motion picture expert group 2 - transport stream* (MPEG2-TS) packets of 188 bytes (fixed length). At the physical layer, MPEG2-TS packets are processed in several steps by using also different modulation and coding combinations in the DVB-S2 case (ETSI - EN 302 307, 2004). An RCST can have assigned slots belonging to the same frequency or to different frequencies with the constraint that only one frequency can be transmitted by an RCST at the same time instant. The NCC is responsible for assigning resources to RCSTs.

Many service providers, satellite operators, system integrators, terminal manufacturers, and technology providers have an interest in the DVB-RCS technology. It is therefore necessary to ensure interoperability between DVB-RCS terminals and systems and to obtain low-cost solutions. Hence, the most important task for manufacturers is to focus on solutions and support *quality of service* (QoS) through interoperability between equipment and protocol layers.

Future satellite networks must support various traffic types with their associated QoS requirements related to the end-to-end delivery of information. The main QoS framework provided by ITU is in Recommendations Y.1541 (ITU-T - Y.1541, 2006) and G.1010. As far as the traffic classification is concerned, we may refer to the categorization in ITU-T Y.1541, which defines 6 QoS traffic classes. It is interesting to note that these traffic classes not only refer to application layer characteristics, but also to connectivity requirements (queuing mechanisms at nodes and routing types) and loss and jitter (delay variation) tolerance.

The aim of the following sub-sections is to provide an overview of the protocol stack and QoS support mechanism for satellite networks with special attention to RRM as performed at layers 3 and 2. Finally, a study is devoted to investigate interconnection problems, when a satellite segment operates with a terrestrial wireless network.

ETSI BSM PROTOCOL STACK

Users' needs for IP-based services are growing, so QoS is an important mechanism for service differentiation, an essential requirement for the support of multimedia applications. Satellite systems, as well as other wireless systems, must allocate capacity carefully, since the radio spectrum is scarce and must be utilized efficiently. This is the reason why there is the need for sophisticated QoS methods closely connected to resource provision and control at different layers of the protocol stack.

Let us focus on satellite IP networks. The ETSI TC-SES/BSM working group has defined the protocol stack architecture shown in Figure 2 (SatLab, 2006), where lower layers depend on satellite system technology (*Satellite-Dependent*, SD, layers) and higher layers are those typical of

the Internet protocol stack (*Satellite-Independent*, SI, layers), as explained by Goodings (2002). These two blocks of stacked protocols are interconnected through the SI-SAP (*Satellite Independent - Service Access Point*) interface. Only a small number of generic functions need to cross the SI-SAP; in particular: address resolution, resource management, traffic classes QoS. SI protocols are characteristic for Internet protocol layers, while SD layers depend on the satellite system implementation (Skinnemoen, Vermesan, Iuoras, Adams, & Lobao, 2005).

At the SI layers, end-to-end QoS over integrated networks is managed by means of several methods with suitable signaling protocols at the session (or application) layer (e.g., based on *session initiation protocol*, SIP) and *differentiated services* (DiffServ), *integrated services* (IntServ), or *next steps in signaling* (NSIS) at the IP layer. SD layers protocols have different QoS characteristics. The aim of the BSM protocol stack is to achieve and maintain the compatibility between these two parts by using generic BSM QoS functions interconnecting higher and lower layers.

Figure 2. Protocol stack by ETSI TC-SES/BSM

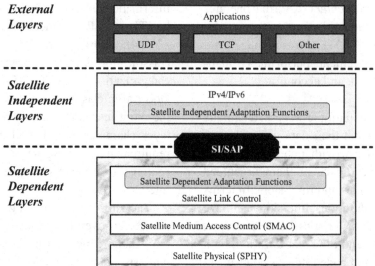

The SI-SAP interface is logically divided into three SAPs, each of them with a suitable function. In particular, we have:

- **SI-U-SAP (*User-SAP*):** Transfer of IP packets between the users;
- **SI-C-SAP (*Control-SAP*):** Transfer of control data and of service signaling for SI-U-SAP;
- **SI-M-SAP (*Management-SAP*):** Transfer of management information.

SI-SAP provides a QoS interface based on the concept of QIDs (*queue identifiers*). QIDs are abstract queues that represent layer 2 queues in a general way to allow the mapping with layer 3 ones (note that using a QoS support mechanism at layer 3, many layer 3 queues are needed). QIDs are a way to hide specific SD layer implementations from the IP layer. Each QID queue is characterized by QoS-specific parameters (flowspecs, path label, marking) and is associated to lower layer transfer capabilities (i.e., capacity allocation methods), including buffer management and policing. The SD layers are responsible for assigning satellite capacity to these abstract queues. The mapping of IP queues to QIDs can in principle be flexible, without being constrained to a one-to-one relationship. If more IP queues correspond to the same QID, a scheduler should be used at layer 3 to determine the service order of the different IP queues to be mapped to the same QID queue; in this case, layer 2 queues are typically used as *First-in First-Out* (FIFO) transmission buffers. The scheduler needs to differentiate the priorities of the IP queues in order to ensure a fair access to QIDs. According to industry current view and standardization, it is accepted that at the IP level (above SI-SAP) between 4 and 16 queues are manageable to support different IP classes. While, below SI-SAP these queues can be mapped into 2-4 satellite-dependent queues within the BSM.

BSM networks use a suitable and general categorization of traffic flows in traffic classes that can be mapped to classical IP QoS classes. The BSM traffic classes are defined at the SI-SAP interface and refer to the IP packets and their class of service (ETSI - TS 102 462, 2006). In particular, 8 BSM traffic classes (i.e., service priority levels) are defined from 0 for emergency services to 7 for low priority broadcast/multicast traffic. BSM classes represent an adaptation of the ITU-T Recommendation Y.1541 classes at the SI-SAP level.

In a BSM *star network* all communications from earth stations are with the NCC station; while, in a BSM *mesh network* also direct connections between earth stations are allowed. A *BSM Resource Controller* function manages the SI services such as BSM Bearer and BSM IP layer QoS, whilst the NCC manages SD services (OSI layer 1 & 2). The *BSM Protocol Manager* (BPM) has been conceived in the BSM protocol stack to maintain QoS and evaluate the BSM performance. BPM resides above the SI-SAP and defines how IP protocols and packet markings are interpreted and transmitted through the BSM, which SI protocols are used and how they in turn trigger SD functions. BPM has interfaces at different levels of the BSM protocol stack. In particular, BPM interacts with a specific middleware to establish transport level and application level PEPs, communicates with bandwidth brokers and potentially with service discovery and security/authentication functions.

One of the main characteristics of the BSM architecture should be allowing services and networks to be realized and offered separately and without any dependence. SI-SAP allows that network and services are independent of the satellite technology. Moreover, there should be open interfaces between services and transport layers. Hence, new services can be independent of the network and the access technology.

The transport layer provides a packet-oriented transport service and the desired network QoS.

The QoS is requested and realized by QoS signaling protocols (like, for instance, *ReSerVation Protocol*, RSVP). Very important possibilities for this architecture are that media path can cross several transport domains that can support different policies and QoS mechanisms.

The application layer provides service to users. Service is requested by signaling protocols. The signaling gives a description of user endpoints of the session and of QoS parameters, like frames per packet, frame size, delay jitter, packet loss, etc. Although QoS signaling is not always required it will be generally needed for guaranteed services.

QoS Building Blocks for BSM Networks

Offering QoS services in an efficient way is a very complex task, because there are some aspects that are interrelated. For example, in case of network resource contention or congestion, to maintain the expected service response and quality requires a lot of functions working at different time-scales, ranging from careful network planning based on traffic patterns over a long period (*management plane*) to differential resource allocation and admission control based on the current network load conditions (*control plane*).

The QoS functions of the BSM network are centralized as far as possible through a client-server model in order to coordinate the control of the whole system performance.

The range of mechanisms involved in QoS provision can be considered as a set of building blocks, or functions that can be combined in different ways to provide different overall objectives (e.g., network type, guaranteed QoS, relative QoS, etc.). These building blocks may be classified in the management, control, and data planes. A comprehensive QoS solution typically employs multiple building blocks across the management plane, control plane, and data plane, but practical implementations may require only a subset of these functions. QoS parameters need to be exchanged among the various building blocks. These

Figure 3. QoS building blocks

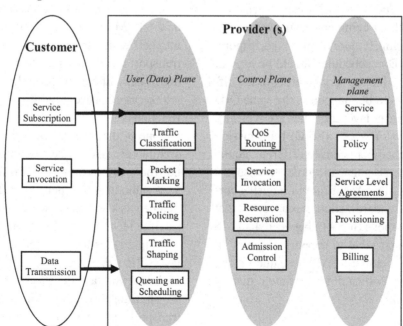

parameters include transaction performance at the packet level (e.g., delay and packet loss) and service reliability/availability expectations in the form of traffic priority levels for specific network functions, such as admission control and traffic restoration. Examples of mechanisms to convey these parameters are signaling and database lookups and include:

- **QoS signaling:** Signaling of QoS parameter requirements per service (or flow) between functional blocks
- **Call signaling:** Service invocation and resource reservation
- **Policy control:** Parameters for admission control, policing, marking etc. (SatLab, 2006)

Figure 3 (ETSI - TS 102 462, 2006) shows the range of QoS functional blocks and message flows between functional blocks at the IP layer and above in the RCST and their interfaces to the rest of the BSM system, split into user, control, and management planes. Figure 3 shows the data flow only in one direction for simplicity (according to ITU Y.1291 Recommendation) that is from the RCST towards network service providers.

QOS CLASSES AND MECHANISMS

IP Layer QoS Support

Internet engineering task force (IETF) is proposing two different ways to handle QoS in IP networks, namely IntServ (IETF - RFC 1633, 1994) and DiffServ (IETF - RFC 2475, 1998). The IntServ approach is based on resource reservation on a per-flow basis, while DiffServ classifies traffic into groups and provides QoS support to aggregated traffic flows.

In IntServ, focus is on providing QoS on a per-flow basis of a single user. A flow of packets is a unidirectional traffic associated with a given connection or a connectionless stream having the same source host, destination host, class of service, and session identification. IntServ routers must maintain per-flow state information and must reserve end-to-end resources for individual flows in order to provide QoS. The major drawback of this approach is that it can be too complex in practice and may not scale well for large volumes of network traffic. Note that the amount of control signals is very high to maintain state information at routers.

On the other hand, with DiffServ, traffic flows are aggregated into classes: all the flows in one class will be treated in the same way in the network. For example, when multiple voice connections are sent over the network, the same QoS provision scheme will be applied to all these connections by using DiffServ, while IntServ will treat each voice stream separately (i.e., per traffic class queuing at nodes with DiffServ and per traffic flow queuing with IntServ). DiffServ is simple and easy to implement and supports a range of network services that are differentiated on the basis of performance.

Because it is more convenient, DiffServ has been adopted as the model of choice for most satellite systems. DiffServ is replacing per-flow service with a *per-hop behavior* (PHB), applicable to traffic aggregates, and per-flow states in network nodes are no longer required. End-to-end performance is then provided by the concatenation of multiple PHBs. DiffServ defines six PHB classes, namely *expedited forwarding* (EF), four *assured forwarding* (AF) classes and the *best effort* (BE) service of the original Internet protocol. At each network node (for example at a router) each IP packet is treated according to its class, as defined by the *type of service* (ToS) bits in the IPv4 packet header.

At a node, DiffServ manages traffic by performing traffic classification, conditioning, shaping, dropping, marking, queuing and scheduling. These mechanisms need proper QoS parameters and policies, set up statically or dynamically.

Traffic packets will be mapped into PHB classes; for instance, packets containing voice stream will be mapped in EF class and will be transmitted before data with lower priority classes (AF, BE). Moreover, each AF class allocates a certain amount of forwarding resources (buffer space and bandwidth). Within each AF class, IP packets are marked with one of three possible drop precedence values. In case of congestion, the drop precedence of a packet determines the relative importance of the packet within the AF class. A congested node tries to protect packets with a lower drop precedence value from being lost by preferably discarding packets with a higher drop precedence value.

Table 1 presents one mapping between BSM traffic classes and DiffServ traffic classes (ETSI - TS 102 462, 2006).

As previously mentioned, a typical QoS-support protocol architecture could be based on queues at IP and *medium access control* (MAC) layers. The active management of queues for QoS

support is performed at the IP layer, while the queues in the MAC layer are only used as simple FIFO transmission buffers. Referring to the DiffServ case, there can be different IP-layer queues: one EF queue, 4 AF queues and one BE queue, and additional traffic management queues (ETSI - TS 102 462, 2006). MAC queues are associated with MAC QoS classes of service. The next sub-Section deals with layer 2 RRM techniques and mapping issues from layer 3 classes to MAC classes and then capacity allocation methods in the DVB-RCS case.

DVB-RCS Capacity Allocation Methods and Layer 2 QoS Mechanisms

In DVB-RCS satellite networks, resources are subject to contention among RCSTs. *Demand assignment multiple access* (DAMA) protocols can be used to allow resources to be assigned on the basis of the requests made by RCSTs. MAC layer

Table 1. Mapping of BSM traffic classes to DiffServ ones

BSM traffic class	Service category	Node mechanism	PHB
0	Emergency services, essential network services	Pre-empts any traffic that has allocated bandwidth	EF
1	Real-time, jitter-sensitive, high interactive fixed size cells VoIP	Separate queue with preferential servicing, traffic grooming, strictly admitted	EF
2	Real-time, jitter sensitive, interactive, variable rate cells	Separate queue with preferential servicing, traffic grooming, loosely admitted	EF
3	Highly interactive, transaction data	Separate queue, drop priority, strictly admitted	AF
4	Interactive, transaction data	Separate queue, drop priority, flow controlled	AF
5	Low loss only	Long queue, drop priority, flow controlled	AF
6	Medium loss, higher delay	Separate queue, flow controlled	BE
7	Not specified, low priority broadcast/multicast traffic or storage networks	Separate queue	BE

QoS support consists in capacity request calculation and generation and scheduling/dispatching of packets from the queues.

DVB-RCS provides a number of different *capacity categories* as described below:

- **Constant Rate Assignment (CRA):** This is a guaranteed capacity assignment. It is used for jitter-intolerant applications, like *voice over IP* (VoIP) or for signaling.
- **Volume-Based Dynamic Capacity (VBDC):** This is a dynamic capacity assignment that is based on traffic volume. Requests are cumulative. VBDC is used for non-real time applications, like *file transfer protocol* (FTP).
- **Rate-Based Dynamic Capacity (RBDC):** This is a dynamic capacity assignment that is based on input bit-rate estimation. Requests are absolute. RBDC is used for real-time jitter-tolerant applications such as video streaming.
- **Free Capacity Assignment (FCA):** This is a variable capacity assignment that is based on free capacity, if there is any left (which will not be used otherwise). This capacity is not requested by an RCST, but simply assigned by the system on the basis of spare resources left available after previous categories have been served.

Note that CRA is a fixed capacity allocation: capacity is reserved and guaranteed during the whole logon time of the terminal (i.e., an RCST) and a terminal does not have to ask for capacity. Even in case when a terminal has no traffic, capacity is allocated. While, RBDC and VBDC are dynamic bandwidth allocation schemes (DAMA schemes): capacity allocation is based on explicit requests sent by the RCST to the NCC that provides suitable resource allocation notification via the broadcast *terminal burst time plan* (TBTP) message, sent once every MF-TDMA superframe. This approach permits an efficient management of the shared resources, but the DAMA signaling exchange needed to reserve capacity entails an additional end-to-end delay contribution, called *access delay*, that is composed of framing delay, processing delay, signaling delay (TBTP transmission) and round-trip propagation delay. Every MF-TDMA superframe, transmission resources (i.e., slots) are assigned by the NCC to RCSTs in an orderly manner on the basis of both the request category (i.e., CRA > RBDC > VBDC > FCA) and the *service level agreements* (SLAs) between operator and customers.

A very important parameter is the *request class* (RC), which is a representation of a PHB at the MAC layer (in the DAMA controller). It defines a behavior of the MAC layer for a given traffic aggregation. The RC is a combination of capacity category and priority level. As an example, an RCST can have two RCs, both using VBDC: one has priority over the other. RC is a concept similar to PHB, but applied at the MAC layer instead of the IP layer: the RCST maps each PHB onto an RC. It shall be possible to map any PHB to any RC.

It is important that different capacity categories on the DVB-RCS air interface be efficiently mapped in order to maximize QoS and return link efficiency. Various mapping options from DiffServ PHBs onto the DVB-RCS capacity categories are possible, combining the following elements:

IP QoS Class (PHB) → **Capacity Request Strategy** → **Capacity Category**

where on one side we have DiffServ QoS traffic types (i.e., EF, AF and BE), while, on the other side, we have different capacity categories (CRA, RBDC, VBDC, and FCA). In between, there are different capacity request strategies that represent a combination of one or more capacity categories (e.g., *rate-based low grade*, RB_LG, *rate-based medium grade*, RB_MG, *rate-based high grade*, RB_HG, *volume-based performance*, VB_PERF, *volume-based utilization*, VB_UTIL) in order to achieve different performance-utilization trade-offs.

An example of mapping is shown in Figure 4 (Skinnemoen et al., 2005).

The correct capacity request strategy for various applications depends on the service needed by them. For a quality-critical application, the RB_HG scheme would be the most appropriate strategy, trading bandwidth for performance and delivering high QoS (i.e., voice), regardless of the congestion level.

Non-critical VoIP applications could be mapped to a cost-aware RB_MG strategy where RBDC and VBDC are combined to achieve an acceptable trade-off between QoS and cost. In particular, while RBDC provides sustained assignments during VoIP activity periods, VBDC is used to maintain ("keep-alive") request opportunities when there is no traffic, in order to improve the transitions from silence to activity.

The DVB-RCS standard (ETSI - EN 301 790, 2002; ETSI - TR 101 790, 2003) defines 6 traffic classes (i.e., *profile classes*, PCs) that are differentiated in terms of QoS characteristics (e.g., delay, jitter, packet loss ratio, application types):

1. Real-time priority traffic (e.g., voice-based applications)
2. Variable rate priority traffic, not jitter tolerant (e.g., real-time TV-cast, interactive TV)
3. Variable rate priority traffic, jitter tolerant (e.g., real-time transaction data)
4. Jitter tolerant priority traffic (e.g., Web browsing, interactive games)
5. Other priority traffic (e.g., file transfer)
6. Best effort (e.g., e-mail, fax)

The standard recommends the following mappings between the DVB-RCS allocation method and the DVB-RCS profile classes:

Figure 4. Example of mapping QoS traffic classes (i.e., PHBs), capacity strategies, and capacity categories

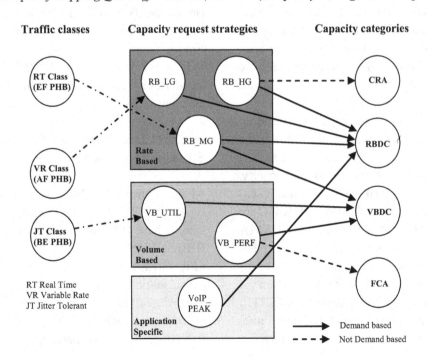

- CRA method (with different bandwidth needs) for profile classes 1 and 2, since they cannot tolerate delay jitter.
- CRA+RBDC+FCA methods for profile classes 3 and 4 (i.e., a minimum guaranteed bandwidth provided by CRA, plus a variable bandwidth negotiated through RBDC when needed and an extra portion of bandwidth obtained automatically with FCA).
- CRA+RBDC+VBDC+FCA methods for profile class 5: as this profile class has less stringent requirements than profile class 4, a combination of RBDC and VBDC can substitute RBDC, thus reducing the guaranteed bandwidth.
- VBDC+FCA methods for profile class 6: such profile class has no requirements so that a VBDC assignment can be used together with an extra bandwidth.

RESOURCE MANAGEMENT TECHNIQUES

RRM is a crucial aspect in satellite networks (Giambene, 2007). RRM techniques consist of transmitted power, time and frequency resource allocation. The aim is to manage the quantity of resources assigned to each user in order to maximize some performance indicators, such as the total network throughput and the total resource utilization, or to minimize the real-time transmission jitter and the end-to-end delay subject to some system constraints. Many RRM techniques and optimization methods have been proposed in the literature for satellite communication systems (Barsocchi et al., 2005; Davoli, Marchese, & Mongelli, 2005). Several system aspects are very important for the selection of the RRM technique, such as traffic types, interference issues, user mobility, channel quality variations due to weather conditions, etc. It is evident that air interface RRM design plays a significant role in the support of QoS in satellite networks.

RRM techniques, operating at layer 3 and/or layer 2 of the protocol stack (Giambene, 2007), are used for both:

- Scheduling of downlink transmissions from the hub earth station to RCSTs via the satellite (*forward path*).
- Allocating capacity for uplink RCSTs transmissions to an earth hub station through the satellite (*return path*).

Hence, two essential RRM components are DAMA schemes and scheduling techniques (Le-Ngoc, Leung, Takats, & Garland, 2003; Giambene, Giannetti, Parràga, Ries, & Sali, in press). In the following sub-sections, we will present some examples of DAMA and packet scheduling techniques, respectively for uplink and downlink transmissions via satellite. Before concluding this part, it is worth mentioning that a scheduler typically operates on short or medium time scales and related adaptivity, while DAMA deals with medium and long-term adaptivity.

Survey on Packet Scheduling Techniques for DVB-S2

In a broadband satellite access system, *user terminals* (UTs) usually receive bursty multimedia traffic from the network; a UT can coincide with an RCST; however, many UTs can refer and be linked to the same RCST. Suitable scheduling schemes are needed on the network side in order to achieve an efficient sharing of resources among different traffic flows towards UTs (Le-Ngoc et al., 2003). These techniques are typically centrally coordinated by a resource manager that decides transmissions on the basis of traffic flow priorities, QoS requirements, channel conditions, etc. Intuitively, on-board scheduling requires the use of a regenerative satellite payload that can also support on-board processing and on-board switching functionalities. In this case, the delay of scheduling decisions is minimized, thus permitting to adapt better to traffic flow and channel fluctuations. However, such implementation approach is more complex and entails additional computational requirements for the payload. Hence, a typical choice is that the scheduler is located in the earth hub station and the GEO satellite is bent-pipe.

In the presence of *adaptive coding and modulation* (ACM) at the physical layer as in the DVB-S2 case (ETSI - EN 302 307, 2004), channel state information has to be sent from UTs to the scheduler in the earth station to notify the current UT's forward channel conditions. However, due to the high *round trip propagation delay* (RTD) of the GEO satellite scenario, the scheduler on the earth uses outdated information on the channel state when scheduling traffic to UTs. Hence, there is a misalignment between the ModCod (*modulation and coding*) scheme used by the scheduler and the channel conditions that will be experienced by the UT when it will receive the transmitted data (Giambene et al., in press). A simple approach to address this problem is to select the ModCod by using margins on the signal-to-noise ratio. However, this method reduces the available capacity. Hence, an improved solution is to make use of channel predictors that permit to transmit data with a ModCod level that takes into account the possible channel evolution when data will be received.

In order to manage both the QoS needs and the available ModCods, it is possible to use a two-stage scheduling approach (Párraga, Kissling, & Lutz, 2005). Considering a reduced set of ModCods of the DVB-S2 standard, a possibility is to have different layer 3 queues for the different available ModCods. Then, in a first stage, a resource manager classifies the IP packets to be transmitted in terms of the ModCod available for the related UT and sends them to the related layer 3 queue. In a second stage, a scheduler is used to decide each time (i.e., for each resource allocation interval) which queue has to be served; once the queue has been selected, some IP packets are delivered to the layer 2 FIFO buffer for framing and transmission.

Different techniques can be adopted to implement a channel-aware layer 3 packet scheduler. Some important channel-aware schedulers are *proportional fairness* (PF) (Kolding, 2003) and *proportional fairness with exponential rule* (PF-ER) (Entrambasaguas, Aguayo-Torres, Gomez, & Paris, 2005). The PF scheduling algorithm has been originally developed to achieve a trade-off between user fairness and cell capacity. The *relative channel quality index* (RCQI) is used for measuring such trade-off. In particular, RCQI represents the ratio between the maximum data rate currently supported by the UT (depending on its channel conditions, and, hence, the assigned ModCod) and the mean UT throughput. The scheduler serves (during the resource allocation interval) the flow with the highest RCQI value. PF-ER scheduler introduces enhancements to the PF scheme in order to balance the weighted delay of all backlogged flows when the differences of weighted queue delay among UTs become significant. This procedure is obtained by adding a multiplicative exponential parameter to the RCQI parameter. Such exponential function is related to the weighted instantaneous delay; if there is the detection of a noticeable delay increase, RCQI increases and the related UT achieves higher priority. It has been shown in the literature that the PF-ER scheme permits lower mean delays than PF and that there is lower variance of delay among different UTs, thus achieving a higher fairness degree. In both PF and PF-ER cases, scheduling decisions can be taken at layer 3 on the basis of the RCQI parameter values that are computed according to layer 2 service parameters (e.g., service delay, deadlines, encapsulation) and layer 1 UT conditions notified through the feedback channel (Giambene et al., in press). This is a classical example of cross-layer approach for resource management.

Survey on DAMA Techniques for DVB-RCS

In order to distribute dynamically the satellite capacity among remotely accessing RCSTs, DAMA techniques have been introduced in the DVB-RCS standardization. In particular, RCSTs request capacity to the NCC that allocates resources on the basis of a coarse time granularity, the superframe time interval. Assigned transmission slots are notified through the TBTP messages sent on a superframe basis over the forward channel. DAMA schemes have been extensively studied for satellite networks in order to improve the utilization of satellite air interface resources in the presence of bursty traffic flows (Le-Ngoc et al., 2003). As previously described, most common DAMA schemes in the DVB-RCS standard are RBDC and VBDC.

In the literature, there are many proposed DAMA techniques that permit to achieve a high multiplexing efficiency, adaptivity to the channel and QoS support for differentiated traffic flows (Abramson, 1993; Tasaka, 1986). Recently, new DAMA techniques have been proposed that assign traffic capacity to requesting UTs taking into account the status of the protocols at different layers of the protocol stack, according to a multi-layer, cross-layer approach (Kota, 2005). In the literature, it is possible to find several examples of cross-layer DAMA schemes for DVB-RCS networks (Astuti & Kojo, 2004; Chini, Giambene, Bartolini, Luglio, & Roseti, 2006; Guainella & Pietrabissa, 2003; Sooriyabandara & Fairhurst, 2003; Yang & de Veciana, 2002). Some relevant DAMA examples are surveyed below.

Bursty multimedia traffic comprises both real-time and non-real-time traffic with different transfer durations, peak-to-average ratios, and QoS requirements (Le-Ngoc et al., 2003). Moreover, during the connection lifetime, the needed capacity is rapidly variable. For this reason, an enhanced DAMA scheme, called *combined-free DAMA* (CFDAMA) has been proposed in order

to support multimedia traffic burstiness and to achieve high channel utilization (Le-Ngoc & Mohammed, 1998). In CFDAMA, the scheduler can allocate resources (i.e., time-frequency slots, typical of an MF-TDMA air interface) to RCSTs every MF-TDMA superframe. The CFDAMA scheduler maintains a reservation request table and a free assignment table. The reservation request table queues RCST requests for demand-assigned slots. When a request is received, the scheduler fills the table with the identification number and the corresponding amount of requested slots of the RCST. The free assignment table takes into account only the identification numbers of all the connected RCSTs. First of all, the CFDAMA scheduler serves the requests starting from the top of the reservation request table by assigning contiguous slots to the corresponding RCSTs, on the basis of the number of slots they requested and according to some predefined priorities (*demand-assignment part*). Then, when such requests are exhausted, the CFDAMA scheduler can freely assign remaining available resources in the superframe to RCSTs according to a round robin scheme without explicit requests made by them (*free allocation part*). Free assigned capacity does not need a reservation and the setup phase is not present. Hence, the traffic related to the free capacity can be transferred with a minimum delay of 1 RTD (similar to random access schemes), which is typically half of the delay of traffic carried out with reservation requests. In conclusion, the CFDAMA scheme is like VBDC+FCA, referring to the previously introduced notations.

In Le-Ngoc et al. (2003), a comparison study is made, in terms of channel utilization and average delay, between a standard DAMA scheme (VBDC-like scheme) where time slots are assigned to RCSTs on a demand basis and the above CFDAMA technique. In case of low-to-medium channel utilization, it has been shown that the free assigned capacity in CFDAMA permits that a greater amount of packets be transmitted without reservation, thus experiencing a delay of

1 RTD much lower than that in the DAMA case. When the traffic load increases, more packets are transmitted by means of the demand-assignment mechanism that entails longer transfer times, but permits to achieve a high throughput equivalent to DAMA.

HYBRID SYSTEMS

The interconnection between satellite and wireless networks is important for permitting the access to broadband services (e.g., wireless broadband Internet access, VoIP service, broadcast TV, etc.) for wireless users (Andrikopoulos et al., 2005; Evans et al., 2005). In this section, we focus on the interconnection of DVB-RCS interactive networks with WiFi networks, according to the IEEE 802.11b/g standards (IEEE 802.11, 1999). A possible scenario is that where the satellite network is interconnected with a *wireless local area network* (WLAN), providing a local coverage

on a plane, a train, or a ship: a WiFi *access point* (AP), connected to the satellite network through a suitable RCST, allows a mobile broadband access to passengers.

The WiFi IEEE 802.11 standard defines MAC and physical layers for WLANs; in particular, IEEE 802.11b allows several data rates (i.e., 1, 2, 5.5 and 11 Mbit/s) in the 2.4 GHz band, while IEEE 802.11g permits data rates up to 54 Mbit/s. In WiFi networks, QoS support is specified in the IEEE 802.11e standard that enhances the existing IEEE 802.11 b/g MAC protocol (Mangold, Choi, Hiertz, Klein, & Walke, 2003).

In this section, we consider a scenario with a WiFi system interconnected to a satellite network (see Figure 5). The former is composed of an AP and some wireless users transmitting at 11 Mbit/s. The latter is composed of a GEO regenerating satellite, an earth hub station, an RCST connected to the AP and an NCC that manages the dynamic resource allocation in terms of portions of bandwidth and time. In this scenario, we consider

Figure 5. Mesh network architecture envisaged for our satellite-WiFi hybrid scenario (the link to the NCC is only used for signaling purposes)

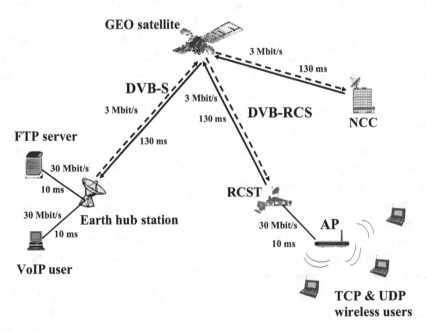

wireless users exchanging both bidirectional VoIP traffic and FTP traffic with sources connected to the satellite network. Hence, both UDP (*user datagram protocol*) and TCP have been considered at transport level. In the envisaged study, all the satellite links are bidirectional at 3 Mbit/s with RTD equal to 560 ms.

Our interest is to study the mapping of resource management schemes and QoS classes in the WiFi network and in the satellite side and investigate the impact that a choice made in one network segment can have on the whole (end-to-end) system performance. An important example of mapping is described in Figure 6. For what concerns the satellite segment, bidirectional VoIP is served with CRA on both the forward and return paths; while, FTP downlink traffic is supported by VBDC on the forward path and shares CRA on the return path with VoIP that has a higher priority. Moreover, in the WiFi segment, the priority increases from TCP uplink flows (i.e., TCP ACKs in our scenario), to FTP downlink data, to uplink VoIP and to downlink VoIP. The mapping scheme adopted on the WiFi side permits to address the *unfairness problem* of WiFi access (see the following sub-Section) and allows good performance, as proved by the results shown at the end of this chapter.

In the earth station, there are separated layer 3 queues for each traffic type to which different allocation methods correspond. For instance, in our study we have a queue for VoIP traffic flows managed according to CRA and another queue for FTP traffic flows that is served with VBDC method. The CRA capacity allocation has priority over the VBDC one in sharing the resources of the forward path. Note that also the WiFi network has layer 2 queues to support different traffic types. Other queues are also needed in the AP as well as in the RCST.

The following part deals with an overview of the WiFi QoS support specified in the IEEE 802.11e standard. Then, some simulation results are presented in order to investigate traffic map-

ping issues for our scenario where WiFi and satellite networks are interconnected.

WiFi Access Characteristics and QoS Support

In IEEE 802.11e, the QoS mechanism is controlled by the *hybrid coordinator* (HC), an entity that implements the so-called *hybrid coordination function* (HCF). The HC is typically located in the AP and uses two modes according to a superframe structure: a contention-based access method, called *enhanced distributed channel access* (EDCA) and a contention-free (polling-based) transfer, named *HCF controlled channel access* (HCCA).

Figure 6. An example of traffic class mapping between satellite and wireless networks. The meaning of some acronyms will be clarified in the chapter

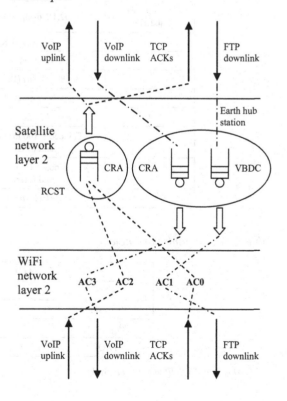

In this study, we refer to the EDCA method. MAC layer parameters depend on the *access category* (AC) that permits to regulate the access urgency. The minimum interval between two transmitted frames is determined by the *arbitration inter-frame spacing* (AIFS) that has a smaller value for ACs with higher priority. If the access is to a free channel, there is no contention and a direct transmission after AIFS is possible. Otherwise, after AIFS a *contention period* (CP) starts. Inside the wireless terminal, each AC starts a back-off counter and contends for a *transmission opportunity* (TXOP). The initial value of the back-off counter ranges between 0 and the minimum *collision window* (CW_{min}). Note that CW_{min} should have a smaller value for traffic with higher priority. Moreover, if a collision occurs, the collision window is multiplied by a *persistence factor* that is smaller for higher priority traffic.

The contention window cannot be increased beyond a maximum value (CW_{max}) that is smaller for higher priority traffic. Service differentiation among ACs is achieved by setting different CW_{min}, CW_{max}, AIFS, and TXOP values.

In EDCA, there are 4 ACs, each of them corresponding to a layer 2 queue in a wireless terminal, here called *QoS-enhanced station* (QSTA). Moreover, traffic flows are categorized according to 8 *user priorities* (UPs), as defined in the IEEE 802.1 D specifications (IEEE 802.1d, 1998). Hence, one or more UPs are mapped to the same AC queue, as shown in Table 2 (IEEE 802.1d, 1998). In particular, AC3 and AC2 are used for real-time applications (i.e., voice and video transmissions), whereas AC1 and AC0 are used for best effort and background traffic, for instance, e-mail, and FTP traffic (Alocci, Giambene, & Koucheryavy, 2007).

Table 2. User priorities for IEEE 802.11e (UP = 7 has the higher urgency)

UPs from IEEE 802.1D	802.1D designation	802.11e AC	Service type
1	*Background* (BK)	AC0	Best Effort
2	Not defined	AC0	Best Effort
0	*Best Effort* (BE)	AC0	Best Effort
3	*Excellent Effort* (EE)	AC1	Video Probe
4	*Controlled Load* (CL)	AC2	Video
5	VI (Video < 100 ms latency and jitter)	AC2	Video
6	VO (Video < 10 ms latency and jitter)	AC3	Voice
7	*Network Control* (NC)	AC3	Voice

Table 3. ACs default parameters

	AC3	AC2	AC1	AC0
AIFS	2	2	3	7
CW_{min} [slots]	3	7	31	31
CW_{max} [slots]	7	15	1023	1023
TXOP	3.264 ms	6.016 ms	0 (*)	0 (*)

(*) The 0 value of TXOP means one packet

The AC parameters can be selected on the basis of the characteristics of higher layers protocols, the adopted applications, the related QoS requirements, the traffic load, and the number of users. A default allocation scheme for CW_{min} and CW_{max} of the four ACs has been defined in the standard (IEEE 802.11, 1999) and described in Table 3. Note that:

- The CW_{min} and CW_{max} values have a rough granularity; in fact, their values must belong to the set $\{2^X - 1$, where X is a number with 4 binary digits$\}$.
- By means of beacon frames, the AP can update the QSTAs with new values for AIFS, TXOP, CW_{min}, and CW_{max} for the different ACs to adapt to variable system conditions.

WiFi is characterized by unfairness problems between downlink and uplink flows. This is particularly important for applications (like FTP and VoIP) that are characterized by bidirectional flows. In order to explain the unfairness problem, let us consider a case with n wireless QSTAs and one AP; by assuming an equal sharing of transmission time among wireless nodes, each of them is able to obtain $1/(n+1)$ of the transmission opportunities. Hence, there is a transmission sharing of $1/n$ on downlink (AP to QSTAs transmissions) and a transmission sharing of $n/(n+1)$ on uplink (QSTAs to AP transmissions). A basic approach to overcome this unfairness problem is to assign a higher priority AC to downlink traffic flows than that for the corresponding uplink flows, as discussed in the following part.

Simulation Results for the Interconnection of WiFi and DVB-RCS with QoS Support

We have simulated the scenario previously described in Figure 5 in the ns-2 environment (NS-2 - 2.29, 2006). We have implemented new classes in C++ to create the DVB-RCS capacity allocation methods in the earth station and to support the NCC functionalities to manage the resource allocation. In our scenario, each wireless user has an active FTP download session from the network and a bidirectional VoIP flow. In this study, the main interest is to investigate the impact on TCP-based traffic due to different RRM mapping options. UDP-based traffic is only used to evaluate the effect of this high priority traffic on TCP.

We have considered two traffic types (i.e., DVB-RCS profile classes) and the following mapping to allocation methods:

- VoIP of profile class 1, managed by CRA.
- FTP of profile class 5, supported by VBDC for the forward path and by CRA for the return path.

The FTP traffic is ACK-clocked (i.e., for each received ACK, the TCP sender has always available new data to send); the TCP segment size has been set to 1500 bytes. Referring to Figure 5, the FTP server sends packets to the earth station that puts them in its VBDC queue. The earth station creates a request related to the number of packets in its queue and transmits it to the NCC that manages dynamic capacity allocation. Transmitted TCP segments are acknowledged through the return path. We have considered in this study the TCP NewReno version as in IETF RFC 3782.

As for VoIP, the G.729/A codec has been used with a constant bit-rate of 8 kbit/s; one packet is generated every 10 ms (frame size), thus 10 bytes are available every 10 ms with added the RTP/UDP/IP header of 40 bytes. Referring to Figure 5, the VoIP traffic (UDP-based flow) arrives to the earth station (where it is delivered to the related queue) then to the satellite, to the RCST, and, finally, to the AP that directs the flow to wireless users. The reverse path is followed by the VoIP traffic generated by the wireless terminals.

A TCP flow experiences a *round trip time*, RTT (from the instant the FTP server sends the packets to the earth station up to the instant it receives the ACK), of 1080 ms plus some variable delays, due to the multiplexing delay imposed by the presence of other flows and the framing delay. The product of the available bandwidth (3 Mbit/s) and the RTT, called *delay bandwidth product* (DBP), is equal to 140 packets.

VoIP traffic flows have a higher priority than FTP ones, with CRA capacity rigidly allocated at call set-up. Whereas, the NCC assigns a variable amount of resources by means of VBDC on a superframe basis to FTP flows. Table 4 provides an example of mapping between traffic flows, DVB-RCS capacity categories and WiFi ACs.

We have compared three mapping schemes on the WiFi side with an earth station buffer size of 280 IP packets (i.e., two times the DBP to exploit the link in the best way taking into account the added delay due to the VBDC request loop). The DVB-RCS superframe duration is 560 ms. Results in Figure 7 are for the following mapping cases: (*i*) FTP data on AC1 and TCP ACK on AC0 (as shown in Table 4 and in Figure 6); (*ii*) both FTP data and TCP ACK on AC1; (*iii*) FTP data in AC0 and TCP ACK on AC1. The values of the AC parameters are detailed in Table 3. The obtained results are for 4 users, each of them has an FTP download and a VoIP bidirectional flow. This graph also shows the results for the case where the 4 users have active only FTP flows. We can note that:

- The best mapping option for the support of the FTP traffic is that in Table 3, even if such advantage is not much evident with 4 users. A more significant advantage could be obtained for a higher number of users (i.e., FTP traffic flows). Therefore, the mapping in Table 3 is a possible approach to deal with the WiFi unfairness problem.
- The introduction of 4 VoIP bidirectional flows causes a reduction in the aggregated TCP goodput due to the fact that, even if the capacity that these flows use on the satellite link is negligible with respect to the whole assigned capacity of 3 Mbit/s, they increase significantly the number of collisions in the WiFi segment, thus delaying the transmission of lower priority TCP data packets (downlink) and TCP ACKs (uplink).

CONCLUSION

Satellite communications play a significant role in supporting next-generation IP-based networks, also reaching those regions that lack of terrestrial telecommunication infrastructures. Efficient utilization of satellite radio resources and end-to-end QoS support are mandatory requirements in order

Table 4. Mapping between traffic flows, DVB-RCS capacity categories and WiFi ACs

Traffic flows	DVB capacity categories	WiFi access categories
VoIP downlink	CRA@40kbit/s	AC3
VoIP uplink	CRA@40kbit/s	AC2
FTP data	VBDC for the remaining capacity after VoIP CRA allocation	AC1
TCP ACK	CRA@3Mbit/s (*)	AC0

(*) The uplink capacity at the RCST that is available for TCP traffic is the capacity that is left after VoIP traffic allocation in the 3 Mbit/s bandwidth.

to implement future satellite-based services. This is the reason why this chapter has focused on QoS issues and RRM techniques for the support of IP-based traffic in satellite networks. Our interest has focused on the BSM network architecture and the reference protocol stack. Then, we have addressed the DVB-S/-S2/-RCS standard by highlighting the network structure, layer 3 QoS mechanisms and layer 2 capacity categories to manage several traffic classes in a differentiated way. Finally, hybrid scenarios integrating a satellite segment and wireless local area networks have been investigated since they represent a very interesting solution to provide mobile broadband services on trains, ships and planes. QoS techniques for an integrated network scenario have been studied showing different possible traffic classes mapping and the potential impact on system performance. Some promising areas for future research activities are: investigation of RBDC schemes and related traffic estimation, comparison of different QoS classes mapping schemes for performance optimization, cross-layer techniques to improve scheduling and DAMA techniques performance.

ACKNOWLEDGMENT

This work has been carried out within the framework of the European-funded network of excellence SatNEx II (contract No. IST-027393).

REFERENCES

Abramson, N. (1993). *Multiple access communications foundations for emerging technologies.* IEEE Press.

Alocci, I., Giambene, G., & Koucheryavy, Y. (2007). Optimization of IEEE 802.11e Access class parameters with cross-layer approach. *International Symposium on Wireless Pervasive Computing 2007 (ISWPC 2007).* San Juan, Puerto Rico.

Andrikopoulos, I., Pouliakis, A., Mertzanis, I., Karaliopoulos, M., Narenthiran, K., Evans, B., Gallet, T., Durand, M., Mazzella, M., Vandermot, J., Dieudonné, M., Roullet, L., Bourdin, E., & Wolf, M. (2005). Demonstration with field trials of a satellite-terrestrial synergistic approach for

Figure 7. Comparison among several mapping methods

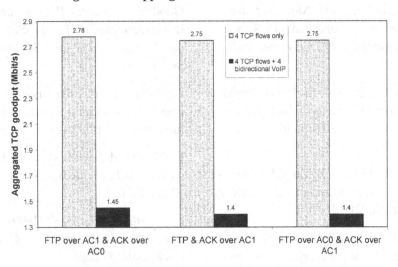

digital multimedia broadcasting to mobile users. *IEEE Wireless Communications, 12*(5), 82-90.

Astuti, D., & Kojo, M. (2004). TCP and link layer enhancements in DVB-S/DVB-RCS satellite systems. *4th Berkeley-Helsinki Ph.D. Student Workshop on Telecommunication Software Architectures - Summer 2004.* University of Berkeley, USA.

Barsocchi, P., Celandroni, N., Ferro, E., Gotta, A., Davoli, F., Giambene, G., González-Castaño, F. J., Moreno, J. I., & Todorova, P. (2005). Radio resource management across multiple protocol layers in satellite networks: A tutorial overview. *International Journal of Satellite Communications and Networking, 23*(5), 265-305.

Chini, P., Giambene, G., Bartolini, D., Luglio, M., & Roseti, C. (2006). Dynamic resource allocation based on a TCP-MAC cross-layer approach for DVB-RCS satellite networks. *International Journal of Satellite Communications and Networking, 24*(5), 367-385.

Davoli, F., Marchese, M., & Mongelli, M. (2005). Optimal resource allocation in satellite networks: Certainty equivalent approach versus sensitivity estimation algorithms. *International Journal of Communication Systems, 18*(1), 3-36.

Entrambasaguas, J. T., Aguayo-Torres, M. C., Gomez, G., & Paris, J. F. (2005). Multiuser capacity and fairness evaluation of channel/QoS aware multiplexing algorithms. *4th COST 290 MCM:* Wurzburg, Germany.

ETSI - EN 300 421. (1997). *Digital video Broadcasting (DVB): Framing structure, channel coding and modulation for 11/12 GHz satellite services.* V1.1.2.

ETSI - EN 301 790. (2002). *Digital video broadcasting (DVB): Interaction channel for satellite distribution systems.* V1.3.1.

ETSI - EN 302 307. (2004). *Digital video broadcasting (DVB): Second generation fram-ing structure, channel coding and modulation systems for broadcasting, interactive services, news gathering and other broadband satellite applications (DVB-S2).* V1.1.1.

ETSI - TR 101 790. (2003). *Digital video broadcasting (DVB): Interaction channel for satellite distribution systems, guidelines for the use of EN 301 790.* V1.2.1.

ETSI - TR 101 985 (2002). *Satellite earth stations and systems (SES): Broadband satellite multimedia, IP over satellite.* V1.1.2.

ETSI - TS 102 462 (2006). *Broadband satellite multimedia services and architectures: QoS Functional architecture.* V0.4.2 (Draft Version).

Evans, B., Werner, M., Lutz, E., Bousquet, M., Corazza, G. E., Maral, G., Rumeau, R., & Ferro, E. (2005). Integration of satellite and terrestrial systems in future multimedia communications. *IEEE Wireless Communications, 12*(5), 72-80.

Giambene, G. (2007). *Resource management in satellite networks. Optimization and cross-layer design.* New York: Springer.

Giambene, G., Giannetti, S., Parràga, C., Ries, M., & Sali A. (in press). Traffic management in HSDPA via GEO Satellite. To appear in the *Space Communications Journal.*

Goodings, R. (2002). IP over satellite: Standardization activities in ETSI/TC-SES. *ITU Workshop on Satellites in IP and Multimedia.* Geneva, Switzerland.

Guainella, E., & Pietrabissa, A. (2003). TCP-friendly bandwidth-on-demand scheme for satellite networks. *ASMS 2003 conference.*

IEEE 802.1d (1998). *Part 3: Medium access control (MAC) bridges, ANSI/IEEE Std. 802.1D.* 1998 edition.

IEEE 802.11 standard. (1999). Available online at the URL: http://standards.ieee.org/get-ieee802/802.11.html

IETF - RFC 1633. (1994). *Integrated services in the Internet architecture.*

IETF - RFC 2475. (1998). *Architecture for differentiated services.*

ITU-T-Recommendation Y.1541. (2006). *Network performance objectives for IP-based services.*

Kolding, T. (2003). Link and system performance aspects of proportional fair scheduling in WCDMA/HSDPA. *IEEE VTC-Fall 2003.* Orlando, Florida, USA.

Kota, S. (2005). Broadband satellite networks: Trends and challenges. *IEEE Communications Society WCNC 2005* (Vol. 3, pp. 1472-1478).

Le-Ngoc, T., & Mohammed, I. J. (1998). Performance analysis of CFDAMA-PB protocol for packet satellite communications. *IEEE Transactions on Communications, 46,* 1206-1214.

Le-Ngoc, T., Leung, V., Takats, P., & Garland, P. (2003). Interactive multimedia satellite access communication. *IEEE Communications Magazine, 41*(7), 78-85.

Mangold, S., Choi, S., Hiertz, G. R., Klein, O., & Walke, B. (2003). Analysis of IEEE 802.11e for QoS Support in Wireless LANs. *IEEE Wireless Communication Magazine, 10*(6), 40-50.

NS-2: Network Simulator, Vers. 2.29. (2006). Available on-line at the URL: http://www.isi.edu/nsnam/ns/ns-build.html

Párraga, C., Kissling, C., & Lutz, E. (2005). Design and performance evaluation of efficient scheduling techniques for second generation DVB-S systems. In *The 23rd AIAA International Communications Satellite System Conference (ICSSC-2005).* Rome, Italy.

SatLab. (November, 2006). *SatLab system recommendations v2 QoS.* Web site with URL: http://satlabs.org/

Skinnemoen, H., Vermesan, A., Iuoras, A., Adams, G., & Lobao, X. (2005). VoIP over DVB-RCS with QoS and bandwidth on demand. *IEEE Wireless Communications, 12*(5), 46-53.

Sooriyabandara, M., & Fairhurst, G. (2003). Dynamics of TCP over BoD satellite networks. *International Journal of Satellite Communications and Networking, 21,* 427-449.

Tasaka, S. (Ed.). (1986). *Performance analysis of multiple access protocols.* MIT Press.

Yang, S., & de Veciana, G. (2002). Size-based adaptive bandwidth allocation: Optimizing the average QoS for elastic flows. *In IEEE INFO-COM.*

Chapter XVI
End–to–End Support for Multimedia QoS in the Internet

Panagiotis Papadimitriou
Democritus University of Thrace, Greece

Vassilis Tsaoussidis
Democritus University of Thrace, Greece

ABSTRACT

An increasing demand for multimedia data delivery coupled with reliance in best-effort networks, such as the Internet, has spurred interest on effective quality of service (QoS) management for multimedia streams. Since today's multimedia applications are expected to run in physically heterogeneous environments composed of both wired and wireless components, we assess the efficiency of transport-layer solutions for multimedia traffic in heterogeneous networks. In order to quantify the performance on media delivery, we investigate the multimedia application requirements vs. the QoS provided by the underlying network. The chapter also provides means for the perceptual QoS assessment of voice and video streams. In the sequel, we describe some representative end-to-end congestion control schemes, identifying the mechanisms that are most suitable for multimedia traffic. Our analysis is complemented with conclusive performance studies which quantify video delivery, within the context of transport protocol support and efficiency.

INTRODUCTION

In recent years, Internet has been experiencing an increasing demand for multimedia services, typically involving audio and video delivery. Media-streaming applications yield satisfactory performance only under certain *quality of service* (QoS) provisions, which may vary depending on the application task and the type of media involved. Unlike bulk-data transfers, multimedia flows require a minimum and continuous bandwidth guarantee, while they are also affected by reliability factors, such as packet drops due to congestion or link errors.

Today's multimedia applications are expected to run in physically heterogeneous environments composed of both wired and wireless components. Wireless links exhibit distinct characteristics, such as limited bandwidth, bit errors, and potential handoff operations. Bit errors typically occur when the signal to interference and noise ratio is not high enough to decode information correctly. Furthermore, wireless channels are hard to model and predict, and designing an error-free communication link generally entails sacrificing significant capacity. QoS requirements in wireless networking essentially remain stringent and complicated, taking additionally into account the influencing mobile device characteristics and limitations. For example, a considerable number of mobile devices offer limited buffer capacities, being unable to smooth the fluctuations in the receiving rate. In this case, the task of smooth media delivery is primarily delegated to the transport protocol.

Several independent mechanisms have been proposed, which normally interact with the transport protocol and provide reliable transmission over wireless links (Balakrishnan, 2002; Hu & Sharma, 2002). Most of them operate on the link layer and generally are considered more efficient than physical-layer techniques, such as spread-spectrum and OFDM modulation, or channel coding. However, link-layer approaches may degrade performance, especially in the presence of highly variable error rates. Local error recovery may alter the characteristics of the network affecting the functionality of higher layer protocols. For example, local retransmission, such as *automatic repeat request* (ARQ) (Hu et al., 2002), could result in packet reordering or in considerable *round trip time* (RTT) fluctuations. In addition, concurrent responses from both local and end-to-end error control may result in undesirable interactions, causing inefficiencies and potentially instability. Considering real-time traffic where data packets bear information with a limited useful lifetime, retransmissions are often a wasted ef-

fort (Papadimitriou & Tsaoussidis, 2006). In such conditions, unfruitful retransmissions deliver delayed packets which are either discarded, or at the worst they obstruct the proper reconstruction of oncoming packets.

Transmission control protocol (TCP) is basically designed to provide a reliable service for wired Internet. The *additive increase multiplicative decrease* (AIMD) algorithm (Chiu & Jain, 1989), incorporated in standard TCP versions, achieves stability and converges to fairness when the demand of competing flows exceeds the channel bandwidth. TCP is further enhanced with a series of mechanisms for congestion management, including *congestion avoidance* (Jacobson, 1988), *slow start*, *fast retransmit,* and *fast recovery* (Stevens, 1997). Despite these features, TCP demonstrates inadequate performance in heterogeneous wired/wireless environments. Tsaoussidis and Matta (2002a) outline three major shortfalls of TCP: (i) ineffective bandwidth utilization, (ii) unnecessary congestion-oriented responses to wireless link errors (e.g., fading channels) and operations (e.g., handoffs), and (iii) wasteful window adjustments over asymmetric, low-bandwidth reverse paths. The difficulty of the task that TCP has to perform is further enhanced, when the protocol provides services for delay-sensitive applications. Standard TCP induces oscillations in the achievable transmission rate, with an adverse effect on the playback quality of multimedia applications. Furthermore, the protocol introduces arbitrary delays, since it enforces reliability and in-order delivery.

In this context, several TCP protocol extensions (Mascolo, Casetti, Gerla, Sanadidi, & Wang, 2001; Tsaoussidis & Badr, 2000; Zhang & Tsaoussidis, 2001) have emerged to overcome the standard TCP limitations providing more efficient bandwidth utilization and sophisticated mechanisms for congestion control. *TCP-friendly* protocols, proposed in Floyd, Handley, Padhye, and Widmer (2000), Yang, Kim, and Lam (2001), and Yang and Lam, 2000), achieve smooth window adjustments while they manage to compete fairly with TCP flows. In order to achieve smoothness, they use gentle backward adjustments upon congestion. However, this modification has a negative impact on protocol responsiveness (Tsaoussidis & Zhang, 2005).

User datagram protocol (UDP) has been widely used instead of TCP by multimedia applications. UDP lacks all basic mechanisms for error recovery and flow/congestion control. Thus, it allows for transmission attempts at application speed. That said, UDP cannot guarantee reliability, and certainly is not able to deal with network delays either. Papadimitriou, Tsaoussidis, and Tsekeridou (2005) showed that UDP may perform worse than TCP in several occasions.

This study is concentrated on transport layer mechanisms. An overview of Internet's current congestion control paradigm reveals that routers play a relatively passive role: they merely indicate congestion through packet drops or *explicit congestion notification* (ECN). It is the end-systems that perform the crucial role of responding appropriately to these congestion signals. Therefore, significant performance gains can be achieved without any support from intermediate nodes in the network. Considering efficiency on the basis of application requirements, we provide an overview of the influencing factors that affect media delivery and subsequently user-perceived quality. In addition, we include means for the perceptual QoS assessment of voice and video streams. We investigate the supportive role of a solution-framework composed of representative end-to-end mechanisms, including TCP-like, rate-based, and equation-based congestion control. We circumscribe the potential gains and undesirable implications on throughput performance, intra-protocol fairness, and especially media delivery. Based on simulations, we identify the mechanisms that manage to alleviate most of the impairments caused by limited bandwidth, contention and wireless links.

We organize the remainder of this chapter as follows. Section 2 overviews the most critical factors that affect multimedia QoS, including application requirements, influencing network QoS parameters, and user-perceived QoS. Section 3 provides a taxonomy and description of end-to-end congestion control schemes with emphasis on the performance on media delivery. In Section 4, we demonstrate comprehensive performance studies based on simulations, assessing protocol efficiency. Finally, in Section 5 we highlight our conclusions.

MULTIMEDIA QOS ISSUES AND LIMITATIONS

We hereby provide an overview of QoS requirements and issues that are critical for media delivery. Among other applications, multimedia applications require a more sophisticated management of QoS. That is, apart from certain application and network parameters, application requirements may be determined by specific user preferences and perception of QoS, as well. Therefore, we separately discuss: (i) multimedia application requirements, (ii) network QoS parameters, and (iii) user-perceived QoS.

Not All Applications Require the Same Service: Requirements and Taxonomy

The network status reflected by its QoS parameters significantly affects multimedia application performance. For example, long delays in the network path have a direct impact on the application latency. However, a user is not able to directly evaluate the network QoS performance and should not be concerned with the specifics of how a network service is implemented. If a user receives streaming video with jitter (e.g., freezing frames), he is not certain whether the network (delay variation) or the application (e.g., the video is not decoded adequately due to application or hardware constraints) is responsible for this inconvenience. What is actually obvious, from the end-user perspective, is the overall application performance. Thus, it should be expressed in terms of *user-perceived metrics*. The relation of application-level QoS parameters with network QoS parameters depends basically on the type of the application and the type of multimedia content involved. After a thorough study of the last two aspects, we hereby present a taxonomy of this nature (Clark, Shenker, & Zhang, 1992), where applications are classified in the following categories:

Elastic vs. Inelastic

Elastic applications tolerate delay and throughput variations, without considerable performance degradation. Although unfavorable network conditions, such as long delays, usually degrade application performance, the actual outcome of the data transfer is not affected. Traditional data transfer applications, such as http traffic, e-mail service, and file transfer, compose typical elastic applications.

Inelastic are real-time applications, which are comparatively intolerant to delay and variations of throughput and delay. They are also affected by reliability parameters, such as packet loss and bit errors. Inelastic applications deliver satisfactory performance only under certain QoS provisions, which may vary depending on the application task and the type of media involved.

Tolerant vs. Intolerant

Tolerant are usually inelastic applications, which tolerate certain levels of QoS degradation and operate satisfactory within a range of QoS values. Most multimedia streaming applications fall into this category, as they have specific QoS requirements, but they are not extremely sensitive to delays, jitter and packet loss. For example, a video streaming application tolerates a specific level of packet loss with slight visual impairments. Tolerant applications are further characterized by their adaptability:

- Tolerant adaptive applications incorporate mechanisms in order to adapt to certain network conditions, such as increased traffic, variable delays, packet loss, and congestion. An adaptive application may be able to reduce its transmission rate at periods of limited bandwidth availability or build a buffer in order to smooth out jitter.
- Tolerant non-adaptive applications cannot adapt in the same fashion, but still tolerate some network QoS variation.

Intolerant applications operate only under strict QoS requirements. If these QoS demands are not met, the outcome is unacceptable and the application task fails. While intolerant applications do not tolerate the distortion of delay adaptivity, they may be able to take advantage of rate adaptivity. These applications are called rate-adaptive, since they are able to adapt their rate to instantaneous changes in throughput.

Network QoS Parameters

The task of specifying the effects of network QoS parameters on video quality is challenging. Transmission rate fluctuations, increased delays, jitter, and packet loss commonly deteriorate the perceived quality or fidelity of the received video content. In the sequel, we discuss the effects of network parameters on multimedia delivery. Although we refer to these parameters individually, we note that they do not affect quality in an independent manner; they rather act in combination or cumulatively, and ultimately, only this joint effect is detected by the end-user. However, studying the effects of network parameters in an isolated fashion is a more tractable approach.

End-to-End Delay

End-to-end delay is introduced at the network and during the encoding/decoding and packetization process. Network delay is expressed by the summation of propagation and transmission delays, and the variable queuing and processing delays at the intermediate routers along the path. The typical delay guidelines for streaming video are shown in Table 1. End-to-end delays exceeding 250 ms affect the timely delivery of data and have an influencing impact on perceptual quality. Generally, increased delays may cause data unavailability and unintelligible real-time interaction with frustrating consequences to the application user.

Delay Variation

Delay variation is usually caused by the variable queuing and processing delays on routers during periods of increased traffic and occasionally by routing changes. Delay variation is responsible for the phenomenon called network jitter. Generally, jitter has unpleasant effects on a multimedia application, as packets often reach the receiver later than required. In addition, delay variation may result in temporal inconsistency of the multimedia presentation, such as freezing video frames. The playback quality of multimedia applications is notably degraded when delay variation exceeds 75 ms.

The use of buffering can eliminate the effects of delay variation by smoothing out jitter. In this situation, an additional delay is incurred to the multimedia presentation. However, buffering exhibits certain limitations, such as application delay tolerance and buffer memory constraints. Even in the presence of a deep playback buffer, the overall effort to overcome excessive jitter may still result in intolerable delays.

Wireless error-prone links may induce considerable sending rate fluctuations and the resulting delay variation has an adverse effect on media playback quality. Cashing incoming packets at link-layer buffers (e.g., TCP-aware Snoop protocol (Balakrishnan, Padmanabhan, Seshan, & Katz, 1997)) may introduce arbitrary delays that cause perceptible variations in RTT and disturbing fluctuations in the receiving rate. Papadimitriou et al. (2006) showed that local error control degrades the performance on media delivery in a wide range of network dynamics and regardless of the transport protocol used.

Packet Loss

Packet loss composes an impairment factor, since it causes a perceptible degradation on playback quality. The specific impact is particularly disruptive on compressed video streams, since packet drops induce distortions on the visual quality, which are typically more annoying to the human viewer than most types of impairments (e.g., encoding artifacts). In MPEG, for example, dropping packets from an independently encoded I (*intra* picture) frame causes the following dependent P (*predictive*), and B (*bidirectional*) frames not to be fully decodable. In practice, inter-frame dependencies may convert a 3% packet loss rate up to a 30% frame loss rate.

Table 1. Typical delay guidelines for streaming video

Delay	Effect in perceived quality
Less than 150 ms	Delay is not noticeable
150 - 250 ms	Acceptable quality with slight visual impairments
Over 250 - 300 ms	Video quality is degraded

Packet loss is typically the result of excessive congestion in the network. However, in heterogeneous wired/wireless environments, apart from congestion, hand-offs and fading channels may result in packet loss. Most transport protocols (e.g., TCP) are not able to detect the cause of packet loss, invoking congestion-oriented responses to all types of errors. Apart from a wasteful rate decrease, further undesirable implications may take place since the flows that reduce their rates can be *suppressed* by competing flows that do not experience wireless loss.

Numerous systems use error correction codes (ECC), such as *forward error correction* (FEC) (Hu et al., 2002), in order to ameliorate the impact of packet loss on stream quality. Despite the presence of such mechanisms, the perceived quality is inevitably diminished, when the transport protocol is unable to restrict packet drops. Furthermore, the use of FEC or retransmission introduces additional delays that delay-sensitive flows cannot withstand (Papadimitriou et al., 2006).

Packet loss rate itself is not always enough to assess the impact of loss on the efficiency of the application. A significant parameter that should be taken into account is loss pattern (or loss period). In the Internet, loss patterns have a bursty nature, as losses often appear in the form of small bursts. Depending on the loss pattern, packet loss may just cause minor distortions or affect at a greater level the quality of the multimedia application. Paxson (1999) provides evidence for correlated packet loss. Isolated losses may occur as well, which cannot be modeled in a specific loss pattern.

Users' Perception of QoS Differs

QoS management for media-streaming applications includes aspects further than application and network parameters. A significant issue is how the end-user perceives the quality of the multimedia application. It is obvious that user-oriented QoS requirements arise and whenever the application priorities strictly converge to the client satisfaction (in user-centric multimedia services), user requirements should be taken seriously into consideration. Below, there is a list of the most common user-perceived QoS parameters (Chalmers & Sloman, 1999):

- Picture/video detail (pixel resolution)
- Picture color accuracy (color information / pixel)
- Audio quality (audio sampling rate and bit rate)
- Video frame rate (playback time, delay)
- Video smoothness (affected by jitter)
- Video/audio stream synchronization

Different users are not expected to have equal levels of perception. A user's perception may be more sensitive to video smoothness than video/audio synchronization. Furthermore, users may exhibit tolerance to a high degree of impairments for some cases but not for others. For example, a user may tolerate certain video distortion but requires the delivery video of relatively high resolution, so that he is able to make out specific video details.

Perceptual QoS Assessment for Voice

In voice communications, several quality evaluation methods have been proposed (Takahashi & Yoshino, 2004). The *mean opinion score* (MOS) provides a numerical measure of human speech quality at the receiving end. *MOS* virtually indicates the speech quality perceived by the listener on a scale from 1 (worst) to 5 (best). The most popular objective measurements include *perceptual evaluation of speech quality* (PESQ) (ITU-T Recommendation P.862, 2001) and *E-model* (ITU-T Recommendation G.107, 1988).

PESQ is an objective measurement tool that predicts the results of subjective listening tests on telephony systems. PESQ score is estimated by processing both the input reference and the degraded output speech signal. PESQ takes into account coding distortions, errors, packet loss, delays and variable delays, and filtering in analogue network components. The resulting quality score is analogous to the subjective MOS and ranks on a scale from 0 (worst) to 5 (best).

E-model is a computational model that uses transmission parameters to predict the subjective quality of packetized voice. It has several input parameters that represent the terminal, network, and environmental quality factors. *E-model* assumes that the perceived effect of impairments, such as echo, delay or distortion, is additive. Based on this principle, *E-model* outputs a single rating (R) on a scale from 0 to 100, which can be further translated into MOS. Table 2 includes a classification of MOS and *R* ratings, along with the corresponding user perception.

Perceptual QoS Assessment for Video

End-to-end delays, packet loss and especially delay variation compose critical factors in the performance on video delivery. We provide selected means for the perceptual QoS assessment of streaming video, including packet jitter, peak signal-to-noise ratio (PSNR) and video delivery index (Papadimitriou et al., 2005). Most of them are computed based on reception statistics.

Packet jitter is the delay variation experienced by packets in a single session. Let D(i, j) denote the value of packet spacing at the receiver compared with packet spacing at the sender for a pair of packets *i* and *j*. D(i, j) is represented as:

$$D(i, j) = (R_j - R_i) - (S_j - S_i) = (R_j - S_j) - (R_i - S_i) \quad (1)$$

where S_i, S_j, R_i and R_j denote the sending and receiving times for packets *i* and *j*, respectively. In the absence of jitter, the spacings will be the same and D(i, j) will be zero. Packet jitter is calculated continuously as a weighted average of the observed values of D(i,j):

$$J(i, j) = \frac{15}{16} J(i, j) + \frac{1}{16} |D(i, j)| \quad (2)$$

PSNR compares the maximum possible signal energy to the noise energy between a source and destination image, I_S and I_D respectively. PSNR is defined as:

$$PSNR(I_D, I_S) = 20 \log_{10} \frac{V_{peak}}{MSE(I_S, I_D)} \quad [db] \quad (3)$$

where $MSE(I_S, I_D)$ is the mean square error of the two images and $V_{peak} = 2^h - 1$, with *h* the bit color depth. We note that representing PSNR frame by frame is more tractable than calculating the average of PSNR values of all frames, since an average PSNR may not map well to the overall subjective impression during video playback.

Video delivery index captures the joint effect of jitter and packet loss on perceptual quality. The metric monitors packet inter-arrival times and distinguishes the packets that can be effectively used by the client application (i.e., without caus-

Table 2. Voice quality classification

User perception	MOS Score	R
Very satisfied	4.3 - 5.0	90 - 100
Satisfied	4.0 - 4.3	80 - 90
Some users satisfied	3.6 - 4.0	70 - 80
Most users dissatisfied	3.1 - 3.6	60 - 70
Almost all users dissatisfied	2.6 - 3.1	50 - 60
Not recommended	1.0 - 2.6	0 - 50

ing interruptions) from delayed packets according to a configurable packet inter-arrival threshold. Video delivery index is defined as the ratio of the number of *jitter_free* packets over the total number of packets sent by the application:

$$\text{Video Delivery Index} = \frac{\#\text{jitter\_free packets}}{\#\text{sent\_packets}} \leq 1$$

$$(4)$$

TRANSPORT-LAYER SOLUTIONS FOR MEDIA DELIVERY AND WIRELESS LINKS

Considering the importance of congestion control (as well as the impending threat of free-transmitting protocols), we provide a classification of end-to-end congestion control schemes, identifying the mechanisms that are well suited to multimedia applications. Furthermore, we discuss selected end-to-end mechanisms that enhance protocol efficiency and application performance over heterogeneous wired/wireless networks.

End-to-End Congestion Control

TCP and TCP-Friendly Congestion Control

Today's Internet is dominated by TCP flows which enforce specific rules (i.e., AIMD) in order to achieve system stability and fairness. Essentially, the goal of AIMD algorithms is to prevent applications from either overloading or under-utilizing the available network resources. Although TCP provides reliable and efficient services for bulk-data transfers, several design issues render the protocol a less attractive solution for multimedia applications. More precisely, the process of probing for bandwidth and reacting to observed congestion causes oscillations to the achievable transmission rate. With TCP's increase-by-one and decrease-by-half control strategy, even an

adaptive and scalable source coding scheme is not able to conceal the flow throughput variation. Possible transmission gaps hurt the performance of multimedia applications, which experience jitter and degraded throughput. Furthermore, TCP's insistence on reliable delivery without timing considerations has an adverse effect on the performance of the system, especially for time-sensitive applications where data packets bear information with a limited useful lifetime.

Beyond standard TCP congestion control and the undesirable multiplicative decrease with a factor of ½ (in terms of media delivery), several TCP-friendly protocols (Floyd et al., 2000; Yang et al., 2000, 2001) enable smooth window adjustments, by invoking gentle backward adjustments on the occurrence of congestion. We consider as TCP-friendly any protocol whose long-term arrival rate does not exceed the one of any conformant TCP in the same circumstances (Floyd & Fall, 1999). In order to attain TCP friendliness, these protocols compromise responsiveness through moderated upward adjustments.

Essentially, the differences between standard TCP and TCP-friendly congestion control lie in the specific values of additive increase rate α and multiplicative decrease β; their similarities lie in their AIMD-based congestion control (a characteristic that enables us to include them both in the family of TCP (α, β) protocols). Standard TCP is therefore viewed as a specific case of TCP (α, β) with $\alpha = 1$ and $\beta = 0.5$. On the other hand, numerous TCP-friendly protocols are designed to satisfy the requirements of delay-sensitive applications. However, they may exhibit further weaknesses, when bandwidth becomes available rapidly (Tsaoussidis et al., 2005). Apparently, the tradeoff between responsiveness and smoothness can be controlled to favor some applications, but it will cause some other damages. The choice of parameters α and β has a direct impact on the responsiveness of the protocols to conditions of increasing contention or bandwidth availability.

GAIMD is a TCP-friendly protocol that generalizes AIMD congestion control by parameterizing the additive increase rate α and multiplicative decrease ratio β. For the family of AIMD protocols, Yang et al. (2000) derives a simple relationship between α and β in order to be friendly to standard TCP:

$$\alpha = \frac{4\,(1-\beta^2)}{3} \qquad (5)$$

Based on experiments, they propose an adjustment of $\beta = 0.875$ as an appropriate smooth decrease ratio, and a moderated increase value $\alpha = 0.31$ to achieve TCP friendliness.

TCP-Real (Tsaoussidis & Zhang, 2002b; Zhang et al., 2001) is a high-throughput transport protocol that incorporates a congestion avoidance mechanism in order to minimize transmission gaps. As a result, the protocol is suited for real-time applications, since it enables improved performance and reasonable playback timers. TCP-Real approximates a receiver-oriented approach beyond the balancing trade of the parameters of additive increase and multiplicative decrease. The protocol introduces another parameter, namely γ, which determines the window adjustments during congestion avoidance. More precisely, the receiver measures the data-receiving rate and attaches the result to its acknowledgments (ACK), directing the transmission rate of the sender. When new data is acknowledged and the congestion window (*cwnd*) is adjusted, the current data-receiving rate is compared against the previous one. If there is no receiving rate decrease, *cwnd* is increased by 1 *maximum segment size* every RTT. If the magnitude of the decrease is small, the *cwnd* remains temporarily unaffected; otherwise, the sender reduces the *cwnd* multiplicatively by γ. Tsaoussidis et al. (2002b) suggest a default value of $\gamma = 1/8$. However, this parameter can be adaptive to the detected conditions. Generally, TCP-Real can be viewed as a TCP (α, β, γ) protocol,

where γ captures the protocol's behavior prior to congestion when congestion boosts up.

Rate-Based Congestion Control

Considering TCP's limitations and the impending threat of unresponsive UDP, rate-based congestion control (Papadimitriou & Tsaoussidis, 2007a; Rejaie, Handley, & Estrin, 1999) composes a plausible candidate for media-streaming applications. Rate-based protocols control directly the transmission rate of the connection and typically generate a smoothed flow by spreading the data transmission across a time interval. Hence, the burstiness induced by the window-based mechanisms is avoided.

Rate adaptation protocol (RAP) (Rejaie et al., 1999) is a rate-based protocol which employs an AIMD algorithm for the transmission of real-time streams. The sending rate is continuously adjusted by RAP in a TCP-friendly fashion, using feedback from the receiver. RAP attempts to resemble TCP's functionality, leaving out only the undesired reliability. The RAP source receives ACK infrequently and exploits the redundant information on a single incoming ACK to detect packet loss, inline with TCP's *fast recovery* algorithm (Stevens, 1997). However, some aspects of TCP design that do not favor smooth delivery are incorporated into RAP. For example, the multiplicative decrease by a factor of ½ invokes abrupt rate reductions upon congestion, compromising smoothness.

Scalable streaming video protocol (SSVP) (Papadimitriou et al., 2007a) is an end-to-end TCP-friendly protocol optimized for unicast video streaming applications. SSVP operates on top of the light-weight UDP which is already preferred by the majority of streaming applications and Internet telephony. The protocol employs AIMD-oriented congestion control and adapts the sending rate by adjusting the inter-packet-gap. SSVP applies modifications only in the sending and receiving host. The recipient uses control packets in order to send feedback of reception statistics to the sender. In accordance with the relaxed packet loss requirements of streaming video and considering the delays induced by retransmitted packets, SSVP does not integrate reliability into UDP datagrams. Hence, control packets do not trigger retransmissions. However, they are effectively used to determine bandwidth and RTT estimates, and properly adjust the rate of the outgoing video streams.

SSVP enables a smoothness-oriented modulation of AIMD parameters in order to reduce the magnitude of AIMD oscillation and allow for smooth transmission patterns, without compromising TCP-friendliness. More precisely, SSVP's congestion control employs an additive increase rate $\alpha = 0.31$ and a multiplicative decrease ratio $\beta = 0.875$. On the occurrence of packet loss, the protocol infers congestion and the sender immediately reduces the transmission rate via the multiplicative increase of IPG. If congestion has not been detected, the SSVP source increases the transmission rate by decreasing IPG additively. The sender adjusts the transmission rate once per RTT in order to maintain a smoothed flow, especially at sudden changes of bandwidth availability.

Equation-Based Congestion Control

Equation-based congestion control enables bandwidth estimation based on statistics of RTT and packet loss probability. In response to the bandwidth estimates obtained, the source adjusts the transmission rate accordingly. *TCP-friendly rate control* (TFRC) (Floyd et al., 2000) is a representative equation-based protocol, which adjusts its transmission rate in response to the level of congestion, as estimated based on the calculated loss rate. Multiple packet drops in the same RTT are considered as a single loss event by TFRC and hence, the protocol follows a more gentle congestion control strategy. The TFRC sender uses the following TCP response function:

$$T(p, RTT, RTO) = \frac{1}{RTT\sqrt{\frac{2p}{3}} + RTO \left(3\sqrt{\frac{3p}{8}}\right) p \left(1 + 32p^2\right)}$$

(6)

where p is the steady-state loss event rate and RTO is the retransmission timeout value. Equation (6) enforces an upper bound on the sending rate T.

According to Floyd et al. (2000), TFRC's increase rate never exceeds 0.14 packets per RTT (or 0.28 packets per RTT when history discounting has been invoked). In addition, the protocol requires five RTTs in order to halve its sending rate. Consequently, the instantaneous throughput of TFRC has a much lower variation over time. TFRC eventually achieves the smoothing of the transmission gaps and therefore, is suitable for applications requiring a smooth sending rate. However, this smoothness has a negative impact, as the protocol becomes less responsive to bandwidth availability (Tsaoussidis et al., 2005). TFRC has another major constraint: it is designed for applications transmitting fixed sized packets, and consequently its congestion control is unsuitable for applications that use packets with variable size. In order to overcome this inconvenience, a TFRC variant, called *TFRC-PacketSize* (TFRC-PS), has been proposed.

End-to-End Enhancements for Wireless Links

We hereby present several end-to-end enhancements for heterogeneous wired/wireless networks (Hu et al., 2002). *TCP Westwood* (Mascolo et al., 2001) is a TCP-friendly protocol that emerged as a sender-side-only modification of TCP Reno congestion control. TCP Westwood exploits end-to-end bandwidth estimation in order to adjust the values of slow-start threshold and *cwnd* after a congestion episode. The protocol incorporates a recovery mechanism which avoids the blind halving of the sending rate of TCP Reno after packet losses and enables TCP Westwood to achieve a high link-utilization in the presence of wireless errors. Papadimitriou et al. (2005) showed that TCP Westwood tends to overestimate the available bandwidth, due to ACK clustering. TCP Westwood+ is a recent extension of TCP Westwood, based on an *additive increase/adaptive decrease* mechanism. Unlike the initial version of Westwood, TCP Westwood+ computes one sample of available bandwidth every RTT, using all data acknowledged in the specific RTT.

Tackling TCP's inefficiency over wireless links, split connection protocols, such as *Indirect-TCP* (Bakre & Badrinath, 1995), split a TCP connection into two separate connections by installing an agent at every base station (BS) in the entire wireless communication system. Apparently, split connection protocols cannot be easily deployed, while they also violate TCP's end-to-end semantics. Alternatively, existing end-to-end loss algorithms can be applied to decouple congestion from wireless errors, based on packet inter-arrival times (Cen, Cosman, & Voelker, 2003). However, inferring a specific behavior from inter-arrival times or packet pair may be inaccurate, due to the variation and complication of traffic patterns in the Internet.

Capone, Fratta, and Martignon (2004) presents and analyzes the bandwidth estimation schemes implemented at the sender side of a TCP connection, including the estimation algorithms of TCP Vegas and TCP Westwood. In addition, they propose *TIBET* (*time intervals based bandwidth estimation technique*), a new bandwidth estimation scheme implemented within the TCP congestion control procedure, which enhances TCP performance over wireless links. *Freeze-TCP* (Goff, Moronski, Phatak, & Gupta, 2000) distinguishes handoffs from congestion through the use of the advertised window. *WTCP* (Sinha, Venkitaraman, Sivakumar, & Bharghavan, 1999) implements a rate-based congestion control replacing entirely the ACK-clocking mechanism. *TCP Probing* (Tsaoussidis et al., 2000) grafts a probing cycle and an *immediate recovery strategy*

into standard TCP in order to control effectively the throughput/overhead trade-off. *MULTFRC* (Chen & Zakhor, 2004) is a recent extension of TFRC for wireless networks, establishing multiple TFRC connections on the same path when a single connection is not able to utilize the wireless resources efficiently.

Papadimitriou, Tsaoussidis, and Zhang (2007b) presented a *loss differentiation algorithm* (LDA), which decouples wireless from congestion loss based on queue length. The proposed LDA is a pure end-to-end mechanism and does not require any modifications in the network infrastructure or the underlying network protocol. Queue length is estimated by RTT measurements. More precisely, the LDA interacts with the protocol monitoring the minimum and maximum RTT, RTT_{min} and RTT_{max} respectively. Queuing delay can be derived by deducting RTT_{min} from the last RTT measured. In the absence of wireless loss, RTT_{max} is normally observed before congestion control is triggered. Practically, upon packet loss if the last RTT is close to the RTT_{min}, the bottleneck is not congested and the loss is due to a link error. On the other hand, a measured RTT substantially larger than RTT_{min} and close to RTT_{max} indicates a congestive loss. Therefore, the protocol's congestion control is complemented with the following algorithm. Upon the detection of packet loss, the transmission rate is decreased only when the following condition is satisfied:

$$\frac{qdelay}{qdelay_{max}} = \frac{RTT - RTT_{min}}{RTT_{max} - RTT_{min}} \geq qthresh \qquad (7)$$

Threshold *qthresh* in equation (7) specifies the point of queue length where packet loss is considered to be congestion-induced. This threshold can be adjusted differently in order to modify the protocol's error-recovery strategy.

If condition (7) does not hold, the experienced loss is classified as wireless, and the sending rate remains unaffected. Such recovery does not endanger packet loss by increasing the transmission rate, and concurrently does not enforce a rate decrease that might be unnecessary and harmful (degrading flow throughput and smoothness). Note that if both queuing delay and wireless loss exist, differentiation capability is limited. However, in the presence of long queuing delay, differentiation is not necessary: packet loss should trigger a rate reduction anyway. Therefore, the LDA classifies the loss as congestive, allowing the flow to recover from congestion, even if wireless loss has also been experienced.

PERFORMANCE STUDIES

In this section, we provide conclusive performance studies of selected transport protocols based on simulations. We also investigate potential performance gains from the collaboration of congestion control with end-to-end enhancements for wireless links. Efficiency is considered on the basis of application requirements, as well as on the underlying network characteristics.

Experimental Environment

The evaluation plan was implemented on the *NS-2* network simulator. Simulations were conducted on a single-bottleneck *dumbbell* topology (Figure 1) with a bottleneck capacity of 10 Mbps and a round-trip link delay of 64 ms. The bottleneck link is shared by competing MPEG and TCP connections. The capacity of all access links to the sink nodes is set to 1 Mbps. The routers are drop-tail with buffer size adjusted in accordance with the *bandwidth-delay* product. We set the packet size to 1000 bytes for all system flows and the maximum congestion window to 64 KB for all TCP connections. Each simulation lasts for 60 sec, and diverse randomization seeds were used in order to reduce simulation dynamics. All the results are collected after 2 sec in order to avoid the skew introduced by the startup effect.

We used a link error model in the access links to the MPEG sink nodes. The error model was configured on both directions of the link traffic. In order to model temporally correlated loss observed in a fading wireless channel, we used the correlated *Bernoulli* model which characterizes the loss pattern as a Bernoulli distribution of loss rounds. Each round consists of a group of consecutive packets, the length of which is approximated by a geometric distribution. The first packet in the round is lost with probability p. Every other packet is lost with probability p, if

Figure 1. Simulation topology

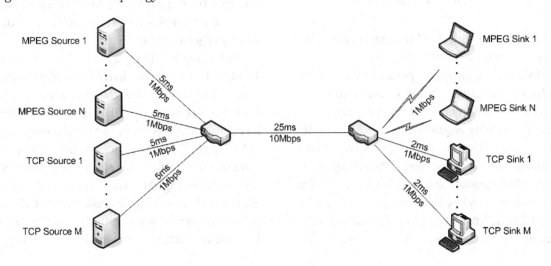

the previous packet has not been lost; otherwise, the loss probability is *q*. In our simulations, we adjusted $p = 0.01$ and $q = 0.15$.

In order to simulate MPEG traffic, we developed an *MPEG-4 Traffic Generator*. The traffic generated closely matches the statistical characteristics of an original MPEG-4 video trace. The compression initiates by encoding a single I frame, followed by a group of P and B frames. P frames carry the signal difference between the previous frame and motion vectors, while B frames are interpolated; the encoding is based on the previous and the next frame. The model developed is based on *Transform Expand Sample* (TES). We used three separate TES models for modeling I, P, and B frames, respectively. The resulting MPEG-4 stream is generated by interleaving data obtained by the three models.

We hereby refer to the performance metrics supported by our simulation model. Since the simulation topology includes competing MPEG and FTP connections, our performance metrics are applied separately to the MPEG and FTP traffic. *Throughput* is used to measure the efficiency in link utilization. Long-term fairness is measured by the *fairness index*, derived from the formula given in Chiu et al. (1989), and is defined as:

$$\text{Fairness Index} = \frac{(\sum_{i=1}^{n} \text{Throughput}_i)^2}{n(\sum_{i=1}^{n} \text{Throughput}_i^2)}$$

where Throughput$_i$ is the throughput of the ith flow and *n* is the total number of flows.

In order to quantify the performance on video delivery, we exploit *Video Delivery Index*, as defined in subsection 2.3.2. In accordance with video streaming requirements, we adjusted the packet inter-arrival threshold at 75 ms. For a system with multiple flows, we present the average of the Video Performance Index of each MPEG flow. The proportion of delayed packets (i.e., with packet inter-arrival times exceeding this threshold) is denoted as *delayed packets rate*. Since MPEG

traffic is sensitive to packet loss, we additionally define *packet loss rate*, as the ratio of the number of lost packets over the number of packets sent by the application.

Results and Discussion

We carried out a series of experiments in order to assess the performance of selected end-to-end mechanisms, in terms of throughput, fairness and video delivery. Particularly we evaluated TFRC, GAIMD, TCP Westwood+ (TCPW+) and SSVP augmented with the LDA (SSVP-LD) presented in (Papadimitriou et al., 2007b). Both TFRC and SSVP are designed for remarkable efficiency on media delivery over a wide range of network and session dynamics. TCPW+ targets at improved performance over wireless links, while GAIMD (0.31, 0.875) composes a smoothness-oriented version of general AIMD congestion control. Threshold *qthesh* is adjusted experimentally at 0.5 for SSVP-LD. Hence, when the queue occupies less than half of the buffer size, packet drops do not trigger congestion control invocations.

In this context, we simulated a diverse range of MPEG flows (10-60) over (i) SSVP-LD, (ii) TFRC, (iii) GAIMD, and (iv) TCPW+ competing with 5 FTP connections of TCP Reno, successively. We measured *throughput, fairness index, video delivery index*, and we additionally demonstrate statistics from delayed and lost packets, which compose influencing factors for perceptual video quality (Figures 2-4).

According to Figure 2, both SSVP-LD and TFRC utilize a high fraction of the available bandwidth. SSVP-LD remains relatively immunized by the wireless errors, as well as by the interfering FTP flows. SSVP is augmented by the integrated LDA, which allows the protocol to utilize wireless resources more efficiently, especially during high link-multiplexing. Although the integrated LDA alleviates most of the undesirable effects induced by the link errors, we note that throughput degradation is sometimes inevitable, since wireless

Figure 2. Throughput of MPEG flows

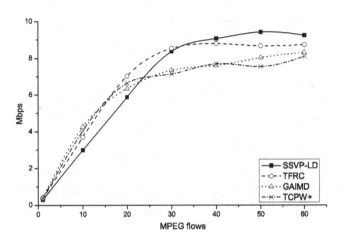

errors may occur while the queue length is close to the buffer size. SSVP-LD performs downward adjustments primarily in response to congestion, abolishing the adverse impact of unnecessary multiplicative decrease on throughput performance. Therefore, loss differentiation is significant, preventing a considerable amount of throughput degradation. Note that SSVP incorporates a gentle decrease ratio (i.e., $\beta = 0.875$), and therefore the impact of an unnecessary multiplicative decrease is not destructive on throughput performance. Indeed, a protocol with conventional congestion control parameters (i.e., $\alpha = 1$, $\beta = 0.5$), such as TCP, would experience higher throughput degradation. Therefore, incorporating the proposed LDA to other protocols may result in more gains, depending on the selection of the AIMD parameters.

TFRC responds adequately to the link errors, estimating the loss rate and adjusting the sending rate approximately. Essentially, the protocol exhibits unnecessary congestion-oriented responses to the wireless errors, since it is not able to detect the nature of the error. However, TFRC's gentle downward adjustments do not diminish significantly the throughout rate. GAIMD fails to adapt

to the network dynamics, since it cannot decouple congestive from wireless loss. Furthermore, its small increase rate does not allow the protocol to allocate rapidly network resources, after a window reduction. Hence, downward adjustments have an adverse effect on throughput performance. Despite the improvements over the initial version of Westwood, TCPW+'s algorithm still does not obtain accurate estimates in heterogeneous environments, failing to achieve full utilization of the available bandwidth (Figure 2). This observation is profound in the case of scarce bandwidth (high contention), where the sending rate is diminished. Apparently, the protocol is sensitive to the disturbances caused by the interfering flows.

Figure 3 illustrates that AIMD-oriented SSVP-LD and GAIMD achieve high levels of fairness. The AIMD-based responses during congestion enforce competing flows to converge to the fairness point for both protocols. In the case of SSVP-LD, the presence of the LDA notably improves fairness and system stability, as shown in Papadimitriou et al. (2007b). The measurement-based TCPW+ also exhibits a fair behavior among its flows. On the other hand, we observe that the *Fairness Index* for TFRC degrades abruptly, reflecting a

Figure 3. Fairness index

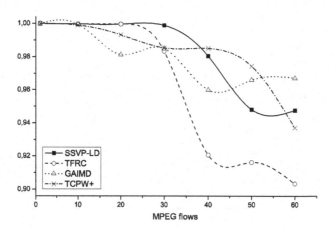

throughput imbalance between the connections. Apparently, TFRC's equation-based responses to packet loss undermine long-term fairness, along with contention increase.

In terms of video delivery, packet errors occasionally induce interruptions in the sending rate and the perceptual video quality inevitably deteriorates. SSVP-LD exhibits remarkable efficiency, delivering smooth video which is only slightly affected by wireless loss and contention (Figure 4a). According to Figure 4b, SSVP-LD achieves the timely delivery of video packets maintaining an uninterrupted and smooth sending rate. This combined approach effectively enforces an upper bound to the magnitude of delay variation, providing a possible guarantee for streaming applications that can efficiently operate within this QoS provision. Papadimitriou et al. (2007a) showed that SSVP maintains a smoothed flow in accordance with the requirements of video streaming applications. The incorporated LDA further refines transmission rate fluctuations, abolishing the damage of error-induced multiplicative decrease on flow throughput and smoothness. As a result, SSVP-LD delivers a smoother video flow, especially when link errors are the primary cause of the observed packet loss (i.e., 10-40 flows).

In contrast, TFRC's random downward adjustments induce oscillations in the sending rate, and subsequently delay variation of a considerable magnitude. GAIMD's performance on video delivery may as well frustrate the end-user. In dynamic environments with wireless errors, the protocol's congestion-oriented responses to all types of errors counterbalance the potential gains from a gentle decrease ratio (that could favor smoothness in a static and error-free network). TCPW+ exhibits increased packet drops (Figure 4c), while a considerable proportion of the packets that are not dropped, reach the recipient later than required (Figure 4b). Besides TCPW+'s tendency to overestimate the available bandwidth, the protocol slows down the transmission in response to the link errors. Consequently, the resulting transmission gaps induce interruptions in the receiving and playback rate of the video stream. The overall effect is long and variable delays, which degrade the perceived video quality.

CONCLUSION

We studied the effects and implications of end-to-end congestion control on media delivery in wire-

Figure 4. Performance on video delivery

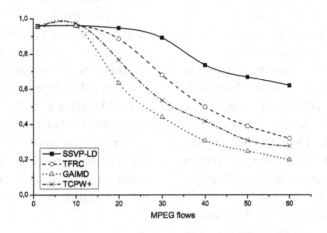

(a) Average video delivery index

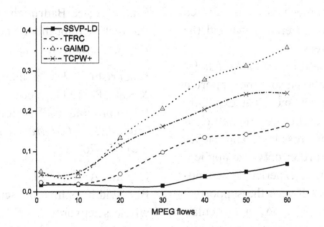

(b) Delayed packets rate

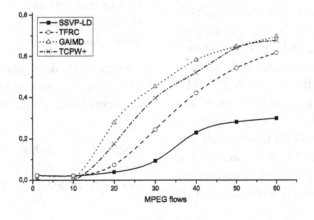

(c) Packet loss rate

less Internet environments. Efficient congestion control should minimize the undesirable effects of the underlying network characteristics and contention conditions, bridging the gap between the stringent multimedia application requirements and the network capabilities. However, congestion control may as well result in considerable implications, such as throughput fluctuations that cause transmission gaps and essentially interruptions in the stream playback. The effects of wireless links render multimedia QoS management even more challenging. Media-streaming applications usually experience limited performance and perceptible quality degradation in the presence of random wireless errors, as the underlying congestion control typically interprets packet loss as the outcome of congestion. In such conditions, the assistance of supportive mechanisms is required in order to enable loss differentiation and the appropriate error recovery.

Since congestion control is arguably mandatory, multimedia applications should be supported by congestion control schemes that explicitly anticipate smoothness and detect the nature of the error. Combined or cross-layer approaches (e.g., SSVP-LD) may further optimize application performance and user experience, depending on the interactions between the supportive mechanisms. The proposed LDA, in particular, renders the underlying transport protocol less susceptible to random wireless loss. Consequently, a wasteful rate reduction in response to a wireless error is usually prevented with notable gains in terms of flow throughput. We incorporated the LDA into SSVP, concentrating on the interactions between the two mechanisms. We showed that SSVP-LD reduces the magnitude of AIMD oscillation inline with the requirements of media-streaming applications for smooth patterns of data transmission. SSVP-LD composes one of the few available end-to-end schemes that achieve efficient performance on video delivery in wired/wireless networks, without requiring the support from lower-layer feedback or *active queue management* mechanisms.

On the other hand, TFRC exploits equation-based congestion control in order to sustain a smoothed flow that favors delay-sensitive traffic. However, the considerable amount of packet loss inevitably degrades the perceptual quality. Both GAIMD and TCPW+ are unable to provide acceptable levels of multimedia QoS, especially at increased contention. The magnitude of delay variation and packet loss cause significant impairments in the quality of the received media streams, with frustrating consequences to the end-user.

REFERENCES

Bakre, A., & Badrinath, B. R. (1995). I-TCP: Indirect TCP for mobile hosts. *Proceedings 15th IDCS*, Vancouver, Canada.

Balakrishnan, H., Padmanabhan, V., Seshan, S., & Katz, R. (1997). A comparison of mechanisms for improving TCP performance over wireless links. *IEEE/ACM Transactions on Networking, 5*(6), 756-769.

Capone, A., Fratta, L., & Martignon, F. (2004). Bandwidth estimation schemes for TCP over wireless networks. *IEEE Transactions on Mobile Computing, 3*(2), 129-143.

Cen, S., Cosman, P. C., & Voelker, G. M. (2003). End-to-end differentiation of congestion and wireless losses. *IEEE/ACM Transactions on Networking, 11*(5), 703-717.

Chalmers, D., & Sloman, M. (1999). A survey of quality of service in mobile computing environments. *IEEE Communication Surveys, 2*(2), 2-10.

Chen, M., & Zakhor, A. (2004). Rate control for streaming over wireless. *Proceedings IEEE INFOCOM 2004*, Hong Kong, China.

Chiu, D., & Jain, R. (1989). Analysis of the increase/decrease algorithms for congestion avoidance in computer networks. *Journal of Computer Networks and ISDN, 17*(1), 1-14.

Clark, D. D., Shenker, S., & Zhang, L. (1992). Supporting real-time applications in an integrated services packet network: Architecture and mechanism. *Proceedings ACM SIGCOMM 1992*, Baltimore, USA.

Floyd, S., & Fall, K. (1999). Promoting the use of end-to-end congestion control in the Internet. *IEEE/ACM Transactions on Networking, 7*(4), 458-472.

Floyd, S., Handley, M., Padhye, J., & Widmer, J. (2000). Equation-based congestion control for unicast applications. *Proceedings ACM SIGCOMM 2000*, Stockholm, Sweden.

Goff, T., Moronski, J., Phatak, D., & Gupta, V. (2000). Freeze-TCP: A true end-to-end enhancement mechanism for mobile environments. *Proceedings IEEE INFOCOM 2000*, Tel-Aviv, Israel.

Hu, F., & Sharma, N. K. (2002). Enhancing wireless Internet performance. *IEEE Communications Surveys and Tutorials, 4*(1), 2-15.

ITU-T Recommendation G.107. (1988). *The E-model, a computational model for use in transmission planning.*

ITU-T Recommendation P.862. (2001). *Perceptual evaluation of speech quality (PESQ).*

Jacobson, V. (1988). Congestion avoidance and control. *Proceedings ACM SIGCOMM*, Stanford, USA.

Mascolo, S., Casetti, C., Gerla, M., Sanadidi, M., & Wang, R. (2001). TCP Westwood: Bandwidth estimation for enhanced transport over wireless links. *Proceedings ACM MOBICOM 2001*, Rome, Italy.

Papadimitriou, P., & Tsaoussidis, V. (2006). Performance evaluation of real-time transport with link-layer retransmissions in wired/wireless networks. *Journal of Mobile Multimedia, Rinton Press, 2*(4), 327-343.

Papadimitriou, P., Tsaoussidis, V., & Tsekeridou, S. (2005). The impact of network and protocol heterogeneity on application QoS. *Proceedings 10th IEEE International Symposium on Computers and Communications (ISCC)*, Cartagena, Spain.

Papadimitriou, P., & Tsaoussidis, V. (2007a). SSVP: A congestion control scheme for real-time video streaming. *Computer Networks, Elsevier, 51*(15), 4377-4395.

Papadimitriou, P., Tsaoussidis, V., & Zhang, C. (2007b). Enhancing video streaming delivery over wired/wireless networks. *Proceedings 13th European Wireless Conference (EW 2007)*, Paris, France.

Paxson, V. (1999). End-to-end packet dynamics. *IEEE/ACM Transactions on Networking, 7*(3), 277-292.

Rejaie, R., Handley, M., & Estrin, D. (1999). RAP: An end-to-end rate-based congestion control mechanism for realtime streams in the Internet. *Proceedings IEEE INFOCOM 1999*, New York, USA.

Sinha, P., Venkitaraman, N., Sivakumar, R., & Bharghavan, V. (1999). WTCP: A reliable transport protocol for wireless wide-area networks. *Proceedings ACM MOBICOM '99*, Seattle, Washington, USA.

Stevens, W. (1997). TCP slow start, congestion avoidance, fast retransmit, and fast recovery algorithms. *RFC 2001.*

Takahashi, A., & Yoshino, H. (2004). Perceptual QoS assessment technologies for VoIP. *IEEE Communications Magazine, 42*(7), 28-34.

Tsaoussidis, V., & Badr, H. (2000). TCP-probing: Towards an error control schema with energy and throughput performance gains. *Proceedings 8th IEEE International Conference on Network Protocols*, Osaka, Japan.

Tsaoussidis, V., & Matta, I. (2002a). Open issues on TCP for mobile computing. *Journal of Wireless Communications and Mobile Computing, 2*(1), 3-20.

Tsaoussidis, V., & Zhang, C. (2005). The dynamics of responsiveness and smoothness in heterogeneous networks. *IEEE Journal on Selected Areas in Communications (JSAC), 23*(6), 1178-1189.

Tsaoussidis, V., & Zhang, C. (2002b). TCP Real: Receiver-oriented congestion control. *Computer Networks, Elsevier, 40*(4), 477-497.

Yang Y. R., & Lam S. S. (2000). General AIMD Congestion Control. *Proc. 8th IEEE International Conference on Network Protocols (ICNP)*, Osaka, Japan.

Yang, Y. R., Kim, M. S., & Lam, S. S. (2001). Transient behaviors of TCP-friendly congestion control protocols. *Proceedings IEEE INFOCOM 2001*, Anchorage, Alaska, USA.

Zhang, C., & Tsaoussidis, V. (2001). TCP Real: Improving real-time capabilities of TCP over heterogeneous networks. *Proceedings 11th IEEE/ACM NOSSDAV*, Port Jefferson, New York, USA.

Chapter XVII
Cross–Layer Radio Resource Management Protocols for QoS Provisioning in Multimedia Wireless Networks

Tarek Bejaoui
University of Carthage, Tunisia

Nidal Nasser
University of Guelph, Canada

ABSTRACT

This chapter introduces the cross layer design for resource allocation over multimedia wireless networks. Conventional layered packet scheduling and call admission control schemes are presented and a number of cross-layered protocols that are recently proposed are investigated. The chapter highlights the QoS improvement and the performance gain obtained while considering the interlayer dependencies concept for various real-time and non-real-time applications. The authors hope that this chapter will assist in the understanding of the cross layering and its enhancement of the layered design for QoS provisioning in future multimedia wireless networks.

INTRODUCTION

Future communication systems are expected to provide a broad range of multimedia services with guaranteed quality of service (QoS). Therefore, effective management of the limited radio resources is important to enhance the network performance. Cross-layered radio resource management algorithms are some of the protocols that being designed to optimally adapt to channel conditions and specific applications requirements. Their purpose is to solve the issue of the lack of built-in mechanisms for protocol layers that makes it very difficult to provide guaranteed QoS for multimedia applications. This chapter intends to provide an overview of the various QoS requirements in next generation wireless multimedia networks, and some of the proposed solutions for effective management of the limited radio resources to enhance the network performance.

In this context, the chapter concentrates on the packets scheduling and admission control schemes proposed for QoS provisioning in such networks. As data communication through the air interface faces the hardest challenges, the chapter attempts to focus on the radio channel conditions and to explore the novel approaches based on cross-layered radio resource management protocols while presenting an overview on such protocols presented in literature.

BACKGROUND

Radio Resource Management for Wireless Systems

The next generation wireless systems are deemed to support a broad spectrum of multimedia services with quality of service (QoS) guarantees. However, in a wireless environment QoS provisioning is a challenging task. The wireless link with its particular characteristics and the user mobility renders QoS provisioning difficult and complicated, especially in such communication systems developed to support simultaneously and efficiently a broad range of heterogeneous multimedia services. Indeed, the wireless channel varies over time and space and has short-term (or small-scale) memory due to multipath (Shakkottai, 2003). These variations are caused either due to motion of the wireless device, or due to changes in the surrounding physical environment, and lead to detector errors. This causes *bursts of errors* to occur during which packets cannot be successfully transmitted on the link. Fast chan-

nel variations due to fading are such that states of different channels can asynchronously switch from "good" to "bad" within a few milliseconds and vice-versa. Further, very strong forward error correction codes (i.e., very low rates) cannot be used to eliminate errors because this technique leads to reduced spectral efficiency. In addition to small-scale channel variations, there are also spatio-temporal variations on a much greater time-scale (Liu, Karol, El Zarki, & Eng, 1996). Large-scale channel variation means that the average channel state condition depends on user locations and interference levels. Thus, due to small-scale and large-scale changes in the channel, some users may inherently demand more channel access time than others based on their location or mobile velocity, even if their data rate requirement is the same as or even less than other users.

One of the most important elements in such wideband wireless systems is the resource access protocol. It defines how a common resource such as the wireless medium is shared among contending users, and hence determines the overall performance of the system. For multimedia cellular networks, the access protocol must ensure efficient and timely access to multi-rate applications with different communications requirements. This implies that the protocol must be able to handle a wide range of information bit rates as well as various types of real-time and non-real-time service classes with different traffic characteristics and QoS guarantees. In addition, the protocol must operate under different constraints of moving users, dynamic traffic load variations, and highly sensitive wireless links.

Within the next generation wireless network architecture, radio resource management (RRM) entity is responsible for utilization of the air interface resources, covering, call admission control (CAC), packet scheduling, and handoff. This chapter investigates the CAC and packet scheduling techniques for next generation wireless networks.

The admission control (CAC) constitutes a fundamental RRM technique for QoS provisioning that limits the amount of traffic accepted by the network, in order to provide better service to existing connections. An admission control policy decides whether the connection request is to be admitted into the system based on some criteria. In a wireless network supporting heterogeneous traffic, an efficient admission control scheme is required to guarantee good performance to admitted users while operating the system at its maximum capacity. In addition, in order to improve system performance and capacity, admission control strategies should exploit the adaptability of certain services to give priority to non-adaptive service. Although the real-time service may have higher priority for the use of radio resources, the non real-time services also impose certain QoS requirements in terms of delay and throughput. Admission control decisions can be based on QoS requirement, link quality, current network load, anticipated traffic characteristics, and tradeoffs according to service provider's choice based on revenue targets. Packet scheduling techniques, on the other hand, control the allocation of channels to users within the coverage area of the system and, to a large extent; it determines the overall behavior of the system.

The most of CAC functions and packet scheduling protocols proposed in literature focus on different layers separately. Indeed, the hierarchy of layers provides natural abstractions to deal with the hierarchy present in networks. In this networking framework each layer communicates with its peer using a set of rules and conventions collectively known as layered protocol. Each layer should perform its own defined functions, shielding it from the details of how the services are implemented in the other layers. In implementing protocols in these layers, control is passed from one layer to the next. The interactions between layers are controlled, each layer has the property that it only uses the functions of the layer below, and only exports functionality to the layer above.

In wireless networks, wireless channels and networks are dynamic in behavior, such as temporal and spatial changes quality and user distribution. Furthermore, meeting the end-to-end performance requirements of demanding applications is extremely challenging without interaction between protocol layers. The conventional layered protocol architecture is inflexible and unable to adapt to such dynamically changing network behaviors, since the various protocol layers can only communicate with each other in a strict and primitive manner. In such a case, the layers are most often designed to operate under worst condition, rather than adapting to changing conditions. This eventually leads to inefficient use of spectrum and energy.

Conventional Layered Packet Scheduling Protocols

One of the key issues in packet radio networks is providing a mechanism for controlled sharing of available radio resources. Scheduling can achieve this objective for packet flows belonging to different applications. The scheduling discipline is used to determine which user will be allowed to transmit in the next time interval. It provides guarantees related to packet transmission delay and bit error rate (BER), and is generally applied when there is contention for an output channel.

So, to achieve a high coverage and a high system capacity for the demanding multimedia wireless services in cellular context, an intelligent packet scheduling algorithm is needed to judiciously manage the precious bandwidth under realistic constraints such as considering both downlink and uplink, multiple antenna signal processing, fairness, QoS, channel adaptation (to exploit the multipath fading and shadowing effects), as well as the soft handover effects.

For packet scheduling in CDMA context, a pioneering work is presented in that authors proposed a unified bandwidth-on-demand fair-sharing platform together with the maximum capacity power allocation (MPCA) criterion (Liu et al., 1996). The principle of MCPA is that the maximum capacity power allocation is obtained when the power assigned to each code among multi-rate mobile terminals is minimized with, at the same time, fulfilling the target signal-to-interference ratio (SIR) at the base station. From the results of the maximum capacity power allocation, the system capacity (the number of basic rate mobile terminals that the system can accommodate) of a multi-code CDMA system can be obtained and the users requests are scheduled iteratively. The proposed work in Liu et al. (1996) and subsequent ones, for example, Choi and Shin (1999), fails to make use of the channel state information to take more accurate scheduling decisions. Furthermore, fairness is largely ignored in that only round robin sharing is implemented in the code distribution (i.e., bandwidth allocation) algorithm.

In the context of wideband CDMA (WCDMA), Kumar and Nanda (1999, 2000) reported their performance evaluation work on simple scheduling methods (first-come-first-served and equal sharing), without regard to fairness.

However, some other research has been done on devising new scheduling algorithms for fair queuing in wireless networks (Cao & Li, 2001), especially for TDMA based systems, taking into account the channel state. Several algorithms have been proposed. The general idea of wireless scheduling algorithms is as follow: the scheduler simulates an error free system running a wired packet scheduling algorithm when the sessions (i.e., the mobile devices' active connections) have good channel states. When the session that is scheduled to transmit data encounters a bad channel state, it will give up the transmit opportunity to other error free sessions (i.e., with a good channel state), then these error free ones will give their transmit rights back to the error session to compensate when it escapes from a bad channel state. Thus, in fact, the scheduler tries to swap the allocated time slots between error free sessions and error prone sessions when sessions

encountering error. The goal is to hide the short-term channel burst from the end users. The system maintains long-term fairness at the expense of instantaneous fairness between sessions.

Notable scheduling algorithms include *WPS (wireless packet scheduling)* (Lu, Bharghavan, & Srikant,, 1999), *IWFQ (idealized wireless fair queuing algorithm)* (Lu et al., 1999), *CIF-Q (channel-condition independent fair queuing)* (Hg, Stoica, & Zhang, 1998), *SBFA (server based fairness algorithm)* (Ramanathan & Agrawal, 1998), *CS-WFQ (channel state independent wireless fair queuing)* (Lin, Bensaou, Ding, & Chua, 2000), and *WFS (wireless fair service)* (Nandagopal, Lu, & Bharghavan, 2002). A scrutiny of these current scheduling and resource allocation algorithms for cellular wireless networks reveals that there are three common major deficiencies: The channel model is too simple and not realistic. Only a two state (good or bad) model is used; there is few analysis for sessions, which have bad channel states; and the applicability in a real wireless network is not demonstrated.

A number of protocols were proposed for multiuser OFDM (orthogonal frequency division multiplexing) systems and addressed the issue of resource assignment in these networks. These systems are promising interface solution for their excellent performance over multipath fading channels (Liu et al., 1996). Their inherent multicarrier nature provides enormous opportunities for fast adaptive transmission and resource allocation (Choi et al., 1999; Cao et al., 2001). For recall, OFDM is a modulation technique on which is on based the orthogonal frequency division multiple access (OFDMA), widely considered one of the most promising multiple access solutions for next generation high-speed wireless networks. In Kumar et al. (1999) and Cao et al. (2001) for example, authors propose adaptive subcarrier-bit-and-power allocation algorithms. Mainly confined to the PHY layer, these algorithms are designed with an assumption of deterministic traffic arrival and do not reflect the dynamic queueing behaviors observed in the MAC layer. As a result, they fail to appropriately allocate the resources in packet networks since traffics usually arrive according to some random processes in these systems (Ben Letaief).

All algorithms previously presented are mainly focused on isolated layers of the overall network protocol. Therefore, the inflexibility of the strict layering structure results in an inefficient utilization of the resources (Hg et al., 1998; Ramanathan et al., 1998).

Conventional Layered Admission Control Algorithms

The admission control becomes a complex problem, especially in the context of the next generation cellular wireless systems characterized by their soft capacity and the support of multiple heterogeneous services with diverse quality requirements. Recent works on radio link management in wireless networks highlights the importance of access control techniques (Goria, Agusti, & Sallent, 2001).

A considerable research effort has been devoted to CAC because of its prime importance and a number of different approaches to this problem have appeared in the literature. Chahed and Elayoubi (2004) have listed only few of them, they are presented as follows.

CAC Algorithms Based on a Maximal Number of Users

The first CAC algorithms were designed for 2G systems, especially GSM, and were based on a maximal predetermined number of users in the system, or equivalently on a fixed capacity. In fact, for systems based on time division multiple access (TDMA) or Frequency Division Multiple Access (FDMA), users can be accepted as long as there are channels (time slots or frequencies) available. This is called NCAC and corresponds to a hard capacity allocation, which is not the case

in 3G systems, whose capacity varies dynamically with the quality of the air channel and mobility of users.

Nevertheless, this simplistic assumption makes it possible to introduce several classes of traffic (Leong & Zhuang, 2001) and (Bartolini & Chlamtac, 2002), based on the limited fractional guard channel (LFGC) policy, first proposed by Ramjee et al. (1996) for 2G systems. They thus obtain important performance measures as the blocking probability (i.e., the probability that a call is blocked due to the lack of resources), or the handoff blocking probability (i.e., the probability that a mobile), accepted in a given cell and moving towards an adjacent one, fails to continue its connection in the new cell.

CDMA-Oriented CAC Algorithms

The first CDMA-oriented algorithms were designed for 2G systems using CDMA as access protocol on the radio interface, like the IS95 system. These earlier algorithms considered interference as the limiting factor when making a CAC decision. In fact, in contrast with the hard capacity allocation, CDMA systems are characterized by a soft capacity where there is no hard theoretical limit on the number of users. A user can then be accepted if its admission does not cause an excessive degradation for already connected users due to a high level of interference (Badia, Lindstrom, Zander, & Zorzi, 2003).

There are three classes of CDMA-oriented CAC in the literature, namely the Interference-CAC, the Power-CAC, and the SIR-CAC.

Interference-CAC
In interference-CAC (ICAC) algorithms, the decision is based on a predetermined interference threshold at the base station (Capone & Redana, 2001; Huang & Yates, 1996). For this kind of CAC, a call is accepted if the resulting interference remains acceptable. Let us note that, by definition, ICAC algorithms are designed for the

reverse link (uplink) as they consider the interference at the base station and not at the mobile. Furthermore, ICAC algorithms developed in the literature do not take into consideration multiple classes of traffic.

Power-Based CAC

When accepting a call, the effect of the transmission power on QoS cannot be neglect. In fact, the power that can be emitted by a mobile or a base station is not infinite, but is limited to a maximal value Pmax. In the downlink, this power is considered as the limiting factor, as presented by Huang et al. (1996) and Capone et al. (2001), because each new user will consume a part of the base station power. The call is then blocked if the base station cannot increase its power to support it.

SIR-Based CAC

An SIR-based CAC scheme is an algorithm that accepts or not a new arrival on the basis of its effect on the SIR of existing users. This choice is based on the fact that SIR is an important measure of the QoS in CDMA radio interface: it can be mapped into corresponding bit rates, bit error rates, or bit energy to interference ratio (Eb/N0) (Chahed, Canton, & Elayoubi, 2003). This approach, combined with an adequate power control mechanism, makes it possible to consider the maximal transmission power of mobile stations that is an important issue in the uplink.

The first SIR-CAC algorithm was presented by Liu and Elzarki (1994). It is based on the idea that SIR is inversely proportional to the capacity. The overall residual capacity is then the minimal residual capacities between all the adjacent cells, and the new call is accepted if this quantity is positive.

One can see that this other-cell interference estimation is not very accurate and does not take into account the various intercell interference conditions. Kim, Shin, and Lee (2000) proposed an extension of Liu et al. (1994) with more realistic assumptions on the interference, as they consider

not only the interference between adjacent cells, but also between cells that are not adjacent, but close to each other. Again, the algorithm is designed for a single class of traffic, and no coverage constraints were taken into account.

Class-Based and Hybrid CAC Schemes

A combined SIR- and power-CAC algorithm was developed by Elayoubi, Chahed, and Hébuterne (2004). It is an effective-based CAC algorithm that insures the required SIR while taking into account the both the maximal transmission power and the coverage constraints. This algorithm also followed a flexible model that can handle handover requests and multimedia traffic, in addition to possible extensions to deal with shared channels that remain a possible solution for data traffic, or the case of limited capacity in the UMTS Terrestrial RAN (UTRAN).

Many other representative CAC schemes were proposed and presented in the literature. Floyd and Jacobson (1995) assign effective bandwidth to a given user according to its traffic profile. Admission requests are grouped into different classes and interference from each class is characterized. New users are assigned their effective bandwidth based on QoS targets according to their classes and call admission control module admits new users of a particular class if total interference of all the classes is less than threshold. Hierarchical priority schemes have been studied by Iera, Marano, and Molinaro (1996) for multimedia services requiring soft and strict QoS requirements to set priorities at call level and burst level. In Goria et al. (2001), they present two different principles on which the CAC can be based. The first one indicates that admission control is performed according to the type of required QoS. In this case, the CAC is performed only for some types of service, like conversational and interactive. It is not performed for background class since no guaranteed QoS is required. For the second principle, the CAC is based on the current system load and the required service. In this way, if none of the suitable cells can efficiently provide the service required by the user equipment (*UE*) at call set up, the call should be blocked avoiding that the required service leads to increase the interference level to an unacceptable value. This action ensures that the *UE* avoids wasting power affecting the quality of other communications. In this case, it is also possible that the network initiates a re-negotiation of resources of the ongoing calls in order to reduce the traffic load.

CAC Schemes Design and Recommendations

Various CAC schemes based on some of the most important criteria including efficiency, complexity, overhead, adaptivity, and stability have been compared by Ghaderi and Boutaba (2005). It was proven that many assumptions about mobility and traffic characteristics made in CAC related research are often not practical. Therefore most of the schemes proposed in the literature are difficult to deploy in current and future cellular systems. Furthermore, most of the researchers in the area developed their own simulation environments, making it difficult to reproduce and compare the results, as there is a clear lack of implementation and testing of CAC schemes in more realistic situations. According to the lessons learned from surveying and analyzing the literature, some recommendations were drawn that must be taken into consideration while designing a new CAC scheme. These recommendations are as follows (Ghaderi et al., 2005):

- To use more realistic (non-exponential) mobility and traffic (packet-based) models in designing and analyzing CAC schemes. New mobility models may not necessarily preserve the Markovian property. Meanwhile, new traffic modeling and engineering techniques are aiming at a more accurate description of traffic dynamics not only at call level but at packet level as well. To avoid

complex schemes and eliminate impractical assumptions about traffic and mobility, measurement-based CAC schemes (Jamin et al., 1997; Jamalipour & Kim, 2003) must be further studied for wireless cellular networks.

- To apply cross layer design (Carneiro, Ruela, & Ricardo, 2004) in order to improve the performance of CAC schemes and achieve bit-level, packet-level and call-level QoS. In particular, scheduling mechanisms at packet level and control mechanisms at call level can benefit from the information about the state of the wireless channel to achieve a superior performance.

- To design CAC schemes for multiple services networks so as to support emerging multimedia services. Efficient sharing of wireless resources between multiple services is of paramount importance. However, the design and analysis of efficient CAC schemes for such multiple services networks is much more complicated than that of single service networks.

- To consider heterogeneous networks and interoperability issues in order to achieve global roaming and quality of service end-to-end. A key aspect is seamless handoff among possibly different networks ranging from reliable and managed cellular networks to unreliable and unmanaged wireless LANs. A CAC scheme must be able to communicate with other control components of the network through standard mechanisms to provide end-to-end QoS guarantees.

Summarizing, the most challenging problems to be solved are mobility and wireless channel effects, particularly when considering multiple services networks. Mobility and wireless channel impacts on call-level, packet-level and bit-level system dynamics complicate significantly the modeling of cellular networks traffic which is essential for devising the appropriate CAC schemes.

THE CROSS-LAYER DESIGN FOR SUPPORTING MULTIMEDIA SERVICES IN WIRELESS

The Concept of Cross-Layer Design

The introduction of independent layers has proven to be a robust and efficient design approach, and has served extremely well in the development and implementation of both past and current communication systems. Layered architectures have certain desirable properties; Other than the reduced design complexity, such architectures exhibit a high degree of modularity, which allows an easy replacement and theoretically an arbitrary combination of protocols. This is important for rapidly updating or replacing protocols. It also plays an important role in maintaining a system.

In next generation wireless networks, guaranteed services will involve mechanisms, algorithms and schemes at physical (PHY), MAC, Internet protocol (IP) and transport layers in the protocol stack, interacting dynamically with each other. This is central to cross-layer design. The cross-layer design concept (cf. Figure 1) does away with the rigid structure of the layered protocol architecture, where each layer is responsible to serve only the higher layer. It is a way of achieving information sharing between all the layers. Each of them is characterized by some key parameters that are passed to the adjacent layers to help them to determine the best operation mode that best suit the current channel, network and application conditions.

These parameters have to be exchanged interactively to cope with the robust characteristics and constraints a multimedia traffic and wireless networks. Thus, with the cross-layer design active exploration of the various synergies of exchanging information between the MAC and PHY layers with the upper layer are emphasized. Their main purpose is to help to improve the end-to-end performance given networks resources by meeting the challenging data rates, higher performance

gains, and QoS requirements for various real-time and non-real-time applications.

However, the interlayer dependencies, which are introduced by the proposed cross-layer design should therefore be kept to a minimum, to preserve the layered structure as much as possible. So instead of a mere replacement, cross-layering should be viewed as an enhancement or a complement, not an alternative, to layered design (Khan, Peng, Steinbach, Sgroi, & Kellerer, 2006). The ultimate goal is to preserve the key characteristics of a layered architecture and in addition to allow for performance improvements and a new form of adaptability.

Cross-layer approaches are more adaptive compared to purely layered architectures. From an architectural view, they are also preferable to approaches that combine functionality from different layers into one functional entity. This is due to the fact that this approach is highly complex when many functions are combined. This kind of approach might also lead to frequent updates as new protocols are introduced. Ultimately, it might lead towards a small layered architecture where a layer exposes the drawbacks of a monolithic stack.

One other important issue in cross-layer design is the amount of the required information exchange between the layers and the time scale that has to be optimized. In general, the lower the amount of information exchange and the longer the timescales are, the more robust and implementable the design becomes.

In the practice, the cross-layer design has many applications: QoS support in the 3GPP2 (3rd generation-general project partnership 2), ad-hoc networks for real time video streaming, QoS mapping architecture for video delivery in wireless networks, multimedia over wireless and multi-hop wireless networks. The goal is either to optimize the use of bandwidth through RRM algorithms in cellular networks, as in the wireless local area networks (WLAN), or to enhance the path selection process and to achieve minimum

Figure 1. The general concept of cross-layer design

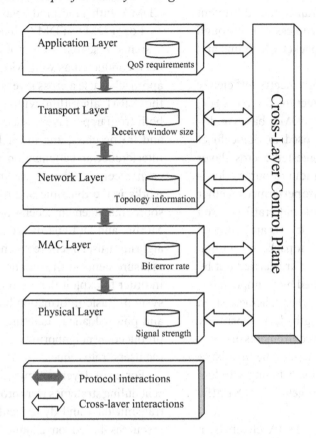

energy consumption in ad-hoc and in wireless sensor networks.

Cross-Layered Resource Allocation Protocols

Recently several researches have been conducted on cross-layer design for resource allocation over multimedia wireless networks. Considering the inflexibility and sub-optimality of the strict-layered design, many resource allocation protocols have been then proposed for the different radio access networks, considering different approaches. These protocols overcome the major deficiencies

presented in the previous sections. In Ben Letaief for example, it has been proposed a novel cross MAC-PHY layer resource allocation algorithm for wireless packet networks with OFDM signaling. In this algorithm, packet scheduling, power distribution, and subcarrier allocation are not designed in isolation, but rather within an integrated framework to take advantage of the inter-dependencies between the MAC and PHY layers. The proposed methodology exploits system diversities due to the channel variation along with the randomness of packet arrival and queueing behaviors. Moreover, it seeks to provide QoS guarantees specified by packet delay, throughput, and fairness instead of those observed in the PHY layer such as data rate and BER. It is able to guarantee the fulfillment of QoS and fairness over wireless links through a joint optimization of the packet scheduling and PHY layer transmissions.

In order to achieve a high spectral efficiency and throughput, an architecture for the PHY, MAC, and LL layers of an OFDMA-based multi-cell system has been proposed in Baiocchi et al. (2006). It has been suggested a cross-layer implementation, in which radio resource allocation and packet scheduling are performed together by exploiting both channel and traffic-related information. Cross-layer trade-offs are achieved with a modular approach, where packet scheduling and radio resource allocation are carried out by independent modules coupled by a simple interface. In the same context, other schemes based on the received power-strength, delay sensitivity and predicted BER as QoS requirements of every user, were proposed. It is the case of the cross layer packet scheduling in multipath fading wireless CDMA networks with heterogeneous QoS traffic (Abd El-Atty, 2006).

Over the time-varying CDMA channels, a pioneering work was provided by Jiang et al. (2005). A cross-layer approach for wireless video resource allocation with service differentiation was proposed and was given the name of dynamic weight generalized processor sharing (DWGPS). This cross-layer algorithm benefits from information in both the application and physical layers to implement a joint source/channel coding called unequal error protection (UEP). For each session, defined as an active batch in the transmission queue, is assigned a weight according to which is defined the priority classes and how many packets that could be transmitted from the active batch of the relative mobile station. DWGPS is originally designed for video transmission in the uplink, as resource allocation in the multiple access uplink is much more complex than that in the broadcasting downlink. It can also be applied

to real-time voice applications such as VoIP over CDMA with a required delay bound.

For FDMA-TDMA based multicellular systems, researches on cross-layer design have been conducted as well. Most of the performed approaches use a cross layer interaction, feeding the RRM algorithm with parameters coming both from upper layers, such as the rate demand and traffic class, and lower layers, such as the interference and attenuation levels estimated for each receiver. One of the most representative works is the dynamic and distributed radio resource management scheme presented by Zanella, Merlin, and Di Lenarda (2005). In the proposed algorithm, user interference and channel condition measurements at the mobile terminals are used in order to exploit the multiuser diversity of the system. Basic information bearers are allocated and power loaded, adapting to the interference produced by neighboring cells, in order to satisfy the users' rate request.

For cross-layer optimization, channel-aware scheduling strategies were proposed to adaptively transmit data and dynamically assign wireless resources based on channel state information (CSI). The key idea of channel-aware scheduling is to choose a user with good channel conditions to transmit packets (Viswanath, Tse, & Laroia, 2002). Taking advantage of the independent channel variation across users, channel-aware scheduling can substantially improve the network performance through multiuser diversity, whose gain increases with the number of users (Knopp & Humblet, 1995; Viswanath et al., 2002).

PROTOCOLS DESIGNS: CONSTRAINTS AND SOLUTIONS

Cross–Layered Scheduling Protocols Architecture

The adaptation of most of the proposed algorithms to the instantaneous variation of the physical channel is not proven although they take into account parameters coming from PHY layer. This is due to the fact that they are not tested under realistic constraints in dynamic scenarios.

Recently, only few cross-layered resource allocation protocols have been proposed and evaluated under realistic behavior of traffic and environment conditions. The most pioneering of such cross-layered protocols are developed by Bejaoui et al. (2006). It consists of a CAC scheme and Packet scheduling algorithm, originally developed for 4G-cellular networks, and could be taken as an example of cross-layer RRM design and simulation. These protocols are dynamically adapted to the state of the system and designed to overcome the shortages of some of simple layer packet scheduling and resource allocation policies presented in previous sections.

Their main objective is to maximize the rate of satisfied users of real-time services and to minimize their session outage rate.

The proposed approach uses a cross-layer interaction, feeding these algorithms with parameters coming from different layers. The algorithm takes into consideration parameters coming both from upper layers, such as the rate demand and traffic class, and lower layers, such as the interference and attenuation levels estimated for each mobile terminal. The system is tested in a dynamic scenario.

This protocol uses the link-sharing mechanism, which is based on the hierarchical class-based resource management referred to as CBQ (class-based queueing) (Callinan, Witwit, & Ball, 2000; Floyd et al., 1995). Focus is on the set of timeslots and codes that represent the radio transmission resource in UTRA-TDD, available periodically, and related to the radio interface of each base station.

CBQ achieves both partitioning and sharing of link bandwidth by hierarchically structured classes. Each class has its own queue and is assigned its share of bandwidth. CBQ is non-work conserving and can regulate bandwidth use of a class. A child class can be configured to borrow bandwidth from its parent class as long as excess bandwidth is available. A key feature of the link-sharing framework is the ability to share bandwidth between classes with different priority.

However, the full details of the comparative evaluation of CBQ and WFQ packet scheduling policies and its results, given in Callinan et al. (2000), showed that generally, continuous media will be best served by a simple CBQ system at times of heavy loads. Non-real-time data would be, however, likely controlled by WFQ and CBQ policies. This motivates the investigation of combination of CBQ with a priority function, integrated within each queue of packets relative to each class of service. The cross-layered packet scheduling policy is therefore given the acronym *ECBQ* for *enhanced class-based queueing*.

Priority Function Model

As conventional simple layered scheduling policies do not take into account several parameters that inevitably affect the level of fairness that can be achieved, this motivated a new notion of fairness governed by an appropriately designed utility objective function that has been developed by Bejaoui et al. (2006). The idea is that, requests belonging to several mobile stations will be queued according to their class of service. After, they will be served according to CBQ algorithm after being adjusted with a priority function, as presented in Figure 2. This one, integrated within the scheduling algorithm, is defined with parameters coming from application and physical layers. It depends on both the instantaneous waiting time and the QoS evolution in term of average waiting time. Furthermore, it takes into account the carrier-to-interference ratio affected by the environment propagation conditions.

At the same time, this priority takes into consideration the precedence class of the data users, negotiated with the network, in order to maintain the required QoS when the network is close to the

Figure 2. Structure of ECBQ scheduler

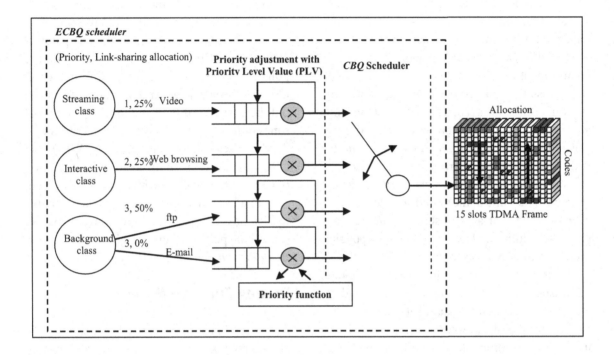

congestion. It is considered that each class in the link-sharing structure is assigned a priority level as well as a link-sharing allocation. This scheduler uses strict priority. For classes of the same priority, it uses a variant of weighted fair queueing, with weights proportional to the classes' link-sharing bandwidths. Thus within a priority level the scheduler distributes bandwidth according to the classes' link-sharing allocations.

Considering all these parameters, the network gives to each data user a priority level value (*PLV*) on which the packets channel assignment depends.

It grows from 0 to 44 according to a generated priority function, defined as below:

$$PLV=LDI*PCI+CQI \times (WTI+AWTI)$$

LDI is the system load indicator, which increase the mobile *PLV* when the system is close to congestion. *LDI* has a binary value, multiplied by 12, which is defined to calibrate this priority function. *LDI* depends on the system load (more or less than 70%) defined as the percentage of active users in the global system.

PCI is the precedence class indicator. For mobiles having negotiated a premium service, *PCI* is equal to 2, while for medium and low priorities, it is equal to 1 and 0, respectively. In an UTRA-TDD network, the energy per bit to spectral noise density ratio (E_b/N_0) determines the channel quality between the *UE* and the *Node B*. It has to be taken into account when computing the priority level value to consider the effect of the mobile radio propagation environment on the priority given to each packet.

Box 1.

$$\{ \; If \; ((E_b/N_0)_{dB} < (E_b/N_{0 \; target})_{dB})$$
$$\quad Then \quad CQI = 1$$
$$Else \; if \; ((E_b/N_{0 \; target})_{dB} < (E_b/N_0)_{dB} < (E_b/N_{0 \; target})_{dB} + 0.3)$$
$$\quad Then \quad CQI = 2$$
$$Else \; if \; ((E_b/N_{0target})_{dB} + 0.3 < (E_b/N_0)_{dB} < (E_b/N_{0target})_{dB} + 0.6)$$
$$\quad Then \quad CQI = 3$$
$$Else \; if \; ((E_b/N_0)_{dB} \geq (E_b/N_{0 \; target})_{dB} + 0.6)$$
$$\quad Then \quad CQI = 4 \; \};$$

Box 2.

$$\{ \; If \; (T_{max-serv} * (k-1)/10 < WT \leq T_{max-serv} * k/10)$$
$$\quad Then \quad WTI = 0.25 \; k \quad and \quad WTI = 0 \; If \; WT = 0$$
$$If \; (T_{max-serv} * (k-1)/10 < AWT \leq T_{max-serv} * k/10)$$
$$\quad Then \quad AWTI = 0.25 \; k \quad and \quad AWTI = 0 \; If \; AWT = 0 \};$$

Since incoming packets are differentiated according to their class of service, they will be classified according to their respective carrier-to-interference ratio (CIR). A channel quality indicator (*CQI*) is then integrated in the PLV formula and ranges from 1 to 4 according to the algorithm shown in Box 1.

The instantaneous Packets Waiting Time Indicator in the buffer is denoted WTI, and AWTI is the Average Packets Waiting Time Indicator in the buffer. Both are computed as shown in Box 2.

Where k is a variable that varies between 1 and 10, *WT* is the Instantaneous Packet Waiting Time (s), and *AWT* is the Average Packets Waiting Time (s) .

$T_{max-serv}$ is the Maximum Packets Waiting Time. It depends on the class of service in use. The performance of this algorithm is evaluated while considering *voice, Web browsing, JPEG image transmitting, and e-mail* applications. Over the radio interface, voice calls have priority over all ongoing data calls.

As it is not possible in simulation to consider the delay class defined in Goria et al. (2001), as the end-to-end packets time transfer in the network, the maximum waiting delay in the radio network

controller (RNC) buffer, $T_{max-serv}$, corresponding to each class of service is estimated as: 250 ms for pictures frames, 2s for Web browsing application packets, 10s for image transmission application packets, and 60s for e-mail best-effort application packets.

The priority level (*PLV*) is therefore obtained by combination of values that characterize the priority function parameters, coming from both Application layer, as for the precedence class and PHY layers, as for the signal to interference ratio. This function was calibrated by multiplying the system load binary indicator by 12 in order to optimize the (0,44) values interval. For all types of services, the highest priority is given to users' packets having waited for a longest instantaneous and average time, being transmitted over the channel of better quality and having negotiated the highest priority when the system is closed to congestion.

Since *ECBQ* is operating through the CBQ algorithm, it can borrow bandwidth from queues that can spare it, in order to forward packets from queues that have exceeded (or are about to exceed) their allotted amount of bandwidth.

A CROSS-LAYERED CALL ADMISSION CONTROL ARCHITECTURE

Following a cross-layered admission control algorithm for new call requests (cf. Figure 3) that has been recently proposed. It is an adaptive QoS oriented CAC function. It takes into account the realistic behavior of traffic and the propagation conditions, and its purpose is to meet the rapidly increasing demand for providing multimedia services with diversified quality requirements. This policy based on service class differentiation aims at maximizing the use of available radio resource and meeting the QoS requirement of higher priority users as much as possible while maintaining the minimum requirements of lower priority users, especially when the system suffers from congestion.

This protocol is interference and time-out based CAC scheme, which fundamentally depends on both cells interference levels and waiting time of streaming, interactive and background sessions. Streaming services are very sensitive to access delay and have priority over all ongoing data packets of other traffic classes. They are followed by interactive and background traffics. Voice calls are given the priority over all ongoing connections and the CAC function is not performed for them.

In next generation wireless networks, each new call increases the interference level of all other ongoing calls, affecting their quality. For each class of service, the interference parameter taken into consideration when the access to the network is controlled varies along simulation and is maintained under defined static threshold. For each user equipment, the energy per bit to spectral noise density ratio target is defined as the following:

$$\left(\frac{E_b}{N_0}\right)_k = \left(\frac{W}{D_k}\right) \times \left(\frac{G_0 P_k^0}{\gamma \times \left(G_0 \times \sum_{i \neq k} P_i^0\right) + \sum_{j=1}^{6} G_j \times P^j}\right)$$

$$(1)$$

Figure 3. Architecture of the proposed CAC scheme

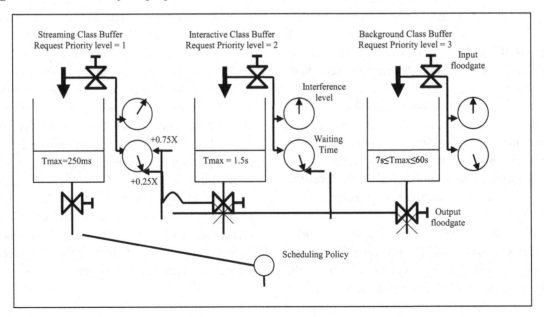

where W is the WCDMA chip rate, P_k^0 (k=1..N) is the received signal power from the user k and N is the number of active users' in the current cell (cell 0), P^j (j=1..6) is the transmit power from the current base station, D_k is the transmission rate, γ is the orthogonality factor and G_j (j=0..6) is the signal attenuation between user and the current base station (Node B). In order to consider all environment effects, G_j is computed using the three-stage propagation model (Parsons, 2001):

$$G_k = Pathloss \times Fast\_Fading \times Slow\_Fading$$
(2)

G_0 is defined as the signal impairment between the user and the current base station. The inter-cells interference can be approximated by $G \times P_n$, where G is the signal attenuation between the current and the interferer base stations, and P_n is the maximum transmit signal power of all base stations. The formula (1) becomes:

$$\left(\frac{E_b}{N_0}\right)_k = \left(\frac{W}{D_k}\right) \times \left(\frac{G_0 P_k^0}{\gamma \times G_0 \times (N-1) \times P_k^0 + G \times P_n}\right)$$
(3)

For each type of service, the maximum number of users depends on the energy per bit to noise density threshold $(E_b/N_0)_{threshold}$. It is defined by:

$$N_{max} = \left\lceil \frac{1}{\gamma + \left(\frac{G}{G_0}\right)} \times \left(\gamma + \left(\frac{W}{D}\right) \times \left(\frac{E_b}{N_0}\right)_{Threshold}^{-1}\right) \right\rceil$$
(4)

The notation $\lceil x \rceil$ designates the whole part of the variable x.

Session packets input floodgate will be closed and the connection will be rejected if the number of admitted users becomes over N_{max}. In this case, the instantaneous ratio (E_b/N_0) becomes lower than $(E_b/N_0)_{threshold}$ relating to the class of the service in use.

Streaming, interactive and background classes are differentiated by the use of a buffer for each, and sessions are rejected when the buffers' filling reach defined thresholds even if the interference level remain low. These thresholds of filling are represented by maximum waiting time $T_{max-service}$ defined for each class and are dynamic along simulation. They vary according to the waiting time of other services having more priority. The algorithm is performed as follows:

- Since background class contains non-real-time services, the output from the buffer of the background session requests is firstly stopped (output floodgate closed) when the streaming packets waiting time become over 75% of $T_{max-streaming}$. The streaming packets have the lowest maximum waiting delay in the buffer, followed by the one of interactive and background requests.

- After 25% of $T_{max-streaming}$, if the average waiting time is still above 75% of $T_{max-streaming}$, the output from the buffer of the interactive request packets is stopped, since they have the highest maximum waiting delay after background session packets.

- Obviously, if this waiting time remains higher then $T_{max-streaming}$, the incoming streaming packets are rejected before entering in the buffer (interactive traffic floodgate closed), until the waiting time become less than $T_{max-streaming}$.

The same reasoning is made for interactive and background session's admissions, while considering their corresponding times $T_{max-service}$ and the packets priority according to their class of service. For each class, the input floodgate will be closed when relative application request waiting time in the buffer still remains over $T_{max\_service}$.

PERFORMANCE EVALUATION OF CROSS-LAYERED RRM PROTOCOLS

The performance evaluation of the cross-layered resource allocation protocol under realistic constraints of traffic and mobility requires the use of an efficient simulation tool that takes into consideration all surrounding effects as well as the traffic and mobility constraints.

In this section, we evaluate the performance of the ECBQ cross-layered scheduling algorithm combined with the proposed call admission control (CAC) and compare it to other existing algorithms. The network configuration, the traffic modeling and the simulation platform are detailed in the next sections to help understanding how surrounding effects and traffic constraints are involved.

Simulation Platform

In order to take into account the signal impairments due to radio propagation in most of cell configurations and surrounding environment, a propagation model, which characterizes the main effects which impact the mobile radio channel as *the path loss, the fast and slow fadings* could be chosen.

The *pathloss*, which represent the signal degradation with distance is given by: $pl=(\lambda/4\pi d)^{\alpha}$, where λ denotes the wave length, d the distance between the mobile terminal and the Node B, and α the path loss exponent, which depends on the environment. The *Fast fading* is the phenomenon whereby the signal amplitude of the multiple signals arriving at the receiver is the vector summation of randomly phased components caused by reflection in the multipath medium. To implement an efficient simulator of the *Fast fading*, the concept of Rice's sum of sinusoids presented by Pätzold, Killat, Laue, and Li (1998a) and Pätzold, and Laue (1998b) was used. The *slow fading (shadowing)*, primarily caused by attenuation in the form of signal-path blocking due to the surrounding environment, is modelled by a log-normal distributed process.

The delay introduced by the propagation channel is assumed negligible, so mobiles will change their transmit power immediately after the signal-to-interference ratio measurement is completed.

The UTRA-TDD-based radio access network has been simulated using a flexible discrete time simulator. It is a pure software solution based on the programming language C++. It has been implemented using as time unit an equal TDMA framework period duration. Both time and spatial dimensions of the traffic variations are taken into account. Time variation of traffic is represented as arrival process, call duration or packet length for various types of services, and spatial variations characterize the user mobility in the cellular area. The simulation includes two time scales: The mobility time scale and the resource allocation time scale.

For the mobility scale, terminal position is computed at every 0.5 s (i.e., 50 units of time). The velocity, which depends on the mobile terminal type, varies randomly and uniformly when changing the direction. In each mobility period of time the energy per bit to spectral noise density ratio (E_b/N_0) belonging to each mobile is compared to the $(E_b/N_0)_{target}$ according to which each mobile can adjust its power transmission by 1 dB steps.

Whereas for the allocation scale, time-slots/codes allocation is performed at each simulation time unit, among the competing mobile terminals currently served in the cell. The resource allocation policy arbitrates among all communication requests that are competing for different services either for new calls or for handovers. Allocation can be effective only for mobile terminals that satisfy to power control conditions. Call arrivals are generated at the end of the loop according to late arrivals mechanism of discrete-time model.

Network System Configuration

The implementation presented here considers 21 micro-cells serving both packet-switched voice and data calls (Bejaoui, 2006). The edges of the network are wrapped around such that the "border effect" is suppressed. In this chapter, base stations use omni-directional antennas and are located at the center of the cells. They have radius value of *500* meters, and they are also parameterized by their transmit power and gains of their antennas. In such cellular configuration, user moves across cells, crossing cells boundaries impacting on the quality of received signal of their resident cell. The radio propagation simulation aims mainly at estimating CIR ratio for each communicating mobile terminal. For the division of slots within a frame, a combination of 8/7 for Downlink (DL)/Uplink (UL) has been chosen.

Mobility Model

The mobility of communicating terminals is taken into account. Depending on their moving speed V, two types of mobile users are considered: vehicles and pedestrians. They are uniformly distributed into the system. They are characterized by their positions in the cell and their directions that are randomly defined and vary each 0.5s. This is to avoid hot spots in the cells. The mobiles initial velocities are respectively 25 km/h and 3km/h, increased or decreased by $\delta V = 0.2*V$ while changing the direction during simulation. In addition, the power transmissions vary from one terminal to another, according to the distance between users and their serving *Node B*. All mobile terminals move across cells and initiate some randomly calls. All data users are assumed to be pedestrians.

During simulation, the mobility model plays a major role in both changes of system state concerning the power control management and handover management. In our UTRA-TDD system, the power control procedure is performed every 0.5 s which acts as the *mobility time unit*.

This procedure takes into account the interference effect, in which intra-cells interferences are neglected. For each interfering mobile, the tool computes the distance that separates it from the current base station and its transmission power on the uplink channel. During 0.5 s, a mobile terminal has moved of a few meters given its speed. At every mobility time unit a handover management is performed and for simplicity reasons, the six neighbouring base stations are considered in the active set regardless of the power level received at each mobile user. Every neighbour base station communicates simultaneously with all mobile terminals moving inside a cell and Inter-cell handovers due to mobility are performed using a hysteresis mechanism. Handovers are then triggered off if the CIR of current base station remains under a defined threshold, while the mobile power transmission reaches its ceiling. At the same time, the target cell power transmission exceeds the one of the current base station of at least the defined hysteresis margin value. It is equal to *-5dBm* in our simulation. The mobile station can finally succeed in its handover only if obviously the target base station has the needed resource for the transfer.

Traffic Model

The traffic generated by each user can be of the following types: voice, video streaming, Web browsing, JPEG image transmitting and e-mail. They are modeled respectively as a conversational, real-time streaming, interactive, and background (image transmitting and e-mail services) traffics as outlined in Goria et al. (2001) and Pâtzold (1998b). The first three types of services are mapped over guaranteed services (GS), while image transmitting and e-mail applications are best effort (BE) traffics having no delay constraint. In the presented simulation campaigns, the system is loaded by the heterogeneous traffic according to the following percentages: voice, 30%; video streaming, 15%; Web browsing, 15%, image transference, 15%; and e-mails, 25%. Thus, While performing CBQ algorithm, the streaming class is reasonably allocated 25% of the link bandwidth, the interactive class is allocated 25% and for the background class 50%.

In this discrete time simulator, the new packet-switched calls are generated with *Bernoulli* distributed process, adopted in most of the traffic models. Only the downlink communication is considered. Speech traffic is modelled with the parameters shown in Table 1.

Internet service traffic is based on the model outlined in Pâtzold (1998b). The traffic model is intended to represent HTTP browsing session by user and calls represent the requests down

loadings. The packet data traffic parameters are exhibited in Table 2.

Video streaming model represents an MPEG-4 streaming data. The service bearer is modelled as a constant bit rate circuit switched data service with 100% activity. The packet sizes vary depending on the type of video frame. There are three types of frames, namely I, P and B frames. The frames are produced periodically and in the deterministic IBBPBBPBBPBBPBB sequence (15 frames per second). Frame generation is done according to (Hughes, 1995) and the video streaming parameters are based on a statistical survey of frame statistics (Tripathi & Krunz, 1997). The size of the video pictures is assumed to be

Table 1. Speech traffic parameters

Voice parameters	Distribution	Mean/value
Inter-arrival of call(s)	Bernoulli	$0 - 120$
Duration of call(s)	Bernoulli	120
Mean talk spurt duration(s)	Geometric	1.35
Codes		2 (SF 16)
Bits per code		61
Max. throughput (kbps)		12.2
$(E_b/N_0)_{target}$ for pedestr./ vehicl.		3.8/5.3

Table 2. WWW interactive traffic parameters

WWW parameters	Distribution	Mean/value
Inter-arrival of calls (s)	Bernoulli	$0 - 120$
UL request size (bytes)	Geometric	180
Packet size (bytes)	Geometric	480
Number of HTML	Geometric	5 pages/session.
Reading time (s)	Neg. Expon.	12
Codes		5 (SF 16)
Bits per code		128
Max. throughput (kbps)		64
Max packet delay $T_{max\text{-}serv}$ (s)		2
$(E_b/N_0)_{target}$ for pedestr./ vehicles		3.3/3.9

QCIF 176×144 pixels. The relative parameters are depicted in Table 3. The parameters of traffic of image transmission and e-mail applications are presented in Table 4.

Discussion

Simulations have been performed while combining either CBQ or WFQ scheduling policy with the priority function. As ECBQ is the acronym given to the cross layered scheduling policy operating

Table 3. Video streaming traffic parameters

Video Streaming parameters			
Frame type	**Distribution**	**Mean (Bytes)**	**Variance**
I -Frame	Log-normal	775	97656
P-Frame	Log-normal	100	4727
B-Frame	Log-normal	63	1405
Codes		max 8 (SF 16)	
Bits per code		144	
Max. throughput (kbps)		115.2	
Max packet delay $T_{max-serv}$ (s)		0.25	
$(E_b/N_0)_{target}$ for pedestr./ vehicl.		1.4	

Table 4. Model parameters of Background JPEG image transmitting and E-mail applications

JPEG image parameters	Distribution	Mean
Inter-arrival of call(s)	Bernoulli	0 – 1200
Images mean size (bytes)	Geometric	4096
Max packet delay $T_{max-serv}$ (s)		10
Codes		5 (SF 16)
Bits per code		128
Max. throughput (kbps)		64
$(E_b/N_0)_{target}$ for pedestr./ vehicl.		1.2/3.0

E-mail parameters	Distribution	Mean
Inter-arrival of call(s)	Bernoulli	0 – 120
E-mails mean size (bytes)	Geometric	18944
Max packet delay $T_{max-serv}$ (s)		60
Max. throughput (kbps)		64
$(E_b/N_0)_{target}$ for pedestr./ vehicles		1.2/3.0

through the CBQ algorithm, the WFQ-based scheduling policy is given the acronym EW²FQ for Enhanced Wireless WFQ scheduling policy (Bejaoui, 2006).

Simulation results obtained while running ECBQ and EW²FQ are compared to those ob-

tained while considering FIFO with priority as a packet scheduling policy. In the following, the acronym "PRIO" is used to designate the *FIFO with priority* scheduling algorithm.

Quality measures reported in this investigation are the percentage of satisfied users and session

Figure 4. Voice and streaming session outage vs. offered load

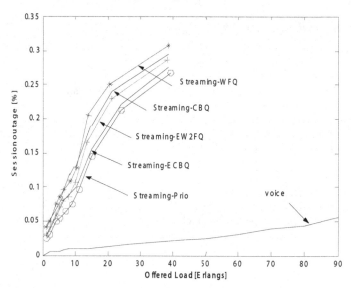

Figure 5. Rates of satisfied video streaming users

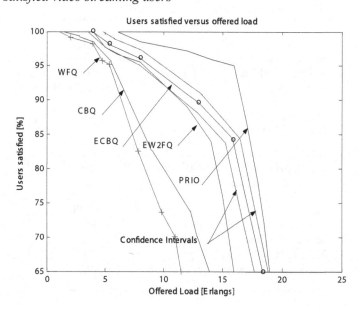

outage for real time (RT) service. Users of video streaming application are satisfied if packets are received in less than 250 ms during 95% of the session duration. For non-real- time (NRT) interactive and background services, focus is on the mean throughput [kbps] and the mean service packet data unit (SPDU) delay [sec].

The QoS parameters of voice and streaming video real time services are reported in Figures 4 and 5.

As streaming video service is very sensitive to access delay, it is given the best performance in term of session output percentage while using FIFO with priority policy. The session output percentage decrease from 21% with WFQ to 16.5% with EW²FQ and from 19% with CBQ to 14% with ECBQ, for a load of 13.5 Erlangs. It decreases respectively from 31% to 28% and from 29% to 26% when the offered load is close to 38 Erlangs. As CBQ gives better performances for RT services than WFQ, ECBQ gives the better performances than those obtained with EW²FQ.

This investigation proved that ECBQ and EW²FQ enhance the QoS performance given by CBQ and WFQ scheduling algorithms for both differentiated background and best-effort services. At the same time, the fair policies, ECBQ and EW²FQ, offer quite similar level of QoS to that obtained using FIFO with priority algorithm, for the streaming and interactive classes of traffic. Furthermore, these results show that ECBQ and EW²FQ give the highest performance when all traffic classes are considered together at the same time, while CBQ and FIFO with priority, followed by WFQ give the best results respectively for both interactive and background traffic on one hand, and for streaming application only on the other hand, as it is very sensitive to access delay.

The rates of satisfied users obtained when using CBQ, ECBQ, WFQ, EW²FQ and PRIO policies are compared and exhibited in Figure 5. As RT services are very sensitive to delay, video streaming sessions are given the priority over all ongoing data sessions while using PRIO scheduling policy. The exhibited results show when the PRIO scheduling policy is performed, the rate of satisfied users remains over 95% if the system load is below 20 Erlangs. These results confirm that at a weak load (less than 6 Erlangs) the rates of satisfied users obtained with CBQ/WFQ and ECBQ/EW²FQ are nearly the same.

Figure 6. Comparison with mean delay of NRT (WWW) packets

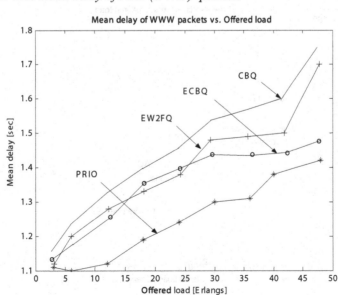

Figure 6 displays curves of mean interactive packets delay versus offered load. At 30 Erlangs The mean delay is decreased from 1.54 s to 1.43 s when ECBQ is performed, from 1.48 s to 1.32 s with EW²FQ, and from 1.32 s to 1.18 s with FIFO with priority policy.

All these results demonstrate the higher performance of the proposed ECBQ scheduling policy through the integration of realistic parameters of traffic within a dynamic priority function.

The rates of satisfied users obtained when using WFQ, EW²FQ and PRIO policies are compared with those obtained while the CAC function is performed (Figure 7). This CAC is based only on maximum delays (scenario 1). In this case, when a user is admitted in the system, the generated interference is not taken into account. As RT services are very sensitive to delay, video streaming sessions are given the priority over all ongoing sessions while using PRIO scheduling policy. The obtained results show that the timeout-based CAC function enhances the rate of satisfied users, with, either PRIO or EW²FQ policies. When the PRIO scheduling policy is performed, the rate

of satisfied users remains over 95% if the system load is below 20 Erlangs. When the interference effects are taken into consideration with maximum delays into the CAC algorithm (scenario 2), 95% of users are satisfied if the system load is about 22 Erlangs.

As shown in Figure 8, under the rate of 8 Erlangs this CAC function has no effects on the offered QoS. Beyond this offered load, the cross-layered CAC function achieved a better performance. When it is performed, the session outage decreases from 24% to 16.5% at 20 Erlangs, and from 29% to 23% at 35 Erlangs when EW²FQ scheduling policy is employed. When using PRIO scheduling algorithm, the session outage decreases from 17.5% to 13% at 20 Erlangs, and from 25% to 20% at 35 Erlangs. However, these results demonstrate that proposed CAC scheme offers slightly better performances for the equitable policy.

The simulation run takes duration of about 10^4 seconds (10^6*Unit of time) to achieve a confidence level of 95%. Beyond this time of simulation, the confidence level remains the same. Confidence

Figure 7. Impact of the CAC function on the satisfied users' percentage using EW²FQ scheduling policies

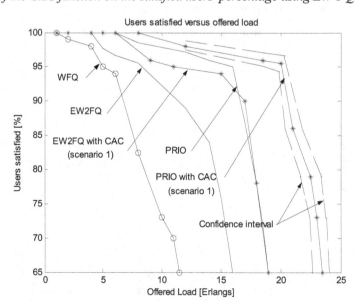

intervals are shown in figures as dash lines. In all curves the arrival rate of voice and data users is varied to study the cellular system under increasing load conditions.

The validation of results by analytical model is very difficult since the full details of a dynamic CAC function with users' mobility and propagation environment cannot be described by formulas usable in practice.

REFERENCES

Abd El-Atty, S. M., (2006). Efficient packet scheduling with pre-defined QoS using cross-layer technique in wireless networks. *11th IEEE Symposium on Computers and Communications (ISCC'06)* (pp. 820-826).

Badia, L., Lindstrom, M., Zander, J., & Zorzi, M. (2003, July). An economic model for the radio resource management in multimedia wireless systems. *Proceedings of IEEE Workshop on Applications and Services in Wireless Networks ASWN*, Bern.

Baiocchi, A., et al. (2006, Sept). *Cross-layer design of optimized packet scheduling and radio resource allocation algorithms for 4th generation cellular wireless systems*. WPMC 2006, San Diego.

Bartolini, N., & Chlamtac, I. (2002). Call admission control in wireless multimedia networks. *Proceedings of IEEE PIMRC*.

Bejaoui, T., Nasser, N., & Vèque, V. (2006, March). Enhanced class-based packet scheduling policy for QoS provisioning in multimedia cellular networks. *4th ACS/IEEE International Conference on Computer Systems and Applications (AICCSA-2006)*, Dubai/Sharjah, UAE.

Bejaoui, T., Vèque, V., & Tabbane, S. (2006, March). Combined fair packet scheduling policy and multi-class adaptive CAC scheme for QoS provisioning in multimedia cellular networks. *International Journal of Communications Systems (IJCS) - WILEY - Special Issue on "Radio Resource Management for Provisioning IP-Based QoS in Wireless Cellular Networks, 19*(2), 121-139.

Figure 8. Impact of the CAC function on the offered RT users' session outage

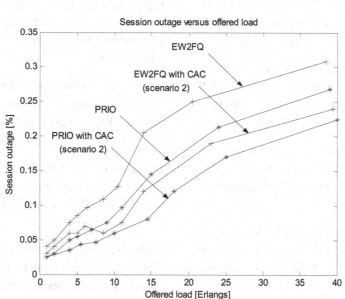

Ben Letaief, K., & Y.J.Z. *Cross-layer Adaptive Resource Management for Wireless Packet Networks with OFDM signalling.* IEEE Transactions in Wireless Communications (Paper TW05-002R1).

Callinan, P., Witwit, M., & Ball, F. (2000, April). A comparative evaluation of sorted priority algorithms and class based queueing using simulation. *Advanced Simulation Technologies Conference ASTC 2000*, Washington DC.

Cao, Y., & Li, V. O. K. (2001, Jan.). Scheduling algorithms in broadband wireless networks. *Proceedings of the IEEE, 89*(1), 76-87.

Carneiro, G., Ruela, J., & Ricardo, M. (2004, April). Cross layer design in 4G wireless terminals. *IEEE Wireless Communications Magazine, 11*(2), 7-13.

Capone, A., & Redana, S. (2001). Call admission techniques for UMTS. *Proceedings of IEEE VTC fall.*

Chahed, T., & Elayoubi, S. E. (2004, August). *QoS in multi-service wireless networks--A state of the art admission control in UMTS--State of the art.* Retrieved from http://www.eurongi.org

Chahed, T., Canton, A. F., Elayoubi, S. E. (2003, May). End-to-end TCP performance in W CDMA/UMTS. *Proceedings of IEEE ICC.*

Choi, S., & Shin, K.G. (1999, Oct.). An Uplink CDMA system architecture with diverse QoS guarantees for heterogeneous traffic. *IEEE/ACM Transactions on Networking, 7*(5), 616-628.

Elayoubi, S. E., Chahed, T., & Hébuterne, G. (2004). Admission control in UMTS in the presence of elastic traffic. *Computer Communications* (pp. 27-11).

Floyd, S., & Jacobson, V. (1995, Aug.). Link sharing and resource management models for packets networks. *IEEE ACM Transactions on Networking. 3*(4).

Ghaderi, M., & Boutaba, R. (2005). *Call admission control in mobile cellular networks: A comprehensive survey.*

Goria, P., Agusti, R., Sallent, O. (2001, April). *System specification radio resource management algorithms: Identification and requirements.* IST-2000-25133: ARROWS, D04.

Hg, T. S. E., Stoica, I., & Zhang, H. (1998). Packet fair queueing algorithms for wireless networks with location-dependent errors. *Proceedings INFOCOM'98* (pp. 1103-1111).

Huang, C., & Yates, R. (1996). Call admission in power controlled CDMA systems. *Proceedings of IEEE VTC.*

Hughes, H. D., Krunz, M., & Sass, R. (1995, April). Statistical characteristics and multiplexing of MPEG streams. *IEEE Infocom 95*, Boston, MA, USA.

Iera, A., Marano, S., & Molinaro, A. (1996). Call level and burst level priorities for effective management of multimedia services in UMTS. *Proceedings of IEEE Infocom'96* (Vol. 3, pp. 1363-1370).

Jamalipour, A., & Kim, J. (2003, May). Measurement-based admission control scheme with priority and service classes for application in wireless IP networks. *Journal of Communication Systems, 16*(6), 535-551.

Jamin, S., et al. (1997, Feb.). A measurement-based admission control algorithm for integrated services packet networks. *IEEE/ACM Transactions on Networking, 5*(1), 524-540.

Jiang, H., et Al (2005, Dec.). Cross-layer design for resource allocation in 3G wireless networks and beyond. *IEEE Communications Magazine*, 120-126.

Khan, S., Peng, Y., Steinbach, E., Sgroi, M., & Kellerer, W. (2006, January). Application driven crosslayer optimization for video streaming over wireless networks. *IEEE Communications Magazine, 44*(1), 122130.

Kim, I., Shin, B., & Lee, D. (2000). SIR-based call admission control by intercell interference prediction for DS-CDMA systems. *IEEE communications Letters*, 4-1.

Knopp, R. & Humblet, P. (1995, June). Information capacity and power controlin single-cell multiuser communications. *Proceedings of the IEEE International Conference on Commun.*, (Seattle, WA).

Kumar, S., & Nanda, S. (1999, March). High data-rate packet communications for cellular networks using CDMA: Algorithms and performance. *IEEE Journal on Selected Areas in Communications, 17*(3), 472-492.

Leong, C., & Zhuang, W. (2001). *Call admission control for voice and data traffic in wireless communications*. Elsevier, computer communications.

Lin, P., Bensaou, B., Ding, Q. L., & Chua, K. C. (2000). A wireless fair scheduling algorithm for error-prone wireless channels. *Proceedings WoWMoM'2000* (pp. 11-20).

Liu, Z., & Elzarki, M. (1994, May). SIR-based call admission control for DS-CDMA cellular systems. *IEEE Journal on Selected Areas in Telecommunications*.

Liu, Z., Karol, M. J., El Zarki, M., & Eng, K. Y. (1996). Channel access and interference issues in multicode DS-CDMA wireless packet (ATM) Networks. *Wireless Networks, 2*, 173-196.

Lu, S., Bharghavan, V., & Srikant, R. (1999, Aug.). Fair scheduling in wireless packet networks. *IEEE/ACM Trans. Networking, 7*(4), 473-489.

Nanda, S., Balachandran, K., & Kumar, S. (2000, Jan.). Adaptation techniques in wireless packet data services. *IEEE Communications Magazine*, 54-64.

Nandagopal, T., Lu, S., & Bharghavan, V. (2002). A unified architecture for the design and evaluation of wireless fair queueing algorithms. *Wireless Networks, 8*, 231-247.

Parsons, J. D. (2001). T*he mobile radio propagation channel (2nd ed)*. WILEY Ed.

Pätzold, M., Killat, U., Laue, F. & Li, Y. (1998a, Feb.). On the statistical properties of deterministic simulation models for mobile fading channels. *IEEE Transactions on Vehicular Technology, 47*(1), 254-269.

Pätzold, M., & Laue, F. (1998b, July). Level-crossing rate and average duration of fades of deterministic simulation models for rice fading channels. *IEEE Tran. On Vehicular Technology, 48*(4).

Ramanathan, P., & Agrawal, P. (1998). Adapting packet fair queueing algorithms to wireless networks. *Proceedings MOBICOM'98* (1-9).

Ramjee, R., Nagarajan, R., & Towsley, D. (1996). On optimal call admission control in cellular networks. *Proceedings of IEEE Infocom'96*.

Shakkottai, S., Rappaport, T. S., & Karlsson, P. C. (2003, Oct.). Cross-layer design for wireless networks. *IEEE Communications Magazine, 41*(10), 74-80.

Tripathi, S. K., & Krunz, M. (1997, June). On the characterization of VBR MPEG streams. *ACM-SIGMETRICS Conference on Measurement and Modeling of Computer Systems, Performance Evaluation Review 25*, Seattle WA. USA.

Viswanath, P., Tse, D. N. C., & Laroia, R. L. (2002, June). Opportunistic beamforming using dumb antennas. *IEEE Trans. Inform. Theory, 48*, 1277-1294.

Zanella, A., Merlin, S., & Di Lenarda, F. (2005). An efficient and adaptive resource allocation scheme for next generation cellular systems. *Proceedings of WPMC 2005*, Aalborg, DK.

Chapter XVIII
Transport Protocols and QoS for Wireless Multimedia

Gürkan Gür
Satellite Networks Research Laboratory (SATLAB), Boğaziçi University, Turkey

Suzan Bayhan
Satellite Networks Research Laboratory (SATLAB), Boğaziçi University, Turkey

Fatih Alagöz
Satellite Networks Research Laboratory (SATLAB), Boğaziçi University, Turkey

ABSTRACT

This chapter introduces the QoS issues and support in transport protocols for wireless multimedia transmission. After an overview of the transport layer functionalities in a transmission and the multimedia characteristics, conventional transport layer protocols: transmission control protocol (TCP), and user datagram protocol (UDP) are described. In this chapter, some of the proposed modifications to these protocols in order to improve multimedia transmission quality in wireless networks are also summarized. Particulary, UDP Lite, TCP friendly rate control protocol (TFRC), and real-time transport protocol (RTP)--real-time transport control protocol (RTCP) are mentioned. Finally, the chapter is concluded with some discussions on the current trends in transport protocols for wireless multimedia transmission and on some of the ongoing research issues.

INTRODUCTION

Recently, there has been an unprecedented increase in the demand for wireless multimedia applications. However, the type of network access technologies has varied a lot. These network access technologies of the present and future are envisioned to range from body area networks to satellite wide area networks (WANs) as can be seen in Figure 1. These networks are being developed to transport high-speed multimedia content for streaming, interactive, peer-to-peer and content distribution services to network segments as well as to individual users. With the recent explosion of YouTube™ and similar multimedia-based services, it has become more crucial to deliver multimedia services with an acceptable quality. These quality of service (QoS) demands for multimedia traffic are compounded in the case of a wireless network, where new problems arise due to the implied mobility of the users as well as due to the nature of the current IP protocols that support IP-based mobility, combined with a lossy and interrupt/outage-prone nature of the communications channel. Therefore, the traditional protocol stacks have to be re-engineered, by designing more flexible and generic communication protocols (Argyriou, 2005).

TCP (transmission control protocol) is the most commonly used protocol at the transport layer of the network stack in the all-IP networks, originally developed in wired networks with low bit error rate (BER) in the order of less than 10^{-8}.

In this context, any wireless network with Internet service needs to be compatible with the protocol used in the wired network (i.e., mainly the TCP/IP protocol). However, future wireless all-IP networks, while offering the promise of these exciting broadband applications, are expected to consist of several, potentially incompatible, wireless access technologies that would be offered by a number of competing service providers. The diversity of access technologies, however, may drastically affect the QoS for multimedia services.

Additional issues arise when considering the widely differing types of services that the user may use: streaming media, real-time communications, interactive communications, VoIP, just to name a few. Each of these services imposes its distinct QoS requirements. Thus, it is a formidable challenge to provide multimedia services which have strict quality-of-service (QoS) requirements on bandwidth, delay and delay jitter over wireless networks. This challenge has been amplified with

Figure 1. Heterogeneous network access technologies

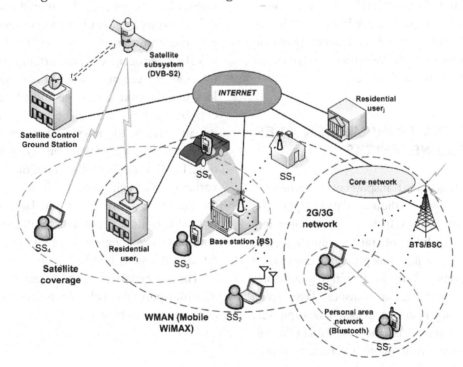

the omnipresent proliferation of heterogeneous wireless systems and networks. In order to provide services with satisfying levels of user experience, QoS can be supported in different layers such as application and transport layer (Zhang, Yang, Zhu, 2005, p. 207-219). Additionally a recent trend has been to go beyond the layered protocol architecture and adapt cross-layer solutions. In this context, we believe that transport layer is a crucial area with respect to the promise that it offers for improvement of QoS in wireless multimedia.

In this chapter, QoS issues and support in transport protocols for wireless multimedia transmission are introduced. After an overview of the transport layer functionalities in a transmission and the multimedia characteristics, conventional transport layer protocols transmission control protocol (TCP) and user datagram protocol (UDP) are described. In this chapter, some of the proposed modifications to these protocols in order to improve multimedia transmission quality in wireless networks are also summarized. Particulary, UDP Lite, TCP friendly rate control protocol (TFRC), and real-time transport protocol (RTP)--real-time transport control protocol (RTCP) are mentioned. Finally, the chapter is concluded with some discussions on the current trends in transport protocols for wireless multimedia transmission and on some of the ongoing research issues.

MULTIMEDIA TRANSMISSION OVER WIRELESS NETWORKS

Main function of the transport layer is to process the data coming from the upper layer (application layer) before passing to the network layer and it has the capability of transferring data from one node to another, thus providing some level of transparency from the underlying network. Generally speaking, the transport layer splits data into smaller packets, dispatch those packets and at the receiver reassemble the data in the correct sequence. Furthermore, the transport layer

may provide the following services: flow control between the two ends so called "end-to-end" services, dividing the streams of data into chunks or packets and reassembling at the receiving end, error-checking to guarantee error-free data delivery, with losses or duplications.

Data transport protocols can be loosely grouped into two classes: *reliable transport protocols* and *unreliable transport protocols. Reliable protocols* ensure that all data are delivered to the receiver at the maximum throughput. However, these protocols do not take the delay issues into account and may deliver data in a long time. *Unreliable protocols* on the other hand do not guarantee the delivery of all packets. However, they provide less delay in the data transmission and therefore provide fewer burdens on the system resources. Considering the nature of these two types of transport protocols, unreliable protocols suit more to the needs of multimedia applications.

Existing transport protocols, which are initially designed for wired networks, have limitation for the use in wireless networks. For instance, multimedia applications (Figure 2) need congestion control but not necessarily ordered and reliable delivery--this combination is not offered by conventional transport protocols TCP or UDP. TCP has also been designed with certain assumptions in mind; for example, when a data segment is lost, it assumes that this was most likely due to congestion. However, it can be due to transmission impairments in the physical layer experienced by the receiver rather than the network congestion. To alleviate this issue, a multitude of TCP variants have been proposed. TCP survived the days of low bandwidth and low latency, but for several reasons it is not able to efficiently cope with today's evolving wireless environments (Iren, Amer, & Conrad, 1999).

The basic challenges and issues in the design of a transport protocol for wireless multimedia applications can be listed as:

Figure 2. An example wireless multimedia transport scenario

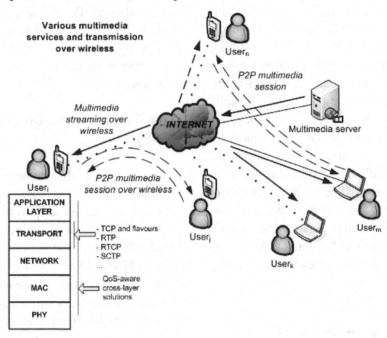

- **Packet loss differentiation and estimation:** Traditional transport protocols assume that a packet loss is encountered due to congestion in the network. However, this assumption may mislead to performance degradation in wireless networks where the packet losses due to transmission errors are more probable in error-prone links. Therefore, the transport mechanism must distinguish between the packet losses experienced due to network congestion and losses due to link errors.

- **Available bandwidth estimation:** To handle the severe bandwidth and delay fluctuation in wireless IP networks, available network condition estimation and congestion control are key issues needed to be addressed in the transport layer. Network information such as packet error rate, delay, and delay jitter is quite useful for high-quality media delivery. Various congestion and rate control schemes can be performed so that multimedia such as video and audio can adapt to the estimated

network information in a smooth way (Zhang et al., 2005, p. 207-219).

- **Mobility management:** Mobility has also significant impact on perceived QoS during multimedia streaming. There is a plethora of research on how to manage the handoffs while there is an ongoing multimedia transmission.

- **Inherent QoS support:** The QoS issue has become more vital with the increasing proliferation of wireless networks and multimedia services. For higher QoS level, QoS support mechanisms embedded in transport layer are beneficial.

Multimedia applications in the widest sense can be grouped as *real-time* and *non-real time* multimedia. Each type of multimedia service and user in wireless networks have different QoS requirements and brings the issue of addressing a set of problems at layers of protocol stack as seen in Figure 2. These problems, specially applied to multimedia and wireless networks, can be summarized as limited bandwidth, high packet loss rate and BER, need for mobility management, heterogeneity among users and networks (WMAN (IEEE 802.16 WiMAX), WLAN (IEEE 802.11x), PAN (IEEE 802.15, Bluetooth), cellular networks (GPRS, UMTS)), security, and most importantly QoS guarantees. Due to the aforementioned problems, providing QoS guarantees is a challenging task, and new and adaptable QoS solutions at the transport layer for these diverse issues are imperative. Real-time traffic (e.g., video and voice) is highly delay sensitive, while non-real-time traffic (e.g., TCP packets and text data transfers) can tolerate large delays. Table 1 enumerates various applications and their traffic classes along with some typical parameters values like bandwidth, connection time, etc.

TRANSPORT PROTOCOLS

In this part, the most common transport layer protocols are described. Additionally, some of the proposed modifications to these protocols in order to improve the quality-of-service of multi-

media applications in wireless access networks are mentioned. Particularly, TCP, UDP, UDP Lite, TCP friendly rate control protocol (TFRC), and real-time transport protocol (RTP)—real-time transport control protocol (RTCP) are introduced.

The Transmission Control Protocol (TCP)

In this part, brief information on TCP (RFC 793, 1981) is provided to make the reader have the notion of general issues of transport protocols. In order to have a notion on transport layer issues, it is essential to understand the fundamental concepts behind TCP and how it is used to transport data between two endpoints. Please see Iren et al. (1999) for an extensive overview of transport protocols. TCP is often described as a connection-oriented, reliable delivery transport layer protocol. TCP residing between the application layer and the network layer, takes the data from an application in 8-bit byte streams. Then TCP manages the byte stream to segment or delineate in order to

Table 1. Traffic classes and their QoS requirements (Marchese, 2007)

Traffic Class	Components	QoS characteristics
Real-time conversational (telephony, teleconference, video telephony and videoconference)	Speech, audio, video, multimedia	Delay and delay variation sensitive, limited tolerance to loss and errors, constant and variable bit rate
Real-time streaming (e.g. audio and video broadcast, surveillance, graphics)	Audio, video, multimedia	Tolerant to delay, delay variation sensitive, limited tolerance to loss and errors, variable bit rate.
Near real-time interactive (e.g. web browsing)	Data	Delay sensitive, tolerant to delay variation, error sensitive, variable bit rate
Non- real-time background	Data	Not delay and delay variation sensitive, error sensitive, best effort

transmit data in manageable pieces which is so called "byte stream delivery service."

TCP provides a connection oriented service by creating a virtual connection between the end points of a transmission. During the connection establishment, end nodes exchange messages in what is known as the *"three-way handshake."* The three-way handshake mechanism is shown in Figure 4a. Before giving a brief summary of connection establishment phase, TCP header fields should better be explained. The TCP header format can be seen in Figure 3. Some of the header fields that are of high importance to understand the TCP basics are summarized in the figure and in the following paragraphs.

The 6 bits control bits field consists of six control flags which are placed from left to right

as URG, ACK, PSH, RST, SYN, and FIN. If *acknowledgement (ACK)* bit is set, the acknowledgement number field is valid. If *reset the connection (RST)* bit is set, it signals the receiver that the sender is aborting the connection and all queued data and allocated buffers for the connection can be freely relinquished. The *synchronize (SYN)* bit field signifies that sender is attempting to "synchronize" sequence numbers. This bit is used during the initial stages of connection establishment between a sender and receiver. The *no more data from sender (FIN)* bit field tells the receiver that the sender has reached the end of its byte stream for the current TCP connection. So it is used in connection termination phase.

The 16-bit checksum field is used to check if the data is to provide basic protection against

Figure 3. TCP header format

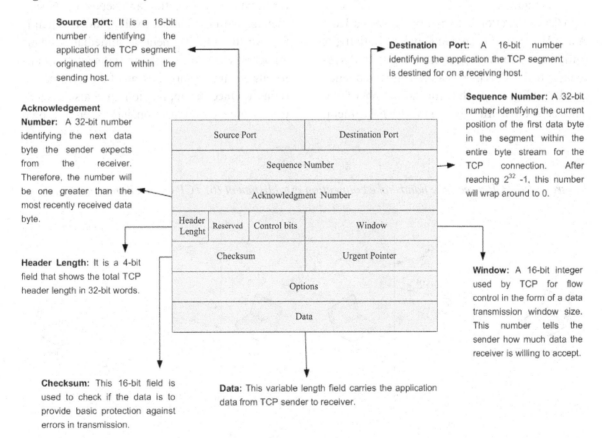

Source Port: It is a 16-bit number identifying the application the TCP segment originated from within the sending host.

Destination Port: A 16-bit number identifying the application the TCP segment is destined for on a receiving host.

Acknowledgement Number: A 32-bit number identifying the next data byte the sender expects from the receiver. Therefore, the number will be one greater than the most recently received data byte.

Sequence Number: A 32-bit number identifying the current position of the first data byte in the segment within the entire byte stream for the TCP connection. After reaching $2^{32} - 1$, this number will wrap around to 0.

Header Length: It is a 4-bit field that shows the total TCP header length in 32-bit words.

Window: A 16-bit integer used by TCP for flow control in the form of a data transmission window size. This number tells the sender how much data the receiver is willing to accept.

Checksum: This 16-bit field is used to check if the data is to provide basic protection against errors in transmission.

Data: This variable length field carries the application data from TCP sender to receiver.

Source Port	Destination Port
Sequence Number	
Acknowledgment Number	

Header Lenght	Reserved	Control bits	Window
Checksum			Urgent Pointer
Options			
Data			

errors in transmission. A TCP sender computes a value based on the contents of the TCP header and data fields. The computed value is compared with the value the receiver generates using the same computation. If the values match, the receiver can conclude that the segment arrived as it has been sent. If the values do not match, then there has been some errors during the transmission.

Options field is used in order to provide additional functionality, and several optional parameters may be used between a TCP sender and receiver. Depending on the option(s) used, the length of this field will vary in size, but it cannot be larger than 40 bytes due to the size of the header length field (4 bits). Using the Options field, a TCP receiver tells the TCP sender the *maximum segment size (MSS)* it is willing to accept through the use of this option. MSS may be 64 KB at maximum. Other options are often used for various flow control and congestion control techniques.

TCP connection between two hosts as Host A and Host B is depicted in Figure 4. Initially, A initiates the connection by sending a TCP segment with the SYN flag set and an initial sequence number (SEQ = x) in the sequence number field. The receiver-B, after getting this SYN segment,

processes it and responds with a TCP segment. The response from B contains the SYN control bit set and the sequence number set to y (SEQ = y). B also sets the ACK flag (control bits field) to indicate the next expected byte from A should contain data starting with sequence number x+1. When A receives B's sequence number and ACK, it finishes the connection establishment phase by sending a final acknowledgement segment to. Finally, A sets the ACK flag and sends the next expected byte from B by placing acknowledgement number (ACK = y+1) in the acknowledgement field.

The connection termination phase is shown in Figure 4(b). As opposed to three segments in connection establishment phase four segments are required to completely close a connection. This is caused by the TCP's full-duplex nature. Therefore each end must terminate the connection independently. In Figure 4(b), A wants to terminate the connection and sends a FIN segment signaling its intent to shut down. When B receives the FIN segment, it immediately sends an acknowledgement for the segment and notifies its destination application of the termination request. Once the application on B also decides to shut down the connection, it then sends its own

Figure 4. (a) TCP three-way handshake connection establishment (b) TCP connection termination

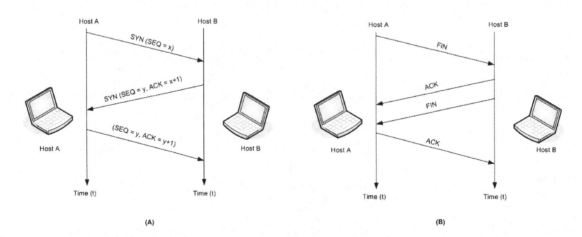

FIN segment, which A will process and respond with an acknowledgement.

TCP (Chaudhary & Jacob, 2003, p. 559-602) has two fundamental control mechanisms; *flow control* and *congestion control*. Flow control determines the rate at which data is transmitted between a sender and receiver. Its main purpose is to properly match the transmission rate of sender to that of the receiver. Congestion control defines the methods for implicitly interpreting signals from the network in order for a sender to adjust its rate of transmission preventing the overflow of both at the receiver and at the intermediate network nodes.

TCP is a sliding window protocol, which utilizes three windows to control the flow; *congestion window, advertised window,* and *transmission window.* Congestion window determines the maximum number of packets that can be transmitted without acknowledgment signaling that they have been received at the receiving end. This number is determined by the sender based on the feedback from the network. *Advertised window,* however, is specified by the receiver and it indicates to the sender the amount of data the receiver is ready to receive in the future. Normally, it equals to the available buffer size at the receiver in order to prevent buffer overflow. *Transmission window* means the maximum number of segments that the sender can transmit at one time without receiving any ACKs from the receiver. Its lower edge indicates the highest numbered segment acknowledged by the receiver. Obviously, to avoid network congestion and receiver buffer overflow, the size of transmission window is determined as the minimum of the congestion window and the receiver's advertised window.

TCP's sliding window is used to achieve several aims; guaranteed delivery of data, ordered delivery and the flow control between the two ends. Since each byte has a sequence number and acknowledgments are cumulative, the data can be sent in a reliable and in-sequence manner. The sending end assigns a sequence number to each byte transmitted. The receiving end sends an acknowledgement to indicate that the byte till that sequence number is received. Upon the receipt of an ACK, the sender knows that all previously transmitted data segments with a sequence number less than the one indicated in the ACK are correctly received at the receiver. In the case that an out-of-order segment (identified on the basis of sequence numbers) arrives at the receiver, a duplicate ACK is generated and sent back to the sender. If a sent byte is not acknowledged in a timeout interval, then the unacknowledged data is retransmitted. The out-of-order delivered data can be rearranged by using the sequence number of the data. If three duplicate cumulative ACKs are received, the sender will assume the packet is lost. A packet loss is also assumed if the sender does not receive an ACK for the packet within a timeout interval called *retransmission timeout* (RTO). RTO value significantly affects the TCP performance; setting it to a high value results in long delay in case of lossy links. Setting it to shorter values than round trip time (RTT) would result in early retransmissions although the ACK is on the way to the sender. To manage this issue; TCP sender tries to estimate the RTT and according to that value it sets the RTO value using the following formulas (Hassan & Jain, 2004, p. 17-20):

$$RTT_{estimate} = (1-\alpha) * RTT_{estimate} + \alpha * RTT_{mean} \qquad (1)$$

$$RTO = RTT_{estimate} + 4*deviation \qquad (2)$$

where $RTT_{estimate}$ and RTT_{mean} stand for the estimated and mean of measured RTT values, respectively. Changing the α value changes the weight of the $RTT_{estimate}$ and RTT_{mean}, and typical value for α is 0.125. *Deviation* is calculated using Formula 3.

$$deviation = (1-\alpha) * deviation + \alpha * | RTT_{mean} - RTT_{estimate} | \qquad (3)$$

By retransmitting the lost packet, TCP achieves reliable data delivery. It is important to note that as opposed to wired networks where an out-of-order delivery usually implies a packet loss, in wireless networks packet loss may be caused by the transmission errors. Therefore, it is a challenge to differentiate the loss caused by the transmission errors and that caused by the congestion. Additionally, TCP responds to packet losses by invoking its congestion control mechanism.

Basically, TCP has two congestion control algorithms--slow start and congestion avoidance. Slow start is a mechanism to avoid sending more data than the network's capacity of transmitting. The slow start algorithm initializes a congestion window *(cwnd)* to one segment, which is the maximum segment size (MSS) initialized by the receiver during the connection establishment phase and is incremented by one MSS on each new acknowledgement. Thus, the sender can transmit the minimum of the congestion window and the advertised window of the receiver, which is actually the *transmission window* (Kristoff, 2002). The slow start phase may cause bandwidth inefficiency in high bandwidth-delay product systems

like satellite networks. Therefore, this phase must be modified to adapt to the high bandwidth-delay product networks. Receiving an ACK for each segment, the cwnd value is doubled therefore resulting in exponential increase in the window size. After *cwnd* reaches a preset threshold (*ssthresh*), the congestion avoidance starts and it is increased linearly (i.e., it is increased by one segment for each RTT). Upon a timeout, *ssthresh* is set to the half of the current transmission window size (but at least two segments) and the congestion window is reduced to 1 MSS. Then slow start mechanism starts again. This procedure is also called the *additive increase and multiplicative decrease* algorithm (AIMD). Figure 5 summarizes the TCP operation and the changes in *cwnd*.

Enhancing TCP to reliably handle loss, minimize errors, manage congestion and go fast in very high-speed environments are ongoing areas of research and standards development. TCP is not very preferable for multimedia transmissions since reliable transmission is inappropriate for delay-sensitive data such as real-time audio and video. Due to the fact that the TCP transmission mechanism is driven by the acknowledgments

Figure 5. The change in the TCP congestion window size

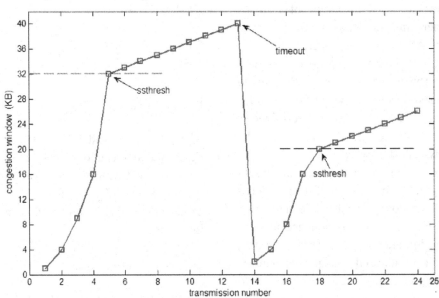

from the receiver node, it takes a long time for the sender to discover the lost packet. Moreover, TCP provides the receiver with the lost packet by retransmissions. The receiver either waits for the retransmission, increasing delay and incurring an audible gap in play-out or it just discards the lost packet. These drawbacks constitute major factor on the perceived QoS.

User Datagram Protocol (UDP)

As opposed to reliable nature of TCP, UDP (Postel, 1980) is a connectionless protocol that does not guarantee in-order packet delivery or reliable transmission. However, UDP provides faster delivery and preserves the boundaries of the messages it transports. Furthermore, UDP has a low protocol overhead of 8 bytes, where fixed part of TCP header is 20 bytes long. UDP has properties that make it suitable for delay and jitter sensitive applications:

- The data rate is defined by the sending application.
- Incoming packets are delivered immediately to the receiving application, even if they arrive out of order.
- Lost packets will not cause retransmissions by the transport layer.
- The checksum field can be utilized to verify the UDP headers and the data payload (Larzon, Degermark, & Pink, 1999).

However, in the noisy wireless channels, UDP checksum mechanism may result in high packet loss rate and finally results in unqualified media transmission. By the checksum field in the UDP header (Figure 6), damaged packets will be discarded if these contain any transmission errors. Real-time multimedia streaming may use audio and video codecs that are robust to channel errors. Therefore, rather than a lost packet, a corrupted packet would be preferred by these

multimedia applications. UDP datagrams are always discarded when their checksum (which is a simple one's complement bit sum) does not pass. In other words even in case of corruption of just one byte, the whole packet is dropped. The effect of the loss packet becomes more significant in case of large packets. One way for an application to allow delivery of damaged packets is to disable the UDP checksum. Also, although header checksum is optional in IPv4, it is mandatory in IPv6. To solve this issue, a slight modification is made to UDP header, which resulted in UDP Lite (Larzon, Degermark, & Pink, 2004) protocol. *UDP Lite* makes it possible to reuse useful information in such cases by limiting the scope of the checksum length.

The difference between the UDP and UDP Lite headers can be seen in Figure 6. The major difference between UDP and UDP-Lite is the *length* and *coverage* fields as shown in the figure. UDP Lite divides each packet into two parts: sensitive and insensitive. The length field in UDP is replaced by the checksum coverage length, with a minimum of the UDP-Lite header length i.e. 8 bytes. UDP Lite is designed to provide a partial checksum that only covers as much of the user data that the sending application specifies as necessary. Errors in the rest of the packet are ignored because they are assumed to be acceptable for the destination application. This increased flexibility is achieved while maintaining the simplicity of UDP. UDP Lite can be easily integrated into or derived from most existing UDP implementations. With a partial checksum such as the one provided by UDP Lite, it is undesirable that link layers drop packets due to errors that are acceptable according to the sender. Various multimedia applications could benefit from using UDP Lite instead of UDP. By reflecting the UDP Lite policy with a partial checksum onto the link layer, the gain can be even higher (Larzon et al., 1999). UDP Lite with a partial checksum field in the header provides the flexibility to accept partially damaged packets.

In Chaudhary et al. (2003, p. 559-602), throughput of UDP and UDP-Lite are compared with the increasing packet corruption rate. The performance of UDP over UDP-Lite can be seen in Figure 7. UDP Lite making it possible to receive the partially damaged packets results in an increase in the throughput when compared to the traditional UDP.

TFRC: TCP Friendly Rate Control

As previously mentioned, real-time multimedia applications such as video conferencing are sensitive to both packet delay and jitter. Therefore connection-oriented transport protocols such as TCP do not fit well to the performance requirements of these applications. Moreover, the sudden changes (decreases) of the rates in the case of congestion cause large oscillations in transmission rates. In the case of a video stream, this degrades the smoothness, resulting in low end-to-end quality of service for the end-users. In order to avoid the congestion collapse, non-TCP (audio/video) traffic should make less extreme changes in the sending rates. Therefore, realtime multimedia applications prefer UDP in order to avoid the unacceptable delay introduced by packet retransmissions. Against the network congestion TCP decreases its transmission rate, whereas UDP does not have such control mechanisms. With the increasing number of real-time multimedia applications, TCP traffic will experience more severe performance degradation due to the more greedy nature of competing UDP-based applications. To ensure fairness between the TCP and UDP transmissions, TCP friendly rate control (TFRC) protocol is proposed. TFRC (Handley, Floyd, Padhye, & Widmer, 2003) is a congestion control mechanism for unicast flows operating in a best-effort Internet environment. It is reasonably fair when competing for bandwidth with TCP flows, but has a much lower variation of throughput over time compared with TCP, making it more suitable for applications such as streaming media where a relatively smooth sending rate is of importance.

The basic idea of TFRC is to split the bandwidth equally between TCP and non-TCP connections. TCP-friendly rate control (TFRC) proposed by Floyd, Handley, Padhye, and Widmer (2000) is a rate-control method, which means that the transmission rate is explicitly calculated based on the information on the current packet loss rate in the network. Main TRFC scheme is depicted in Figure 8. As the RFC 3448 specifies, for managing the congestion TFRC directly uses a throughput equation for the allowed sending rate as a function of the loss event rate and round-trip time. In order to compete fairly with TCP, TFRC uses the TCP throughput equation, which roughly describes TCP's sending rate as a function of the loss event rate, round-trip time, and packet size. As shown in

Figure 6. UDP and UDP Lite headers

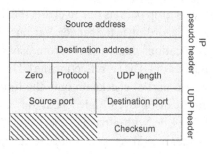

UDP header

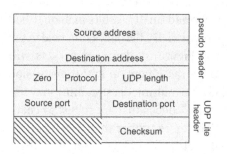

UDP Lite header

Figure 7. Throughput comparison between UDP and UDP Lite

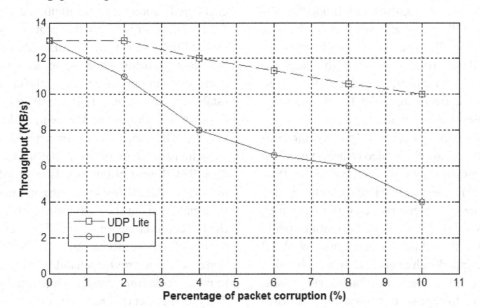

Figure 8, the multimedia receiver measures both the loss event rate and received bit rate and feeds this information back to the multimedia sender. The sender also uses these feedback messages to measure RTT. The loss event rate and RTT are then fed into TFRC's throughput equation, giving the acceptable transmit rate. Next, using this calculated transmission rate the sender adjusts its transmit rate. For a complete source for the details of TRFC, please see Floyd et al. (2000).

The applicability of TFRC protocol to multimedia transmissions has been an area of research and some modifications are proposed to improve the performance of multimedia transmission on wireless links. TFRC is originally designed for wired links, it accounts wireless losses also as congestion losses. TFRC also suffers from degraded performance due to packet reordering in the Internet. Suggestions have been made to have a rate control mechanism based on *Explicit Congestion Notification (ECN)* marking, which works well in wireless scenarios. ECN allows advance notification of congestion by placing an ECN bit in the IP header to explicitly notify the

transmitter that the network link is congested. Chaudhary et al. (2003, p. 559-602) proposed an ECN-based TFRC protocol that can also be robust to packet reordering. In their work, they first tested a combination of UDP-Lite and loss based TFRC for wireless streaming. Subsequently, several experiments are performed to study the robustness of ECN based TFRC to both the losses over wireless hop and packet reordering in the Internet. Similarly, Bae and Chong (2004, p. 405-419) utilizes ECN marking in order to adapt the TFRC mechanism to the wireless environment. The main idea behind this scheme is that by using ECN marking in conjunction with random early detection (RED) queue management scheme intelligently, it is possible that not only the degree of network congestion is notified to multimedia sources explicitly in the form of ECN-marked packet probability but also wireless losses are hidden from multimedia sources. After calculating the TCP-friendly rate based on ECN-marked packet probability instead of packet loss probability, thereby effectively eliminating the effect of wireless losses in flow control and thus preventing throughput degradation of multimedia flows traveling through wireless links, the performance of the proposed transport mechanism for wireless MPEG-4 transmission is evaluated. The simulation results show that the proposed mechanism significantly enhances the video quality while maintaining the TCP-friendliness in a wireless environment.

Another friendly rate control protocol for wireless networks, so called video transport protocol (VTP) is proposed by Yang, Sun, and Gerla (2006, p. 109-126). The proposed scheme has a new and unique end-to-end rate control mechanism that aims to avoid drastic rate fluctuations while maintaining friendliness to legacy protocols. VTP is also equipped with an achieved rate estimation scheme and a loss discrimination algorithm, both end-to-end, to cope with random errors in wireless networks efficiently. VTP consists of two key components: an achieved rate (AR)-based rate control mechanism and a loss discrimination algorithm (LDA). It is shown by analysis that VTP preserves most of the convergence properties of AIMD and converges to its fair share fast.

Real Time Protocol (RTP) and Real Time Control Protocol (RTCP)

RTP can carry any data with real-time characteristics, such as interactive audio and video. Streaming multimedia is a client-server application in which a user (the client) views the media using a media viewer application such as Crystal

Player and the server application provides all the client applications with the multimedia content. Network protocols are used to provide these services, initially a connection is established between the client application and the server application using signaling protocols. Upon the connection establishment phase, RTCP, and RTP (Cranley, Fiard, & Murphy, 2000; Miyazaki, Fukushima, Wiebke, Hakenberg, & Burmeister, 2001) are used in parallel to transmit the actual media data. RTCP most of the time is used with RTP to monitor the quality of service and to convey information about the participating ends. RTCP can be seen as an addendum to RTP that provides quality-of-service mechanisms. The main motivation of RTP is to provide reliability to some extent in multimedia transmission while satisfying the delay requirements of real-time or near real-time multimedia applications. The RTP header format is seen in Figure 9.

Since RTP does not assume that packets will arrive in sequence and so it incorporates packet sequence numbers within its header so that the receiver can sort the sender's packet sequence before decoding (Cranley et al., 2000). The sequence number increments by one for each RTP data packet sent, and may be used by the receiver to detect packet loss and to restore packet sequence. The SSRC field identifies the synchronization source. The source of a stream of RTP packets, identified by a 32-bit numeric SSRC identifier carried in the RTP header so as not to be dependent upon the network address. All

Figure 8. Basic TFRC scheme

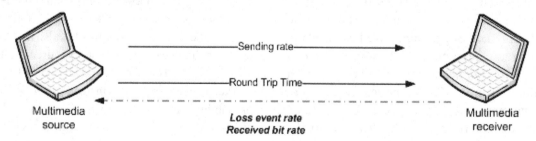

packets from a synchronization source form part of the same timing and sequence number space, so a receiver groups packets by synchronization source for playback. Examples of synchronization sources include the sender of a stream of packets derived from a signal source such as a microphone or a camera, or an RTP mixer. A synchronization source may change its data format (e.g., audio encoding) over time. The SSRC identifier is a randomly chosen value meant to be globally unique within a particular RTP session. A participant need not use the same SSRC identifier for all the RTP sessions in a multimedia session; the binding of the SSRC identifiers is provided through RTCP. If a participant generates multiple streams in one RTP session, for example from separate video cameras, each must be identified as a different SSRC (Postel, 1980). The CSRC list is used to identify the sources of the payload data since a multimedia data may compose of several sources especially in case of videoconferencing applications. This data from multiple sources can be combined in a frame and can be sent by an RTP mixer. This field identifies the contributing sources for the payload contained in this packet. The mixer inserts a list of the SSRC identifiers of the sources that contributed to the generation of a particular packet into the RTP header of that packet. This list is called the *CSRC list*.

RTCP is particularly useful as it enables the integration of some quality of service mechanisms by means of client feedback, thus allowing the server to modify its transmission to the client in response to network conditions. In essence, it is the clients' feedback which dictates the servers' transmission. RTCP has various packet types, which can be listed as sender report packet, receiver report packet, source description RTCP packet, goodbye RTCP packet, and application specific RTCP packets. Basically, RTCP achieves the following (Cranley et al., 2000):

Figure 9. RTP packet header

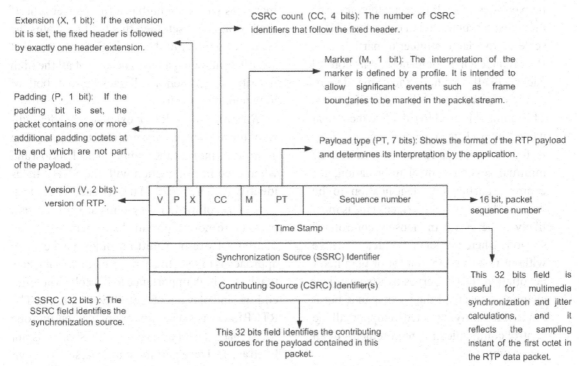

Extension (X, 1 bit): If the extension bit is set, the fixed header is followed by exactly one header extension.

CSRC count (CC, 4 bits): The number of CSRC identifiers that follow the fixed header.

Marker (M, 1 bit): The interpretation of the marker is defined by a profile. It is intended to allow significant events such as frame boundaries to be marked in the packet stream.

Padding (P, 1 bit): If the padding bit is set, the packet contains one or more additional padding octets at the end which are not part of the payload.

Payload type (PT, 7 bits): Shows the format of the RTP payload and determines its interpretation by the application.

Version (V, 2 bits): version of RTP.

| V | P | X | CC | M | PT | Sequence number |

Time Stamp

Synchronization Source (SSRC) Identifier

Contributing Source (CSRC) Identifier(s)

16 bit, packet sequence number

SSRC (32 bits): The SSRC field identifies the synchronization source.

This 32 bits field identifies the contributing sources for the payload contained in this packet.

This 32 bits field is useful for multimedia synchronization and jitter calculations, and it reflects the sampling instant of the first octet in the RTP data packet.

- **QoS Reporting** collects statistics information on a media connection such as bytes sent, packets sent, lost packets, jitter, feedback, and round-trip delay. This information can be utilized to increase the quality of service by changing the transmission properties like limiting the flow or adapting the codec used.

RFC 1889 specifies the RTCP properties as follows:

- RTCP carries a persistent transport-level identifier for an RTP source called the *canonical name or CNAME*. Since the SSRC identifier may change if a conflict is discovered or a program is restarted, receivers require the CNAME to keep track of each participant. Receivers also require the CNAME to associate multiple data streams from a given participant in a set of related RTP sessions, for example to synchronize audio and video.

- The first two functions require that all participants send RTCP packets, therefore the rate must be controlled in order for RTP to scale up to a large number of participants. By having each participant send its control packets to all the others, each can independently observe the number of participants. This number is used to calculate the rate at which the packets are sent.

- A fourth, optional function is to convey minimal session control information, for example participant identification to be displayed in the user interface. This is most likely to be useful in "loosely controlled" sessions where participants enter and leave without membership control or parameter negotiation. RTCP serves as a convenient channel to reach all the participants, but it is not necessarily expected to support all the control communication requirements of an application.

Typically RTP runs over UDP, which degrades the quality of the received media stream, when transmitted over wireless links. Especially compressed streams, such as MPEG video-data, are highly susceptible to packet loss, which will lead to an insufficient video quality at the client. However, retransmitting all the lost packets will deteriorate the quality even worse. Therefore, selective transmission mechanism is added to the RTP mechanism. The idea of selective retransmission is that not all the lost packets but the ones that have high importance need to be retransmitted. The compressed media streams generally consist of data packets of high importance and data packets of lower importance. Therefore, RTP and RTCP headers need some modifications as shown in Figure 10 and 11.

The extension header is used for quality-of-service provisioning. The fields that are of our interest are *PR* and *SNHP fields*. The Priority (PR) bit identifies the priority of the RTP packet. The 6-bit *sequence number of RTP packet with high priority (SNHP)* indicates the sequence number of the RTP packet with high priority. This number increases with each high priority packet sent. If the PR bit is not set, then this field indicates the sequence number of the last high priority packet sent, thus allowing a log to be kept of all the high priority packets sent in all packets sent, both of high and low priority.

RXP field in the RTCP extension header indicates the re-transmission protocol to be used. The control bits indicate the number of packets lost and when used in conjunction with the SNHP fields identify which packets in the sequence were lost. In the case of MPEG-4 systems streams certain packets are more important than others so, instead of arbitrarily re-transmitting all lost packets, the approach is to selectively re-transmit lost packets that have a high importance to the coherence, decoding, and play out of the MPEG-4 stream. The RTCP interval is set to approximately sending one RTCP packet every 5 seconds. This value is not fixed as, if all receivers in a multicast session were

Figure 10. RTP extension header (Postel, 1980)

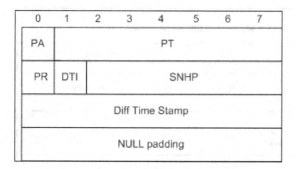

Figure 11. RTCP extension header (Postel, 1980)

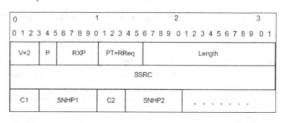

to transmit their control packets at the same time, this could cause flooding at the sever side. In the unicast scenario this is unsuitable as the request for the retransmission of lost packets could take up to 5 seconds and would be useless for real-time or near real-time applications as the retransmitted packet would arrive after the playout time. The RTCP interval should be dynamically adaptable to signal severe packet loss to the server as soon as possible, indicating that there are problems with the network (Handley et al., 2003).

Chiung and Wu (2001, p. 535-546) presents a real time transport protocol called the *burst-oriented transfer with time-bounded retransmission (BTTR)* that works on burst-by-burst basis. BTTR uses a large transmission window for ending/receiving a burst of time-sensitive data and, within this window, another smaller observation window is repeatedly used for error status feedback via the backward channel. There is time limitation on each retransmission such that the burst of data can be received in a timely manner, however, with some degradation on the packet loss rate. An analysis is given in terms of the expectations of delay, throughput, and packet drop rate. A sender can send a burst of data blocks continuously without waiting. The burst length, denoted by W_b, is given in terms of number of packets. Before sending a burst, the station should send a *Burst_Request* packet to the targeting receiver. Then the receiver will issue a *Burst_Confirmed* packet to the transmitting station and grants it

a burst window size Wb. The process will then be followed by transferring the burst of blocks between the sending station and the receiving station. Finally, the sending station will issue an *End_of_Burst* packet to the receiver. With this mechanism, BTTR achieves a very large burst of data transport under a limited transmitting/receiving buffer at both ends while achieving the delay restrictions for real-time multimedia applications. Furthermore, the packet drop rate is kept as low as possible by using smaller dynamic retransmission timer.

Finally, we conclude by a comparison of the aforementioned transport protocols; TCP, UDP, UDP-Lite, TRFC and RTP. Table 2 summarizes the delay, delay variation (jitter), and packet loss characteristics of each protocol.

CROSS-LAYER PROTOCOL APPROACHES

Of late, there has been a tremendous increase in the number of cross-layer design proposals for wireless networks and the popularity of cross-layer design of communication protocols has risen considerably recently due to stricter performance requirements and ubiquitous migration to wireless communications media. Although monolithic approaches may generate "islands of performance" where systems are overtuned for specific applications and only implementable

Table 2. Summary of the mentioned transport protocol characteristics

Comparison of some transport layer protocols for wireless multimedia applications					
	RFC #	Packet Loss	Delay	Jitter	TCP-friendliness
Tranmission Control Protocol (TCP)	793	Reliable, guaranteed delivery	High	High	Friendly
User Datagram Protocol (UDP)	768	Unreliable, checksum field may increase packet loss	Low	Low	Not friendly
The Lightweight User Datagram Protocol (UDP-Lite)	3828	Unreliable, Parial checksum reduces packet loss	Low	Low	Not friendly
TCP Friendly Rate Control Protocol (TFRC)	3448	Reliable, guaranteed delivery	High	High	Friendly
Real-time Transmission Protocol (RTP)	1889	works on UDP	Low	High	works on UDP

with specific hardware, a tighter and more dynamic cooperation of PHY and MAC layers may naturally boost the wireless multimedia system's performance. Moreover, some cross-layer application-optimized profiles for the most popular services, such as streaming video voice over Internet Protocol or (VoIP), may be integrated as optional components into upcoming standard releases. In this part, current research on cross layer protocol design for wireless multimedia applications is discussed.

The conventional layered TCP/IP approach where each layer performs some defined functionalities, only allows the adjacent layers to communicate via some primitives. This layered approach as depicted in Figure 12(a), leads to better understanding of the abstract functionality of layers and thus enables better understanding of the overall system. This led to rapid growth in the development of number of applications that drive the Internet. The fact that the same lower layers may be reused for every application decreases the development cost of the application and enhances the utility of the network architecture. Layering simplifies network design and leads to

robust scalable protocols in the internet. On the other hand, layering suffers from sub-optimality and inflexibility. Layering is suboptimal because each layer has insufficient information about the network since it does not allow the sharing of information among the layers. The interface between the layers is static and independent of individual network constraints and applications (Schaar & Turaga, 2007). As opposed to restrictions in the interactions between the adjacent layers in layered approach, the cross layer (Figure 12(b)) expands the functionalities of the layers by enabling the non adjacent layer interactions. The cross layer design aims to achieve optimal performance by allowing sharing of information across several layers. By the extended sharing of information, each layer has wider information about the network when compared to layered approach. However, several concerns have been raised regarding the flexibility, inter-operability, proliferation and even the performance of the cross layer design. Since cross layer violates the abstraction of the lower layers to the upper layers, it leads to dependencies between various layers. This in turn, leads to challenges in the cross layer

Figure 12. (a) Traditional TCP/IP layered protocol stack (b) Cross-layer protocol stack

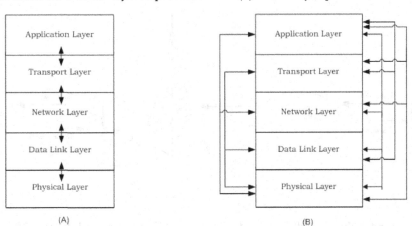

protocol design. All dependency relations must be clearly identified between the layer pairs and then the design framework must be drawn. Therefore, the simplification in the layered protocol approach leaves its place to many challenges in the cross layer approach.

Although there are numerous work and research being conducted on cross-layer design, in the following paragraphs some of these valuable works will be mentioned.

Zhang et al. (2005, p. 207-219) present a framework (Figure 13), which provides QoS support, for multimedia delivery over wireless Internet with cross-layer architecture. In this framework, in order to have efficient QoS support for different types of media, a cross-layer architecture combining the application-level, transport-layer, and link-layer controls are proposed. Specifically, dynamical estimation of the varying channel, adaptive application and link-level error control, efficient congestion control, header compression, adaptive scheduling, as well as the QoS-adaptive proxy caching are explicitly discussed in this architecture. In the transport layer, they introduce an intermediate node (gateway) on the edge of the wireless network domain. The sender performs application-level error control and a TCP-friendly congestion control based on congestion feedback from the mobile host and the gateway and informs

the gateway about packet losses by sending negative acknowledgements (NACKs). Based on the client's feedback packet, the server can adjust the current round-trip time. The gateway retransmits the lost packets if they are still in the buffer. In this scheme, packet losses caused by congestion or by random errors can be discriminated, thus the congestion control and error control can be performed respectively. Network conditions include packet loss ratio and bit error rate (BER) /block error rate (BLER) are reported to multimedia application so that they can adjust their behavior. Retransmission mechanism is incorporated in this scheme to reduce the errors in a packet and the packet losses due to fading. Authors perform performance evaluation by using NS-2 simulator and the simulation results show that both the throughput and received rate change smoothly and stand at a relatively high level when BER and fading probability varies.

Triantafyllopoulou, Passas, and Kaloxylos (2007) focus on the cross-layer optimizations on the physical, MAC and application layers for multimedia traffic in IEEE 802.16 networks by utilizing the adaptive modulation capability of the PHY layer and the multi-rate feature of modern multimedia standards at the application layer. The IEEE 802.16 (commercially known as WiMAX) family of standards specifies the air

Figure 13. System architecture for media over wireless Internet

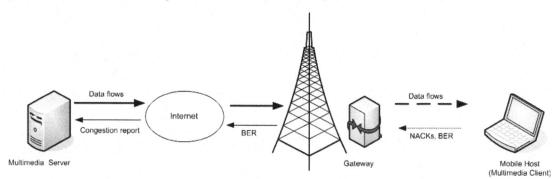

interface of fixed and mobile broadband wireless access (BWA) systems that support multimedia services. The objective of this standardization effort has been to establish the industry standards for broadband radio access for Wireless Metropolitan Networks (WMAN). The WiMAX wireless broadband access standard provides the missing link for the "last mile" connection in metropolitan area networks where DSL, Cable and other broadband access methods are not available or too expensive. The proposed cross-layer optimizer for WiMAX networks is split into two parts, namely the *base station (BS) part* and the *subscriber station (SS) part.* The BS part accepts an abstraction of layer-specific information, regarding the channel conditions and QoS parameters of active connections, provided by the BS PHY and MAC layers. According to this information, a specific decision algorithm determines the most suitable modulation and/or traffic rate of each SS, separately for each direction. Finally, the BS part informs the corresponding layers of the required modifications. If the decision of the BS part involves traffic rate changes, it communicates with the SS part through the SS MAC layer, which instructs the SS Application layer accordingly. The SS part may either accept the BS part's suggestions or refine them, based on its better knowledge of the status of active connections.

Giambene and Kota (2006) present an extensive survey on the cross layer protocol optimization in the protocol stack for satellite communications. As can be seen from the current communications trends, satellites are envisaged as a key component of the next-generation Internet, but have characteristics that differ significantly from those of the wired Internet, therefore providing high quality multimedia services via satellite links needs further research. For instance, in high bandwidth-delay product satellite links, TCP suffers from a number of well-known performance problems, especially for higher data rates and high altitude satellites with longer delays. In response to these difficulties, the satellite and networking research communities have developed a large pool of solutions ranging from architectural modifications to changes to the conventional TCP. Satellites depending on its orbital altitude (LEO, MEO, GEO) have a large footprint serving the users in its footprint at the same cost. This makes satellite based solutions particularly attractive in remote areas that would be very expensive to reach with terrestrial cables or even terrestrial radio links. Satellites are also very good at broadcasting information. Anybody in the coverage area receives all that the satellite transmits, and each user is equipped and configured to decode and use the subset of the information she is interested in and authorized to receive. However, in order to make the upcoming satellite network systems fully realizable, meeting new services and application Quality of Service (QoS) requirements, many technical challenges have to be addressed that are constrained by the layered protocol architecture, typical of both the ISO/OSI reference model and the Internet protocol suite. TCP slow start algorithm wastes a lot of bandwidth on satellite networks. Because of large bandwidth-delay product it takes a large time to increase the congestion window to fill the link and hence effectively utilize the bandwidth. Delayed ACKs also cause wasted bandwidth during this slow start phase. One method to deal with this is to increase the initial value of congestion window. Furthermore, due to the fact that the congestion-control mechanism of TCP relies upon lost packets as indicators of congestion and decreases the transmission rate, high BER satellite links do not fit the TCP's operation scheme. There are a plethora of studies in TCP variants specially designed for satellite networks. Currently, the emerging cross-layer methods offer new opportunities for satellite systems to adapt to the needs of multimedia traffic, allowing performance to be tuned to the needs of specific classes of application. Cross-layer methods can also offer increased information to the transport layer and applications concerning the quality and characteristic of the channel that they are using. This new flexibility provides opportunity for higher-layer protocols to react in appropriate ways.

Another work on satellite multimedia can be found in Fairhurst et al. (2006, p. 471-491). Fairhurst et al. present two methods that can enhance the quality of multimedia applications in satellite links using UDP-Lite. The authors also provide the analytical, simulation and evaluation data for a set of novel techniques based on the UDP-Lite transport protocol and the adaptive coding and modulation (ACM) provided by DVB-S2. Satellite protocol stack defined by the ETSI broadband satellite multimedia (BSM) working group is depicted in Figure 14. The protocol is divided into two parts: the upper part provides IP-based internetworking using a set of common satellite-independent (SI) functions that are applicable to many satellite systems; the lower part provides the satellite-dependent (SD) functions. The BSM reference model has a logical interface between the SI and SD layers provided by the satellite-independent service access point (SI-SAP). To benefit from using UDP-Lite, the changes at the transport layer must be reflected in the design of link (SD) layers. A link must recognize UDP-Lite packets (via their IP Protocol type), and then terminate the frame CRC after checksum processing coverage bytes, rather than the entire frame. This makes UDP-Lite a cross-layer technique utilizing implicit cross-layer signaling. In a satellite system, the SI layers must signal the required coverage to the SD layer, (e.g., via a new parameter/primitive in the SI-SAP or through snooping at lower layers). This signaling also allows a physical layer to be adapted to select differential Forward Error Correction (FEC) coding and modulation for the error-sensitive and error tolerant parts. UDP-Lite can also provide additional information to the receiving end-host, allowing a receiver to assess the level of corruption (via feedback from the media decoder) and to discriminate corruption from congestive loss. This information may be fed back to the media encoder via application signaling (e.g., RTCP), allowing it to adapt the media codec to changes in channel conditions.

Schaar et al. (2007) apply a cross-layer optimization basically focusing on the interactions between application layer and the MAC layer. In this paper, authors deploy a joint application-layer adaptive packetization and prioritized scheduling and MAC-layer retransmission strategy by successfully taking advantage of the available feedback at the MAC about the actual number of times previous packets have been transmitted to correctly determine the number of times the current packet can be retransmitted. Additionally, this algorithm can also successfully adapt on-the-fly to the changing channel conditions or physical layer modulation strategies. The interested reader

Figure 14. Satellite protocol stack architecture (Fairhurst, Berioli, & Renker, 2006, p.471-491)

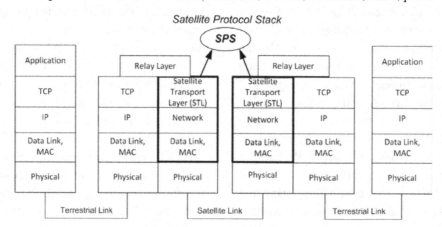

could find the extensive analytical work of the proposed mechanism in Schaar et al. (2007).

CONCLUSION

The next-generation wireless networks are targeted at supporting various applications such as voice, data, and multimedia over packet-switched networks. Providing quality of service (QoS) guarantees for these applications is an important objective in the design of the next generation wireless networks. However, as opposed to wired networks wireless networks are characterized by substantial packet loss due to the imperfection of the radio medium. This increased packet loss disturbs the successful operation of TCP's loss-based congestion control mechanism. Therefore standard TCP has some performance drawbacks in wireless links. Moreover, the quality of wireless multimedia applications comprising audio, video and data, is more sensitive to packet delay and delay jitter rather than packet loss. This is due to the fact that interruption in playback due to packet delay is more annoying for the users than degradation of picture quality due to packet loss. Hence, most of multimedia applications use UDP in transport layer due to un-reliable, connection-

less nature of UDP. UDP incurs no retransmission delay and jitter. However, UDP itself provides no flow control mechanism so that sources cannot adapt its transmission rate to time-varying available bandwidth depending on the network load. Therefore, it is necessary to have an application-layer flow control scheme, which resulted in protocols such as the RTP/RTCP protocol.

In this chapter, some fundamental issues of transport layer in supporting quality of service for wireless multimedia applications have been discussed. In the emerging wireless networks where the transmission of multimedia and IP traffic is a requirement, it is very essential to provision the quality of service at each layer in the protocol stack. The traditional transport layer protocols must be adapted to the wireless multimedia applications to provide satisfying multimedia services. The emerging trend is to apply cross layer approaches in the design of multimedia transport protocols. The deployment of streaming multimedia over the wireless IP networks brings multiple challenges. Cross-layer design methodologies that rely on interaction between the different protocol layers are promising for addressing these challenges and for providing reliable and high-quality end-to-end performance in wireless multimedia communications. Cross-layer architecture is needed, providing these main functionalities at various layers: Adaptive video encoding at the application layer, TCP-friendly congestion control at the transport layer, and efficient error control mechanism at the link layer. Interaction between these three functionalities remains as the crucial design and research issue. However, cross layer protocol design imposes many challenges in the protocol design and implementation; increase in the layer interdependencies, more complex protocol design, and stability issues. Therefore, intense effort and research on the novel cross layer techniques are required.

ACKNOWLEDGMENT

This work is supported by The State Planning Organization of Turkey under projects DPT 2003-K120250 and DPT 2007-K120610.

REFERENCES

Argyriou, A. (2005). *Transport layer optimizations for heterogeneous wireless multimedia networks*. Unpublished doctoral dissertation, School of Electrical and Computer Engineering Georgia Institute of Technology.

Bae, S., & Chong, S. (2004). TCP-friendly flow control of wireless multimedia using ECN marking. *Signal Processing: Image Communication, 19*, 405-419.

Bisnik, N. (2005). *Protocol design for wireless ad hoc networks: The cross-layer paradigm* (Technical Report). Rensselaer Polytechnic Institute, from http://www.rpi.edu/~bisnin/

Chaudhary, R., & Jacob, L. (2003). ECN based TCP-friendly rate control for wireless multimedia streaming. *Proceedings of the 12th International Conference on IEEE Computer Communications and Networks ICCCN 2003* (pp. 599-602).

Chiung, J., & Wu, S. (2001). A real time transport scheme for wireless multimedia communications. *Mobile Networks and Applications* (pp. 535-546). Kluwer Academic Publishers.

Cranley, N., Fiard, L., & Murphy, L. (2000). Quality of service for streamed multimedia over the Internet. *Proceedings of the Irish Signals and Systems Conference 2000* (pp. 181-188).

Fairhurst, G., Berioli, M., & Renker, G. (2006). Cross-layer control of adaptive coding and modulation for satellite Internet multimedia. *International Journal of Satellite Communications, 24*, 471-491.

Floyd, S., Handley, M., Padhye, J., & Widmer, J. (2000). *Equation-based congestion control for unicast applications: The extended version* (ICSI technical report TR-00-003). Retrieved from http://www.icir.org.

Giambene, G., & Kota, S. (2006). Cross-layer protocol optimization for satellite communications networks: A survey. *International Journal of Satellite Communications and Networking*, DOI: 10.1002/sat.853.

Handley, M., Floyd, S., Padhye, J., & Widmer, J. (2003). *TCP-friendly rate control protocol (TFRC): Protocol specification, RFC 3448*. Found at ftp://ftp.isi.edu/in-notes/rfc3448.txt

Hassan, M., & Jain, R. (2004). *High performance TCP/IP networking*. Prentice Hall.

Iren, S., Amer, P. D., & Conrad, P. T. (1999). The transport layer: Tutorial and survey. *ACM Computing Surveys, 31*(4).

Kristoff, J. (2002). *TCP congestion control*. Retrieved from http://condor.depaul.edu/~jkristof

Larzon, L., Degermark, M., & Pink, S. (2004). The *lightweight user datagram protocol (UDP Lite), RFC 3828*. Retrieved from http://tools.ietf.org/html/rfc3828

Larzon, L., Degermark, M., & Pink, S. (1999). *UDP lite for real time multimedia applications.* HP Laboratories Bristol. Retrieved from http://www.hpl.hp.com

Marchese, M. (2007). *QoS over heterogeneous networks.* John Wiley & Sons Ltd.

Miyazaki, A., Fukushima, H., Wiebke, T., Hakenberg, R., & Burmeister, C. (2001). *RTP payload type format to enable selective retransmissions.* Retrieved from http://www.cs.columbia.edu/~hgs/rtp/drafts/draft-miyazaki-avt-rtp-selret-00.txt

Postel, J. (1980). *User datagram protocol, RFC 768.* Retrieved from http://www.ibiblio.org/pub/docs/rfc/rfc768.txt

Rakocevic, V. (2004). Congestion control for multimedia applications in the wireless Internet. *International Journal of Communication Systems, 17,* 723-734) (DOI: 10.1002/dac.662)

Schaar, M., & Turaga, D. S. (2007). Cross-layer packetization and transmission strategies for delay-sensitive wireless multimedia transmission. *IEEE Transactions on Multimedia, 9*(1).

Schulzrinne, H., Casner, S., Frederick, R., & Jacobson, V. (1996). *RTP: A transport protocol for real-time applications, RFC 1889.* Retrieved from http://www.freesoft.org/CIE/RFC/1889/13.htm

Schulzrinne, H., Casner, S., Frederick, R., & Jacobson, V. (2003). *RTP: A transport protocol for real-time applications, RFC 3550.* Retrieved from http://www.ietf.org/rfc/rfc3550.txt?number=3550

Stanislaus, W., Fairhurst, G., & Radzik, J. (2005, September). *Cross layer techniques for flexible transport protocol using UDP-Lite over a satellite network.* Paper presented at the 2nd International Symposium Wireless Communication Systems, Siena, Italy.

Transmission Control Protocol (TCP). *Transmission control protocol, darpa internet program protocol specification, September 1981, RFC 793.* Retrieved from http://www.ibiblio.org/pub/docs/rfc[/rfc793.txt

Triantafyllopoulou, D. K., Passas, N., & Kaloxylos, A. (2007, April). *A cross-layer optimization mechanism for multimedia traffic over IEEE 802.16 networks.* Paper presented at 13th European Wireless Conference, Paris, France.

Yang, G., Sun, T., Gerla, M., Sanadidi, M. Y., & Chen, L. J. (2006). Smooth and efficient real-time video transport in the presence of wireless errors. *ACM Transactions on Multimedia Computing, Communications, and Applications (TOMCCAP), 2,* 109-126.

YouTube. www.youtube.com

Zhang, Q., Yang, F., & Zhu, W. (2005). Cross-layer QoS support for multimedia delivery over wireless Internet. *EURASIP Journal on Applied Signal Processing 2005, 2,* 207-219.

Compilation of References

3GPP TR 22.934. (2002). *Feasibility study on 3GPP system to wireless local area network (WLAN) interworking (Release 6).*

3GPP TR 23.802 (2005). Technical Specification Group Services and System Aspects – Architectural enhancements for end-to-end Quality of Service (QoS).

3GPP TS 22.105. *3GPP TS 22.105 Services and service capabilities, Release 6.*

3GPP TS 23.060. (2006). *3GPP TS 23.060 v7.1.0 General packet radio service (GPRS); Service description; Stage 2.*

3GPP TS 23.107. (2003). *3GPP TS 23.107 quality of service (QoS) concept and architecture V6.0.0 (Release 6).*

3GPP TS 23.228 (2006). Technical Specification Group Services and System Aspects: IP Multimedia Subsystem (IMS), Rel. 7.

3GPP. (2005). *3GPP TS 25.214 V5.11.0 Physical Layer Procedures (FDD).*

3GPP. (2007). *3GPP TS 25.306 V7.4.0 UE Radio Access Capabilities.*

3GPP. (2007). *3GPP TS 25.331 V7.5.0 Radio Resource Control (RRC) Protocol Specification.*

3GPP. (2007). *3GPP TS 25.433 V7.5.0 UTRAN Iub interface Node B application part (NBAP) signalling.*

802.11e. (2003). *Draft supplement to part 11: Wireless medium access control (MAC) and physical layer (PHY) specifications: Medium access control (MAC) enhancements for quality of service (QoS): IEEE 802.11e/D6.0.*

Aad, I., Ni, Q., & Castelluccia, C. (2002). Enhancing IEEE 802.11 performance with slow CW decrease. *IEEE 802.11e working group document 802.11-02/674r0.*

Abd El-Atty, S. M., (2006). Efficient packet scheduling with pre-defined QoS using cross-layer technique in wireless networks. *11th IEEE Symposium on Computers and Communications (ISCC'06)* (pp. 820-826).

Abdrabou, A., & Weihua, Z. (2006). A position-based QoS routing scheme for UWB mobile ad hoc networks. *IEEE Journal on Selected Areas in Communications, 24*(4), 850-856.

Abowd, D. A., Atkeson, C. G., Hong, J., Long, S. & Pinkerton, M. (1996). Cyberguide: A mobile context-aware tour guide. *Wireless Networks, 3*(5), 421-433.

Abramson, N. (1993). *Multiple access communications foundations for emerging technologies.* IEEE Press.

Acquaviva, A., Benini, L., & Ricco, B. (2001). Software-controlled processor speed setting for low-power streaming multimedia. *IEEE Transactions on Computer-Aided Design of Integrated Circuits and Systems, 20*, 1283-1292, November 2001.

Acquaviva, A., Lattanzi, E., & Bogliolo, A. (2004). Design and simulation of power-aware scheduling strategies of streaming data in wireless LANs. *ACM MSWiM 2004 – Proceedings of the 7th ACM Symposium on Modeling, Analysis, and Simulation of Wireless and Mobile Systems* (pp. 39-46).

Ad hoc Multicast Routing protocol utilizing Increasing id-numberS (AMRIS) Functional Specification, (1998).

Adams, J., & Muntean, G. M. (2006). Power-dependent adaptation algorithm for mobile multimedia networking. *IEEE International Symposium on Broadband Multimedia Systems and Broadcasting*, April 2006.

Adams, J., & Muntean, G. M. (2007). Power save adaptation algorithm for multimedia streaming to mobile devices. *IEEE International Conference on Portable Information Devices,* Orlando, Florida, USA, 2007.

Adams, J., & Muntean, G. M. (2007). Adaptive-bu®er power save mechanism for mobile multimedia streaming. *IEEE International Conference on Communications (ICC07),* Glasgow, Scotland, UK, 2007.

Adya A., Bahl, P., & Padhye, J. (2004). A multi-radio unification protocol for IEEE 802.11 wireless networks. *Proceedings of BroadNets* (pp. 344-354), San Jose, California, USA.

Agusti, R. (2006). Radio resource management in beyond 3G systems. *IEEE Melecon*, Malaga, Spain.

Ahmavaara, K., Haverinen, H., & Pichna, R. (2003). Interworking architecture between 3GPP and WLAN systems. *IEEE Communications Magazine, 41*(11), 74-81.

Ahmed, D. F., & Khaled, M. F. (2004). Channel-quality dependent earliest deadline due fair scheduling schemes for wireless multimedia networks. *Proceedings of IEEE/ACM MSWiM '04.* Venice, Italy: ACM Press.

Ahn, G., Campbell, A. T., & Veres, A. (2002). Supporting service differentiation for real-time and best effort traffic in stateless wireless ad hoc networks (SWAN). *IEEE Transactions on Mobile Computing, 1*(3), 192-207.

Akao, Y. (1990). *Quality function deployment: Integrating customer requirements into product design.* Productivity Press Inc.

Akyildiz, I. F., et al. (1999, Aug). Mobility management in next-generation wireless systems. *Proceedings IEEE, 87*(8), 1347-84.

Akyildiz, I. F., Wang, X., & Wang, W. (2005). Wireless mesh networks: A survey. *Elsevier Journal of Computer Networks and ISDN Systems, 47*(4), 445-487.

Al Hanbali, A., Altman, E., & Nain, P. (2005). A survey of TCP over ad hoc networks. *IEEE Communications Surveys & Tutorials*, 22-36.

Aladwani, A. M., & Palvia, P. C. (2002). Developing and validating an instrument for measuring user-perceived Web quality. *Information and Management, 39*, 467-476.

Al-Ali, R. J. S., Rana, O. F. Walker, D. W. (2003). Supporting QoS-based discovery in service-oriented grids. *Proceedings of the International Parallel and Distributed Processing Symposium, 2003.*

Alcaraz, J. J., & Cerdan, F. (2006). Using buffer management in 3G radio bearers to enhance end-to-end TCP performance. *20th International Conference on Advanced Information Networking and Applications, 2006. AINA 2006..*

Alemu, T., & Jean-Marie, A. (2004). Dynamic configuration of RED parameters [random early detection]. *Global Telecommunications Conference, 2004. GLOBECOM '04. IEEE.*

Alkahtani, A. M. S., Woodward, M. E., Al-Begain, K., & Alghannam, A. (2002). *Enhanced best effort QoS routing with multiple prioritised metrics using the analytic hierarchy process (AHP) concept.* Paper presented at the ICAI 2002, Canary Islands. Spain.

Alocci, I., Giambene, G., & Koucheryavy, Y. (2007). Optimization of IEEE 802.11e Access class parameters with cross-layer approach. *International Symposium on Wireless Pervasive Computing 2007 (ISWPC 2007).* San Juan, Puerto Rico.

Alsenmyr, G., Bergström, J., Hagberg, M., Milén, A., Müller, W., Palm, H., Van der Velde, H., Wallentin, P., & Wallgren, F. (2003). Handover between WCDMA and GSM. *Ericsson Review no. 01.*

Ameigeiras, P., Wigard, J., & Mogensen, P. (2004). Performance of the M-LWDF scheduling algorithm for streaming services in HSDPA. *Proceedings of IEEE VTC Fall '04.* Los Angeles, CA, USA: IEEE.

Anastasi, G., Passarella, A., Conti, M., Gregori, E., & Pelusi, L. (2005). A power-aware multimedia streaming protocol for mobile users. *Proceedings of the International Conference on Pervasive Services 2005* (pp. 371-80).

Anderson, J. (2001). *Methods for measuring perceptual speech quality.* White paper, Agilent technologies. Retrieved from www.agilent.com

Andrews, M. (2004). Instability of the proportional fair scheduling algorithm for HDR. *IEEE Transactions on Wireless Communications, 3*(5), 1422-1426.

Andrews, M., Kumaran, K., Ramanan, K., Stolyar, A., Whithing, P., & Vijayakumar, R. (2001). Providing quality of service over a shared wireless link. *IEEE Communications Magazine*, 150-154.

Andrikopoulos, I., Pouliakis, A., Mertzanis, I., Karaliopoulos, M., Narenthiran, K., Evans, B., Gallet, T., Durand, M., Mazzella, M., Vandermot, J., Dieudonné, M., Roullet, L., Bourdin, E., & Wolf, M. (2005). Demonstration with field trials of a satellite-terrestrial synergistic approach for digital multimedia broadcasting to mobile users. *IEEE Wireless Communications, 12*(5), 82-90.

Aniba, G., & Aissa, S. (2004). Adaptive proportional fairness for packet scheduling in HSDPA. *Proceedings of IEEE GLOBECOM '04.* Montreal, Canada: IEEE.

ANSI, (2003). Digital transport of one-way video signals--parameters for objective performance assessment. *ANSI T1.801.03.*

ANSI/IEEE Std 802.11

Aoki, H., Kurashima, A., & Takahashi, A. (2006). Conversational quality estimation model for wideband IP-telephony services. *International Conference on Spoken Language Processing* (pp.1069-1072).

Argyriou, A. (2005). *Transport layer optimizations for heterogeneous wireless multimedia networks.* Unpublished doctoral dissertation, School of Electrical and Computer Engineering Georgia Institute of Technology.

Armitage, G. (2001). *Lag over 150 milliseconds is unacceptable.* Retrieved from http://gja.space4me.com/things/quake3-latency-051701.html

Armitage, G. (2001). *When does the QuakeIII community play?* Retrieved from http://gja.space4me.com/things/quake3-when-051401.html

Ashourian, M., Zhu, J., & Lambadaris, I. (2004). A review on online quality measure for videos. *TENCON 2004, IEEE Region 10 Conference* (pp. 363-366). November.

Astuti, D., & Kojo, M. (2004). TCP and link layer enhancements in DVB-S/DVB-RCS satellite systems. *4th Berkeley-Helsinki Ph.D. Student Workshop on Telecommunication Software Architectures - Summer 2004.* University of Berkeley, USA.

Athuraliya, S., Lapsley, D., et al. (2000). An enhanced random early marking algorithm for Internet flow control. INFOCOM 2000. The *19th Annual Joint Conference of the IEEE Computer and Communications Societies.*

Atkinson, D. J. (1997). Proposed annex to recommendation P.861. *ITU-T Study Group 12 Contribution 24* (Com 12-24 E), International Telecommunication Union, CH-Geneva.

Awerbuch, B., Holmer, D., & Rubens, H. (2004). High throughput route selection in multi-rate ad hoc wireless networks. *In Proceedings of 1st Working Conference on Wireless On-demand Network Systems* (pp. 253-270), Madonna di Campiglio, Italy.

Babulak, E. (2004, Dec). Quality of service provision assessment for campus network. *Journal of Electrical Engineering, 55*(7-8), 221-224

Bachl, R., Gunreben, P., Das, S., & Tatesh, S. (2007). The long term evolution towards a new 3GPP air interface standard. *Bell Labs Technical Journal, 11*(4), 25-51.

Badia, L., Lindstrom, M., Zander, J., & Zorzi, M. (2003, July). An economic model for the radio resource management in multimedia wireless systems. *Proceedings of IEEE Workshop on Applications and Services in Wireless Networks ASWN*, Bern.

Bae, G., Kim, J., Kim, D., & Park, D. (2005). Low-power multimedia scheduling using output pre-buffering. *13th IEEE International Symposium on Modeling, Analysis, and Simulation of Computer and Telecommunication Systems* (pp. 389-96).

Bae, S., & Chong, S. (2004). TCP-friendly flow control of wireless multimedia using ECN marking. *Signal Processing: Image Communication, 19*, 405-419.

Baiocchi, A., et al. (2006, Sept). *Cross-layer design of optimized packet scheduling and radio resource allocation algorithms for 4th generation cellular wireless systems*. WPMC 2006, San Diego.

Bakre, A., & Badrinath, B. R. (1994). *I-TCP: Indirect TCP for mobile hosts*. Rutgers University, Dept. of Computer Science, Laboratory for Computer Science Research.

Bakre, A., & Badrinath, B. R. (1995). I-TCP: Indirect TCP for mobile hosts. *Proceedings 15th IDCS*, Vancouver, Canada.

Balakrishnan, H., & Katz, R. H. (1998). *Explicit loss notification and wireless web performance*. Paper presented at the EEE Globecom Internet Mini-Conference, Sydney, Australia.

Balakrishnan, H., Padmanabhan, V., Seshan, S., & Katz, R. (1997). A comparison of mechanisms for improving TCP performance over wireless links. *IEEE/ACM Transactions on Networking, 5*(6), 756-769.

Ban, S. Y., Choi, J. K., & Kim, H. S. (2006). Efficient end-to-end qos mechanism using egress node resource prediction in NGN network. *ICACT 2006, 1*, pp. 480-483.

Banchs, A., & Pérez, X. (2002). Providing throughput guarantees in IEEE 802.11 wireless LAN. *Proceedings of IEEE Wireless Communications and Networking Conference* (Vol. 1, pp. 130-138). Orlando, Florida, USA.

Banchs, A., Pérez, X., & Qiao, D. (2003). Providing throughput guarantees in IEEE 802.11e wireless LANs. *Proceedings of 18th International Teletraffic Congress*, Berlin, Germany.

Baoxian, Z., & Mouftah, H. T. (2005). QoS routing for wireless ad hoc networks: Problems, algorithms, and protocols. *Communications Magazine, IEEE, 43*(10), 110-117.

Barnes, S., & Vidgen, R. (2000, July 3-5, 2000). *WebQual: An exploration of Web-site quality*. Paper presented at the Proceedings of the 8th European Conference on Information Systems, Viena, Austria.

Barolli, L., Koyama, A., & Shiratori, N. (2003). *A QoS routing method for ad-hoc networks based on genetic algorithm*.

Barry, M., Campell, A. T., & Veres, A. (2001). Distributed control algorithms for service differentiation in wireless packet networks. *Proceedings of IEEE INFOCOM* (Vol. 1, pp. 582-590), Anchorage, Alaska, USA.

Barsocchi, P., Celandroni, N., Ferro, E., Gotta, A., Davoli, F., Giambene, G., González-Castaño, F. J., Moreno, J. I., & Todorova, P. (2005). Radio resource management across multiple protocol layers in satellite networks: A tutorial overview. *International Journal of Satellite Communications and Networking, 23*(5), 265-305.

Bartolini, N., & Chlamtac, I. (2002). Call admission control in wireless multimedia networks. *Proceedings of IEEE PIMRC*.

Bauer, B., & Patrick, A. S. (2004). *A human factors extension to the seven-layer OSI reference model*. Retrieved December 2, 2007, from http://www.andrewpatrick.ca/OSI/10layer.html

Beerends, J. G., Meijer, E. J., & Hekstra, A. P. (1997). Improvement of the P.861 perceptual speech quality measure. *Contribution to COM 12-20 ITU-T Study Group 12*, International Telecommunication Union, CH-Geneva.

Beerends, J., & Stemerdink, J. (1994). A perceptual speech quality measure based on a psychoacoustic sound representation. *Journal of Audio Eng. Soc.*, 115-123.

Bejaoui, T., Nasser, N., & Vèque, V. (2006, March). Enhanced class-based packet scheduling policy for QoS provisioning in multimedia cellular networks. *4th ACS/IEEE International Conference on Computer Systems and Applications (AICCSA-2006)*, Dubai/Sharjah, UAE.

Bejaoui, T., Vèque, V., & Tabbane, S. (2006, March). Combined fair packet scheduling policy and multi-class adaptive CAC scheme for QoS provisioning in multimedia cellular networks. *International Journal of Communications Systems (IJCS) - WILEY - Special Issue on "Radio*

Resource Management for Provisioning IP-Based QoS in Wireless Cellular Networks, 19(2), 121-139.

Bellalta, B., & Meo, M. (2006). Call admission control in WLANs. *Resource, Mobility and Security Management in Wireless Networks and Mobile Communications.* Auerbach Publications, CRC Press.

Bellalta, B., Macian, C., Sfairopoulou, A., & Cano, C. (2007). Evaluation of joint admission control and VoIP codec selection policies in generic multirate wireless networks. *ITC/IEEE NEW2AN'07*, St. Pertersburg, Russia.

Bellalta, B., Meo, M., & Oliver, M. (2007). VoIP call admission control in WLANs in presence of elastic traffic. *IEEE Journal of Communications Software and Systems, 2*(4).

Bellalta, B., Oliver, M., Meo, M., & Guerrero, M. (2005). A simple model of the IEEE 802.11 MAC protocol with heterogeneous traffic flows. In *IEEE Eurocon 2005*, Belgrade, Serbia, and Montenegro.

Bellur, B., & Ogier, R. G. (1999). *A reliable, efficient topology broadcast protocol for dynamic networks.*

Ben Letaief, K., & Y.J.Z. *Cross-layer Adaptive Resource Management for Wireless Packet Networks with OFDM signalling.* IEEE Transactions in Wireless Communications (Paper TW05-002R1).

Berggren, F., & Kim, S. L. (2004). Energy-efficient control of rate and power in DS-CDMA systems. *IEEE Transactions on Wireless Communications, 3*(3), 725–733.

Bergren, F., & Jäntti, R. (2003). Multiuser scheduling over Rayleigh fading channels. *Proceedings of IEEE GLOBECOM '03.* San Francisco, CA, USA: IEEE.

Bernet, Y., Ford, P., et al. (2000). A framework for integrated services operation over Diffserv networks. *IETF RFC 2998.*

Berry, R., & Yeh, E. (2004). Cross-layer wireless resource allocation. *IEEE Signal Processing Magazine, 21*, 59-68.

Bertsekas, D., & Gallager, R. (1987). *Data networks.* Prentice Hall.

Bhatti, N., Bouch, A., & Kuchinsky, A. (2000). Integrating user-perceived quality into Web server design. *Proceedings of the 9th international World Wide Web Conference on Computer Networks: The International Journal of Computer and Telecommunications Networking* (pp. 1-16). North-Holland Publishing Co.

Bianchi, G. (2000). Performance analysis of the IEEE 802.11 distributed coordination function. *IEEE Journal of Selected Areas on Commununications, 18*(3), 535-547.

Bicket, J., Aguayo, D., & Biswas, S. (2005). Architecture and evaluation of an unplanned 802.11b mesh network. *Proceedings of ACM MOBICOM* (pp. 31-42), Cologne, Germany.

Bisnik, N. (2005). *Protocol design for wireless ad hoc networks: The cross-layer paradigm* (Technical Report). Rensselaer Polytechnic Institute, from http://www.rpi.edu/~bisnin/

Blake, S., Black, D., & Carlson, M. (1998). An architecture for differentiated service. *RFC 2475.*

Bluetooth specification part E, service discovery protocol. Retrieved from http://www.bluetooth.com

Bodin, L. D., Gordon, L. A., & Loeb, M. P. (2005). Evaluating information security investments using the analytic hierarchy process. *Communications of the ACM, 48*(2), 79-83.

Bonald, T., May, M., et al. (2000). Analytic evaluation of RED performance. *19th Annual Joint Conference of the IEEE Computer and Communications Societies (INFOCOM 2000).*

Boppana, R. V., & Konduru, S. P. (2001). *An adaptive distance vector routing algorithm for mobile, ad hoc networks.*

Bouch, A., & Sasse, M. A. (1999). Network quality of service: What do users need? *Proceedings of the 4th International Distributed Conference (IDC'99)* (pp. 78-90).

Bouch, A., Kuchinsky, A., & Bhatti, N. (2000). *Quality is in the eye of the beholder: meeting users' requirements for Internet quality of service.* Paper presented at the

SIGCHI Conference on Human factors in computing systems, The Hague, The Netherlands.

Bouch, A., Sasse, M. A., & DeMeer, H. (2000, 5-7 June 2000). *Of packets and people: A user-centered approach to quality of service*. Paper presented at the International Workshop on Quality of Service (IWQOS 2000).

Brad, K., & Kung, H. T. (2000). *GPSR: Greedy perimeter stateless routing for wireless networks*. Paper presented at the Proceedings of the 6th Annual International Conference on Mobile Computing and Networking.

Braden, B., Clark, D., et al. (1998). Recommendations on queue management and congestion avoidance in the internet. *RFC 2309*.

Braden, R., Clark, D., & Shenker, S. (1994). Integrated services in the Internet architecture: An overview. *RFC 1633*.

Braden, R., Zhang, L., & Berson, S. (1997). Resource reservation protocol (RSVP)-version 1 functional specification. *RFC 2205*.

Braden, R., Zhang, L., et al. (1997). Resource ReSerVation Protocol (RSVP). *RFC 2205*.

Broom, S., & Hollier, M. (2003). Speech quality measurement tools for dynamic network management. *Measurement of Speech and Audio Quality in Networks Conference*, Czech Technical University.

Brouwer, F., de Bruin, I., Silva, L. C., Souto, N., Cercas, F., & Correia, A. (2004). Usage of link-level performance indicators for HSDPA network-level simulations in E-UMTS. *Proceedings of the IEEE International Symposium on Spread Spectrum Techniques and Applications (ISSSTA)*. Sydney, Australia: IEEE.

Brueck, S., Jugl, E., Kettschau, H. J., Link, M., Mueckenheim, J., & Zaprozhets, A. (2007). Radio resource management in HSDPA and HSUPA. *Bell Labs Technical Journal, 11*(4), 151-167.

Buddhikot, M., Chandranmenon, G., & Han, S. (2003). Integration of 802.11 and third-generation wireless data networks. *Proceedings of IEEE INFOCOM* (Vol. 1, pp. 503-512), San Francisco, California, USA.

Buranatrived, J., & Vickers, P. (2004). A study of application and device effects between a WAP phone and palm PDA. *6th International Symposium (MobileHCI 2004)* (pp. 192-203).

Burigat, S., & Chittaro, L. (2005). Location-aware visualization of VRML models in GPS-based mobile guides. *Proceedings of the 10th International Conference on 3D Web Technology* (pp. 57-64).

Buxton, W. (1995). Integrating the periphery and context: A new taxonomy of telematics. *Proceedings of Graphics Interface* (Vol. 95, pp. 239-246).

Buyukkokten, O., Garcia-Molina, H., Paepcke, A., & Winograd, T. (2000). Power brower: Efficient Web browsing for PDAs. *Proceedings of ACM CHI 2000* (pp. 430-437), The Hague, Amsterdam.

Cai, L., Xiao, Y., Shen, X., & Mark, J. (2006). VoIP over WLAN: Voice capacity, admission control, QoS, and MAC. *International. Journal of Communication Systems, 19*, 491-508.

Calafate, C. T., Malumbres, M. P., & Manzoni, P. (2004). *Performance of H.264 compressed video streams over 802.11b based MANETs*. Paper presented at the 24th International Conference on Distributed Computing Systems Workshops, 2004. Proceedings.

Callinan, P., Witwit, M., & Ball, F. (2000, April). A comparative evaluation of sorted priority algorithms and class based queueing using simulation. *Advanced Simulation Technologies Conference ASTC 2000*, Washington DC.

Camarillo, G., & García-Martn, M. (2004). *The 3G IP multimedia subsystem (IMS): Merging the Internet and the cellular worlds*. John Wiley and Sons.

Camarillo, G., Kauppinen, T., Kuparinen, M., Ivars, I., & Res, E. (2007). Towards an innovation oriented IP multimedia subsystem [IP multimedia systems (IMS) infrastructure and services]. *IEEE Communications Magazine, 45*(3), 130-136.

Cano, C., Bellalta, B., & Oliver, M. (2007). A simple model of the IEEE 802.11 MAC protocol with heterogeneous traffic flows. In *IEEE Personal, Indoor and Mobile Radio Communications (PIMRC'07)*, Athens, Greece.

Cano-Garcia, J. M., Gonzalez-Parada, E., & Casilari, E. (2006). Experimental analysis and characterization of packet delay in UMTS networks. *Proceedings of NEW2AN '06*. St. Petersburg: Springer.

Cao, Y., & Li, V. O. K. (2001, Jan.). Scheduling algorithms in broadband wireless networks. *Proceedings of the IEEE, 89*(1), 76-87.

Capone, A., & Redana, S. (2001). Call admission techniques for UMTS. *Proceedings of IEEE VTC fall*.

Capone, A., Fratta, L., & Martignon, F. (2004). Bandwidth estimation schemes for TCP over wireless networks. *IEEE Transactions on Mobile Computing, 3*(2), 129-143.

Carneiro, G., Ruela, J., & Ricardo, M. (2004, April). Cross layer design in 4G wireless terminals. *IEEE Wireless Communications Magazine, 11*(2), 7-13.

Cassandras, C. G., & Lafortune, S. (1999). *Introduction to discrete event systems*. Kluwer Academic Publishers.

Cassandras, C. G., Wardi, Y., et al. (2002). Perturbation analysis for online control and optimization of stochastic fluid models. *Automatic Control, IEEE Transactions on, 47*(8), 1234-1248.

Cen, S., Cosman, P. C., & Voelker, G. M. (2003). End-to-end differentiation of congestion and wireless losses. *IEEE/ACM Transactions on Networking, 11*(5), 703-717.

Cesar, A. S., & Ram, R. (2001). Hazy sighted link state routing protocol (HSLS). *BBN Technical Memorandum, 1301*.

Chahed, T., & Elayoubi, S. E. (2004, August). *QoS in multi-service wireless networks--A state of the art admission control in UMTS--State of the art*. Retrieved from http://www.eurongi.org

Chahed, T., Canton, A. F., Elayoubi, S. E. (2003, May). End-to-end TCP performance in W CDMA/UMTS. *Proceedings of IEEE ICC*.

Chai-Keong, T. (1997). Associativity-based routing for ad hoc mobile networks. *4*(2), 103-139.

Chakeres, I. D., & Belding-Royer, E. M. (2004). PAC: Perceptive admission control for mobile wireless networks. *Proceedings of the 1st International Conference on Quality of Service in Heterogeneous Wired/Wireless Networks* (pp. 18-26), Dallas, Texas, USA.

Chakraborty, D., Joshi, A., & Yesha, Y. (2006). Integrating service discovery with routing and session management for ad-hoc networks. *Ad Hoc Networks, 4*(2), 204-224.

Chakravorty, R., Vidales, P., Patanapongpibul, L., Subramanian, K., Pratt, I., & Crowcroft, J., (2003, June). *On inter-network handover performance using Mobile IPv6*. University of Cambridge Computer Laboratory-Technical Report.

Chalmers, D., & Sloman, M. (1999). A survey of quality of service in mobile computing environments. *IEEE Communication Surveys, 2*(2), 2-10.

Chandra, S., & Vahdat, A. (2002). Application-specific network management for energy-aware streaming of popular multimedia formats. *Proceedings of the General Track, USENIX Annual Technical Conference* (pp. 329-42).

Chandrakasan, A., Sheng, S., & Brodersen, R. (1992). Low-power CMOS digital design. *IEEE Journal of Solid-State Circuits, 27*(4), 473-484.

Chandran, K., Raghunathan, S., Venkatesan, S., & Prakash, R. (2001). A feedback-based scheme for improving TCP performance in ad hoc wireless networks. *IEEE Personal Communications, 8*(1), 34-39.

Chandrasekaran, P., & Joshi, A., (2002). MobileIQ: A framework for mobile information access. *3rd International Conference on Mobile Data Management (MDM'02)* (pp. 43-52).

Chane, L. F., & Garcia-Luna-Aceves, J. J. (1995). Floor acquisition multiple access (FAMA) for packet-radio networks. *SIGCOMM Comput. Commun. Rev. %@ 0146-4833, 25*(4), 262-273.

Charles, E. P., & Pravin, B. (1994). Highly dynamic Destination-Sequenced Distance-Vector routing (DSDV) for mobile computers. *24*(4), 234-244.

Charoenpanyasak, S., Paillassa, B., & Jaddi, F. (2007). *Experimental study on TCP enhancement interest in ad hoc networks.* Paper presented at the 3rd International Conference on Wireless and Mobile Communications, 2007. ICWMC '07, Guadeloupe, French Caribbean.

Charzinski, J. (2001a Dec 2001). *Measured HTTP performance and fun factors.* Paper presented at the ITC 2001, Salvador, BA, Brasil.

Charzinski, J. (2001b. *Web performance in practice: Why we are waiting?* Paper presented at the AEÜ International Journal of Electronics and Communications.

Chase, D. (1985). Code combining - a maximum-likelihood decoding approach for combining an arbitrary number of noisy packets. *IEEE Transactions on Communications, 33*(5), 385-393.

Chaudhary, R., & Jacob, L. (2003). ECN based TCP-friendly rate control for wireless multimedia streaming. *Proceedings of the 12th International Conference on IEEE Computer Communications and Networks ICCCN 2003* (pp. 599-602).

Chen, G., & Parsa, V. (2005). Bayesian model based non-intrusive speech quality evaluation. *IEEE International Conference on Acoustics, Speech, and Signal Processing* (pp. I-385-388).

Chen, J., Lee, L., & Tseng, Y. (2006). Integrating SIP and IEEE 802.11e to support handoff and multi-grade QoS for VoIP applications. In *Proceedings of the 2nd ACM International Workshop on Quality of Service & Security for Wireless and Mobile Networks* (pp. 67-74). New York, NY, USA, ACM Press.

Chen, L. J., Sun, T., Chen, B., Rajendran, V., & Gerla, M. (2004). A smart decision model for vertical handoff. *4th ANWIRE International Workshop on Wireless Internet and Reconfigurability (ANWIRE 2004)*, Athens, Greece, 2004.

Chen, L. J., Sun, T., Cheung, B., Nguyen, D., & Gerla, M. (2004). *Universal seamless handoff architecture in wireless overlay networks.* Technical Report TR040012, UCLA CSD.

Chen, L., & Heinzelman, W. (2005). QoS-aware routing based on bandwidth estimation for mobile ad hoc networks. *IEEE Journal on Selected Areas of Communication, 23*(3), 561-572.

Chen, M., & Zakhor, A. (2004). Rate control for streaming over wireless. *Proceedings IEEE INFOCOM 2004*, Hong Kong, China.

Chen, S., & Nahrstedt, K. (1999). Distributed quality-of-service routing in ad-hoc networks. *IEEE Journal on Selected Areas in Communications, Special Issue on Ad-Hoc Networks, 17*(8), 1-18.

Chen, T. W., Tsai, J. T., & Gerla, M. (1997). *QoS routing performance in multihop, multimedia, wireless networks.*

Cheng, J. F. (2003). On the coding gain of incremental redundancy over chase combining. *Proceedings. of IEEE GLOBECOM '03.* San Francisco, CA, USA: IEEE.

Cherkasova, L., Fu, Y., & Tang, W. (2002). Measuring end-to-end Internet service performance: Response Time, caching efficiency and QoS.

Cherkasova, L., Fu, Y., Tang, W., & Vahdat, A. (2003, Dec). Measuring and characterizing end-to-end Internet service performance. *ACM Trans. Inter. Tech., 3*(4), 347-391.

Chi, M., & Yuanyuan, Y. (2005). *A prioritized battery-aware routing protocol for wireless ad hoc networks.* Paper presented at the Proceedings of the 8th ACM International Symposium on Modeling, Analysis, and Simulation of Wireless and Mobile Systems.

Chiang, C. C., Wu, H. K., Liu, W., & Gerla, M. (1997). *Routing in clustered multihop, mobile wireless networks with fading channel*: Computer Science Department, University of California, Los Angeles.

Chien, C. H., & Liao, W. (2003). A self-configuring RED gateway for quality of service (QoS) networks. *2003 International Conference on Multimedia and Expo, 2003. ICME '03.*

Chini, P., Giambene, G., Bartolini, D., Luglio, M., & Roseti, C. (2006). Dynamic resource allocation based on a TCP-MAC cross-layer approach for DVB-RCS satellite networks. *International Journal of Satellite Communications and Networking, 24*(5), 367-385.

Chiu, D., & Jain, R. (1989). Analysis of the increase/decrease algorithms for congestion avoidance in computer networks. *Journal of Computer Networks and ISDN, 17*(1), 1-14.

Chiung, J., & Wu, S. (2001). A real time transport scheme for wireless multimedia communications. *Mobile Networks and Applications* (pp. 535-546). Kluwer Academic Publishers.

Choi, K., Dantu, K., Cheng, W. C., & Pedram, M. (2002). Frame-based dynamic voltage and frequency scaling for a MPEG decoder. *IEEE/ACM International Conference on Computer Aided Design. IEEE/ACM Digest of Technical Papers (Cat. No.02CH37391)* (pp. 732-737).

Choi, S., & Shin, K.G. (1999, Oct.). An Uplink CDMA system architecture with diverse QoS guarantees for heterogeneous traffic. *IEEE/ACM Transactions on Networking, 7*(5), 616-628.

Christiansen, M., Jeffay, K., et al. (2001). Tuning RED for Web traffic. *IEEE/ACM Transactions on Networking, 9*(3), 249-264.

Chrysostomou, C., Pitsillides, A., et al. (2003). Fuzzy logic controlled RED: Congestion control in TCP/IP differentiated services networks. *Soft Computing, 8*(2003) 79-92.

Chuang, H. C., Huang, C. Y., et al. (2004). On the buffer dynamics of scalable video streaming over wireless network. *IEEE 60th Vehicular Technology Conference 2004 (VTC2004-Fall)*.

Chung, H., & Zhao, X. (2004). Effects of perceived interactivity on Web site preference and memory: Role of personal motivation. *Journal of Computer-Mediated Communication, 10*(1).

Chunhung Richard, L., & Jain-Shing, L. (1999). QoS routing in ad hoc wireless networks. *IEEE Journal on Selected Areas in Communications, 17*(8), 1426-1438.

Cicconetti, C., Lenzini, L., & Mingozzi, E. (2006). Quality of service support in IEEE 802.16 Networks. *IEEE Network, 20*(2), 50-55.

Cidon, I., Guérin, R., et al. (1994). On protective buffer policies. *IEEE/ACM Transactions on Networking, 2*(3), 240-246.

Cisco Technical Document 7934. (2006). *Voice over IP--Per call bandwidth consumption.* Updated February 2006. Retrieved from http://www.cisco.com

Clark, A. D. (2003). *Description of VQMON algorithm.* International Telecomm. Union Del. Cont. COM12-D105.

Clark, D. D., & Fang, W. (1998). Explicit allocation of best-effort packet delivery service. *IEEE/ACM Transactions on Networking, 6*(4), 362-373.

Clark, D. D., Shenker, S., & Zhang, L. (1992). Supporting real-time applications in an integrated services packet network: Architecture and mechanism. *Proceedings ACM SIGCOMM 1992,* Baltimore, USA.

Clausen, T., & Jacquet, P. (2003). Optimized link state routing protocol (OLSR). *RFC 3626.*

Clausen, T., Jacquet, P., & Viennot, L. (2002). Comparative study of CBR and TCP performance of MANET routing protocols. *Workshop MESA.*

Cole, R. G., & Rosenbluth, J. H. (2001, May). Voice over IP performance monitoring. *ACM SIGCOMM Computer Communication Review, 31*(2), 9-24.

Commission for Communications. (2007). *Irish communications market: Quarterly key data report.* Tech. Rep., Commission for Communications Regulation, Ireland http://www.comreg.ie, 2007.

Conti, A., Dardari, D., & Pasolini, G. (2003). Bluetooth and IEEE 802.11b coexistence: Analytical performance evaluation in fading channels. *IEEE Journal on the Selected Areas in Communications, 21*(2), 259-269.

Cranley, N., Fiard, L., & Murphy, L. (2000). Quality of service for streamed multimedia over the Internet. *Proceedings of the Irish Signals and Systems Conference 2000* (pp. 181-188).

Cristache, G., David, K., & Hildebrand, M. (2003). Aspects for the Integration of ad-hoc and cellular networks. *3rd Scandinavian Workshop on Wireless Ad-hoc Networks*.

Cronin, J. J., & Taylor, S. A. (1994). SERVPERF vs. SERVQUAL: Reconciling performance-based and perceptions-minus-expectations measurement of service quality. *Journal of Marketing, 58*, 125-131.

D'Ambra, J., & Rice, R. E. (2001). Emerging factors in user evaluation of the World Wide Web. *Information and Management, 38*, 373-384.

Davis, F. D. (1989). Perceived usefulness, perceived ease of use, and user acceptance of information technology. *MIS Quarterly, 13*(3), 319-340.

Davis, F. D., Bagozzi, R. P., & Warshaw, P. R. (1989). User acceptance of computer technology: A comparison of two theoretical models. *Management Science, 35*(8), 982-1003.

Davoli, F., Marchese, M., & Mongelli, M. (2005). Optimal resource allocation in satellite networks: Certainty equivalent approach versus sensitivity estimation algorithms. *International Journal of Communication Systems, 18*(1), 3-36.

de Angelis, F., Habib, I., Giambene, G., & Giannetti, S. (2005). Scheduling for differentiated traffic types in HSDPA cellular systems. *Proceedings of IEEE GLOBE-COM '05*. St. Louis, MO, USA: IEEE.

De Couto, D., Aguayo, D., & Bicket, J. (2003). High-throughput path metric for multi-hop wireless routing. *Proceedings of ACM MOBICOM* (pp. 134-146), San Diego, California, USA.

Deora, V., Shao, J., Shercliff, G., Stockreisser, P. J., Gray, W. A., & Fiddian, N. J. (2004). Incorporating QoS specifications in service discovery. *Web Information Systems – WISE 2004 Workshops* (pp. 252-263).

Dick, M., Wellnitz, O., & Wolf, L. (2005). Analysis of factors affecting players' performance and perception in multiplayer games. *Proceedings of 4th ACM SIGCOMM*

Workshop on Network and System Support for Games. Hawthorne, NY: ACM Press.

Dimitri, B., & Robert, G. (1987). *Data networks*. Prentice-Hall, Inc.

Dixit, S., Guo, Y., & Antoniou, Z. (2001). Resource management and quality of service in third-generation wireless networks. *IEEE Commun. Mag., 39*(2), 125-133.

Dongwoo, K., Chan-Ho, M., & Sehun, K. (2004). On-demand SIR and bandwidth-guaranteed routing with transmit power assignment in ad hoc mobile networks. *Vehicular Technology, IEEE Transactions on, 53*(4), 1215-1223.

Dongyan, X., Klara, N., & Duangdao, W. (2001). *QoS-aware discovery of wide-area distributed services*. Paper presented at the Proceedings of the 1st International Symposium on Cluster Computing and the Grid.

Döttling, M., Michel, J., & Raaf, B. (2002). Hybrid ARQ and adaptive modulation and coding schemes for high speed downlink packet access. *Proceedings of IEEE PIMRC '02*. Lisboa, Portugal: IEEE.

Dovrolis, C., & Ramanathann, P. (2000). Proportional differentiated services, part II: Loss rate differentiation and packet dropping. *2000 Eighth International Workshop on Quality of Service*, 2000. IWQOS.

Drabu, Y. (1999). A survey of QoS techniques in 802.11.

Draves, R., Padhye, J., & Zill, B. (2004). Comparison of routing metrics for static multi-hop wireless networks. *Proceedings of ACM SIGCOMM* (pp. 133-144), Portland, Oregon, USA.

Draves, R., Padhye, J., & Zill, B. (2004). Routing in multi-radio, multi-hop wireless mesh networks. *Proceedings of ACM MOBICOM* (pp. 114-128), Philadelphia, PA, USA.

DSL Forum. (2006). *Triple play services quality of experience (QoE) requirements*. DSL Forum Technical Report, TR-126, December.

Dube, R., Rais, C. D., Wang, K. Y., & Tripathi, S. K. (1997). *Signal stability based adaptive routing (SSA) for ad-hoc mobile networks.*

Dutta-Roy, A. (2000). The cost of quality in Internet-style networks. *IEEE Spectrum, 37*(9), 57-62, September.

Dyer, T. D., & Boppana, R. V. (2001). A comparison of TCP performance over three routing protocols for mobile ad hoc networks. *Proceedings of the 2nd ACM International Symposium on Mobile Ad Hoc Networking & Computing* (pp. 56-66).

Dynamic MANET On-demand (DYMO) routing, (2007).

Elayoubi, S. E., Chahed, T., & Hébuterne, G. (2004). Admission control in UMTS in the presence of elastic traffic. *Computer Communications* (pp. 27-11).

Elizabeth, M. R., & Charles, E. P. (1999). *Multicast operation of the ad-hoc on-demand distance vector routing protocol.* Paper presented at the Proceedings of the 5th Annual ACM/IEEE International Conference on Mobile Computing and Networking.

Engelstad, P., Thanh, D. V., & Egeland, G. (2003). *Name resolution in on-demand MANETs and over external IP networks.* Paper presented at the ICC '03. IEEE International Conference on Communications, 2003.

Entrambasaguas, J. T., Aguayo-Torres, M. C., Gomez, G., & Paris, J. F. (2005). Multiuser capacity and fairness evaluation of channel/QoS aware multiplexing algorithms. *4th COST 290 MCM*: Wurzburg, Germany.

Ergen, M., & Varaiya. P. (2005). Throughput analysis and admission control for IEEE 802.11a. *ACM/Springer Journal of Mobile Networks and Applications, 10*(5), 705-716.

eTForecasts (2005). *Worldwide PDA and smartphone forecasts.* Retrieved April 8, 2006, from http://www.etforecasts.com/products/ES_SP-PDA.htm

ETSI - EN 300 421. (1997). *Digital video Broadcasting (DVB): Framing structure, channel coding and modulation for 11/12 GHz satellite services.* V1.1.2.

ETSI - EN 301 790. (2002). *Digital video broadcasting (DVB): Interaction channel for satellite distribution systems.* V1.3.1.

ETSI - EN 302 307. (2004). *Digital video broadcasting (DVB): Second generation framing structure, channel coding and modulation systems for broadcasting, interactive services, news gathering and other broadband satellite applications (DVB-S2).* V1.1.1.

ETSI - TR 101 790. (2003). *Digital video broadcasting (DVB): Interaction channel for satellite distribution systems, guidelines for the use of EN 301 790.* V1.2.1.

ETSI - TR 101 985 (2002). *Satellite earth stations and systems (SES): Broadband satellite multimedia, IP over satellite.* V1.1.2.

ETSI - TS 102 462 (2006). *Broadband satellite multimedia services and architectures: QoS Functional architecture.* V0.4.2 (Draft Version).

ETSI BRAN TR 101 957. (2001). *Requirements and architectures for interworking between HIPERLAN/2 and 3rd generation cellular systems V1.1.1.*

ETSI ES 282.003 (2006). TISPAN – Resource and Admission Control Sub-system (RACS): Functional Architecture.

ETSI ES 282.004 (2006). TISPAN – NGN Functional Architecture: Network Attachment Sub-System (NASS).

ETSI ES 282.007 (2006). TISPAN – IP Multimedia Subsystem (IMS): Functional architecture.

ETSI TS 185.001 (2005). TISPAN - Next Generation Network (NGN) - Quality of Service (QoS) Framework and Requirements.

ETSI. (1994). *Network Aspects (NA); General aspects of Quality of Service (QoS) and Network Performance (NP).* ETSI.

ETSI. (1998). *Digital cellular telecommunications system (Phase 2+): Adaptive multi-rate (AMR) speech transcoding (GSM 06.90).* European Telecommunications Standards Institue (ETSI)

ETSI. (2001). *ETSI TS 123 107 QoS concept and architecture V4.3.0.*

EURESCOM Project P905-PF (2000, August). *AQUAVIT - Assessment of quality for audio-visual signals over Internet and UMTS - Deliverable 2: Methodology for subjective audio-visual quality evaluation in mobile and IP networks.*

Evans, B., Werner, M., Lutz, E., Bousquet, M., Corazza, G. E., Maral, G., Rumeau, R., & Ferro, E. (2005). Integration of satellite and terrestrial systems in future multimedia communications. *IEEE Wireless Communications, 12*(5), 72-80.

Fairhurst, G., Berioli, M., & Renker, G. (2006). Cross-layer control of adaptive coding and modulation for satellite Internet multimedia. *International Journal of Satellite Communications, 24*, 471-491.

Falowo, O. E., & Chan, H. A. (2005). *Joint call admission control for integrated UMTS-WLAN network.* SATNAC.

Farber, J. (2002). Network game traffic modelling. *Proceedings of the 1st Workshop on Network and System Support for Games* (pp. 53-57). ACM Press.

Feng, W. C., Shin, K. G., et al. (2002). The BLUE active queue management algorithms. *IEEE/ACM Transactions on Networking, 10*(4), 513-528.

Flinn, J., & Satyanarayanan, M. (1999). Energy-aware adaptation for mobile applications. *Operating Systems Review, 33*(5), 48-63.

Floyd, S. & Jacobson, V. (1993). Random early detection gateways for congestion avoidance. *IEEE/ACM Transactions on Networking, 1*(4), 397-413.

Floyd, S. (1994). TCP and explicit congestion notification. *ACM Computer Communication Review, 24*(5), 10-23.

Floyd, S. (1997). *RED: Discussions of setting parameters.*

Floyd, S., & Fall, K. (1999). Promoting the use of end-to-end congestion control in the Internet. *IEEE/ACM Transactions on Networking, 7*(4), 458-472.

Floyd, S., & Jacobson, V. (1995, Aug.). Link sharing and resource management models for packets networks. *IEEE ACM Transactions on Networking. 3*(4).

Floyd, S., Handley, M., Padhye, J., & Widmer, J. (2000). Equation-based congestion control for unicast applications. *Proceedings ACM SIGCOMM 2000*, Stockholm, Sweden.

Floyd, S., Handley, M., Padhye, J., & Widmer, J. (2000). *Equation-based congestion control for unicast applications: The extended version* (ICSI technical report TR-00-003). Retrieved from http://www.icir.org.

Fogg, B. J., Jonathan, M., Othman, L., Alex, O., Chris, V., Nicholas, F., et al. (2001). What makes Web sites credible? A report on a large quantitative study. *Proceedings of the SIGCHI Conference on Human Factors in Computing Systems.* Seattle, WA: ACM Press.

Fox, A., Goldberg, I., Gribble, S. D., Lee, D. C., Polito, A., & Brewer, E. A. (1998). Experience with top gun wingman: A proxy-based graphical Web browser for the 3Com PalmPilot. *Proceedings of Middleware '98*, Lake District, England.

Fox, A., Gribble, S., Chawathe, Y., Brewer, E., & Gauthier, P. (1997, Oct.). Cluster-based scalable network services. *Proceedings of the Symposium on Operating Systems Principles.*

Francoise, S., & Valerie, I. (2005). *Scalable service discovery for MANET.* Paper presented at the Proceedings of the 3rd IEEE International Conference on Pervasive Computing and Communications.

Freire, J., Kumar, B., & Lieuwen, D. (2001). WebViews: Accessing personalized web content and services. *Proceedings of the 10th International Conference on World Wide Web* (pp. 576-586).

Frenger, P., Parkvall, S., & Dahlman, E. (2001). Performance comparison of HARQ with chase combining and incremental redundancy for HSDPA. *Proceedings of IEEE VTC Fall '01.* Atlantic City, NJ, USA: IEEE.

Fu, Z., Greenstein, B., Meng, X., & Lu, S. (2002). *Design and implementation of a TCP-friendly transport protocol for ad hoc wireless networks.* Paper presented at the 10th IEEE International Conference on Network Protocols, 2002., Paris, France.

Furuskär, A., Parkvall, S., Persson, M., & Samuelsson, M. (2002). Performance of WCDMA high speed packet data. *Proceedings of IEEE VTC Spring '02.* Birmingham, AL, USA: IEEE.

G.107 Rec. (2000). *The E-model, a computational model for use in transmission planning.* International Teleco-munications Union (ITU-T) Recommendation.

G.113 Rec. (2001). *Transmission impairments due to speech processing.* International Teleccomunications Union (ITU-T) Recommendation.

Galletta, D., Henry, R., McCoy, S., & Polak, P. (2004). Web site delays: How tolerant are users? *Journal of the Association for Information Systems, 5*(1), 1-28.

Ganguly, S., Navda, V., Kim, K., Kashyap, A., Niculescu, D., Izmailov, R., Hong, S., & Das, S. (2006). Performance optimization for deploying VOIP services in mesh networks. *IEEE Journal on Selected Areas in Communications, 24*(11), 2147-2158.

Gao, D., Cai, J., & Ngan, K. N. (2005). Admission control in IEEE 802.11e wireless LANs. *IEEE Network, special issue on Wireless Local Area Networking: QoS provision & Resource Management, 19*(4), 6-13.

Gao, D., Shu, Y., et al. (2002). Evaluating RED performance in wireless base-station under self-similar traffic. *Canadian Conference on Electrical and Computer Engineering, 2002.* IEEE CCECE 2002.

García-Macías, J., Rousseau, F., Berger-Sabbatel, G., Toumi, L., & Duda, A. (2003). Quality of service and mobility for the wireless Internet. *ACM/Springer Wireless Networks, 9*(4), 341-352.

Gardikis, G., Kourtis, A., & Constantinou, P. (2003). Dynamic bandwidth allocation in DVB-T networks providing IP services. *IEEE Transactions on Broadcasting, 49*(3), 314-318.

Gardner, M., Frost, V., & Petr, D. (2003). Using optimization to achieve efficient quality of service in voice over

IP networks. *IEEE Performance, Computing, and Communications Conference Proceedings* (pp. 475-480).

Garg, S., & Kappes, M. (2003). Can I add a VoIP call? *Proceedings of IEEE ICC* (Vol. 2, pp. 779-783), Anchorage, USA.

Gbaguidi, C., Verscheure, O., & Hubaux, J. P. (1997, Julio 1997). *A new flexible and modular QoS mapping framework based on psychophysics.* Paper presented at the MMNS 97, IFIP/IEEE Conference on Management of Multimedia Networks, Montreal, Canada.

George, A., & Rahim, T. (1999). *RDMAR: A bandwidth-efficient routing protocol for mobile ad hoc networks.* Paper presented at the Proceedings of the 2nd ACM International Workshop on Wireless Mobile Multimedia.

Ghaderi, M., & Boutaba, R. (2005). *Call admission control in mobile cellular networks: A comprehensive survey.*

Ghinea, G. (2000). *Quality of perception: An essential facet of multimedia communications.* PhD thesis, Department of Computer Science, The University of Reading, UK.

Ghinea, G., & Magoulas, G. (2001). Neural network-based interactive multicriteria decision making in a quality of perception-oriented management scheme. *Joint Conference on Neural Networks* (pp. 2536-2541).

Ghinea, G., & Magoulas, G. D. (2001). Quality of service for perceptual considerations: An integrated perspective. *IEEE International Conference on Multimedia and Expo* (pp. 752-755).

Ghinea, G., & Thomas, J. (2005). Improving perceptual multimedia quality with an adaptable communication protocol. *Journal of Computing and Information Technology, 13*(2), 149-161.

Ghinea, G., & Thomas, J. P. (1998). QoS impact on user perception and understanding of multimedia video clips. *Proceedings of ACM Multimedia '98* (pp. 49-54), Bristol UK.

Ghinea, G., & Thomas, J. P. (2005). Quality of perception: User quality of service in multimedia presentations. *IEEE Transactions on Multimedia, 7*(4), 786-789.

Ghinea, G., & Thomas, J. P., (2000). Impact of protocol stacks on quality of perception. *IEEE International Conference on Multimedia and Expo*, New York (Vol. 2, pp. 847-850).

Giambene, G. (2007). *Resource management in satellite networks. Optimization and cross-layer design.* New York: Springer.

Giambene, G., & Kota, S. (2006). Cross-layer protocol optimization for satellite communications networks: A survey. *International Journal of Satellite Communications and Networking*, DOI: 10.1002/sat.853.

Giambene, G., Giannetti, S., Parràga, C., Ries, M., & Sali A. (in press). Traffic management in HSDPA via GEO Satellite. To appear in the *Space Communications Journal*.

Goff, T., Abu-Ghazaleh, N. B., & Phatak, D. S. (2001). Preemptive routing in ad hoc networks. *Proceedings of ACM MOBICOM* (pp. 43-52), Rome, Italy.

Goff, T., Moronski, J., Phatak, D., & Gupta, V. (2000). Freeze-TCP: A true end-to-end enhancement mechanism for mobile environments. *Proceedings IEEE INFOCOM 2000*, Tel-Aviv, Israel.

Goldsmith, A., & Varaiya, P. (1997). Capacity of fading channels with channel side information. *IEEE Transactions on Information Theory, 46*, 1986-1992.

Goodings, R. (2002). IP over satellite: Standardization activities in ETSI/TC-SES. *ITU Workshop on Satellites in IP and Multimedia*. Geneva, Switzerland.

Goodman, D., & Mandayam, N. (2000). Power control for wireless data. *IEEE Personal Communications, 7*, 48-54.

Goria, P., Agusti, R., Sallent, O. (2001, April). *System specification radio resource management algorithms: Identification and requirements*. IST-2000-25133: AR-ROWS, D04.

Grace, K., & Corporation, M. (2000). *Mobile mesh routing protocol (MMRP)*. Retrieved from http://www.mitre.org/tech_transfer/mobilemesh

Gray, P., Hollier, M. P., & Massara, R. E. (2000). Non-intrusive speech quality assessment using vocal-tract models. In *IEEE Proc.-Vis. Image Signal Process* (pp. 493-501).

Gronroos, C. (1983). *Strategic management and marketing in the service sector*. Boston: Marketing Science Institute.

Grossglauser, M., & Tse, D. (2003). A time-scale decomposition approach to measurement-based admission control. *IEEE/ACM Transactions on Networking, 11*(4), 550-563.

Group, I. I. E. T. F. M. W. Mobile Ad-hoc Networks. Retrieved from http://www.ietf.org/html.charters/manet-charter.html

Guainella, E., & Pietrabissa, A. (2003). TCP-friendly bandwidth-on-demand scheme for satellite networks. *ASMS 2003 conference*.

Guangyu, P., Gerla, M., & Tsu-Wei, C. (2000a). *Fisheye state routing: a routing scheme for ad hoc wireless networks*.

Guangyu, P., Mario, G., & Xiaoyan, H. (2000b). *LAN-MAR: Landmark routing for large scale wireless ad hoc networks with group mobility*. Paper presented at the Proceedings of the 1st ACM International Symposium on Mobile Ad Hoc Networking & Computing.

Gulliver, S. R., & Ghinea, G. (2003). How level and type of deafness affects user perception of multimedia video clips. *Universal Access in the Information Society, 2*(4), 374-386.

Gulliver, S. R., Serif, T., & Ghinea, G. (2004). Pervasive and standalone computing: The perceptual effects of variable multimedia quality. *International Journal of Human Computer Studies, 60*, 640-665.

Gunawan, I. P., & Ghanbari, M. (2003). *Reduced-reference picture quality estimation by using local harmonic amplitude information*. Paper presented at the London Communications Symposium 2003.

Guo, C., Guo, Z., Zhang, Q., & Zhu, W. (2004, June). A seamless and proactive end-to-end mobility solution for roaming across heterogeneous wireless networks. *IEEE Journal on Selected Areas in Communications, 22*(5), 834-848.

Gupta, P., & Kumar, P. R. (2000). The capacity of wireless networks. *IEEE Transactions on Information Theory, 46*(2), 388-404.

Gupta, R., Zhanfeng, J., Tung, T., & Walrand, J. (2005). *Interference-aware QoS routing (IQRouting) for ad-hoc networks.*

Guttman, E., Perkins, C., Veizades, J., & Day, M. (1999). *Service Location Protocol, Version 2*: RFC Editor.

Gyasi-Agyei, A. (2002). Service differentiation in wireless Internet using multiclass RED with drop threshold proportional scheduling. *10th IEEE International Conference on Networks*. ICON 2002.

H.323 Rec. (1998). *H. 323, packet-based multimedia communications systems.* International Teleccomunications Union (ITU-T) Recommendation.

Haartsen, J. (1998). BLUETOOTH—The universal radio interface for ad hoc, wireless connectivity. *Ericsson Review.*

Haas, Z. J. (1997). *A new routing protocol for the reconfigurable wireless networks.*

Habib, A., & Abrams, M. (2000). *Analysis of sources of latency in downloading web pages.* Paper presented at the WebNet 2000.

Hammer, F., Reichl, P., & Ziegler, T. (2004). *Where packet traces meet speech samples: An instrumental approach to perceptual QoS evaluation of VoIP.* Paper presented at the IWQOS'04.

Han, Z., & Liu, K. R. (2004). Joint adaptive link quality and power management over wireless networks with fairness constraint and space-time diversity. *IEEE Transactions on Vehicular Technology, 53*, 1138-1148.

Handley, M., Floyd, S., Padhye, J., & Widmer, J. (2003). *TCP-friendly rate control protocol (TFRC): Protocol specification, RFC 3448.* Found at ftp://ftp.isi.edu/in-notes/rfc3448.txt

Hannikainen, M., Hamalainen, T. D., Niemi, M., & Saarinen, J. (2002). Trends in personal wireless data communications. *Computer Communications, 25*, 84-99.

Haratcherev, I., Taal, J., Langendoen, K., Lagendijk, R., & Sips, H. (2005). Automatic IEEE 802.11 rate control for streaming applications. *Wireless Communications and Mobile Computing, 5*(4), 421-437.

Hassan, M., & Jain, R. (2004). *High performance TCP/IP networking.* Prentice Hall.

Hatami, A., et al. (1999, Sept). Analytical framework for handoff in non-homogeneous mobile data networks. *Proceedings PIMRC '99* (pp. 760-64). Osaka, Japan.

Havinga, P. J. M., & Wu, G. (2001). Wireless Internet on heterogeneous networks. *Proceedings of Workshop on Mobile Communications in Perspective*, Enschede, the Netherlands.

Havinga, P., & Smit, G. (2001). Energy-efficient wireless networking for multimedia applications. *Wireless Communications and Mobile Computing, 1*(2), 165-184.

Heavy Heading. (2006). Assuring quality of experience for IPTV. *HeavyReading Whitepaper*, July.

Hedge, N., Proutiére, A., & Roberts, J. (2005). Evaluating the voice capacity of 802.11 WLAN under distributed control. In *IEEE LAN/MAN Conference*, Megalo Arsenali, Chania, Greece.

Heickerö, R., Jelvin, S., & Josefsson, B. (2002). Ericsson seamless network. *Ericsson Review no. 02.*

Heinanen, J., & Guérin, R. (1999). A single rate three color marker. *IETF RFC 2697.*

Heinanen, J., & Guérin, R. (1999). A two rate three color marker. *IETF RFC 2698.*

Heinanen, J., F. Baker, et al. (1999). Assured forwarding PHB group. *RFC 2597.*

Helal, S., Desai, N., Verma, V., & Choonhwa, L. (2003). *Konark: A service discovery and delivery protocol for ad-hoc networks.* Paper presented at the Wireless Communications and Networking, 2003. WCNC 2003. 2003 IEEE.

Henderson, T., & Bhatti, S. (2001, October 5, 2001). *Modelling user behaviour in networked games.* Paper presented at the ACM Multimedia 2001, Ottawa, Canada.

Heusse, M., Rousseau, F., Berger-Sabbatel, G., & Duda, A. (2003). Performance anomaly of 802.11b. In *IEEE INFOCOM*, San Francisco, USA.

Hg, T. S. E., Stoica, I., & Zhang, H. (1998). Packet fair queueing algorithms for wireless networks with location-dependent errors. *Proceedings INFOCOM'98* (pp. 1103-1111).

Ho, Y. C., & Cao, X. R. (1991). *Perturbation analysis of discrete event dynamic systems.* Boston, MA: Kluwer Academic Publishers.

Hoffman, D., Fernando, G., et al. (1998). RTP payload format for MPEG1/MPEG2 video.

Hole, D. P., & Tobagi, F. A. (2004). Capacity of an IEEE 802.11b Wireless LAN supporting VoIP. In *IEEE International Conference on Communications (ICC'04)*, Paris, France.

Holland, G., & Vaidya, N. (2002). Analysis of TCP performance over mobile ad hoc networks. *Wireless Networks, 8*(2), 275-288.

Hollot, C. V., Misra, V., et al. (2002). Analysis and design of controllers for AQM routers supporting TCP flows. *IEEE Transactions on Automatic Control, 47*(6), 945-959.

Holma, H., & Toskala, A. (2004). *WCDMA for UMTS: Radio access for third generation mobile communications* (3rd ed.). John Wiley & Sons.

Holtzman, J. M. (2000). CDMA forward link waterfilling power control. In *Proceedings of the IEEE Vehicular Technology Conference* (pp. 1663-67).

Hosein, P. (2002). QoS control for WCDMA high speed packet data. *Proceedings of 4th International Workshop on Mobile and Wireless Communications Network.* Calcutta, India: Springer.

Hu, F., & Sharma, N. K. (2002). Enhancing wireless Internet performance. *IEEE Communications Surveys and Tutorials, 4*(1), 2-15.

Huang, C., & Yates, R. (1996). Call admission in power controlled CDMA systems. *Proceedings of IEEE VTC.*

Huang, C., Chindapol, A., Ritcey, J., & Hwang, J. (2006). Link layer packet loss classification for link adaptation. In *WLAN. 2006 40th Annual Conference on Information Sciences and Systems* (pp. 603-608).

Hughes, H. D., Krunz, M., & Sass, R. (1995, April). Statistical characteristics and multiplexing of MPEG streams. *IEEE Infocom 95*, Boston, MA, USA.

Hui, S., Bingxin, S., Ling, z., & Huazhi, G. (2003). *A distributed entropy-based long-life QoS routing algorithm in ad hoc network.*

Hung, K., & Zhang, Y. (2003). Implementation of a WAP-based telemedicine system for patient monitoring. *IEEE Transactions on Information Technology in Biomedicine, 7*(2), 101-107.

IEEE 802.11 standard. (1999). Available on-line at the URL: http://standards.ieee.org/getieee802/802.11.html

IEEE 802.11. (2000). *IEEE 802.11: Wireless LAN medium access control (MAC) and physical layer (PHY) specification.* Standard, IEEE.

IEEE 802.11a. (1999). *IEEE 802.11a: High-speed physical layer in the 5GHz band.* Standard, IEEE.

IEEE 802.11b. (2001). *IEEE 802.11b: Higher-speed physical layer (PHY) extension in the 2.4GHz band.* Standard, IEEE.

IEEE 802.11e. (2003). Part 11: Wireless LAN medium access control (MAC) and physical layer (PHY) specifications: medium access control (MAC) enhancements for quality of service (QoS). *IEEE Std 802.11e/D4.3.*

IEEE 802.11e. (2005). *IEEE 802.11e: Medium access control (MAC) quality of service enhancements.* Standard, IEEE.

IEEE 802.11f. (2003). IEEE trial-use recommended practice for multi-vendor access point interoperability via an inter-access point protocol across distribution systems supporting IEEE 802.11 ™ operation. *IEEE Standard.*

IEEE 802.11g. (2003). *IEEE 802.11g: Further higher-speed physical layer extension in the 2.4GHz band.* Standard, IEEE.

IEEE 802.11n. (2006). *IEEE 802.11n: Standard for enhancements for higher throughput.* Standard, IEEE.

IEEE 802.11s. (1998). Draft amendment to standard for information technology, telecommunications and information exchange between systems - LAN/MAN specific requirements - part 11: wireless medium access control (MAC) and physical layer (PHY) specifications: amendment: ESS mesh networking, *IEEE Standard.*

IEEE 802.1d (1998). *Part 3: Medium access control (MAC) bridges, ANSI/IEEE Std. 802.1D.* 1998 edition.

IEEE 802.1Q. (2003). Virtual bridged local area networks, *IEEE Standard.*

IEEE. (1997). IEEE std 802.11--Wireless LAN medium access control (MAC) and physical layer (PHY) specification. *IEEE Standard.*

Iera, A., Marano, S., & Molinaro, A. (1996). Call level and burst level priorities for effective management of multimedia services in UMTS. *Proceedings of IEEE Infocom'96* (Vol. 3, pp. 1363-1370).

IETF - RFC 1633. (1994). *Integrated services in the Internet architecture.*

IETF - RFC 2475. (1998). *Architecture for differentiated services.*

International Telecommunication Union. (1996). Methods for subjective determination of transmission quality. *ITU Recommendation P.800.*

International Telecommunication Union. (1998). Objective measuring apparatus, Appendix 1: Test signals. *ITU-T Recommendation P.50.*

International Telecommunication Union. (2001). Perceptual evaluation of speech quality (PESQ), an objective method for end-to-end speech quality assessment of narrow-band telephone networks and speech codec. *ITU Recommendation P.862.*

International Telecommunication Union. (2003). Mapping function for transforming P.862 raw result scores to MOS-LQO. *ITU Recommendation P.862.1.*

International Telecommunication Union. (2003). Mean opinion score (MOS) terminology. *ITU Recommendation P.800.1.*

International Telecommunication Union. (2004). Single-ended method for objective speech quality assessment in narrow-band telephony applications. *ITU-T Recommendation P.563.*

International Telecommunication Union. (2005). The E-model, a computational model for use in transmission planning. *ITU Recommendation G.107.*

International Telecommunication Union. (2006). Conformance testing for narrowband voice over IP transmission quality assessment models. *ITU-T Recommendation P.564.*

Iren, S., Amer, P. D., & Conrad, P. T. (1999). The transport layer: Tutorial and survey. *ACM Computing Surveys, 31*(4).

Irnich, T. (2000). *Measuring and modelling WWW traffic characteristics in access networks.* Thesis. Aachen University of Technology.

Ishihara, T., & Yasuura, H., (1998). Voltage scheduling problem for dynamically variable voltage processors. *Proceedings, 1998 International Symposium on Low Power Electronics and Design* (pp. 197-202).

Itakura, F., & Saito, S. (1978). Analysis synthesis telephony based on the maximum likelihood method. *Proceedings 6th Int. Congr. Acoust.,* (pp. c17-c20).

ITU-T - Recommendation Y.1541. (2006). *Network performance objectives for IP-based services.*

ITU-T Rec. Y.1291 (2004). Internet protocol aspects – Architecture, access, network capabilities and resource management: An architectural framework for support of Quality of Service in packet networks.

ITU-T Rec. Y.2011 (2004). Next Generation Networks – Frameworks and functional architecture models:

General principles and general reference model for Next Generation Networks.

ITU-T Rec. Y.2111 (2006). Next Generation Networks – Quality of Service and Performance: Resource and admission control functions in Next generation Networks.

ITU-T Recommendation E. 800. (1994). *Terms and definitions related to quality of service and network performance including dependability*. International Telecommunication Union CH-Geneva.

ITU-T Recommendation G.107. (2005). *The E-model, a computational model for use in transmission planning*. International Telecommunication Union CH-Geneva.

ITU-T Recommendation G.113 (2005). Transmission impairments due to speech processing, *ITU-T Standard*.

ITU-T Recommendation G.729 (1996). Annex B, A silence compression scheme for G.729 optimized for terminals conforming to recommendation V.70. *ITU-T Standard*.

ITU-T Recommendation P.562. (2000). *Analysis and interpretation of INMD voice-service measurements*. International Telecommunication Union CH-Geneva.

ITU-T Recommendation P.563. (2004). *Single ended method for objective speech quality assessment in narrow-band telephony applications*. International Telecommunication Union, CH-Geneva.

ITU-T Recommendation P.800. (1996). *Methods for subjective determination of transmission quality*. International Telecommunication Union CH-Geneva.

ITU-T Recommendation P.862. (2001). *Perceptual evaluation of speech quality (PESQ), an objective method for end-to-end speech quality assessment of narrowband telephone networks and speech codecs*. International Telecommunication Union CH-Geneva.

ITU-T. (1993). General aspects of quality of service and network performance in digital networks, including ISDNs. In *Rec. G.1000*. Vol. Rec. I.350, (ITU).

ITU-T. (1994). QoS terms and definitions related to quality of service and network performance including dependability. *ITU-T Recommendation E.800*, August.

ITU-T. (1997). *Methods for subjective determination of transmisión quality*.

ITU-T. (1998). Objective measuring apparatus, appendix 1: Test signals. *ITU-T P.50 (2/1998)*

ITU-T. (1998). Subjective picture quality assessment for digital cable television systems, *ITU-T Recommendation J. 140*, March.

ITU-T. (2000). User requirements for objective perceptual video quality measurements in digital cable television. *ITU-T Recommendation J.143*, May.

ITU-T. (2001). End-user multimedia QoS categories. *ITU-T Recommendation G. 1010*, November.

ITU-T. (2001). Perceptual evaluation of speech quality (PESQ), an objective method for end-to-end speech quality assessment of narrow-band telephone networks and speech codecs. *P.862. (02/2001)*.

ITU-T. (2002). *Internet protocol data communication service - IP packet transfer and availability performance parameters*: International Telecommunication Union.

ITU-T. (2002). Methodology for the subjective assessment of the quality of television pictures, *ITU-T Recommendation BT.500*, June.

ITU-T. (2004). *Handbook on quality of service and network performance*. ITU Press.

ITU-T. (2004). Method for specifying accuracy and cross-calibration of video quality metrics (VQM). *ITU-T Recommendation J.149*, March.

ITU-T. (2004). Objective perceptual video quality measurement techniques for digital cable television in the presence of a full reference. *ITU-T Recommendation J.144*, March.

ITU-T. (2005). Quality of service ranking and measurement methods for digital video services delivered over broadband IP networks. *ITU-T Recommendation J.241*, 2005.

ITU-T. (2005). Wideband extension to recommendation P.862 for the assessment of wideband telephone networks and speech codecs. *P.862.2 (11/2005).*

ITU-T. (2006). Conformance testing for narrowband voice over IP transmission quality assessment models. *P.564 (07/2006).*

ITU-T. P.862.1 (11/2003). *Mapping function for transforming P.862 raw result scores to MOS-LQO.*

ITU-T. Recommendation P.861. (1996). *Objective quality measurement of telephone-band (300-3400 Hz) speech codecs.* International Telecommunication Union, CH-Geneva.

ITU-T. Recommendation P.862.1. (2003). *Mapping function for transforming P.862 raw result scores to MOS-LQO.* International Telecommunication Union, CH-Geneva.

Iwata, A., Ching-Chuan, C., Guangyu, P., Gerla, M., & Tsu-Wei, C. (1999). Scalable routing strategies for ad hoc wireless networks. *IEEE Journal on Selected Areas in Communications, 17*(8), 1369-1379.

Jacobson, V. (1988). Congestion avoidance and control. *Proceedings ACM SIGCOMM,* Stanford, USA.

Jacobson, V., Nichols, K., et al. (1999). An expedited forwarding PHB. *RFC 2598.*

Jacquet, P., Muhlethaler, P., Clausen, T., Laouiti, A., Qayyum, A., & Viennot, L. (2001). *Optimized link state routing protocol for ad hoc networks.*

Jafar, S. A., & Goldsmith, A. (2000). Optimal rate and power adaptation for multirate CDMA. In *Proceedings of the IEEE Vehicular Technology Conference* (pp. 994-1000).

Jain, R. (2004). Quality of experience. *IEEE Multimedia, 11*(1), 96-97.

Jalali, A., Padovani, R., & Pankaj, R. (2000). Data throughput of CDMA-HDR: A high efficiency-high data rate personal communication wireless system. *Proceedings of IEEE VTC Spring '00.* Tokyo, Japan: IEEE.

Jamalipour, A., & Kim, J. (2003, May). Measurement-based admission control scheme with priority and service classes for application in wireless IP networks. *Journal of Communication Systems, 16*(6), 535-551.

Jamin, S., et al. (1997, Feb.). A measurement-based admission control algorithm for integrated services packet networks. *IEEE/ACM Transactions on Networking, 5*(1), 524-540.

Jaseemuddin, M. (2003). An architecture for integrating UMTS and 802.11 WLAN Networks. *Eighth IEEE International Symposium on Computers and Communication (ISCC03).* IEEE Computer Society.

Jaseemuddin, M. (2003). An architecture for integrating UMTS and 802.11 WLAN networks. *Proceedings of IEEE Symposium on Computers and Communications* (pp. 716 -723), Antalya, Turkey.

Jiang, H., et Al (2005, Dec.). Cross-layer design for resource allocation in 3G wireless networks and beyond. *IEEE Communications Magazine,* 120-126.

Jin, C., & Kubichek, R., (1995). Output-based objective speech quality using vector quantization techniques. *Proc. ASILOMAR. Conf. On Signals, Systems and Computers* (pp. 1291-1294).

Joa-Ng, M., & Lu, I. T. (1999). A peer-to-peer zone-based two-level link state routing for mobile ad hoc networks. *IEEE Journal on Selected Areas in Communications, 17*(8), 1415-1425.

Jodra, J. L., Vara, M., Cabero, J. M., & Bagazgoitia, J. (2006). *Service discovery mechanism over OLSR for mobile ad-hoc networks.* Paper presented at the 20th International Conference on Advanced Information Networking and Applications, 2006. AINA 2006.

Johnson, C. (1998). *Why CHI (computer-human interaction) has failed to improve the Web.* Retrieved from www.dcs.gla.ac.uk/~johnson/papers/Web98.html

Johnson, D. B., & Maltz, D. A. (1996). *Dynamic source routing in ad hoc wireless networks.*

Johnson, D. B., Maltz, D. A., & Broch, J. (2001). DSR: The dynamic source routing protocol for multi-hop wireless ad hoc networks. In C. E. Perkins (Ed.), *Ad hoc networking* (pp. 139-172). Addison-Wesley Press.

Johnson, J. (1998). Transform coding of audio signals using perceptual noise criteria. *IEEE J. Select. Areas Comm.*, 314-323.

Jones, M., Marsden, G., Mohd-Nasir, N., Boone, K., & Buchanan, G. (1999). Improving Web interaction on small displays. *8ᵗʰ International WWW Conference* (pp. 51-59).

Ju, H. J., & Rubin, I. (2006). Backbone topology synthesis for multiradio mesh networks. *IEEE Journal on Selected Areas in Communications, 24*(11), 2116-2126.

Jugi's traffic generator. *Summary*. From https://hoslab. cs.helsinki.fi/savane/projects/jtg/

Jun, J., & Sichitiu, M. L. (2003). The nominal capacity of wireless mesh networks. *IEEE Wireless Communications, 10*(5), 8-14.

Jurdak, R. (2007). *Wireless ad hoc and sensor networks: a cross-layer design perspective* (1ˢᵗ ed.). Springer.

Kamal, A. E., & Hassanein, H. S. (2004). Performance evaluation of prioritized scheduling with buffer management for differentiated services architectures. *Computer Networks, 46*(2), 169-180.

Kanodia, V., Li, C., & Sabharwal, A. (2002). Distributed priority scheduling and medium access in ad hoc networks. *ACM Wireless Networks Journal, 8(*5), 455-466.

Kapov, L. S., & Matjasevic, M. (2006). End-to-end QoS signaling for future multimedia services in the NGN. *LNCS*, Vol. 4003. Springer.

Karn, P. (1990). *MACA--A new channel access method for packet radio*. Paper presented at the ARRL/CRRL Amateur Radio 9ᵗʰ Computer Networking Conference.

Kawalek, J. A. (1995). User perspective for QoS management. *Proceedings of the QoS Workshop aligned with the 3ʳᵈ International Conference on Intelligence in Broadband Services and Network (IS&N 95)*, Crete, Greece.

Kazantzidis, M., Gerla, M., & Lee, S. J. (2001). Permissible throughput network feedback for adaptive multimedia in AODV MANETs. *Proceedings of IEEE International Conference on Communications* (Vol. 5, pp. 1352-1356), Helsinki, Finland.

Kazasis, F. G., Moumoutzis, N., Pappas, N., Karanastasi, A., & Christodoulakis, S. (2003). Designing ubiquitous personalized tv-anytime services. In J. Eder, R. Mittermeir, & B. Pernici (Eds.), *The CAISE'03 Workshops* (pp. 136-149). Slovenia: University of Maribor Press.

Keith, E., & Tom, R. (2001). *Jini Example by Example*. Prentice Hall PTR.

Kelly, F. P. (1997). Charging and rate control for elastic traffic. *European Transactions on Telecommunications, 8*, 33-37.

Kelly, F., Maulloo, A., & Tan, D. (1998). Rate control in communication networks: Shadow prices, proportional fairness and stability. *Journal of the Operational Research Society, 49*, 237-252

Kerpez, K., Waring, D., Lapiotis, G., Lyles, J. B., & Vaidyanathan, R. (2006). IPTV service assurance. *IEEE Communications Magazine, 44*(9), 166-172.

Kesidis, G., Singh, A., et al. (1996). Feasibility of fluid-driven simulation for ATM network. *Proc. IEEE Globecom*.

Khan, S., Peng, Y., Steinbach, E., Sgroi, M., & Kellerer, W. (2006, January). Application driven crosslayer optimization for video streaming over wireless networks. *IEEE Communications Magazine, 44*(1), 122130.

Khattab, A. D., & Elsayed, K. M. (2004). Channel-quality dependent earliest deadline due fair scheduling schemes for wireless multimedia networks. *Proceedings of ACM/ IEEE MSWiM*. Venice, Italy: ACM Press.

Khorashadi, B., Chen, A., Ghosal, D., Chuah, C. N., & Zhang, M. (2007). Impact of transmission power on the performance of UDP in vehicular ad hoc networks. *IEEE International Conference on Communications, 2007. ICC'07* (pp. 3698-3703).

Kim, D. S. (2005). ANIQUE: An auditory model for single-ended speech quality estimation. *IEEE Trans. Speech and Audio Process* (pp. 821-831).

Kim, D. S. (2006). Enhanced perceptual model for non-intrusive speech quality assessment. *IEEE Intl. Conf. Acoustics, Speech, and Signal Process* (pp. I-829-832).

Kim, D., Toh, C. K., & Choi, Y. (2001). TCP-BuS: Improving TCP performance in wireless ad hoc networks. *Journal of Communications and Networks, 3*(2), 1.

Kim, I., Shin, B., & Lee, D. (2000). SIR-based call admission control by intercell interference prediction for DS-CDMA systems. *IEEE communications Letters*, 4-1.

Kim, J. O., Tode, H., & Murakami, K. (2005). Service-based rate adaptation architecture for IEEE 802.11 e QoS networks. In *IEEE Global Telecommunications Conference (GLOBECOM'05)*.

Kim, J. B., & Honig, M. L. (2000). Resource allocation of multiple classes of DS-CDMA traffic. *IEEE Transactions on Vehicular Technology, 49*(2), 506-519.

Kim, L., & Albers, M. J. (2001). Web design issues when searching for information in a small screen display. *ACM SIGDOC'01* (pp. 193-200). University of Memphis.

Klein, T., Leung, K., & Zheng, H. (2004). Enhanced scheduling algorithms for improved TCP Performance in wireless IP networks. *Proceedings of IEEE GLOBECOM '04*. Dallas, TX, USA: IEEE.

Knopp, R., & Humblet, P. A. (2000). Information capacity and power control in single-cell multiuser communications. In *Proceedings of the IEEE International Conference on Communications*.

Ko, Y. B., & Vaidya, N. H. *Optimizations for Location-aided Routing (LAR) in Mobile Ad Hoc Networks (A brief note)*.

Kohler, E., Morris, R., & Jannotti, J. (2000). The click modular router. *ACM Transaction on Computer System, 18*(3), 263-297.

Kolding, T. E. (2003). Link and system performance aspects of proportional fair scheduling in WCDMA/HSDPA. *Proceedings of IEEE VTC Fall '03*. Orlando, FL, USA: IEEE.

Kolding, T. E. (2006). QoS-aware proportional fair packet scheduling with required activity detection. *Proceedings of IEEE VTC Fall '06*. Montreal, Canada: IEEE.

Kolding, T. E., Frederiksen, F., & Mogensen, P. E. (2001). Performance evaluation of modulation and coding schemes proposed for HSDPA in 3.5G UMTS networks. *Proceedings of WPMC '01*. Aalborg, Denmark: IEEE.

Kolding, T. E., Frederiksen, F., & Mogensen, P. E. (2002). Performance aspects of WCDMA systems with high speed downlink packet access. *IEEE VTC Fall '02*. Vancouver, CA.

Kopparty, S., Krishnamurthy, S. V., Faloutsos, M., & Tripathi, S. K. (2002). *Split TCP for mobile ad hoc networks*. Paper presented at the IEEE Global Telecommunications Conference, 2002. GLOBECOM'02.

Korhonen, J., & Gurtov, A. (2004). Effect of vertical handovers on performance of TCP-friendly rate control. *SIGMOBILE Mobile Computing and Communications Review, 8*(3), 73-87.

Korhonen, J., & Wang, Y. (2005). Power-efficient streaming for mobile terminals. *Proceedings of the 15th International Workshop on Network and Operating Systems Support for Digital Audio and Video. NOSSDAV 2005* (pp. 39-44).

Kota, S. (2005). Broadband satellite networks: Trends and challenges. *IEEE Communications Society WCNC 2005* (Vol. 3, pp. 1472-1478).

Koumaras, H., Kourtis, A., & Martakos, D. (2005). Evaluation of video quality based on objectively estimated metric. *Journal of Communications and Networks, 7*(3), 235-242.

Koumaras, H., Pallis, E., Xilouris, G., Kourtis, A., Martakos, D., & Lauterjung, J. (2004). *Pre-encoding PQoS assessment method for optimized resource utilization*. Paper presented at the HET-NETs04, Ilkley, West Yorkshire, UK.

Kozat, U. C., & Tassiulas, L. (2004). Service discovery in mobile ad hoc networks: an overall perspective on architectural choices and network layer support issues. *Ad Hoc Networks, 2*(1), 21.

Krashinsky, R., & Balakrishnan, H. (2002). Minimizing energy for wireless Web access with bounded slowdown. *Proceedings of the Annual International Conference on Mobile Computing and Networking, MOBICOM* (pp. 119-130).

Krishna, C., & Lee, Y. H. (2000). Voltage-clock-scaling adaptive scheduling techniques for low power in hard real-time systems. *Proceedings of the 6th IEEE Real-Time Technology and Applications Symposium* (pp. 156-165).

Krishnamurthy, B., & Wills, C. E. (2000, May 2000). *Analyzing factors that influence end-to-end web performance.* Paper presented at the Ninth International World Wide Web Conference, Amsterdam, Netherlands.

Kristoff, J. (2002). *TCP congestion control.* Retrieved from http://condor.depaul.edu/~jkristof

Kroner, H., Hebuterne, G., et al. (1991). Priority management in ATM switching nodes. *IEEE Journal on Selected Areas in Communications, 9*(3), 418-427.

Kumar, S., & Nanda, S. (1999, March). High data-rate packet communications for cellular networks using CDMA: Algorithms and performance. *IEEE Journal on Selected Areas in Communications, 17*(3), 472-492.

Kumaran, K., & Mitra, D. (1998). Performance and fluid simulations of a novel shared buffer management system. *Proceedings of IEEE INFOCOM.*

Kurkowski, S., Camp, T., & Colagrosso, M. (2005). *MANET Simulation Studies: The Incredibles.*

Kushner, H. J., & Clark, D. S. (1978). *Stochastic approximation for constrained and unconstrained systems.* Berlin, Germany: Springer-Verlag.

Kwan, R., Peter, C. H., Poutiainen, E., & Rinne, M. (2003). The effect of code-multiplexing on the high speed downlink packet access (HSDPA) in a WCDMA network. *Proceedings of IEEE WCNC '03.* New Orleans, LA, USA: IEEE.

Kwon, D., Kim, S. S., Park, C. Y., & Jung, C. I. (2005). Experiments on the energy saving and performance effects of IEEE 802.11 power saving mode (PSM). *Lecture Notes in Computer Science* (Vol. 3391, pp. 41-51).

Kwon, T., & Choi, Y. (2003). QoS provisioning in wireless/mobile multimedia networks using an adaptive framework. *Wireless Networks, 9*, 51-59.

Kyun, K. Y., & Prasad, R. (2006). *4G roadmap and emerging communication technologies.* Artech House.

Labrador, M. A., & Banerjee, S. (1999). Packet dropping policies for ATM and IP networks. *IEEE Communications Surveys & Tutorials, 2*(3), 2-14.

Lakshman, T. V., Neidhardt, A., et al. (1996). The drop from front strategy in TCP and in TCP over ATM. IN-FOCOM '96. The *15th Annual Joint Conference of the IEEE Computer Societies.*

Lamont, L., Wang, M., & Villasenor, L. (2003). Integrating WLANs & MANETs to the IPv6 based Internet. *Proceedings of IEEE International Conference on Communications* (Vol. 2, pp. 1090-1095), Anchorage, Alaska, USA.

Lang, D. (2003). *A comprehensive overview about selected ad hoc networking routing protocols.* München: Department of Computer Science, Technische Universität München.

Lapsley, D., & Low, S. (1999). Random early marking: An optimisation approach to Internet congestion control. 67-74.

Larzon, L., Degermark, M., & Pink, S. (1999). *UDP lite for real time multimedia applications.* HP Laboratories Bristol. Retrieved from http://www.hpl.hp.com

Larzon, L., Degermark, M., & Pink, S. (2004). The *lightweight user datagram protocol (UDP Lite), RFC 3828.* Retrieved from http://tools.ietf.org/html/rfc3828

Lavie, T., & Tractinsky, N. (2004). Assessing dimensions of perceived visual aesthetics of Web sites. *International Journal Human-Computer Studies, 60*(3), 269-298.

Lee, C. (1999). *On quality of service management*. PhD thesis. Carnegie Mellon University.

Lee, C., Lehoczky, J., Siewiorek, D., Rajkumar, R., & Hansen, J. (1999). *A scalable solution to the multi-resource QoS problem*. Paper presented at the 20th IEEE Real-Time Systems Symposium.

Lee, L., Gerla, M., Chen, J., Chen, J., Zhou, B., & Caruso, A. (2006). "Direction" forward routing for highly mobile ad hoc networks. *Ad Hoc & Sensor Wireless Networks*.

Lee, S. (2005). Low-power video decoding on a variable voltage processor for mobile multimedia applications. *ETRI Journal, 27*(5), 504-10.

Lee, S. B., Ahn, G. S., & Campbell, A. T. (2001). Improving UDP and TCP performance in mobile ad hoc networks withINSIGNIA. *Communications Magazine, IEEE, 39*(6), 156-165.

Lee, S. B., Ahn, G. S., Zhang, X., & Campbell, A. T. (2000). INSIGNIA: An IP-based quality of service framework for mobile ad hoc networks. *Journal of Parallel and Distributed Computing, 60*(4), 374-406.

Lee, Y. J., & Riley, G. F. (2005). *Dynamic nix-vector routing for mobile ad hoc networks*.

Lei, C., & Heinzelman, W. B. (2005). QoS-aware routing based on bandwidth estimation for mobile ad hoc networks. *IEEE Journal on Selected Areas in Communications, 23*(3), 561-572.

Lenders, V., May, M., & Plattner, B. (2005). Service discovery in mobile ad hoc networks: A field theoretic approach. *Pervasive and Mobile Computing, 1*(3), 343-370.

Le-Ngoc, T., & Mohammed, I. J. (1998). Performance analysis of CFDAMA-PB protocol for packet satellite communications. *IEEE Transactions on Communications, 46*, 1206-1214.

Le-Ngoc, T., Leung, V., Takats, P., & Garland, P. (2003). Interactive multimedia satellite access communication. *IEEE Communications Magazine, 41*(7), 78-85.

Leong, C., & Zhuang, W. (2001). *Call admission control for voice and data traffic in wireless communications*. Elsevier, computer communications.

Li, J., & Mohapatra, P. (2002). *PANDA: An Approach to Improve Flooding Based Route Discovery in Mobile Ad hoc Networks*: CSE.

Li, J., & Sampalli, S. (2006). QoS-guaranteed wireless packet scheduling for mixed services in HSDPA. *Proceedings of ACM/IEEE MSWiM '06*. Terromolinos, Spain: ACM Press.

Li, J., Blake, C., & De Couto, D. S. J. (2001). Capacity of ad hoc wireless networks. *Proceedings of ACM MOBICOM* (pp. 61-69), Rome, Italy.

Li, M., & Prabhakaran, B. (2004). Dynamic priority re-allocation scheme for providing quality of service in IEEE 802.11e WLANs. *Proceeding of SPIE/ACM Conference on Multimedia Computing and Networking* (pp. 83-94), Santa Clara, CA, USA.

Li, M., & Prabhakaran, B. (2005). MAC layer admission control and priority re-allocation for handling QoS guarantees in non-cooperative wireless LANs. *ACM/Springer Mobile Networks and Applications, 10*(6), 947-959.

Li, M., & Prabhakaran, B. (2005). On supporting reliable QoS in multi-hop multi-rate mobile ad hoc networks. *Proceedings of the 1ˢᵗ IEEE International Workshop on Next Generation Wireless Networks*, Goa, India.

Li, M., Prabhakaran, B., & Sathyamurthy, S. (2003). On flow reservation and admission control for distributed scheduling strategies in IEEE 802.11 wireless LANs. *Proceedings of the 6ᵗʰ ACM International Workshop on Modeling, Analysis and Simulation of Wireless and Mobile Systems* (pp. 108-115), San Diego, CA, USA.

Li, M., Zhu, H., Chlamtac, I., & Prabhakaran, B. (2006). End-to-end QoS framework for heterogeneous wired-cum-wireless networks. *ACM/Baltzer Wireless Networks, 12*(4), 439-450.

Li, Q., Aslam, J., & Rus, D. (2001). Online power-aware routing in wireless ad-hoc networks. *Proceedings of the*

Annual International Conference on Mobile Computing and Networking, MOBICOM (pp. 97-107).

Li, Y., & Ephremides, A. (2005). Simple rate control for fluctuating channels in ad hoc wireless networks. *IEEE Transactions on Communications, 53,* 1200-1209.

Liberal, F., Ferro, A., Jodra, J. L., & Fajardo, J. O. (2005). *Application of general perception-based QoS model to find providers' responsibilities. Case study: User perceived Web service performance.* Paper presented at the Joint International Conference on Autonomic and Autonomous Systems and International Conference on Networking and Services (ICAS/ICNS 2005), Tahiti.

Liebeherr, J. O. R., & Christin, N. (2001). JoBS: Joint buffer management and scheduling for differentiated services. *Lecture Notes in Computer Science, 2092,* 404.

Liebl, G., Jenkac, H., et al. (2005). Joint buffer management and scheduling for wireless video streaming. *Lecture Notes in Computer Science, 3420,* 882-891.

Liebl, G., Jenkac, H., et al. (2005). Radio link buffer management and scheduling for wireless video streaming. *Telecommunication Systems, 30*(1-3), 255-277.

Lin, A. Y. M., & Silvester, J. A. (1991). Priority queueing strategies and buffer allocation protocols for traffic control at an ATM integrated broadband switching system. *IEEE Journal on Selected Areas in Communications, 9*(9), 1524-1536.

Lin, C. R., & Gerla, M. (1997). *Asynchronous multimedia multihop wireless networks.*

Lin, P., Bensaou, B., Ding, Q. L., & Chua, K. C. (2000). A wireless fair scheduling algorithm for error-prone wireless channels. *Proceedings WoWMoM'2000* (pp. 11-20).

Lindgren, A., & Schelen, O. (2002). *Infrastructured ad hoc networks.* Paper presented at the Proceedings. International Conference on Parallel Processing Workshops.

Litjens, R., van den Berg, J. L., & Fleuren, M. J. (2005). Spatial traffic heterogeneity in HSDPA networks and its impact on network planning. *Proceedings of the*

19th International Teletraffic Congress. Bejing, China: Elsevier.

Liu, B., Guo, Y., et al. (1999). Fluid simulation of large scale networks: Issues and tradeoffs. *Proceedings of the International Conference on Parallel and Distributed Processing Techniques and Applications.*

Liu, C., & Arnett, K. P. (2000). Exploring the factors associated with Web site success in the context of electronic commerce. *Information and Management, 38,* 23-33.

Liu, J. S., & Lin, C. H. R. (2005). A relay-based MAC protocol for multi-rate and multi-range infrastructure wireless LANs. *Wireless Personal Communications, 34,* 7-28.

Liu, J., & Singh, S. (2001). ATCP: TCP for mobile ad hoc networks. *IEEE Journal on Selected Areas in Communications, 19*(7), 1300-1315.

Liu, P., Zhang, P., Jordan, S., & Honig, M. (2004). Single-cell forward link power allocation using pricing in wireless networks. *IEEE Transactions on Wireless Communications, 3,* 533-543.

Liu, X. (2002). *Opportunistic scheduling in wireless communication networks.* Unpublished doctoral dissertation, Purdue University.

Liu, Z., & Elzarki, M. (1994, May). SIR-based call admission control for DS-CDMA cellular systems. *IEEE Journal on Selected Areas in Telecommunications.*

Liu, Z., Karol, M. J., El Zarki, M., & Eng, K. Y. (1996). Channel access and interference issues in multicode DS-CDMA wireless packet (ATM) Networks. *Wireless Networks, 2,* 173-196.

Lo, C. C., & Lin, M. H. (1998). QoS provisioning in handoff algorithms for wireless LAN. *Proceedings of the International Zurich Seminar on Broadband Communications, Accessing, Transmission, Networking* (pp. 9-16), Zurich, Swissland.

Lou, X., Li, B., & Thng, I. (2002). An adaptive measured-based pre-assignment scheme with connection-level QoS support for mobile networks. *IEEE Transactions on Wireless Communication, 1*(3), 521-530.

Lu, L., Wang, Z., Bovik, A. C., & Kouloheris, J. (2002). *Full-reference video quality assessment considering structural distortion and no-reference quality evaluation of MPEG video*. Paper presented at the IEEE International Conference on Multimedia.

Lu, S., Bharghavan, V., & Srikant, R. (1999, Aug.). Fair scheduling in wireless packet networks. *IEEE/ACM Trans. Networking, 7*(4), 473-489.

Lu, Z., Lach, J., Stan, M., & Skadron, K. (2003). Reducing multimedia decode power using feedback control. *Proceedings 21st International Conference on Computer Design* (pp. 489-96).

Luna, C. E., Kondi, L. P., & Katsaggelos, A. K. (2003). Maximizing user utility in video streaming applications. *IEEE Transactions on Circuits and Systems for Video Technology, 13*(2), 141.

Lundberg, T., de Bruin, P., Bruhn, S., Hakansson, S., & Craig, S. (2005). Adaptive thresholds for AMR codec mode selection. In *IEEE 61st Vehicular Technology Conference (VTC 2005-Spring)*.

Lundevall, M., Olin, B., Olsson, J., Wiberg, N., Wänstedt, S., Eriksson, J., et al. (2004). Streaming applications over HSDPA in mixed service scenarios. *Proceedings of IEEE VTC Fall '04*. Los Angeles, CA, USA: IEEE.

Mäder, A., & Staehle, D. (2007). A flow-level simulation framework for HSDPA-enabled UMTS networks. *ACM/IEEE MSWiM '07*. Chania, Crete Island, Greece: ACM Press.

Mäder, A., Staehle, D., & Barth, H. (2007). A novel performance model for the HSDPA with adaptive resource allocation. *Proceedings of the 20th International Teletraffic Congress*. Ottawa, Canada: Springer.

Mäder, A., Staehle, D., & Spahn, M. (2007). Impact of HSDPA radio resource allocation schemes on the system performance of UMTS networks. *IEEE VTC Fall '07*. Baltimore, MY, USA: IEEE.

Mäder, A., Wagner, B., Hoßfeld, T., Staehle, D., & Barth, H. (2006). Measurements in a laboratory UMTS network with time-varying loads and different admission control strategies. *The 4th International Workshop on Internet Performance, Simulation, Monitoring and Measurement*. Salzburg, Austria: Springer.

Maguolo, F., Pellegrini, F. D., & Zanella, A. (2006). Cross-layer solutions to performance problems in VoIP over WLAN. *Proceedings of EURASIP EUSIPCO*, Florence, Italy.

Mahlke, S. (2002). Factors influencing the experience of Web site usage. *CHI '02 Extended Abstracts on Human Factors in Computing Systems* (pp. 846-847): ACM Press.

Makela, Ylianttila, J., & Pahlavan, M. (2000, Sept). Handoff decision in multi-service networks. *11th IEEE International Symposium on Personal, Indoor and Mobile Radio Communications (PIMRC)*.

Malinen, J. (2006). Host AP driver for Intersil Prism2/2.5/3, Hostapd, and WPA supplicant.

Maltz, D. A. (1999). *Resource Management in Multi-hop Ad Hoc Networks*.

Mangold, S., Choi, S., Hiertz, G. R., Klein, O., & Walke, B. (2003). Analysis of IEEE 802.11e for QoS Support in Wireless LANs. *IEEE Wireless Communication Magazine, 10*(6), 40-50.

Marchese, M. (2007). *QoS over heterogeneous networks*. John Wiley & Sons Ltd.

Markou, M. M., & Panayiotou, C. G. (2006). Dynamic control and optimization of buffer size in multiclass wireless networks. The *49th IEEE GLOBECOM Conference*.

Martin, T. (1999). *Balancing batteries, power, and performance: System issues in CPU speed-setting for mobile computing*. PhD thesis, Carnegie Mellon University, Pittsburgh, USA, August 1999.

Mascolo, S., Casetti, C., Gerla, M., Sanadidi, M., & Wang, R. (2001). TCP Westwood: Bandwidth estimation for enhanced transport over wireless links. *Proceedings ACM MOBICOM 2001*, Rome, Italy.

Masip-Bruin, X., Yannuzzi, M., Domingo-Pascual, J., Fonte, A., Curado, M., Monteiro, E., et al. (2006). Research challenges in QoS routing. *Computer Communications, 29*(5), 563-581.

Masuda, M., & Hayashi, T. (2006). Non-intrusive quality monitoring method of VoIP speech based on network performance metrics. In *IEICE Transactions Communications* (pp. 304-312).

McGovern, P., Murphy, S., & Murphy, L. (2006). Addressing the Link adaptation problem for VoWLAN using codec adaptation. In *IEEE Global Telecommunications Conference (GLOBECOM'06)*.

McGovern, P., Murphy, S., & Murphy, L. (2006). Protection against link adaptation for VoWLAN. In *Proceedings of the 15th IST Mobile and Wireless Communications Summit*.

McNair, J., & Zhu, F., (2004, June). Vertical handoffs in fourth-generation multinetwork environments. *IEEE Wireless Commun., 11*(3), 8-15.

McNair, J., Akyildiz, I. F., & Bender, M. (2000, March). An inter-system handoff technique for the IMT-2000 System. *Proceedings of IEEE INFOCOM 2000*, March 2000.

Meddahi, A., & Afifi, H. (2006). Packet E-model: E-model for VoIP quality evaluation. *Journal of Computer Networks*, 2659-2675.

Mesarina, M., & Turner, Y. (2003). Reduced energy decoding of MPEG streams. *Multimedia Systems, 9*(2), 202-13).

Michael, K., Birgitta, K., Nig, R., & Philipp, O. (2003). *Service rings--A semantic overlay for service discovery in ad hoc networks*. Paper presented at the Proceedings of the 14th International Workshop on Database and Expert Systems Applications.

Min, S., Jiandong, L., & Yan, S. (2003). Routing protocol with QoS guarantees for ad-hoc network. *Electronics Letters, 39*(1), 143-145.

Min, W., & Geng-Sheng, K. (2005). *An application-aware qos routing scheme with improved stability for multimedia applications in mobile ad hoc networks*.

Mirhakkak, M., Schult, N., & Thomson, D. (2000). *Dynamic quality-of-service for mobile ad hoc networks*.

Mishra, M. S. A., & Arbaugh, W. (2003). An empirical analysis of the IEEE 802.11 MAC layer handoff process. *ACM SIGCOMM Computer Communication Review, 33*(2), 93-102.

Misra, A., & Banerjee, S. (2002). *MRPC: maximizing network lifetime for reliable routing in wireless environments*.

Misra, V., Gong, W. B., et al. (2000). A fluid-based analysis of a network of AQM routers supporting TCP flows with an application to RED. *Proceedings of ACM SIGCOMM*.

MIT Roofnet Project. From http://pdos.csail.mit.edu/roofnet/

Miyazaki, A., Fukushima, H., Wiebke, T., Hakenberg, R., & Burmeister, C. (2001). *RTP payload type format to enable selective retransmissions*. Retrieved from http://www.cs.columbia.edu/~hgs/rtp/drafts/draft-miyazaki-avt-rtp-selret-00.txt

Mohapatra, P., Li, J., & Gui, C. (2003). QoS in mobile ad hoc networks. *IEEE wireless communications (IEEE wirel. commun.) ISSN 1536-1284*

Mohapatra, S., & Venkatasubramanian, N. (2003). PARM: Power aware reconfigurable middleware. *Proceedings, International Conference on Distributed Computing Systems* (pp. 312-319).

Mohapatra, S., Cornea, R., Dutt, N., Nicolau, A., & Venkatasubramanian, N. (2003). Integrated power management for video streaming to mobile handheld devices. *Proceedings of the 11th ACM International Conference on Multimedia* (pp. 582-591).

Monfort, J. Y. (2006). *Voice quality assessment, ITU-T Study Group 12*. Retrieved from http://www.etsi.org/plugtests/History/2006STQ_Asia/JYMonfort_SG12_QoSMeasurement.pdf

Moon, B., & Aghvami, A. H. (2004). Quality of service mechanisms in all-IP wireless access networks. *IEEE*

Journal on Selected Areas in Communications, 22(5), 873-888.

Moon, J. W., & Kim, Y. G. (2001). Extending the TAM for a World-Wide-Web context. *Information and Management, 38*(4), 217-230.

Mullin, J., Smallwood, L., Watson, A., & Wilson, G. (2001). *New techniques for assessing audio and video quality in real-time interactive communications.* Paper presented at the 3rd International Workshop on Human Computer Interaction, Lille, France.

Multicast Ad hoc On-Demand Distance Vector (MAODV) Routing, (2000).

Munoz, M. A., Rodriguez, M., Favela, J., Martinez-Garcia, A. I., Gonzalez, V. M. (2003). Context-aware mobile communication in hospitals. *IEEE Computer, 36*(9), 38-46.

Muntean, C. H., & McManis, J. (2004, June 20-24, 2004). *A QoS-aware adaptive Web-based system.* Paper presented at the IEEE International Conference on Communications.

Muntean, G. M., & Cranley, N. (2007). Resource efficient quality-oriented wireless broadcasting of adaptive multimedia content. Accepted, Special Issue on "Mobile Multimedia Broadcasting." *IEEE Transactions on Broadcasting, 53*(1), part II.

Murthy, C. S. R., & Manoj, B. S. (2004). *Ad Hoc Wireless Networks.* Prentice Hall International.

Myers, M. B. (2000), Predicting and measuring quality of service for mobile multimedia. *IEEE 3G Mobile Communication Technologies*, Conference Publication No. 471.

Nah, F. (2004). A study on tolerable waiting time: How long are Web users willing to wait? *Behaviour and Information Technology, 23*(3), 153-163(111).

Nam, D. H., & Park, S. K. (1999). Adaptive multimedia stream presentation in mobile computing environment. TENCON 99. *Proceedings of the IEEE Region 10 Conference.*

Nanda, S., Balachandran, K., & Kumar, S. (2000, Jan.). Adaptation techniques in wireless packet data services. *IEEE Communications Magazine*, 54-64.

Nandagopal, T., Lu, S., & Bharghavan, V. (2002). A unified architecture for the design and evaluation of wireless fair queueing algorithms. *Wireless Networks, 8*, 231-247.

Narbutt, M., & Pomy, J. (2007). The e-model based quality contours for predicting speech transmission quality and user satisfaction from time-varying transmission impairments. *Appendix I to ITU-T Recommendation G.109.*

Nasipuri, A., Zhuang, J., & Das, S. R. (1999), A multichannel CSMA MAC protocol for multihop wireless networks. *Proceedings of IEEE Wireless Communications and Networking Conference* (pp. 1402-1406), New Orleans, Louisiana, USA.

Nasser, N., & Hassanein, H., (2006). Radio resource management algorithms in wireless cellular networks. In A. Boukerch (Ed.), *Handbook of algorithms for wireless networking and mobile computing* (pp. 415-47). Chapman Hall, CRC Press.

National Statistics Website. (2006). *Social trends.* Retrieved January 10, 2006, from http://www.statistics.gov.uk/STATBASE/Expodata/Spreadsheets/D7202.xls

Necker, M. C. (2006). A comparison of scheduling mechanisms for service class differentiation in HSDPA networks. *AEÜ International Journal of Electronic Communication*, 136-141.

Ng, K. T., Chan, S. C., et al. (1996). Buffer control algorithm for low bit-rate video compression. *International Conference on Image Processing*, 1996.

Ni, Q., Romdhani, L., & Turletti, T. (2004). A survey of QoS enhancements for IEEE 802.11 wireless LAN. *Wiley Journal of Wireless Communications and Mobile Computing, 4*(5), 547-566.

Nichols, K., Blake, S., et al. (1998). Definition of the differentiated services field (DS Field) in the IPv4 and IPv6 Headers. *IETF RFC 2474.*

Nidd, M. (2001). Service discovery in DEAPspace. *Personal Communications, IEEE [see also IEEE Wireless Communications], 8*(4), 39-45.

Niebert, N., Schieder, A., Abramowicz, H., Malmgren, G., Sachs, J., Horn, U., et al. (2004). Ambient networks: An architecture for communication networks beyond *3G. IEEE Wireless Communications, 11*(2), 14-22.

Nikaein, N., & Bonnet, C. (2001). HARP-Hybrid Ad Hoc Routing Protocol.

Nikaein, N., Labiod, H., & Bonnet, C. (2000). *DDR-distributed dynamic routing algorithm for mobile ad hoc networks.* Paper presented at the Mobile and Ad Hoc Networking and Computing, 2000. MobiHOC. 2000 First Annual Workshop on

Noble, B., Satyanarayanan, M., Narayanan, D., Tilton, J., Flinn, J., & Walker, K. (1997). Agile application-aware adaptation for mobility. *Operating Systems Review, 31*(5), 276-87.

NS2. (2005). *Network Simulator,* release 2.28. Retrieved from http://www.isi.edu/nsnam/ns/

NS2. (2007). NS2. *The network simulator.* Retrieved from http://www.isi.edu/nsnam/ns/

NS-2: Network Simulator, Vers. 2.29. (2006). Available on-line at the URL: http://www.isi.edu/nsnam/ns/ns-build.html

Ohrtman, F. (2004). *Voice over 802.11.* Arthec House Inc. Press.

Okamoto, T., & Hayashi, T. (2002). *Analysis of service provider's profit by modeling customer's willingness to pay for IP QoS.* Paper presented at the Globecom 2002.

Olga, R., Dipanjan, C., Anupam, J., & Timothy, F. (2002). *Allia: Alliance-based service discovery for ad-hoc environments.* Paper presented at the Proceedings of the 2nd international workshop on Mobile commerce.

Olshefski, D., & Nieh, J. (2006). Understanding the management of client perceived response time. *SIGMETRICS Perform. Eval. Rev., 34*(1), 240-251.

Olson, T. (1994). *In a framework about task-technology fit, what are the tasks features.* Paper presented at the CSCW '94: Workshop on video mediated communication: Testing, Evaluation & Design Implications, North Carolina, US.

Oodan, A. P., Ward, K. E., & Mullee, A. W. (1997). *Quality of service in telecommunications.* The IEE press.

OPNET. (2007). *OPNET* [http://www.opnet.com/].

Optimized Link State Routing Protocol (OLSR), (2003).

Ott, J., Wenger, S., Sato, N., Burmeister, C., & Rey, J. (2004). *Extended RTP profile for RTCP-based feedback (RTP/AVPF).* Internet Engineering Task Force. Technical report, Internet Draft.

P800 Rec. (1996). *P. 800: Methods for subjective determination of transmission quality.* International Telecommunications Union (ITU-T) Recommendation.

Pakdeepaiboonpol, P., & Kittitornkun, S. (2005). Energy optimization for mobile MPEG-4 video decoder. *Mobile Technology, Applications, and Systems, the 2nd International Conference on* (pp. 1-6), November 2005.

Panayiotou, C. G., & Markou, M. M. (2007). Perturbation analysis for stochastic fluid models with respect to parameters of the fluid arrival process. *European Control Conference (ECC'07),* Kos, Greece.

Panayiotou, C. G., Cassandras, C. G., et al. (2004). Control of communication networks using infinitesimal perturbation analysis of stochastic fluid models. In S. Tarbouriech, C. T. Abdallah, & J. Chiasson (Eds.), *Lecture notes in control and information sciences (LCNCIS): Advances in communication control networks.* Springer-Verlag.

Pantel, L., & Wolf, L. C. (2002). *On the impact of delay on real-time multiplayer games.* Miami, FL: ACM Press.

Papadimitriou, P., & Tsaoussidis, V. (2006). Performance evaluation of real-time transport with link-layer retransmissions in wired/wireless networks. *Journal of Mobile Multimedia, Rinton Press, 2*(4), 327-343.

Papadimitriou, P., & Tsaoussidis, V. (2007). SSVP: A congestion control scheme for real-time video streaming. *Computer Networks, Elsevier, 51*(15), 4377-4395.

Papadimitriou, P., Tsaoussidis, V., & Tsekeridou, S. (2005). The impact of network and protocol heterogeneity on application QoS. *Proceedings 10th IEEE International Symposium on Computers and Communications (ISCC)*, Cartagena, Spain.

Papadimitriou, P., Tsaoussidis, V., & Zhang, C. (2007). Enhancing video streaming delivery over wired/wireless networks. *Proceedings 13th European Wireless Conference (EW 2007)*, Paris, France.

Parasuraman, A., Berry, L. L., & Zeithaml, V. A. (1988). SERVQUAL: A multiple-item scale for measuring consumer perceptions of service quality. *Journal of Retailing, 64*(1), 12-40.

Parasuraman, A., Zeithaml, V. A., & Berry, L. L. (1985). A conceptual model of service quality and its implications for future research. *Journal of Marketing, 49*(4).

Parasuraman, A., Zeithaml, V. A., & Berry, L. L. (1991). Refinement and reassessment of the SERVQUAL scale. *Journal of Retailing, 67*(4), 420-450.

Park, H., Yoon, S., & Kim, T. (2002). Vertical handoff procedure and algorithm between IEEE 802.11 WLAN and CDMA cellular network. *Proceedings of Mobile Communications: 7th CDMA International Conference*, Seoul, Korea.

Park, S. et al. (2003). Collaborative QoS architecture between DiffServ and 802.11e wireless LAN. *VTC 2003, 2*, pp. 945-949.

Park, S., Kim, K., & Kim, D. C. (2003). Collaborative QoS architecture between DiffServ and 802.11e wireless LAN. *Proceedings of IEEE VTC'03-Spring* (Vol. 2, pp. 945-949), Jeju, Korea.

Park, V. D., & Corson, M. S. (1997). *A highly adaptive distributed routing algorithm for mobile wireless networks.*

Park, V., & Corson, S. (2001). *Temporally-ordered routing algorithm (TORA) Version 1 Functional Specification.*

Retrieved from http://www.ietf.org/internet-drafts/draft-ietf-manet-tora-spec-04.txt

Párraga, C., Kissling, C., & Lutz, E. (2005). Design and performance evaluation of efficient scheduling techniques for second generation DVB-S systems. In *The 23rd AIAA International Communications Satellite System Conference (ICSSC-2005)*. Rome, Italy.

Parsons, J. D. (2001). *The mobile radio propagation channel (2nd ed)*. WILEY Ed.

Part 11: Wireless LAN Medium Access Control (MAC) and Physical Layer (PHY) Specifications, (1999).

Pasricha, S., Mohapatra, S., Luthra, M., Dutt, N., & Venkatasubramanian, N. (2003). Reducing backlight power consumption for streaming video applications on mobile handheld devices. *ACM/IEEE/IFIP Workshop on Embedded Systems for Real-Time Multimedia* (pp. 11-17).

Patrick, A. S., Singer, J., Corrie, B., Noel, S., El Khatib, K., Emond, B., Zimmerman, T., & Marsh, S. (2004). A QoE sensitive architecture for advanced collaborative environments. *Proceedings of the 1st International Conference on Quality of Service in Heterogeneous Wired/Wireless Networks* (pp. 319-322). IEEE.

Pätzold, M., & Laue, F. (1998, July). Level-crossing rate and average duration of fades of deterministic simulation models for rice fading channels. *IEEE Tran. On Vehicular Technology, 48*(4).

Pätzold, M., Killat, U., Laue, F. & Li, Y. (1998, Feb.). On the statistical properties of deterministic simulation models for mobile fading channels. *IEEE Transactions on Vehicular Technology, 47*(1), 254-269.

Paxson, V. (1999). End-to-end packet dynamics. *IEEE/ACM Transactions on Networking, 7*(3), 277-292.

Pedersen, K. I., & Michaelsen, P. H. (2006). Algorithms and performance results for dynamic HSDPA resource allocation. *IEEE VTC Fall '06*. Montreal, CA: IEEE.

Pedersen, K. I., Lootsma, T. F., Stottrup, M., Frederikson, F., Kolding, T. E., & Mogensen, P. E. (2004). Network performance of mixed traffic on high speed downlink packet access and dedicated channels in WCDMA. *IEEE VTC Fall '04*. Los Angeles, CA, USA: IEEE.

Pedersen, K. I., Mogensen, P. E., & Kolding, T. E. (2006). Overview of QoS options for HSDPA. *IEEE Communications Magazine, 44*(7), 100-105.

Pei, G., Gerla, M., Hong, X., & Chiang, C. C. (1999). *A wireless hierarchical routing protocol with group mobility.*

Perkins, C. E., & Belding-Royer, E. M. (2003). Quality of service for ad hoc on-demand distance vector routing. *Internet Draft, draft-perkins-manet-aodvqos-02.txt.*

Perkins, C. E., & Bhagwat, P. (1994). Highly dynamic destination sequenced distance vector routing (DSDV) for mobile computers. *Proceedings of ACM SIGCOMM* (pp. 234-244), London, UK.

Perkins, C. E., Belding-Royer, E. M., & Chakeres, I. (2003). Ad hoc on demand distance vector (AODV) routing. *IETF Internet draft, draft-perkins-manet-aodvbis-00.txt.*

Pi, R., Song, J., et al. (2004). An integrated scheduling and buffer management scheme for packet-switched routers.

Picovici, D., & Mahdi, A. E. (2004). New output-based perceptual measure for predicting subjective quality of speech. *IEEE International Conference on Acoustics, Speech, and Signal Processing* (pp. 633-636).

Picovici, D., Mahdi, A. E., & Murphy, T. (in press). New output-based objective measure for non-intrusive speech quality evaluation. *Digital Signal Processing Journal.* Elsevier.

Picovici, D., Raja, A., & Flanagan, C. (2006). Real-time non-intrusive VoIP evaluation using second generation network processor. *IEEE International Conference on Acoustic, Speech, and Signal Processing Proceedings,* published on DVD, IEEE Cat No.:06CH37812C.

Pillai, P., & Shin, K. G. (2002). Real-time dynamic voltage scaling for low power embedded operating systems. *ACM Operating Systems Review, 35*(5), 89-102.

Pilosof, S., Ramjee, R., Raz, D., Shavitt, Y., & Sinha, P. (2003). *Understanding TCP fairness over wireless LAN.* Paper presented at the INFOCOM 2003. The 22nd Annual Joint Conference of the IEEE Computer and Communications Societies.

Pong, D., & Moor T. (2003). Call admission control for IEEE 802.11 contention access mechanism. *Proceedings of IEEE GLOBECOM* (Vol. 1, pp. 174-178), San Francisco, California, USA.

Postel, J. (1980). *User datagram protocol, RFC 768.* Retrieved from http://www.ibiblio.org/pub/docs/rfc/rfc768.txt

Pouwelse, J., Langendoen, K., & Sips, H. (2003). Application-directed voltage scaling. *IEEE Transactions on Very Large Scale Integration (VLSI) Systems, 11*(5), 812-826.

Prabhakar, B., Biyikoglu, E., & El Gamal, A. (2001). Energy-efficient transmission over a wireless link via lazy packet scheduling. *Proceedings IEEE INFOCOM* (Vol. 1, pp. 386-394).

Prasad, A. R., Esmailzadeh, R., Winkler, S., Ihara, T., Rohani, B., Pinguet, B., et al. (2001). *Perceptual quality measurement and control: Definition, application, and performance.* Paper presented at the 4th International Symposium on Wireless Personal Multimedia Communications, Aalborg, Denmark.

Qiang Ni, L. R. T. T. (2004). A survey of QoS enhancements for IEEE 802.11 wireless LAN (Vol. 4, pp. 547-566).

Qiao, Z., Sun, L., Heilemann, N., & Ifeachor, E. (2004). A new method for VoIP quality of service control use combined adaptive sender rate and priority marking. In *IEEE International Conference on Communications.*

Quackenbush, S. R., Barnawell, T. P., & Clements, M. A. (1988). *Objective measures of speech quality.* Prentice Hall Press.

Quality of Service for Ad hoc On-Demand Distance Vector Routing, (2001).

Quality of Service for Ad hoc Optimized Link State Routing Protocol (QOLSR), (2006).

Quatieri, T. E. (2002). *Discrete-time speech signal processing: Principles and practice.* Prentice Hall Press.

R.John. (1999). *UpnP, Jini and Salutation. A Look at some popular Coordination Frameworks for Future Network Devices*: California software Labs.

Raake, A. (2006). *Speech quality of VoIP assessment and prediction.* John Wiley & Sons, Ltd Press.

Radhakrishnan, S., Racherla, G., Sekharan, C. N., Rao, N. S. V., & Batsell, S. G. (1999). *DST-A routing protocol for ad hoc networks using distributed spanning trees.*

Raju, J., & Garcia-Luna-Aceves, J. J. (1999). *A new approach to on-demand loop-free multipath routing.*

Rakocevic, V. (2004). Congestion control for multimedia applications in the wireless Internet. *International Journal of Communication Systems, 17*, 723-734) (DOI: 10.1002/dac.662)

Raman, B. (2006). Channel allocation in 802.11-based mesh networks. *Proceedings of IEEE INFOCOM* (pp. 1-10), Barcelona, Spain.

Ramanathan, P., & Agrawal, P. (1998). Adapting packet fair queueing algorithms to wireless networks. *Proceedings MOBICOM'98* (1-9).

Ramjee, R., Nagarajan, R., & Towsley, D. (1996). On optimal call admission control in cellular networks. *Proceedings of IEEE Infocom'96.*

Ramsay, J., Barbesi, A., & Preece, J. (1998). A psychological investigation of long retrieval times on the World Wide Web. *Interacting with Computers, 10*(1), 77-86(10).

Ranganathan, C., & Shobha, G. (2002). Key dimensions of business-to-consumer Web sites. *Information and Management, 39*, 457-465.

Reddy, T. B., Karthigeyan, I., et al. (2006). Quality of service provisioning in ad hoc wireless networks: A survey of issues and solutions. *Elsevier Ad Hoc Networks, 4*, 83-124.

Rejaie, R., Handley, M., & Estrin, D. (1999). RAP: An end-to-end rate-based congestion control mechanism for realtime streams in the Internet. *Proceedings IEEE INFOCOM 1999*, New York, USA.

Richards, A., Rogers, G., Antoniades, M., & Witana, V. (1998, Nov). *Mapping user level QoS from a single parameter.* Paper presented at the International Conference on Multimedia Networks and Services (MMNS '98).

Riva, O., Saarto, J., & Kojo, M. (2004). *Performance analysis on HTTP traffic and traffic mixtures with competing TCP and UDP flows.* University of Helsinki - Department of Computer Science.

Rix, A. W., & Hollier, M. P. (2000). The perceptual analysis measurement system for robust end-to-end speech quality assessment. *IEEE International Conference on Acoustics, Speech, and Signal Processing* (pp. 1-4).

Rix, A., Beerends, J. G., Kim, D. S., Kroon, P., & Ghitza, O. (2006). Objective assessment of speech and audio quality-technology and applications. *IEEE Transactions on Audio, Speech, and Language Processing* (pp. 1890-1901).

Roach, A. (2001). *SIP-specific event notification.* draft-sip-events-00 (work in progress), July.

Romdhani, L., Ni, Q., & Turletti, T. (2003). Adaptive EDCF: Enhanced service differentiation for IEEE 802.11 wireless ad hoc networks. *IEEE Wireless Communications and Networking Conference* (Vol. 2, pp. 1373-1378), New Orleans, USA.

Romero, J. P., Sallent, O., Agusti, R., & Diaz-Guerra, M. A. (2005). *Radio resource management strategies in UMTS.* John Wiley & Sons.

Rosenberg, J., Schulzrinne, H., Camarillo, G., Johnston, A., Peterson, J., Sparks, R., Handley, M., & Schooler, E. (1998). *SIP: Session Initiation Protocol.*

Rubin, I., & Liu, Y. C. (2003). *Link stability models for QoS ad hoc routing algorithms.*

Sachs, J., Wiemann, H., Lundsjo, J., & Magnusson, P. (2004). Integration of multi-radio access in a beyond

3G network. *IEEE Personal, Indoor, and Mobile Radio Communications, 15th PIMRC.*

Sailhan, F., & Issarny, V. (2005). *Scalable Service Discovery for MANET.*

Saliba, A. J., Beresford, M. A., Ivanovich, M., & Fitzpatrick, P. (2005). User-perceived quality of service in wireless data networks. *Personal Ubiquitous Comput., 9*(6), 413-422.

Samaraweera, N. K. G., & Fairhurst, G. (1998). Reinforcement of TCP error recovery for wireless communication. *ACM SIGCOMM Computer Communication Review, 28*(2), 30-38.

Sanzgiri, K., Chakeres, I. D., & Belding-Royer, E. M. (2004). Determining intra-flow contention along multihop paths in wireless networks. *Proceedings of IEEE BROADNETS Wireless Networking Symposium* (pp. 611-620), San Jose, CA.

Sasikanth, A., Anupam, J., & Timothy, F. (2002). Enhanced service discovery in bluetooth (Vol. 35, pp. 96-99): IEEE Computer Society Press.

SatLab. (November, 2006). *SatLab system recommendations v2 QoS.* Web site with URL: http://satlabs.org/

Schaar, M., & Turaga, D. S. (2007). Cross-layer packetization and transmission strategies for delay-sensitive wireless multimedia transmission. *IEEE Transactions on Multimedia, 9*(1).

Schaefer, C., Enderes, T., Ritter, H., & Zitterbart, M. (2002, April 2002). *Subjective quality assessment for multiplayer realtime games.* Paper presented at the Workshop on Network and System Support for Games.

Schubert, P. (2003). Evaluation of electronic commerce applications from the customer's viewpoint. *International Journal of Electronic Commerce, 7.*

Schubert, P. D. W. (2002, January 07-10). *Extended Web assessment method (EWAM): Evaluation of e-commerce applications from the customer's viewpoint.* Paper presented at the 35th Annual Hawaii International Conference on System Sciences (HICSS'02), Big Island, Hawaii.

Schubert, P., & Dettling, W. (2001). *Web site evaluation: Do Web applications meet user expectations? Music, consumer goods and e-banking on the test bed.* Paper presented at the 14th International Bled Electronic Commerce Conference, Bled, Slovenia.

Schubert, P., & Leimstoll, U. (2001). *The extended Web assessment method (EWAM) applied: Do Web sites for consumer goods stand the test?* Paper presented at the Eighth Research Symposium on Emerging Electronic Markets RSEEM 01, Maastricht, The Netherlands.

Schulzrinne, H., Casner, S., Frederick, R., & Jacobson, V. (1996). *RTP: A transport protocol for real-time applications, RFC 1889.* Retrieved from http://www.freesoft.org/CIE/RFC/1889/13.htm

Schulzrinne, H., Casner, S., Frederick, R., & Jacobson, V. (2003). *RTP: A transport protocol for real-time applications, RFC 3550.* Retrieved from http://www.ietf.org/rfc/rfc3550.txt?number=3550

Schulzrinne, H., Rao, A., et al. (1998). Real Time Streaming Protocol (RTSP).

Sears, A., Jacko, J. A., & Borella, M. S. (1997). *Internet delay effects: How users perceive quality, organization, and ease of use of information.* Atlanta, GA: ACM Press.

Seeling, P., Reisslein, M., & Kulapala, B. (2004). Network performance evaluation using frame size and quality traces of single layer and two layer video: A tutorial. *IEEE Communications Surveys & Tutorials, 6*(3), 58-78.

Seet, B. C., Liu, G., Lee, B. S., Foh, C. H., Wong, K. J., & Lee, K. K. (2004). A-STAR: A Mobile Ad Hoc Routing Strategy for Metropolis Vehicular Communications: Springer.

Selz, D., & Schubert, P. (1997). Web assessment: A model for the evaluation and the assessment of successful electronic commerce applications. *Electronic Markets, 7*(3).

Servetti, A., & De Martin, J. (2003). Adaptive interactive speech transmission over 802.11 wireless LANs.

In *Proceedings of the IEEE International Workshop on DSP in mobile and Vehicular Systems.*

Sevcik, P. J. (2002). Understanding how users view application performance. *Business Communication Reviews--Net Forecasts, 32*(7).

Sfairopoulou, A., Macián, C., & Bellalta, B. (2006). QoS adaptation in SIP-based VoIP calls in multi-rate 802.11 environments. In *ISWCS 2006*, Valencia, Spain.

Shah, R. C., & Rabaey, J. M. (2002). *Energy aware routing for low energy ad hoc sensor networks.*

Shah, S. H., Chen, K., & Nahrstedt, K. (2004). Dynamic bandwidth management for single-hop ad hoc wireless networks. *ACM/Kluwer Mobile Networks and Applications, Special Issue on Algorithmic Solutions for Wireless, Mobile, Ad Hoc and Sensor Networks, 10*(1-2), 199-217.

Shakkottai, S., & Stolyra, A. L. (2001). Scheduling algorithms for a mixture of real-time and non-real-time data in HDR. *Proceedings of the 17ᵗʰ International Teletraffic Congress.* Salvador da Bahia, Brazil: Elsevier.

Shakkottai, S., Rappaport, T. S., & Karlsson, P. C. (2003, Oct.). Cross-layer design for wireless networks. *IEEE Communications Magazine, 41*(10), 74-80.

Shankar, S., & Choi, S. (2002). QoS signaling for parameterized traffic in IEEE 802.11e wireless LANS. *Lecture Notes in Computer Science, Vol. 2402*, 67-84.

Sheldon, N., Girard, E., Borg, S., Claypool, M., & Agu, E. (2003). *The effect of latency on user performance in Warcraft III.* Paper presented at the 2ⁿᵈ Workshop on Network and System Support for Games. Redwood City, California.

Shigang, C., & Nahrstedt, K. (1999). Distributed quality-of-service routing in ad hoc networks. *IEEE Journal on Selected Areas in Communications, 17*(8), 1488-1505.

Shim, H., Chang, N., & Pedram, M. (2004). A backlight power management framework for battery-operated multimedia systems. *IEEE Design and Test of Computers, 21*(5), 388-396.

Shin, M., Lee, S., & Kim, Y. (2006). Distributed channel assignment for multi-radio wireless networks. *Proceedings of International Conference on Mobile Adhoc and Sensor Systems* (pp. 417-426), Vancouver, Canada.

Shin, S., Forte, A., & Rawat, A. (2004). Reducing MAC layer handoff latency in IEEE 802.11 wireless LANs. *Proceeding of ACM MobiWAC* (pp. 19-26), Philadelphia, Pennsylvania, USA.

Shree, M., & Garcia-Luna-Aceves, J. J. (1996). An efficient routing protocol for wireless networks. *Mob. Netw. Appl. %@ 1383-469X, 1*(2), 183-197.

Shuping, R. (2003). A model for web services discovery with QoS (Vol. 4, pp. 1-10): ACM Press.

Siller, M., & Woods, J. (2003). Improving quality experience for multimedia services by QoS arbitration on a QoE framework. *Proceedings of the 13ᵗʰ Packed Video Workshop 2003*, Nantes, France.

Simcock, T., Hillenbrand, S. P., & Thomas, B. H. (2003). Developing a location based tourist guide application. *Australasian Information Security Workshop Conference on ACSW Frontiers* (Vol. 21, pp. 177-183).

Sinha, A., & Chandrakasan, A. (2000). Energy aware software. *VLSI Design 2000, Proceedings of 13ᵗʰ International Conference on VLSI Design* (pp. 50-55).

Sinha, P., Venkitaraman, N., Sivakumar, R., & Bharghavan, V. (1999). WTCP: A reliable transport protocol for wireless wide-area networks. *Proceedings ACM MOBICOM '99*, Seattle, Washington, USA.

Sirisena, H., Haider, A., et al. (2002). Auto-tuning RED for accurate queue control. *Global Telecommunications Conference, 2002. GLOBECOM '02. IEEE.*

Sivakumar, R., Sinha, P., & Bharghavan, V. (1999). CEDAR: A core-extraction distributed ad hoc routing algorithm. *IEEE Journal on Selected Areas in Communications, 17*(8), 1454-1465.

Skehill, R., Barry, M., O'Callaghan, M., Gawley, N., Kent, W., & McGrath, S. (2007). Common RRM approach to admission control for converged heterogeneous wireless networks. *Special Issue of IEEE Wireless Communica-*

tions Magazine on Technologies on Future Converged Wireless and Mobility Platform.

Skinnemoen, H., Vermesan, A., Iuoras, A., Adams, G., & Lobao, X. (2005). VoIP over DVB-RCS with QoS and bandwidth on demand. *IEEE Wireless Communications, 12*(5), 46-53.

So, J., & Vaodya, N. (2004). Multi-channel MAC for ad hoc networks: Handling multi-channel hidden terminals using a single transceiver. *Proceedings of ACM MobiHoc* (pp. 222-233), Roppongi, Japan.

Song, G., & Yang, O. W. (2002). *Performance of backup source routing in mobile ad hoc networks.*

Song, L., & Mandayam, N. B. (2001). Hierarchical SIR and rate control on the forward link for CDMA data users under delay and error constraints. *IEEE Journal on Selected Areas in Communications, 19*, 1871-1882.

Sooriyabandara, M., & Fairhurst, G. (2003). Dynamics of TCP over BoD satellite networks. *International Journal of Satellite Communications and Networking, 21*, 427-449.

Staehle, D., & Mäder, A. (2007). A model for time-efficient HSDPA simulations. *IEEE VTC Fall '07.* Baltimore, MY, USA: IEEE.

Stanislaus, W., Fairhurst, G., & Radzik, J. (2005, September). *Cross layer techniques for flexible transport protocol using UDP-Lite over a satellite network.* Paper presented at the 2nd International Symposium Wireless Communication Systems, Siena, Italy.

Std. 802.11 (1999). *Wireless LAN medium access control (MAC) and physical layer (PHY) specifications.* IEEE Std 802.11.

Std. 802.11e (2005). *Wireless LAN medium access control (MAC) and physical layer (PHY) specifications; Amendment: Medium access control(MAC) quality of service enhancements.* IEEE Std 802.11e.

Stefano, B., Imrich, C., Violet, R. S., & Barry, A. W. (1998). *A distance routing effect algorithm for mobility (DREAM).* Paper presented at the Proceedings of the 4th

Annual ACM/IEEE International Conference on Mobile Computing and Networking.

Stemm, M., & Katz, R. (1997). Measuring and reducing energy consumption of network interfaces in hand-held devices. *IEICE Transactions on Communications,* E80-B, pp. 1125-1131, August 1997.

Stevens, W. (1997). TCP slow start, congestion avoidance, fast retransmit, and fast recovery algorithms. *RFC 2001.*

Stine, J. A., & de Veciana, G. (2004). A paradigm for quality-of-service in wireless ad hoc networks using synchronous signaling and node states. *IEEE Journal on Selected Areas in Communications, 22*(7), 1301-1321.

Sun, G., Cassandras, C. G., et al. (2004). Perturbation analysis of multiclass stochastic fluid models. *Journal of Discrete Event Dynamic Systems: Theory and Applications, 14*(3), 267-307.

Sun, L., & Ifeachor, E. (2006). Voice quality prediction models and their application in VoIP networks. *IEEE Transactions on Multimedia, 8*(4), 809-820.

Svoboda, P., & Rupp, M. (2005). *Online gaming models for wireless networks.* Paper presented at the 9th IASTED International Conference, Internet and Multimedia Systems and Applications, Grindelwald, Switcherland.

Tafazolli, L. H. I. A. R. (2007). A survey of QoS routing solutions for mobile ad hoc networks.

Taivalsaari, A., (1999) *The event horizon user interface model for small devices* (Tech. Report No. SMLI TR-99-74). Sun Microsystems.

Takahashi, A., & Yoshino, H. (2004). Perceptual QoS assessment technologies for VoIP. *IEEE Communications Magazine, 42*(7), 28-34.

Takahashi, A., Kurashima, A., & Yoshino, H. (2006). Objective assessment methodology for estimating conversational quality in VoIP. *IEEE Transactions on Audio, Speech, and Language Processing* (pp. 1984-1993).

Takahata, K., Uchida, N., et al. (2004). Optimal data rate control for video stream transmission over wireless network. *18ᵗʰ International Conference on Advanced Information Networking and Applications*, 2004. AINA 2004.

Talucci, F., Gerla, M., & Fratta, L. (1997). *MACA-BI (MACA By Invitation)--A receiver oriented access protocol for wireless multihop networks*. Paper presented at the The 8th IEEE International Symposium on Personal, Indoor, and Mobile Radio Communications, 1997. 'Waves of the Year 2000'. PIMRC '97.

Tasaka, S. (Ed.). (1986). *Performance analysis of multiple access protocols*. MIT Press.

Taylor, L., Titmus, R., & Lebre, C. (1999). The challenges of seamless handover in future mobile multimedia networks. *IEEE Personal Communications*, Special Issue on "Advanced Mobile Communication Systems – Managing Complexity in a Competitive and Seamless Environment."

TeleManagement Forum. (2005). Enhanced Telecom Operations Map (eTOM): The business process framework for the information and communications services industry, Release 6 v6.1, *TeleManagement Forum GB921*.

Temporally-Ordered Routing Algorithm (TORA) Version 1, (2001).

The Adaptive Demand-Driven Multicast Routing Protocol for Mobile Ad Hoc Networks (ADMR), (2001).

The Interzone Routing Protocol (IERP) for Ad Hoc Networks, (2002).

The Intrazone Routing Protocol (IARP) for Ad Hoc Networks, (2002).

The Zone Routing Protocol (ZRP) for Ad Hoc Networks, (2002).

Tian, Y., Xu, K., & Ansari, N. (2005). TCP in wireless environments: Problems and solutions. *Communications Magazine, IEEE, 43*(3), S27-S32.

Toh, C. K., Guichal, G., & Bunchua, S. (2000a). *ABAM: On-demand associativity-based multicast routing for ad hoc mobile networks*.

Toh, C. K., Vassiliou, V., Guichal, G., & Shih, C. H. (2000b). *MARCH: A medium access control protocol for multihop wireless ad hoc networks*. Paper presented at the MILCOM 2000. 21st Century Military Communications Conference Proceedings.

Tong, L., & Ramanathan, P. (2004). Adaptive power and rate allocation for service curve assurance in DS-CDMA network. *IEEE Transactions on Wireless Communications, 3*(2), 555-564.

Topology Dissemination Based on Reverse-Path Forwarding (TBRPF), (2004).

Trad, A., Ni, Q., & Afifi, H. (2004). Adaptive VoIP transmission over heterogeneous wired/wireless networks. *Lecture Notes in Computer Science, 3311* (pp. 25–36). Springer.

Transmission Control Protocol (TCP). *Transmission control protocol, darpa internet program protocol specification, September 1981, RFC 793*. Retrieved from http://www.ibiblio.org/pub/docs/rfc[/rfc793.txt

Triantafyllopoulou, D. K., Passas, N., & Kaloxylos, A. (2007, April). *A cross-layer optimization mechanism for multimedia traffic over IEEE 802.16 networks*. Paper presented at 13ᵗʰ European Wireless Conference, Paris, France.

Tripathi, S. K., & Krunz, M. (1997, June). On the characterization of VBR MPEG streams. *ACM-SIGMETRICS Conference on Measurement and Modeling of Computer Systems, Performance Evaluation Review 25*, Seattle WA. USA.

Tsao, S. L., & Lin, C. C. (2002). Design and evaluation of UMTS-WLAN interworking strategies. *Vehicular Technology Conference, 56th IEEE VTC*.

Tsaoussidis, V., & Badr, H. (2000). TCP-probing: Towards an error control schema with energy and throughput performance gains. *Proceedings 8ᵗʰ IEEE International Conference on Network Protocols*, Osaka, Japan.

Tsaoussidis, V., & Matta, I. (2002). Open issues on TCP for mobile computing. *Journal of Wireless Communications and Mobile Computing, 2*(1), 3-20.

Tsaoussidis, V., & Zhang, C. (2002). TCP Real: Receiver-oriented congestion control. *Computer Networks, Elsevier, 40*(4), 477-497.

Tsaoussidis, V., & Zhang, C. (2005). The dynamics of responsiveness and smoothness in heterogeneous networks. *IEEE Journal on Selected Areas in Communications (JSAC), 23*(6), 1178-1189.

Tschudin, C., Gold, R., Rensfelt, O., & Wibling, O. (2004). LUNAR: a Lightweight Underlay Network Ad-hoc Routing Protocol and Implementation.

Tsu-Wei, C., & Gerla, M. (1998). *Global state routing: a new routing scheme for ad-hoc wireless networks.*

TV-Anytime. (2003). *TV anytime forum Web site.* Retrieved June 15, 2003, from http://www.tv-anytime.org

Understanding Web Services: XML, WSDL, SOAP, and UDDI. (2002). Addison-Wesley Longman Publishing Co., Inc.

Vaduvur, B., Alan, D., Scott, S., & Lixia, Z. (1994). *MACAW: A media access protocol for wireless LAN's.* Paper presented at the Proceedings of the Conference on Communications Architectures, Protocols and Applications.

Vaidya, N. H., Bahl, P., & Gupta, S. (2000). Distributed fair scheduling in wireless LAN. *Proceedings of ACM MOBICOM* (pp. 167-178), Boston, USA.

Valaee, S., & Li, B. (2002). Distributed call admission control in wireless ad hoc networks. *Proceedings of IEEE Vehicular Technology Conference* (Vol. 2, pp. 1244-1248), Vancouver, British Columbia.

Valera, A., Seah, W. K. G., & Rao, S. V. (2002). *CHAMP: A highly-resilient and energy-efficient routing protocol for mobile ad hoc networks.*

van der Heijden, H. (2003). Factors influencing the usage of Web sites: The case of a generic portal in The Netherlands. *Information and Management, 40*(6), 541-549.

van der Mei, R. D. (2004). *Performance analysis of communication networks.* Course syllabus, Faculty of Science: Vrije Universiteit.

Varadhan, K., Estrin, D., & Floyd, S. (1998). *Impact of network dynamics on end-to-end protocols: case studies in reliable multicast.*

Varshavsky, A., Reid, B., & de Lara, E. (2005). *A cross-layer approach to service discovery and selection in MANETs.* Paper presented at the Mobile Adhoc and Sensor Systems Conference, 2005. IEEE International Conference.

Veaux, C., & Barriac, V. (2002). Perceptually motivated non-intrusive assessment of speech quality. In *Proceedings On-line Workshop on Measurement of Speech and Audio Quality in Networks.* Retrieved from http://wireless.feld.cvut.cz/mesaqin 2002/full11.pdf

Verma, R., Iyer, A., et al. (2003). Towards an adaptive RED algorithm for achieving delay-loss performance. *Communications, IEE Proceedings.*

Viswanath, P., Tse, D., & Laroia, R. (2002). Opportunistic beamforming using dumb antennas. *IEEE Transaction on Information Theory, 48*(6), 1277-1294.

Voran, S. (1994). Techniques for comparing objective and subjective speech quality tests. *Proc. IEEE Workshop on Speech Quality Assessment* (pp. 59-64).

Voran, S. (1999). Objective estimation of perceived speech quality--Part I: Development of the measuring normalizing block technique. *IEEE Trans. On Speech and Audio Process* (pp. 371-382).

VQEG. (2000). *Final report from the video quality experts group on the validation of objective models of video quality assessment.* Retrieved from http://www.vqeg.org

Wang, B., Kurose, J., Shenoy, P., & Towsley, D. (2004). Multimedia streaming via TCP: An analytic performance study. *Proceedings of the 12th Annual ACM International Conference on Multimedia* (pp. 908-915).

Wang, C. H. (2003 June). *A dynamic resource allocation for vertical handoff on heterogeneous wireless networks.* Department and Graduate Institute of Information Management, Master's Thesis.

Wang, F., & Zhang, Y. (2002). Improving TCP performance over mobile ad-hoc networks with out-of-order detection and response. *Proceedings of the 3rd ACM International Symposium on Mobile Ad Hoc Networking & Computing* (pp. 217-225).

Wang, H., & Bovik, A. C. (2004). Video quality assessment based on structural distortion measurement. *Signal Processing: Image Communication, special issue on Objective video quality metrics, 19*(2), 121-132.

Wang, H., Bovik, A. C., Sheikh, H. R., & Simoncelli, E. P. (2004). Image quality assessment: From error visibility to structural similarity. *IEEE Transactions on Image Processing, 13*(4), 1-14.

Wang, H., Katz, R., & Giese, J. (1999). Policy-enabled handoffs across heterogeneous wireless networks. WMCSA.

Wang, S., Sekey, A., & Gersho, A. (1992). An objective measure for predicting subjective quality of speech coders. *IEEE J. Select. Areas Comm.*, 819-829.

Wang, X. (2004). Wide-band TD-CDMA MAC with minimum-power allocation and rate- and BER-scheduling for wireless multimedia networks. *IEEE/ACM Transactions on Networking, 12*, 103-116.

Wang, Z. (2001). *Internet QoS: Architectures and mechanisms for quality of service.* Morgan Kaufmann Publishers.

Wang, Z., Bovik, A. C., & Lu, L. (2002). *Why is image quality assessment so difficult?* Paper presented at the IEEE International Conference on Acoustics, Speech, and Signal Processing.

Wang, Z., Sheikh, H. R., & Bovik, A. C. (2003). Objective video quality assessment. In B. Furht & O. Marqure (Eds.), *The handbook of video databases: Design and applications* (Vol. 41, pp. 1041-1078). CRC Press.

Want, R., Hopper, A., Falcao, V., & Gibbons J. (1992). The active badge location system. *ACM Transactions on Information Systems, 10*(1), 91-102.

Want, R., Schilit, B. N., Adams, N. I., Gold, R., Petersen, K., Goldberg, D., Ellis, J. R., & Weiser, M. (1995). *The ParcTab ubiquitous computing experiment* (Tech. Report No. CSL-95-1). Xerox Palo Alto Research Centre, March 1995. Also appears in Korth, H. F., & Imielinski, T. (Eds.), *Mobile computing.* Kluwer Academic Press, 1996.

Wardi, Y., Melamed, B., et al. (2002). On-line IPA gradient estimators in single-node stochastic fluid models. *Journal of Optimization Theory and Applications, 115*(2), 369-405.

Watson, A., & Sasse, M. A. (1998). *Measuring perceived quality of speech and video in multimedia conferencing applications.* Paper presented at the ACM Multimedia.

Watson, A., & Sasse, M.A. (1997). Multimedia conferencing via multicasting: Determining the quality of service required by the end user. *Proceedings of AVSPN '97* (pp. 189-194). Aberdeen, Scotland.

Wei, Y., Bhandarkar, S. M., & Chandra, S. (2006). A client-side statistical prediction scheme for energy aware multimedia data streaming. *IEEE Transactions on Multimedia, 8*(4), 866-874.

Weiser, M. (1991). *The computer for the 21st century.* Scientific American, September 1991.

Weiser, M. (1993). Some computer science issues in ubiquitous computing. *Communications of the ACM, 36*(7), 74-84, July 1993.

Weiser, M. (1998). The future of ubiquitous computing on campus. *Communication of the ACM, 41*(1), 41-42.

Wolfgang, K., & Martin, M. (2007). A survey on real-world implementations of mobile ad-hoc networks (Vol. 5, pp. 324-339): Elsevier Science Publishers B. V.

Wong, T., Mark, J., & Chua, K. C. (2003). Joint connection level, packet level, and link layer resource allocation for variable bit rate multiclass services in cellular DS-CDMA networks with QoS constraints. *IEEE Journal on Selected Areas in Communications, 21*, 1536-1545.

Woolley, R. D. (2000). *Web performance measurement & capacity planning: Briefing paper.* Chief Information Officer's Section. Office of the Governor. State of Utah.

Wroclawski, J. (1997). *RFC 2210* - The use of RSVP with IETF integrated services.

Wu, H., Peng, Y., & Long, K. (2002). Performance of reliable transport protocol over IEEE 802.11 wireless LANs: Analysis and enhancement. *Proceedings of IEEE INFOCOM* (pp. 599–607), New York, USA.

Wu, K., & Harms, J. (2001). On-demand multipath routing for mobile ad hoc networks. *Proceedings of EPMCC*.

Wu, K., & Harms, J. (2001). *Performance study of a multipath routing method for wireless mobile ad hoc networks*. Paper presented at the IEEE Int'l Symposium on Modeling, Analysis and Simulation of Compute and Telecommunication Systems (MASCOTS).

Wu, P., Tseng, Y., & Lee, H. (2005). Design of QoS and admission control for VoIP Services over IEEE 802.11e WLANs. In *National Computer Symposium*.

Xiao Y., & Li, H. (2004). Local data control and admission control for ad hoc wireless networks. *IEEE Transactions on Vehicular Technology, 53*(5), 1558-1572.

Xiao Y., & Li, H. (2004). Voice and video transmissions with global data parameter control for the IEEE 802.11e enhance distributed channel access. *IEEE Transactions on Parallel and Distributed Systems, 15*(11), 1041-1053.

Xiao, M., Shroff, N. B., & Chong, E. K. (2003). A utility-based power-control scheme in wireless cellular systems. *IEEE/ACM Transactions on Networking, 11*, 210-221.

Xiao, Y. (2005). Performance analysis of priority schemes for IEEE 802.11 and IEEE 802.11e wireless LANs. *IEEE Transactions on Wireless Communications, 4*(4), 1506-1515.

Xiao, Y., Li, H., & Choi, S. (2004). Protection and guarantee for voice and video traffic in IEEE 802.11e wireless LANs. *Proceedings of IEEE INFOCOM* (pp. 2153-2163), Hong Kong, China.

Xilouris, G., Kourtis, A., & Stefanou, G. (2005). A mesh topology DVB-S network architecture for node interconnection, featuring QoS capabilities. *Computer Networks, 48*(1), 45-56.

Xipeng, X., & Ni, L. M. (1999). Internet QoS: A big picture. *Network, IEEE, 13*(2), 8-18.

Xu, Y., Heidemann, J., & Estrin, D. (2001). Geography-informed energy conservation for ad hoc routing. *Proceedings of the International Conference on Mobile Computing and Networking MOBICOM* (pp. 70-84).

Xue, Q., & Ganz, A. (2003). Ad hoc QoS on-demand routing (AQOR) in mobile ad hoc networks. *Journal of Parallel Distributed Computing, 63*(2), 154-165.

Xylomenos, G., & Polyzos, G. C. (1999). *TCP and UDP performance over a wireless LAN*. Paper presented at the INFOCOM'99. The 18th Annual Joint Conference of the IEEE Computer and Communications Societies, New York, USA.

Xylomenos, G., Polyzos, G. C., Mahonen, P., & Saaranen, M. (2001). TCP performance issues over wireless links. *Communications Magazine, IEEE, 39*(4), 52-58.

Yaling, Y., & Kravets, R. (2005). Contention-aware admission control for ad hoc networks. *IEEE Transactions on Mobile Computing, 4*(4), 363-377.

Yamori, K., & Tanaka, Y. (2004, August 2004). *Relation between willingness to pay and guaranteed minimum bandwidth in multiple-priority service*. Paper presented at the 10th Asia-Pacific Conference on Communications (APCC 2004), Beijing, China.

Yan, A., & Gong, W. B. (1999). Fluid simulation for high-speed networks with flow-based routing. *IEEE Transactions on Information Theory, 45*, 1588-1599.

Yang Y. R., & Lam S. S. (2000). General AIMD Congestion Control. *Proc. 8th IEEE International Conference on Network Protocols (ICNP)*, Osaka, Japan.

Yang, G., Sun, T., Gerla, M., Sanadidi, M. Y., & Chen, L. J. (2006). Smooth and efficient real-time video transport in the presence of wireless errors. *ACM Transactions on Multimedia Computing, Communications, and Applications (TOMCCAP), 2*, 109-126.

Yang, S., & de Veciana, G. (2002). Size-based adaptive bandwidth allocation: Optimizing the average QoS for elastic flows. *In IEEE INFOCOM*.

Yang, W. (1999). *Enhanced modified bark spectral distortion (EMBSD).* PhD Thesis, Temple University, Philadelphia.

Yang, W., Benbouchta, M., & Yantorno, R. (1997). Performance of a modified bark spectral distortion measure as an objective speech quality measure. *IEEE Proc. International Conference on Acoustics, Speech, and Signal Processing* (pp. 541-544).

Yang, X., Bigham, J., & Cuthber, L. (2005, March). Resource management for service providers in heterogeneous wireless networks. *IEEE Wireless Communications and Networking Conference, 3*, 1305-1310.

Yang, Y. R., Kim, M. S., & Lam, S. S. (2001). Transient behaviors of TCP-friendly congestion control protocols. *Proceedings IEEE INFOCOM 2001*, Anchorage, Alaska, USA.

Yang, Y., & Kravets, R. (2005). Contention-aware admission control for ad hoc networks. *IEEE Transactions on Mobile Computing, 4*(4), 363-338.

Yavatkar, R., & Bhagawat, N. (1994). Improving end-to-end performance of TCP over mobile internetworks. *Mobile Computing Systems and Applications, 1994. Proceedings., Workshop on*, 146-152.

Yavatkar, R., Hoffman, D., & Bernet, Y. (2000). SBM (subnet bandwidth manager): A protocol for RSVP-based admission control over IEEE 802-style networks. *RFC2814.*

Ylianttila, M., Mäkelä, J., & Mähönen, P. (2002). Supporting resource allocation with vertical handoffs in multiple radio network environment. *IEEE International Symposium on Personal Indoor and Mobile Radio Communications.*

Ylianttila, M., Mäkelä, J., & Mähönen, P., (2002, Sept). Optimization scheme for mobile users performing vertical handoffs between IEEE 802.11 and GPRS/EDGE networks. *IEEE PIMRC, 1*, 15-18.

Ylianttila, M., Pichna, R., Vallström, J., & Mäkelä, J. (1999). Handoff procedure for heterogeneous wireless networks. *Global Telecommunications Conference.*

Young-Bae, K., & Nitin, H. V. (2000). Location aided routing (LAR) in mobile ad hoc networks. *Wireless Networks, V6*(4), 307-321.

YouTube. www.youtube.com

Zander, S., & Armitage, G. (2004). *Empirically measuring the QoS sensitivity of interactive online game players.* Paper presented at the Australian Telecommunications Networks & Applications Conference 2004 (ATNAC 2004), Sydney, Australia.

Zanella, A., Merlin, S., & Di Lenarda, F. (2005). An efficient and adaptive resource allocation scheme for next generation cellular systems. *Proceedings of WPMC 2005*, Aalborg, DK.

Zapater, M. N., & Bressan, G. (2007). A proposed approach for quality of experience assurance for IPTV. *Proceedings of the 1st International Conference on the Digital Society 2007*, Guadeloupe, French Caribbean.

Zhai, H., Chen, X., & Fang, Y. (2006). A call admission and rate control scheme for multimedia support over IEEE 802.11 wireless LANs. *ACM Wireless Networks, 12*(4), 451-463.

Zhang, C., & Tsaoussidis, V. (2001). TCP Real: Improving real-time capabilities of TCP over heterogeneous networks. *Proceedings 11th IEEE/ACM NOSSDAV*, Port Jefferson, New York, USA.

Zhang, F., & Chanson, S. (2005). Proxy-assisted scheduling for energy-efficient multimedia streaming over wireless LAN. *Networking 2005. Networking Technologies, Services and Protocols; Performance of Computer and Communication Networks; Mobile and Wireless Communication Systems. Proceedings of the 4th International IFIP-TC6 Networking Conference.* (LNCS vol. 3462, pp. 980-91).

Zhang, G., & Mouftah, H. T. (2001). End-to-end QoS guarantees over Diffserv networks. *The 6th IEEE Symposium on Computers and Communications*, 2001.

Zhang, L. Y., Ge, Y., & Hou, J. (2003). Energy-efficient real-time scheduling in IEEE 802.11 wireless LANs.

Proceedings - International Conference on Distributed Computing Systems (pp. 658-667).

Zhang, P. (2005). *Utility-based resource allocation in wireless multimedia CDMA networks.* Unpublished doctoral dissertation, University of California, Irvine.

Zhang, P., & Jordan, S. (2006). Throughput guarantee targeted hybrid scheduling for downlink WCDMA data networks. In *Proceedings of the IEEE Wireless Communications and Networking Conference.*

Zhang, P., & von Dran, G. (2001, January 03-06). *Expectations and rankings of Website quality features: results of two studies on user perceptions.* Paper presented at the 34th Annual Hawaii International Conference on System Sciences (HICSS-34).

Zhang, P., & von Dran, G. (2001). User expectations and rankings of quality factors in different Web site domains. *International Journal of Electronic Commerce, 6*(2), 9.

Zhang, Q., Guo, C., Guo, Z., & Zhu, W. (2003, Nov.). Efficient mobility management for vertical handoff between WWAN and WLAN. *IEEE Communications Magazine, 41*(11), 102-108.

Zhang, Q., Yang, F., & Zhu, W. (2005). Cross-layer QoS support for multimedia delivery over wireless Internet. *EURASIP Journal on Applied Signal Processing 2005, 2,* 207-219.

Zhenyu, Y., & Garcia-Luna-Aceves, J. J. (1999). *Hop-reservation multiple access (HRMA) for ad-hoc networks.* Paper presented at the INFOCOM '99. The 18th Annual Joint Conference of the IEEE Computer and Communications Societies. Proceedings. IEEE.

Zhong, F. (2004). *QoS routing using lower layer information in ad hoc networks.*

Zhou, C., Honig, M., & Jordan, S. (2005). Utility-based power control for a two-cell CDMA data network. *IEEE Transactions on Wireless Communications, 4,* 2764 - 2776.

Zhou, C., Zhang, P., Honig, M., & Jordan, S. (2004). Two-cell power allocation for downlink CDMA. *IEEE Transactions on Wireless Communications, 3,* 2256-2266.

Zhu, F., & McNair, J., (2004, March). Optimizations for vertical handoff decision algorithms. *IEEE Wireless Communications and Networking Conference (WCNC)* (pp. 867-872).

Zhu, H., & Cao, G. (2004). A power-aware and QoS-aware service model on wireless networks. *IEEE INFOCOM* (Vol. 2, pp. 1393-1403).

Zhu, H., & Cao, G. (2005). On supporting power-efficient streaming applications in wireless environments. *IEEE Transactions on Mobile Computing* (Vol. 4, pp. 391-403).

Zhu, H., & Chlamtac, I. (2003). An analytical model for IEEE 802.11e EDCF differential services. *Proceedings of the 12th International Conference on Computer Communications and Networks* (pp. 163-168), Dallas, Texas, USA.

Zhu, H., Li, M., Chlamtac, I., & Prabhakaran, B. (2004). Survey of quality of service in IEEE 802.11 networks. *IEEE Wireless Communications, Special Issue on Mobility and Resource Management, 11*(4), 6-14.

Zviran, M., Glezer, C., & Avni, I. (2006). User satisfaction from commercial Web sites: The effect of design and use. *Information and Management, 43*(2), 157-178.

About the Contributors

Nicola Cranley received her BSc in applied physics with French from Dublin City University in 1998, MSc in computing for commerce and industry from the Open University in 2004, and a PhD in computer science from University College Dublin in 2004. Dr. Cranley has published over 25 refereed journal and conference papers in the areas of video quality analysis, QoS for multimedia streaming and wireless multimedia. Her research interests include wireless video streaming, video adaptation and wireless networks.

Liam Murphy received a BE in electrical engineering from University College Dublin in 1985, and MSc and PhD in electrical engineering and computer sciences from the University of California, Berkeley in 1988 and 1992 respectively. He is currently an associate professor in computer science at University College Dublin, where he is director of the Performance Engineering Laboratory. Prof. Murphy has published over 100 refereed journal and conference papers on various topics, including multimedia transmissions, dynamic and adaptive resource allocation algorithms, and software development. His current research projects involve mobile and wireless systems, computer network convergence issues, and web services performance issues. Prof. Murphy is a member of the IEEE and a fellow of the Irish Computer Society.

***

Janet Adams was a researcher with the Performance Engineering Laboratory, School of Electronic Engineering, Dublin City University, Ireland, university from which she obtained her BEng degree in telecommunications engineering (2005) and an MEng degree by research (2007). Adams's research focuses on power saving solutions for mobile and wireless-enabled devices in relation to multimedia streaming. Currently she works with Ericsson Ireland.

Fatih Alagöz is an associate professor in the Dept. of Computer Eng., Bogazici University, Turkey. From 2001 to 2003, he was with the Dept. of Electrical Eng., United Arab Emirates University, AlAin, UAE. In 1993, he was a research engineer in a missile manufacturing company, Muhimmatsan AS, Turkey. He received the BSc degree in electrical engineering from Middle East Technical University, Turkey (1992), and MSc and DSc degrees in electrical engineering from The George Washington University, USA (1995 and 2000, respectively). His current research interests are in the areas of satellite networks and wireless/mobile networks, UWB communications. He has contributed/managed to seven research projects for various agencies/organizations including US Army of Intelligence Center, Naval Research

Laboratory, State Planning Organization of Turkey, Turkish Research Council TUBITAK, BAP, etc. He has edited five books and published more than 60 scholarly papers in selected journals and conferences. Alagöz is the satellite systems advisor to the Kandilli Earthquake Research Institute, Istanbul, Turkey. He has served on several major conferences technical committees, and organized and chaired many technical sessions in many international conferences. He is a member of the IEEE Satellite and Space Communications Technical Committee. He has numerous professional awards.

Michael Barry received his BEng and MEng degrees in computer engineering from the University of Limerick, Ireland (1995 and 1999, respectively). From 1998-2001, he worked at Broadcom Eireann Research Limited in Dublin, Ireland. In 2000, he was a visiting Scholar with the COMET group at the University of Columbia, New York, NY. Since 2001 Michael has been a member of the Wireless Access Research Centre at the University of Limerick. His research interests include Mobile IP, IP QoS, and wireless access mechanisms.

Suzan Bayhan received her BSc and MSc degrees from the department of computer engineering, Bogazici University (2003 and 2006, respectively). Currently, she is a PhD student in the same department. She has been a member of Satellite Networks Research Laboratory (SATLAB). Her main research interests are satellite communications, dynamic spectrum access networks, 3G/4G networks, and IP Multimedia Subsystem (IMS) applications.

Tarek Bejaoui is an assistant professor at the Institut Supérieur des Sciences Appliquées et de Technologies, University of Carthage, Tunisia. He has graduated from Ecole Nationale d'Ingénieurs de Tunis in 1999 and got a PhD of Paris-Sud 11 University, France, in 2005. His current research interests include wireless multimedia, QoS service provisioning, sensor networks, mobile ad hoc networks, mobile and pervasive computing, performance evaluation of communication networks and communication protocols. Bejaoui has published several research papers in these areas. Bejaoui has organized and served on the program committee of a numerous international conferences and workshops.

Boris Bellalta received his MSc degree in telecommunications from the Technical University of Catalonia (2002) and the PhD in computer science from the Universitat Pompeu Fabra (2007). Since 2002, he is an assistant professor at Universitat Pompeu Fabra. His research interests are in the field of performance analysis and dimensioning of multiservice wireless networks, with special interests in Internet traffic modelling and MAC/PHY cross-layer design.

Janez Bester received his PhD degree in the field of telecommunications from the University of Ljubljana, Slovenia. He is currently the head of the Laboratory for Telecommunications and is an associate professor at the Faculty of Electrical Engineering in Ljubljana. His work focuses on planning, realization, and management of telecommunication systems and services as well as applying information and communication technologies to education. He is a member of several national committees--AAATE, IEEE, IFIP, ACM, and IEICE.

Bego Blanco received BS and MS degrees in telecommunications engineering from the University of the Basque Country, Spain (2000). In 2001 she completed a postgraduate in networking, telematic services, and Internet at the same University. She currently works as a lecturer in the Faculty of Technical Engineering of Bilbao and is doctoral student of the Department of Electronics and Communications of the University of the Basque Country. His research interests include quality management and multicriteria optimization in MANETs and NGNs.

Graça Bressan has a PhD in electronic engineering (1986) from Escola Politecnica of University of Sao Paulo (EPUSP). At Scopus Tecnologia she was the head of the software department where coordinated the development of operating systems, computers network middleware and firmware and software for teller machines and ATM. She is professor at Computer Engineering Department at EPUSP, where coordinates researches on computer network and internetworking multimedia. Her current research interests includes modeling and performance analysis of networks, middleware, distributed systems, computer networks, QoS mechanisms, collaborative virtual environment, middleware for Digital TV, interactive digital TV, and distance education as an application for multimedia delivery system. She received the Decio Leal de Zagotis award from EPUSP(2001).

Paolo Chini was born in Siena, Italy, in 1972. He received the Dr Ing degree in telecommunications engineering in 2005 from the University of Siena, Italy, with a thesis entitled "Cross-layer management of resources in an interactive DVBRCS-based satellite network" in the framework of the SatNEx "Satellite Communications Network of Excellence," in FP6 network of excellence, in cooperation with the University of Rome "Tor Vergata." Since 2005, he has performed research activities at the University of Siena as a CNIT fellowship recipient; his fields of interests include satellite communications, DVB-RCS standards, TCP and MAC layer protocols, mobile and wireless networks.

Imrich Chlamtac is the president of Create-Net, a non-profit international research institute and the Honorary Bruno Kessler Professor at the University of Trento, Italy. In the past, he was with Technion and UMass, Amherst, and DEC Research and helped found several successful technology firms, including Consip Ltd and BCN Inc, one of the largest system integrators in central Europe. In his academic life, he has held various chaired professorships in USA and Europe including the distinguished chair in Telecommunications Professorship at the University of Texas at Dallas, Sackler Professorship at Tel Aviv University, "University Professorship" at the Budapest University of Technology and Economics, and Honorary Professorship from the Beijing University of Posts and Telecommunicatrions. Chlamtac is the recipient of various professional award including Fellow of the IEEE, Fellow of the ACM, Fulbright Scholar, the ACM Award for Outstanding Contributions to Research on Mobility and the IEEE Award for Outstanding Technical Contributions to Wireless Personal Communications. Chlamtac published over 400 refereed journals and conference articles and is listed among ISI's highly cited researchers in computer science. He is the co-author of several books, including the first book on local area networks (1980) and the Amazon.com best seller, *Wireless and Mobile Network Architectures* (John Wiley and Sons). He has widely contributed to the scientific community as chair of ICST Scientific Council, founder and chair of ACM Sigmobile, founder and steering committee chair of several leading conferences, including ACM Mobicom, IEEE/ICST/CreateNet Broadnets, IEEE/ICST/CreateNet Tridentcom, IEEE/ICST/CreateNet Securecomm, and IEEE/ICST/Create-Net Comsware. He also serves as the founding editor in chief of the ACM/Springer Wireless Networks (WINET), and the ACM/Springer Journal on Special Topics in Mobile Networks and Applications (MONET).

Giovanni Giambene received his PhD degree in telecommunications and informatics from the University of Florence, Italy (1997). He contributed to the following EU projects, most of them on satellite communications: (*i*) COST 227; (*ii*) SAINT RACE 2117; (*iii*) COST 252; (*iv*) CNR "*Multime-dialità*" project; (*v*) PALIO FP5 EU Project. Since 1999, he is with the Information Engineering Dept. of the University of Siena, Italy, where he is currently assistant professor (qualification of "confirmed researcher and adjunct professor"), teaching the course of Telecommunication Networks II. At present, he is involved in the SatNEx FP6 network of excellence as leader of 2 working groups on cross-layer air interface design for satellite systems (www.satnex.org). He is vice-chair of the COST 290 Action (www.cost290.org, "Traffic and QoS Management in Wireless Multimedia Networks").

Gheorghita Ghinea received his BSc and BSc (Hons) degrees in computer science and mathematics(1993 and 1994, respectively), and his MSc degree in computer science (1996) from the University of the Witwatersrand, Johannesburg, South Africa. He then received his PhD degree in computer science from the University of Reading, UK (2000). He is a lecturer in the School of Information Systems, Computing and Mathematics at Brunel University. His research interests pervasive computing, telemedicine, quality of service and multimedia resource allocation, as well as computer networking and security issues.

Gürkan Gür received a BSc degree in electrical engineering (2001) and an MSc degree in systems and control engineering (2005), both from the Bogazici University, Istanbul, Turkey. Currently he is pursuing a PhD degree in computer engineering, and working as a researcher at Satellite Networks Research Laboratory (SATLAB) in the Bogazici University. He has been involved in development of various telecom products in industry as a software developer. His research interests include multimedia over wireless networks, 3G and Beyond-3G heterogeneous networks, signal processing for communications, transport protocols over wireless networks, and performance evaluation and design of computer networks.

Snezana Hadzic was born in Belgrade, Serbia in 1980. She received her Dipl. Ing. degree from electro-technical Faculty, University of Belgrade, Serbia (2006). Since 2006, she has been a PhD student with the Department of Information Engineering at the University of Siena, Italy. The topics of her PhD research activity deal with cross-layer optimization for wireless networks, traffic flow differentiation and interconnection via satellite. Since July 2007, she is also recipient of a one-year CNIT fellowship for the AMUSE project "Interconnected Satellite Network for Multimedia Service Provision with Differentiated Quality of Service Levels."

Jose Luis Jodra received his BS and MS degrees in computer sciences from the University of the Basque Country, Spain (2001). In 2002 he completed a MBA from Uniactiva attached to UPC (Technical University of Catalonia). He currently works as a lecturer in the Faculty of Engineering of Bilbao and cooperates in different national and European R&D projects. His research interests include quality management and multicriteria optimization in MANETs and NGNs.

Scott Jordan received his BS/AB, MS, and PhD degrees from the University of California, Berkeley (1985, 1987, and 1990, respectively). From 1990 until 1999, he served as a faculty member at Northwestern University. Since 1999, he has served as a faculty member at the University of California,

Irvine. During 2006, he served as an IEEE congressional fellow, working in the United States senate on Internet and telecommunications policy issues. His research interests currently include pricing and differentiated services in the Internet, resource allocation in wireless multimedia networks, and telecommunications policy.

William Kent received his BEng and MEng from the University of Limerick (2004 and 2007, respectively). He has worked on both national and European funded projects including SFI NCNRC and Celtic Gandalf project. His research interests include scheduling in wireless systems, heterogeneous network architectures, and radio resource management.

Andrej Kos graduated from the University of Ljubljana, Slovenia (1996) and was awarded his PhD degree in telecommunications (2003). At present, he works as an assistant professor at the Faculty of Electrical Engineering in Ljubljana. He has extensive research and industrial experience in the analysis, modeling, and design of advanced telecommunications elements, networks, systems, and services. His current work and research focus on managed broadband packet switching and next generation intelligent converged services. He is a member of IEEE, IEICE, and Telemanagement Forum.

Harilaos Koumaras was born in Athens, Greece in 1980. He received his BSc degree in physics (2002) from the University of Athens, Physics Department, his MSc in electronic automation and information systems (2004), being scholar of the non-profit organization Alexander S Onassis, from the University of Athens, Physics and Informatics Department, and his PhD (2007) on digital video quality prediction from the University of Athens, Informatics Department, having granted the four-year scholarship of NCSR "Demokritos." He has received the Greek State Foundations (IKY) scholarship twice for excellent performances during the academic years 2000-01 and 2003-04. He has also granted with honors the classical piano and harmony degrees from the classical music department of Attiko Conservatory. He joined the Digital Telecommunications Lab at the National Centre of Scientific Research "Demokritos" in 2003 and since then he has participated in the EU funded projects SOQUET, ENTHRONE and national funded project PYTHAGORAS with presentations and publications at international conferences, scientific journals and book chapters. At the same time, he is a principal lecturer at the Business College of Athens (BCA) and City University of Seattle, teaching modules related to Information Technology, Data Networks, and Mathematics. His research interests include objective/subjective evaluation of the perceived quality of multimedia services, video quality and picture quality evaluation, video traffic modeling, digital terrestrial television and video compression techniques. Currently, he is the author or co-author of more than 20 scientific papers in international journals, technical books, and conference proceedings, numbering 16 non-self citations. He is a member of IEEE, SPIE, and National Geographic Society.

Ming Li has been a faculty in the Department of Computer Science, California State University, Fresno, since August 2006. He received his MS and PhD degrees in computer science from The University of Texas at Dallas (2001 and 2006, respectively). His research interests include QoS strategies for mobile ad-hoc networks and multimedia streaming over wireless networks. His research works have been published in several journals and conferences, including ACM TOMCCAP, ACM/Springer MONET, and ACM/Springer/URSI WINET. He is the recipient of the Best Student Paper Award in the

First IEEE International Workshop on Next Generation Wireless Networks (WoNGeN'05). He has served the technical program committees of several international conferences such as ISM'07, ICCCN'07, and ROBOCOMM'07. Li is a member of ACM, IEEE, and Upsilon Pi Epsilon (UPE).

Fidel Liberal received his BS and MS degrees in telecommunications engineering from the University of the Basque Country, Spain (2001). In 2005, he received his PhD in telecommunications engineering from the same University for his work in the area of holistic management of quality (both NQoS and PQoS-QoE) in telecommunications services. He currently works as a lecturer in the Faculty of Engineering of Bilbao and cooperates in different national and European R&D projects. His research interests include quality management and multicriteria optimization in MANETs and NGNs.

Carlos Macián obtained his MSc in electrical engineering from the Polytechnic University in València (Spain) (1997). Afterwards he joined the Institute of Communication Networks and Computer Engineering (IKR) at the University of Stuttgart (Germany), where he was a scientific staff member while pursuing his PhD in computer networks, which he finished in 2004. In 2002, he stayed at the Washington University in St. Louis (USA) as an invited scholar. In 2004, he joined the Universitat Pompeu Fabra in Barcelona (Spain) as a visiting professor. During these years, he has participated in a number of research projects, both public and corporate, in the areas of QoS in IP networks, router architecture, fixed-mobile network convergence and overlay network architectures. His current areas of interest include distributed multimedia over IP protocols and architectures, fixed-mobile network convergence, alternative telecommunication operator models, and telecommunication policy and techno-economic impact.

Andreas Mäder received his degree in computer science in 2003 at the University of Wuerzburg. Since then he is working as a research fellow at the Department of Distributed Systems towards his Doctoral degree (PhD). He has published several papers on the performance of 3.5G mobile communication systems like HSDPA and HSUPA. His current research interests are on UTRAN LTE and the influence of user traffic models on the performance of wireless networks.

Michael M. Markou has received a diploma in computer engineering and informatics from University of Patras, Greece (2003). He is currently pursuing PhD at the Department of Electrical and Computer Engineering, University of Cyprus, Cyprus. Since 2003, he has been a Researcher at the University of Cyprus and is funded by the Cyprus Research Promotion Foundation. He has published several journal and conference articles concerning control and optimization of network parameters in communication networks. His research interests include optimization and control of discrete-event systems with applications to wirelined and wireless communication networks, design and implementation of distributed algorithms. Markou served as a chair of IEEE Student Branch at University of Cyprus from 2005 to 2007.

Sean McGrath received his MSc from Heriot-Watt University (1986) and his PhD from the University of Limerick (1992) in the area of indoor wireless data communication systems. He has worked in mobile communication research for the last 12 years. He lectures in telecommunication systems and digital communication. He is a member of the Committee of the IEEE Communications Chapter and IEEE Committee on Information Theory. His research interests include mobile communications, communication theory and applications, satellite systems. Mc Grath is the director of the Wireless Access Research Centre at the University of Limerick.

Gabriel-Miro Muntean is a lecturer with the School of Electronic Engineering, Dublin City University (DCU), Ireland, institution, which has also awarded him a PhD degree for research in quality-oriented adaptive multimedia streaming (2003). His research interests include QoS and performance-related issues of adaptive solutions for multimedia delivery over wired and wireless networks and performance-aware adaptive hypermedia systems. He has published a book, three book chapters and over 60 papers in prestigious international journals and conferences. He is a member of the IEEE and co-director of DCU Performance Engineering Laboratory.

Nidal Nasser is an assistant professor at the Department of Computing and Information Science, University of Guelph, Ontario, Canada. He received his BSc and MSc degrees with Honors in Computer Engineering from Kuwait University (1996 and 1999, respectively). He completed his PhD in the School of Computing at Queen's University, Canada (2004). His current research interests include, heterogeneous wireless data networks, wireless sensor networks and multimedia wireless cellular networks with special emphasis on the following topics, radio resource management techniques, performance modeling and analysis and provisioning QoS. Nasser has authored five book chapters and has several publications in reputable journals, conferences and workshops in the areas of wireless and mobile system and networks and performance evaluation. Nasser has organized and served on the program committee of a numerous international conferences and workshops. Nasser is a member of the IEEE, Communications Society, and Computer Society. He received Fund for Scholarly and Professional Development Award in 2004 from Queen's University.

John Nelson is a senior lecturer in electronic and computer engineering at the University of Limerick, Ireland. He is one of the cluster investigators in the Science Foundation Ireland funded National Communications Network Research Centre (NCNRC), which is primarily investigating measurement driven quality of service in wireless networks. From 2000 to 2004, he held the position of engineering director in the Wireless Division at Parthus/Ceva Inc where he undertook major system level projects in the areas of Bluetooth, GPS, and 802.11. His interests in wired and wireless networks include architecture, performance, power management, network measurement, and test-bed construction.

Christos G. Panayiotou has received his PhD degree in electrical and computer engineering from the University of Massachusetts at Amherst, USA (1999). Between 1999-2002, he was a research associate at Boston University. Currently, he is an assistant professor in electrical and computer engineering at UCY. His research interests include distributed control systems, wireless, ad hoc and sensor networks, computer communication networks, quality of service (QoS) provisioning, optimization and control of discrete-event systems, resource allocation, simulation. Panayiotou is an associate editor for the Conference Editorial Board of the IEEE Control Systems Society and a senior member of the IEEE.

Panagiotis Papadimitriou obtained a BSc in computer science from University of Crete, Greece and an MSc in information technology from University of Nottingham. He is currently a PhD candidate in electrical and computer engineering in Democritus University of Thrace, Greece. Papadimitriou is a visiting lecturer in the Information Management Department of Technological Educational Institute (TEI) of Kavala, Greece. His research interests include transport protocols for multimedia applications, video and voice over IP, congestion control, and satellite/space communications.

Francesco De Pellegrini was born in 1974 in Belluno, Italy. He received his Laurea degree (2000) and his PhD degree (2004), both in telecommunication engineering, from the University of Padova. He is currently a senior researcher at Create-Net. His research interests are location detection in sensor networks, multirate systems, turn-prohibition routing, WLAN VoIP, delay tolerant networks and bio-inspired networking. During 2001/2002, he spent one year at Boston University as a visiting scholar. De Pellegrini is a member IEEE and serves as a reviewer for several international networking conferences, among which IEEE INFOCOM and several Journals IEEE Transactions on Wireless Communications and IEEE Transactions on Vehicular Technology. Francesco serves as Steering Programm Commitee of Mobiquitous 2007 and is the programm vice chair of IEEE/ACM Robocomm. Francesco is cited in Marquis Who's Who.

Dorel Picovici received his BSc in electronic engineering from Technical University of Cluj-Napoca, Romania (1999). He received his master of engineering and PhD from University of Limerick, Ireland (2000 and 2004, respectively). He is affiliated with the Department of Electronic and Computer Engineering at University of Limerick. Picovici's research interests are in the area of non-intrusive objective voice quality assessment and to date he has one patent application pending, authored and co-authored more than 38 book chapters, refereed journals, and international conference articles.

Roberto Riggio received his masters degree in telecommunication engineering at the School of Engineering of the "University degli Studi Mediterranea" of Reggio Calabria, Italy (July 2004). He is currently working towards the PhD degree in University of Trento, Italy. From May 2007 to November 2007, he was a visiting researcher at the Computer Science Department of the University of Florida. His main research interests lie in field of wireless mesh networks with a particular focus on cross-layer design and QoS.

Tacha Serif received the BSc (Hons) degree in information systems engineering (2000), M.Phil. degree in computing (2002), from UMIST, and PhD in information systems and computing form Brunel University, United Kingdom. He is currently a research fellow in the School of Information Systems, Computing, and Mathematics at Brunel University. His research interests include mobile health systems, pervasive computing, distance learning, mobile infotainment, wireless networks, as well as location-based and context-aware systems.

Anna Sfairopoulou graduated computer science from the University of Ioannina, (Greece) in 2000. She received her MSc degree in computer science and digital communications from the Universitat Pompeu Fabra (Spain) (2002) and she is currently working on her PhD thesis at the same university, while being a full-time researcher at the Network Technologies and Strategies (NeTS) research group. During these years, she has participated in a number of research projects in the areas of 3G/UMTS and 802.11 networks, neutral networks architecture and VoIP. Her research interests are in the field of VoIP performance, optimization, and QoS in 802.11 WLANs, signalling and cross-layer design.

Ronan Skehill received his BEng., MEng., and PhD from University of Limerick (1999, 2001, and 2004 respectively). Since 1999, when he joined the Wireless Access Research Centre, he has worked on several European projects namely the IST HARMONICS, IST ARROWS projects and Celtic Gandalf project. He has also worked on several National Projects such as the EI REALM and IONOS project and currently is working on the SFI NCNRC project. His primary research deals with mobility and radio resource management issues of users in cellular networks.

Dirk Staehle is assistant professor at the Department of Distributed Systems at the University of Würzburg, Germany. He received his degree in computer science from the University of Würzburg (1999) and his doctoral degree (PhD) from the same university (2004). His research interests include radio network planning and radio resource management of mobile and wireless networks. He has published numerous papers on the analysis of coverage and capacity of UMTS networks. His current research focus is on adaptive resource allocation in cellular and mesh OFDMA networks.

Lingfen Sun received her PhD degree in computing and communications from the University of Plymouth UK in 2004. She holds an MSc in communication and electronics system (1988) and BEng in telecommunications engineering (1985), both from the Institute of Communications Engineering, Nanjing, China. She is now a lecturer in computer networks in the School of Computing, Communications, and Electronics, University of Plymouth, UK. She has published over 40 papers in peer-refereed journals and conference proceedings. Her main research interests include VoIP, QoS, voice and video quality prediction and control for voice and video over packet, wireless ad-hoc and cellular networks, grid computing and applications in eHealthcare.

Vassilis Tsaoussidis received a BSc in applied mathematics from Aristotle University, Greece, a diploma in statistics and computer science from the Hellenic Institute of Statistics, and a PhD in computer networks from Humboldt University, Berlin, Germany (1995). Vassilis held faculty positions in Rutgers University, New Brunswick, SUNY Stony Brook, and Northeastern University, Boston. In May 2003, Vassilis joined the Department of Electrical and Computer Engineering of Democritus University of Thrace, Greece. His research interests lie in the area of transport/network protocols (i.e., their design aspects and performance evaluation). Tsaoussidis is editor-in-chief in the Journal of Internet Engineering and editor for IEEE Transactions in Mobile Computing, the Journal of Computer Networks (Elsevier), the Journal of Wireless Communications and Mobile Computing, and the Journal of Mobile Multimedia. He participates in several Technical Program Committees in his area of expertise, such as INFOCOM, GLOBECOM, ICCCN, ISCC, EWCN, WLN, and several others.

Mojca Volk achieved her BSc degree from the University of Ljubljana, Slovenia (2004). She is currently with the Laboratory for Telecommunications as a PhD student. In addition to topics related to next generation networks, protocol and dedicated mechanisms, her current research interests involve design, deployment and testing of broadband IP multimedia infrastructures and services within convergent service delivery solutions. She is a member of IEICE and Telemanagement Forum.

Marcio Nieblas Zapater holds BS and MSc degrees in electrical engineering from Escola Politecnica of Universidade de Sao Paulo. His research areas include telecommunications services and networking, combining technology and business perspectives. As consultant at Promon Tecnologia he works on projects for local and foreign telecom service providers and large corporations. He performed several projects in telecom field (e.g., Broadband access and portals, Mobile VAS, IP Telephony, Managed Security Services), including new services creation and development, portfolio evaluation and reformulation, business plan creation and evaluation (to support new services or rollout of infrastructure), corporate telecom infrastructure optimization. International experience includes engagements of strategy and business plan evaluation for South America and Middle East operators.

Peifang Zhang received her BS and MS degrees in physics from Tsinghua University, Beijing (1996 and 1999 respectively), and received her PhD degree in electrical engineering from the University of California, Irvine (2005). Her research focused on cross layer design, radio resource management, multiple access control, and QoS provisioning in wireless communication networks. Since 2006, she has been working in Nextwave Broadband Inc., San Diego, California, on the emerging wideband wireless technology WiMAX.

Index